BT652.B99 I45 2005
Images of the Mother of God
: perceptions of the
Theotokos in Byzantium
39090013261470

IMAGES OF THE MOTHER OF GOD

To the memory of Nicolas Oikonomides

Images of the Mother of God

Perceptions of the Theotokos in Byzantium

Edited by Maria Vassilaki

ASHGATE

© The contributors 2005

All rights reserved. No part of this publication may be reproduced, stored in a retrieval system, or transmitted in any form or by any means electronic, mechanical, photocopying, recording or otherwise without the prior permission of the publisher.

Maria Vassilaki has asserted her moral right under the Copyright, Designs and Patents Act, 1988, to be identified as the Editor of this Work.

Published by
Ashgate Publishing Limited
Gower House
Croft Road
Aldershot
Hants GU11 3HR
England

Ashgate Publishing Company
Suite 420
101 Cherry Street
Burlington,
VT 05401-4405
USA

Ashgate website: http://www.ashgate.com

British Library Cataloguing in Publication Data
Images of the Mother of God: perceptions
 of the Theotokos in Byzantium
 1. Mary, Blessed Virgin, Saint – Art 2. Icons,
 Byzantine 3. Byzantine Empire – Religion
 I. Vassilaki, Maria
 704.9'4855'09495'0902

Library of Congress Cataloging-in-Publication Data
Images of the Mother of God: perceptions of the Theotokos in Byzantium / edited by Maria Vassilaki.
   p.   cm.
  Includes bibliographical references and index.
  ISBN 0-7546-3603-8 (alk. paper)
  1. Mary, Blessed Virgin, Saint—Devotion to—Byzantine Empire—Congresses. 2. Byzantine Empire—Religious life and customs—Congresses. I. Vassilaki, Maria. II. Title.

BT652.B99I45 2004
232.91—dc22

2004000031

ISBN 0 7546 3603 8

Typeset in Garamond by Bookcraft Ltd, Stroud, Gloucestershire.
Printed and bound in Great Britain by Biddles Ltd, King's Lynn, Norfolk.

Contents

List of Illustrations		ix
List of Contributors		xvii
Foreword *Angelos Delivorrias*		xix
Preface *Evangelos Chrysos*		xxi
Acknowledgements *Maria Vassilaki*		xxiii
List of Abbreviations		xxv
Introduction *Averil Cameron*		xxvii

I Early cult and representations

1	Isis and Mary in early icons *Thomas F. Mathews and Norman Muller*	3
2	The enigmatic Coptic Galaktotrophousa and the cult of the Virgin Mary in Egypt *Elizabeth S. Bolman*	13
3	Icons and sites. Cult images of the Virgin in mediaeval Rome *Gerhard Wolf*	23
4	Theotokos and *Logos*: the interpretation and reinterpretation of the sanctuary programme of the Koimesis Church, Nicaea *Charles Barber*	51

II The theology of the Theotokos

5	The Virgin as the true Ark of the Covenant *† Michel van Esbroeck*	63
6	The Theotokos in Byzantine hymnography: typology and allegory *Christian Hannick*	69
7	Use and abuse of the 'image' of the Theotokos in the political life of Byzantium (with special reference to the iconoclast period) *Nike Koutrakou*	77
8	From poetry to liturgy: the cult of the Virgin in the Middle Byzantine era *Niki Tsironis*	91

9	Exchanging embrace. The body of salvation Ioli Kalavrezou	103
10	The symbolism of the censer in Byzantine representations of the Dormition of the Virgin Maria Evangelatou	117
11	The Portaitissa icon at Iveron monastery and the cult of the Virgin on Mount Athos Kriton Chryssochoidis	133

III Female authority and devotion

12	The empress and the Virgin in early Byzantium: piety, authority and devotion Liz James	145
13	Female piety in context: understanding developments in private devotional practices Brigitte Pitarakis	153
14	The eyes of the Mother of God Robin Cormack	167
15	Zoe's lead seal: female invocation to the Annunciation of the Virgin Vasso Penna	175

IV Public and private cult

16	Byzantine domestic art as evidence for the early cult of the Virgin Henry Maguire	183
17	The 'activated' icon: the Hodegetria procession and Mary's *Eisodos* Bissera V. Pentcheva	195
18	Picturing the spiritual protector: from Blachernitissa to Hodegetria Christine Angelidi and Titos Papamastorakis	209
19	The image of the Virgin Zoodochos Pege: two questions concerning its origin Natalia Teteriatnikov	225
20	The cult of the Virgin Zoodochos Pege at Mistra Rhodoniki Etzeoglou	239
21	The Virgin, the Christ-child and the evil eye Vassiliki Foskolou	251
22	Praying for the salvation of the empire? Maria Vassilaki	263

V Between East and West

23	Thoughts on Mary east and west *Annemarie Weyl Carr*	277
24	The Kahn and Mellon Madonnas and their place in the history of the Virgin and Child Enthroned in Italy and the East *Rebecca W. Corrie*	293
25	Representations of the Virgin in Lusignan Cyprus *Sophia Kalopissi-Verti*	305
26	The legacy of the Hodegetria: holy icons and legends between east and west *Michele Bacci*	321
27	A Byzantine icon of the *dexiokratousa* Hodegetria from Crete at the Benaki Museum *Nano Chatzidakis*	337

Epilogue *Maria Vassilaki*	359
Index	363

List of Illustrations

Colour plates

between the Introduction and Part 1

1. Wadi Natrun, Monastery of the Virgin Mary (so-called Syrian Monastery), Church of the Virgin Mary. *Khurus*, painted column, encaustic. Virgin Mary Galaktotrophousa
2. Rome, S. Maria Maggiore, Cappella Paolina. The Virgin 'Salus Populi Romani'
3a. Rome, S. Maria Maggiore, Cappella Paolina. The Virgin 'Salus Populi Romani' (detail)
3b. Rome, S. Maria Maggiore, Cappella Paolina. The Virgin 'Salus Populi Romani' (detail)
4. Athens, Benaki Museum. Icon of the Lamenting Virgin
5. Rome, Biblioteca Apostolica Vaticana. Rebecca giving birth (late 11th c.)
6. Cyprus, Lagoudera, church of the Virgin Arakiotissa, view of the south wall. Dormition of the Virgin
7. Mt Athos, Holy Monastery of Iveron. Icon of the Virgin 'Portaitissa'
8. Athens, Benaki Museum. Bronze ring (6th–7th c.)
9. Turkey, Aphrodisias, wall painting at the theatre. St Michael (6th c.)
10. Paris, Bibliothèque nationale. Zoe's lead seal (11th c.)
11. Poreč, Basilica of Eufrasius. Apse mosaic. The Virgin and Child with bishop Eufrasius and the child Eufrasius (detail)
12a. Ohrid, church of St Clement (the Virgin Peribleptos). Two-sided icon: front side, the Virgin Hodegetria
12b. Ohrid, church of St Clement (the Virgin Peribleptos). Two-sided icon: back side, the Crucifixion
13. Cyprus, Paphos, Enkleistra of St Neophytos (late 12th c.). St Stephen the Younger holding the icon of the Virgin
14. Cyprus, Trikomo, church of the Virgin. Apse conch
15. Mistra, church of the Hodegetria (Aphendiko). The Virgin Zoodochos Pege
16. Aigina, Omorphi Ekklesia (1289). The Nativity
17. The Freising 'Lukasbild'
18a. The Freising 'Lukasbild' (detail)
18b. Mt Athos, Pantokrator monastery. Detail from a two-sided icon of the Virgin and Child

19	Cyprus, Kalopanagiotis, Monastery of St John Lampadistes, Icon Museum. Diptych; *Pietà* (detail)	
20	Washington, National Gallery of Art. Enthroned Madonna and Child (13th c.)	
21	Asinou, church of the Virgin Phorbiotissa. Narthex, south conch	
22	Calabria, Polistena, parish church. Panel of the *Madonna dell'Itria* (c. 1530)	
23	Athens, Benaki Museum. Icon of the Virgin Hodegetria *dexiokratousa*, with the Deesis and Saints on the border (after conservation)	
24a	Christ, detail of Plate 23	
24b	The Angel on the right, detail of Plate 23	

Black and white illustrations

1.1	Alexandria, Kom el-Dikka, House D. Mary enthroned	10
1.2	Karanis, House B50. Watercolour from the original mural. Isis and Harpocrates	10
1.3	Berlin, Staatliche Museen, Ägyptisches Museum. Isis	11
1.4	The J. Paul Getty Museum. Panel with painted image of Isis	11
1.5	Dakhleh Oasis, Kellis, temple of Tutu. Isis	11
2.1	Cairo, Coptic Museum. Monastery of Apa Jeremiah, Saqqara, Cell A, east wall, secco. Virgin Mary Galaktotrophousa	20
2.2	Wadi Natrun, Monastery of the Virgin Mary (so-called Syrian Monastery), Church of the Virgin Mary. *Khurus*, painted column, encaustic. Virgin Mary Galaktotrophousa	21
2.3	Dendera, Temple Complex of Hathor. *Mammisi* (Birth House) of Nero and Trajan (c. 1st – early 2nd c.). General view of the south-west side	22
2.4	Dendera, Temple Complex of Hathor. *Mammisi* (Birth House) of Nero and Trajan (c. 1st – early 2nd c.). Nursing Scene	22
3.1	Rome, S. Maria Nova. Icon of the Virgin with Christ-child	42
3.2	Rome, view of the Forum Romanum	43
3.3	Rome, drawing of the Pantheon	43
3.4	Rome, Pantheon. Icon of the Virgin with Christ-child	44
3.5	Rome, S. Maria Maggiore, Cappella Paolina. The Virgin 'Salus Populi Romani'	45
3.6	Rome, S. Maria Maggiore, Cappella Paolina. The Virgin 'Salus Populi Romani' (detail)	46
3.7	Rome, S. Maria Maggiore, Cappella Paolina. The Virgin 'Salus Populi Romani' (detail)	46
3.8	Rome, S. Maria in Trastevere, Cappella Altemps. The *Madonna della Clemenza*	47
3.9	Rome, S. Maria del Rosario, Monte Mario. The *Madonna Advocata*	48
3.10	Rome, S. Maria in Aracoeli. The Madonna *Advocata*	49
4.1	Nicaea (Iznik), Koimesis church. Apse mosaic. Standing Theotokos (late 7th, 8th and 9th c.)	57

4.2	Nicaea (Iznik), Koimesis church. Mosaic in the bema. Angels (late 7th and 9th c.)	58
4.3	Nicaea (Iznik), Koimesis church. Mosaic in the bema. Angels (late 7th and 9th c.)	58
4.4	Nicaea (Iznik), Koimesis church. Mosaic in the bema. *Hetoimasia* (late 7th c.)	59
8.1	Constantinople, Hagia Sophia, the apse mosaic. The Virgin enthroned with Christ-child	100
8.2	Athens, Benaki Museum. Icon of the Lamenting Virgin	101
8.3	Cappadocia, Tokalı kilise, wall painting with the Virgin Eleousa	101
8.4	Phokis, Monastery of Hosios Loukas, narthex. The Crucifixion	102
9.1	Rome, S. Maria ad Martyres. Icon of the Virgin and Child	110
9.2	Moscow, Tretyakov Gallery. Icon of the Virgin of Vladimir (12th c.)	110
9.3	Nerezi, Church of St Panteleemon. Fresco of the scene of the Threnos (1164)	111
9.4	Kastoria, Byzantine Museum. Two-sided icon with the Man of Sorrows and the Virgin Hodegetria (12th c.)	111
9.5	Rome, Biblioteca Apostolica Vaticana. Rebecca giving Birth (late 11th c.)	112
9.6	St Petersburg, The State Hermitage Museum. Ivory diptych with the Crucifixion and the Koimesis (12th c.)	113
9.7	Ravenna, Museo Nazionale. Ivory diptych with the Nativity and the Deposition and Threnos (12th c.)	113
9.8	London, private collection. Ivory panel icon with four scenes: Crucifixion, Threnos, Anastasis, Koimesis	114
9.9	Mt Sinai, Monastery of St Catherine. Icon of the Virgin and Child (detail) (mid-12th c.)	115
10.1	Cyprus, Lagoudera, church of the Virgin Arakiotissa, view of the south wall. Upper register: Dormition of the Virgin. Lower register: Virgin and Child and Archangel Michael	126
10.2	Cyprus, Lagoudera, church of the Virgin Arakiotissa. Dormition of the Virgin; officiating hierarch holding a censer (detail)	127
10.3	Mt Sinai, Monastery of St Catherine. Miniature with the Dormition of the Virgin	127
10.4	Mt Sinai, Monastery of St Catherine. Icon with the Dormition of the Virgin	128
10.5	Mt Sinai, Monastery of St Catherine. Icon with the Dormition of the Virgin	129
10.6	Mt Sinai, Monastery of St Catherine. Icon with the Dormition of the Virgin; officiating hierarch holding a censer (detail)	129
10.7	Cyprus, Lagoudera, church of the Virgin Arakiotissa, view of the dome	130
10.8	Cyprus, Lagoudera, church of the Virgin Arakiotissa. The Annunciation; the Virgin (detail)	130
10.9	Kastoria, church of the Virgin Mavriotissa. Icon with the Dormition of the Virgin	131

11.1	Mt Athos, Holy Monastery of Iveron. Icon of the Virgin 'Portaitissa'	142
13.1	Athens, Benaki Museum. Bronze ring (6th–7th c.)	163
13.2	Bulgaria, Silistra. Bronze pectoral reliquary cross (11th c.)	163
13.3	Washington, DC, Dumbarton Oaks Collection. Gold reliquary cross (9th–10th c.)	164
13.4	Washington, DC, Dumbarton Oaks Collection. Bronze votive cross (7th c.)	164
13.5	Former A. Veglery Collection. Silver solidus pattern of Constantine VII and Zoe	165
13.6	Paris, Bibliothèque nationale, Cabinet des médailles. Gold ring (7th c.)	165
13.7	Paris, Bibliothèque nationale, Cabinet des médailles. Cameo (7th c.) on obverse and intaglio (10th c.) on reverse	165
13.8	Maastricht, Onze Lieve Vrouw. Enkolpion (late 11th–12th c.)	165
13.9	Cambridge, Massachusetts, Fogg Art Museum (on loan to Dumbarton Oaks Collection). Seal of the Sebaste Irene Synadene (12th c.)	166
13.10	Washington, DC, Dumbarton Oaks Collection. Bronze cross (6th–7th c.)	166
14.1	Mt Sinai, Monastery of St Catherine. Icon of the Virgin and Child between Archangels accompanied by two Saints (6th c.)	172
14.2	Turkey, Aphrodisias, wall painting at the theatre. St Michael (6th c.)	173
15.1	Paris, Bibliothèque nationale. Zoe's lead seal. Annunciation and inscription (11th c.)	179
16.1	Washington, DC, Dumbarton Oaks Collection. Gold medallion. Virgin and Child with the Nativity and the Adoration of the Magi	191
16.2	Toronto, Royal Ontario Museum. Silver armband. Virgin and Child	191
16.3	Washington, DC, Dumbarton Oaks Collection. Gold marriage ring. Christ and the Virgin between the groom and the bride	191
16.4	Richmond, Virginia Museum of Fine Arts. Gold marriage ring. Christ between the groom and the bride	191
16.5	London, British Museum. Tapestry-woven medallion. The Adoration of the Magi	192
16.6	New York, The Metropolitan Museum of Art. Tapestry-woven medallion. Scenes from the life of Joseph	192
16.7	Poreč, Basilica of Eufrasius. Apse mosaic. The Virgin and Child with bishop Eufrasius and the child Eufrasius (detail)	193
16.8	Washington, DC, The Textile Museum. Tapestry-woven panel. 'Wealthy woman'	193
17.1	Arta, Blacherna monastery. Tuesday ceremony with the Hodegetria	203

17.2	Washington, DC, Dumbarton Oaks Collection. Seal. Pre-iconoclast visual type of the Virgin (7th c.)	203
17.3	Cambridge, Massachusetts, Fogg Art Museum (on loan to Dumbarton Oaks Collection). Seal, showing the Hodegetria type identified with the name *Nikopoios* (second half of the 11th c.)	203
17.4	Ohrid, church of St Clement (the Virgin Peribleptos). Two-sided icon: front side, the Virgin Hodegetria	204
17.5	Ohrid, church of St Clement (the Virgin Peribleptos). Two-sided icon: back side, the Crucifixion	205
17.6	Vatican City, Biblioteca Apostolica Vaticana, Basil II's *Menologion*. Liturgical procession	206
17.7	Vatican City, Biblioteca Apostolica Vaticana, sermons of James of Kokkinobaphos. The *Eisodos* of Mary	206
17.8	Milan, Museo del Duomo. Ivory book-cover (detail). The *Eisodos* of Mary	207
17.9	Vatican City, Biblioteca Apostolica Vaticana, Basil II's *Menologion*. Presentation of Mary in the Temple	207
18.1	Moscow, State Historical Museum, Khludov Psalter, fol. 86v (9th c.)	218
18.2	Constantinople, Hagia Sophia. South-west vestibule, mosaic lunette over the doorway into the inner narthex (10th c.)	219
18.3	Madrid, National Library. John Tzimiskes' triumph (12th c.)	219
18.4	Sinai, Monastery of St Catherine, Hexaptych (12th c.). The Virgin Blachernitissa (detail of the upper zone)	220
18.5	Cyprus, Paphos, Enkleistra of St Neophytos (late 12th c.). St Stephen the Younger holding the icon of the Virgin	220
18.6	Moscow, Tretyakov Gallery. The Virgin of Vladimir (Constantinople, c. 1130)	221
18.7	Venice, San Marco. The Virgin *Nikopoios* (Constantinople, 12th c.)	221
18.8	London, British Museum. Icon of the Triumph of Orthodoxy (Constantinople, c. 1400)	222
18.9	Skopje, Markov Manastir (14th c.). 23rd stanza of the Akathistos Hymn, procession with the icon of the Virgin Eleousa	223
18.10	Skopje, Markov Manastir (14th c.). 24th stanza of the Akathistos Hymn, procession with the icon of the Virgin Hodegetria	223
19.1	Mistra, church of the Aphendiko. Narthex	234
19.2	Cyprus, Trikomo, church of the Virgin. Apse conch	234
19.3	Istanbul, Archaeological Museum. Marble relief. The Virgin orans	235
19.4	Zacos Collection. Lead seal of the nun Maria	236
19.5	Moscow, Tretyakov Gallery. Jasper cameo	236
19.6	Mt Athos, Hilandar Monastery Treasury. *Panagiarion*	236
19.7	Washington, DC, Dumbarton Oaks Collection. Coin of Andronikos II Palaiologos	236
19.8	Peć, monastery church. East wall of the narthex, lunette above the main door	237
19.9	Istanbul, Kariye Çamii. Narthex, north wall, *arcosolium*	238

20.1	Mistra, church of the Hodegetria (Aphendiko). The Virgin Zoodochos Pege	246
20.2	Mistra, church of the Hodegetria (Aphendiko). The Virgin Zoodochos Pege (detail)	246
20.3	Mistra, church of the Hodegetria (Aphendiko). Sts Anargyroi	246
20.4	Mistra, church of the Hodegetria (Aphendiko). Christ and the woman of Samaria; the Marriage at Cana	247
20.5	Mistra, church of the Hodegetria (Aphendiko). Healing of the man blind from birth; healing of Peter's wife's mother	247
20.6	Mistra, church of the Hodegetria (Aphendiko). Healing of the man with dropsy	248
20.7	Mistra, church of the Hodegetria (Aphendiko). Healing of the paralytic at Bethesda; cure of the woman with issue of blood	248
20.8	Mistra, chapel of Ai-Yannakis. The Virgin Zoodochos Pege	249
20.9	Mistra, church of Sts Theodore. The Virgin Zoodochos Pege	249
21.1	Aigina, Omorphi Ekklesia (1289). The Nativity	259
21.2	Otranto, San Pietro. The Nativity; barking dog (detail) (third quarter of the 13th c.)	259
21.3	Crete, Kouneni, Church of Archangel Michael. The Nativity	260
21.4	Moscow, State Historical Museum, Khludov Psalter	260
21.5	Paris, Bibliothèque nationale, Homilies of James of Kokkinobaphos. 'How the Virgin was preserved unharmed from the weapons of evil by an unseen power'	261
21.6	Egypt, Bawīt, Monastery of St Apollo. St Sisinnios piercing a female demon (6th c.)	262
21.7	Paris, Bibliothèque nationale, Cabinet des médailles. Bronze amulet. The Holy Rider, a female demon and the 'much-suffering eye'	262
22.1	The Freising 'Lukasbild'	271
22.2	The Freising 'Lukasbild'. X-ray photograph	271
22.3	Paris, Musée du Louvre. Département des Objets d'Art, MR 416, fol. 2	272
22.4	The Freising 'Lukasbild' in its baroque setting	273
22.5	Mt Athos, Pantokrator monastery. Detail from a two-sided icon of the Virgin and Child	274
22.6	Moscow, Tretyakov Gallery. Detail from an icon of the Virgin and Child	274
23.1	Cosenza, Cathedral. *Madonna del Pilerio*	287
23.2	Lyon, Bibliothèque municipale. Opening of Song of Songs	288
23.3	Washington, DC, Dumbarton Oaks Collection. Gold nomisma. The empresses Zoe and Theodora	289
23.4	London, British Library. Opening of *Liber Vitae* of New Minster and Hyde Abbey, Winchester	289
23.5	Siena, Museo del Opera del Duomo. Duccio, *Maestà*; Mary from the central panel (detail)	290
23.6	Siena, Palazzo Pubblico. Simone Martini, *Maestà*; Mary (detail)	291

23.7	Kalopanagiotis, Monastery of St John Lampadistes, Icon Museum. Diptych; *Pietà* (detail)	292
23.8	Florence, Accademia. Giovanni da Milano, *Pietà*	292
24.1	Washington, DC, National Gallery of Art. Enthroned Madonna and Child (13th c.)	301
24.2	Washington, DC, National Gallery of Art. Madonna and Child on a Curved Throne (13th c.)	302
24.3	Washington, DC, National Gallery of Art. Enthroned Madonna and Child (13th c.) (detail)	303
24.4	St Petersburg, The State Hermitage Museum. Icon with the Dormition of the Virgin (first half of the 14th c.)	303
25.1	Asinou, church of the Virgin Phorbiotissa. Narthex, east wall	315
25.2	Asinou, church of the Virgin Phorbiotissa. The Virgin Eleousa, in the Paraklesis type	315
25.3	Asinou, church of the Virgin Phorbiotissa. Narthex, south conch	316
25.4	Asinou, church of the Virgin Phorbiotissa. The Virgin of Mercy with donors	316
25.5	Jerusalem, Armenian Patriarchate. The Virgin of Mercy (*della Misericordia*) praying for Prince Vasak and his sons	317
25.6	New York, Pierpont Morgan Library. The Virgin of Mercy with Marshal Ōshin and his sons	317
25.7	Nicosia, Byzantine Museum of the Archbishop Makarios III Foundation. Icon of the enthroned Virgin with a group of Carmelite monks	318
25.8	Nicosia, Byzantine Museum of the Archbishop Makarios III Foundation. Icon of the enthroned Virgin with a family of donors and a dead girl	318
25.9	Mt Sinai, Monastery of St Catherine. Hexaptych; the Virgin Blachernitissa (detail)	319
25.10	Turin, Galleria Sabauda. The Virgin and Child, known as 'Madonna Gualino'	319
25.11	Novoli, church of the Virgin Immacolata. The Virgin and Child	319
26.1	Sardinia, Gavoi, the hill of *sa Itria*. The annual feast day (31 July)	332
26.2	Sardinia, Gavoi, the hill of *sa Itria*. Prehistoric menhir known as *Nostra Signora del Buon Cammino*	332
26.3	Rossano Calabro, Museo Diocesano. Two-sided icon of *Our Lady the Neodigitria*. The Virgin and Child (obverse, late 15th c.)	333
26.4	Rossano Calabro, Museo Diocesano. Two-sided icon of *Our Lady the Neodigitria*. The Crucifixion (reverse)	333
26.5	Padua, Benedictine Abbey of S. Giustina. Icon of the *Madonna Costantinopolitana* (late 13th c.)	334
26.6	Agrigento, Cathedral. Fresco of the *Madonna dell'Itria* (late 14th c.)	334
26.7	Calabria, Polistena, parish church. Panel of the *Madonna dell'Itria* (c. 1530)	335

26.8 Umbria, Bugian Piccolo, parish church.
Panel of the *Madonna di Costantinopoli* (early 17th c.) — 335
26.9 Messina, church of S. Caterina di Valverde
(from the church of Santissima Trinità).
A. Riccio, *Madonna di Costantinopoli*, oil on canvas (*c.* 1570) — 336
26.10 Engraving with the icon of the *Madonna d'Itria* church
in Messina (17th c.) — 336

27.1 Athens, Benaki Museum. Icon of the Virgin Hodegetria
dexiokratousa with the Deesis and Saints on the border
(before conservation) — 351
27.2 Athens, Benaki Museum. Icon of the Virgin Hodegetria
dexiokratousa with the Deesis and Saints on the border
(after conservation) — 352
27.3 Christ, detail of Fig. 27.2 — 353
27.4 The Angel on the right, detail of Fig. 27.2 — 353
27.5 St Peter, detail of Fig. 27.2 — 354
27.6 St John Chrysostom, detail of Fig. 27.2 — 354
27.7 St Basil, detail of Fig. 27.2 — 354
27.8 St Gregory the Theologian, detail of Fig. 27.2 — 354
27.9 Cyprus, Hagios Theodoros.
Icon of the Virgin Hodegetria *dexiokratousa* — 355
27.10 Bari, Pinacoteca Provinciale. Icon of the Virgin Hodegetria — 355
27.11 Padua, S. Giustina.
Icon of the Virgin *dexiokratousa*, *Madonna Costantinopolitana* — 355
27.12 Cyprus, formerly in the church of St Chrysostomos Koutsovendis.
Icon of the Virgin *Faneromeni* — 355
27.13 Crete, Kritsa, Panagia Kera, wall painting. Christ from the Deesis. — 356
27.14 Crete, Kritsa, Panagia Kera, wall painting.
Angel from the Prayer of Joachim. — 356
27.15 Crete, Kritsa, Panagia Kera, wall painting. Unidentified saint — 356
27.16 Crete, Kritsa, Panagia Kera, wall painting.
St Anne holding the Virgin — 356

E1 The 'Hodegetria' football team. At the training grounds — 361
E2 The 'Hodegetria' football team. In the dressing room — 361

List of Contributors

Christine Angelidi, Research Professor, Institute for Byzantine Research, National Hellenic Research Foundation, Athens
Michele Bacci, Associate Professor of Iconography and Iconology, University of Siena
Charles Barber, Associate Professor of the History of Art, University of Notre Dame, Notre Dame, IN
Elizabeth S. Bolman, Associate Professor, Tyler School of Art, Temple University, Philadelphia, PA
Averil Cameron, Warden, Keble College, Oxford
Annemarie Weyl Carr, Distinguished Professor of Art History, Southern Methodist University, Dallas, TX
Nano Chatzidakis, Professor in Byzantine Archaeology, University of Ioannina, Greece
Kriton Chryssochoidis, Research Professor, Institute for Byzantine Research, National Hellenic Research Foundation, Athens
Robin Cormack, Professor in the History of Art, Courtauld Institute of Art, University of London
Rebecca W. Corrie, Phillips Professor of the History of Art, Bates College, Lewiston, ME
† **Michel van Esbroeck**, Professor of Philology of the Christian East, Ludwig Maximilian University of Munich
Rhodoniki Etzeoglou, Ministry of Culture, Greece
Maria Evangelatou, Independent Scholar, Athens
Vassiliki Foskolou, Independent Scholar, Athens
Christian Hannick, Professor of Slavic Philology, University of Würzburg
Liz James, Reader in the History of Art, University of Sussex
Ioli Kalavrezou, Dumbarton Oaks Professor of Byzantine Art, Harvard University
Sophia Kalopissi-Verti, Professor in Byzantine Archaeology, University of Athens
Nike Koutrakou, Faculty Adviser and in charge of the Art and History Programme, NATO Defense College, Rome
Henry Maguire, Professor of the History of Art, Johns Hopkins University, Baltimore, MD
Thomas F. Mathews, John Langeloth Loeb Professor of the History of Art, Institute of Fine Arts, New York University
Norman Muller, Conservator, Princeton University Art Museum, Princeton, NJ
Titos Papamastorakis, Assistant Professor of the History of Art, University of the Aegean
Vasso Penna, Teaching Fellow in Byzantine History, University of Peloponnese
Bissera V. Pentcheva, Assistant Professor, Stanford University, Stanford, CA

Brigitte Pitarakis, Researcher, Centre d'histoire et civilisation de Byzance, CNRS-Collège de France

Natalia Teteriatnikov, Curator of Byzantine Photograph and Fieldwork Archives, Dumbarton Oaks

Niki Tsironis, Researcher, Institute for Byzantine Research, National Hellenic Research Foundation, Athens

Maria Vassilaki, Associate Professor of the History of Byzantine Art, University of Thessaly and Benaki Museum, Athens

Gerhard Wolf, Director, Kunsthistorisches Institut, Max-Planck-Institut, Florence

Foreword

Angelos Delivorrias

Although the Millennium celebrations passed untroubled by the shadows of the ominous events to come – these emerged only later – the year 2000 was to set a decisive mark on the dark landscape of the new era. Yet we should not forget that this was also the year in which Greece experienced two events of deep spiritual significance, two safeguards of its pre-postmodern humanitarian values: the inauguration of the renovated Benaki Museum and the superb 'Mother of God' exhibition. While the remodelling of the Museum's Greek collections aimed at a dynamic presentation of the cultural parameters of the past, emphasizing the vital role of historical memory in enabling us to 'know ourselves' today, the 'Mother of God' exhibition ventured to broadcast a message of consolation, a message which I would call universal in its scope. For the sanctity of motherhood, the supreme symbolic expression of human feeling, far transcends the time and space of Byzantium and the specific landmarks of Christian iconography to touch such chords of sensitivity as may still vibrate in the globalized conditions of today's world.

To the receptive, or rather the informed visitor, the international character of the exhibition must have been evident from the selection of material on display, which contained a wealth of objects representing countries from all over the world. This international aspect was also to the fore in the associated 'Mother of God' conference, in whose papers the sensitive reader may look beyond the immediate justification of specialized scholarship and perceive the ecumenical dimension of a subject which transcends specific issues and activates intellectual processes of a different order. If the publication of the exhibition catalogue by Skira Editori fulfilled the hopes of the organizers for the diffusion of its message beyond the frontiers of Greece, the involvement of Ashgate Publishing Ltd in this edition of the conference proceedings is a vindication of the spirit which animated the entire enterprise at its deepest level.

On behalf of the Trustees of the Benaki Museum I would like to express thanks to Maria Vassilaki for supervising the preparation of this volume with the dedication and sense of responsibility that she brings to every task she undertakes; also to Yannis Varalis for editorial assistance and for compiling the index, to Panorea Benatou for secretarial support and the handling of the photographic material, to Maria Kretsi for word-processing and to John Avgherinos for translating the articles written in Greek. Averil Cameron deserves a special mention for her willingness to take on the writing of the introduction, as does Evangelos Chrysos for hosting the conference at the Hellenic National Research Foundation in accordance with the wishes of the late Nicolas Oikonomides. Gratitude is naturally due to all those who attended the conference, the speakers who played an active role in its proceedings, and especially the authors of the papers included in the present volume. But most of all I would like to thank Ashgate for this fruitful collaboration with the Benaki Museum, and specifically John Smedley, who ungrudgingly shouldered the burden of the editorial process, and contributed immeasurably to the quality of the final product.

Preface

Evangelos Chrysos

When an institution such as the Benaki Museum – whose position at the forefront of Greek cultural life has recently been recognized with the award of a prize from the Academy of Athens – collaborates with the Hellenic National Research Foundation, something remarkable may be expected. And 'remarkable' is the word I would use to describe the 'Mother of God' conference – an academic forum which took place against the background of the magnificent exhibition with the same title. It reflects the high aesthetic and academic sensibilities and the scholarly acumen of the organizers who arranged the programme, complemented by the intellectual distinction of the scholars from far and near who accepted the invitation to take part in the colloquium and place on record the distillation of their research.

This tribute to the organizers of the conference represents the public acknowledgement of a debt which can be expressed freely and unstintingly by the present writer, who did not have the good fortune to make any personal contribution to the preparations; for when I succeeded the late Nicolas Oikonomides as Director of the Institute for Byzantine Research the basic concept, the choice of topics and of speakers, the sponsorship and the organizational details were virtually complete. For this reason the dedication of the conference was never in doubt. The untimely death of this great scholar, eminent Byzantinist and indefatigable administrator made it unthinkable that the conference, and now this volume, should be dedicated otherwise than to the memory of Nicolas Oikonomides.

Many important conclusions were reached during the conference on particular aspects of Byzantine art history relating to the portrayal of the Virgin Mother and to her glorification through hymnography. The present volume, together with the superb catalogue of the exhibition, provides an authoritative record of the current state of scholarship on all these issues. There are, however, two further topics that I suggest would merit further research, in the wider context of studies dedicated to the Mother of God.

The first of these concerns the clues that may be extracted from representations of the Theotokos as to the perception which Byzantine society held or cultivated regarding the archetypal Woman, Mother, Life-companion and Intercessor. How did they visualize the external form of the ideal woman, what aesthetic predilections are projected by the images of the Mother of God in her various identities as 'Brephokratousa', 'Galaktotrophousa', 'Glykophilousa', 'Virgin Kykkotissa', 'Virgin of the Passion', 'Hodegetria', 'Deomene', 'Platytera' and 'Regina'?

Bishop Theodotos of Ankyra, who played an active role in the Third Ecumenical Council, where the Mother of God was pronounced to be 'truly the Theotokos', described the appearance and the attributes of the Virgin in terms which are clearly indicative of the general sensibilities, moral and aesthetic, of the Byzantines towards the archetypal Woman and Mother, and which indirectly suggest how Mary should be depicted. In the translation of Dr Niki Tsironis a typical passage on the subject reads as follows:

> The Virgin, not casting her eyes to any inappropriate view, not dishonouring her natural beauty by covering colours, not sheathing her cheeks with the fake colour of the Phoenicians, not making conspicuous her honourable head by adding vain ornaments, not making her neck glitter by adding jewellery made of precious stones, not allowing her hands and her feet to be spoiled by golden chains … but full of the smell of the Holy Spirit, being dressed by the Holy Grace as with a garment, keeping the thought of God in her soul, having God as a wreath over her heart, her eyes shining of holiness … her lips dripping wax, beautiful in her way of walking, even more beautiful in her manners and so to speak, all good (ὅλη καλή).

It may be that further study will confirm the proposition that all the manifestations of the central and symbolic figure of the Virgin Mary in Byzantine art are indirect but incontestable evidence of Byzantine criteria of morality and taste regarding the ideal woman.

Secondly, and in the same context, it would be useful to have a comparative study of the depiction of the Theotokos in eastern and western art. The basic guidelines of her portrayal developed in parallel in East and West and scholarship has drawn attention to instances of mutual influence and interdependence. A well-known and appropriate example is the role of the Byzantine princess Theophano, when empress of the Frankish-Saxon Empire, in the introduction and diffusion of the cult and iconography of the Virgin as *bona angelorum imperatrix augusta*. In the words of Krijnie Ciggaar,

> Theophano was raised in a religious ambience where the Virgin was venerated daily. By bringing images of the Virgin to the West and by venerating these she contributed to the popularity of the Virgin Mary in the West. Images were important in the Middle Ages because they carried a message and so the Virgin became a carrier of culture, of Byzantine culture, to the West.

It is a truism that in the West the cult of the Virgin acquired a distinctive form, fundamentally dissociated from honorific veneration, and culminated in the divinization of Mary with the doctrines of the Immaculate Conception and of her corporeal Assumption into heaven. As Konstantinos Kalokyris remarks:

> The East accepted and rehabilitated the female *persona* to the extent of human equality with Christ, and honoured the woman primarily in the fulfilment of her role as mother, while the West went to the limits of sensuality in a manner unknown and unacceptable to Orthodoxy, celebrating her in forms of erotic adoration: for monastic orders it is the Virgin Mary, not the Mother of God, who becomes the symbol of sacred love for the archetypal female.

This is why certain women – often the artist's *inamorata*, as in the case of Lippi, Raphael, Rubens and Titian – with blatant sensual attractions, lent their charms to serve as a model for depictions of the chaste Virgin.

Here we have an example of a situation that the scholar often chances on, and which is indeed one of the delights of scholarship: for while the subject of the 'Mother of God' illuminates the world of Byzantine faith and ideas, the aesthetics and the self-knowledge of the society that created the works of art and used them in their day-to-day devotions, it also reflects our present-day aesthetic, academic and intellectual interests and inclinations. And thus it serves as a mirror to assist us in our own self-understanding.

Acknowledgements

Maria Vassilaki

One of my most pleasant tasks as editor of this volume is to thank all those who have contributed to its preparation. In doing this, I have the formidable responsibility of ensuring not only that no names are omitted, but also that my gratitude is expressed in the most appropriate terms. Dr Yannis Varalis and Panorea Benatou shared with me all the anxieties and the joys involved in such an enterprise. Yannis provided the editorial assistance and I shall never forget the innumerable hours he spent poring over these texts, checking them with his characteristic dedication. He is also responsible for the list of abbreviations and the index. Panorea acted as secretarial assistant and was responsible for all the work of preparing the illustrations for the book. John Avgherinos translated the texts written in Greek and also took an active role in the entire editorial process, reading and re-reading all the papers. With his talent for penetrating to the essence of the texts and evaluating their merits (and also their weaknesses), he was involved with us at every stage of the journey in our efforts to produce the best possible result. His knowledge of Ancient Greek and Latin enabled him to make invaluable comments which contributed towards the faithful rendering of passages from original sources. I believe I am expressing not only my own sentiments but also those of all the authors when I say how fortunate we were to have John dealing with our texts. Maria Kretsi handled the word-processing. This was not the first time that we had worked together, and once again I appreciated her skills, her dedication and her ability to focus her attention on a pile of papers for hours on end without ever losing her cheerful smile. Dr Judith Gilliland translated Christian Hannick's paper from the German, a text with a highly specialized vocabulary. Dr Olga Karageorgiou helped us over certain practical details.

Averil Cameron agreed to write the Introduction. I am especially grateful to her not only for finding a window in her busy timetable to do this, but also for providing such an interesting text on a subject which she knows particularly well.

I must also express my gratitude to the Institute for Byzantine Research, which hosted the 'Mother of God' conference, the fruit of which is the collection of papers included in this volume. It is a tragedy that Nicolas Oikonomides is no longer with us. I shall never forget the alacrity with which he responded to the idea of collaborating on a conference against the background of the 'Mother of God' exhibition. Thanks are due to his successor, Professor Evangelos Chrysos, for his readiness to assume the obligations of the Institute towards the conference and for the warm hospitality with which he received us. All this is fully described in the Preface which he has himself written for this book, for which I am most grateful.

I would especially like to thank the publishers, and in particular John Smedley, for accepting this volume for inclusion in Ashgate's list of publications. They have shared with me the responsibilities of producing a book which is handsome as well as scholarly, and I hope that we have succeeded in this aim.

Finally I should acknowledge my greatest debt, which is to the Director of the Benaki Museum, Professor Angelos Delivorrias, and the Trustees of the Museum, for demonstrating their confidence in me, first over the 'Mother of God' exhibition and then over the conference associated with it. I should also mention their generosity in bearing the greater part of the expenses of this book.

This volume is dedicated to the memory of Nicolas Oikonomides as a small token of recognition for all he contributed while he was with us. His departure leaves a gap that is impossible to fill.

List of Abbreviations

AA	*Archäologischer Anzeiger*
AASS	*Acta Sanctorum*
ActaNorv	*Acta ad Archaeologiam et Artium Historiam Pertinentia, Institutum Romanum Norvegiae*
AD	*Αρχαιολογικόν Δελτίον*
AE	*Αρχαιολογική Εφημερίς*
AnBoll	*Analecta Bollandiana*
ArtB	*Art Bulletin*
BCH	*Bulletin de Correspondance hellénique*
BF	*Byzantinische Forschungen*
BHG	*Bibliotheca Hagiographica Graeca*
BMGS	*Byzantine and Modern Greek Studies*
BollGrott	*Bolletino della Badia Greca di Grottaferrata*
BSl	*Byzantinoslavica*
Byz	*Byzantion*
BZ	*Byzantinische Zeitschrift*
CahArch	*Cahiers archéologiques*
CCSG	*Corpus Christianorum, Series Graeca*
CorsiRav	*Corsi di cultura sull'arte ravennate e bizantina*
CSCO	*Corpus Scriptorum Christianorum Orientalium*
DChAE	*Δελτίον της Χριστιανικής Αρχαιολογικής Εταιρείας*
DOP	*Dumbarton Oaks Papers*
DOS	*Dumbarton Oaks Studies*
EEBS	*Επετηρίς Εταιρείας Βυζαντινών Σπουδών*
EEThSPTh	*Επιστημονική Επετηρίς της Θεολογικής Σχολής του Αριστοτελείου Πανεπιστημίου Θεσσαλονίκης*
EO	*Échos d'Orient*
Hell	*Ελληνικά*
ItMedUm	*Italia medioevale e umanistica*
JbAC	*Jahrbuch für Antike und Christentum*
JEChSt	*Journal of Early Christian Studies*
JÖB	*Jahrbuch der Österreichischen Byzantinistik*
JÖBG	*Jahrbuch der Österreichischen Byzantinistischen Gesellschaft*
JThSt	*Journal of Theological Studies*
JWarb	*Journal of the Warburg and Courtauld Institutes*
KretChron	*Κρητικά Χρονικά*
KyprSp	*Κυπριακαί Σπουδαί*
LCI	*Lexikon der christlichen Ikonographie*, ed. E. Kirschbaum
NE	*Νέος Ελληνομνήμων*

ODB	*Oxford Dictionary of Byzantium*
PG	*Patrologiae Cursus Completus, Series Graeca*, ed. J.-P. Migne
PL	*Patrologiae Cursus Completus, Series Latina*, ed. J.-P. Migne
PLP	E. Trapp (ed.), *Prosopographisches Lexikon der Palaiologenzeit* 1–12 (Wien, 1976–1994)
PO	*Patrologia Orientalis*, eds R. Graffin and F. Nau
PrOC	*Proche-Orient chrétien*
RAC	*Reallexikon für Antike und Christentum*
REArm	*Revue des Études arméniennes*
REB	*Revue des Études byzantines*
RendPontAcc	*Atti della Pontificia accademia romana di archeologia. Rendiconti*
RIASA	*Rivista dell'Istituto Nazionale d'Archeologia e Storia dell'Arte*
RSBN	*Rivista di studi bizantini e neoellenici*
SC	*Sources chrétiennes*
TM	*Travaux & Mémoires*
VTIB	*Veröffentlichungen der Kommission für die Tabula Imperii Byzantini*
VV	*Vizantijskij Vremennik*
ZKirch	*Zeitschrift für Kirchengeschichte*
ZLU	*Zbornik za Likovne Umetnosti*
ZRVI	*Zbornik Radova Vizantološkog Instituta*

Angelidi, 'Un texte patriographique'	Chr. Angelidi, 'Un texte patriographique et édifiant: le "discours narratif" sur les Hodégoi', *REB* 52 (1994), 113–49
Evans and Wixom, *Glory of Byzantium*	H. C. Evans and W. D. Wixom (eds), *The Glory of Byzantium: Art and Culture of the Middle Byzantine Era, A.D. 843–1261*, exh. cat., The Metropolitan Museum of Art (New York, 1997)
Janin, *Églises CP*	R. Janin, *La géographie ecclésiastique de l'empire byzantin, Première partie: Le siège de Constantinople et le patriarchat oecuménique, 3. Les églises et les monastères* (Paris, 1969)
Mango, *Art of the Byz. Empire*	C. Mango, *The Art of the Byzantine Empire, 312–1453* (Englewood Cliffs, NJ, 1972; Toronto, 1986)
Mango, 'Blachernae Shrine'	C. Mango, 'The Origins of the Blachernae Shrine at Constantinople', in *Actes du XIIIe Congrès international d'Archéologie chrétienne* II (Vatican City and Split, 1998), 61–76
Mango, 'Theotokoupolis'	C. Mango, 'Constantinople as Theotokoupolis', in Vassilaki, *Mother of God*, 17–25
Vassilaki, *Mother of God*	M. Vassilaki (ed.), *Mother of God. Representations of the Virgin in Byzantine Art*, exh. cat., Benaki Museum (Milan and Athens, 2000)
Xanthopoulos, *Logos*	Nikephoros Kallistos Xanthopoulos, Περὶ συστάσεως τοῦ σεβασμίου οἴκου τῆς ἐν Κωνσταντινουπόλει Ζωοδόχου Πηγῆς καὶ τῶν ἐν αὐτῷ ὑπερφυῶς τελεσθέντων θαυμάτων, ed. A. Pamperis (Leipzig, 1802)

Introduction

Averil Cameron

The collection of essays in this volume comes at a particularly appropriate moment. Arising from a conference held in January 2001 in association with the important exhibition of representations of the Theotokos at the Benaki Museum, Athens,[1] the present volume takes a wide sweep, both chronologically and also thematically. 'Byzantium' in the title is interpreted to include the whole period of the Byzantine empire from the fourth and especially the fifth century to the end of Constantinople, and including later Orthodox theological and liturgical tradition. It also includes 'western' material from the very important early icons of the Virgin in Rome to the images and cult practices of south Italy and Sicily in late mediaeval and even modern times which show a clear Byzantine inspiration. Equally, while the impetus for the volume came from an exhibition, and thus from visual art – even from a particular form of visual art – the development of the cult of the Virgin must be studied in relation to a range of wider issues, whether historical, textual, liturgical or social, all of which receive treatment here. At the same time the subject of Mary has attracted the attention of other scholars, not least in a volume arising from another conference with a rather different but clearly related scope.[2] Much consideration has also been given to the fifth-century context in which the Virgin became for the first time a real focus of attention, with a number of studies relating to the context of the Council of Ephesus in AD 431, when the Theotokos title became the issue in contention.[3] An international research project has been initiated by Professor Pauline Allen, Dr Leena Mari Peltomaa and others which will collect in a database all references to Mary in the period up to Ephesus, which is indeed the most obscure part of the history of Mary.[4] Further work is planned by Dr Mary Cunningham on the important Marian hymnography and homiletic of the eighth century.[5]

The topic of this volume is therefore of considerable current interest, as well as being of obvious inherent importance, not least because Roman Catholic scholarship accounts for such

---

[1] The catalogue of this exhibition (Vassilaki, *Mother of God*) contains a series of substantial essays and is itself a major contribution to recent scholarship.

[2] R. N. Swanson (ed.), *Mary and the Church* (*Studies in Church History*, forthcoming).

[3] For instance, N. F. Constas, '"Weaving the Body of God": Proclus of Constantinople, the Theotokos and the Loom of the Flesh', *JEChSt* 3.2 (1995), 169–94. Id., *Proclus of Constantinople and the Cult of the Virgin in Late Antiquity* (Leiden, 2003). For the role of Cyril of Alexandria in the controversy, see J. A. McGuckin, *Cyril of Alexandria, The Christological Controversy: its History, Theology and Texts* (Leiden, 1994). L. M. Peltomaa, *The Image of the Virgin Mary in the Akathistos Hymn* (Leiden, 2001) offers a detailed content analysis of the Akathistos hymn and dates it to the period between the Councils of Ephesus (AD 431) and Chalcedon (AD 451). Another notable recent book is S. J. Shoemaker, *Ancient Traditions of the Virgin Mary's Dormition and Assumption* (Oxford, 2002).

[4] See A. M. Cameron, 'The Early Cult of the Virgin', in Vassilaki, *Mother of God*, 3–15.

[5] See also the useful recent volume by B. E. Daley SJ, *On the Dormition of Mary. Early Patristic Homilies* (Crestwood, NY, 1998).

a large percentage of the vast existing bibliography on Mariology. Much progress has been made, but as several contributors point out, there is still a great deal of work to be done on the disentangling of the often difficult and even contradictory evidence. The first puzzle is why Mary was so slow in becoming recognized as a figure of central importance for the early church, or as a figure in her own right: before the later fourth century, references are sparse indeed, and this is all the more strange in comparison with the enormous attention given to the Theotokos in the Byzantine period and her very central role in the Orthodox tradition. It is becoming more and more clear that in the later centuries her role in the earlier period was elaborated, and anachronistic stories and details developed to give her more of a history. This is especially the case with the late sources spelling out the early history of her robe and girdle at Constantinople and the alleged role of the Empress Pulcheria in relation to the veneration of the Virgin;[6] the same phenomenon is found in connection with the prehistory of the lost Hodegetria icon, which was so important in the life of Constantinople in the Middle Byzantine and Palaiologan periods. The erroneous statements which recur frequently in the scholarly literature show that we have not yet arrived at a full understanding of all these developments, but the essays in this volume and in its predecessor together make a most important contribution, and bring the possibility of a full history of the Theotokos in Byzantium very much nearer.

It is important to recognize the late date at which attention began to be paid to the Virgin as a figure in her own right, as opposed to an essential component in Christological argument. This seems to happen very slowly, and to begin to find full expression only with the events surrounding the Council of Ephesus. Earlier Christian writers saw the importance of Mary in relation to Christ, and also to Eve, but so far as we can tell it seems to be with Ambrose (d. 397) and others from the later fourth century that she begins to be assigned a more central role. In part this is in the context of the controversies about asceticism and the virginal life. However, in Syriac literature Ephrem (d. 373) was already foreshadowing the vividly imaginative and poetic approach to the subject of the Virgin which we find in the homilies of Proklos just before the Council of Ephesus. If the Akathistos hymn in its first stage does date from the fifth century, as argued by Leena Mari Peltomaa in her recent book, its context must be this developing discourse about Mary. Its approach can be seen as essentially Christological, with the incorporation of the repeated *chairetismoi* (greetings) to Mary, and it does not develop the scenes of Mary's own childhood which were already expressed in the second-century apocryphal *Protevangelium of James*.[7] Nevertheless the Akathistos later became, as it still is, the touchstone for Orthodox devotion to the Virgin, and this should perhaps lead us not to make too strong a distinction between the Christological and the more emotional and personal aspects of veneration of the Theotokos.

A set of questions raised by several of the contributors to this volume concerns the relation between the public, or 'official', and private elements of the cult of the Virgin, and the relation between doctrine and personal devotion. I would suggest that the balance varies within the time limits set by the volume, and indeed according to the surviving evidence. But religious history is

---

[6] See L. James in this volume, 145–152. Angelidi, 'Un texte patriographique'. Ead., *Pulcheria. La castità al potere (c.399–c.455)* (Milan, 1998). A. M. Cameron, 'The Cult of the Virgin in Late Antiquity: Religious Development and Myth-making', in Swanson, *Mary and the Church*.

[7] For which see J. K. Elliott, *The Apocryphal New Testament* (Oxford, 1993).

dynamic and not static, and does not depend on a single factor at any particular time. Thus, important as the Council of Ephesus was, it was not the sole critical element in the development of veneration of the Theotokos, for, as Michel van Esbroeck has shown, there was regional variety in the development of Marian feasts, and the same post-Ephesus period saw the evolution of apocryphal (and hardly Christological) accounts of the 'Dormition' or *Koimesis* of Mary in the set of texts known as the *Transitus Mariae*. It was perhaps the possibilities offered by the secure position of Christianity in the empire from the later fourth and fifth centuries as much as the particular doctrinal concerns culminating in the clash between Cyril of Alexandria and Nestorios at Ephesus which allowed and encouraged the rich and varied developments in attention to Mary which we see more clearly in the sixth century and later. By that time, as we learn from the contributions of Henry Maguire and Brigitte Pitarakis, the signs of popular attachment to the Theotokos are becoming as well established as the more 'official' representations on the walls of churches. Similar issues arise at all periods once devotion to the Theotokos is established, and this in itself indicates that we should not be looking for a single explanation for its development. Any history of the cult of the Virgin would have to allow for multiple developments and a high degree of social and regional variety.

The title of this volume carefully refers to 'perceptions of the Theotokos', rather than to her cult, or to her place in the religious history of Byzantium, and this is of course appropriate for a volume which focuses to a large extent on visual art. Nevertheless it encourages us to ask the questions addressed by several contributors about the factors – public, official or private – which caused the Theotokos to assume such a central place in Byzantine religious life, and in the broader development of Orthodoxy. Here we may pause to consider terminology. The term 'cult' is widely used in connection with the Virgin, but it is usually so used without further definition; moreover, as Niki Tsironis rightly points out, it is strictly incorrect, certainly in Orthodox terms. However, historians of late antiquity are used to using the term in relation to saints[8] and it is perhaps legitimate to use it here in this sense, while certainly implying veneration rather than actual worship. But we are in need of a more nuanced definition of what is meant by 'cult'. The term 'devotion', currently much used in relation to the Theotokos, seems to indicate something personal rather than Christological or doctrinal, but this term too is usually left undefined. Maguire's use of 'private' and 'public' avoids some of the problems while leaving the term 'public' in need of closer analysis. That would take us into the question of how Byzantine religious life actually worked in the context of the Byzantine state, and what factors were key in encouraging specific developments. We see some of these issues illustrated during the iconoclast period, as set out in the contribution by Nike Koutrakou, and Niki Tsironis interestingly points to the importance in Orthodox theology of popular reception, demonstrated in liturgical expression. A study of the role of the Theotokos against these backgrounds would constitute a different kind of endeavour, and this volume demonstrates how exciting that could be.

Related to the issue of public versus private is the question of the relation between the cult of the Theotokos and women's piety. After all, since the Virgin was held out as a model for all women (albeit an unattainable one) it seems reasonable to ask how women reacted, or even to

---

[8] Cf. P. Brown, *The Cult of the Saints. Its Rise and Function in Latin Christianity* (Chicago, 1981).

assume that she had a special appeal for women. The same assumption has been made in relation to icon veneration in a more general sense,[9] and if that connection has validity, then surely it would be even more likely that women would be drawn to the Theotokos. After all, apart from the obvious gender connection, women in traditional societies belonged to the private sphere, from which we have a good deal of evidence of devotion to the Theotokos. However, Brigitte Pitarakis and Henry Maguire both show how difficult it is to argue from this evidence to an unequivocal position about female attitudes to the Virgin. If stories about the Virgin's intervention often feature women,[10] just as women appear in iconophile texts as fervent iconophiles, we cannot take them simply at face value without considering the agendas operating in the relevant texts; equally, for every story about the Virgin involving a woman there is at least one involving a man. On another note, it is interesting that the 'feminine' weaving imagery applied to the Virgin in the fifth-century homily of Proklos is the work of a male writer who belonged to the top of the church hierarchy.[11] Some women were of course themselves empresses, or belonged to the imperial family of the day. Liz James ably argues in this volume against the assumption that Byzantine empresses as a class were somehow specially devoted to the Theotokos; nevertheless some may well have been, and others will naturally have included the Theotokos in their patronage of churches or their commissioning of objects. Only occasionally do we have specific information about the personal religious attachments of individual empresses. That did not stop Byzantine writers from ascribing such sentiments or acts of patronage to them, as we have seen in the case of Pulcheria. Another case is the Empress Sophia, wife of Justin II (565–578), who is credited by the Latin panegyrist Corippus with a long prayer to the Virgin, perhaps because this was thought appropriate for her as empress, following her husband's prayer to God.[12] At the same time it is not surprising if individual empresses, like their husbands, showed favour or even enthusiasm for what was increasingly established as a central part of Byzantine religious life; Irene, for example, was associated with the monastery of the Virgin on Prinkipo, where she was banished in 802 and later buried, and restored the church of the Virgin *tes Peges* in Constantinople, and Theodora (830–842) was a regular visitor to the Blachernai church of the Theotokos.[13] Finally, Judith Herrin has connected the rising cult of the Virgin with an 'imperial feminine' on which empresses could draw for their authority and legitimacy.[14] The relation of empresses with the cult of the Virgin in Byzantium could therefore be ambiguous, which is perhaps what one would have expected. Conversely, it has also been argued that the different development of the Virgin's cult in East and West, and in particular her portrayal in icons, was influenced by the existence of an empress in Byzantium, affording a rival queenly model.[15] In this regard the very early Roman icons of Mary discussed

---

[9] See however R. Cormack, 'Women and Icons, and Women in Icons', in L. James (ed.), *Women, Men and Eunuchs. Gender in Byzantium* (London, 1997), 24–51, esp. 31–8.
[10] For some of these, see Cameron, 'The Cult of the Virgin in Late Antiquity'.
[11] See Constas, 'Weaving the Body of God'.
[12] Corippus, *In Laudem Iustini Augusti Minoris*, ed. and tr. A. M. Cameron (London, 1976), II.47–71: Sophia goes to a church of the Virgin to pray before Justin's coronation and seems to pray standing before an icon (II.50: 'ante pios vultus expansis ... palmis').
[13] See J. Herrin, *Women in Purple. Rulers of Medieval Byzantium* (London, 2001), 104–5, 193; cf. also ead., 'The Imperial Feminine in Byzantium', *Past and Present* 169 (2000), 3–35, at 25–8.
[14] Herrin, *Women in Purple*, 241–3; ead., 'The Imperial Feminine'.
[15] Herrin, 'The Imperial Feminine', 14–18.

by Gerhard Wolf would mainly conform to the 'eastern' model, in which Mary is not depicted in imperial dress but with a simple robe and veil covering her head. On the other hand there are examples of the enthroned Virgin from both East and West.[16] It remains true that the West did not see the vast growth in iconic depictions of the Virgin that took place in Byzantium, and in fact one might suggest that the latter may possibly have drawn benefit from the continued role of the empress in the Byzantine state and society.

Whatever exact date should be attributed to the Akathistos hymn, it is clear that hymns and invocations to the Virgin as well as the first stages of liturgical development existed at an early stage in tandem with the doctrinal debates. Moreover the basic doctrinal issues surrounding the Virgin were settled at the Council of Ephesus, so that the subsequent path was clear for developments in iconography, liturgy, church building and general consciousness. This is indeed what seems to have taken place, to judge from our evidence, by and during the sixth century, so that even if we were to agree with Leslie Brubaker and Bissera Pentcheva[17] that the cult of icons and the special association of icons of the Theotokos with Constantinople belong only later, even after iconoclasm, it is clear that the Virgin had already acquired a role in religious consciousness quite different from what had been the case in the early centuries of Christianity. One of the most intriguing and difficult current problems for the scholar of Marian development in Byzantium is to match up the evidence of practical religion – belief and liturgy – with that for public cult and with what is known or can be deduced about the great surviving Marian icons. Different though often overlapping layers have to be investigated, from the pattern of regular liturgical life in ordinary churches and monasteries, with the evidence of the *theotokaria*, to the public rituals of Middle and Late Constantinople centring on the Hodegetria icon.[18] It is difficult in itself to put such disparate and often sparse evidence together, and especially so when so many of the necessary sources still even now lack critical treatment. As for the essential evidence from homiletic and poetry, especially hymnography, this has only recently begun to be appreciated as contributing in an important way towards the overall development of attention to the Theotokos.[19] But this may also be one of the perhaps rare cases when the rule of *lex orandi, lex credendi*, i.e. that doctrine follows the existing practice of faith, does not hold, at any rate for the early stages, for as Henry Maguire notes in his contribution, there certainly was, in the circumstances of Byzantium as a Christian state, a strong impetus from the top in such matters at

---

[16] On these issues see R. Cormack, 'The Mother of God in Apse Mosaics', in Vassilaki, *Mother of God*, 91–105 at 93; with J.-M. Spieser, 'Impératrices romaines et chrétiennes', in *Mélanges Gilbert Dagron, TM* 14 (2002), 593–604.

[17] See L. Brubaker, 'Icons before Iconoclasm?', in *Morfologie sociali culturali in Europa fra tarda antichità e alto medioevo*, Settimane di studio del Centro italiano di studi sull'alto Medioevo 45 (Spoleto, 1998), 1215–54. B. V. Pentcheva, 'The Supernatural Protector of Constantinople: the Virgin and her Icons in the Tradition of the Avar Siege', *BMGS* 26 (2002), 2–41.

[18] In addition to the contributions here and in Vassilaki, *Mother of God*, see N. P. Ševčenko, 'Icons in the Liturgy', *DOP* 45 (1991), 45–57. Ead., 'Servants of the Holy Icon', in C. Moss and K. Kiefer (eds), *Byzantine East, Latin West. Studies in Honor of Kurt Weitzmann* (Princeton, NJ, 1995), 547–53. On icons in processions see especially G. Wolf, below, and Pentcheva, 'The Supernatural Protector of Constantinople', 15–22, denying the possibility of Marian icon processions in Constantinople until after iconoclasm.

[19] See N. Tsironis below, with her PhD thesis, 'The Lament of the Virgin Mary from Romanos the Melode to George of Nicomedia: an Aspect of the Development of Marian Cult', King's College, London, 1998. P. Allen, 'Severus of Antioch and the Homily: the End of the Beginning?', in P. Allen and E. Jeffreys (eds), *The Sixth Century: End or Beginning?* (*Byzantina Australiensia*, 10) (Brisbane, 1996), 163–75, at 165–74 (seeing a 'blend

various times. That interaction, of 'official' policy and individual piety, is difficult for scholars to grasp adequately from the disparate material available, and yet it is one of the factors which make the history of the Theotokos in Byzantium so fascinating.

In the textual evidence we find many traces of the imaginative and emotional attitude to icons which was typical of Byzantium. Icons were often believed to be active; they could cure, or perform miracles, or defend themselves against arrows or other attack. They also had the power of movement, and could fly from one place to another for safety or should a need arise, as is illustrated by the supposed exploits of the Madonna di S. Sisto and of the Hodegetria retold here by Gerhard Wolf and Michele Bacci. These projections onto famous icons of very human wishes and fears are paralleled by the many tales and claims concerning old or miraculous icons which attached themselves in later centuries to places as far apart as Palestine and south Italy. These cannot be ascribed to the 'official' sphere, and nor can the spread of the Constantinopolitan tradition of the Virgin's saving of the city when under siege into the mediaeval collections of Marian miracles, as described by Bacci. Stories of Mary miracles had started much earlier, in the context of the miracles of saints and in the need to fill out in the warmth of the imagination the bare details of Christian doctrine. Significantly, icons of the Virgin occupied a major role in the lists of miraculous images which were drawn up in the ninth century under the impetus of the experience of iconoclasm.[20] We should think of the Virgin's fame, and that of her images, as spreading even more luxuriantly after iconoclasm, with the stories becoming ever more complex and more imaginative – Nike Koutrakou aptly writes of the 'inventiveness' of the Byzantines in this regard; indeed this very luxuriance of imagination is one of Byzantium's characteristic but unsung achievements. The important role of emotion in the Byzantine reaction to the Mother of God in literature, art and piety has been emphasized in a well-known paper by Ioli Kalavrezou,[21] and this accounts a great deal for the attraction today of icons of the Theotokos. It was combined however with a doctrinal and theological discourse of considerable complexity, without which many icons cannot be fully expounded or appreciated. Giving due weight to both these aspects of the role of the Theotokos in Byzantium is the challenge to which the contributors to this volume have risen so admirably.

---

of formal and "popular" theology' in the Marian homilies of Severus). M. B. Cunningham, 'The Mother of God in Early Byzantine Homilies', *Sobornost* 10.2 (1988), 53–67. Ead., 'The Meeting of the Old and the New: the Typology of Mary the Theotokos in Byzantine Homilies and Hymns', in Swanson, *The Church and Mary*.

[20] See for these lists Ch. Walter, 'Iconographical Considerations', in J. A. Munitiz, J. Chrysostomides, E. Harvalia-Crook and Ch. Dendrinos, *The Letter of the Three Patriarchs to Emperor Theophilos and Related Texts* (Camberley, 1997), li–lxxviii, with J. Munitiz, 'Wonder-working Icons in the Letter to Theophilus', in L. Garland (ed.), *Conformity and Non-conformity in Byzantium, Papers given to the 8th Conference of the Australian Association of Byzantine Studies*, BF 24 (1997), 115–23.

[21] I. Kalavrezou, 'Images of the Mother. When the Virgin Mary became *Meter Theou*', *DOP* 44 (1990), 165–72; cf. her contribution 'The Maternal Side of the Virgin', in Vassilaki, *Mother of God*, 41–5.

Colour Plates

PLATE 1   Wadi Natrun, Monastery of the Virgin Mary
(so-called Syrian Monastery),
Church of the Virgin Mary. *Khurus*, painted column, encaustic.
Virgin Mary Galaktotrophousa
(source: E. Bolman; courtesy of Karel Innemée)

PLATE 2 Rome, S. Maria Maggiore, Cappella Paolina.
The Virgin 'Salus Populi Romani' (source: G. Wolf)

PLATES 3a, 3b
Rome, S. Maria Maggiore, Cappella Paolina.
The Virgin 'Salus Populi Romani', details
(source: G. Wolf)

PLATE 4   Athens, Benaki Museum, inv. no. 36363.
Icon of the Lamenting Virgin
(source: Benaki Museum)

PLATE 5   Rome, Biblioteca Apostolica Vaticana, MS. gr. 747, fol. 46v. Rebecca giving birth (late 11th c.) (source: Biblioteca Apostolica Vaticana)

PLATE 6 Cyprus, Lagoudera, church of the Virgin Arakiotissa, view of the south wall. Dormition of the Virgin
(source: Sophocleous, *Panagia Arakiotissa*, Pl. 17, b)

PLATE 7 Mt Athos, Holy Monastery of Iveron.
Icon of the Virgin 'Portaitissa'
(source: Holy Monastery of Iveron)

PLATE 8   Athens, Benaki Museum,
inv. no. 11519.
Bronze ring (6th–7th c.)
(source: Benaki Museum)

PLATE 9   Turkey, Aphrodisias,
wall painting at the theatre.
St Michael (6th c.) (source: R. Cormack)

PLATE 10 Paris, Bibliothèque nationale, inv. no. BnF 3233.
Zoe's lead seal (11th c.).
Annunciation (obverse) and inscription (reverse)
(source: J.-Cl. Cheynet)

PLATE 11 Poreč, Basilica of Eufrasius. Apse mosaic.
The Virgin and Child with bishop Eufrasius and
the child Eufrasius (detail)
(source: A. Terry)

PLATE 12a Ohrid, church of St Clement (the Virgin Peribleptos).
Two-sided icon: front side, the Virgin Hodegetria
(source: Vocotopoulos, *Βυζαντινές εικόνες*, Fig. 67)

PLATE 12b Ohrid, church of St Clement (the Virgin Peribleptos).
Two-sided icon: back side, the Crucifixion
(source: Vocotopoulos, *Βυζαντινές εικόνες*, Fig. 68)

PLATE 13 Cyprus, Paphos, Enkleistra of St Neophytos (late 12th c.).
St Stephen the Younger holding the icon of the Virgin
(source: G. Philotheou, Dept. of Antiquities, Cyprus)

PLATE 14　Cyprus, Trikomo, church of the Virgin.
Apse conch
(source: G. Philotheou, Dept. of Antiquities, Cyprus)

PLATE 15　Mistra, church of the Hodegetria (Aphendiko).
The Virgin Zoodochos Pege (source: R. Etzeoglou)

PLATE 16 Aigina, Omorphi Ekklesia (1289).
The Nativity
(source: V. Foskolou)

PLATE 17 The Freising 'Lukasbild'
(source: Munich, Bayerisches Nationalmuseum;
photo: Walter Haberland)

PLATE 18a
The Freising 'Lukasbild' (detail)
(source: Munich,
Bayerisches Nationalmuseum;
photo: Walter Haberland)

PLATE 18b
Mt Athos, Pantokrator monastery.
Detail from a two-sided icon of the
Virgin and Child
(source: Pantokrator monastery)

PLATE 19　Cyprus, Kalopanagiotis,
Monastery of St John Lampadistes, Icon Museum.
Diptych; *Pietà* (detail)
(source: G. Philotheou, Dept. of Antiquities, Cyprus)

PLATE 20   Washington, National Gallery of Art, 1949.7.1.
(1048)/PA. Enthroned Madonna and Child (13th c.).
Gift of Mrs Otto H. Kahn
(Image © Board of Trustees, National Gallery of Art, Washington)

PLATE 21 Asinou, church of the Virgin Phorbiotissa.
Narthex, south conch
(source: S. Kalopissi-Verti)

PLATE 22 Calabria, Polistena, parish church.
Panel of the *Madonna dell'Itria* (*c.* 1530)
(source: M. Bacci)

PLATE 23   Athens, Benaki Museum.
Icon of the Virgin Hodegetria *dexiokratousa* with the
Deesis and Saints on the border (after conservation)
(source: Benaki Museum)

PLATE 24a Christ, detail of Plate 23
(source: Benaki Museum)

PLATE 24b The Angel on the right, detail of Plate 23
(source: Benaki Museum)

I

Early cult and representations

Isis and Mary in early icons

Thomas F. Mathews and Norman Muller

At the start of the exhibition 'Mother of God' there stands the eloquent yet enigmatic Sinai icon of the enthroned Mary – eloquent in the strength of its refined painting style and its quasi-miraculous state of preservation, and enigmatic in its lack of documentation.[1] Nothing is known of its place of manufacture, the patron who commissioned it, or its original destination – that is, the setting where it was meant to be used.

In the Orthodox world the cult of icons has had two principal settings. One is the church building where the Divine Liturgy is always preceded by a pre-liturgy of icon veneration. On arriving in church, the faithful begin their devotions by making a circuit of the icons, which they venerate according to ancient tradition with *proskynesis* (reverential bowing) and *aspasmos* (kissing and touching). Before some icons they light candles. When the official liturgy begins, the priest seals the people's icon veneration with incense, making his own tour of the icons on the templon screen and elsewhere in the church.[2] The second setting is domestic. Whether in the mansions of the wealthy or the cabins of the lowly, everyone had a corner for the display and veneration of icons, where they performed the same rituals as in church: *proskynesis*, *aspasmos*, candle lighting, incense.

Since Ernst Kitzinger's fundamental study of the rise of icons, the church setting has been given priority,[3] but I believe that historically the development of Christian icon use started in the home, where it had the weight of a centuries-old pagan tradition of icon cult behind it. The earliest references to Christian icon cult – in the *Acts of John* and Irenaeus' *Against the Heresies* in the second century and in Eusebios in the early fourth – all situate the practice in the home and mention its pagan precedents.[4] The veneration of icons in church represented the intrusion of private cult into the official ecclesiastical realm, where it came into sharp conflict with the primary business of community worship. Originally the Divine Liturgy had nothing to do with painted images but consisted basically of (1) instruction by reading and preaching, and (2) communion by commemorating the Last Supper. Eusebios asserts that icons are 'banished and excluded from churches all over the world'.

The Sinai Mother of God, flanked by angels, sits on a gilded throne, magenta-cushioned and ornamented with pearls and jewels, with a footstool attached. While the military guards who flank her stare boldly at us, Mary refuses eye contact and looks slightly to our right. Her child sits on her left thigh with his feet on her right. While documentation is lacking on the place of

---

[1] See Vassilaki, *Mother of God*, no. 1, 262–3 (R. Cormack).
[2] Th. F. Mathews, 'The Sequel to Nicaea II in Byzantine Church Decoration', *Perkins Journal of Theology* 41.3 (1988), 11–21, repr. in id., *Art and Architecture in Byzantium and Armenia* (Aldershot, 1995), XII.
[3] E. Kitzinger, 'The Cult of Icons in the Age before Iconoclasm', *DOP* 8 (1954), 83–150.
[4] Th. F. Mathews, 'The Emperor and the Icon', *ActaNorv* 15 (2001), 167–8.

manufacture of this magisterial painting, its find spot in Sinai is itself important evidence. Weitzmann wanted to link the painting to Constantinople, but Sinai is geographically much closer to Alexandria, Bawīṭ and the Fayyūm, and in the early Byzantine period Sinai was intimately tied to the church in Egypt.[5]

To investigate the origins of Marian icons one must turn to Egypt. It is in Egypt that the term 'Theotokos' first appears as an Alexandrine *theologoumenon* for the mystery of the Incarnation.[6] Popularized by Origen, it was vindicated by Cyril of Alexandria and became the foundation of the dogma of the two natures in Christ. Moreover, behind this Christian cult of the Theotokos lies the rich Egyptian background of the cult of Isis, from whom Mary took the title Theotokos. Isis had been called both the 'Mother of the God', meaning the mother of the divine Horos (Harpocrates), and the 'Great Virgin'. By Late Antiquity Isis had become the most widely venerated divinity of the Graeco-Roman world as she was gradually identified with the most popular and most powerful goddesses of the whole Mediterranean, from the Magna Mater to Aphrodite (Venus) to Tyche (Fortuna). Witt talks of Isis' identification with Mary as the last in a series.[7] But whether one describes Mary as another manifestation of Isis, or a competitor of Isis who had to assume her attributes in order to win over her followers, it is clear that Christian churchmen found reasons to appropriate popular Isiac language and practice for their own purposes.[8]

They also appropriated her imagery. Early icons present important evidence of the Isis–Mary continuity, which has not yet been properly evaluated. In the earliest icons of Mary of the sixth century, the virgin of Nazareth was given the look of Isis, as witnessed by surviving icons of the great goddess, dated to the second and third centuries. A number of archaeological facts can be strung together to connect the two.

First is the fact that in the Late Antique house 'D' in Kom el-Dikka, Alexandria, Mieczysław Rodziewicz discovered a wall painting (Fig. 1.1), which, however fragmentary, has much in common with the Sinai icon.[9] The painting was situated in the principal hallway of an extensive multi-storeyed house, which included workshops for the production of ivory and bone carvings of traditional Dionysiac subjects. The mural painting of Mary was much larger than the Sinai panel, measuring about 150 cm across. Though her face did not survive, one can see that Mary sat on a great throne and was accompanied by angels. The Child in frontal pose was seated on her left knee. A donor, perhaps the owner of the house, appeared in smaller scale to the left, and metal hooks for lamps flanked the image. Dated by the excavator to the early sixth century, the image is important testimony to veneration of Marian images in a domestic setting in early Byzantine Egypt. A domestic setting for the Sinai Mother of God is certainly in the range of possibilities.

---

[5] K. Weitzmann, *The Monastery of Saint Catherine at Mount Sinai. The Icons, I. From the Sixth to the Tenth Century* (Princeton, NJ, 1976), no. B3, 18–21.
[6] J. McGuckin, 'The Paradox of the Virgin-Theotokos: Evangelism and Imperial Politics in the 5th-Century Byzantine World', *Maria, A Journal of Marian Theology* 3 (2001), 5–23.
[7] R. E. Witt, *Isis in the Ancient World* (Baltimore, 1977), originally published as *Isis in the Graeco-Roman World* (Ithaca, NY, 1971).
[8] McGuckin, 'Virgin-Theotokos', 11.
[9] M. Rodziewicz, *Les habitations romaines tardives d'Alexandrie à la lumière des fouilles polonaises à Kom el-Dikka* (*Alexandrie*, 3) (Warsaw, 1984).

In addition, many of the Bawīṭ niches that are commonly labelled apses are further examples of the domestic cult of Marian images, for they were located not in churches but in private cells, in the living quarters of the monks. For example, a niche in Room '30' of the monastery of St Apollo presented an image of Mary nursing her divine Son, the Isis antecedents of which have been much discussed.[10]

The veneration of Isis in domestic shrines is a critical link in this chain of evidence. The Christian domestic shrines had precedents in pre-Christian Egypt, whose importance has been underscored by David Frankfurter's recent study of religion in Late Antiquity.[11] The second and third centuries witnessed a steep decline in traditional public religions. State financing of the official priesthoods dried up, temple sacrifices fell into disuse, and the processions that had filled the streets with colour and movement gradually retreated. Religion, however, did not disappear; it was privatized. The rites and observances that were thought to guarantee prosperity, fertility, health and security were now observed privately in the intimacy of the home.

Striking archaeological evidence of these domestic observances was discovered at the beginning of the last century by Otto Rubensohn.[12] In Theadelphia in the Fayyūm he found a house of the early fourth century with a series of wall niches containing paintings of pagan divinities. The gods included Demeter and her daughter Kore, an enthroned male god of Zeus type, a pair of nude male gods (perhaps the Dioscuri), and an Isis. At Tebtunis another Rubensohn house yielded two important panel paintings of the ancient gods; one can only call these icons since they are panel paintings of gods in static, non-narrative poses for the viewer's veneration. The better preserved (unfortunately lost in Berlin in World War II) came complete with its frame and the hemp cord by which it hung from a nail on the wall. It presented the Nile god Seknebtynis on the left and perhaps Amon, the great father-god of Egypt.[13] Their radiant haloes and their placement on a high-backed throne offer interesting precedents for the Sinai Mother of God. The compositional similarities are reinforced by physical similarities. Measuring 63 by 60 cm, it is very close to the Sinai icon's 69 by 50 cm. Furthermore the Sinai icon has a reserved edge on all sides where the thin board fitted into a grooved frame, as Weitzmann observed, which is exactly the framing that was found still intact on the Tebtunis icon. The second icon discovered by Rubensohn at Tebtunis showed a pair of military figures, Heron and Lykourgos.[14]

In domestic shrines Isis reigned supreme, offering numerous parallels to the enthroned Mother of God. In the houses of Karanis in the Fayyūm, niches and shelves were provided to accommodate cult figures.[15] Clay figurines of Isis were found in the hundreds, her commonest pose being her fertility image nursing her divine son Horos (Harpocrates). Furthermore, in one home a painting of Isis and her son was recorded, dated to the fourth century (Fig. 1.2).[16]

---

[10] On the Isis lactans and Mary, see E. S. Bolman's contribution in this volume, 13–22.
[11] D. Frankfurter, *Religion in Roman Egypt, Assimilation and Resistance* (Princeton, NJ, 1998).
[12] O. Rubensohn, 'Aus griechische-römischen Häusern des Fayyūm', *AA* 20 (1905), 1–25.
[13] Rubensohn's identification of the figure as Athena and my own identification of it as Isis (Fig. 3 in Mathews, 'The Emperor and the Icon') have been questioned by V. Rondot, who proposes Amon in a study now in progress.
[14] V. Rondot, 'Le dieu à la bipenne, c'est Lycurgue', *Revue d'Égyptologie* 52 (2001), 219–36.
[15] E. K. Gazda, *Karanis, An Egyptian Town in Roman Times* (Ann Arbor, 1983).
[16] Ibid., Fig. 68.

Though it is commonly classified as an 'Isis lactans', in fact the mother is not actually nursing. Her mantle is tied in a traditional Isis knot, which in this case leaves both breasts exposed, and she offers her left breast with her fingers. But Horos does not take the breast; rather he holds his right first finger to his lips, a gesture referring to his role in opening the mouth of the dead for the passage of the soul. Like the Marys of Sinai and of Kom el-Dikka, Isis holds the child on her left thigh. She sits on a cushioned wooden throne with an upholstered back, and she tilts her head and gazes slightly to our right with a smile that Tran Tam Tinh describes as 'coquettish'.[17] Sculptures of Isis sometimes offer even closer precedent for the icon composition of Mary and the Christ-child. A full-size limestone statue in Berlin represents the seated mother carrying the child on her left thigh but with her breasts modestly covered the way Mary generally appears.[18]

In Late Antique Egypt Isis was also venerated in icons, that is, in panel paintings. The existence of a sizeable corpus of Late Antique panel paintings of the ancient gods has gone largely unnoticed in literature on Christian icons, but they are in fact the most convincing antecedents for Christian icons in construction, composition, and use. A new interdisciplinary project has forty such panels under study from the second to the fourth century. The project team consists of Egyptologist Vincent Rondot (University of Lille), paintings conservator Norman Muller (Princeton University), and myself, a historian of early Christian art. The first published instalment of this project will be a volume under Professor Rondot's direction on the panel paintings from Tebtunis in the Fayyūm.

It is dangerous to draw conclusions at this preliminary stage of our research, but there are three rather well preserved panels of Isis, which seem to establish a kind of 'Isis look', with important connections to the appearance of the Mother of God. These paintings will be examined further in the projected publication of the corpus of Late Antique icons, but they can be discussed in a preliminary fashion here.

The oldest, as far as its museum history is concerned, was acquired over a century ago by the Egyptian Museum in Berlin, which allowed us to examine and photograph it (Fig. 1.3).[19] Hitherto unpublished, it measures 24.5 by 7 cm, and it consists of a single board 5 mm thick, which is roughly broken at the bottom but true across the top, where the reserved border shows how it fitted into a grooved framing piece. The figure seems to have been standing, and her incomplete condition right and left implies additional boards, perhaps with additional figures on either side. Though she lacks the knotted mantle, she is identified by the crescent moon above a crown of greenery, by the stalks of grain in her raised left hand, and by the yellow sceptre, which disappears into the folds of her garments. Her head is ringed by a grey halo with a white border, her hair falls in loose ringlets in front of her left shoulder, and around her neck she wears one necklace of emeralds and another of gold wire with a single red stone. The torso turns slightly to the viewer's right while her head turns to the left.

In sharp contrast with the everyday faces of the Fayyūm mummy portraits, this is unmistakably the face of a goddess. Lacking the veristic details of the portraits, Isis is generalized in features as a youthful but mature, robust woman with a double chin. Her superhuman dignity and reserve are conveyed in her eyes, which do not engage the common spectator. The eyes are

---

[17] Tran Tam Tinh, *Isis Lactans. Corpus des monuments greco-romains d'Isis allaitant Harpocrate* (Leiden, 1973), 33.
[18] Berlin Staatliche Museen, inv. no. 41136. For the illustration, see Tran Tam Tinh, *Isis Lactans*, Fig. 30.
[19] Accession no. 14443, catalogued as 'Holzbrettchen griechischen Stil. 1899 durch Reinhardt-Zugabe'.

very important. In the mummy portraits the eyes go twinkle, twinkle with a white spot of reflected light. The figures are modelled in the quotidian light and shade of the world in which we dwell, and you might imagine yourself at home with them, the bright glow of the atrium reflected in their moist eyes. Isis, however, dwells in another ambience entirely; there is no reflected light in her eyes; the halo tells us that she has the source of light in herself.

Further panels of Isis confirm these observations of an 'Isis look'. The J. Paul Getty Museum purchased in 1974 a panel with a bust image of Isis (Fig. 1.4) and a matching panel of Sarapis, which have corner pintles for hinging into some sort of frame, suggesting they belonged to a triptych. They have accordingly been associated with a male portrait acquired at the same time as the centrepiece.[20] However, in a recent article Klaus Parlasca observed a dowel hole on the right edge of the Isis panel, to which a knob was attached, whose use is evident in the wear around the hole.[21] This would make the panels not triptych wings but doors of a shrine of some sort with the images on the outside, the Isis being the left valve. The male portrait must be entirely disassociated from the pair of panels for reasons of measurements. The Isis panel measures 37.2 by 19.5 cm, exclusive of the pintles, and 1 cm thick. In addition to the knob hole noticed by Parlasca, Norman Muller observed dowel holes along the leading edge of each panel, indicating that another strip of board was attached, meaning the panels were originally wider than they now are.[22] Therefore the cumulative width of the panels, at least 50 cm, would have been considerably greater than that of the portrait, which measures 36 by 37.5 cm. The height is also wrong, for in ancient triptych construction the wings must be shorter than the centrepiece to fit into its frame, whereas in fact they are more than a centimetre higher. The mid-third-century date of the portrait therefore has nothing to do with the dating of the panels of Isis and Sarapis, which are probably late second century.

Isis' identity is established by her more customary disc-and-horns crown, which contains a cobra, or uraeus, as well as by the knot in her mantle. Again she wears a pair of necklaces, one a string of blue stones, the other a gold strap with a fringe of pendants. In her loose, shoulder-length hair one sees ears of grain and pink flowers. Though more broadly modelled and more sculptural than the Berlin panel, in general she has the same 'Isis look': the sturdy columnar neck, the plump, healthy face, the double chin, the wide eyes and the remote, averted gaze. Now she looks toward our right, that is, toward her companion Sarapis, who in turn gazes toward her. The flecks in her eyes are loss of pigment, not reflected light.

A newly discovered icon fragment, perhaps of the late second century, from Kellis in the Dakhleh oasis constitutes a third document of this 'Isis look' (Fig. 1.5). Our team has not yet examined the piece at first hand, but it has been reported by its discoverer Colin Hope and Helen Whitehouse.[23] This is the only one of the three Isis panels under discussion that has

---

[20] D. L. Thompson, 'A Painted Triptych from Roman Egypt', *The J. Paul Getty Museum Journal* 6/7 (1978/9), 185–92.
[21] Kl. Parlasca, 'Eine sepulkrale Schreintür römischer Zeit aus Ägypten', in Kr. M. Cialowicz and J. A. Ostrowski (eds), *Les civilisations du bassin méditerranéen, Hommages à Joachim Sliwa* (Cracow, 2000), 293–8.
[22] Further details to be published subsequently.
[23] C. Hope, 'Objects from the Temple of Tutu', in *Egyptian Religion the Last Thousand Years, II. Studies Dedicated to the Memory of Jan Quaegebeur* (Louvain, 1998), 826–8. H. Whitehouse and C. Hope, 'A Painted Panel of Isis', in C. A. Hope and A. J. Mills (eds), *Dakhleh Oasis Project: Preliminary Reports on the 1992–1993 and 1993–1994 Field Seasons* (Oxford, 1999), 95–100.

precise archaeological provenance. Stratigraphy indicates that the panel was lost or discarded in the mid-fourth century in the main temple of Tutu in the Dakhleh oasis. Whitehouse supposes, however, that the painting dates to the late second century and that it had domestic use before being offered as a votive-offering at the temple.

This is the smallest of the panels, measuring only 18.2 by 4.7 cm, the board being 1.5–2.5 cm thick. The unpainted borders along the top and bottom edges indicate that the painting had a grooved frame. The other edges indicate that it was originally wider: the right edge is irregularly broken and, while the left edge is straight, the paint reaches the edge, meaning another panel rather than a frame piece was here. Hence other figures may have accompanied Isis. As in the Getty piece, the haloed Isis wears her disc-and-horns crown, painted in red and yellow, with a cobra on the disc and ears of grain on either side. Beneath this she wears a yellow (gold) diadem and floral wreath. The goddess has a somewhat younger appearance here, holding her head high on a longer neck. Her hair is arranged in tight curls on her forehead and looser on the sides, where it falls to her shoulders. While her face turns slightly to the left the direction of her gaze seems to be slightly to our right; the 'apparent highlighting … is in fact due to loss of paint here', according to Whitehouse. Her cloak is knotted on her right shoulder and a gold necklace with a dark pendant ornaments her neck.

These three 'icons' of Isis are an important documentation of the private cult of Isis in Late Antique Egypt at a time when her official temple cult was in steep decline. But they also offer a tantalizing glimpse of what might have been the starting point for icons of Mary, which exhibit many points of similarity. And it must be kept in mind that while the surviving material evidence presents us with a gap of some centuries before the first surviving icons of Mary, the literary sources attest to the existence of Christian icons during this interval.

Like Isis, the Sinai Mother of God has none of the portrait specificity of the mummy faces. Her features are generalized to make her appear 'divine', and her look is remote and serene, above human problems. The friendly twinkle of reflected light is missing in her eyes, as indeed it is in Christian icons in general. Moreover, Mary refrains from looking directly at us – a detail often noted with puzzlement, which however makes perfectly good sense in the context of an Isiac background. Indeed this detached 'Isis look' is characteristic of most of the early images of Mary. From Egypt itself one can cite the famous Cleveland tapestry icon, which is the closest surviving relative of the Sinai enthroned Mary.[24] While the Sinai enthroned Mary has not so full a face, the tapestry image has a very full face with marked double chin. Both of these Marys hold the child on the left thigh. The same averted, superior glance characterizes the second icon in the 'Mother of God' exhibition, a Sinai icon numbered B2, now in Kiev,[25] as well as the Sinai icons B40 and B48.[26] Further it is characteristic of the oldest Roman icon of Mary, that of S. Maria Nova.[27] This averted gaze can be followed in countless Byzantine examples of later date, but most significant is certainly its use in 'her most frequently viewed representation

---

[24] See M.-H. Rutschowscaya, 'The Mother of God in Coptic Textiles', in Vassilaki, *Mother of God*, 218–25, Pls 163, 170.

[25] Weitzmann, *The Monastery of Saint Catherine*, no. B2, 15–18. Vassilaki, *Mother of God*, no. 2, 264–5 (R. Cormack).

[26] Weitzmann, *The Monastery of Saint Catherine*, no. B40, 67 and no. B48, 77–8.

[27] P. Amato (ed.), *De Vera Effigie Mariae. Antiche Icone Romane*, exh. cat. (Rome, 1988), 18–21. Ch. Barber, 'Early Representations of the Mother of God', in Vassilaki, *Mother of God*, 252–61.

in the Byzantine world', namely the apse mosaic of Hagia Sophia in Constantinople (Fig. 8.1), executed in 867.[28]

The connection between Isis enthroned and Mary enthroned is also highly suggestive, for the throne is a proper attribute of Isis, whereas it is hardly what one would expect for Mary of Nazareth. Isis' name seems to have meant 'throne', her hieroglyph was a throne, and she was protector of the pharaoh's throne. Mary acquired the throne to demonstrate that she was equal to, and indeed replaced, the ancient Mother of the God. This competition of the Christian pantheon with the divinities they replaced is a process observed frequently in the formation of Christian iconography. Along with the throne, Mary acquired the halo, common on icons of the ancient gods, and a military guard. It should be noted that alongside the Karanis enthroned Isis was a representation of the Thracian military god Heron.[29]

One could go a step further, although this is highly speculative, and suggest a connection between Isis lactans and the icon type of Mary Hodegetria.[30] The latter image is traditionally read as if Mary were gesturing toward the Child with her open right hand while holding him with her left, but a pointing gesture ought to be made with the index finger, not with an open hand. Against the background of countless images of Isis lactans, it might be possible to read Mary's gesture as holding her breast with her hand as if to offer it to the Child. The Karanis Isis could be seen as prototype of the Hodegetria. When in Byzantine art the breast was covered in the spirit of Christian modesty, the nurturing meaning of the gesture was obscured over time and thus came to be reinterpreted as a pointing gesture.

One final connection with Mary's icons is suggested by the left placement of the Getty Isis door panel in relation to the Sarapis panel, as established by Parlasca. What lay inside the twin doors of this shrine is unknown, but the fact that they are door images is an important observation, for in Byzantine art the most important Mary and Christ icons were also door images, namely the *proskynetarion* icons of the icon screen, which are located left and right respectively of the door to the sanctuary. The parallel is strengthened by the relationship of the traditional Christ Pantocrator type iconography with Sarapis iconography, in that both share Zeus' cast of face. A considerable gap in time separates the Getty shrine doors from the earliest firm evidence of icons on the chancel screen, but left and right have profound psychological resonance and the Isis precedent must be connected, however obscure the link.

---

[28] R. Cormack, 'The Mother of God in the Mosaics of Hagia Sophia at Constantinople', in Vassilaki, *Mother of God*, 106–23.
[29] Gazda, *Karanis*, Fig. 68.
[30] Ch. Baltoyanni, 'The Mother of God in Portable Icons', in Vassilaki, *Mother of God*, 144–9.

1.1 Alexandria, Kom el-Dikka, House D. Mary enthroned (source: Rodziewicz, *Les habitations romaines*, Fig. 236, drawing by H. Lewak)

1.2 Karanis, House B50. Watercolour from the original mural. Isis and Harpocrates (source: photo by courtesy of the Kelsey Museum of Archaeology, Ann Arbor, Michigan)

ISIS AND MARY IN EARLY ICONS   11

1.3 Berlin,
Staatliche Museen,
Ägyptisches Museum,
inv. no. 14443.
Isis
(source: photo by courtesy
of the Staatliche Museen
zu Berlin)

1.4 The J. Paul Getty Museum,
no. 74.AI.22.
Panel with painted image of Isis
(© The J. Paul Getty Museum)

1.5 Dakhleh Oasis,
Kellis, temple of Tutu,
inv. no.
31/420-D6-1/D/1/152.
Isis
(source: photo
by courtesy of
Colin A. Hope)

2

The enigmatic Coptic Galaktotrophousa and the cult of the Virgin Mary in Egypt

Elizabeth S. Bolman

> We wish that you would 'deign to give us a little milk from [your] ... breast, so that we might drink it and never die. For we have riches in abundance, and innumerable possessions, but no one to inherit them.'[1]
>
> A request made of the Virgin Mary, by a family of wealthy magicians, from the Coptic *History of Aur*

Images of the Virgin Mary nursing Jesus have been a minor but persistent subject in Christian art.[2] Called the Galaktotrophousa, or 'she who nourishes with milk' in the eastern Christian tradition, examples appear throughout the mediaeval world, as Late Antique Coptic secco paintings (Plate 1, Figs 2.1–2.2), post-Byzantine Cretan icons, thirteenth-century Armenian manuscript illuminations and a German statuette of *c.* 1300, to name only a few. The earliest significant body of representations of this subject comes from Late Antique Egypt.[3] Among these we have established contexts only for the wall paintings, which were intended for an audience of monks.

The powerful emotional significance of the nursing subject, as it has been constructed in the modern West, has complicated the study of this iconographic type. A historiographic commonplace has been the move to impose on the pre-modern image associations of mother and child bonding, supreme maternal responsibility and love. Questions about the Virgin Mary's role in the nursing image overlap readily with issues about her cult, and pose the same dangers to the

---

[1] E. A. Wallis Budge, *Egyptian Tales and Romances* (London, 1931; repr. New York, 1980), 250.

[2] This article draws on my PhD dissertation, 'The Coptic Galaktotrophousa as the Medicine of Immortality', Bryn Mawr College, 1997. I have presented aspects of this larger project at the Byzantine Studies Conference (University of Wisconsin, Madison, 1997), and at the International Association for Coptic Studies Congress (Leiden, 2000). The Leiden paper will appear in the published Congress Proceedings. Funding for this work comes from multiple sources. I am grateful to the many institutions that funded my research, as a dissertation and beyond, including the Samuel H. Kress Foundation, the American Research Centre in Egypt, Bryn Mawr College, and Temple University.

[3] Catalogue: (1) Woman Nursing Child; possibly an early Galaktotrophousa; grave stele; limestone; Medinet el-Fayyūm?; 4th c.?; Berlin, Museum für Spätantike und Byzantinische Kunst, inv. 4726. (2) Galaktotrophousa; stele, perhaps a stone icon; limestone; Fayyūm?; 7th c.?; Cairo, Coptic Museum, inv. 8006. (3) Galaktotrophousa; papyrus fragment; Antinoe; *c.* 500–550; Florence, Istituto Papirologico G. Vitelli, inv. PSI XV 1574. (4) Galaktotrophousa; secco wall painting; Cell A, Monastery of Apa Jeremiah, Saqqara; 6th–7th c.?; Cairo, Coptic Museum, inv. 8014. (5) Galaktotrophousa; secco wall painting; Cell 1725, Monastery of Apa Jeremiah, Saqqara; 6th–7th c.?; Cairo, Coptic Museum, inv. 7987. (6) Galaktotrophousa; secco wall painting; Cell 1807, Monastery of Apa Jeremiah, Saqqara; 6th–7th c.?; no longer extant, to my knowledge never photographed. (7) Galaktotrophousa; secco wall painting; Cell 30, Monastery of Apa Apollo, Bawīṭ; 6th–7th c.?; no longer extant. (8) Galaktotrophousa; secco wall painting; Cell 42, Monastery of Apa Apollo, Bawīṭ; 6th–7th c.?; no longer extant. (9) Galaktotrophousa; secco wall painting, Monastery of the Virgin Mary (so-called Syrian Monastery), in situ in the *khurus*, 7th–10th c. (10) Galaktotrophousa; MS frontispiece, fol. 1v; Monastery of the Archangel Michael, Hamouli, Fayyūm; 892–893; New York, Pierpont Morgan Library, M612. (11) Galaktotrophousa; MS frontispiece, fol. 1v; Monastery of the Archangel Michael, Hamouli, Fayyūm; 897–898; New York, Pierpont Morgan Library, M574. (12) Galaktotrophousa; MS frontispiece, fol. 1v; Hamouli, Fayyūm; 905–906; New York, Pierpont Morgan Library, M600. (13) Galaktotrophousa, MS frontispiece, fol. 1v; possibly Sohag; 989–990; London, British Library, BMO 6782.

scholar, those of assuming that a phenomenon powerful in later periods must have inspired or at least affected the production and meaning of the nursing image.[4] My purpose in this paper is to explore the historical meaning of the Galaktotrophousa within a narrowly defined Coptic, male and monastic environment, and to evaluate the possibility that a relationship existed between the cult of the Virgin Mary and the appearance of the Galaktotrophousa in Coptic art.

Lucia Langener has contributed most significantly to our knowledge about the Egyptian evidence. In her dissertation of 1996 she amassed an impressive catalogue of Egyptian nursing types, both pagan and Christian, and also a large quantity of textual sources of relevance to this subject. Prior to this extensive work, eminent specialists in Coptic art such as Klaus Wessel and Paul van Moorsel had wrestled with the subject.[5] The essential quandary facing scholars was why an image of Christ at his most human, nursing at his human mother's breast, would be so prevalent in Late Antique Egyptian monasteries. Coptic monks are known for their tenacious adherence to a doctrinal position referred to by others as Monophysite, and by Copts simply as orthodox. Questions about how many Egyptian Christians in the period after the decisive Council of Chalcedon (451) were Coptic Orthodox, and how many were not, are difficult to evaluate. It is generally accepted that the majority was Coptic Orthodox, and that the six known wall paintings of the Galaktotrophousa found in Coptic monastic cells were produced in this environment.[6] I will proceed with this assumption.

The interpretative problem, then, has been why that most human image of the Christ-child, at Mary's breast, would have been a fairly common, even a popular choice among Coptic Orthodox monks.[7] This audience emphasized the divine aspect of Christ's manifestation in a human body.[8] No scholar approaching this subject has questioned the historical construction of nursing in our own period and in Late Antique Egypt. This new approach from gender studies corrects the methodological error.

---

[4] The most extensive publication of the Coptic nursing Virgin is a dissertation by L. Langener, *Isis Lactans – Maria Lactans. Untersuchungen zur koptischen Ikonographie* (Altenberge, 1996). Langener's interpretation of the importance of Mary in early Christian Egypt raises a historiographic problem. She followed an established tradition of unproblematically interpreting the designation of Mary as Theotokos as proof of devotion to her. According to Langener, the depiction of the Galaktotrophousa is an expression not only of Christ's human nature, but also of the Copts' devotion to Mary, since nursing is one of the ways in which she contributed to Christ's incarnation. Langener, *Isis Lactans – Maria Lactans*, 133–5, 145–6.

[5] K. Wessel, *Coptic Art*, tr. J. Carroll and S. Hatton (New York, 1965). Id., 'Eine Grabstele aus Medinet el-Fajum: Zum Problem der Maria Lactans', *Wissenschaftliche Zeitschrift der Humboldt-Universität zu Berlin. Gesellschafts- und sprachwissenschaftliche Reihe 3*, 4 (1954/5), 149–54. Id., 'Zur Ikonographie der Koptischen Kunst', in K. Wessel (ed.), *Christentum am Nil. Internationale Arbeitstagung zur Ausstellung 'Koptische Kunst', Essen, Villa Hügel*, 23–5 July, 1963 (Recklinghausen, 1964), 233–9. P. P. van Moorsel, 'Galactotrophousa', in A. Atiya (ed.), *Coptic Encyclopedia* (New York, 1991), 531–5. Id., 'Die stillende Gottesmutter und die Monophysiten', in E. Dinkler (ed.), *Kunst und Geschichte Nubiens in christlicher Zeit* (Recklinghausen, 1970), 281–8.

[6] Marlia Mundell assembled fragmentary evidence for the possibility that the monasteries at Bawīṭ and Saqqara were in the possession of Melkites while the majority of the paintings were done. See M. Mundell, 'Monophysite Church Decoration', in A. Bryer and J. Herrin (eds), *Iconoclasm* (Birmingham, 1977), 59–74. While the possibility remains, it seems a slender one to me, and more plausible to assume that the paintings of the Galaktotrophousa (now known in three and not two monastic environments) were made for monks participating in the majority doctrinal position.

[7] Wessel, 'Zur Ikonographie', 233–9. G. A. Wellen, *Theotokos* (Utrecht, 1961), 164.

[8] W. H. C. Frend, *The Rise of the Monophysite Movement* (Cambridge, 1972), x, 5.

Breast-feeding is without question a biologically natural act for female mammals. Images of nursing, on the contrary, are not produced by nature. Beyond their reference to one of the biological functions of a woman's body, there is nothing natural about such depictions. They are expressions of their makers' and their societies' ideas about nursing and milk. In the modern West, the concept of nursing enshrines a cluster of ideas about mothers and children. Common constructions of the subject, found in publications for young mothers, present the nursing pair with a soft focus and pastel colours, posed in intimate proximity.[9] Such representations convey a series of interconnected messages. The child is helpless and trusting, held protectively in the arms of his or her mother. The child and mother bond, in this moment of what is an all-too-short period in an infant's life. We know that the milk itself could easily be replaced by infant formula, but the emotional link cannot. We invest the youngest among us with the most worth, as innocents who have yet to realize their individual potential. We also place the most intense value on the mother's role at the beginning of the child's life cycle. Nursing is a choice, not a necessity, and resonates with associations of maternal devotion, as the title of one book on the subject makes clear: *The Tender Gift: Breast-feeding.*[10]

Among all of its members, Late Antique and early Byzantine societies valued new-born children the least. Suzanne Dixon has shown that the ideal Roman mother played a very important part in her child's upbringing. However, her role did not come into being until the child was about seven years old and was ready to be trained in morality, an important subject which was the mother's responsibility. Prior to this, slaves and hired staff were seen as sufficient to care for most of the child's needs.[11] John Boswell has estimated that in the first three centuries of the Christian era between twenty and forty per cent of children born in urban areas were abandoned at birth.[12] In the fourth century, Gregory of Nyssa wrote that the deaths of the large majority of young children were caused by exposure, smothering, drowning or 'natural removal by illness'.[13] While it has been demonstrated that Christianity gradually affected ideas about the value of children's lives, killing a new-born child was a legal act, at least in Byzantium, until Justinian's reforms.[14]

In Late Antique and early Byzantine Egypt the duration of nursing was usually two to three years, and the woman who breast-fed a child was often not the child's mother. Certainly in the fourth century, and probably later, many new-born children were sent away from their families for this extended period, to live with a wet nurse.[15] Sporadic textual evidence from the fourth century on presents a picture of continuity.[16]

---

[9] A characteristic example is on the cover of a book published by the La Leche League: *The Womanly Art of Breast-feeding* (Franklin Park, 1991).
[10] D. Raphael and F. Davis, *The Tender Gift: Breast-feeding* (Westport, 1985). L. M. Blum, *At the Breast* (Boston, 1999), 4–6 and elsewhere.
[11] S. Dixon, *The Roman Mother* (London, 1988), 114–7.
[12] J. Boswell, *The Kindness of Strangers* (New York, 1988), 135.
[13] Gregory of Nyssa, *De Infantibus Praemature Abreptis*, PG 46, 168B. M.-H. Congourdeau, 'Regards sur l'enfant nouveau-né à Byzance', REB 51 (1993), 165–9.
[14] *Digest*, XXV.3–4. Congourdeau, 'Regards sur l'enfant', 164 n. 17.
[15] K. Bradley, 'The Nurse and the Child at Rome', *Thamyris* 1/2 (1994), 137–56.
[16] See my forthcoming publication in the Proceedings of the International Association for Coptic Studies Congress, Leiden, for more discussion of this point. I will also expand upon this in a planned book on the Galaktotrophousa in eastern Christian art.

This brief overview shows that an image of a woman nursing a child was not a symbol of mother and child intimacy, since the nurse was often not the child's mother. The average period of nursing was two to three years, so the nursling was not always a helpless, pre-verbal infant. A mother's role was not most important shortly after birth, and neither did a person's life have its greatest value then. By demonstrating that the act and image of nursing were not the charged repositories of maternal intimacy and infant frailty in Late Antique and early Byzantine Egypt that they are for us, I have divested the iconography of the Galaktotrophousa of its presumed meaning. If I am correct, and it was not made to assert Christ's human nature, then what did it mean? Why did Coptic monks choose it for inclusion in their cells and churches? One possibility is that early devotion to the Virgin Mary motivated its selection. Characterizations of Mary's importance in Egypt vary considerably, making the relationship of the Galaktotrophousa and the cult of the Virgin Mary difficult to assess.[17]

Averil Cameron and Vassiliki Limberis have convincingly demonstrated that the doctrinal controversies of the fifth century and the designation of the Virgin Mary as 'Theotokos' were not motivated by the cult of the Virgin.[18] We know, however, that the cult of the Virgin existed unofficially in this time period. One attestation is the Kollyridians, a group of women who lived in the fourth century in the eastern Mediterranean. They baked cakes, dedicated them to the Virgin Mary, and then ate them. They acted as their own priests, and worshipped Mary as a goddess.[19]

As I observed above, the known contexts for the Coptic Galaktotrophousa are all monastic and male. If a survey of the principal textual source for the monastic life in late antique Egypt is any indication, early Coptic monks were certainly not devoted to the Virgin Mary. The alphabetical collection of the *Apophthegmata Patrum*, compiled between the fourth and the sixth centuries, includes only two mentions of Mary. In neither is she a focus of special attention.[20] In another version of the *Apophthegmata*, devotion to Mary is explicitly addressed. Satan asked a chaste widow why she prayed like a man, to the Father, the Son, and the Holy Ghost, suggesting instead that she should glorify Mary, the mother of Christ. She responded by asking why she should 'forsake the Lord and worship a hand maiden?' At this Satan disappeared.[21]

Explicit evidence of her construction as a powerful entity capable of providing magical healing and protection appears outside of a monastic context in Egypt by the fifth or sixth century, in spells written for women.[22] One undated summoning spell seems to invoke magic in part through identification with the suckling Christ. 'My mother is Mary. The breast ... the

---

[17] S. Kent Brown sees little evidence for it, in: 'Coptic and Greek Inscriptions from Christian Egypt: A Brief Review', in B. Pearson and J. Goehring (eds), *The Roots of Egyptian Christianity* (Philadelphia, 1986), 36. Dorothy Shepherd Payer expresses the opposite view, in 'Virgin Enthroned', in Atiya, *Coptic Encyclopedia*, 542.
[18] A. M. Cameron, 'The Early Cult of the Virgin', in Vassilaki, *Mother of God*, 3–15. V. Limberis, *Divine Heiress: The Virgin Mary and the Creation of Christian Constantinople* (London, 1994), 109–11 and elsewhere.
[19] S. Benko, *The Virgin Goddess* (Leiden, 1993), 170–95 (ch. 5: 'The Women who Sacrificed to Mary: The Kollyridians'). Limberis, *Divine Heiress*, 118–20.
[20] *The Sayings of the Desert Fathers: The Alphabetical Collection*, ed. and tr. B. Ward (Kalamazoo, 1975), 47, 57.
[21] *The Paradise of the Holy Fathers*, tr. E. A. Wallis Budge (London, 1907), II, no. 575, 269–70. My search in the *Apophthegmata* for references to the Virgin Mary has not been exhaustive.
[22] Florence, Istituto Papirologico G. Vitelli, no. 365, and London, University College, Edwards Collection, amulet, tr. in M. Meyer, R. Smith and N. Kelsey (eds), *Ancient Christian Magic: Coptic Texts of Ritual Power* (San Francisco, 1994), 38, 48.

breast from which our lord Jesus Christ drank.'²³ A thin papyrus codex of *c*. 950 includes what may be evidence for a significant shift in perceptions of Mary. It is called *The Magical Book of Mary and the Angels*.²⁴ Using this text and others like it, the magical practitioner identified with Mary as an unambiguous source of power: 'I am Mary, I am Mariham, I am the Mother of the Life (of) the whole world, I myself (am) NN.'²⁵

Some epigraphic material suggests devotion to Mary from within at least one Coptic monastery at around the seventh century. Many of the monastic tombstones found at the Monastery of Apa Jeremiah actually include reference to her, and this is particularly interesting for our study, because three paintings of the nursing Virgin were discovered at this site.²⁶ But consideration of evidence for the cult of the Virgin Mary within and outside of monasteries yields uneven results, and does not provide clear evidence for the genesis of the Galaktotrophousa. Texts attesting to the significance of milk and the ritual of the baptismal Eucharist suggest that the concept of the nursing Virgin pre-dated her cult. In the second century Clement of Alexandria wrote that the milk in Mary's breasts had its origin in God and not the Virgin's own body. According to Clement, as a virgin, Mary's body is incapable of generating this milk. Clement tells us that the milk is actually the *Logos*, because it has the same composition as the flesh and blood of Christ. Drawing on contemporary medical knowledge, Clement explains that blood is simply 'liquid flesh' and that milk is blood coloured white, 'so as not to frighten the little child'. Of these three 'milk is the most succulent and subtle part of the blood'.²⁷ 'No one should be surprised if we say that milk allegorically designates the blood of Christ: isn't this blood equally symbolized by the allegory of wine?'²⁸ According to Clement, milk is 'the drink of immortality', Christ is the nurse, and 'it is again milk which the Lord promises the just, to show clearly that the *Logos* is at one and the same time the alpha and omega, the beginning and the end.'²⁹

In the fifth century another Alexandrine, Cyril, reiterated these points, explaining both that God gave Mary the milk in her breasts 'in the heavens',³⁰ and that, by nursing Christ with this milk, Mary deserves to have the flesh and blood of Christ placed in her mouth.³¹ Cyril's fifth-century text is copied and bound with three others in a late tenth-century manuscript now in the British Library, BMO 6782.³² This manuscript is illustrated with a frontispiece of

---

[23] John Rylands University Library of Manchester, Coptic 103, tr. in Meyer *et al.*, *Ancient Christian Magic*, 231.
[24] M. Meyer, 'The Magical Book of Mary and the Angels (P. Heid. Inv. Kopt. 685)', in S. Emmel, M. Krause, S. G. Richter and S. Schaten (eds), *Ägypten und Nubien in Spätantike und christlicher Zeit, Akten des 6. Internationalen Koptologenkongresses* (Wiesbaden, 1999), 287–94.
[25] Ibid., 291.
[26] For examples see nos 12, 27, 43, 44, 48, 53, 54 and 65 in J. E. Quibell, *Excavations at Saqqara 1907–1908* (Cairo, 1909), 32, 36–7, 42–3, 45, 47–8.
[27] Clement of Alexandria, *Paed.*, I.VI, 39, 2 – 40, 1, ed. H.-I. Marrou, *Clément d'Alexandrie, Le pédagogue* (SC, 70) (Paris, 1960), 183–5. Hippocrates articulated the medical belief that milk is blood in *Glands*, 16, tr. P. Potter (*Loeb Classical Library*, VIII) (Cambridge, 1988), 123.
[28] Clement of Alexandria, *Paed.*, I.VI, 47, 2, ed. Marrou, 194–5.
[29] Id., *Quis Divus Salvetur*, 24, 3 and 29; *Paed.*, I.VI, 36, 1, ed. Marrou, 174–5.
[30] Cyril of Alexandria, 'Discourse on the Virgin Mary', BMO 6782, fol. 31a, 1–2. E. A. Wallis Budge, *Miscellaneous Coptic Texts in the Dialect of Upper Egypt* (London, 1915), 719.
[31] BMO 6782, fol. 33a2–33b1. Wallis Budge, *Miscellaneous Coptic Texts*, 721.
[32] BMO 6782, fol. 1v. B. Layton, *Catalogue of Coptic Literary Manuscripts in the British Library Acquired Since the Year 1906* (London, 1987), no. 151, 174–6. *Ägypten. Schätze aus dem Wüstensand: Kunst und Kultur der Christen am Nil*, exh. cat., Gustav-Lübcke-Museum der Stadt Hamm, Wiesbaden (Wiesbaden, 1996), no. 270, 252.

the Galaktotrophousa, accompanied by John the Evangelist. Clement's discussion of milk focused on its character, divine origins and symbolism, and barely at all on the Virgin Mary. Likewise Cyril has been shown to characterize Mary as a tool for salvation, but not as an active protagonist.[33]

Numerous references to milk exist in diverse textual sources disassociated from the Virgin Mary. Rivers of milk and honey refer to the Promised Land and to Paradise in the Old Testament and in the early Christian *Apocalyptic Vision of Esdras* of c. 150.[34] Milk is given as a reward to Christian martyrs and to the just at the Last Judgement.[35] Accounts of the martyrdom of St Paul and St Catherine of Alexandria tell us that milk gushed forth in place of blood from their decapitated remains.[36] It attested to their instantaneous salvation and attainment of immortality in Christ.

Additional information about the significance of milk for our understanding of the Galaktotrophousa comes from the early liturgy. The ritual practice of the church included a significant expression of the importance of milk and its close ties to blood and flesh, specifically the blood and flesh of Christ. The newly baptized were offered a special Eucharist, designed for this moment of rebirth in Christ. In between the wine and bread of the standard ceremony they were given a cup of milk mixed with honey.[37] The *Canons of Hippolytus*, which originated in Egypt c. 350, give the cup of milk and honey a complex symbolic significance. Its type is the milk small children consume after birth, underlining the fact that baptism marks a new beginning. At the ritual birth of baptism, the *Canons* tell us that the milk and honey *is* the flesh of Christ, which 'dissolves the bitterness of the heart through the sweetness of the *Logos*'.[38] Finally, it is also a promise of the food that the faithful will consume in heaven when they die and are reborn for the last time into everlasting life.[39]

The Coptic Christian images of nursing are actually only the last in an exceptionally long tradition of similar depictions from pagan Egypt. Most prominent among these are the Birth Houses or *Mammisi*, which attain an independent form within temple complexes beginning in the fourth century BC.[40] The Roman-period *Mammisi* at Dendera is covered inside and out with images of goddesses nursing the divine child, who is also the Pharaoh, and in this case the Roman Emperor (Figs 2.3–2.4). These Birth Houses were the sites of the ritual birth of the Pharaoh. The act of consumption helps the king assimilate to the young god, and also gives him the authority to rule. It shows him at a moment of ritual rebirth, with parallels to Christian

---

[33] Limberis, *Divine Heiress*, 109–11.
[34] Exodus 3:17; 13:5. 2 Esdras 2:19. B. Metzger (ed.), 'The Apocrypha of the Old Testament', in *The New Oxford Annotated Bible* (Oxford, 1977), 23.
[35] *Passio Sanctarum Perpetuae et Felicitas*, 4. R. Kraemer, *Maenads, Martyrs, Matrons, Monastics* (Philadelphia, 1988), 98–9. *Passio Montani*, VIII. M. Meslin, 'Vases sacrés et boissons d'éternité dans les visions des martyrs africains', in J. Fontaine and C. Kannengiesser (eds), *Epektasis. Mélanges patristiques offerts au Cardinal Jean Daniélou* (Paris, 1972), 149. Clement of Alexandria, *Paed.*, I.IV, 34, 3 – 36, 1, ed. Marrou, 173–5.
[36] *Acts of Paul* (c. AD 185–195). See 'The Martyrdom of the Holy Apostle Paul', in E. Hennecke (ed.), *New Testament Apocrypha* II (Philadelphia, 1964), 351, 386. R. Coursault, *Sainte Catherine d'Alexandrie: le mythe et la tradition* (Paris, 1984), 14, 42, 50, 121.
[37] H. Unserer, 'Milch und Honig', *Rheinisches Museum für Philologie* 57 (1902), 177–95.
[38] W. Till and J. Liepoldt, *Der koptische Text der Kirchenordnung Hippolyts* (Berlin, 1954), 22–3.
[39] A. J. Butler, *The Ancient Coptic Churches of Egypt* II (Oxford, 1884), 272–3.
[40] D. Arnold, *Temples of the Last Pharaohs* (Oxford, 1999), 285–8.

baptism.⁴¹ The example at Dendera dates to the first and early second centuries AD, only a few decades before Clement of Alexandria wrote that the milk in Mary's breasts was the *Logos*.

While the extant *exempla* are somewhat later, the concept and the meaning of the nursing Virgin were formulated between the second and fourth centuries, drawing on long-standing Egyptian associations between royalty and nursing. This Christian formulation had a continued relevance in the following centuries, both in church ritual and after the Islamic conquest of Egypt in 641. The pagan Egyptian images of nursing, the sources which describe Mary's milk as the *Logos*, which comes from God in heaven, and the ritual inclusion of a cup of milk and honey in the baptismal Eucharist add up to a very different interpretation of the Coptic Galaktotrophousa than has been offered to date. It is not about human frailty but about life after death, and shows one of the principal means of attaining this state – drinking the *Logos*. Even shown as a small child, the divine aspect of Christ is emphasized as he suckles divine food provided by God and not everyday mother's milk. It was never included in a narrative context, its formal, iconic presentation underscoring its symbolic significance.⁴²

At a certain point, the cult of the Virgin affected at least some perceptions about the Galaktotrophousa. A mediaeval Egyptian tale called the *History of Aur* is illuminating. One day a family of wealthy magicians decided to cast a spell to call up the Virgin Mary. When she appeared, the magicians addressed her, saying: We wish that you would 'deign to give us a little milk from [your] … breast, so that we might drink it and never die. For we have riches in abundance, and innumerable possessions, but no one to inherit them.'⁴³ The milk in Mary's breast is the *Logos*, the word of God, a food that makes one immortal. In this miracle, the Virgin can provide the milk if she wishes, although incidentally she does not give it to the wicked magicians, but what interests me particularly is that she has it, and also has power over it. The emphasis is on Mary here, and there is no mention of God, Christ, or the act of nursing.

In its early Coptic contexts, the Galaktotrophousa reads unambiguously as a metaphor for the Eucharist. Its genesis as a concept, first expressed by Clement of Alexandria, pre-dates evidence for the cult of the Virgin Mary in Egypt. The proliferation of depictions of the Galaktotrophousa in monastic contexts may have been partially motivated by devotion to her, but the intended message of this iconographic type was one which divested Mary of power, while showing Christ drinking the *Logos* provided by God. At some later point, as suggested by the *History of Aur*, devotion to the Virgin refashioned at least some people's reception of the early configuration, shifting the emphasis from Christ to the Virgin Mary herself.

---

⁴¹ J. Leclant, 'Le rôle de l'allaitement dans le cérémonial pharaonique du couronnement', *Proceedings of the IXth International Congress for the History of Religions, Tokyo and Kyoto, 27 August – 9 September 1958* (Tokyo, 1960), 135–45.

⁴² Langener sees the *Adoration of the Magi* scene in Paris B.N. copte 13 as including nursing, but I do not. Langener, *Isis Lactans – Maria Lactans*, 167–8.

⁴³ Wallis Budge, *Egyptian Tales*, 250. Clara ten Hacken is working on these manuscripts for her doctoral dissertation (Leiden University). In a paper presented at the Fayyūm Symposium (February 2004) she said that all the manuscripts are in Arabic, and the earliest is dated to AD 1380.

2.1 Cairo, Coptic Museum, inv. no. 8014.
Monastery of Apa Jeremiah, Saqqara, Cell A, east wall, secco.
Virgin Mary Galaktotrophousa (source: J. E. Quibell,
Excavations at Saqqara, 1906-1907 II (Cairo, 1908), Pl. XL)

2.2 Wadi Natrun, Monastery of the Virgin Mary
(so-called Syrian Monastery), Church of the Virgin Mary.
Khurus, painted column, encaustic.
Virgin Mary Galaktotrophousa
(source: author; courtesy of Karel Innemée)

2.3   Dendera, Temple Complex of Hathor. *Mammisi* (Birth House) of Nero and Trajan (*c.* 1st – early 2nd c.). General view of the south-west side (source: author)

2.4   Dendera, Temple Complex of Hathor. *Mammisi* (Birth House) of Nero and Trajan (*c.* 1st – early 2nd c.). Nursing Scene (source: author)

3

Icons and sites.
Cult images of the Virgin in mediaeval Rome*

Gerhard Wolf

Icons are not by definition transportable. 'Eikon' merely means 'image' (the corresponding Latin word is *imago*), a term with a rich semantic field in both Classical culture and the Christian tradition.¹ In the case of the latter, this extends from the theological concept that Christ is the co-substantial *eikon* of the Father and that man is created in his image and likeness (κατ' εἰκόνα καὶ καθ' ὁμοίωσιν) to the material pictures representing the protagonists of the history of Salvation, namely Christ, Mary and the saints. The legitimization of such painted objects in Byzantium in fact drew on the richness of the term, emphasizing the bridging of heaven and earth by means of the Incarnation, with the *Logos* becoming flesh (and thus becoming the subject of icons). The complex relationship between the image and the represented body or face on the one hand and the dynamics of the access to spiritual truth by means of images on the other was at the heart of the issue. Picturing the Annunciation could thus become an iconic treatise on the mystery of Incarnation, as for example in the spectacular late twelfth-century Sinai panel² where Mary is shown seated in front of her house – in other words the house in which Christ makes his dwelling; the transparent *sagoma* of the child is projected onto her mantle in an extreme attempt at painting the invisible, pre-incarnate form. This is a subject concerned with the origin of the icon in the Christian era, but obviously not with the historical origins of the cult of icons, or, to put it more cautiously, the rise of icons in the Oecumene.³

The Annunciation became an 'icon' much earlier than the Sinai panel in the form not only of a transportable object, but also, for example, of mural paintings such as those in the church of

---

* I would like to thank Julia Triolo for revising my English and Maria Vassilaki for the careful editing of the text.
¹ See the classic study G. B. Ladner, 'The Concept of the Image in the Greek Fathers and the Byzantine Iconoclast Controversy', *DOP* 7 (1953), 1–34. M. Barasch, *Icon. Studies in the History of an Idea* (New York and London, 1992). Cf. H.-G. Thümmel, *Die Frühgeschichte der ostkirchlichen Bilderlehre* (*Texte und Untersuchungen*, 139) (Berlin, 1992). R. Cormack, *Writing in Gold. Byzantine Society and its Icons* (London and New York, 1985). H. Belting, *Bild und Kult. Eine Geschichte des Bildes vor dem Zeitalter der Kunst* (Munich, 1990); trans. into English as *Likeness and Presence. A History of the Image Before the Era of Art* (Chicago and London, 1994). H. Maguire, *The Icons of their Bodies. Saints and their Images in Byzantium* (Princeton, NJ, 1996).
² K. Weitzmann, 'Eine spätkomnenische Verkündigungsikone des Sinai und die zweite byzantinische Welle des 12. Jahrhunderts', in G. von der Osten and G. Kauffmann (eds), *Festschrift für Herbert von Einem zum 16. Februar 1965* (Berlin, 1965), 299–312. Evans and Wixom, *The Glory of Byzantium*, no. 246, 374–5 (A. W. Carr). G. Wolf, 'La vedova di Re Abgaro', in J.-C. Schmitt and J.-M. Sansterre (eds), *Les images dans les sociétés médiévales: pour une histoire comparée, Actes du colloque international organisé par l'Institut Historique Belge de Rome en collaboration avec l'École Française de Rome et l'Université Libre de Bruxelles (Rome, 19–20 juin 1998)*, *Bulletin de l'Institut belge de Rome* 69 (1999), 215–43.
³ Even if later, one may add, it was not by chance that the Annunciation-evangelist St Luke became the archetypal painter of the Madonna. M. Bacci, *Il pennello dell'Evangelista. Storia delle immagini sacre attribuite a San Luca* (Pisa, 1998).

S. Maria Antiqua in Rome (dated from the late sixth to the mid-seventh century). Here we also encounter other wall icons, which may reflect objects brought to Rome from Palestine or the Greek East, as has been recently postulated by Beat Brenk.[4] If so, differences would not so much be a sign of changing styles and stylistic modes, as Kitzinger and others have argued,[5] but rather result from association with particular iconic models, and not from artistic or programmatic selection. In this case, the 'icons' would have been placed on the wall as ex-votos.[6] They obtain an iconic identity through the process of framing or through their stylistic mode; thus in the early eighth-century Theodotus chapel, the patron and his family are shown venerating an icon of the martyr saints Quiricus and Julitta.[7]

In the following remarks I will, however, restrict myself to icons as transportable objects and in particular to those that may be considered as ideal portraits of the Virgin Mary in her role as the Mother of God. The ways in which these images were displayed, 'transported', 'moved' or activated in any fashion over the centuries may be defined as forms of veneration ranging from personal devotion to public cult. By display we mean everything from the ritual veiling and unveiling of the image to exhibitions such as those of the recent past which have brought some of the oldest of all icons to the eyes of the modern viewer. Given that this paper was written for a conference accompanying an exhibition, the marvellous 'Mother of God' at the Benaki Museum in Athens,[8] I would like to begin by considering this form of transport and display of icons, and subsequently to take a brief look at the early history of Marian icons in the city of Rome.

In 1988 an unusual exhibition was briefly held in the apse of the basilica of S. Maria Maggiore in Rome.[9] The five oldest images of the Virgin Mary in Rome came together for the first time since the Middle Ages – if indeed they had ever met before. The public was unsure how to behave in front of these icons, and reactions oscillated between devotion and curiosity, scholarly and otherwise. In the Jubilee year of 2000, several of these images met again, this time not in a church but in the Palazzo delle Esposizioni in Rome, for an exhibition entitled 'Aurea Roma. Dalla città pagana alla città cristiana'.[10] The Madonnas from the Pantheon and the church of S. Maria Nova were present, whereas the Madonna della Clemenza from S. Maria in Trastevere was represented by a photographic replica, thus equating original and copy in a place – the museum – where the focus is usually aesthetic identity rather than cultic evocation. Absent was the small S. Maria del Rosario image from Monte Mario, often called the 'Madonna

---

[4] B. Brenk, 'Kultgeschichte versus Stilgeschichte. Von der *raison d'être* des Bildes im 7. Jahrhundert in Rom', in *Settimane di studio del Centro italiano di studi sull'alto Medioevo* 50 (Spoleto, 2003), 971–1054. I would like to thank the author for allowing me to read the manuscript of this article before its was published.

[5] See the bibliography in Brenk, 'Kultgeschichte versus Stilgeschichte', and especially E. Kitzinger, 'Römische Malerei vom Beginn des 7. bis zur Mitte des 8. Jahrhunderts', Ph. Diss., University of Munich, 1934. P. J. Romanelli and P. J. Nordhagen, *Santa Maria Antiqua* (Roma, 1964). E. Kitzinger, *Byzantine Art in the Making. Main Lines of Stylistic Development in Mediterranean Art, 3rd–7th Century* (London, 1977).

[6] See also Belting, *Bild und Kult*. P. J. Nordhagen, 'Icons Designed for the Display of Sumptuous Gifts', *DOP* 41 (1987), 453–60. Cf. A. Weis, 'Ein vorjustinianischer Ikonentypus in S. Maria Antiqua', *Römisches Jahrbuch für Kunstgeschichte* 8 (1958), 19–61.

[7] H. Belting, 'Eine Privatkapelle im frühmittelalterlichen Rom', *DOP* 41 (1987), 55–69.

[8] Vassilaki, *Mother of God*.

[9] P. Amato (ed.), *De Vera Effigie Mariae. Antiche icone romane*, exh. cat. (Milan and Rome, 1988).

[10] S. Ensoli and E. La Rocca (eds), *Aurea Roma. Dalla città pagana alla città cristiana*, exh. cat. (Rome, 2000).

di S. Sisto', which is still housed today in a convent with a strict rule of enclosure, and also the icon which had been the centrepiece of the meeting in 1988 – its host, so to speak – the Madonna of S. Maria Maggiore, known since the nineteenth century as 'Salus Populi Romani'. What created a link between the 'Mother of God' exhibition in Athens and those in Rome (that on Late Antiquity was joined in the same place by another on the Face of Christ[11]) was that after its stay in Athens the early Sinai Virgin (now in Kiev) joined its Roman 'sisters' for several weeks in an even more unusual encounter than that of the Roman images themselves.

As is well known, the icons of Rome and those of Sinai are the oldest 'collections' of Christian panel paintings. They were discovered during the 1950s and 1960s under rough overpainting and sometimes below a quite different pictorial surface. One of the most spectacular instances is that of the Madonna of S. Maria Nova, which had been covered by a thirteenth-century Hodegetria. There is a substantial difference between the group of Sinai icons and those of Rome. The icons of St Catherine's at the foot of Mt Sinai[12] are the only surviving remnant of the sacred treasuries accumulated by important monasteries in the Holy Land over the course of the centuries. It is a particularly appealing fact that the richest icon collection is to be found in precisely the place where tradition has it that Moses in his first theophany saw the Burning Bush and heard God say 'I am that I am',[13] where the first commandment written by the finger of God was entrusted to Moses and where the Israelites were at the same time venerating the golden calf, made by melting down their jewellery. Whether one sees it as a protecting wall against idolatry or as a reversion to idolatrous practices, the Sinai icon collection had certainly acquired a specific liturgical and devotional role in the monastery. At the same time, however, it was a treasury, a sacred collection with strong associations with holy images venerated in Constantinople and other centres. Many of the icons were undoubtedly gifts or ex-votos from prominent visitors. Perhaps it may be said that the treasury was more a site of 'copies' than of originals. We do not hear of an 'acheiropoietos' or image of St Luke in the monastery, and it seems symptomatic that one of the Marian paintings from St Catherine's shows a kind of painted collection of the most venerable Virgins of the Byzantine world.[14]

The situation in Rome is rather different. To a certain degree it still preserves a sacred topography that can be traced back to the Middle Ages. Nearly all the icons of the Mother of God in Rome were housed for centuries in important sanctuaries. Associated with legends and miracles, the images constituted sites of veneration or, more precisely, were indispensably bound to their locations in a reciprocal relationship: they were in a sense iconic contractions of their churches, providing a focus of attraction (both spiritual and as symbols of various communities) while also acquiring importance from the site itself. Not by chance were the names of the

---

[11] G. Morello and G. Wolf (eds), *Il Volto di Cristo*, exh. cat. (Milan, 2000).
[12] G. and M. Soteriou, Εικόνες της Μονής Σινά I–II (Athens, 1956–1958). K. Weitzmann, *The Monastery of Saint Catherine at Mount Sinai. The Icons, I. From the Sixth to the Tenth Century* (Princeton, NJ, 1976).
[13] See the Mariological exegesis of the Burning Bush in Gregory of Nyssa, *De Vita Moysis*. N. Zchomelidse, 'Das Bild im Busch. Zu Theorie und Ikonographie der alttestamentlichen Gottesvision im Mittelalter', in B. Janowski and N. Zchomelidse (eds), *Die Sichtbarkeit des Unsichtbaren. Zur Korrelation von Text und Bild im Wirkungskreis der Bibel, Tübinger Symposion 1999* (Arbeiten zur Geschichte und Wirkung der Bibel, 3) (Stuttgart, 2002), 164–89.
[14] Soteriou, Σινά I, Figs 146–9 and II, 125–8. Belting, *Bild und Kult*, 13. N. P. Ševčenko, 'Icons in the Liturgy', *DOP* 45 (1991), 76–98.

images often toponymic, as in the case of the so-called Madonna of the Pantheon. It is against this background that the vicissitudes of the 'biography' of these images must be seen, and part of this is their material survival within a long history of over-paintings or restorations. Given these premises, reconstructing the Marian cult topography of Rome in the earlier Middle Ages promises to be a fascinating endeavour, if we agree that there is indeed a small group of images dating more or less from the sixth to the eighth/ninth centuries. The problem, however, is the near-total lack of written sources referring to those images and to a cult surrounding them in the city before the eleventh or twelfth century. The sources only become truly eloquent in the thirteenth century. Consequently, in a project I undertook around the time of the Roman Madonnas exhibition in 1988, I decided to concentrate strictly on the reception history of the images, and on their ritual or devotional 'life' as far as it could be reconstructed by means of written or visual sources.[15] In this context the dating of legends was in a sense more important than that of the images themselves. The epicentre of the project was thus the period from the eleventh to thirteenth centuries. It remained a speculative endeavour in which it was possible to postulate the pre-existence of such beliefs and practices during earlier centuries. The discovery of a late ninth-/early tenth-century Greek source published by Alexakis in 1996 throws new light on this earlier period,[16] but the modality of the rise of the cult of icons in Rome is still a highly debated subject. This is even more true given that in recent years scholars have expressed strong doubts regarding the existence of an elaborate cult of icons of the Virgin in pre-iconoclast Constantinople. No icon has survived, and many of the sources thought to date to the pre-iconoclast, or even iconophile, period have proven to be (or are claimed to be) later interpolations. This has been developed into the rather radical position on the part of some scholars that there was no cult of images before the iconoclast period, which in turn greatly alters the character of that period.[17] The remarks which follow certainly do not aim to contribute to this discussion in one direction or the other. Concentrating on Rome, we can maintain that there, too, virtually no written sources exist attesting to a cult of images before the eighth century. The *Liber Pontificalis* does not speak about images except when a Pope is donating gold and silver to an image or is commissioning an image of the Virgin in such precious materials. In Rome, however, there was no iconoclasm, and several icons of Mary and one of Christ have survived: the question is what these images themselves can tell us about their 'life' in the city, or how we can contextualize our observations. All I can offer here is a brief look at the five Roman Madonnas which I consider, with due caution, to have been painted before the end of the first millennium, as well as a few remarks on their 'biography', insofar as we know it.[18]

---

[15] G. Wolf, *Salus Populi Romani. Die Geschichte römischer Kultbilder im Mittelalter* (Weinheim, 1990).

[16] See below, n. 66. I discuss the sources at some length in G. Wolf, '*Alexifarmaka*. Aspetti del culto e della teoria delle immagini tra Roma, Bisanzio e la Terra Santa', in *Roma fra Oriente e Occidente, Settimane di studio del Centro italiano di studi sull'alto Medioevo* 49 (Spoleto, 2002), 755–96.

[17] See L. Brubaker, 'Icons before Iconoclasm', in *Morfologie sociali e culturali in Europa fra tarda antichità e alto Medioevo, Settimane di studio del Centro italiano di studi sull'alto Medioevo* 45 (Spoleto, 1998), 1215–54, with recent bibliography. Cf. for a more critical view of this position the recent work of J.-M. Sansterre, 'Entre deux mondes. La vénération des images à Rome et en Italie d'après les textes des VIe – XIe siècles', in *Roma fra Oriente e Occidente*, 993–1052.

[18] The following comments overlap with some of the arguments put forward in my article mentioned in n. 16 but adopt a different perspective. See now also M. Andaloro, 'Le icone di Roma in età preiconoclasta', in *Roma fra Oriente e Occidente*, 719–53.

I. S. Maria Nova

It has often been maintained that this icon (Fig. 3.1) was identical with an 'imago antiqua' mentioned in the life of Gregory III (731–741) in the *Liber Pontificalis*, and was originally housed in the church of S. Maria Antiqua. In the restoration by Pico Cellini, encaustic fragments of the heads of Mary and the child were discovered.[19] The subtle modulation of the flesh tones and the small mouth of the Virgin are the best testimony to the original state of the image, which was of the highest quality, whereas the somewhat sharp outlines of the eyes that hieratically gaze into the far distance may be the result of the depletion of the surface finish of the painting during later restorations and coverings. For its dating the traditional reference is to the palimpsest wall of S. Maria Antiqua, with the hieratic Maria Regina on the first layer and the Bel Angelo of the Annunciation of the second layer.[20] The Maria Regina (venerated by two angels with the *aurum coronarium*) was partially destroyed and covered by the Annunciation in the context of the construction of the apse, after 570. If the icon, which draws on the tradition of imperial portraiture, was originally housed in that church (or even painted on the occasion of its consecration) it would have been the 'temple image' of a church in the old political and religious centre of Rome. One must not, however, forget the hypothetical nature of this argument, even if it is a rather attractive one. The location of the 'imago antiqua' embellished by Gregory with a metalwork cover was unfortunately not indicated by the *Liber Pontificalis*. And even if we agree that it came from this church (called S. Maria Antiqua even before the construction of its 'descendant', S. Maria Nova),[21] the date of its construction and that of its wall paintings are highly controversial. The dates suggested range from the reign of the Emperor Justin II (565–578) to the pontificate of Theodore (640–650), the first Greek pope, who came from Jerusalem during the Arab occupation of the Holy Land.[22] The dynamics of the byzantinization of Rome and in particular its possible artistic impact is still an open question.[23] For the rest the definition of the wall paintings of S. Maria Antiqua as 'Constantinopolitan' tends to involve a circular argument, given that we hardly have any knowledge of the latter. Is the 'hellenistic' style a reference to the capital of the Byzantine empire, or is it an iconic style (copying encaustic paintings but using other techniques) without a precise geographical reference, given the sparse remains in the Oecumene? I do not want to enter into this discussion here, whereas I will return to the 'Maria Regina' later in my paper.

What we can say with more certainty is that in the Forum context the icon in question played a major role in the church that was the juridical and religious descendant of S. Maria

---

[19] P. Cellini, 'Una Madonna molto antica', *Proporzioni* 3 (1950), 1-6. See also the entry of M. Andaloro, in Ensoli and La Rocca, *Aurea Roma*, no. 375, 660–1, with bibliography, and her study as quoted in n. 18.

[20] Belting, *Bild und Kult*, 142 ff.

[21] See the 7th-c. catalogue from Salzburg (C. Hülsen, *Le chiese di Roma nel Medio Evo. Cataloghi ed appunti* (Florence, 1927), 3) and the inscription in the chapel of Sts Quiricus and Julitta commissioned by primicerius Theodotus in the early 8th c.: '[...] semperque Virgo Maria quae appellatur antiqua'.

[22] R. Krautheimer, 'Sancta Maria Rotunda', in id., *Corpus Basilicarum Christianarum Romae* II (Rome, 1962), 251–70 and the critical discussion in Brenk, 'Kultgeschichte versus Stilgeschichte'. See also *S. Maria Antiqua. Cent' anni dopo lo scavo*, Proceedings of the Conference held in Rome, May 2000 (forthcoming).

[23] See also J.-M. Sansterre, *Les moines grecs orientaux à Rome aux époques byzantine et carolingienne* (*Mémoires de la Classe des Lettres de l'Académie royale de Belgique*, 65.1-2) (Brussels, 1983).

Antiqua (destroyed in an eighth-century earthquake), S. Maria Nova, which was still called 'S. Maria nuova quae antiqua vocabatur' in the eleventh century.[24] During the procession of the *transitus* (Koimesis) of the Virgin on the night of 14 to 15 August, the Saviour icon of the Lateran, an encaustic panel showing the figure of the enthroned Christ and dating to the sixth–seventh centuries, was carried in procession from the Papal palace through the Forum Romanum (Fig. 3.2) to S. Maria Maggiore.[25] The procession was mentioned for the first time as early as the ninth century. As we learn from an *Ordo* and an accompanying poem of the late tenth to early eleventh century, in front of the church of S. Maria Nova the Saviour icon met the icon of the Virgin in a kind of *synthronon*.[26] In later sources the image is sometimes mentioned as painted by St Luke, but we do not know much about its 'fortune' in the later Middle Ages, when the remaining fragments were incorporated into and then covered by a new picture, taking some essential features of the morphological structure of the original icon but changing, for example, the angles of the heads of Mary and the Christ-child, which were more inclined in the old image.[27]

II. The Madonna of the Pantheon

In the case of the Pantheon there is a higher degree of certainty regarding the existence from the very beginning of a relation between image and sacred building. The dedication of the Pantheon to Mary (Fig. 3.3) and to all martyrs is a crucial moment in the Christianization of the heritage of pagan Rome, and it became a prototype of the Christian concept of the temple inhabited by an image. As is well known the Pantheon was donated by Emperor Phokas to Pope Boniface IV on 13 May 609.[28] There is in fact little doubt that the icon of the Virgin housed therein dates to the same period, or that the passage from pagan to Christian temple was effected by the removal of the pagan deity figures, regarded as idols inhabited by demons, and 'her' introduction into the 'Rotunda' together with the erection of an altar dedicated to Christ.

---

[24] Wolf, *Salus Populi Romani*, 264 ff. with references.

[25] For the icon (restored in 1994–1996 in the laboratories of the Musei Vaticani), its cult and its copies, see the section with the contributions of M. Andaloro, S. Romano, W. Angelelli and E. Parlato, in Morello and Wolf, *Il Volto di Cristo*, 39 ff. See now also S. Romano, 'L'icône acheiropoiete du Latran: fonction d'une image absente', in N. Bock *et al.* (eds), *Art, cérémonial et liturgie au Moyen Âge* (*Études lausannoises d'Histoire de l'art*, 1) (Rome, 2002), 301–19.

[26] For the procession see Wolf, *Salus Populi Romani*, 29 ff. with bibliography and discussion of the sources. For the *Ordo* and the text of the hymn see M. Andrieu (ed.), *Ordines Romani* V (Louvain, 1961), 358–61. For the year 1000, see G. Wolf, ' "Sistitur in Solio." Römische Kultbilder um 1000', in *Bernward von Hildesheim und das Zeitalter der Ottonen* I (Hildesheim and Mainz, 1993), 81–9. For the imperial connotations of the hymn, cf. I. Frings, ' "Sancta Maria Quid est?" Hymnus, Herrscherlob und Ikonenkult im Rom der Jahrtausendwende', *Analecta Cisterciensia* 52 (1996), 224–50. Cf. E. Kitzinger, 'A Virgin's Face. Antiquarianism in Twelfth-Century Art', *ArtB* 62 (1980), 6–19.

[27] See nn. 18 and 19, in particular the reconstruction by Andaloro, 'Le icone di Roma in età preiconoclasta'.

[28] H. Grisar, 'Il Pantheon in Roma e la sua dedicazione fatta da Bonifazio IV (608–615)', *Civiltà Cattolica* 10 (1900), 210–24. M. V. Schwarz, 'Eine frühmittelalterliche Umgestaltung der Pantheon-Vorhalle', *Römisches Jahrbuch der Bibliotheca Hertziana* 26 (1990), 1–29. P. Virgilio, 'Strutture altomedievali sulla fronte del Pantheon', *RendPontAcc* 70 (1997/8), 197–207.

It is, however, rather improbable that at this early point large quantities of martyrs' relics were introduced into this church *intra muros*.[29]

The Madonna of the Pantheon[30] is a tempera painting (Fig. 3.4); as it appears today it represents a half-length figure of Mary cut around her nimbus and shoulders and truncated at the lower end. The Virgin carries her son on her left side, in a gesture which oscillates between holding and pointing to him. Her hands are painted gold: the power of intercession resides in them. The shifting of the attention from Mother to Son (at the same time highlighting her role) is performed by the painting itself. The figure of Mary seems roughly painted with rapid strokes:[31] her asymmetrical face and eyes and slightly turning body retrocede, opening a space, whereas, as has often been noted, Christ appears as a Dionysiac God-child actively but not directly addressing the beholder. The tempera technique certainly does not allow for the subtle transitions of the encaustic (as is obvious if one compares it with the Madonna of S. Maria Nova), but in the modelling of the face of the child by light and shadow and in its high crown of hair it marvellously establishes its own icon aesthetics. Bertelli has proposed the reconstruction of the panel as a full-length figure whose dimensions would be approximately 2.50 m,[32] but I doubt whether this corresponds to the nature of this icon, the subtle focusing of the relation between Mother and Son. The Madonna of the Pantheon is a field of grace created by means of the gazes, the gestures, the gold hands and the interplay of monumentality and intimacy in the image.

Turning from the icon to the Christianized temple, I do not want to enter into the discussion of S. Maria Rotunda as an example of the reception of earlier or contemporary Constantinopolitan models of Marian shrines like the circular reliquary chapel of the Blachernai church, which housed the maphorion, one of the major *palladia* of the city and the empire.[33] It is important, however, to underline that Constantinople had no such pagan temples to be christianized, and that from this point of view the situation in Rome is quite different.[34] Beyond this, if we can trust the *Liber Pontificalis*, the gift of the Pantheon was less the result of spontaneous generosity on the part of Phokas than of the Pope's explicit request. Given that Rome and its church remained the only ally of Phokas, who was in the midst of an extremely difficult political and military situation, his gesture is quite comprehensible. In any case, there is little reason to

---

[29] I would like to thank Caroline Goodson, Columbia University, for discussion on this point. For the relation of relic and icon, see now E. Thunoe, *Image and Relic. Mediating the Sacred in Early Medieval Rome* (Rome, 2002).

[30] C. Bertelli, 'La Madonna del Pantheon', *Bolletino d'arte* 46 (1961), 24–32. Belting, *Bild und Kult*, 141. Ensoli and La Rocca, *Aurea Roma*, no. 376, 661–2 (M. Andaloro). Brenk, 'Kultgeschichte versus Stilgeschichte'. The format is 100 × 47.5 cm.

[31] Bertelli, 'La Madonna del Pantheon', 102: 'dal colore povero e poco variato e gli effetti del modellato ottenuti subito e senza gradazione di tinte'. For the characterization of the Christ-child see, for example, Belting, *Bild und Kult*, 142. Andaloro, 'Le icone di Roma in età preiconoclasta', 736.

[32] Bertelli, 'La Madonna del Pantheon'.

[33] A. M. Cameron, 'The Theotokos in Sixth-Century Constantinople. A City Finds it Symbol', *JThSt* 29 (1978), 79–108. Mango, 'Theotokoupolis'. For the history of the icons, see Bacci, *Il pennello*. See also Krautheimer, 'Sancta Maria Rotunda'. I find it rather misleading that even in recent literature the early Roman Madonnas are called Hodegetrias. Beyond the fact that we have no sources from this early period for this famous Constantinopolitan icon, this denomination suggests a Byzantine provenance for the images in Rome, whereas I would prefer to speak of the rise of the cult of images as a phenomenon of the whole Oecumene in which local tradition (in Rome obviously rather strong) interferes with that of other centres.

[34] See also Andaloro, 'Le icone di Roma in età preiconoclasta', 751 ff.

doubt that there was a strong papal interest in taking over the central imperial monument of the *Campus Martius*, a building that was a symbol par excellence of the pagan world.

The account of the life of Boniface in the *Liber Pontificalis* is rather brief; after the usual formula it proceeds with the statement that during his times Rome was troubled by terrible famine, plague and floods, followed immediately by the news of his petition to Phokas for papal control of the Pantheon.[35] The transformation into a church of the major temple in the city centre, which was dangerously exposed to the continuous flooding of the Tiber, seems not least to be an attempt to ward off such calamities and to provide a strong Christian cult centre at a time when – as mentioned above – the translation of relics *intra muros* had not yet begun on a grand scale. The Madonna of the Pantheon could thus become a sacred protector of the *Populus Romanus* in the heart of the early mediaeval *urbs*, and could be defined as a cult image even if we know nothing about such a cult.[36]

On the occasion of the Christianization of England by Augustine, who arrived on the shores of the British Isles with an icon of Christ only a few years before the pontificate of Boniface, Gregory the Great had insisted that temples should not be destroyed, but only the idols which were worshipped within them.[37] And in a letter of 599 to the bishop of Cagliari, Gregory had criticized the forcible conversion of a synagogue into a church by means of the introduction of an image of the Virgin, a cross and other 'venerable' objects.[38] Cross and image are mentioned on the same level; the term 'veneratio' can be seen in contrast to 'adoratio imaginum', which was prohibited in Gregory's view, as he maintains in his famous letters to Serenus of Marseilles, destined to become basic texts for the image theory of the western Church.[39] While it is true that the *Liber Pontificalis* mentions 'multa dona' given by Phokas to the new church, and one cannot exclude that among them was an icon of the Virgin, in my view the introduction of the icon into the temple was not the foundation moment of a cult of images in early mediaeval Rome, imported on this occasion from Byzantium, but should rather be seen in the context of an already established 'tradition' on the basis of other instances more difficult to date, but presumably earlier. I agree, however, that the later sixth and early seventh century was a crucial moment for the introduction of such a cult of images. It is interesting that this seems to have happened during or around the time of the pontificate of Gregory the Great, and that it was hardly a phenomenon which could escape the attention of the bishop of the city; indeed he was actively engaged in it, as seems obvious in the case of the Pantheon.

---

[35] Despite the fact that the vitae in the *Liber Pontificalis* are organized in the form of a catalogue, the sequence seems in this case to be symptomatic. The high walls erected in the intercolumnia of the Pantheon, fortifying the church, may also have functioned as a protection against flooding.

[36] See in this sense also Brenk, 'Kultgeschichte versus Stilgeschichte', despite the scepticism he shows in relation to the term 'cult image'.

[37] Beda, *Historia Anglorum*, I.30.

[38] Gregorius Magnus, *Epistula IX*, 196, in id., *Registrum Epistularum* I (*Corpus Scriptorum Ecclesiasticorum Latinorum*, 140a) (Turnholt, 1982), 750–2, esp. 751.

[39] For the afterlife of Gregory's 'theory of images', see J.-Cl. Schmitt, 'L'Occident, Nicée II et les images du VIIIe au XIIIe siècle', in F. Boespflug and N. Lossky (eds), *Nicée II (787–1987). Douze siècles d'images religieuses* (Paris, 1987), 271–301. For a critical discussion on studies of Gregory's letters, see L. Duggan, 'Was Art Really the "Book of the Illiterate"', *Word and Image* 5 (1989), 227–51. C. M. Chazelle, 'Pictures, Books, and the Illiterate: Pope Gregory I's Letters to Serenus of Marseilles', *Word and Image* 6 (1990), 138–53. Cf. Wolf, '*Alexifarmaka*', 772, and also Brenk, 'Kultgeschichte versus Stilgeschichte' (for *adorare – venerari*).

We see Gregory interacting with images on the occasion of the *adventus* of the imperial image(s) of Phokas and his wife Leontia, which were welcomed to Rome in April 603, brought to the Lateran basilica and finally translated to the chapel of St Caesarius in the imperial *palatium* on the Palatine Hill. It is with this act that the good relations between the popes and Phokas began.[40] In 607 the emperor conceded to Boniface III the sovereignty of the bishop of Rome over all churches.[41] In fact Gregory I had been extremely critical of the title 'ecumenical patriarch', which the bishops of Constantinople had adopted for nearly a hundred years. Thus the gift of the Pantheon and the erection of an honorary column on the Forum Romanum by the exarch of Ravenna, Smaragdus, were the final monumental testaments of an alliance between Emperor and Pope. These years may also have offered a climate favourable to the construction of the church of S. Maria Antiqua on the Forum at the foot of the Palatine Hill.[42]

I will return to the pontificate of Gregory in the next section when discussing the history of the Virgin of S. Maria Maggiore, but on the subject of the Pantheon icon almost no later written source adds anything substantial to its 'biography'. It is thus all the more surprising that it is mentioned once in the *Liber Pontificalis*, during the papacy of Stephanus III, when in an often quoted story a Lombard priest tries to take refuge from his persecutors in the Pantheon while holding the image of the Mother of God ('portante eodem Wadiperto imaginem ipsius Dei genetricis'), but is unable to save himself.[43]

III. S. Maria Maggiore

The *Liber Pontificalis* reports another vain attempt to gain asylum in a church of the Virgin during the pontificate of Theodore (642–649).[44] The rebellious *chartoularios* Mavrikios, looking for protection from the exarch Isaac, fled into the basilica of S. Maria Maggiore 'ad praesepe'. There he was taken by Isaac's men and killed. Did he try to gain protection from an icon, and, more generally, can we be sure that there was an icon of the Virgin in the basilica during this period? If we look at the 'Salus Populi Romani', the most important Marian image of the church (Plate 2, Fig. 3.5), venerated since the early seventeenth century in the Cappella Paolina, we become engaged with a somewhat problematic case of dating. The dates proposed by various authors (often in an apodictic way) stretch from the fifth to the thirteenth century.[45]

My own remarks are based on a close examination of the icon in 1987, when it was taken out of its tabernacle and brought for a few days to the Vatican conservation laboratories. To be somewhat apodictic myself, I would say that I have little doubt about the relatively early date of

---

[40] Gregorius Magnus, *Registrum Epistularum II* (App. VIII), 1101.
[41] *Liber Pontificalis*, I.316 (Life of Bonifatius III). In general see J. Richards, *The Life and Times of Gregory the Great* (London, 1980). R. A. Markus, *Gregory the Great and His World* (Cambridge, 1997).
[42] In this case the church could be considered in a certain sense to be a product not of hostility but of friendship between the Greeks and Romans. I do not want to argue for an alternative hypothesis for the date of the construction of this church, but only to emphasize that there is more than one historical moment during which such construction would have been possible.
[43] *Liber Pontificalis*, I.472.
[44] Ibid., I.331.
[45] J. Wilpert, *Die römischen Mosaiken und Malereien der kirchlichen Bauten vom 4. bis ins 13. Jahrhundert* (Rome, 1916), 1134–8. Amato, *De Vera Effigie Mariae*, 52–60. M. Andaloro, 'L'icona della Vergine "Salus Populi

this painting, even if the panel is the only icon never to have been restored apart from a short and problematic 'ritocco' in 1931. In contrast to the Madonna of S. Maria Nova, the panel does not display an over-painting superimposed on an early image which could be liberated from under later layers, but is rather a kind of palimpsest icon, which was restored from time to time in different areas and thus documents the survival and coexistence of various modifications to the same pictorial surface (Plate 3a, Fig. 3.6). It is evident that the nimbus and the dirty green colour of the face of the Virgin are the product of late restorations, as is the distorted contour of her shoulders. Especially revealing in the same context is the contrast between the two hands of Christ: while the left hand holding the book is sharply outlined in black and is schematically coloured, the right hand raised in a gesture of blessing over the dark ground of Mary's robe appears modulated with the use of tones of green and white, creating an impressionistic effect (Plate 3b, Fig. 3.7). The craquelure indicates that this is not part of a Renaissance restoration, but is an older fragment of the painting, indicative of the Late Antique character of the icon. In my view, the morphology of the image also points in this direction: Mary's gesture of crossing her hands as she holds the child does not correspond to any known mediaeval model. If we compare the icon with the small early Virgin of Mt Sinai (today in Kiev)[46] or with the Madonna of the Pantheon, concrete stylistic affinities cannot be singled out; what we find are different solutions to the same artistic 'problem', namely the representation of the Divine Child in the arms of the human Mother, with a play of gazes and gestures that simultaneously convey both an extraordinary sensuality and great spirituality. The Sinai Virgin, an icon for private devotion, has a more intimate character, while the Madonna of S. Maria Maggiore, whose hieratic solemnity was perhaps comparable to that of the Madonna of S. Maria Nova, became at some point the official cult image of the papal basilica. In a mural painting in S. Maria Antiqua we find a Mother and Child in nearly the same position, including the motif of the crossed hands of the Virgin, presumably copied from the original in S. Maria Maggiore as a votive image.[47] The frame of the icon has often been dated to the Cosmatesque period, which in turn has operated as a strong criterion for a late dating. Some years ago, I compared it with the frame of an icon of S. Panteleemon which was preserved in Kiev (but seems to have been lost) together with other panels from Sinai: both show the same combination of ornamental rhombs and concentric circles. Wulff and Alpatoff dated the Panteleemon icon to the ninth century and defined it as a work of the so-called 'Macedonian Renaissance'.[48] I do not want to draw definitive conclusions from this comparison, but rather aim to counterbalance the apodictic certainty of Wilpert and others in attributing the frame to the Cosmati. In my view the ornament consists of motifs common in antiquity.

There are several good reasons for placing the 'Salus Populi Romani' among the other early Roman icons of the Virgin. While it would be too audacious to date the image to the period of

---

Romani"', in C. Pietrangeli (ed.), *Santa Maria Maggiore a Roma* (Florence, 1988), 124–9. Wolf, *Salus Populi Romani*, 24 ff. Belting, *Bild und Kult*, 79 ff.

[46] For the Sinai icon (35.4 × 20.6 cm), today in Kiev, Bogdan and Varvara Khanenko Museum of Arts, inv. 112 ZK, see Weitzmann, *The Monastery of Saint Catherine*, 32–5. Belting, *Bild und Kult*, 82 ff. Vassilaki, *Mother of God*, no. 2, 264–5 (R. Cormack). Ensoli and La Rocca, *Aurea Roma*, no. 374, p. 660 (E. N. Roslavec).

[47] W. de Grüneisen, *Sainte-Marie-Antique* (Rome, 1911).

[48] O. Wulff and M. Alpatoff, *Denkmäler der Ikonenmalerei in kunstgeschichtlicher Folge* (Hellerau bei Dresden, 1925), 48–52. Wolf, *Salus Populi Romani*, 256.

the consecration of the basilica by Sixtus III, I have no hesitation in seeing it as part of the group of icons extant by the late sixth and early seventh centuries. Indeed, by this time it may already have become the 'temple' image of the basilica as we encounter it in later mediaeval sources. It is important to note, however, that the cult of the Virgin (and her Son) in S. Maria Maggiore did not and could not have a single focus. The same source which recounts the story of Mavrikios mentions the title of the basilica 'Sancta Maria ad praesepe' for the first time (and perhaps not by chance at a time when Bethlehem had come under Islamic control).[49] Indeed, the crib of Christ was to become the major relic of the church. There was at least one Marian image present in the context of this oratory of the *praesepe*: a metalwork icon (probably in relief) depicting Mary embracing her Son.[50] This precious image was the gift of Pope Gregory III (731–741), and was a visualization adapted to the *praesepe* shrine, an iconic 'inhabitant' of the relic site and certainly not a movable image with an important role in ritual performances. By contrast we know for certain from twelfth- and thirteenth-century sources that the so-called 'Salus Populi Romani' functioned in this way. It was that icon which the Lateran Saviour came to visit on the night of the Dormition and Assumption of the Virgin. This procession was one of the major ritual events of mediaeval Rome, as mentioned above in the discussion of the encounter between the images of Mother and Son at the church of S. Maria Nova. Presumably in the ninth century it grew out of a group of four processions on Marian feast days (i.e. Purification, Annunciation, Nativity and Dormition) introduced or institutionalized by Sergius I (678–701), processions that went from S. Adriano (the Christianized *curia* on the Forum Romanum and former *collecta* meeting-place) to S. Maria Maggiore. Once in the twelfth century we hear of the participation of eighteen Marian icons in the Purification procession as symbols of the *diaconiae* in the Forum, but we have no further details about this event.[51]

The dynamics of the Assumption procession, which became a ritual in its own right, and especially the role played by icons of the Virgin in it, were very much the subject of debate several years ago.[52] I do not intend to return extensively to this controversy now. The important point here is to remain close to the sources, which confirm that on this occasion there was only one image carried in procession, namely the Lateran Saviour, and that we have reports of only two images of the Virgin, those of S. Maria Nova and S. Maria Maggiore, involved in the ritual within or in front of their respective churches. The presence of any other icon at this event is merely speculative.[53] It may seem puzzling that both icons show Mary with her son, since the meeting of such an image with a Saviour icon appears less comprehensible to modern eyes than

---

[49] *Liber Pontificalis*, I.331 (and the comment in this sense by Duchesne, 33). See for the following Brenk, 'Kultgeschichte versus Stilgeschichte'.

[50] *Liber Pontificalis*, I.418; it is a few lines before the mention of the adornment of an/the 'imago antiqua': '… ibidem in oratorio sancto quod praesepe dicitur imaginem auream Dei genetricis amplectendem Salvatorem dominum Deum nostrum in gemmis diversis, pens. lib. V'.

[51] *Ordo of Albinus*, ed. in *Liber Censuum*, II (Paris, 1910), 128. Wolf, *Salus Populi Romani*, 327 (Q.12).

[52] On the Assumption procession see the references in nn. 20 and 21. Also H. Belting, 'Icons and Roman Society in the Twelfth Century', in W. Tronzo (ed.), *Italian Church Decoration of the Middle Ages and the Early Renaissance: Functions, Forms and Regional Traditions* (Villa Spelman Colloquia, 1) (Bologna, 1989), 27–41. W. Tronzo, 'Apse Decoration, the Liturgy, and the Perception of Art in Medieval Rome. S. Maria in Trastevere and S. Maria Maggiore', ibid., 167–93. See now also Romano, 'L'icône acheiropoiete du Latran'.

[53] See the 12th-c. treatise of Nicolaus Maniacutius, *Historia Imaginis Salvatoris* (Rome, 1709), partly republished in Wolf, *Salus Populi Romani*, 321 ff., and the analysis of this text, 61 ff., esp. 65 ff.

does an encounter with an icon showing the Virgin alone (see below, section V).[54] We must remember, however, that what we would like to see is less important than what the sources tell us, and from that point of view the encounter of the icons as mentioned above also corresponds to the puzzling theological *mysterium* that Mary is the mother and the bride of Christ (*mater et sponsa*) – and, one may add, when he takes her soul in his arms at her death, according to the Koimesis iconography, also his daughter. Thus, the *synthronon* or ritual encounter of the Saviour with the two icons of the Madonna (representing Mary as the Mother of God), however it was performed,[55] has rich theological and devotional connotations, including that of the corporeal assumption of the Virgin.

Another important point is that by the twelfth century the procession was no longer a papal ritual. The Pope (if he was in Rome in August) celebrated Mass in S. Maria Maggiore on the morning of the Feast of the Assumption, but did not take part in the procession from the Lateran through the Roman Forum up to the Esquiline Hill. It thus became a communal event,[56] and this consideration invites a short reflection on the way in which icons work as symbols of communities. In the papal palace chapel, the icon of the enthroned Christ (called 'acheropita' by the *Liber Pontificalis*, that is, not made by human hands)[57] represented the *Rex Regum* to the Pope and thus played a role in papal liturgy: on Easter Sunday morning the shrine of the icon in the Sancta Sanctorum was ritually opened and the Pope kissed the feet of Christ,[58] whose image stood on relics and earth from the Holy Land. As a twelfth-century author maintains, because of its presence in the Lateran the prophetic words would be fulfilled: 'See, I come and will live in the midst of you.'[59] From this perspective one could define the icon as a symbol of papal authority, as one may also view its numerous copies found throughout Latium. However, during the Assumption procession – once it was no longer a papal event – for one night the icon, even if transported and accompanied by clerics, was welcomed by the *Populus Romanus* as its judge and sovereign, and became a symbol of the community itself. If we turn to the icons of the Virgin we may observe a similar passage in the symbolic process. The Madonna is certainly a 'partner' for private and collective devotion, and an intercessor on the occasion of political or natural calamities. Unfortunately we know little about the mounting of the icons in their churches, but the sources indicate that by at least the twelfth–thirteenth century the Madonna of S. Maria Maggiore was called 'Regina Coeli' and mounted over the door of the

---

54 Tronzo, 'Apse Decoration, the Liturgy, and the Perception of Art'.
55 Frings, 'Sancta Maria Quid est?', visualized the two images on one throne, a ritual I find difficult to imagine, given that the Saviour icon was certainly carried on a heavy 'machina', as perhaps was also the 'Virgin' when she emerged from 'her' church.
56 See for this transformation of the nature of the procession Wolf, *Salus Populi Romani*, 37 ff. with respective sources (esp. the *Ordo XI* of *c*. 1145, ed. in *Liber Censuum*, II (Paris, 1910), 158 ff.). For the typology of processions in general, see S. de Blaauw, 'Contrasts in Processional Liturgy: A Typology of Outdoor Processions in Twelfth-Century Rome', in Bock *et al.*, *Art, cérémonial et liturgie au Moyen Âge*, 357–96.
57 It is not by chance that the epithet appears in the life of Stephanus II, in 752 (*Liber Pontificalis*, I.443) during the iconoclast period. For the terminology in general, see M. Andaloro, 'Il *Liber Pontificalis* e la questione delle immagini da Sergio I e Adriano I', in *Roma e l'età carolingia* (Rome, 1976), 69–77. Ead., 'L'acheropita nell'ombra del Laterano', in Morello and Wolf, *Il Volto di Cristo*, 43–5. Wolf, 'Alexifarmaka'.
58 For this rite see now Romano, 'L'icône acheiropoiete du Latran', 309 with discussion of the sources.
59 Maniacutius, *Historia Imaginis Salvatoris*, in Wolf, *Salus Populi Romani*, 323, following Zechariah 2:10. For the implications of this concept of presence constituted by the image, see ibid., 64.

Baptistery.⁶⁰ In this way she represented the union of Maria and Ecclesia.⁶¹ Thus the icon of the Virgin, too, could function as a symbol of the people and of the *Ecclesia Romana*, the Papal church; in any case the two spheres interpenetrated in various ways as the historical situation changed.

To sum up, the icons of Mary and Christ were the central *palladia* of the city of Rome, with a wide range of possible 'instrumentalizations'. Their specific connotations were defined, though not exhausted, by their contexts (i.e. iconography, display technique, adornment, ritual, etc.) as well as by the individuals or groups who gathered around them. These icons were thus bound no less to their sites and to the complex interplay between them than to their communities. Not only were they a veil or membrane for an osmotic exchange of the divine and the terrestrial sphere, but also a mirror or magnifying/burning glass that focused the energy projected onto them by the public who venerated them. I have referred to this phenomenon on another occasion as 'the two bodies of images'.⁶² This terminology was not meant as a simple explanation of the miraculous power of these icons but as an attempt to understand some of the aspects of the transfer of energy that the icon field offers. One may view the encounter between the Saviour icon and the Madonna of S. Maria Maggiore which took place, at least in the later Middle Ages, in the early morning of 15 August in front of the basilica as a ritual *concordia* between the Papal or ecclesiastical authority and the *Populus Romanus*. According to my interpretation, however, the two icons could 'stand' for both sides; the icons are themselves fields of tensions and pretensions, in which different positions may meet, neutralize, fertilize or enter into conflict. Both Church and community groups, whose cohabitation characterizes Rome itself, needed to participate in the icons, whose 'chora' was a field of encounter.

At the same time that the liturgical texts tell us that the Assumption procession had become a major communal ritual, the legends arise that the Madonna of S. Maria Maggiore was painted by the hand of St Luke, and that it was the protagonist of a miracle during a procession instituted by Gregory the Great immediately following his election to the papal throne.⁶³ The latter refers to the famous story, widely diffused by the *Legenda aurea* and the *Rationale Divinorum Officiorum* of Durantus,⁶⁴ that during the great plague of 590 the icon of Mary was carried to the basilica of St Peter's and by means of the intercession of the Virgin the plague – a sign of the wrath of God – ceased. In fact, when the procession crossed the bridge of the Tiber, whose floods full of demons were believed to have given rise to the epidemic, Archangel Michael appeared over the mausoleum of Hadrian and returned his sword to its sheath while angels hovered around the Madonna, greeting her with the antiphon 'Regina Coeli'. Thus the legend also became an aetiology of the name of the icon, which was seen as the sacred protector of the city. The plague of 590 is a historical fact as well as being coincident with the institution of a penitential procession; both are mentioned by Gregory of Tours, whereas the register of Pope

---

⁶⁰ Ibid., 93 ff., 106 ff.
⁶¹ For the concept, see A. Müller, *Ecclesia – Maria. Die Einheit Marias und der Kirche* (*Paradosis. Beiträge zur Geschichte der altchristlichen Literatur und Theologie*, 5) (Fribourg, 1954).
⁶² Wolf, *Salus Populi Romani*, viii.
⁶³ Ibid., 102 ff.
⁶⁴ *Guillelmi Duranti Rationale divinorum officiorum I–IV* (*Corpus Christianorum*, 140), ed. A. Davril and T. M. Thibodeau (Turnholt, 1995), VII.89. Jacobus de Voragine, *Legenda Aurea, Vita Gregorii*, ed. Graesse (Leipzig, 1890), 190. For extensive discussion of the sources, see Wolf, *Salus Populi Romani*, 138 ff.

Gregory contains the indication of the so-called *laetania septiformis*, that is, seven processions with different social groups departing from different churches according to the seven church districts of the city, which met at the basilica of S. Maria Maggiore.[65] Certainly, these sources make no allusion to the involvement of an icon in the procession(s), carried in the hope of placating the wrath of God by means of the intercession of his Mother. Nevertheless, I would like to argue that it is possible to antedate the legend to at least the ninth century on the following grounds. In the above-mentioned list of nine images 'not made by human hands' in a Greek iconophile anthology of the late ninth or early tenth century, we find the following entry:

> The icon not painted by hands ('acheirographa') of the Most Holy Mother of God in Rome. At the time when the plague pervaded all the cities, precisely in August for the Feast of the Dormition of the Virgin, the Roman people in penitence and submission (prostrating themselves in *proskynesis*) solemnly carried the icon around the city as an antidote to all spiritual and corporal disease.[66]

There can be little doubt that this entry refers to the Madonna of S. Maria Maggiore, and it seems to fuse the memory of the Assumption procession with the salvation from the plague, when the image of Christ was brought to the church of his mother. The epithet of the icon, 'acheirographa', not mentioned by any other source, in fact places the image on the same level as that of the Lateran Saviour. Thus to my eyes the legend of the salvation of the city of Rome by a procession with an icon of Mary seems not to be a product of the period of the eleventh- or twelfth-century reform, but, in whatever earlier form, to go back to the time when legends served as arguments in the debates on images. The codex Marcianus gr. reads like a pamphlet emphasizing the need for an 'acheiropoieta' for the city of Constantinople, a requirement that was fulfilled in the year 944 with the triumphal entry of the Mandylion from Edessa.[67] Weak as the bridge offered by this Greek source may be, it is nonetheless tempting to think that we here encounter an older tradition with traces going back to the period of natural calamities during the reign of Pope Gregory and his disciple Boniface IV. More generally, these calamities could have played an important role in the rise of the cult of images in Rome, presenting occasions on which

---

[65] Gregorius Turonensis, *Libri Historiarum XII*, ed. R. Buchner, II (Darmstadt, 1956), 321 ff. Cf. F. Graus, *Volk, Herrscher und Heiliger im Reich der Merowinger, Studien zur Hagiographie der Merowingerzeit* (Prague, 1965). See above n. 41.

[66] A. Alexakis, *The Codex Parisinus Graecus 1115 and Its Prototype* (Washington, DC, 1996), 348–50: cod. Marcianus gr. 573, fols 23v–26 (esp. fol. 25v); see also Wolf, '*Alexifarmaka*', 790 f. Cf. the discussion of his reconstruction of the iconophile anthologies as 8th-c. Roman compilations: E. Lamberz, 'Studien zur Überlieferung der Akten des VII. Ökumenischen Konzils: Der Brief Hadrians I. an Konstantin VI. und Irene (JE 2448)', *Deutsches Archiv für die Erforschung des Mittelalters* 53 (1997), 1–43. K.-H. Uthemann, 'Ein griechisches Florileg zur Verteidigung des Filioque aus dem 7. Jahrhundert? Eine Bemerkung zum Parisinus graecus 1115', *BZ* 92 (1999), 502–11, and the reaction of A. Alexakis, 'The Epistula *Ad Marinum Cypri Presbyterum* of Maximos the Confessor (*CPG* 7697.10) Revisited: A Few Remarks on Its Meaning and Its History', *BZ* 94, (2001) 545–54. This discussion does not touch on the list of 'acheiropoieta' in the cod. Marcianus and its dating.

[67] For the entry of the Mandylion, see E. Patlagean, 'L'entrée de la Sainte Face d'Édesse à Constantinople en 944', in *La religion civique à l'époque médiévale et moderne, Chrétienté et Islam, Actes du colloque organisé par le centre de Recherche sur l'Histoire sociale et culturelle de l'Occident, XIIe–XVIIIe siècle* (Collection de l'École française de Rome, 213) (Rome, 1995), 21–35. In general, see most recently A. M. Cameron, 'The Mandylion and Byzantine Iconoclasm', in H. Kessler and G. Wolf (eds), *The Holy Face and the Paradox of Representation* (Milan, 1999), 33–54. H. L. Kessler, 'Il Mandilion', in Morello and Wolf, *Il Volto di Cristo*, 67–76.

the need arose for supernatural protectors or mediators from the demons liberated by the wrath of God, and the dedication of the Pantheon with the abolition of the idols and the introduction of an icon of the Virgin would certainly have met with Gregory's full approval, if indeed the plan to christianize the Rotunda was not developed during his pontificate.

IV. The Madonna della Clemenza

The Virgin icons which we have looked at up to now could be called 'temple images'. I would briefly like to discuss two other early images that correspond to a somewhat different iconic logic: the Madonna della Clemenza of S. Maria in Trastevere (Fig. 3.8) and the so-called Madonna di S. Sisto. The first of these, a monumental encaustic painting (164 × 116 cm),[68] has the character of a 'mediated' icon through the different strata of temporality and reality within the image itself, also palpable by means of different *modi* or conventions of style: the hieratically enthroned Maria Regina, the human expression of the incarnate child on her lap, the more ethereal angel guardians (*silentiarii*) flanking the throne, and finally the almost completely effaced figure of a Pope who simultaneously kneels within and in front of the image. Corresponding to this liminal position is the cross staff held by Mary, which was applied to the image as a votive gift.[69] Proposed datings fluctuate between the occasion of the dedication of the *titulus Julii et Callistii* to S. Maria, presumably in the late sixth century, and the ninth century, and more particularly the pontificate of John VII (705–707), who has been seen as an appropriate candidate for the donor pope, who devotedly touches the red shoes of the Virgin while gazing out from the image.[70] In a mosaic in the chapel erected by John on the right side of Old St Peter's, the Pope is shown as a small donor figure before the monumental Maria Regina orans (preserved in the church of S. Marco, Florence).[71] The style of the Madonna della Clemenza (or its use of stylistic modes) does not allow for a firm dating, given that these conventions were known and used in Rome from at least the late sixth to the eighth centuries. For the dating we must therefore look for a more stringent historical contextualization. In his monograph Bertelli develops the hypothesis that the icon demonstrates the claims of papal autonomy with respect to the Byzantine emperor, showing that the Pope submits himself only to the divine empress and to Christ. I do not want to enter into the discussion of this

---

[68] The essential bibliography is C. Bertelli, *La Madonna di S. Maria in Trastevere. Storia-iconografia-stile di un dipinto romano dell'ottavo secolo* (Roma, 1961). M. Andaloro, 'La datazione della tavola di S. Maria in Trastevere', *RIASA*, n.s., 19/20 (1972/3) 135–215. E. Russo, 'L'affresco di Turtura nel cimitero di Comodilla, l'icona di S. Maria in Trastevere e le più antiche feste della Madonna a Roma', *Bulletino storico italiano per il medio evo e archivio muratoriano* 88 (1979), 35–85; 89 (1980/1), 73–150. Ensoli and La Rocca, *Aurea Roma*, no. 377, 662–3 (M. Andaloro). Andaloro, 'Le icone di Roma in età preiconoclasta', 740 ff. For the history of the church, see D. Kinney, *S. Maria in Trastevere from its Foundings to 1215* (Ann Arbor, 1982). B. Kuhn-Forte, 'Die Kirchen innerhalb der Mauern Roms, S. Teodoro bis Ss. Vito'; 'Modesto e Crescenzia'; 'Die Kirchen in Trastevere', in W. Buchowiecki (ed.), *Handbuch der Kirchen Roms* (Wien, 1997), 699 ff.

[69] See Nordhagen, 'Icons Designed for the Display of Sumptuous Gifts'. Ch. Barber, 'Early Representations of the Mother of God', in Vassilaki, *Mother of God*, 253–61.

[70] Bertelli, *La Madonna di S. Maria in Trastevere*.

[71] See P. J. Nordhagen, 'The Mosaics of John VII (705–707). The Mosaic Fragments and their Technique', *ActaNorv* 2 (1965), 121–66.

hypothesis here, nor of those for an earlier dating proposed by Maria Andaloro and Eugenio Russo.[72]

The iconography of Maria Regina which we first encounter in S. Maria Antiqua draws on imperial schemata and has parallels in paintings in which Mary is flanked by saints or angels without being vested as a queen. In the present context, whether that particular iconography was a Greek or a Latin invention is less important than the fact that it was appropriated in Papal Rome over the centuries with specific connotations, and that already by the Carolingian period the Madonna della Clemenza had become an authoritative prototype, used in papal propaganda in the investiture controversy and during the Counter-Reformation.[73]

An intriguing problem arises when we turn to the sources, which in this case are extremely limited throughout the centuries. Surprisingly, it is an icon in S. Maria in Trastevere that is mentioned in one of the earliest, quite summary descriptions of Roman churches, the *De Locis Martyrum* of the mid-seventh century.[74] Here we read, 'basilica quae appellatur Sancta Maria Transtiberis; ibi est imago sanctae Mariae quae per se facta est.' ('There is an image of Mary which has been made by itself.') How can this refer to the 'mediated' icon we are discussing here? Does the reference perhaps point not to this icon but to an earlier image, on the basis of a dating of the Madonna della Clemenza to the early eighth century – for example, a mural painting of Maria Regina, later 'copied' in the monumental icon? It would be easier to accept this hypothesis if it were not for the confirmation in a later, independent source of the concept of the 'imago quae per se facta est', for the list of 'acheiropoieta' in the codex Marcianus of *c*. 900 mentions a second icon of the Virgin in Rome to be found in S. Maria in Trastevere, which at this date must be seen to indicate the Madonna della Clemenza.[75] The entry, which is somewhat difficult to translate, speaks of the Virgin (using the epithets 'acheiropoietos' and 'acheirographos') coming to appropriate the house dedicated to the martyrs, desiring that it be dedicated to her and taking possession of it with her child on her breast (obviously a reference to the icon), not through the help of human hands but acting as a lord and honourable servant: 'in fact the servant too receives honour when his lord truly decides to live in his house.' The text is constructed around the relation between 'acheiropoieton' and house, the argument being that Mary selects her house as Christ has selected her as a *habitaculum*. Mary is the Mother of God

---

[72] See the references above, n. 68.

[73] U. Nilgen, 'Maria Regina – Ein politischer Kultbildtypus', *Römisches Jahrbuch für Kunstgeschichte* 19 (1981), 1–33. For a recently discovered early mediaeval Maria Regina in a sepulchral context (at S. Susanna), see ead., 'Eine neu aufgefundene Maria Regina in Santa Susanna, Rom: ein römisches Thema mit Variationen', in K. Möseneder and G. Schüssler (eds), *Bedeutung in der Bildern, Festschrift für Jörg Traeger zum 60. Geburtstag* (Regensburg, 2002), 231–45. In the year 2000 the icon returned to the altar of the Cappella Altemps, which is a celebration of the council of Trent; see the remarks on this in Andaloro, 'Le icone di Roma in età preiconoclasta', 728 ff.

[74] R. Valentini and G. Zucchetti (eds), *Codice topografico della città di Roma* II (Rome, 1942), 122. Bertelli, *La Madonna di S. Maria in Trastevere*, 17 ff. Kinney, *S. Maria in Trastevere*, 67 ff. H. Geertman, *More veterum. Il Liber Pontificalis e gli edifici ecclesiastici di Roma nella tarda antichità e nell'alto medioevo* (Groningen, 1975), dated the catalogue to the end of the 8th c., but see the detailed criticism of that hypothesis by F. A. Bauer, 'Das Bild der Stadt Rom in karolingischer Zeit. Der Anonymus Einsidelensis', *Römische Quartalschrift* 92 (1997), 190–228. Id., 'Roma come meta di pellegrinaggio', in *Carlo Magno a Roma* (Rome, 2000), 67–80. See also R. Santangeli Valenzani, 'Le più antiche guide romane e l'itinerario di Einsiedeln', in M. D'Onofrio (ed.), *Romei e giubilei. Il pellegrinaggio medievale a San Pietro (350–1350)* (Milan, 1999), 195–8.

[75] Alexakis, *The Codex Parisinus Graecus 1115 and Its Prototype*, 349 (Marcianus gr. 573, fol. 24v).

but she also represents the Church, a concept frequent in the patristic literature which we have already encountered in the case of S. Maria Maggiore, and which was later also applied to the symbolism of the church building.[76]

At this point I would like to look again at the Madonna della Clemenza. How can the quoted text refer to this icon? Its frame bears a somewhat corrupt inscription which contains the formula 'natum... ds quod per se factum est'.[77] This clearly refers to the child born from the Virgin without human/male intervention. The entry in *De Locis Martyrum* has been understood as a misinterpretation of this inscription.[78] Rather then defining the remark in *De Locis Martyrum* as a misreading of a theological subject inscribed on the frame, I would like to consider it as an insight into the nature of the image in the reference to the prototype, not in the sense that the 'acheiropoieta' of Christ (the Mandylion or the Veronica) were created by means of the touch of a towel to the face of Christ but by means of a theophanic presence.[79] In this way, the text seems to highlight the image within the image which is put between the figure of the Pope and the applied cross staff held by the Virgin, thus breaking down the levels of reality at the same moment, or even through the same process by which they were constructed. If we accept that both sources refer to the same icon, the question of the dating again arises, and the Maria Regina in the chapel of John VII would not be a contemporary parallel to the Madonna della Clemenza but the first 'papal' reception of this icon, which must then most probably date to the early seventh century, if not to the period of Gregory I or the 'moment' of the transformation of the *titulus Julii et Callistii* into a Marian church. I do not want to elaborate such a hypothesis here, but only to note the existence of the tradition emphasized in the codex Marcianus, that the church in Trastevere, founded as the *titulus* of two martyr Popes, was transformed into a Marian church by means of an 'acheiropoite' act, through the 'inhabitation' of an icon. Again, this confirms the intrinsic connection of icon and site, and we may define this icon as a temple image in its own right.

V. The Madonna di S. Sisto

For the last icon I want to examine briefly here, this connection of image and site is strictly speaking not applicable. It may seem unjust to dedicate only a few lines to the small Madonna di S. Sisto (75.5 × 42.5 cm), for it is perhaps the most beautiful icon of the Virgin in Rome (Fig. 3.9), and has attracted the devotion of art historians since its uncovering in the

---

[76] Cf. the adoption of this theological *topos* in the inscription of the apse of S. Maria in Trastevere, showing the *synthronon* of Christ and Mary vested as a queen (according to Kitzinger, a reference to the encounter of the icons in front of S. Maria Nova on Assumption eve), discussed in Nilgen, 'Maria Regina'.

[77] Bertelli, *La Madonna di S. Maria in Trastevere*, 34 ff. The inscription as far as it is readable runs: 'ASTANT STYPENTES ANGELORUM PRINCIPES – GESTARE NATUM ... A ... / DS QYOD IPSE FACTUS EST'; some fragments suggest the reading 'YTERO TUO'. Bertelli proposes the following reconstruction: 'poiché Dio stesso si fece dal tuo utero, ... i principi degli angeli ristanno e stupiscono di Te che porti in grembo il Nato...'.

[78] Kinney, *S. Maria in Trastevere*, 67 ff.

[79] For the 'acheiropoieta' in the former sense cf. Kessler and Wolf, *The Holy Face and the Paradox of Representation*, and Morello and Wolf, *Il Volto di Cristo*. For the distinction between different types of 'acheiropoieta' in this sense, see Bacci, *Il pennello*, 72 ff. In the context of the Greek list, cf. the more extensive arguments in Wolf, 'Alexifarmaka', and Barber, 'Early Representations of the Mother of God'.

1960s.[80] While the monumental Madonna of S. Maria in Trastevere binds the iconic dimension to historical time, and presents the image of the Virgin within a complex interplay of different 'levels of (un)reality', the Madonna di S. Sisto distances itself from this concept and the other temple icons by moving in the opposite direction. In other words, it opens an imaginary dialogue on two levels: with the unrepresented Son by means of the intercessory address of the Virgin-advocate with her raised gold hands, and with the observers by means of her merciful gaze turned to them, placing the icon in a sphere between realities outside the image. Differentiated even in technique from the other icons, this encaustic painting with its incredibly subtle modulation of colour and light may in fact be an imported icon, as has often been maintained by scholars since the publication of the restoration report. The hypothesis that it came to Rome in the period of iconoclasm is tempting, and Bertelli even speculated that it might have been the pre-iconoclast 'Hagiosoritissa' icon itself, which would thus have been preserved in Rome.[81] A dating from the sixth or, perhaps better, the eighth century seems to be reasonable, but the issue cannot be discussed here. It appears to me symptomatic that this image had a quite well-developed legend already documented by the eleventh century, which defines it as a painting begun by St Luke and coloured (who could not believe it!) by angels: a semi-'acheiropoietic' act, so to speak.[82] The legend emphasizes its Constantinopolitan provenance. At first it was kept in the small church of S. Maria in Tempulo, from where it was transferred to S. Sisto Vecchio, a convent of Benedictine nuns to which the former church belonged. There, according to the legend, it resisted a papal attempt to bring it into the Sancta Sanctorum to be with her son (that is, the above mentioned 'Lateran Saviour') by flying back at night. In the thirteenth century the convent became Dominican, and the icon moved with the nuns on two further occasions, as a transportable icon bound less to a place than to a religious community. Since the 1930s it has been enclosed in a Dominican convent on Monte Mario in Rome.

The early evolution of the legend on the one hand seems to indicate that the icon required propagation of its specific power within the city, which had such a well-established cult of images of the Virgin, while on the other hand the legend explicitly affirms its attraction as a mobile and resistant icon as compared with the old temple Madonnas which reside in their *aulae regiae*. Not by chance, in the twelfth century the Madonna di S. Sisto became the most copied icon of the Virgin in the city, particularly as a symbol for female convents or with a communal identity, while during the same period the Madonna della Clemenza was used as a papal political image.[83]

The basic difference between these two groups of copies (which leads us to a brief conclusion) lies in the fact that in the latter case the copies use the formula of the image for the purposes of papal propaganda, and thus refer to the iconic legitimization given by the authoritative model of the Madonna della Clemenza 'herself', whereas in the case of the Madonna di S.

---

[80] C. Bertelli, 'L'immagine del "Monasterium tempuli" dopo il restauro', *Archivium Fratrum Praedicatorum* 31 (1961), 82–111. Amato, *De Vera Effigie Mariae*. Belting, *Bild und Kult*.

[81] C. Bertelli, 'Pour une évaluation positive de la crise iconoclaste byzantine', *Revue de l'art* 80 (1988), 9–16.

[82] See the legend in the 11th-c. cod. Biblioteca Apostolica Vaticana, Fondo S. Maria Maggiore 122, fols 141v–143, ed. in Wolf, *Salus Populi Romani*, 161 ff., 318 ff. with further bibliography. See especially V. Koudelka, 'Le "Monasterium Tempuli" et la fondation dominicain de San Sisto', *Archivium Fratrum Praedicatorum* 31 (1961), 5–61.

[83] Belting, 'Icons and Roman Society in the Twelfth Century'.

Sisto the copies tend to have a 'life' in their own right. This means that they themselves became centres of cults as symbols of their communities. As we have seen in the discussion of the Assumption procession, the 'range' of an icon embracing the whole city depended on the fact that the main partners could share in it. From this point of view, the horizon of the Madonna di S. Sisto as a symbol of the identity or relative liberty of a specific group became restricted, as its power was spread by means of copies which in a way became independent (or even competitors) of each other. The most important of the copies is the Madonna of Aracoeli (Fig. 3.10), a twelfth-century icon, present at the heart of the communal movement, the Capitoline hill.[84] In the thirteenth century the church became Franciscan (and the Madonna di S. Sisto in its turn Dominican), and by this time it was claimed that the icon had been painted by St Luke and had saved the city from the plague in the procession of St Gregory. It was by these claims that the Aracoeli icon attempted to become (or proved to be) a symbol of the whole city in competition with the 'Salus Populi Romani', and because of this its relationship to the Madonna di S. Sisto changed. The Aracoeli icon became the Roman prototype of the Madonna Advocata type until the 1960s restoration, when the 'true' original was rediscovered. And the barely accessible Madonna di S. Sisto was sometimes mentioned in the late mediaeval sources in connection with a miracle which is in complete accordance with the subtle modulation of the flesh tones (though we must doubt that they were still visible at this period): on Good Friday the face of the Virgin changed colour, and became pale.[85]

Given the lack of sources, the early history of the cult of images in early Christian and mediaeval Rome remains a field of conjecture and speculation, and we must confess in the papal words: 'ignoramus et ignorabimus'. In this paper I have not aimed at a firm hypothesis regarding this period but rather at emphasizing the complex relations between the icons and their locations – temples on the one hand, and the cult topography of the city as a whole on the other: *Roma Mariana*. The consecration of the Pantheon is certainly a central moment in its early history, at least in terms of what we believe we know about it. During the great flood and pestilence of 590, as well as those of previous and subsequent years, so vividly described in Gregory's homilies on Ezekiel, scores of ancient monuments on the *Campus Martius* were ruined, and stinking pestilent demons emerged from the waters and flew about, but the Pantheon still stood firm.[86] Its consecration and the expulsion of the idols thus converted it, and it would be indeed interesting to contextualize these events through a reading of Gregory's demonology. If I tend to see Gregory as the central figure in this history, as a destroyer of pagan idols and even as one who favoured the icons as an antidote, it is perhaps because I have become too involved with the mediaeval legends surrounding the Pope-Saint: at a certain point it becomes difficult not to believe them.

---

[84] Wolf, *Salus Populi Romani*, 228 ff. The icon was described by 14th- and 15th-c. sources as a portrait of the Virgin praying under the cross (as Mater Dolorosa).

[85] See ibid., 232. In a few sources (admittedly Dominican) the Madonna of S. Sisto was also described as the Virgin brought in procession by Gregory; some texts tend to accept more than one icon in it.

[86] See the 'classic' description in F. Gregorovius, *Geschichte der Stadt Rom im Mittelalter* I (Munich, 1978), 246 ff. I will return to Gregory's demonology and concept of images on another occasion. For the legend of the anti-idolatrous activities of Gregory, see T. Buddendieg, 'Gregory the Great as a Destroyer of Pagan Idols', *JWarb* 28 (1965), 44–65.

3.1 Rome, S. Maria Nova.
Icon of the Virgin with Christ-child
(source: author)

3.2   Rome, view of the Forum Romanum (source: author)

3.3   Pantheon, Rome. Berlin, Kupferstichkabinett,
Heemskerck, Erstes römisches Skizzenbuch, fol. 10r, drawing
(16th c.) (source: Berlin, Kupferstichkabinett)

3.4 Rome, Pantheon.
Icon of the Virgin with Christ-child
(source: author)

3.5 Rome, S. Maria Maggiore, Cappella Paolina.
The Virgin 'Salus Populi Romani' (source: author)

3.6

3.6–3.7 Rome, S. Maria Maggiore, Cappella Paolina.
The Virgin 'Salus Populi Romani', details
(source: author)

3.8 Rome, S. Maria in Trastevere, Cappella Altemps.
The *Madonna della Clemenza* (source: author)

3.9　Rome, S. Maria del Rosario, Monte Mario. The *Madonna Advocata* (source: author)

3.10 Rome, S. Maria in Aracoeli.
The *Madonna Advocata* (source: author)

4

Theotokos and *Logos*: the interpretation and reinterpretation of the sanctuary programme of the Koimesis Church, Nicaea

Charles Barber

One of the more compelling moments in the reinterpretation of a visual text is offered by the reconfiguration of the well-known late seventh-century sanctuary programme in the Koimesis Church at Nicaea during the iconoclast crisis of the eighth and ninth centuries (Fig. 4.1).[1] In the exchange between the Theotokos and the Cross that is proposed within the common framework of this decoration, we will find competing claims on the origins of Christian representation.

The programme was focused on a ninth-century standing Theotokos and Child in the apse. They replaced an iconoclast cross, which had replaced an original Theotokos and Child.[2] In effect, we are seeing a 'restoration'. Above them were three rays of light that were variously bright pink, bright grey and bright green. An inscription ran through these rays. Adapted for this location from Psalms 2:7 and 109(110):3, it read: 'I have begotten thee in the womb before the morning star.' The rays of light emerge from three concentric bands of blue, whose shades darken towards the outer ring. A hand of God is visible at the centre of these bands. Between the bema vault and the conch of the apse is a second inscription. This faces towards the naos of the church and is framed by monograms of the monastery's founder, Hyakinthos. This inscription is from Psalms 92(93):5: 'Holiness becomes thine house, O Lord, forever.' In the bema in front of the apse are four of the ranks of angels – Principality, Virtue, Dominion, Power (Figs 4.2–4.3).[3] These ninth-century restorations are dressed in courtly costume and carry banners that show the *trisagion* hymn. A repeated inscription from Odes 2:43, which is Deuteronomy 32:43, runs beneath them: 'And let all the angels of God worship him.'[4] Above these angels is the *Hetoimasia* (Fig. 4.4). This shows the jewelled prepared throne of the Apocalypse bearing a

---

[1] This paper is very close to the paper given at the conference. It draws heavily upon the following pages of my book *Figure and Likeness: On the Limits of Representation in Byzantine Iconoclasm* (Princeton, NJ, 2002), 63–9, 83–4, 94–8, 103–5 and 120–1.

[2] O. Wulff, *Die Koimesiskirche in Nicäa und ihre Mosaiken nebst den verwandten kirchlichen Baudenkmälern* (Strassbourg, 1903). Th. Schmit, *Die Koimesis-kirche von Nikaia, Das Bauwerk und die Mosaiken* (Berlin and Leipzig, 1927). Ed. Weigand, review of Th. Schmit's book, in *Deutsche Literaturzeitung* (1927), 2601–11. P. Underwood, 'The Evidence of Restoration in the Sanctuary of the Church of the Dormition at Nicaea', *DOP* 13 (1959), 235–44. F. de' Maffei, *Icona, pittore e arte al Concilio Niceno II* (Rome, 1974). Ead., 'L'Unigenito consostanziale al Padre nel programma trinitario dei perduti mosaici del bema della Dormizione di Nicea e il Cristo trasfigurato del Sinai', *Storia dell'Arte* 45 (1982), 91–116; 46 (1982), 185–200. Ch. Barber, 'The Koimesis Church, Nicaea: The Limits of Representation on the Eve of Iconoclasm', *JÖB* 41 (1991), 43–60. C. Mango, 'Notes d'épigraphie et d'archéologie: Constantinople, Nicée', *TM* 12 (1994), 349–57. Id., 'The Chalkoprateia Annunciation and the Pre-Eternal Logos', *DChAE* 17 (1993/4), 165–70. G. Peers, 'Patriarchal Politics in the Paris Gregory (B.N. gr. 510)', *JÖB* 47 (1997), 51–71. Id., *Subtle Bodies: Representing Angels in Byzantium* (Berkeley, 2001).

[3] These orders are listed together at Ephesians 1:21.

[4] It is unnecessary to link this passage to Hebrews 1:6 as Cyril Mango in his somewhat problematic reading (or anti-reading?) of these mosaics proposes: Mango, 'Chalkoprateia Annunciation', 168–70.

closed Gospel book, a Latin cross, and a dove with a cruciform halo. This is set against a circle of three concentric bands of blue, paralleling those of the apse itself. Seven rays of light emanate from the cross and the dove.

This programme, in all its states, provides a brief essay on the origins of Christian representation. A reading may begin with the *Hetoimasia* in the bema vault. This is a traditional representation of the Christian Godhead, one that we would usually define as symbolic in nature. First signalled in the three concentric circles of blue,[5] the Godhead is also represented by three things: the Gospel book, the dove, and the cross. Every part of this figures the Godhead by indirect yet sanctioned means. This form of representation continues at the crown of the apse, where the hand of God emerges from the centre of the three concentric circles of blue.[6] This may be read as God's voice, which utters the prophecy inscribed below: 'I have begotten thee in the womb before the morning star.' It is this prophetic text that marks a boundary between a symbolic and verbal knowledge of the divinity and an incarnate and iconic form of knowing. In this regard, it is significant that the inscription is carefully inserted into the image, rather than being placed at its perimeter. Early eighth-century exegesis of the passages from which this inscription derives underlines their importance as prophecies of the Incarnation. As such they speak of a healing of the divide that has separated heaven from the earth.[7] The movement from verbal prophecy to an iconic economy is then completed beyond the written text by the representation of the Theotokos and Child. For the first time in the mosaic the human body enters representation, and one of the Godhead becomes visible in the flesh.

This sense of a particular transition is underlined by the remarkable rays of light that are included within the apse design. In the *Hetoimasia* mosaic, the rays that emerge from the cross and the dove end at the edge of the outermost circle of blue. Although marked by a different and uniform colour, they respect the limits set by this circle. In the apse itself the rays of light are presented differently. Each is marked by a distinct colour: bright pink, bright grey, and bright green. At the end of each ray vertical lines of tesserae introduce a second colour, announcing the end of the ray of light. Each finishes in a concave arc. The arc of the central ray hugs the halo of the Theotokos. The ray and the halo fit one another, suggesting that the manner of concluding the rays of light in the bema was determined by the shape of the Theotokos' halo. As such, it is striking that the two outermost rays finish in the same manner as the central ray, even though neither meets a visible haloed body. It appears, therefore, that these outermost rays announce a space for that which cannot become visible in an image such as this.

The difference between the treatment of the central ray and the treatment of the outer rays is crucial. Our interpretation of this is aided by a perhaps contemporary homily on the Koimesis by Patriarch Germanos.[8] In this, he draws a link between the principal Psalms text found in the apse inscription (Psalms 109(110):3) and the idea of Christ's generation from divine light. Christ is characterized as 'light born from light', co-eternal with the Father, yet begotten.[9] The

---

[5] This is defined as a symbol of the Trinity by John of Gaza: P. Friedländer, *Johannes von Gaza und Paulus Silentiarius* (Leipzig and Berlin, 1912), 137–8 lines 41–4.
[6] M. Kirigin, *La Mano Divina nell'iconografia cristiana* (Studi di antichità cristiana, 31) (Vatican City, 1976).
[7] Barber, 'Koimesis Church', 53–4.
[8] *First Homily on the Koimesis*, PG 98, 341C–344B. Germanos of Constantinople, *Omelie Mariologiche*, tr. V. Fazzo (*Collana di Testi Patristici*, 49) (Rome, 1985), 105 ff.
[9] PG 77, 1121A–1145B. The Trinitarian aspect of this decoration is discussed at length in Barber, 'Koimesis Church', 53–7.

light metaphor thus serves to maintain the Trinitarian doctrine of one God manifest in three hypostases. In the Koimesis decoration each ray represents one of the hypostases of the deity (Father, Son and Holy Spirit). The difference between these hypostases is intimated in their different colours. Yet they share the same form and the same origin. Of these three hypostases only this, which touches the Theotokos, who is fully human and therefore visible in the flesh, can give rise to a God who is also visible in the flesh. The outer rays thus underline that two members of the trinity remain hidden beyond direct human perception. They are only available to the human intelligence by means of symbols.[10]

This is a complex image that operates through several levels of representation. It begins from a symbolic presentation of the Trinitarian Godhead, then underlines verbal prophecy by including text within the image, and finally inserts the iconic presentation of one of the Godhead. This is shown to be a consequence of the Incarnation, and was made possible by the Theotokos. It is a christological exploration of the Christian God *opening himself* to representation, drawing a theoretical distinction between the visible and the invisible. Thanks to the extraordinary apparatus that frames the rather more commonplace image of the Theotokos and Child, this mosaic has become both an account of the meaning of the Incarnation and an essay on the origins of Christian iconic representation.

It is noteworthy that when iconoclasts replaced the Theotokos and Child with a cross they retained this framing apparatus. It is too easy to characterize iconoclasm as an absolute destruction that completely erases existing imagery. Yet here we are confronted by a rather more interesting phenomenon, namely the adaptation of an existing visual text to an iconoclast programme. It suggests some common ground between these antagonists, a point that can be masked by our customary and somewhat rhetorical invocation of destruction.

Let me now try to define this iconoclast programme. To begin with, it is important to understand the iconoclasts' cross. Given its evident value to the iconoclasts, there is surprisingly little iconoclast writing on the cross itself that survives, the main source being the sequence of poems that framed the ninth-century iconoclast cross in the Chalke Gate of the Great Palace. I will quote just one of these. It is attributed to Ignatios,[11] and can be translated:

> O *Logos*, in order to strengthen the piety of those below,
> and to show a clear and more complete knowledge of yourself,
> you gave a law that only the cross be depicted.
> You disown being pictured on the walls here by means of
> material artifice, as clearly now as before.
> Behold the great rulers have inscribed
> it as a victory-bringing figure.[12]

---

[10] Barber, 'Koimesis Church', 57–60.
[11] There has been some discussion of the identity of this figure. One might compare the opinions of W. Wolska-Conus, 'De Quibusdam Ignatiis', *TM* 4 (1970), 351–7, and P. Speck, 'Die ikonoklastischen Jamben an der Chalke', *Hell* 27 (1974), 376–80.
[12] *PG* 99, 436B–437A. A different translation can be found at S. Gero, *Byzantine Iconoclasm During the Reign of Leo III with Particular Attention to the Oriental Sources* (CSCO, 346) (Louvain, 1973), 121. The text is:
Ἵνα κρατύνῃς τοῖς κάτω σέβας, Λόγε.
Γνῶσίν τε τὴν σὴν ἐμφανῆ δείξῃς πλέον·

This text is addressed to the *Logos*. As such it complies with the theocentric language of all of the iconoclast poems in the Chalke decoration. The poem also reiterates an opposition between the cross and material depictions, when it points to a law that allows the depiction of the cross, while denying depiction on the walls by means of 'material artifice (τεχνικῆς ὕλης)'. The poem then develops this opposition into the claim that the cross is the appropriate means of showing 'a clear and more complete knowledge (γνῶσίν τε τὴν σὴν ἐμφανῆ δείξῃς πλέον)' of the *Logos*. Such a conception might surprise us, if we assume that the cross is understood to operate in an entirely symbolic economy.

The crucial term in this text is the definition of the cross as a figure (τύπος). This is an absolutely consistent usage in iconoclast writings and, as we shall see, the use of this terminology was much disputed by the iconophiles.[13] The value of the term is brought forward in Theodore of Stoudios' ninth-century refutation of these iconoclast poems on the Chalke cross. Let me quote a somewhat difficult but very rich passage from this:

> On the one hand the *Logos* has indeed given the cross to us for salvation as a support of the faithful and as an object of divine veneration, this is clear to all. On the other hand it does not follow that this is the life-giving figure (τύπος) of the Passion, O loquacious one. For how in the design (σχήματι) of the cross is Christ to be figured (τυπωθήσεται) being arrested, being bound, being beaten, festering, being crucified, being speared, or some other happening? Not in any way at all. For the cross signifies Christ, it does not figure him (σημαίνει γὰρ Χριστὸν ὁ σταυρός, οὐ τυποῖ). Hence it is also called a sign (σημεῖον) in holy scripture. It says that Moses made the serpent as a sign (σημεῖον). This is for the cross. But a sign is one thing and a figure is another (ἀλλ' οὖν σημεῖον καὶ ἕτερον τύπος). Hence the morning star only signifies (σημαίνει) the day, while the sun itself figures (τυποῖ) when it indicates (δείκνυσι) the day. This then is how Christ is signified (σημαινόμενος) in the cross, even as he is himself figured in icons (ἐν ... εἰκόνι τυπούμενος). For the archetype is manifest in the icon (ἐν γὰρ τῇ εἰκόνι τὸ ἀρχέτυπον ἐμφαίνεται), as the divine Dionysios says.[14] And indeed the icon (ἡ εἰκών) and the figure (ὁ τύπος) have been spoken of by him and other fathers in a comparable manner. Clearly Christ's icon (εἰκών) is the life-giving figure (τύπος) of the Passion; which you wish to conceal, not wishing to have this revealed. The figure of the cross is the signifier of these things (ὁ δὲ τοῦ σταυροῦ τύπος, ἡ τούτων σημασία). If therefore the signifier (ἡ σημασία) is the support of the faithful and veneration, then how much greater [a support of the faithful and veneration] is the representation in the work of the icon (ἡ ἐκτυπωτικὴ εἰκονουργία). This therefore is really the true discourse. Not the false argument offered by you.[15]

The text is complex, but goes directly to the idea of 'figure'. Theodore deploys a twofold strategy in relation to this term. First he argues that the iconoclasts' use of the term in relation to the cross is inappropriate. The form of the cross cannot show the historical Christ. Indeed it is

---

        Νόμον δέδωκας σταυρὸν ἐγγράφειν μόνον,
        Ἀπαξιοῖς δὲ τεχνικῆς ὕλης ὕπο
        τοιχογραφεῖσθαι, δῆλον ὡς πρὶν ἐνθάδε.
        Ἰδοὺ γὰρ αὐτὸν οἱ μέγιστοι δεσπόται
        ὡς νικοποιὸν ἐγχαράττουσιν τύπον.

[13] Its perhaps problematic nature can be suggested by the fact that this same term was used by Anastasios of Sinai to define the illustration of the Crucifixion that accompanies his refutation of Theopaschism: K. H. Uthemann, *Anastasii Sinaitae Opera, Viae Dux* (CCSG, 8) (Turnhout, 1981), XII.3, 13–15.
[14] *Ecclesiastical Hierarchy*, IV.3, 1. PG 3, 473.
[15] PG 99, 457B–C.

better conceived as a sign, a term that belongs to the discourse of Old Testament prefiguration. These signs are absolutely arbitrary in relation to that which they indicate. Second, the term 'figure' is properly treated as an aspect of the term icon. Any figure becomes manifest in the icon. The figure is thus directly connected to the icon, coming before it. Theodore then privileges the icon because, implicitly, it is the final manifestation of that which is potential in the cross.

If we turn to Theodore's *Three Refutations* of the iconoclasts we find similar notions in play. Theodore's basic tactic in his addresses to the cross is to use it as a model from which to establish comparisons with the icon. For example, in the twenty-third chapter of the second *Refutation*, Theodore explores the relation of icon and figure:

> For what is better as a paradigm for the icon (εἰκών) of Christ than the figure (τύπος) of the cross, since the icon bears the same resemblance (ἐμφερείας) as the representation (ἐκτύπωμα)? We can as readily speak of the icon of the life-giving cross as of a figure of the same, and of Christ's figure as well as of his icon. For in terms of etymology εἰκών derives from ἐοικός and ἐοικός means likeness (ὅμοιον). Likeness has been perceived, spoken of, and beheld in both the figure and the icon.[16]

Theodore here underlines the point that he considers 'figure' and 'icon' to be interchangeable terms. In this case he uses this similarity to argue that the beliefs held regarding the cross, as a form of representation, must also apply to the icon. It is an analogy that the token iconoclast consistently rejects, arguing that 'icon' and 'figure' are distinct terms.[17] This is an important point that is not taken up by Theodore, in part because it reveals the different patterns of thought that at times make these fictional dialogues impossible. What Theodore leaves us with is his need to maintain 'figure' and 'icon' as equivalents. In so doing, he seeks to give to the iconoclasts the term 'sign', substituting this for their own use of the term 'figure'.[18]

The iconoclasts' use of the term 'figure' should be read alongside the use of the person of the *Logos* as the primary person addressed by the iconoclast poems at the Chalke Gate. In using this term the iconoclasts emphasize the Trinitarian discourse that shapes their image theory.[19] The issue is identified by Theodore of Stoudios in his refutation of the iconoclast poems. Theodore writes:

> The bastard is shameful, but not the legitimate child. This [distinction] is beyond nature, not according to nature. If, as you say, there can be an icon of the pre-incarnate *Logos*, then this claim is indeed shameful, as it is absolutely extraordinary to place the unincarnate *Logos* in the flesh: it resembles nothing, while all icons resemble man. Hence God has said this: 'With what likeness have you compared me?' Indeed this is idolatry, as he has clearly himself defined it.[20]

Having rejected the possibility of a pre-incarnate icon of the *Logos*, Theodore then proceeds to argue for the post-incarnation representation of Christ. Interestingly he does not use *Logos* again in this passage, using Christ for the post-incarnate God. As such he discloses the significance of

---

[16] Ibid., 368B–C.
[17] Ibid., 368B, 368C.
[18] Ibid., 368A.
[19] Barber, *Figure and Likeness*, 61–81.
[20] *PG* 99, 457D.

the iconoclasts' consistent use of the term *Logos*. This is most clearly indicated in the poem by Ignatios, where the strongest claim for the value of the cross as a means of showing the *Logos* is made, when the poem states that the cross makes available 'a clear and more complete knowledge (γνῶσίν τε τὴν σὴν ἐμφανῆ δείξῃς πλέον)' of the *Logos*.

We can now consider why these iconoclast texts insist upon the term τύπος. Figure is, as Theodore points out, an equivalent of icon. As such, it represents something that exists. What needs to be underlined at this point is that the iconoclasts also share this iconic notion of the figure. For them, it also indicates the representation of something that exists. If the iconoclast cross were simply the representation of the cross found in Christianity's narratives, then this definition would present an unproblematic if severely limited instance of Christianity's visual repertoire. But the iconoclasts understood the figure of the cross in a second manner. It both represented the true cross and, as Constantine V puts it, is a representation of him who was crucified on that cross. For iconophiles, such a declaration amounts to an admission of a symbolic order of representation, the cross being essentially and formally different from the incarnate God crucified upon it. But for the iconoclasts, the figure of the cross was an appropriate figurative icon of the *Logos*. The 'he' to whom Constantine V referred in his interpretation of the cross is crucial to the definition of the operation of the cross in representation. The iconoclasts understand the 'he' as the *Logos*, the iconophiles understand this 'he' as Christ. For the iconoclasts, the cross was not only sanctioned by God, it also made the Godhead visible in a system of representation that was other than the one founded upon the body of Christ. For them, this is not a symbolic or signifying economy of representation (as these terms are defined by the iconophiles). Rather they have chosen a term, 'figure', which is appropriate to a non-corporeal form of representation of a non-corporeal subject. It is an aniconic order, that retains the representational possibilities of the icon, but displaces the iconophile regime of likeness with that of iconoclast figuration.

In insisting upon the term τύπος the iconoclasts return us to the language of Canon 82 of the Quinisext Council of 691–692. There, the concept of the figure was rejected, as it had connotations of the pre-incarnational. It is apparent that in their use of the term the iconoclasts were exploring a distinctly aniconic figuration. They have used the 'aniconic' quality of the cross to develop an anti-materialistic theory of appropriate Christian representation, one that stands in opposition to the material body of the Theotokos.

If we now return to the Koimesis Church at Nicaea we can see how it was possible for the cross to be inserted into the pre-existing programme. The cross was a direct replacement of the Theotokos and Child. In the original programme they had functioned to demonstrate the entry of one member of the Trinity into visibility through the intervention of the Theotokos' body in the Incarnation. In rejecting this christocentric and materialistic account of Christian representation, the iconoclasts at Nicaea were able to adopt and adapt the same conceptual framing. But whereas the iconophiles identified a moment of transformation and difference at the Incarnation, the iconoclasts used the figure of the cross to emphasize a fundamental continuity. Where the iconophile apse marked a change from the figurative order of the Trinitarian representations by introducing the iconic body, the iconoclast apse replaced this point of disruption with a figure that presents the *Logos* in a visual language that is unchanged by the fact of the Incarnation. It is a crucial change of emphasis: one that must efface the Theotokos, as it is she who marks the very possibility of this icon's being.

THEOTOKOS AND LOGOS 57

4.1 Nicaea (Iznik), Koimesis Church. Apse mosaic.
Standing Theotokos (late 7th, 8th and 9th c.)
(source: Schmit, *Die Koimesis-Kirche von Nikaia*, Pl. 20)

4.2 Nicaea (Iznik), Koimesis Church.
Mosaic in the bema.
Angels (late 7th and 9th c.)
(source: Schmit,
Die Koimesis-Kirche von Nikaia, Pl. 13)

4.3 Nicaea (Iznik), Koimesis Church.
Mosaic in the bema.
Angels (late 7th and 9th c.)
(source: Schmit,
Die Koimesis-Kirche von Nikaia, Pl. 14)

4.4 Nicaea (Iznik), Koimesis Church.
Mosaic in the bema. *Hetoimasia* (late 7th c.)
(source: Schmit, *Die Koimesis-Kirche von Nikaia*, Pl. 15)

Part II

The theology of the Theotokos

5

The Virgin as the true Ark of the Covenant

† Michel van Esbroeck

In this paper I should like to draw attention to some features of the cult of Mary in the context of the liturgy of the Dormition in the fourth and fifth centuries. For this purpose, I will first refer to a Marian exegesis which was written down in 393 by Epiphanios of Cyprus,[1] but surely existed much earlier in some – perhaps only oral – Palestinian catechesis. Secondly, I shall quote some passages from the literature on the Dormition which are clarified by this exegesis. Thirdly, I shall consider the independent testimony of John Rufus, who around 520 wrote the *Plerophories*, a résumé of which has been preserved in Syriac. Finally, having presented the evidence from the years around 451, I shall show the impact of the Marian liturgy of the Dormition on the imperial politics of Anastasios (491–518) and Justinian (527–565).

I

The Bible contains a strange translation in the passage of the book of Exodus where Moses tells Aaron to put a vessel with the Manna of the desert into the Ark of the Covenant (Exodus 16:33). The Greek translation from the Hebrew runs as follows: 'Λαβὲ στάμνον χρυσοῦν ἕνα καὶ ἔμβαλε εἰς αὐτὸν πλῆρες τὸ γομὸρ τοῦ μᾶν καὶ ἀποθήσεις αὐτὸ ἐναντίον τοῦ Θεοῦ εἰς διατήρησιν εἰς τὰς γενεὰς ὑμῶν' ('Take one golden urn, and put an omer of manna in it and lay it up before the Lord, to be kept for your generations'). In the patristic typology, ἡ στάμνος, with its irregular feminine, is generally considered to represent Mary herself within the Ark of the Covenant. But verse 36 from the same chapter adds והעמד עשרת האיפה הוא ('one omer is the tenth part of one eipha'), and this is rendered in the Septuagint as follows: 'τὸ δέκατον τῶν τριῶν μέτρων ἦν' ('one omer was the tenth part of three measures'). Consequently, three measures are equal to a single eipha, and this is rendered by Epiphanios by the Greek word μόδιον, which in the Gospel of St Matthew means the amphora with a capacity near to ten litres of corn, the 'bushel' under which the light should not be put (Matthew 5:15). How can one eipha be the equivalent of three measures? Epiphanios answers this question with a large-scale theological discussion, in which the role of Mary is further developed. He first tells the story of the translation of the Septuagint, which confirms the spiritual inspiration behind the accuracy of this translation. He then comments on the Modios as a sacred measure which emphasizes the

---

[1] Epiphanios of Cyprus, III.21–35, ed. M. van Esbroeck, *Les versions géorgiennes d'Épiphane de Chypre. Traité des poids et des mesures* (*CSCO*, 461) (Louvain, 1984), 39–42. The Greek and the Syriac versions of this treatise have lost the original date of the document. The note on 'Epiphanius' in R. Bäumer and L. Scheffczyk, *Marienlexikon* 2 (1989), 375–6 does not mention this Marian exegesis.

plenitude of the faith and the complete fulfilment of the Law (§§22–4). The three measures are also those which were prepared by Sara for the three angels of the Lord (§30), and then became the four *xestoi* which were put into the urn of Manna in the Ark of the Covenant. They contain not only the four books plus Deuteronomy, but also the four Gospels plus the living Law, the twenty-two letters of the alphabet, the twenty-two books of the Bible and the twenty-two elements of the universe (§42).

We may here comment on the reasoning behind the cakes Sara prepared for her heavenly hosts: Genesis 18:6 becomes the object of a remarkably expansive commentary. Abraham says to Sara: 'σπεῦσον καὶ φύρασον τρία μέτρα σεμιδάλεως καὶ ποίησον ἐγκρυφίας' ('Quickly make ready three measures of fine meal, knead it and make hidden cakes'). Since Epiphanios is about to draw from what is hidden a sign of the future Incarnation, it is necessary to translate here 'hidden' cakes. We have already seen that we are dealing with the sacred measure of the Manna whose nature is explained by the Pharisees' question about Jesus: 'מ׳ הו׳' ('who is he?'), or about 'Manna' ('what is that?'), and by the answer of Jesus: 'I am the living bread which came down from heaven' (John 6:51). Let me here quote the text of Epiphanios himself and comment on it afterwards.

> These three measures are a single *modios*, which is a sacred measure, for it is not possible for three people to eat so much. However, this occurred so that there should not be a lacuna in the name of the Trinity, for such is the measure of the Trinity, and the *modios* is the confession of the one substance, and the three are the expression of the one communion of the Trinity. And his words 'Make *hidden* cakes' denote the true bread which is not yet revealed to the whole universe, for he is the Word of God who came down from heaven and still remains hidden in the lineage of Abraham, hidden by its own advent. The fact that the bread was hidden under the heap of ashes is the reason it acquired its name 'hidden'. It still lies within coal and ashes, and this occurred as an omen. Caleb, the son of Jephonias, his first wife Gazuba having died, married Ephrata, a widow, and he received from Joshua bar Nun as an inheritance the town of Kaphrata, which means 'the celebrated'. He then built a second town near the first one and named it Ephrata after his wife, which means 'plentifulness of fruits'. And after the birth of Elamon, Zara and others, he begot a son and gave him the name Bethlehem. He loved him and built another town near the first ones, to which he gave the name of his son, which means 'the house of bread'. This was the name of the house, but its meaning was only revealed after the descent from heaven of him who was born of the Virgin Mary in Bethlehem, 'the house of Bread' – of him who said 'I am the living bread which came down from heaven'. The place had long had the name, but the bread had not yet been revealed, for it was hidden, as previously mentioned.[2]

This excerpt, which comments on the Scripture at such length, is explained adequately, if not in every detail, by the Book of Joshua and by chapter 2 of 2 Chronicles. First the problematic Kaphrata must be identified as Hebron from Joshua 15:13. The Semitic meaning 'hidden' is quite clear, and the Georgian rendering 'celebrated' must be corrupt. The name in Joshua 15:13 is rendered as 'Arbok' by the Septuagint and 'Arba' in the Hebrew text. The whole exegesis indeed starts from the oak of Mamre in Hebron. In 1 Chronicles 2:19 it is said that after the death of Gazouba, Caleb married Ephrata, but it adds that he had a son called Ôr or Ḥûr in Hebrew. Later, in verse 51, 'Salomon, father of Bethlehem' is mentioned among the lineage of Ôr, while the preceding verses refer to other wives of Caleb, namely Gaipha and

---

[2] Van Esbroeck, *Les versions géorgiennes*, 39–40.

Mocha. The Hebrew text gives Salma as father of Bethlehem, while the names Elamon and Zara, which appear in the text of Epiphanios, must arise from errors of transcription or more from mere typological simplification. The main message of the exegesis is clear, however: Caleb son of Jephonias provides the authority for the passage of the bread hidden at Hebron to the bread hidden at Bethlehem.

II

Let us now consider some features in the liturgy and the literature of the several texts on the *Transitus Mariae*. Around the year 451, on 2 or 3 December, the church of the Kathisma ('Κάθισμα') or 'Rest of Mary' was inaugurated, or rather enlarged, at the third mile from Bethlehem,[3] halfway between Bethlehem and Jerusalem. This church commemorates the place where Mary rested on the way to the census as she was awaiting the birth of Jesus. Juvenal of Jerusalem consecrated the church, which had been founded by Hikelia. This is a clear indication that the foundation was associated with the group at Jerusalem favourable to the Council of Chalcedon, that is the Palaea Lavra or St Chariton, for which Epiphanios of Cyprus was the main theological authority. However, the feast of the Kathisma occurred on 13 August, against the background of the Dormition and the Assumption of the Virgin Mary. Fortunately, the liturgical reading for this day has been preserved in a Georgian version in the ancient Mravalthavi.[4]

The main theme of this reading is Mary as the true Ark of the Covenant, and it uses the *Life of Prophet Jeremiah*, which is attributed to Dorotheos bishop of Tyre. It contains a prophecy according to which salvation will come from him who will be born of a Virgin and laid down in a manger. This crib, into which the child is placed from one year to another for the visit of the Magi, is the sign of the Ark of the Covenant. The Ark had been saved by Jeremiah before the destruction of the first temple and sealed in the rock, so that nobody was able to use or to interpret the tables of the Law that lay concealed there, but, according to Psalms 131:8, the new Covenant will shine in Sion, and the Ark is thus the body of the Virgin: 'Ἀνάστηθι, Κύριε, εἰς τὴν ἀνάπαυσίν σου, σὺ καὶ ἡ κιβωτὸς τοῦ ἁγιάσματός σου' ('Arise O Lord to your resting place, You and the ark of your holiness!').[5] The same verse is quoted by Epiphanios of Cyprus to explain the leap of John the Baptist in the womb of Elisabeth when Mary visited her.[6] According to the *Life of Prophet Jeremiah*, Mary will be the first to arise after Jesus, for in fulfilment of the prophecy, Jeremiah was placed next to Moses and Aaron beside the Ark, which is henceforth Mary. Psalms 131:8 is explained as follows: 'It is the holy Virgin Mary who is passing from this world to God, she to whom the apostles proclaimed in Sion the praise of Myrrh saying: Today the Virgin is being guided from Bethlehem to Sion, and today from earth to heaven!'[7] The text immediately adds, quoting the *Life*: 'All the saints are gathered together

---

[3] G. Garitte, *Le calendrier palestino-géorgien du Sinaiticus 34 (Xe siècle)* (Brussels, 1958), 301, 401.
[4] M. van Esbroeck, 'Nouveaux apocryphes de la Dormition conservés en géorgien', *AnBoll* 90 (1972), 364–9, repr. in id., *Aux origines de la Dormition de la Vierge* (Aldershot, 1995), IV.
[5] Id., 'Nouveaux apocryphes', 369 (section 9).
[6] Id., *Les versions géorgiennes*, 42.
[7] Id., 'Nouveaux apocryphes', 369 (section 10).

around her and wait for the Lord, putting to flight the enemy who aims to destroy them.' It would hardly be possible to provide a better commentary for the feast of the Dormition than this combination of Bethlehem and Sion, especially in a pro-Chalcedonian context. The enemy who aims to harm Mary exists in two somewhat different contexts. The most frequent can be traced in the family of texts where Bethlehem has not yet obtained its place.[8] At the moment when the body of Mary was being taken from Sion to the tomb of Gethsemane, the high priest Jephoniah tried to destroy it. But at the very moment when his hands touched the shroud, an angel of God cut them off with an oath: only through the intercession of the apostles did Mary herself heal Jephoniah, who would thereafter believe in Christ.[9] This event cannot be understood except as an allusion to the attempt of Oziah against the Ark of the Covenant in 2 Kings 6:6–8. As for the hands which alone are cut off, the parallel must be sought in the *Protevangelium* of James. There the hand of the midwife Salome withered completely for having attempted to verify the virginity of Mary after the birth.[10] There is however a second narration in which Bethlehem has a role. Here the house where Mary lies is attacked; this occurs in Jerusalem, when the apostles have just returned from Bethlehem, where the Virgin was previously. I quote the story according to the third Book of the so-called *Six Books' Redaction*, which is preserved in Syriac:

> Then the people of Jerusalem assembled, and took fire and wood, and they went to the court in which the blessed one dwelt; and the Governor was standing at a distance looking on. And when they came to the court, they found the doors shut. And they lifted their hands to pull them up, and straightway the angel of the Lord struck on their faces with his wings, and fire was kindled from the door and the flame blazed forth, which no man had kindled, and the faces and heads of those people who had arrived at the door of the Blessed one's court were burnt, and many of them died.[11]

To understand this passage, one must refer to another story attributed to Cyril of Jerusalem, in which he describes the efforts of the Jews to reconstruct the temple of Jerusalem during the reign of Julian the Apostate: after an earthquake they were astonished and went to the synagogue in which they usually gathered, 'and they found the synagogue doors closed. They were greatly amazed at what happened and stood around in silence and fear when suddenly the synagogue doors opened of their own accord, and out of the building there came forth fire, which licked up the majority of them, and most of them collapsed and perished in front of the building.'[12] The meaning of both narratives emphasizes that the temple of the Lord, the holy Virgin, is irreplaceable. In the Syriac *Transitus*, the story continues by saying that Caleb, the chief of the Sadducees, who was secretly a Christian, converted the crowd. In the same story, Jephoniah is not the high priest but only a scribe. In any case, if we go back to the exegesis of Epiphanios of Cyprus, the two names Jephoniah and Caleb acquire in this

---

[8] For the various families of the legend, see M. van Esbroeck, 'Les textes littéraires sur l'Assomption avant le Xe siècle', in F. Bovon *et al.*, *Les Actes apocryphes des apôtres* (Geneva, 1981), 265–85, repr. in id., *Aux origines de la Dormition*, I.
[9] K. von Tischendorf, *Apocalypses Apocryphae* (Leipzig, 1866), 110.
[10] E. de Strycker, *La forme la plus ancienne du Protévangile de Jacques* (Brussels, 1961), 158–66.
[11] A. Smith Lewis, *Apocrypha Syriaca. The Protevangelium Jacobi and Transitus Mariae* (London, 1902), 38.
[12] S. P. Brock, 'A Letter Attributed to Cyril of Jerusalem on the Rebuilding of the Temple', *Bulletin of the School of Oriental and African Studies* 40 (1977), 267–86, esp. 275.

context their full significance. They are the unconscious guardians of the urn containing the true Manna, and thus of Mary who gave the bread of life. Jephoniah did not believe that Joshua conquered the Promised Land, but Caleb his son obtained it directly from Joshua together with many towns.

III

The *Plerophories* of John Rufus is a violent polemic against the Council of Chalcedon. It collects testimonies of several personalities from the spiritual worlds of the time, including two important bishops, Peter the Iberian and Timotheos Ailouros. But it relates dozens of other stories, mostly from Palestine, in order to exalt the virtues of the heroes who opposed the accursed Council that established the two fully independent natures of Christ. The extant Syriac résumé is much abbreviated, as a fragment in Coptic demonstrates that the earlier version must have been considerably more expansive. However, it still retains much of its earlier passion. It was probably first published *c.* 505, when the Council of Chalcedon began to be publicly criticized after the first period of the Henotic politics of Emperor Zeno. In chapter 55, John Rufus recalls the feelings of those few persons who, right at the beginning, felt it their duty to oppose the 636 bishops' decision at the famous Council. He then shows how they defended their thesis:

> Remember how many thousands of people went out from Egypt and how many miracles and epiphanies they saw. With the exception of two people, they all prevaricated and rebelled and they died in the desert; not only did they yield to temptation without obtaining the eternal reward, but also through their lack of faith they even lost the privilege of entering into the promised land. The great legislator and prophet Moses gave warnings and said: Do not participate in evil with the multitude! In the same way in Persia, when the captives were invited to adore the statue of the king, only the three children remained without weakening and did not prevaricate and by this refusal alone, they not only have been glorified by the God they previously praised, but also they gave the king and the many persons who were present the benefit of the true knowledge of God! Whom do you wish to join and with whom will you fight? With Joshua son of Nun, with Caleb son of Jephoniah and the three children of Babylon, or with all the crowd that adored the golden statue? Think on this in connection with the huge crowd that was in Chalcedon for the Council of the renegades![13]

This somewhat lengthy quotation shows the importance which Caleb son of Jephoniah acquired at the very beginning of the opposition to the Council of Chalcedon, when only a small minority sought to resist the mass of bishops who signed its dogmatic definition of the natures of Christ. The exegesis of Epiphanios regarding Caleb must have played a similar role in the theological ideas of the opponents to the Council.

One should also observe how the cult of the three Children of Babylon developed in Egypt at exactly the same time, giving the quiet Monophysite-oriented *Life of John Kolobos* and the orthodox answer with a translation of the relics of the three Children of Babylon. The convergence of this new cult on both sides of the great dogmatic contestation about the Council is reflected in the parallel emergence of Jephoniah on the opposite side in relation to the

---

[13] John Rufus, *Plerophories*, ed. F. Nau, *PO* 8 (1912), 109–10.

Dormition of the Virgin. Caleb rather belongs to the family of texts in which the narrative of the Dormition begins with the palm of Life being given to the Virgin by the angel on the Mount of Olives in Jerusalem. To complete this simpler conception of the events, another representation on the last issue of the Virgin developed. There Bethlehem was the first meeting place of the apostles, and the use of incense becomes more important than the palm of Life. The inauguration or enlargement of the church in the Kathisma, where 13 August is related more to the transfer of the Ark of the Covenant from Bethlehem to Jerusalem than to the Virgin's rest on her journey from Jerusalem to Bethlehem before the birth of Jesus, is associated with the Chalcedonian party under Juvenal of Jerusalem. Nevertheless, it must have been a response to the new liturgy of their opponents, who could not use Jerusalem for the celebration of the Dormition. Both conceptions converged at the time of the *Henotikon* under Emperor Zeno, and they resulted in the Syriac composition in six books with only one celebration in Jerusalem and in Bethlehem. When the criticism of Chalcedon recurred *c.* 505, the celebration must have developed into a coherent liturgy in harmony with the political views of Emperor Anastasios and Severos of Antioch, at a time when in Constantinople itself Timotheos in 512 promoted a clear opposition to the Council.

The relics of the Virgin in the church of the Blachernai and in the Chalkoprateia have a notable parallel in Jerusalem in the two churches of the Holy Sion on the hill where the Virgin died, and the church of Gethsemane below, in the valley where she was buried. Timotheos of Constantinople copied the rites of Jerusalem in the Byzantine capital with a procession from one church to the other.[14] But when the opposition to Justinian was annihilated in the 'Nika' revolt in 532, Justinian established a new liturgy in Jerusalem as well as in Constantinople, in the hope of obtaining public unanimity in favour of his religious views. For this purpose he built in Jerusalem the 'Nea' Maria near the Holy Sion, which was inaugurated in 543 on 17 August during the week of the Dormition. A special reading for the Dormition from this foundation has been preserved, though only in Georgian: the liturgy began on Tuesday in Bethlehem, showing that Justinian wished to associate with his celebration all the concepts which had already appeared in that liturgical cycle.[15] Later, in 591, after Emperor Maurice had conquered Armenia and divided its Catholicossate, he built a new church in Gethsemane, the place most closely associated with the first repression of the Monophysites under Juvenal. He fixed the feast of 15 August with a *triduum* in which the main features of the episodes which had developed from the time of the Council onwards disappeared. Bishop John of Thessaloniki then reinstated what was in danger of being lost from the Greek tradition. The date of 15 August was accepted by the Latin Church from the time of Maurice, but Gregory of Tours still knew something about 18 January, according to the Coptic tradition and the opposition in Gethsemane in 453.

In conclusion, I hope that I have succeeded in my aim of illustrating how the Virgin as the Ark of the Covenant was introduced into the liturgy of the Dormition and became deeply rooted in the religious politics of the Byzantine Empire in the fifth and sixth centuries.

---

[14] M. van Esbroeck, 'Le culte de la Vierge de Jérusalem à Constantinople aux 6e–7e siècles', *REB* 46 (1988), 181–90, repr. in id., *Aux origines de la Dormition*, X.

[15] That text is edited in M. van Esbroeck, 'L'Assomption dans un *Transitus* pseudo-basilien', *AnBoll* 92 (1974), 125–63, repr. in id., *Aux origines de la Dormition*, VI.

6

The Theotokos in Byzantine hymnography: typology and allegory

Christian Hannick

Hymns in honour of the Theotokos are sung, according to the cycles of the Byzantine liturgical year, both for the feasts of the Mother of God (Θεομητορικαὶ ἑορταί) and as theotokia, following the cycle of the Oktoechos, especially on Wednesday and Friday each week. This explains the large number of such hymns in Byzantine hymnography – a treasury of hymns some of which belong to the most ancient strata of Greek ecclesiastical poetry. Almost a century ago, Anton Baumstark, the great historian of liturgy, drew attention to similarities between Byzantine and Coptic hymnography,[1] which indicate a very early circulation of Byzantine hymns in honour of the Theotokos in Egypt, certainly before the eighth century. The oldest collections of Greek hymns, whose composition is closely associated with the Tropologion in the developments around the mid-ninth century following the Council of Nicaea II (787), already contain numerous theotokia, both as stichera and as troparia within the kanon. In this ancient collection of liturgical books in the form of the Tropologion, the kanons include up to fourteen troparia, as, for example, in the so-called 'Paracletice sinaitica antiqua' (Sin. gr. 776, Lond. B.M. Add. 26113, Sin. gr. 1593).[2] Hymns in honour of the Theotokos also have their place in the Sticherokathismatarion, a non-musical collection of hymns known only from Greek manuscripts of the tenth and eleventh centuries.

Alongside hymnography, homiletics also form part of liturgical worship. However, as far as texts in honour of the Theotokos are concerned, a fundamental difference between homiletics and hymnography is discernible: homilies in honour of the Theotokos are connected with the feasts of the Mother of God, and can therefore be evaluated more easily than hymns, which are scattered throughout the entire liturgical year.

To talk of theotokia in terms of hymns to Mary is to address the content very imprecisely. Certainly many texts belonging to the genre of ecclesiastical poetry and designated as theotokia or staurotheotokia are simply *laudes marianae*: a string of epithets in praise of the Ever-Virgin (ἀειπάρθενος). The student of forms of devotion in Byzantium can find highly useful information in the kanon of Theosteriktos of Stoudios (probably ninth–tenth century) of the fourth plagal mode without acrostic,[3] which forms the central element of the *Mikra Paraklesis*, particularly popular in Orthodox community life. In reading this text, one cannot remain unmoved

---

[1] A. Baumstark, 'Ein frühchristliches Theotokion in mehrsprachiger Überlieferung und verwandte Texte des ambrosianischen Ritus', *Oriens Christianus* 9 (1920), 36–61.
[2] Cf. Ch. Hannick, 'Le texte de l'Oktoechos', in *Dimanche-Office selon les huit tons* (*La prière des églises de rite byzantin*, 3) (Chevetogne, 1972), 48. On the Tropologion in general, cf. H. Husmann, 'Hymnus und Troparion. Studien zur Geschichte der musikalischen Gattungen von Horologion und Tropologion', in *Jahrbuch des Staatlichen Instituts für Musikforschung Preußischer Kulturbesitz* (1971), 7–86.
[3] Παρακλητική, ἤτοι Ὀκτώηχος ἡ μεγάλη (Rome, 1885), 737–41.

before the pleasing sound of the poetic imagery; it represents an expression of personal experience of devotion, unconnected to salvation history and therefore largely expressed in the first person.

Historians of doctrine have long recognized the value of homiletics in honour of the Theotokos.[4] As a rule, homilies bear an author's name, even if often pseudepigraphical, and are datable on this basis. Further, it is known that the context in which some homilies were produced was the formulation of Conciliar decrees – for example, the *Homilies on the Nativity of Christ* composed by Theodotos of Ankyra (*BHG*, 1901–2; *CPG*, 6125–6) on the occasion of the Council of Ephesus (431).[5] They are therefore an expression of doctrinal understanding, and belong to the most important branch of theological literature, which formulates the content of faith as the basis of ecclesiastical life. This precise definition is necessary in order to characterize the strength of doctrinal writings, for instance by comparison with mysticism. In mystical writings or in *Πνευματικαὶ νουθεσίαι*, it is possible to emphasize concerns which have little perceptible connection with revelation and the sacramental life of the community of the faithful. Such subjective judgement is not permissible in dogmatics.

In this respect hymnography, and (in particular) church poetry in honour of the Theotokos, is in an ambiguous situation. In many cases it is not immediately clear whether the author of a given hymn to the Theotokos, who is in any case writing in poetic language, intends to make a doctrinal declaration or to elicit feelings of devotion from his audience. This ambivalence explains why in theological studies less attention is given to hymnography than to homiletics. To give an explicit example: in the preparations for the proclamation of the doctrine of *Assumptio Mariae in corpore* in the Roman Catholic Church by Pope Pius XII in 1950, the French theologian and byzantinist Martin Jugie undertook the task of unearthing statements relating to this doctrine in the homilies of Greek Church Fathers up to George Scholarios in the fifteenth century.[6] The purpose of this investigation was obvious: to analyse Greek homiletics in terms of the history of doctrine. The aims of the monks of Grottaferrata, Toscani and Cozza were similar when, at the time of the Vatican Council I, they collected Greek hymnographic material on the 'immaculate conception' of the Mother of God, and equipped it with a first-rate patristic apparatus.[7] It is undoubtedly the case that this doctrinal development in the Roman Catholic Church – the legitimacy of which is not under discussion here – provided an impetus for patristic studies in the Greek world as well as in the Latin; in this context one need only mention Roberto Caro's examination of homiletic texts in honour of the Theotokos.[8]

---

[4] For example, the Catholic theologian René Laurentin presented a 'Table rectificative des pièces mariales inauthentiques ou discutées contenues dans les deux Patrologies de Migne', in his *Court traité de théologie mariale* (Paris, 1954), 119–73.

[5] Cf. O. Bardenhewer, *Geschichte der altkirchlichen Literatur* IV (Freiburg i. B., 1924; repr. Darmstadt, 1962), 198 ff.

[6] M. Jugie, *Homélies mariales byzantines. Textes grecs édités et traduits en latin I–II*, PO 16.3 (1921); 19.3 (1925) (repr. Turnhout, 1990).

[7] Th. Toscani and I. Cozza, *De Immaculata Deiparae Conceptione, Hymnologia Graecorum ex Editis et Manuscriptis Codicibus Cryptoferratensibus* (Rome, 1862). On G. Cozza-Luzi (1837–1905), later Abbot of Grottaferrata, and the work mentioned here, see S. Parenti and E. Velkovska (eds), *L'abate Giuseppe Cozza-Luzi, archeologo, liturgista, filologo. Atti della giornata di studio, Bolsena, 6 maggio 1995* (Ἀνάλεκτα Κρυπτοφέρρης, 1) (Grottaferrata, 1998), esp. the article by M. Petta, 'Attività liturgica di Giuseppe II Cozza-Luzi', ibid., 173–84.

[8] R. Caro, *La homilética mariana griega en el siglo V I–II* (*Marian Library Studies*, 3–4) (Dayton, OH, 1971–1972).

Byzantine hymnography on the subject has remained very much in the background in comparison with scholarly work on homiletics.⁹ Since the epoch-making work of Sophronios Eustratiades, Metropolitan of Leontopolis, about seventy years ago, nothing comparable has appeared in this field. Now as then, the thematic work of Eustratiades, *Η Θεοτόκος εν τη υμνογραφία* [*The Mother of God in Hymnography*] (Paris, 1930) remains an indispensable reference book, although the material which it comprises is only partially edited. Indeed one year later, in 1931, Eustratiades published the first volume of his *Θεοτοκάριον*, which presents 106 kanons in the first three modes. Nothing further was published, although from *Η Θεοτόκος εν τη υμνογραφία* it is clear that the entire work for the eight modes had been completed in manuscript, which explains the numerous references to texts in the remaining modes. Eustratiades included in it only kanons and kathismata which appear in the kanons. Stichera and kathismata transmitted outside the kanons are not included, in contrast to the earlier work of Filippo Vitali¹⁰ in 1738, which is, however, difficult to find, and therefore rarely used.¹¹ More recently, new material has been published and philologically appraised both in Greece and elsewhere. Nevertheless much remains unedited in manuscripts. It is not my task here to emphasize once again the uncontested richness of Byzantine hymnography in honour of the Theotokos, and even less to attempt an overview of the surviving material, on a chronological or any other basis. Rather it is my concern to develop criteria for theological – or, rather, historico-theological – evaluation.

Let us leave to one side all those texts in which the poetic form or the devotional content is subject to question, and confine ourselves to those hymns which can be given a theological interpretation within a historical dimension. In order to avoid misunderstandings, I would again emphasize that in this examination I am excluding such branches as Ποιμαντική, Ηθική and Μυστική θεολογία, since as a rule these belong outside the historical dimension and therefore do not necessarily have a temporal connection with the historical sources. The material in question here is, in contrast, temporally situated within the sphere of Greek literature: these historical components become all the more clear when one considers that hymnography has a clear connection with homiletics and the history of doctrine. One need only recall the term Theotokos itself and the debates of the era of the Council of Ephesus (431). On the other hand, common expressions such as 'τῶν πιστῶν τὸ στήριγμα' (support of the faithful), 'τὸν ἀρχηγὸν τῆς γαλήνης τὸν Χριστὸν ἐκύησας' (you bore Christ, the Prince of Peace) from the kanon of Theosteriktos,¹² mentioned above, are without specific historical or theologico-historical connections.

As far as the term theotokion¹³ – hymn in honour of the Theotokos – is concerned, the first thing to emphasize is that such a hymn does not necessarily contain an address to the

---

⁹ Cf. M. Lattke, *Hymnus. Materialien zu einer Geschichte der antiken Hymnologie* (Fribourg and Göttingen, 1991), 368.
¹⁰ *Παρακλητικὸν σὺν Θεῷ ἁγίῳ τῆς Ὑπεραγίας Θεοτόκου, ποίημα τοῦ ὁσίου πατρὸς ἡμῶν Ἰωάννου τοῦ Δαμασκηνοῦ* (Rome, 1738).
¹¹ Georg Olms (Hildesheim) has announced a forthcoming reprint.
¹² *Παρακλητική*, 737.
¹³ The earliest evidence for this *terminus technicus* of hymnography is found in the 7th–8th c. in the works of Andrew of Crete and John of Damascus – that is to say, in the region of Jerusalem. See G. W. H. Lampe, *A Patristic Greek Lexicon* (Oxford, 1968), 639. J. C. Suicerus, *Thesaurus Ecclesiasticus e Patribus Graecis* (Amsterdam, 1682),

Theotokos. Indeed there are examples in which hymns designated as theotokia explicitly address Christ as 'σωτὴρ ἡμῶν' (our Saviour), for example, the theotokion ''Ο δι' ἡμᾶς γεννηθεὶς' (he who was born for us)[14] of the anastasimon apolytikion of the fourth plagal mode, 'Ἐξ ὕψους κατῆλθες' (you descended from on high), and the address 'Υἱὲ Θεοῦ' (Son of God) in the theotokion of the sixth ode of the kanon to the Apostles on the Thursday of the second plagal mode.[15] There is a double reason for this. On the one hand, theotokia often commemorate the Incarnation of Christ as the high point of salvation history. On the other hand, theotokion is the name given to the closing hymn of a series which, depending on the liturgical framework, can include two or more hymns and which does not always exhibit a clear 'Marian' content.

The dogmatika theotokia of Saturday vespers form a category in themselves, following the cycle of the Oktoechos. These texts, some of which are distinguished by their unusual length, present short dogmatic tracts on the theme of the Incarnation and the union of the divine and human natures in Christ – that is to say, the central theme of Christology.[16] Since they are metrically and musically constructed as idiomela, they are preserved in the Sticherarion, a genre of manuscripts documented from the tenth/eleventh centuries.[17] Accordingly, the dogmatika theotokia, together with other idiomela from the Sunday office of the eighth mode, are preserved – in part also with commentary – in the transcripts of the Byzantine musical arrangement of each part of the Oktoechos.[18] The dogmatika theotokia are considered to be the work of John of Damascus, an attribution which, linguistically speaking, is supported by their use of unusual expressions such as 'αὐθυπάρκτως' (existent in itself) in the theotokion of the *tonus gravis*: 'Φρικτὸν καὶ ἄρρητον ὄντως' (terrible and inexpressible indeed)[19] – an expression which is used only by authors of the seventh to eighth centuries, such as Anastasios of Sinai, Leontios of Jerusalem or John of Damascus.

The thematic variety of the hymns to the Theotokos is demonstrated by the work of Eustratiades mentioned earlier, *Η Θεοτόκος εν τη υμνογραφία*, which indicates the range of metaphors and poetic images applied to Mary. This material can be divided into two categories, which contribute further towards our arguments. The first of these consists of typological images from the Old Testament such as 'ὁ πόκος τοῦ Γεδεών' (Gideon's fleece; Judges 6:37), 'ἡ κλίμαξ τοῦ Ἰακώβ' (Jacob's ladder; Genesis 28:12), 'ἡ κεκλεισμένη πύλη' (the closed gate; Ezekiel 44:2), 'ἡ στάμνος ἡ τὸ μάννα φέρουσα' (the jar of manna; Exodus 16:33). These are

---

1386–7, gives, under the entry for 'Theotokion', only one passage, from the commentary on the typikon of Markos hieromonachos, probably from the turn of the 13th–14th c. See *PLP* 7 (1985), no. 17084. An important manuscript of the *Σύνταγμα ποιηθὲν εἰς τὰ ἀπορούμενα τοῦ τυπικοῦ* is the cod. Vind. theol. gr. 285 from the year 1459: H. Hunger, W. Lackner and Ch. Hannick, *Katalog der griechischen Handschriften der Österreichischen Nationalbibliothek, Teil 3.3: Codices theologici 201–337* (Wien, 1992), 285.

[14] *Παρακλητική*, 618.
[15] Ibid., 506.
[16] Compare the introduction by Ch. Hannick in *Dogmatika in den acht Tönen aus einer Handschrift aus dem Ende des 16. Jahrhunderts (Anthologie zur ukrainischen sakralen Monodie,* 1) (L'vov, 2002), 3–4.
[17] The cod. Athos Laura Γ.67 (according to Chartres notation) from the beginning of the 11th c. is among the earliest witnesses to the dogmatika; C. Floros, *Universale Neumenkunde* I (Kassel, 1970), 53–4.
[18] *The Hymns of the Oktoechos* I–II, tr. H. J. W. Tillyard (Copenhagen, 1940–1949). L. Tardo, *L'Ottoeco nei mss. melurgici. Testo semiografico bizantino con traduzione sul pentagramma* (Grottaferrata, 1955).
[19] *Παρακλητική*, 533.

found, for example, in the following hymns: 'πόκον προεώρα Γεδεὼν τὴν ἄχραντον γαστέρα σου δρόσον οὐράνιον, παρθένε, δεξαμένην' (in the fleece Gideon foresaw your spotless womb, Virgin, receiving the divine dew; ode of the kanon in honour of the martyr Basiliskos, 22 May: MR V 146);[20] 'κλίμακα θεωρήσας Ἰακὼβ πρὸς ὕψος ἐστηριγμένην εἰκόνα μεμύηται τῆς ἀπειρογάμου σου' (Having seen the ladder reaching on high, Jacob had a foretaste of the image of your virgin birth; ode of the kanon in honour of the Virgin, Sunday of the seventh mode);[21] 'πύλην ἀδιόδευτον ὁ προφήτης βλέπει σέ, παρθένε πανάχραντε, ἣν μόνος διώδευσεν ᾧ πάντες μελωδοῦμεν' (The prophet sees you as the impenetrable door, spotless Virgin, which he alone entered whom we all sing; seventh ode of the kanon in honour of the Prophet Nahum, 1 December: MR II 349); 'στάμνον σὲ τὸ μάννα κεκτημένην τῆς θεότητος ἔγνωμεν, κόρη, κιβωτὸν καὶ λυχνίαν, θρόνον Θεοῦ καὶ παλάτιον καὶ γέφυραν μετάγουσαν πρὸς θείαν ζωήν' (we know you as the jar which held the manna of the Godhead, Maiden, as the Ark and the Candle, as the Throne and Palace of God, as Bridge leading to eternal life; eighth ode of the kanon in honour of the martyr Cecilia, 22 November: MR II 247). The second category comprises allegories, where a more profound meaning is to be discovered, such as 'ὁ λογικὸς τοῦ δευτέρου Ἀδὰμ παράδεισος' (the spiritual paradise of the second Adam), in a dogmatikon theotokion of the first mode, alluding to 1 Corinthians 15:45,[22] and 'ἱστὸς Χριστοῦ θεοΰφαντος ἐξ οὗ στολὴν τοῦ σαρκὸς τὸ θεαρχικώτατον πνεῦμα ἐξύφανεν' (loom of Christ, woven by God, from which the spirit of divine origin wove the garment of flesh), from the ninth ode of a kanon by Metrophanes of the third mode.[23] Both these allegories are taken from homilies of Patriarch Proklos.[24]

The typological method, which is very frequently used – not just in the case of hymns in honour of the Theotokos, but also in hymns honouring the Apostles – gives an insight into the exegetical methods of mediaeval Byzantium; it should be borne in mind though that typology is only distantly related to metaphor. Typology means the recognition of a foreshadowing in the Old Testament of a stage of salvation history.[25] A classic example occurs in the episode of the Crossing of the Red Sea, when, according to Exodus 14:16, Moses raised his staff ('ῥάβδος'), through which Israel sought salvation. The raising of the staff is typologically interpreted as a foreshadowing of the raising of the cross of Christ. To the Old Testament biblical text it is added that Moses stretched out the staff 'σταυροειδῶς' (in the form of a cross), that is to say, he inscribed the 'character' of the cross with the staff, 'ῥάβδος τὸν χαρακτῆρα τοῦ σταυροῦ ἐχάραξε' (the staff inscribed the character of the cross); here the expression 'χαρακτὴρ' (character) recalls the tablets of stone ('πλάκες') which were 'inscribed' by the finger of God when he revealed himself on Mt Sinai (Exodus 31:18). This phrasing is also included in a well-known heirmos of the fourth plagal mode for the feast of the Elevation of the Cross: 'Σταυρὸν χαράξας Μωσῆς * ἐπ' εὐθείας ῥάβδῳ * τὴν Ἐρυθρὰν διέτεμε * τῷ Ἰσραὴλ πεζεύσαντι * τὴν δὲ ἐπιστρεπτικῶς * Φαραὼ τοῖς ἅρμασι

---

[20] *Μηναία τοῦ ὅλου ἐνιαυτοῦ* I–VI (Rome, 1888–1901).
[21] *Παρακλητική*, 544.
[22] Ibid., 1.
[23] S. Eustratiades, *Θεοτοκάριον* (Chennevières-sur-Marne, 1931), 271 (83.185).
[24] D. M. Montagna, *La lode alla Theotokos nei testi greci dei secoli IV–VII* (Rome, 1963), 64–5, with reference to Homily I: *De Laudibus S. Mariae* (*BHG*, 1129; *CPG*, 5800), *PG* 65, 681A–B.
[25] Cf. Ch. Hannick, 'Exégèse, typologie et rhétorique dans l'hymnographie byzantine', *DOP* 53 (1999), 207–18.

* κροτήσας ἥνωσεν * ἐπ' εὔρους διαγράψας * τὸ ἀήττητον ὅπλον' (When Moses made the sign of the cross on the calm water with his staff, he divided the Red Sea for Israel, who walked through it on foot; on the other bank, turning to the other side, when he hit the sea again, he united the waters and drowned Pharaoh's chariots; [the cross is] the invincible weapon),[26] etc. It is even more significant that in the seventh–eighth century John of Damascus uses this typology in chapter 88 ('On the Cross') of his Ἔκθεσις ἀκριβὴς τῆς ὀρθοδόξου πίστεως (*Demonstratio fidei orthodoxae*): 'Ῥάβδος Μωσαϊκὴ σταυροτύπως τὴν θάλασσαν πλήξασα καὶ σώσασα μὲν τὸν Ἰσραήλ, Φαραὼ δὲ βυθίσασα' (The staff of Moses struck the sea in the form of the cross, saving Israel and drowning the Pharaoh).[27] This episode of salvation history does not lend itself to application to the Theotokos. However, in a kanon of the first mode, ascribed to the Emperor Theodore II Laskaris (1254–1258) and composed according to the method of the *Chairetismoi*,[28] one does, however, find a typological comparison with the staff of Moses, although without further biblical elaboration: 'χαῖρε θεία ῥάβδος, παθῶν πελάγη ἡ ῥήσσουσα' (rejoice, divine staff, which breaks through the sea of passion).[29]

However, the use of typology as an exegetical method presupposes more than the simple mention of an Old Testament foreshadowing of a stage of salvation history which corresponds to New Testament material. It is, in other words, more than a protyposis. The Theotokos is not infrequently addressed typologically as 'πλὰξ θεόγραφος' (tablet inscribed by God), in a reference to the tablets which God gave to Moses on Mt Sinai (Exodus 13:18). In the theotokion of the ninth ode of the kanon in honour of the Departed of the second plagal mode, we read: 'Σκηνὴν ἁγίαν, ἁγνή, γινώσκομεν, καὶ κιβωτὸν καὶ πλάκα σὲ τοῦ νόμου τῆς χάριτος' (As Sacred Tent, Spotless One, we know you, as Ark and Tablet of the Law of Grace).[30] The order is not coincidental: the Tablet (*plax*) was kept in the Ark (*kibotos*: Deuteronomy 10:5), and the Ark was placed in the Tent (*skene*: Exodus 26:33); the Theotokos is in this manner 'ἀστέκτου θεότητος χωρίον' (Vessel of the inextinguishable Godhead),[31] as in a kanon of the fourth mode, reminiscent of the 'ἄστεκτον πῦρ ἐν τῇ βάτῳ' (inextinguishable fire in the burning bush) of Exodus 3:2, or the 'χωρίον εὐρύχωρον τῆς ἀχωρήτου φύσεως' (spacious Vessel of incomprehensible nature) from a kanon of John Thekaras of the first mode.[32] More important to the construction of the typology is, however, the designation of the *plax* as 'πλὰξ τοῦ νόμου τῆς χάριτος' (Tablet of the Law of Grace),[33] which provides the transition to the New Testament (John 1:17): 'The Law was given through Moses, grace and truth came through Jesus Christ'.

The opposition of *nomos* and *charis* with reference to Old Testament prefigurations (προτυπώσεις) – models which are used in many hymns to the Theotokos – is given the widest possible significance in the dogmatikon theotokion of the second mode which is given

---

[26] S. Eustratiades, Εἱρμολόγιον (Chennevières-sur-Marne, 1932), 224 (322.1).
[27] Cited after E. Weiher, *Die Dogmatik des Johannes von Damaskus in der kirchenslavischen Übersetzung des 14. Jahrhunderts* (Monumenta Linguae Slavicae Dialecti Veteris, 25) (Freiburg i. B., 1987), 503 (352 b 11).
[28] Cf. *RAC* 2 (1954), 993–1006 (A. Baumstark).
[29] Eustratiades, Θεοτοκάριον, 39 (11.11).
[30] Παρακλητική, 530.
[31] Ibid., 284.
[32] Eustratiades, Θεοτοκάριον, 82 (25.49).
[33] This theotokion on the ninth ode of the kanon in honour of the Departed for Saturday in the second plagal mode links concepts which have already been mentioned: 'Σκηνὴν ἁγίαν, ἁγνή, γινώσκομεν, καὶ κιβωτὸν καὶ πλάκα σὲ τοῦ νόμου τῆς χάριτος'. Παρακλητική, 530.

here in its full text: 'Παρῆλθεν ἡ σκιὰ τοῦ νόμου, τῆς χάριτος ἐλθούσης * ὡς γὰρ ἡ βάτος οὐκ ἐκαίετο καταφλεγομένη, οὕτω παρθένος ἔτεκες καὶ παρθένος ἔμεινας * ἀντὶ στύλου πυρὸς δικαιοσύνης ἀνέτειλεν ἥλιος * ἀντὶ Μωϋσέως Χριστὸς ἡ σωτηρία τῶν ψυχῶν ἡμῶν' (The shadow of the Law passed when Grace came. As the burning bush in flames was not consumed, so you, Virgin, gave birth and yet remained Virgin. In the place of the pillar of fire appeared the sun of righteousness; in the place of Moses, Christ, the salvation of our souls).[34]

It is characteristic of the typological method of exegesis that different terms can be connected in more than one way. If a connection between 'πλὰξ θεόγραφος' (Tablet inscribed by God) and the Theotokos can be established, so too can connections be made with other concepts by bringing in different interpretative elements; in our case, for example, the apostles. A troparion of the sixth ode of the kanon in honour of the Apostles sung on the Thursday of the second plagal mode makes this clear: ' Ὡς πλάκες θεόγραφοι, τὰς τοῦ πνεύματος σαφῶς νομοθεσίας, ἔνδοξοι, ἐν ταῖς ψυχαῖς ἐσχήκατε ἀψευδῶς * δι' ὧν τὸν ἐν γράμματι κατηργήσατε νόμον, κόσμον σώσαντες' (You are as Tablets inscribed by God, glorious ones, without deception possessing the commands of the spirit in your souls; through them, you have destroyed the Law written in words and saved the world).[35] Here reference is made to Pauline theology, with its opposition *pneuma–gramma* in relation to the *nomos*, as, for example, in 2 Corinthians 3:6.

In order to investigate the deeper sense of allegories, it is occasionally necessary to refer to apocryphal texts, as in the case of the term *histos* (loom) mentioned above, which comes from the *Protevangelium* of James.[36] A second example of an allegory proves to have several levels. 'Λογικός' (spiritual), in the sense of νοερός, νοητός, πνευματικός, is contrasted with 'φυσικός' (physical). The Theotokos is the spiritually blooming paradise ('παράδεισος λογικὸς εὐθαλής'), from which Christ springs as blossom, Christ the New Adam, in accordance with 1 Corinthians 15:45 or with a kathisma of the first mode of a kanon by Theodore of Stoudios: 'Παράδεισον ἐν γῇ λογικόν σε φυτεύσας ὁ Χριστὸς ὁ φυτουργὸς παραδείσου τοῦ πρώτου ἐν μέσῳ σου, δέσποινα, ὡς ζωῆς ξύλον ἔφυσεν' ?(Christ, the planter of the first paradise, has planted you on earth as spiritual paradise, and planted in your centre, Lady, something like a tree of life).[37]

The scope of this essay prohibits further elaboration and examples. I will focus my conclusions on one point. Often, particularly from a western European perspective, criticism is made of the lack of exegetical development in Byzantine theology. When placed alongside the great exegetes of the Latin Middle Ages and those of Syrian and Armenian origin, it is true that theologians such as Theophylaktos of Ohrid in the eleventh century appear somewhat modest.[38] The fame of Archbishop Theophylaktos is based more on his letters than on his commentaries on the Gospels, which are less original. The lack of exegetical development is even more evident in Slavic Orthodox literature, whether Bulgarian, Serbian or Russian.[39] On the other hand, what is often overlooked is that hymnography reached a level in Byzantine Orthodoxy which

---

[34] *Παρακλητική*, 101. Tardo, *L'Ottoeco*, 26.
[35] *Παρακλητική*, 506.
[36] E. de Strycker, *La forme la plus ancienne du Protévangile de Jacques* (*Subsidia Hagiographica*, 33) (Brussels, 1961), 112 (X.2). *Los Evangelios apocrifos*, ed. A. de Santos Otero (Madrid, 1956), 164.
[37] Eustratiades, *Θεοτοκάριον*, 86 (26.150).
[38] Cf. *Theologische Realenzyklopädie* 33 (2001), 371–5 (Ch. Hannick).
[39] Cf. Ch. Hannick, 'Christlich-orientalisches Denken in slavischer Umformung – Traditionsbewahrung und

far surpasses Latin church poetry. Both genres of theological writing (or, rather, both branches of theological thought), exegesis and church poetry, complement each other. The major commentaries on individual books of Scripture, such as those of Cyril of Alexandria or Hesychios of Jerusalem, originated in the period of the great Church Fathers. This theological strand later becomes confined to commentary and exegesis of individual, selected passages of Scripture, *loca difficiliora*, as in, for example, the Περὶ διαφόρων ἀπόρων τῆς θείας Γραφῆς (*On difficulties of Holy Scripture*) of Maximos the Confessor (*CPG*, 7705), or the *Amphilocheia* of Patriarch Photios. Parallel to this – and at the same time – hymnography flourishes, reaching its high point at the end of the first millennium.

If one proceeds from the idea that it is in liturgical space that Holy Scripture is expounded in its entirety, with all its complexities and internal relationships, it is but a small step to the recognition of hymnography as the privileged bearer of scriptural exegesis. In terms of the history of liturgy, hymnography grew out of the singing of the Psalter, and afterwards of non-biblical refrains ('ἐφύμνια') and antiphons. The kontakion of the sixth to seventh centuries presents an independent form of biblical commentary, in which the poet uses dialogue and elaboration of the text to convey to his audience the content of Holy Scripture.[40]

In hymnography, from the time of John of Damascus, and to a lesser extent from that of Sophronios of Jerusalem, the distinguishing features which set patristic homily apart from patristic scriptural commentary – namely, typology and allegory, which are far more than simply rhetorical devices – are developed and lead to an independent method of exegesis. Hymnography has its own rules, but it also adopts many taken from homiletics and develops them further. For the homily, a particular point in the liturgical proceedings was prescribed. Hymnography, on the other hand, includes without exception all biblical readings, and, using the format of the troparia and stichera to provide a commentary on individual verses of the psalms, applies a method which breaks down divisions between individual books of Scripture and between the Old and New Testaments, in order to reconstruct the entirety of salvation history in relation to the *telos*, the *teleiosis*.

Typology and allegory are the two principal exegetical methods employed by hymnography. Only in this genre of theological literature were these methods so abundantly and widely applied, and in this way hymnography assembled a content of incomparable exegetical value. If one considers the names which have contributed to the development of hymnography within theological writing, one can speak without hesitation of a method of exegesis which rendered purely exegetical-philosophical writing, unconnected with the liturgical understanding of Holy Scripture as a whole, effectively superfluous.

To assess the exegetical achievements of the mediaeval Greek Orthodox Church, the exegetical method employed in hymnography must be taken into account. I trust that the examples quoted here in honour of the Theotokos have succeeded in demonstrating this.

Entwicklung eigener Züge', in R. Taft (ed.), *The Christian East. Its Institutions and Its Thought* (*Orientalia Christiana Analecta*, 251) (Rome, 1996), 107–27.

[40] J. Koder, 'Romanos Melodos und sein Publikum. Überlegungen zur Beeinflussung des kirchlichen Auditoriums durch das Kontakion', *Anzeiger der phil.-hist. Klasse der Österreichischen Akademie der Wissenschaften* 134 (1999), 63–94.

Use and abuse of the 'image' of the Theotokos in the political life of Byzantium (with special reference to the iconoclast period)

Nike Koutrakou

There is nothing new in the idea that in Byzantium political differences were often expressed through religious arguments or, conversely, that theological and doctrinal disputes found expression in political conflict.[1] A mere glance at Byzantine history and at the role played in it by heresies is enough to furnish a number of examples[2] which emphasize the place of Christianity in the empire's politics and in its history generally.[3]

The iconoclast period is particularly well suited to such theorizing since iconoclasm itself was, even by contemporaries, perceived as an 'imperial' heresy or, in the words of Theosteriktos, author of the *Life of Abbot Niketas of Medikion* at the end of the second iconoclast dispute,[4] one arising 'ἐκ βασιλικῆς δυναστείας' (from imperial coercion),[5] i.e. a heresy which had its origins in imperial power. Indeed Theosteriktos makes a clear distinction between the heresy of his own times and those of the past, declaring to his readers: 'understand how different are the Elders of the church and monarchs. Earlier heresies were established by teaching and counter-argument, and gathered strength gradually in this way. But this latest heresy derives from imperial coercion',[6] before continuing his narrative with a description of the origins of the iconoclast dispute.

Against this background the image of the Theotokos, as fashioned at the time of the first Ecumenical Councils on the nature of Christ, and disseminated mainly through hymnography, was exploited to the full in the political life of Byzantium. But here a caveat is required. A study of the use of the verbal 'image' of the Theotokos in the political life of

---

[1] This theory is perhaps best expressed by H. G. Beck, *Das byzantinische Jahrtausend* (Munich, 1978), 87–108, esp. 106; Greek tr. (Athens, 1990), 119–46, esp. 143. On the same subject, with special reference to the political aspect of the origins of the iconoclastic dispute, see P. Yannopoulos, 'Aux origines de l'Iconoclasme: une affaire doctrinale ou une affaire politique?', in *La spiritualité de l'univers byzantin, le verbe et l'image, Hommages offerts à Edmond Voordeckers* (Instrumenta Patristica, 30) (1997), 383–4.

[2] Beck, *Das byzantinische Jahrtausend*, 102; Greek tr., 139.

[3] A. Toynbee, *A Study in History* (2nd edn, London, 1976), 180 ff.

[4] Between 842 and 844. See I. Ševčenko, 'Hagiography of the Iconoclast Period', in A. Bryer and J. Herrin (eds), *Iconoclasm* (Birmingham, 1975), 113–31, esp. 118 and n. 42. The *Life* was written while the former Emperor Michael I was still alive, i.e. before 844–845, and certainly after 824, the year of Niketas' death.

[5] Βίος Νικήτα Μηδικίου, in *AASS*, Aprilis I, XII–XXXIII, esp. XXVIIIA. On the attribution of the iconoclast heresy exclusively to Leo III, see S. Gero, *Byzantine Iconoclasm During the Reign of Leo III, with Particular Attention to the Oriental Sources* (CSCO, 346; Subsidia, 41) (Louvain, 1973), 89 ff. Id., 'Notes on Byzantine Iconoclasm in the Eighth Century', *Byz* 44 (1974), 21–42, esp. 41–2. D. Stein, *Der Beginn des byzantinischen Bilderstreites und seine Entwicklung bis in die 40. Jahre des 8. Jahrhunderts* (Miscellanea Byzantina Monacensia, 25) (Munich, 1980), 177. See also P. Schreiner, 'Der byzantinische Bilderstreit: kritische Analyse des zeitgenössischen Meinungen und das Urteil der Nachwelt bis heute', in *Bisanzio, Roma e l'Italia nel'alto Medioevo*, Settimane di studio del Centro italiano di studi sull'alto Medioevo 34.1 (Spoleto, 1988), 338, and E. Kountoura-Galaki, *Ο βυζαντινός κλήρος και η κοινωνία των 'σκοτεινών αιώνων'* (Athens, 1996), 116.

[6] Βίος Νικήτα Μηδικίου, XXVIIIA.

Byzantium need not involve an examination of the theological aspect of the arguments employed – especially during the iconoclast dispute – even though these arguments were basically theological in nature. Our interest lies not in whether they accord with Orthodox doctrine, but in how they were exploited in the promotion of a specific policy or in the reaction to it, and, in so far as we can judge, how they were perceived and understood by the public to whom they were addressed. Additionally, we should be aware from the outset that this exploitation generally takes the form not of a logical sequence of arguments but of indirect reference, through allusion and allegory.

This political use of the image of the Theotokos began with her elevation as the supreme archetype. This led to the indirect association of the image in the popular consciousness with contemporary Byzantine noblewomen (as in the phrase in the *Oneirokritika* 'seeing a lady (in a dream), perceive her to be the Theotokos'[7]) and thence to the application of epithets such as 'σεμνή', 'σεμνοτάτη δέσποινα' not to the Theotokos but, by analogy, to Byzantine noblewomen and empresses, for whom the Mother of God served as model. One instance is the 'σεμνοτάτη' noblewoman of the miracles of St Theodore at Euchaita who appears in the fifth miracle as the recipient of visions,[8] while the crowning example occurs in certain letters of St Theodore of Stoudios. Consciously or not, Theodore, when writing to Empress Irene the Athenian, uses Marian appellations – not, admittedly, 'the temple of the Lord, the living spring' and other epithets from the Akathistos Hymn, but certainly some of those belonging to the typology of the Theotokos. In a letter of gratitude sent to the empress after, in the words of Theophanes,[9] 'she had remitted the civic taxes for the inhabitants of Byzantium and alleviated the so-called *kommerkia* of Abydos and Hiero', Theodore alludes to this event using biblical expressions such as 'Our most virtuous lady, angels appearing from your holy palace and proclaiming to us all the songs of praise for your actions ... abundant prayers circling like clouds worship God on account of your holy deeds';[10] and he audaciously borrows phrases from the chapter in Isaiah on the Nativity of Christ such as 'the heavens above rejoiced ... [and] ... the Lord had mercy on his people on your account'[11] – in other words the conventional

---

[7] Fr. Drexl, 'Das Traumbuch des Patriarchen Nikephoros', in *Festgabe Albert Ehrhard zum 60. Geburtstag* (Bonn and Leipzig, 1922), 104, verse 75: 'δέσποιναν ἰδών, τὴν Θεοτόκον νόει'.

[8] H. Delehaye, *Les légendes des saints militaires* (Paris, 1909), 198. On St Theodore Teron, St Theodore Stratelates and the city of Euchaita, see N. Oikonomidès, 'Le dédoublement de St. Théodore et les villes d'Euchaïta et d'Euchaïna', *AnBoll* 104 (1986), 327–35.

[9] Theophanes, *Chronographia* (Bonn, 1839), 737 lines 5–6. Theophanes, *Chronographia*, I, ed. de Boor (Leipzig, 1883–1885), 475 line 16. C. Mango and R. Scott (eds), *The Chronicle of Theophanes the Confessor. Byzantine and Near Eastern History AD 284–813* (Oxford, 1997). For an analysis of the writing of the *Chronographia*, see B. Coulie and P. Yannopoulos, *Thesaurus Theophanis Confessoris Cronographia, Thesaurus Patrum Grecorum* (Turnhout, 1998), XXVIII ff., and recently L. Brubaker and J. Haldon (eds), *Byzantium in the Iconoclast Era (ca. 680–850): The Sources. An Annotated Survey* (Birmingham Byzantine and Ottoman Monographs, 7) (Aldershot, 2001), 168–71. On Irene's fiscal policy, A. Christophilopoulou, *Βυζαντινή Ιστορία, Β1 (610–867)* (2nd edn, Thessaloniki, 1993), 150, and N. Oikonomidès, 'De l'impôt de distribution à l'impôt de quotité: à propos du premier cadastre byzantin', *ZRVI* 26 (1987), 9–19, esp. 14 ff. On the *kommerkia* around the year 800 and their – not always obvious earlier – relationship with the responsibilities of the *kommerkiarioi*, N. Oikonomides, 'Silk Trade and Production from the 6th to the 9th Century: The Seals of *kommerkiarioi*', *DOP* 40 (1986), 33–53, esp. 48–9. On the tax exemptions of Irene according to Theodore of Stoudios, cf. N. Oikonomidès, *Fiscalité et exemption fiscale à Byzance (IXe–XIe s.)* (Athens, 1996), 30–3, esp. nn. 22–4.

[10] Theodore of Stoudios, *Epistulae*, ed. G. Fatouros (Berlin and New York, 1992), I.24; *PG* 99, 929C–D.

[11] Isaiah 44:23.

phraseology referring to the Theotokos. This suggests an indirect, quasi-identification of Irene with the Mother of God, which both flatters her[12] and makes a political statement in its allusion to the Restoration of the Icons in 787: Irene is being presented as the new Mother of God who brings about the salvation of the world from iconoclasm.

The application of Marian epithets, in particular to imperial figures, represents, in the context of the *Imitatio Dei* of Byzantine ideology, an indirect reference to the Theotokos archetype. The purpose of these comparisons is to add prestige to the figure concerned, a concept which is found mainly in court literature. A typical example is the poem *To the Lady Theophano*, written after the death of the first wife of Emperor Leo VI, the future St Theophano, and probably inspired by this event. Even if the poem may be taken as a rhetorical exercise, it includes expressions such as 'the shelter and table of the poor' to describe the empress's tomb[13] – language which suggests a comparison with 'the living table, containing the bread of life' and the 'table holding the abundance of favours', which are used to describe the Theotokos in the Akathistos Hymn.

Although Theophano's undeniably virtuous life might anyway have justified the use of such epithets, which also hint at a political message by creating the image of an empress who has the welfare of her subjects at heart, this still remains a 'political' use of appellations and expressions relating to the Mother of God in the context of the political activity of the time. And if the poem is read in conjunction with another marginal poem, entitled *To the Poor Leo*, on the same page of the manuscript[14] – again probably a rhetorical exercise – which refers to the quasi-'apostolic' poverty of Leo VI at the time of his quarrel with his father Basil I and his confinement in the palace, the 'political' colour becomes clear: the anonymous author or – more probably – copyist of the second poem, who achieves this nuance by placing these verses on the same page, discredits Leo's political opponents by emphasizing that he had the support not only of his wife but also, through the application to her of expressions associated with the Mother of God, of

---

[12] On Theodore's inclination to exaggeration, if not flattery, when referring to political figures involved in his affairs, E. Koundoura-Galaki, 'Ὁ Μάγιστρος Θεοστήρικτος καὶ ὁ Θεόδωρος Στουδίτης. Μοναστηριακὸς Βίος καὶ πολιτική', *Σύμμεικτα* 12 (1998), 43–55, esp. 45 n. 16. On his political involvement in various issues, P. Karlin-Hayter, 'A Byzantine Politician Monk: Saint Theodore the Studite', *JÖB* 44 (1994), 229 ff., and P. Hatlie, 'Theodore of Studios and the Joseph Affair (808–812)', *Orientalia Christiana Periodica* 61/2 (1995), 412 ff. On the position of Theodore and the Stoudites generally as representatives of pure monasticism and the attitude of the ecclesiastical and imperial authorities to them, recently Kountoura-Galaki, *Ὁ βυζαντινὸς κλῆρος*, 223 ff., with relevant bibliography.

[13] Madrid, Palacio Real 43 (now at Salamanca), fol. 11v, ed. I. Ševčenko, 'La civiltà byzantina dal IV al IX secolo. Aspetti e Problemi. Storia Letteraria', *Corsi di Studi* I (Bari, 1977), 89–127, esp. 127: 'σκέπη τε καὶ τράπεζα τῶν πενεστέρων'.

[14] Madrid, Palacio Real 43, fol. 11v, in Ševčenko, 'La civiltà byzantina', 127:
Ἀχαλκος ὤν,
ἄραβδος ἐμβάδων δίχα,
σὺν πᾶσι τούτοις οὐ στολὰς ἔχων δύο
ἀποστόλου ζῇς, μὴ θέλων βίον, Λέον.

This poem has also been attributed to the 11th-c. (first half) poet Christophoros Mytilenaios, who was particularly well known for his talent at versified hagiography (see E. Follieri, 'Le poesie di Cristoforo Mitileneo come fonte storica', *ZRVI* 8.2 (1964), 133–48). If this is so, it argues for the survival of Leo VI's political persona through associative imagery well beyond his time. See also R. Cantarella, *Poeti bizantini* II (2nd edn, Milan, 2000), 688. On Leo VI as a popular subject of poetry, see, among others, I. Ševčenko, 'On the Death of Leo VI and Constantine VII in the Madrid manuscript of Skylitzes', *DOP* 23/4 (1969/70), 185–228.

the Theotokos as well. We find the same pro-Leo position in the *Life of St Theophano*, where Emperor Basil I's behaviour towards his son meets with popular disapproval.[15]

This form of use – or abuse – of the 'image' of the Mother of God was exploited by both sides in the context of the politics of the iconoclast period. This becomes apparent when we examine its place in the arguments of each faction – not from the theological perspective, as we have said, but from the perspective of political action defining a political position. And this is so despite the problems that arise, at least as regards the iconoclast arguments, from the dearth of strictly iconoclast sources, and from the dependence of the surviving texts mainly on the Definition of the Council of Nicaea II and on certain basic iconophile texts such as the *Antirrhetics* of Patriarch Nikephoros, the works of Theodore of Stoudios and the *Life of St Stephen the Younger* which from the ninth century onwards[16] represent, if not primary, at least secondary sources for those who write about iconoclasm. At the same time any examination of the political use of the Mother of God must take into account the fact that on the level of political semantics each side in presenting its own views gave to certain words and arguments a particular meaning – biased or otherwise – and imposed its own interpretation on words and arguments employed by the opposition in responding to them.[17]

At the level of political semantics, there is an interesting use of the Theotokos image in the context of 'refutation' ('ἔλεγχος', i.e. the demonstration of error) and 'contradiction' ('ἀντιλογία', i.e. the iconophile refutation of the iconoclast arguments), as expressed in various public or supposedly public debates between the two sides, usually between saints and (iconoclast) emperors or representatives of authority.[18] This is particularly apparent if we examine it in the

---

[15] *Βίος Θεοφανούς*, ed. E. Kurtz, 'Zwei griechische Texte über die heilige Theophano die Gemahlin Kaisers Leo VI', *Zapiski Imperatorskoi Akademii Nauk po istoriko-filologicheskomu otdeleniiu* series VIII, III/2 (1898), 1–24, esp. 12 lines 23–4: 'πᾶσα ἡ σύγκλητος ἅμα τῇ πόλει καταβοᾶ σου τοῦ κράτους'.

[16] According to the *Life* itself, it was written by Stephen the Deacon 42 years after the death of the saint, which occurred in 764 or 765 according to the *Chronographia* of Theophanes (Theophanes, *Chronographia*, ed. Bonn, 674) – i.e. in 806–807 (Ševčenko, 'Hagiography', 115, n. 15). However in her recent edition, M.-F. Auzépy places the death of the saint in 766–767 on the basis of internal evidence in the *Life*, and dates the writing of the Life to 809: M.-F. Auzépy, *La vie d'Étienne le Jeune par Étienne le Diacre, Introduction, édition et traduction* (Birmingham Byzantine and Ottoman Monographs, 3) (Birmingham, 1997), 18. See also ead. (*sub nom.* M.-F. Rouan), 'Une lecture "iconoclaste" de la Vie de St. Étienne le Jeune', *TM* 8 (1981), 421–3.

[17] As regards the language used, this was naturally restricted by each side's view of what was 'politically correct', and by the freedom of expression available to those using it: G. Weiss, 'Publizistik in Byzanz. Ein Beitrag zur Kommunikationsforschung in Byzanz', *BZ* 89 (1996), 79–93, esp. 81. This freedom in the use of language might be self-evident as regards the emperor, but it would barely be acceptable for others. The problem was compounded by difficulties of communication – mainly through letters – and often by difficulties in the comprehension and further dissemination of complex ideas such as Theodore of Stoudios' 'of everything depicted, not the nature but the hypostasis is depicted' (*PG* 99, 405B). N. Tomadakis, 'Εἰκονογραφικά (εἰκονόφιλοι–εἰκονομάχοι–ὁρολογία)', in *Βυζάντιον. Ἀφιέρωμα στον Ἀνδρέα Ν. Στράτο* II (Athens 1986), 673–710, esp. 676–80, 692.

[18] A practice that follows the common topos in the lives of saints in which the saint is confronted with the persecutor/tyrant: H. Delehaye, *Les légendes hagiographiques* (Subsidia Hagiographica, 18) (3rd edn, Brussels, 1927), 21–2 ff. Id., *La passion des martyrs et les genres littéraires* (Subsidia Hagiographica, 13bis) (Brussels, 1962), 171 ff. In the opinion of Ševčenko ('Hagiography', 115), perhaps the best example of such a confrontation during the iconoclast period is the scene involving St Stephen the Younger and Constantine V, which became the model for similar confrontations between other saints (see the lives of Makarios of Pelekete and the brothers Theophanes and Theodore Graptos) and Emperors Leo V and Theophilos. See the analysis of S. Gero, *Byzantine Iconoclasm During the Reign of Constantine V (with Particular Attention to the Oriental Sources)* (CSCO, 384, Subsidia, 52) (Louvain, 1977), 129 ff. For an overview of the use of topoi in hagiography, see the

light of the formally expressed position of the iconoclast Council of Hiereia. A basic source is thus the iconoclast Definition (*Horos*) of 754 and not the Council of Blachernai of 815, which, at least as regards the Theotokos, merely ratified the Definition of Hiereia and restricted itself to anathematizing the Council of Nicaea II (787) for restoring the icons: according to the Blachernai text 'it [the Council of 787] also heedlessly stated that lifeless portraits of the most-holy Mother of God and the saints who share in his (Christ's) form should be set up and worshipped, thereby coming into conflict with the central doctrine of the Church'.[19]

We now come to the arguments themselves, in their most widely publicized form – the famous *Canon of Orthodoxy* of Patriarch Methodios (843). As is well known, with the ending of iconoclasm the *Canon of Orthodoxy* defined the Orthodox position on the Theotokos in two regards: the first concerns the Virgin Birth and the doctrine of the Incarnation of the *Logos*, as already formulated at the Council of Ephesus in 431, which declared that the Theotokos is 'truly the Mother of God' (third ode)[20] and that 'through her the *Logos* was incarnated'. The Patriarch addresses her: 'Pure city, glorified by God ... from whom your maker was born, preserving you after birth in your former state' (sixth ode).[21] The second, which is basically consequent on the first, consists of references to the Mother of God as intercessor with her son and as helper of man. The Patriarch addresses 'the much hymned, much praised, Virgin mother, Mother of God' and requests her 'to redeem from grave misdeeds those who honour your Virgin Birth. For we have no other help but you, bride of God' (seventh ode).[22] And he beseeches 'Help, shelter and succour of all, show that you can intercede ... with the power of your son', because 'as a mother you are all-powerful' (ninth ode).[23] This is a synoptic and exceptionally poetic expression of the iconophile response to the iconoclast position on the Theotokos, i.e. to the rejection of pictorial representation as a dual statement of the mortal and divine natures of the *Logos*, the consequent rejection of the depiction of the mortal nature alone, as contravening the indivisibility of the two natures of Christ, and the logical further rejection of both matter, which leads to the Incarnation of the *Logos* through the Virgin, and of her entire role as intercessor for mankind.

But let us return to the iconoclast arguments themselves. The introduction to the iconoclast Definition of the Council of Hiereia has a conventional reference to the church 'of our holy, pure lady the Mother of God and ever-virginal Mary',[24] where the Council met in 754. After expressing the basic iconoclast position that 'the image of his flesh delivered by God, the divine bread, was filled with the holy spirit together with the cup of life-giving blood from his side. This is accepted as the true image of God's incarnated plan, Christ our Lord'[25] (i.e. that the only

---

most recent study, N. Delierneux, 'L'exploitation de "topoi" hagiographiques. Du cliché à la réalité codée', *Byz* 70 (2000), 57–90.
[19] P. Alexander, 'The Iconoclast Council of St. Sophia (815) and its Definition (*Horos*)', *DOP* 7 (1953), 35–66, esp. 59.
[20] *PG* 99, 1772A.
[21] Ibid., 1776A.
[22] Ibid., 1776D.
[23] Ibid., 1780B.
[24] J. D. Mansi, *Sacrorum Conciliorum Nova et Amplissima Collectio* XIII (Paris–Leipzig, 1920), 209C–D; H. Hennerhof, *Textus Byzantini ad Iconomachiam Pertinentes* (Leiden, 1969), frg. 201, 61. See also G. Ostrogorsky, *Studien zur Geschichte des byzantinischen Bilderstreites* (Breslau, 1929), 51.
[25] Mansi, *Collectio* XIII, 264B–C; Hennerhof, *Textus*, frg. 226, 68.

acceptable representation of the Divine is the divine Eucharist) it returns to the Mother of God in order to explain through a rhetorical question (*aporia*) why portrayals of the Theotokos are forbidden: 'the *aporia* of why we prohibit the creation of images of the unblemished and supremely glorious Mother of God, the prophets, apostles and martyrs, who are mere mortals and not of two natures – human and divine – in one substance like Christ alone'.[26] This was a logical *aporia*, since no one was presenting the Theotokos as a spirit, to need 'veneration in spirit and truth' according to iconoclast arguments.[27] The explanation in this case employs an argument of Monophysite inspiration: 'How can the all-hymned Mother of God, on whom the fullness of the divinity cast its shadow, through whom the unapproachable light shone, higher than the heavens and holier than the Cherubim, be depicted in the vulgar art of the Greek?', and it repeats this in connection with the portrayal of saints[28] i.e. that because matter cannot reproduce her grandeur, any representation must be an offence to the Mother of God.

Furthermore, the iconoclast Definition, which forbade representation of the *Logos* as 'ἰδιοϋπόστατος' (self-subsistent), and anathematized anyone who by depicting his mortal form only 'divides the one Christ into two subsistent entities, making him on the one hand the son of God and on the other the son of the Virgin Mary, and not one and the same'[29] emphasizes the intercessory role of the Theotokos: 'if anyone does not admit the Ever-Virgin Mary to be primarily and truly the Mother of God and higher than all things created both visible and invisible and with genuine faith does not implore her intercession, since she has freedom of speech with the son who was born of her, let him be anathema'.[30] Thus in the most formal iconoclast text, the Definition of 754, the Theotokos plays such a major role that some scholars argue that exaggerated honours were paid to her by the iconoclasts,[31] though according to others these honours remained on the purely verbal level. In reality, however, it appears that in the context of the use of matter practices associated with the expression of faith in the Mother of God directly conflicted with basic iconoclast credos.[32]

Thus the use of the 'image' of the Theotokos in Byzantine political life is a two-way mirror which reflects both sides – iconoclast and iconophile – and focuses on certain basic elements:

1. The Theotokos as the personification of the destruction of idols.
2. The Theotokos in the context of the dialectic of light and darkness.
3. Refusal to pay honours to the Theotokos through the denial of her name and her person.
4. Denial of the intercessory role of the Theotokos and of her mediation with the Son on behalf of mankind.

The 'image' of the Theotokos as the personification of the destruction of idols was consistently exploited at this time. To the iconoclasts, the Mother of God was the figure responsible for the destruction of the idolatry of antiquity, and by the same token the idolatry of icon

---

[26] Mansi, *Collectio* XIII, 272; Hennerhof, *Textus*, frg. 228, 68–9.
[27] Mansi, *Collectio* XIII, 216B–C.
[28] Ibid., 277; Hennerhof, *Textus*, frg. 232, 70–1: 'ἀδόξῳ καὶ νεκρᾷ ὕλῃ καθυβρίζειν'.
[29] Mansi, *Collectio* XIII, 341C–D; Hennerhof, *Textus*, frg. 254, 75.
[30] Mansi, *Collectio* XIII, 345A–B; Hennerhof, *Textus*, frg. 257, 76.
[31] K. Parry, *Depicting the Word. Byzantine Thought of the Eighth and Ninth Centuries* (Leiden, New York and Cologne, 1996), 191.
[32] N. Tsironis, 'The Mother of God in the Iconoclastic Controversy', in Vassilaki, *Mother of God*, 27–39, esp. 28.

veneration through the Incarnation of the *Logos*-Spirit.³³ For the iconophiles, she represented the embodiment of their basic argument, since depiction of the *Logos* found its ultimate justification in its Incarnation through the Mother of God, 'whence' in the words of Patriarch Germanos 'the stone not cut by hand rolled and destroyed the idolatrous altars'.³⁴

It is precisely for this reason that the iconophiles persisted in the use of the verbal image of the Theotokos in their confrontation with idolatry. A typical instance is the argument of the Old Man in the Νουθεσία γέροντος περὶ τῶν ἁγίων εἰκόνων,³⁵ the oldest extant text of anti-iconoclast polemic, during his public debate³⁶ with the iconoclast bishop: 'Whose idols do I worship, those of Artemis the mother of demons, or the image of the Mother of God and eternal Virgin Mary, the mother of our Lord?'³⁷ This goes rather further than mere denial of the charges of idolatry which were being levelled at the iconophiles. The juxtaposition of the Theotokos and Artemis which is repeated in the *Life of St Stephen the Younger*³⁸ (and, almost a century later, in the *Life of Michael Synkellos*),³⁹ and, more specifically, the antithesis 'Artemis – the mother of demons' and 'Mother of God' allude to a second interpretation. Artemis herself derives from the demonology – in an amalgam of Jewish, Graeco-Egyptian and gnostic beliefs and apocryphal gospels – of early Christian texts, such as the sixth-century *Acts of St Marina of Antioch*.⁴⁰ A struggle with devils is a common topos of such texts; indeed St Marina herself overcomes a demon and compels him to explain the origin of demons from the union of his father Satan and the Daughter of Zeus. What are of particular interest here are the exegetic scholia on the text by Patriarch Methodios: the heroine is modelled on the Theotokos in her persona as *the Redeemer of Eve* who, armed with Divine Grace in the form of a bronze hammer, prevails over the serpent Satan.⁴¹ On another level, the reference to the 'mother of demons' in texts of the

---

33 For the ambiguity of the term 'idolatry' in the iconoclast period when it was applied to the iconophiles by the iconoclasts, see G. Ostrogorsky, *Studien zur Geschichte des byzantinischen Bilderstreites* (Breslau, 1929), 49, where iconoclast emperors are shown as responsible for the 'καθαίρεσιν δαιμονικῶν ὀχυρωμάτων', 'destruction of demonic forts'. See also M.-F. Auzépy, 'L'analyse littéraire et l'historien: l'exemple des vies de saints iconoclastes', *BSl* 53 (1992), 57–76, as well as P. Speck, 'Ich bin's nicht, Kaiser Konstantin ist es gewesen: die Legenden vom Einfluss des Teufels des Juden und des Moslem auf den Ikonoklasmus', in his Ποικίλα Βυζαντινά 10 (Bonn, 1990), 362 ff.
34 *PG* 98, 308A.
35 Attributed to AD 755–760. See M. B. Melioranskii, 'Georgii Kiprianin i Ioann Ierosalimlianin, dva maloizvestnykh borca za pravoslavie v VIII veke', *Zapiski Istoriko-Filologicheskogo Fakulteta Imp. S.-Peterburgskogo Universiteta* 59 (1901), v–xxxix. A. Metsides, Η παρουσία της εκκλησίας Κύπρου εις τον αγώνα υπέρ των εικόνων (Nicosia, 1989), 153–200.
36 Melioranskii, 'Georgii Kiprianin i Ioann Ierosalimlianin', XXIX.
37 Metsides, Η παρουσία της εκκλησίας Κύπρου, 170 lines 461–3.
38 Auzépy, *Vie d'Étienne*, 156 lines 11–12, and 254.
39 Th. J. Schmitt, 'Βίος καὶ πολιτεία καὶ ἀγῶνος τοῦ ὁσίου πατρός ἡμῶν καὶ ὁμολογητοῦ Μιχαὴλ πρεσβυτέρου καὶ συγκέλλου γεγονότος τῆς πόλεως Ἱεροσολύμων', in *Kakhrie-džami. Istoriia Monastyria Khory*, *IRAIK* 11 (1906), 227–94, esp. 240. M. Cunningham, *The Life of Michael the Synkellos. Text, Translation and Commentary* (Belfast, 1991), 80: 'εἴδωλον ἔστιν ὡς Ἀπόλλωνος καὶ τῆς μητρὸς αὐτοῦ τῆς εὐλογημένης Θεοτόκου ὡς Ἀρτέμιδος …'.
40 *BHG*, 1165–6. *Acta S. Marinae et S. Christophori*, ed. K. H. Usener, *Festschrift zur fünften Säcularfeier der Carl-Ruprechts-Universität zu Heidelberg, überreicht von Rector und Senat der Rheinischen Friedrich-Wilhelm-Universität* (Bonn, 1886).
41 *Acta S. Marinae et S. Christophori*, ed. Usener, *Festschrift*, 48; see P. Boulhol, 'Hagiographie antique et démonologie. Notes sur quelques passions grecques (*BHG* 962z, 964 et 1165–66)', *AnBoll* 112 (1994), 255–302, esp. 260 n. 25.

period itself contains the seeds of her own defeat and that of the idolatry of antiquity through the indirect allusion to the Incarnation of the Word through the Theotokos, the main foundation of the iconophile argument. At the same time the chastisement of demons is yet another contemporary political nuance in a religious guise, as in the eyes of the iconophiles the iconoclasts themselves were frequently to be identified as demons. For example, iconophile saints such as Andrew, 'who crossed himself'[42] at his trial before Constantine V, often behaved in front of iconoclasts as if they were faced by men possessed by devils, and had to resort to exorcism through the sign of the cross! In this context the political colour in the use of the image of the demon-destroying Theotokos, albeit indirect, is a striking expression of the opposition to iconoclast imperial power.

The second element mentioned above is the dialectic of light and darkness. By the eighth century epithets of the Mother of God which exploit the imagery of light – starting with the 'bright dawn' of the *Akathistos Hymn* (widely disseminated in the previous century) and the 'east which heralds the never-setting lamp' in the words of Patriarch Germanos[43] – had already been established as a conventional topos involving yet another reference to the doctrine of the Incarnation and to the Mother of God as the conceptual gate of light, who through the Incarnation of the *Logos* banishes the darkness of idolatry. Accordingly there is nothing remarkable about the use of the light–darkness dialectic during the iconoclast dispute. The iconoclasts referred to the Theotokos 'through whom the unapproachable light shone', in accordance with the iconoclast Definition of 754.[44] At the same time they projected themselves as redeemers from the darkness of the second idolatry/iconolatry. The *Life of St Stephen the Younger* refers to the formal acclamations paid by the people of Constantinople to Constantine V: 'you, O emperor, delivered us from the idols',[45] while the Definition of 754 praises the emperors 'for destroying every trace of idolatry'.[46] Moreover the term 'darkness' is used ad nauseam in contemporary polemic, in the context of demonizing one's opponent.[47] Epithets such as 'clothed in darkness'[48] were applied by the iconoclasts to monks in an attempt to associate them with 'demonic' darkness (demons often appear as creatures painted in black)[49] and thus to discredit them. The iconophiles made a similar attempt in the use of expressions such as 'the dense darkness of heresy' and 'dense darkness (σκοτόμαινα) of error'[50] in the *Apologeticus Major* of Patriarch Nikephoros, and in the splendid pun ἐπίσκοτοι (men of darkness) for

---

[42] *Passio Andreae in Crisi*, in *AASS*, Octobris VIII (1853), 135–42, esp. 138F. See also N. Koutrakou, *La propagande impériale byzantine, persuasion et réaction (VIIIe–Xe siècles)* (Athens, 1994), 280–1.
[43] *PG* 98, 308A.
[44] Mansi, *Collectio* XIII, 277C; Hennerhof, *Textus*, frg. 232, 69.
[45] Auzépy, *Vie d'Étienne*, 128 lines 9–10, and 223.
[46] Mansi, *Collectio* XIII, 353C; Hennerhof, *Textus*, frg. 263, 77–8.
[47] Koutrakou, *Propagande impériale*, 288–90.
[48] Auzépy, *Vie d'Étienne*, 141 line 19: 'σκοτένδυτον'.
[49] A striking example of the black demon-enemy in the context of the light–darkness dialectic of the texts is the vision of the Ethiopian enemy of the Church who invaded Hagia Sophia with the (iconoclast) emperor while the Church itself appeared as a 'woman encircled by the sun', which occurs in the letter of the three Patriarchs to Emperor Theophilos. *Epistula Synodica ad Theophilum Imperatorem (BHG 1386)*, ed. J. A. Munitiz, J. Chrysostomides, E. Harvalia-Crook and Ch. Dendrinos, *The Letter of the Three Patriarchs to Emperor Theophilos and Related Texts* (Camberley, 1997), 73–5.
[50] *PG* 100, 597D.

iconoclast ἐπίσκοποι (bishops) in the *Life of St Stephen the Younger*.[51] In the context of this polemic the use of the image of the Theotokos as light involved a de facto identification of the exploiting faction with the party of sanctity while simultaneously discrediting its rival as the instrument of demonic darkness.

The third element, the refusal to render honour to the Mother of God with which the iconoclasts were charged by their iconophile opponents, places even greater emphasis on the political colour in the use of the Theotokos image. It is no longer a question of failing to render honour to her image but rather of insulting the name and indeed the person of Mother of God herself.[52] Most iconophile texts after the Council of Nicaea II in 787 concentrate not only on the 'insult to the holy icons'[53] but mainly on the outrage committed by the iconoclasts – in particular Emperor Constantine V, who is portrayed as the archetypal iconoclast – against the Theotokos 'whom', according to the *Life of Abbot Niketas of Medikion*, 'Christ chose and honoured as his dwelling place' (i.e in refutation of the doctrine of the Incarnation of the *Logos* and thus of the portrayal of Christ) – and whose 'reverend name he [Constantine V] tried to banish from the church in many ways'.[54] This is accordingly a specific instance of the iconoclast aniconic doctrine expressed in terms of the Mother of God. In similar fashion, Patriarch Nikephoros in his *First Antirrhetic* refers to the Theotokos as 'dishonoured in many ways'[55] by the iconoclasts. Apart from the denial of intercession by the Mother of God, the form this 'dishonour' took is not exactly clear. Nor is it obvious how the iconoclast emperor intended to banish the use of her name from the church. It does not seem to have been some conjectural prohibition e.g. of hymns to the Mother of God, which our iconophile sources would certainly not have failed to emphasize. Theodore of Stoudios, for example, says that during the second iconoclast dispute 'Psalms handed down of old which sang of icons were set aside and new doctrines were sung in their place'.[56] And the same Patriarch Nikephoros insists that Constantine V dares 'to remove 'Θεοτόκον φωνήν', the name of the Mother of God, entirely from the tongue of Christians', and he continues 'then he perverts and distorts whatever had been invoked in her name'.[57] iconoclast practice regarding the Theotokos thus appears as an orchestrated attack conforming to the well-known practice of prohibiting the mention of the name of a particular person or object, a form of *damnatio memoriae* with the ultimate aim of denying its existence. This practice found particular expression in the nickname 'unmentionables' which was often used by the iconoclasts in connection with iconophile monasticism.[58] In the case of the Theotokos however, this 'unmention' was not a literal one except as far as portrayal is concerned, and this in line with the denial of a name which leads not to disappearance but to disrepute, thus constituting a political position. References to the Theotokos in the beautiful epithets of the Akathistos Hymn, e.g. 'the living and plentiful spring' or 'the bright dawn' could easily have given sustenance to both iconophile and iconoclast arguments (e.g. in the context of the

---

[51] Auzépy, *Vie d'Étienne*, 126 line 7.
[52] Tsironis, 'The Mother of God in the Iconoclastic Controversy', 31.
[53] Βίος Νικήτα Μηδικίου, XXVIIIB–C.
[54] Ibid., XXVIIIC.
[55] Patriarch Nikephoros, *First Antirrhetic*, *PG* 100, 216D.
[56] Theodore of Stoudios, *Epistulae*, ed. Fatouros, II, 411; *PG* 99, 1164B.
[57] Patriarch Nikephoros, *Second Antirrhetic*, *PG* 100, 341C–D.
[58] Βίος Νικήτα Μηδικίου, XXVIIID.

dialectic of light and darkness mentioned above), something which explains the iconophile reactions. This political use of the image of the Theotokos by the iconoclasts is perceived in the opposing camp as bringing it into dishonour.

The same leitmotif of using an offence against the Mother of God to discredit the offender politically (in an even more obvious and simplistic, one might even say Manichean, manner) lies behind the episode from the *Chronographia* of Theophanes in which the iconophile patriarch Anastasios swears on the holy Cross that Emperor Constantine V had told him, 'Do not regard Mary's offspring, who is called Christ, as the Son of God, but as a mere man. For Mary gave birth to Him just as my mother Mary gave birth to me'[59] – and also behind the anecdotes on the discrediting of the Theotokos by the same emperor. One of these tells how in a didactic moment Constantine decided to demonstrate his assertions about the Mother of God by giving a visual parallel:

> Taking a purse full of gold in his hands and showing it to the audience, he asked them 'What is this worth?' And when they said 'A lot', he poured out the gold and again asked 'What is the purse worth now?' 'Nothing', they replied, and the villain said 'It is the same with the Theotokos' (for the infamous man did not wish to say holy). 'When she had Christ within her she was due all honour, but once she had given birth, she was no different from anyone else.'[60]

If the argument has a clear theological colour, the use of the image of the Theotokos is political. The story of Anastasios' oath is set against the background of a purely political event, Artabasdos' revolt of 742. From the point of view of dynastic legitimacy Artabasdos was a usurper – to gain acceptance from the people of Constantinople he had, through a supporter of his, falsely informed them that Constantine V was dead[61] – and the patriarch's action is an apparent attempt at legitimizing the usurper, on the grounds that as an iconophile (which may not even have been the case)[62] Artabasdos rejoices in the favour of God from which the heretical Constantine had fallen. The patriarch's motive is obviously political, and he uses the story of the emperor's denial of the doctrine of the Incarnation for political ends. The second anecdote also has a political colour. It shows the emperor using a form of stagecraft – something which accords with Constantine's known behaviour, in particular his habit (according to his enemies) of organizing sham public wedding ceremonies between monks and nuns.[63] Constantine's

---

[59] Theophanes, *Chronographia*, ed. Bonn, 640; ed. de Boor, I.415, lines 26–27. Mango and Scott, *The Chronicle of Theophanes the Confessor*, 576.
[60] *Βίος Νικήτα Μηδικίου*, XXVIIIC–D.
[61] Theophanes, *Chronographia*, ed. Bonn, 639; ed. de Boor, I.415, line 7. Mango and Scott, *The Chronicle of Theophanes the Confessor*, 575: 'πείθει πάντας ὡς ὁ βασιλεύς τέθνηκεν'.
[62] Probably this is an appropriation of an enemy of the iconoclast emperor by the iconophile faction. On Artabasdos' revolt, P. Speck, 'Artabasdos der rechtgläubige Vorkämpfer der göttlichen Lehren. Untersuchungen zur Revolte des Artabasdos und ihrer Darstellung in der byzantinischen Historiographie', in his *Ποικίλα Βυζαντινά* 2 (Bonn, 1981), 97–8. There are also several instances of iconoclast adherents of Artabasdos, particularly from the Theme of Opsikion which supported him (V. Vlysidou, E. Kountoura, S. Lambakis, T. Loungis and A. Savvidis, *Η Μικρά Ασία των Θεμάτων* (Athens, 1998), 170–1), such as the iconoclast general who, during the siege of Nicaea by the Arabs, threw a stone at the icon of the Virgin and the next day during an Arab attack was killed by a stone thrown by one of the enemy (Theophanes, *Chronographia*, ed. Bonn, 624). This gave rise to doubts about his (belated) iconophilia, which was not apparent while he was a general of Leo III.
[63] Theophanes, *Chronographia*, ed. Bonn, 688. These sham marriages aimed at ridiculing monasticism based on the

exploitation of the rules of logical argument is also consistent with the rumours which gathered around him, accusing him of using persuasion 'which obtained the consent of the audience by coercion through the use of elaborate and contrived words: this is a Hellenic device',[64] according to the *Third Antirrhetic* of Patriarch Nikephoros, and of a 'Hellenizing kingship'.[65] In spite of the perfectly plausible way in which Constantine V is presented, the 'propagandist' use of the story is clear. It shows the iconoclast emperor coming into direct conflict with the Nicene Creed, which the iconoclast Definition of 754 firmly restates: 'if anyone does not admit ... that for our salvation he came down from the heavens and was incarnated of the Holy Spirit and the Virgin Mary ... anathema', and 'if anyone does not admit that God is truly the Emmanuel and therefore that the holy virgin is the Mother of God – for she bore of the flesh the incarnated *Logos* of God – anathema'.[66] Moreover, in the second story, the heretical nature of the emperor's behaviour, in relation to views already condemned by the first ecumenical councils, seems obvious. But mainly it contradicts the views spelt out by the iconoclasts about the attribution of due honours to the Theotokos as Mother of God, whose representation in base matter is an offence. The whole story thus performs a political function: the insult to the Theotokos from the iconoclast emperor makes him not only a heretic but also inconsistent towards the official credos of his party.

Finally, in the denial of the intercessory role of the Mother of God we have perhaps the most blatantly 'political' exploitation of her image during this period. Indeed the only concrete example of 'dishonour' towards the Theotokos, the only *damnatio memoriae*, which is mentioned for example in the *Life of Niketas of Medikion*, relates to intercession, mediation by the Theotokos on behalf of mankind: 'her intercessions, through which the world is established, he did not even want to be mentioned, saying that she had no power to help'.[67] The *Chronographia* of Theophanes and the *Logos on the Inventio of the Relics of the blessed martyr Euphemia*[68] impute the denial of intercession by the Mother of God to Leo III.[69] In the same context, the iconophile party appears to subscribe to a form of 'oath of allegiance' to mediation by the Theotokos, as found for example in the putative doctrinal letter of Patriarch Nikephoros to Pope Leo III.[70]

It is, however, significant that the charges made against the iconoclasts of denying the Theotokos' mediation on behalf of the faithful, which led to the appropriation of intercession

---

segregation of the sexes: D. Abrahamse, 'Women's Monasticism in the Middle-Byzantine Period. Problems and Prospects', *BF* 9 (1985), 33–58. G. Huxley, 'Women in Byzantine Iconoclasm', in J.-Y. Perreault (ed.), *Women in Byzantine Monasticism* (Athens, 1991), 11–24. At the same time however they underlined the importance of marriage in iconoclast policy, as opposed to the iconophile monastic model of chastity: see A. Kazhdan, 'Η βυζαντινή οικογένεια και τα προβλήματά της', *Βυζαντινά* 14 (1988), 223–36, esp. 224–5. Note also Patriarch Nikephoros' use of the word 'triumphed' in this context (*Third Antirrhetic*, *PG* 100, 524A), which places the monks in the position of the defeated. See the analysis of Auzépy [Rouan], 'Une lecture', 415 ff., esp. 419, 433.

[64] *PG* 100, 377C.
[65] Theodore of Stoudios, Ἐγκώμιον Πλάτωνος ἡγουμένου, *PG* 99, 824B.
[66] Mansi, *Collectio* XIII, 333E, 336A–D; Hennerhof, *Textus*, frg. 249, 74.
[67] Βίος Νικήτα Μηδικίου, XXVIIIC.
[68] Written between 796 and 806. Constantinos Tios, Λόγος εἰς τὴν εὕρεσιν τοῦ τιμίου λειψάνου τῆς ἁγίας καὶ πανευφήμου μάρτυρος Εὐφημίας, ed. Fr. Halkin, *Ste Euphémie de Chalcédoine* (*Subsidia Hagiographica*, 41) (Brussels, 1965), 81–106, esp. 82.
[69] Theophanes, *Chronographia*, ed. Bonn, 625. Halkin, *Ste Euphémie de Chalcédoine*, 96.
[70] *PG* 100, 189.

by the iconophile party, appear in texts later than the Council of Nicaea II. Earlier texts such as the *Νουθεσία* do not mention it, while the iconoclast Definition of 754 threatens with excommunication those who do not invoke the Theotokos' intercession. The charge against the iconoclasts of denying mediation by the Theotokos obscures the fact that what they actually denied was mediation through her image and her portrayal. Her name continued to be invoked, even in front of iconoclasts, without offence being taken.[71] A possible explanation for the iconophiles' insistence that the iconoclasts introduced an 'interdict' on intercessions and on the Theotokos' intercessory role might be that it represented a counter-argument to a basic issue of contemporary imperial theology, the 'intercessory role' of emperors. This cannot be proved, of course, but it seems a plausible theory in the context of contemporary polemic and the silence and the contradictions of the texts.

This is not the place to elaborate on the admittedly broad subject of imperial intercession as expressed in the phrase attributed to Leo III 'I am priest and *basileus*'.[72] The fact that it occurs in forged *Letters of Pope Gregory II*[73] is sufficient to emphasize that here again we are looking at iconoclast views through an iconophile prism. However, a clearly genuine, official text, the *Ecloga* of the Isaurians, refers to the emperor in its introduction as 'Shepherd to the most faithful flock',[74] and the use of epithets such as 'θεόσοφος'[75] and 'σοφός'[76] in the context not only of imperial designation but also of the iconophile–iconoclast dialectic reflects the concept of imperial intercession. The most formal expression of this can be found in the popular acclamations addressed to Constantine V: 'today the world is saved because you, O emperor, redeemed us from the idols',[77] with its obvious reference to the Easter message of Christ the Saviour,[78] and in the phrase attributed to Leo V: 'I shall hear as intercessor.'[79]

Against this background the attribution to the iconoclasts of the denial of intercession by the Mother of God plays a double role from the political perspective. It shifts the argument from imperial mediation to imperial calumniation, thus raising the charge of insulting a generally accepted symbol, the Theotokos, and stressing the weaknesses of the imperial position on intercession. Secondly, by laying emphasis on the generally accepted intercession between Mother and Son, it reminds the iconoclast imperial faction of the apostolic 'one intercessor between God and men, Jesus Christ the man' (1 Timothy 2:5).

The use of the entire Theotokos 'package' for political ends serves to devalue the aspirations for a wider acceptance of intercession by an emperor-priest. Furthermore, by restricting

---

[71] e.g. the invocation of the name of the Mother of God by the Graptos brothers in their interrogation by Theophilos: PG 116, 676A.
[72] See the excellent analysis by G. Dagron, based on the *Νουθεσία γέροντος περὶ τῶν ἁγίων εἰκόνων*, in his *Empereur et prêtre. Étude sur le 'césaropapisme' à Byzance* (Paris, 1996), 193 ff.
[73] J. Gouillard, 'Aux origines de l'Iconoclasme. Le témoignage de Gregoire II', *TM* 3 (1968), 243–307, esp. 299.
[74] I. and P. Zepos, *Jus Grecoromanum* II (Athens, 1931), 11.
[75] Theognostos, *Περὶ ὀρθογραφίας*, ed. K. Alpers, *Theognostos, Περὶ ὀρθογραφίας. Überlieferung, Quellen und Text des Kanones* (Hamburg, 1964), 68, with reference to Leo V.
[76] Alpers, *Theognostos, Περὶ ὀρθογραφίας*, 68.
[77] Cf. above, n. 45.
[78] Koutrakou, *Propagande impériale*, 202–3.
[79] *Βίος Νικήτα Μηδικίου*, XXIXE: 'τέκνον εἰμὶ τῆς Ἐκκλησίας καὶ ὡς μεσίτης ἐπακροάσομαι ... συγκρίνας ἑκάτερα τἀληθῆ γνώσομαι'.

imperial authority to 'Christomimic'[80] intercession – not between God and men but between fellow-citizens – it already outlines the path which imperial ideology would follow in the post-iconoclast period.

The exploitation of the image of the Mother of God during and after the iconoclast dispute provides a vivid portrait of the inventiveness and flexibility to be found on both sides and also of the stability of religious symbols among the Byzantines. It thus establishes a link between the theological arguments and the political and state objectives of the era, something which in the final analysis is characteristic of the entire political life of Byzantium.

---

[80] Cf. the terms used in the *Life of Theodore of Stoudios* regarding Michael I, who brought back the Stoudites from exile (*PG* 99, 272D): 'and he becomes an envoy in imitation of Christ and an intercessor for the dissidents.'

8

From poetry to liturgy:
the cult of the Virgin in the Middle Byzantine era

Niki Tsironis

Until a few years ago, and certainly before the publication of the collective volume which formed the catalogue of the 'Mother of God' exhibition, it would have been difficult to make definitive statements about the role of the Virgin in the Middle Byzantine era.[1] Now scholars in various fields have recorded their views on the Virgin cult[2] and have made a decisive contribution to establishing a picture of the significant role she played at this time, in particular between the eighth and the eleventh centuries. Although her cult began in the early Christian era, it took centre stage when it became identified with the cult of icons during the period which conventionally we term as iconoclasm.[3] As recent research has shown, it was at this time that the human image of the Virgin as Mother of God came to the fore.[4]

Other scholars have elaborated on the origins of the cult of the Theotokos as it emerged during the first Christian centuries, and hence set the scene for the developments of the Middle Byzantine period.[5] In this paper, therefore, I will focus on the Middle Byzantine era itself. It was during this period that the Virgin became established, through the perpetually evolving traditions of the Church, as a symbol of Orthodoxy.

In this period, moreover, we can see a striking shift in the images and symbols associated with the Theotokos or Mother of God, a transition from one genre to another. I refer in particular to the emergence, in word and image, of the theme of the Virgin as Christ's tender mother. This theme makes its first appearance in poetry; it then passes over into iconography, and finally enters the liturgical life of the Church. While following strictly the conventions laid down for each medium of expression – literary, iconographic and so on – the Byzantines introduced this new theme gradually, grafting it carefully onto preceding ones, and in this

---

[1] As Averil Cameron writes in her article, 'The Early Cult of the Virgin', in Vassilaki, *Mother of God*, 3–15, n. 1, the bibliography on the Theotokos is vast, but most authors approach the subject from the Roman Catholic position.
[2] The term 'cult' is employed here in the meaning used (correctly, in my view) by Maria Vassilaki, editor of the *Mother of God* catalogue. From the strictly theological point of view the word 'cult' (in Greek, λατρεία) can only refer to God, while the correct term as regards the Virgin and icons is 'honour' or 'veneration'.
[3] This is independently of the studies that are continually adding new pieces of information to change the image of iconoclasts and iconophiles which existed until recently. It seems probable that the two sides had no clear ideological frontiers and certainly did not constitute a formal ideological movement.
[4] Ioli Kalavrezou was the first to describe this important role in her article 'Images of the Mother: When the Virgin Mary became *Meter Theou*', *DOP* 44 (1990), 165–72. See also ead., 'The Maternal Side of the Virgin', in Vassilaki, *Mother of God*, 41–5.
[5] Apart from H. Graef, *Mary: A History of Doctrine and Devotion* (New York, 1963) and M. Carroll, *The Cult of the Virgin Mary, Psychological Origins* (New Jersey, 1986), see the classic articles by A. M. Cameron, 'The Theotokos in Sixth-Century Constantinople: A City Finds its Symbol', *JThSt* 29 (1978), 79–108, and 'The Virgin's Robe: an Episode in the History of Early Seventh-Century Constantinople', *Byz* 49 (1979), 42–56.

way a hierarchy of genres was created. There is nothing haphazard about this process: a new theme first emerges in the free images of poetry; it then moves over into the language of religious homilies, which is also poetical but is closer to the liturgical style; it appears next in iconography; and only when the new theme has been fully integrated within all those media can it be adopted and assimilated into liturgical texts – a process which signifies the full incorporation and consolidation of this new theme into the main body of Orthodox religious practice.

Poetry and homiletics

The theme of Theotokos as the tender Mother of God appears both in Middle Byzantine poetry and in religious discourse; this reflects the fact that writers associated with the beginning of the iconoclastic period – before Leo III became emperor – wrote verse as well as prose homilies. In any case, these two mediums of expression had, during the period in question, certain similarities of tone and content; both employed strikingly vivid images, designed to stir the emotions, and made extensive use of rhetorical figures of speech. Let us look in particular at two of the primary writers of the iconoclastic period: Andrew of Crete, who is known as the composer of the *Great Canon*, and Patriarch Germanos I of Constantinople. Both men were involved in the acceptance of the teaching of monothelitism, which they were obliged to adopt after a decree issued by Philippikos Bardanes in 712. After the fall of that emperor, Germanos declared his opposition to the doctrine, and he became Patriarch of Constantinople under Emperor Leo III. In 730 he lost the patriarchal throne because of his iconophile beliefs which forced him to withhold support from the emperor's iconoclastic policy. The literary oeuvre of Germanos I has not yet been fully established, as some of his bibliographical details remain unclear, and his writings on the Mother of God are often confused with those of Germanos II, who also wrote poems and homilies on the Virgin.[6] We can, however, say that in his surviving works Germanos presents the Theotokos in a manner that differs from that of previous works of poetical prose.

By way of comparison, let us look briefly at a representative sample of the work of one of the strongest defenders of the Virgin in the early Byzantine period, namely Proklos of Constantinople. The first difference is simply one of proportion: among the extant homilies of Proklos, a relatively small number are dedicated to the Virgin.[7] As for their content, what we see in Proklos is an insistence on the principle of typology; in other words, the practice of singling out certain events from the New Testament in conjunction with events and images from the Old Testament.[8] Although not absent from the work of later writers, in the homilies of Proklos

---

[6] A. Kazhdan (L. F. Sherry and Ch. Angelidi coll.), *A History of Byzantine Literature (650–850)* (Athens, 1999), 59–64.

[7] Of the 115 homilies mentioned in *CPG* III, 5800–5915, only four refer to feasts of the Virgin: 5800, *De Laudibus S. Mariae*; 5804, *In S. Virginem ac Dei Genitricem Mariam*; 5805, *Laudatio S. Dei Genitricis Mariae*; 5875, *In Annuntiatione Beatissimae Dei Genitricis*.

[8] It is in this way that Christian thinkers, particularly in early centuries, testify to the New Testament as the continuation and the fulfilment of the Old. See F. Young, *Biblical Exegesis and the Formation of Christian Culture* (Cambridge, 1997), 192–5, esp. 194. On the use of the typology by Proklos of Constantinople, see N.

typology forms the basic structure on which he develops his theme.⁹ The Christological background of his era is apparent in the author's attempt to substantiate the nature of Christ and to observe a distance between his divine and human hypostases. A typical passage reads: 'He enlisted his own servant as a mother, the one who is in essence motherless, and according to God's plan on earth fatherless. Then how is he, according to Paul, motherless and fatherless? If a simple man, he is not motherless, for he has a mother. If pure God, he is not fatherless, for he has a father. But as a creator he has no mother, and as a man he has no father.'[10] And in the same spirit he writes: 'For according to God's plan there is no other such, nor has there been, nor will there be, apart from the one born both God and Man from a Virgin.'[11] This gives the main emphasis to Christ himself rather than to the figure of the Theotokos, let alone her identity as Mother of God. More specifically, Proklos places the Theotokos within the context of the Christological disputes of the time, as in his homily *On the Incarnation of the Lord*: 'Let Arius and Eunomios, Makedonios and Nestorios be shamed … I shall tell you a mystery. Being God, he was seen on the earth, and through the Virgin he was present and came to dwell here and birth did not diminish him nor did labour corrupt his uncreated nature, but the created form moulded the creator and the world contained the uncontainable incarnated one'.[12]

Poetry and homilies of the iconoclastic period display a shift of emphasis in their treatment of the Virgin. In his customary poetic style Germanos stresses the Theotokos' human qualities and her identity as Mother of God, innovatively linking this with the Passion of Christ. The Passion underlines the fully human nature of Christ, on which iconophile writers founded their defence of icon veneration, but it is also of great significance to the Virgin's image as Mother of God, since her presence at the Crucifixion of her *Son and God* brings her human qualities to the fore. Both of these concepts share a common denominator in their emphasis on the Incarnation, with, in the background, the affirmation of matter and its consequent link with the veneration of icons.

These concepts, which are also found in other contemporary texts, are perhaps the most striking instances of the phenomenon of the hierarchy of genres; for, as we shall later discover, it is precisely these themes which will be adopted by the iconography of the period after the Triumph of Orthodoxy and which will eventually be chosen for incorporation in liturgical texts.

A typical example is Germanos' homily on the burial of Christ, where he states: 'she endured his Passion and death in human fashion.'[13] This homily shows the Theotokos dramatically giving way to the grief that only a mother can feel: 'The mother reaches a peak in her lamentations. She conceives still greater sighs. She gives birth to more extensive weeping. For now she no longer has sight of her son. The sun knew its setting, going below the earth, and it became night for the mother of the Sun. A night of heavy sorrow and disaster.'[14] She prolongs her

---

P. Constas, 'Weaving the Body of God: Proklos of Constantinople, the Theotokos and the Loom of the Flesh', *JEChSt* 3.2 (1995), 169–94.
[9] See for example the homily *De Laudibus S. Mariae*, PG 65, 679–92, esp. 680–4.
[10] Ibid., 685A.
[11] Ibid., 685D.
[12] *De Incarnatione Domini nostris*, PG 65, 691B–704C, esp. 693B–C.
[13] *In Dominici Corporis Sepulturam*, PG 98, 269A.
[14] Ibid., 269B.

maternal lamentation using the epithets applied to her in Old Testament typology: lamp, fleece, bush, ladder, bright cloud, gold jar of manna.[15] Similar references are also found in Germanos' homily *On the Presentation of the Virgin to the Temple*, which again emphasizes her role as mother: 'the all-golden jar, which holds the sweetest delight of our souls, Christ, the manna ... you surpassed all created things, O gift of God. Untilled earth, unploughed field, vine with fair branches, delightful cup, bubbling fountain, Virgin who gave birth and Mother who knew no man, treasure of innocence and pride of holiness.'[16] And he goes on to indicate the indissoluble link between this role and the Theotokos' intercessionary powers: 'with your well-received and maternally persuasive prayers to your Son, born of you without a father and to God, the creator of all things'.[17]

In introducing a theotokion at the end of each strophe of his *Great Canon*, Andrew of Crete also presents the Virgin as an intercessor whose *parresia* (directness of speech) arises from her close relationship with Christ: 'She intercedes in the height of divinity and in the lowliness of the flesh and becomes a mother of the creator.'[18] The homilies of the same author, most of which are dedicated to various feasts of the Theotokos, emphasize not only the mystery of the Incarnation of the *Logos* but also the assumption of human nature from the Virgin: for example 'the emptied nature, God and Man, and the deification of what is assumed',[19] and: 'the birthday is the feast day, and [celebration of the] regeneration of the race. For a Virgin is now born and feeds at the breast and is fashioned, and is made ready to be mother to God the all-powerful king of the centuries.'[20]

The same images, and a similar emphasis on the Virgin as a mother, are also found in the work of other authors of the period such as John of Damascus, Kosmas of Maiouma, the Graptoi brothers, Theodore of Stoudios and George of Nikomedeia.[21] Henry Maguire has shown how George's homily *On the great and holy Friday and on the bodily burial of our Lord Jesus Christ* was used by icon-painters as a model in the emergence of the theme of the Lamentation.[22] The emotional charge of the Virgin, at the foot of the Cross, is echoed in the immediate post-iconoclastic iconography of the Crucifixion where, in contrast to the earlier version, the Virgin is depicted at the foot of the Cross together with John, 'the disciple whom Jesus loved'.[23] The iconography of the Deposition, which elaborates the theme of the Lamentation and gives fullest expression to the Virgin's pain, represents a still later development.[24]

---

[15] Ibid., 269D–270A. On the typology, see M. Warner, *Alone of All Her Sex, the Myth and the Cult of the Virgin Mary* (London, 1976). Mgr Kallistos Ware, *Mary in the Orthodox Tradition* (Wallington, Surrey, 1997). Young, *Biblical Exegesis*, 192–5. Archim. Ephrem Lash, 'Mary in the Eastern Christian Literature', *Epiphany* (1989) 310–21.

[16] *In Presentationem SS. Deiparae* II, PG 98, 308C.

[17] Ibid., 308C.

[18] Andrew of Crete, *In Nativitatem B. Mariae* I, PG 92, 805–20, esp. 808B.

[19] Ibid., 808A.

[20] Ibid., 808B.

[21] For a detailed assessment of their work in so far as it concerns the Virgin, see N. Tsironis, *The Cult and the Lament of the Virgin in the Iconoclastic Period* (Oxford, forthcoming).

[22] H. Maguire, *Art and Eloquence in Byzantium* (Princeton, NJ, 1981). Id., 'The Depiction of Sorrow in Middle Byzantine Art', *DOP* 31 (1977), 123–74.

[23] M. Vassilaki and N. Tsironis, 'Representations of the Virgin and their Association with the Passion of Christ', in Vassilaki, *Mother of God*, 453–63.

[24] H. Belting, *Likeness and Presence. A History of the Image Before the Era of Art* (Chicago and London, 1994),

From the wealth of images found in the poetry and homiletics of the iconoclastic period, this is the example which I have singled out in order to trace its progress in the ensuing centuries through iconography and liturgical texts.

Iconography

The iconoclastic dispute, during which the defenders of icon veneration composed the voluminous corpus of Marian hymns and homilies, ended in the Triumph of Orthodoxy, which was celebrated by the creation of the famous mosaic which still adorns the apse of Hagia Sophia (Fig. 8.1). In his tenth homily, written for the inauguration of this mosaic representation of the Virgin and Child, Patriarch Photios, a close friend and collaborator of George of Nikomedeia, describes something which has no connection with what the viewer actually sees. Avoiding a realistic *ekphrasis*, he chooses to reveal the deeper conceptual plane of the iconography, most notably in his reference to the tenderness with which the Virgin gazes at Christ, when in reality she is portrayed with her eyes turned towards the viewer. At this period the Virgin of Tenderness was not yet established as a common type in Byzantine art, which partly explains why Photios' description does not accord with the mosaic;[25] but what particularly interests us here is to observe the gradual transference of the model from one genre to another, for in the iconography of later centuries the poetic description would be used as the basis for portrayals of the Virgin of Tenderness, culminating in the Late Byzantine period with the passionate embrace of Mother and Child.

The model which passes into the iconography of the post-iconoclastic period is that of the Mother of God, and in particular the Lamenting Virgin.[26] Ioli Kalavrezou has rightly noted the correspondence between the Mother's embrace of the new-born Child and her embrace of her dead Son in later depictions of the Deposition.[27] The notions of maternity and sorrow at the death of a child are thus indissolubly linked in rendering the human dimension of the Theotokos, which in theological terms represents the affirmation of the human element in God's plan for the salvation of mankind (Plate 4, Fig. 8.2). The introduction of the new iconographic type in the period after the Triumph of Orthodoxy begins with the addition of the title 'Mother of God', which is later reflected in modifications to the Virgin's pose and features. Her pose acquires a distinct humanity and tenderness, the embrace of Mother and Son makes its appearance, and physical contact later receives further emphasis with the Virgin pressing her cheek against that of Jesus. Her features are dominated by sorrow at the coming death of Christ, despite her joy at the Incarnation of the Messiah. The eyes take on a pained expression, the whole body crumples, the hands seem to cling in yearning to the Son who is predestined to die,

---

120–3 and *passim*. R. Cormack, *Painting the Soul. Icons, Death Masks and Shrouds* (London, 1997), 57, 113.

[25] On the discrepancy between description and image, see the excellent study by L. James and R. Webb, '"To Understand Ultimate Things and Enter Secret Places": Ekphrasis and Art in Byzantium', *Art History* 14.1 (1991), 1–17.

[26] Kalavrezou, 'Images of the Mother', and ead., 'The Maternal Side of the Virgin'. Maguire, 'The Depiction of Sorrow', and id., *Art and Eloquence*, 101 ff.

[27] Kalavrezou, 'The Maternal Side of the Virgin', 43.

and the mouth is contracted by grief. All these elements would find a permanent place in the iconography of all other types of the Virgin.

This conspicuous maternal tenderness, marked with sorrow at the Passion, makes a striking contrast with the imperial style of pre-iconoclastic portrayals of the Enthroned Virgin and the Hodegetria. In the New Church of Tokalı an early example depicts the Virgin with the child resting against her cheek; she gazes fixedly at the viewer (Fig. 8.3), and the eyes have not yet taken on the sorrowful expression which we shall see in later representations.

From the tenth century onwards there is a proliferation of portrayals emphasizing the tender maternal aspect of the Virgin. The whole development may thus be summarized as a gradual transition from the classic Hodegetria of the pre-iconoclastic period to the representation of the Virgin as Mother of God, ending with the widespread diffusion of the Glykophilousa in the Late Byzantine era.

The transmission of models from literature to art is a process recognized by scholars working on the history and art of Byzantium. Unlike his counterpart in Europe, where from the Renaissance onwards individual creativity was exalted and artistic development was motivated by the creator in his role of *secundus deus*,[28] the Byzantine artist was obliged by the conventions of his genre to follow models already current in literature.

In post-iconoclastic depictions of the Crucifixion, where as noted the Virgin stands with John by the Cross, we find images of a suffering shared between Jesus and his mother, who with the pain like a sword in her side looks on at the Crucifixion of her only son.[29] The mosaic in the narthex of Hosios Loukas in Phokis (Fig. 8.4), for example, shows the Virgin holding a kerchief, which symbolizes her grief. The contracted facial features express her sorrow: the wide eyes are cast downward, the lips are pursed and she clutches her hands to her breast in a gesture of pain.

Liturgy

We now turn to the liturgical corpus – a field where studies are still at an early stage – and specifically to the incorporation of the Mother of God within liturgical texts of the Orthodox Church. This is a subject about which we know little, as the material is voluminous, inaccessible and demanding.[30] The formation of the Divine Liturgy broadly coincides with the beginnings of the iconoclastic dispute. The *Exegesis of the Liturgy, Ecclesiastical History and Mystical Theory* of Germanos of Constantinople reflect the changes which have come over the Byzantine tradition, as the main emphasis is now given to popular devotion rather than the strictly theological approach.

The study of the *Triodion*, to which Theocharis Detorakis has made a major contribution, is still incomplete,[31] but our present knowledge suggests that it was during the eleventh century

---

[28] On western ecclesiastical art and the different concepts in East and West, see A. Louth, 'Orthodoxy and Art', in A. Walker and C. Carras (eds), *Living Orthodoxy in the Modern World* (London, 1996), 159–77, esp. 160–1.
[29] See the homily by George of Nikomedeia, *Oratio in Sepulturam Jesu Christi*, PG 100, 1457–89.
[30] See the introduction by R. Taft to his *Liturgy in the Byzantine World and Beyond* (Variorum Reprints, Aldershot, 1995), vii–viii.
[31] Th. Detorakis, 'Ἀνέκδοτα μεγαλυνάρια τοῦ Μεγάλου Σαββάτου', EEBS 47 (1987/9), 221–46.

that hymns to the Theotokos became integrated within Orthodox liturgical books. Further evidence for this development is found in the ever-increasing number of 'diataxeis' which were produced from the twelfth century onwards, to form a virtually new 'genre' in Byzantine ecclesiastical literature.[32] Most of the kontakia and even the theotokia and staurotheotokia found in the *Triodion* and the *Menaia* are anonymous or attributed erroneously, but leaving aside the question of provenance, it is a relatively easy task to identify the images, most of which derive from the hymnography of the iconoclastic and immediate post-iconoclastic period. However, on a few occasions extracts from a particular hymn or homily are included in the liturgical texts in their original form. This suggests an interesting procedure, a kind of 'selection process' taking place within the day-to-day practices of the Church, whereby the most beautiful – that is, the most poetic and emotionally charged – images from hymns and homilies were detached from their original contexts, set to music, and then incorporated in liturgical texts such as the *Triodion*. This would be analogous to the workings of the oral tradition;[33] in any case, as it is improbable that a *melourgos* would have set out to make a selection of images from hymns and homilies destined for the Church, it is difficult to come up with any alternative theory.

The images contained in Orthodox liturgical texts summarize the development of the cult of the Theotokos, with its emphasis on her paradoxical maternal role, her intercessory function on behalf of the faithful and her human conduct at the Crucifixion of her only son. Among the multitude of theotokia and staurotheotokia contained in the *Triodion* is an interesting theotokion for the Sunday of Orthodoxy which directly links the Virgin's identity as Mother of God with icon veneration: 'To those who honour your holy Image, O reverend one, and with one accord proclaim you as the true Mother of God and faithfully venerate you'.[34] Her role as intercessor becomes apparent immediately afterwards: 'Appear, O guardian and powerful protector, averting every difficulty far from these people, since you are all-powerful,'[35] and later: 'Help of all, protection and shelter, conceiver of God, show that you can intercede for all who take refuge in you and that you drive away the impious men through the power of your Son, since as Mother you are all-powerful.'[36] Such passages show that it is her identity as a Mother which gives the Theotokos her directness of speech: this emphasis is not found in earlier texts, and in conjunction with the homily of George of Nikomedeia it demonstrates how the Virgin becomes Christ's representative on earth and intercessor through her unique maternal role.[37]

The theotokia and staurotheotokia of the *Triodion* are characterized by themes of virginity, the paradoxical birth and the mystery of the Incarnation, as well as by typological references and by images which echo the poetry and homiletics of the iconoclastic period. They abound in the

---

[32] R. Taft, 'The Liturgy of the Great Church: an Initial Synthesis of Structure and Interpretation on the Eve of Iconoclasm', *DOP* 34/5 (1980/1), 45–74, esp. 49.

[33] On the theory of orality, see W. J. Ong, *Orality and Literacy* (3rd edn, London and New York, 1990), 20–40. On the application of Lord and Parry's theory of oral tradition to texts of the late Byzantine period, see E. and M. Jeffreys, *Popular Literature in Late Byzantium* (Variorum Reprints, London, 1983), esp. IV ('The Nature and Origins of the Political Verse').

[34] Τριώδιον Κατανυκτικόν (Athens, 1960), 136. The Theotokos is also linked to the veneration of icons elsewhere: 'they have departed from their wicked heresies. For, gazing respectfully, we now rejoice in your church, decorated with icons, O holy pure one.'

[35] Ibid., 136.

[36] Ibid., 143.

[37] See George of Nikomedeia, *PG* 100, 1477A–B.

images discussed above in the context of iconography, in which the Theotokos is portrayed uttering mournful laments at Golgotha: 'Your unwedded Mother, when she saw you raised on the Cross, spoke these words, in pained lamentation: What is this new, strange miracle, my Son? How did the lawless people nail you to the Cross, you the life of all, my sweetest light?',[38] and later: 'As she saw you raised on the Cross, the Mother who bore you without birth pangs wept bitter tears and cried out: Alas my sweetest Son! I am now wounded in my soul, seeing you nailed to the Cross between two criminals, like a criminal.'[39] These images of the lamenting Virgin which were woven into the homilies of the iconoclastic period draw on those found in the kontakia of Romanos the Melode, the first poetical works of the genre, which date from the sixth century.[40] However, the iconology of the Crucifixion in its full dramatic intensity was further developed in the Middle Byzantine era, in particular by Germanos of Constantinople, as noted earlier, and by George of Nikomedeia.

It is in the relationship between the texts incorporated in Orthodox liturgy, Church doctrine and popular piety that we may find the reason why the Virgin as Mother of God is not included in these texts earlier than the eleventh century. We should note that the fully-fledged doctrinal formulations characteristic of other Christian denominations are not a feature of Orthodoxy: the decrees of the various Ecumenical Councils mainly dealt with the condemnation of heresies expounded and creating problems within the Church.

Alexander Schmemann, perhaps the greatest liturgiologist of the twentieth century, uses the expression 'lex orandi est lex credendi' in connection with the liturgical tradition whereby the highest theological statements are found in the language of the liturgy. The tradition of the eastern Church was indeed built on popular belief, in the experiential meaning of the term. As Schmemann remarks on the process of conversion to the new religion at the time of its origins in the fourth century: 'The meeting of the new and now more peaceable approach of the new religion and the world can be described as a meeting which took place on the basis of worship. The conversion of this world was primarily a liturgiological conversion,' and as the author develops his theme it becomes clear that this process involved a succession of worship practices.[41]

Each parameter of what we call Orthodox doctrine was tested by the faithful; that is, by the Church – in other words by the people, in the literal meaning of the Greek word *ekklesia*. Only after receiving their affirmation and approval was a doctrine entrusted to the liturgy and incorporated within the tradition. This 'filtration process' for the acceptance or rejection of dogma involved the whole Church, clergy and laity as a single body, and it is fully consistent with the procedures described or suggested in the present article – the adoption of the experimental imagery of poetry and homiletics by religious art, and its subsequent transference through the agency of the *melourgos* into the liturgical life of the Church, where, once established, it would remain alive and unchallenged throughout the centuries. The theoretical background to this

---

[38] Τριώδιον Κατανυκτικόν, 170.
[39] Ibid.
[40] See N. Tsironis, 'Ο θρήνος της Θεοτόκου στη βυζαντινή παράδοση', addendum to her Ω Γλυκύ μου Έαρ, Ο Επιτάφιος Θρήνος (Athens, 2001), 79–98.
[41] Th. Fish (ed.), *Liturgy and Tradition. Theological Reflections of Alexander Schmemann* (Crestwood, NY, 1990), 11–20.

process is in complete harmony with Orthodox theory and practice since it confirms the 'power' of the people in the life of the Church.

One significant conclusion to be drawn from this transition from one genre to the other is the extent to which, precisely because of the lack of well-defined dogma, Orthodox liturgy and cult do not accept models imposed from above, but rather follow the devotional customs of the faithful and adopt whatever the Church – the people – sanctifies through practice. The Virgin herself perhaps best exemplifies this process as it is the contrast between the striking absence of ecclesiastical doctrine and the devotion – equally striking – on the part of the faithful which finally elevates the Mother of God to become the very symbol of the Orthodox Church.

The images surrounding the Virgin which project her as a symbol of doctrine were constructed over the centuries, but mainly during the period marked by the iconoclastic dispute. Through her identification with the material hypostasis of the divine, she became synonymous with the advocacy of icon veneration, and she emerges from the poetry and homiletics of the period in her persona as Mother of God, associated with the Passion of the Lord which she witnesses at Golgotha, thus emphasizing the two defining moments of her son's earthly life – his Nativity and his Death. These images were adopted into art in the ninth and tenth centuries, creating new iconographic types such as that of the Mother of God, which would subsequently evolve into the Glykophilousa and the Lamenting Virgin. And from the eleventh century onwards it was the most dramatically and emotionally intense of these images which were eventually selected for incorporation in liturgical writings.

This transition from one genre to another, which we have been examining in the context of the Mother of God and of the Lament, testifies to the interaction between genres and to the dialectical relationship which they maintain in the complex pattern of symbolism and hierarchy in the Byzantine world. It also serves to reveal the respective status of each genre in the life of the Church; in this hierarchical scheme, the most prestigious is liturgical literature, and the incorporation of the Mother of God in Orthodox liturgical texts represents the final stage in the journey – the crowning moment when the centuries-long evolution of her cult attained its consummation.

8.1 Constantinople, Hagia Sophia, the apse mosaic.
The Virgin enthroned with Christ-child
(source: E. J. W. Hawkins, Courtauld Institute of Art)

8.2 Athens, Benaki Museum, inv. no. 36363. Icon of the Lamenting Virgin (source: Benaki Museum)

8.3 Cappadocia, Tokalı kilise, wall painting with the Virgin Eleousa (source: A. J. Wharton)

8.4   Phokis, Monastery of Hosios Loukas, narthex.
The Crucifixion
(source: Melissa Publishing House)

9

Exchanging embrace. The body of salvation

Ioli Kalavrezou

The centrality of the image in Byzantine life and culture is obvious, but the individual response to this visual experience is difficult to detect from the object itself. A close examination of the subject depicted is essential if we are to reach an understanding of the religious optical experience. This paper will focus on the image as such and will argue that by viewing what is depicted, whether iconic or narrative, the viewer becomes involved at an emotional level in responding to what he or she sees. The image provides the guides or symbols for a meditation on the importance of life, death, and possible salvation offered through Christ and the Virgin. This paper is driven by the visual, and in this way parallels the proposed reception of these images by the Byzantine viewer. I would like to explore how the physical manifestation of love exchanged between the Virgin and her Son becomes a material experience of the salvific plan. The main focus of my discussion is the type of image that symbolizes the Incarnation of Christ, as developed during the centuries after iconoclasm, and especially in the late eleventh and twelfth centuries. Like the earlier representations of the Virgin and Child of the pre-iconoclast period these images carry the message of the salvation that Christ brought to the world through the Virgin Mary. It is however highly revealing to observe the changes which have occurred in the presentation of that salvation. The visual means by which this is now displayed are utterly different and would have been unacceptable if used in the first millennium of the Christian church.[1]

Representations of the Virgin Mary begin to proliferate after the fifth century. The earliest images depict scenes that recount her role in the story of Christ's Incarnation. As a narrative they consist of events that lead up to the birth of Christ, beginning with the apocryphal stories of Mary's own early life, and followed by the gospel references themselves: the Annunciation, the Visitation, the Nativity and the Adoration of the Magi. They establish Mary's own descent and they emphasize the miraculous events connected with the Incarnation. They are found on a great variety of objects, especially in the category of personal or private objects: medallions, small reliquaries and other enkolpia, rings and bracelets and pieces of clothing with these scenes woven into the textile. When on private objects or worn on the body these scenes seem to acquire quasi-healing and protective powers for the individual who wears them.[2] However, the

---

[1] It is fascinating to follow the development of Christian iconography through the centuries in its relation to theological debates and dogmas. Although the basic theological positions of the Church remain the same, their visual counterparts, influenced by what could be labelled as the literary texts (hymns, homilies, etc.) of Christian theology, develop and take Christian images in new directions.

[2] H. Maguire, 'The Cult of the Mother of God in Private', in Vassilaki, *Mother of God*, 279–89. A. Walker, 'Marriage. Wife and Husband: "A Golden Team"', in I. Kalavrezou (ed.), *Byzantine Women and their World*, exh. cat., Arthur M. Sackler Museum, Harvard University Art Museum, 25 October 2002 – 27 April 2003 (Cambridge, MA, 2003), 215–21 and 227–8.

increasingly prominent place of the Virgin in the Christological debates of the late fourth and fifth centuries brings about another type of representation of the Virgin Mary. With the exception of the Annunciation and Nativity, which were incorporated into the developing Christological cycle, these simple narrative images lose their importance and popularity in private devotional practices. They become secondary and are dominated by compositions giving the Virgin Mary the central role which she will come to play throughout the Middle Ages, that of intercessor for mankind. These new images are also evidence of the increasing recognition of her role as the human virgin through whom the union of the two natures of Christ was made possible. They testify to the establishment of a cult in her own right, a development that took place after the Council of Ephesus in 431, where her status as the Theotokos was recognized.[3] Depictions of her mediating role were already beginning to appear – she is portrayed without Christ, either turned to the side in a gesture of supplication or in a frontal pose with her hands outstretched or in front of her breast in prayer. Yet the most important representations that gave recognition to her title as Theotokos and her official place in the church were those where she is represented holding the Christ-child[4] (Fig. 9.1).

Although it took some time for Mary to achieve this recognition, by the sixth century these images firmly show her as the prime female figure of Christian devotion. In these she is removed from any narrative content. She is shown frontally, presenting the Christ-child for the world's salvation. She holds Christ either on her left arm with her right directing the viewers' eyes towards him, or enthroned on her lap in front of her.[5] These representations do not derive from a specific text but are the so-called symbolic or abstract images of church authority and dogma. What is dramatically new and what makes these compositions special and theologically important is the bringing together of the Virgin and the child in her arms in one visual form. The union of these two figures in one image gives visual expression to the mystery of the Incarnation, and in addition, through their close relationship, it testifies to God's planned role for Mary in the salvation of the world. What appears to us to be a self-evident image of Mother and Child, whose meaning is familiar to all human beings, took quite some time to be recognized as the most appropriate visual symbol to project the incomprehensible and complex Christological and Marian mysteries. Both these types of image, the enthroned Virgin and Child and the standing Virgin with the Child on her left arm, which can also be shown in bust length and became the famous Hodegetria type, are the ones used by the Church for the most formal and doctrinal purposes. They are given an important place in sixth-century church programmes, which will have a lasting presence throughout the Middle Ages. The choice of location, usually the apse, makes fully apparent the direct way to salvation through the juxtaposition of the

---

[3] For a discussion of the early theological and literary developments of Marian spirituality see A. M. Cameron, 'The Early Cult of the Virgin', in Vassilaki, *Mother of God*, 3–15.

[4] There are numerous examples of these 6th-c. iconographic types. For example, see in Vassilaki, *Mother of God*, no. 1, 262–3 (R. Cormack) (the icon of the Virgin and Child enthroned at Sinai), Pls 170 (the textile wall-hanging in the Cleveland Museum of Art), 199 (the Pantheon icon), 201 (the S. Maria in Trastevere icon) and numerous other pieces.

[5] In the early narrative scenes she holds the child only in the scene of the Adoration of the Magi, where she is usually depicted from the side. In some Coptic examples she may be depicted as the Galaktotrophousa (Isis influence?); see, for example, the limestone icon of the Museum für Spätantike und Byzantinische Kunst, Berlin: Vassilaki, *Mother of God*, Pl. 185.

Incarnation of Christ in the images with the rite of the Eucharist which takes place on the altar just below them.[6] They also are chosen to decorate objects of official use in the church, for example liturgical diptychs and book covers.[7] It is also significant that the famous miraculous icons of the early Church display this type of image.

After the tenth century, however, depictions of Mary, from wall paintings to manuscripts to icons, began to present in a visual language what had long been a tradition in the key literary texts of Marian spirituality. From as early as the fourth century in the writings of the Church Fathers, in particular of figures like Ephraim the Syrian,[8] a devotional language expressive of personal emotions and feelings begins to be felt in hymns to the Virgin Mary. In the fifth and sixth centuries these find stronger expression in the poetry of Romanos the Melode and later in the Akathistos Hymn, culminating in the homilies of George of Nikomedeia in the ninth century.[9]

The iconographic development to which this path led created highly impressive representations of the Virgin Mary as a divine human being and an understanding mediator for mankind. From the late eleventh century onwards the Virgin is associated more and more with the Passion of Christ. In the strongest terms possible she expresses feelings of love for her son, resignation towards his inevitable future and grief at his suffering and death. These sentiments are vividly expressed in the art of this period, especially in the twelfth century, in churches, icons and manuscripts. One of the most famous surviving examples is the depiction of the Lamentation or Threnos and the preparation of Christ's burial in the fresco at Nerezi of 1164 (Fig. 9.3). The active gesture of embrace and the overtly emotional expressions of her suffering face are found not only in the narrative scenes of Christ's Passion, but also in the portrait-type icons where she holds the Child. In this new type of composition, narrative elements penetrate the iconic image. The Vladimir icon (Fig. 9.2) is the best-known example but icons such as the two-sided Kastoria icon, with on the one side the Virgin holding the Child on her arm in the manner of the Hodegetria and on the other the dead Christ as 'King of Glory', is another innovative example (Fig. 9.4).[10] Although in this case there is no tender embrace, the Hodegetria brings out in the suffering expression of her frowning eyes and brows the pain of death in the soul of a mother who can foresee her son's future as depicted on the reverse. The innovation here is the creation of images that combine iconic elements together with narrative elements from the Passion cycle. The result is a double image of two portrait icons: in the Virgin Hodegetria, emotion and lament are manifested through facial expressions; in the image of

---

[6] Two important examples of precisely such apse programmes are the Church of the Virgin Angeloktisti at Kition on Cyprus with the standing figure of Virgin and Child (Vassilaki, *Mother of God*, Pls 3, 49), and the apse of the basilica Eufrasiana in Parenzo (Poreč) with the enthroned Virgin and Child (Plate 11 in this volume).

[7] The ivory diptych in Berlin in the Museum für Spätantike und Byzantinische Kunst, and the ivory plaque in the British Museum with the depiction of the Adoration of the Three Magi which has here been transformed into such an official frontal image. Vassilaki, *Mother of God*, Pl. 12 and no. 3, 266–7 (A. Eastmond).

[8] Cameron, 'The Early Cult of the Virgin', 8–10.

[9] On the influence of George of Nikomedeia's homilies in the shifting iconography of the Theotokos as Mother of God and her lament, see I. Kalavrezou, 'Images of the Mother: When the Virgin Mary became *Meter Theou*', *DOP* 44 (1990), 165–72, esp. 169–70, and M. Vassilaki and N. Tsironis, 'Representations of the Virgin and Their Association with the Passion of Christ', in Vassilaki, *Mother of God*, 457–60.

[10] Vassilaki, *Mother of God*, no. 83, 484–5 (E. Tsigaridas), with bibliography. H. Belting has explained this image through its liturgical function. He sees in it the ideal icon that encompasses the entire Passion cycle from the Crucifixion to the Lamentation. See his *Likeness and Presence. A History of the Image Before the Era of Art* (Chicago and London, 1994), 262–5.

Christ as a dead man the iconographic elements that come from the narrative context of the Crucifixion and Lamentation have been drastically removed to create a bust in the manner of a portrait-type icon.

The close relationship between Mother and Child becomes the means which, as in the pre-iconoclast period, leads the way to salvation. In this period, however, the focus is on the exchange between Christ's death on the cross – proof of his human nature and Incarnation leading to redemption through his sacrifice – and the Virgin's human love, suffering and lament. Together with the role of the Mother of God given to her in the post-iconoclast period,[11] the visual expression centres on the theme of love and pain in that relationship.

The theology of images was consolidated during the iconoclast period and the justification of icons rested on the concept of the Incarnation. In a manner similar to the *Logos* acquiring material form, the image offered the material form, the physical representation, through which salvation was made comprehensible. Icons work like the body of the Virgin; they are the conduit through which God's Divine Economy is expressed. Thus the icon presented this vehicle for salvation in a visual form. With this in mind, I would like to discuss how iconic depictions as well as narrative scenes provided the visual means to interpret love, the binding love between mother and child, as leading to human redemption.

The Vladimir icon of the twelfth century (Fig. 9.2) is a prime example of the exchange of embrace and love between mother and child. The Virgin holds the Christ-child high enough for his head to reach her cheek, while actually supporting the child only with her right arm. The left barely touches his garments, in a gesture similar to that of the Hodegetria directing our gaze to the *Logos* incarnate in her arm. Her severe gaze is also directed at the viewer to lead him into the image. Christ's love for his mother is unconditional.[12] His physical response to her motherly love is a tender embrace, in which his small arm reaches up and around her neck to touch her cheek. Through her knowledge of his love she can be assured of his response to her appeal for the salvation of mankind. In this privileged relationship she provides the access to the economy of intercession.

Another complex representation of the binding love between mother and son is expressed in the scene of the Threnos, the Lamentation of Christ (Fig. 9.3). In the fresco at Nerezi dating from the second half of the twelfth century, Christ, already taken down from the cross, lies in his mother's embrace, surrounded by the grieving mourners and the angels above. The majority of the iconic images where the Virgin holds Christ as a child in her arms express her sorrow at the knowledge of his impending death; however, in this narrative scene the Virgin's face expresses her grief at its fulfilment. She is seated on the ground, embracing Christ with both her arms, thus mirroring his loving embrace as a child in her arms. Just as once he stretched out one arm around her neck and the other across her body, so she does now, at the same time pressing her cheek against his. Of particular interest in this scene is the placement of her body in relation to that of her dead son. The posture of her legs framing Christ is most unusual. They are separated and wide apart so that the upper part of Christ's body rests on her limbs. Her feet come

---

[11] Kalavrezou, 'Images of the Mother', esp. 169–72.
[12] As observed by B. Pentcheva while discussing this icon in her dissertation 'Icons and Image of the Virgin and Their Public in Middle Byzantine Constantinople', Harvard University, 2000, 189–95, and further discussion in her *Icons and Power: the Mother of God in Byzantium* (University Park, PA, forthcoming), ch. V.

together again at the level of his thighs. This highly original positioning of the figures would seem to allude to the act of giving birth.

A number of events relating to unexpected or unusual births are narrated in the Old Testament. Famous examples such as Rebecca giving birth to Esau and Jacob were illustrated in the series of Octateuchs that were produced and illustrated in the eleventh and twelfth centuries.[13] One such scene, which is still well preserved, can be seen in the eleventh-century Vatican Octateuch gr. 747 on fol. 46v (Plate 5, Fig. 9.5).[14] Rebecca is shown twice in the scene. On the left she is seated pensive and sad next to her husband, who is praying to God to make them fertile; she wears a long dress and her hair is covered with a scarf typical of married women.[15] On the right she is depicted within the house wearing a short simple gown and without her scarf. She supports herself in a seated position with her legs parted at the moment of giving birth, and the child becomes visible as its head appears between her legs. What we see is the birth of Jacob, while Esau already born lies at her side. The depiction of such a very private moment is remarkable; however it is not the only such birth but one of several found in the Octateuchs.[16] The placement of the Virgin's legs in the Nerezi fresco cannot be accidental and must be intended to bring together in one image the whole divine plan. Through the visual references to Christ's human birth and Incarnation on the one hand and to his death on the other, the complete cycle of spiritual salvation is established iconographically.

The Byzantine image where the salvation of the soul is made pictorially comprehensible is the scene of the Virgin's Koimesis. I have chosen to discuss this image of Salvation in connection with a representation of the Koimesis from a twelfth-century ivory panel that is the right wing of a diptych (Fig. 9.6). The left panel shows the Crucifixion with an abbreviated depiction of the Resurrection below.[17] In the Koimesis composition, well established by the tenth century, the Virgin, already dead, is shown lying on the bier surrounded by the mourning apostles.[18] By far the most astonishing figure here is Christ, who stands next to her outstretched body, holding in his arms her soul in the traditional form of a small child or swaddled infant. Although it is a scene of death, with expressions of sorrow and lament very much present through the crowd of

---

[13] K. Weitzmann, M. Bernabò and R. Tarasconi, *The Illustrations in the Manuscripts of the Septuagint, 2. The Byzantine Octateuchs* I–II (Princeton, NJ, 1999).

[14] Vatican city, Biblioteca Apostolica Vaticana, MS. gr. 747, fol. 46v: Weitzmann, Bernabò and Tarasconi, *The Byzantine Octateuchs*, Fig. 355. In a number of the other Octateuchs the areas where the child was visible have been erased, as for example ibid., Figs 358, 479, 481 and 482, an indication of the 'embarrassing' subject matter depicted.

[15] In these representations we should not expect a realistic depiction of the female body. As Hutter has observed, by the Middle Byzantine period there is a loss of definition in the illustration of female forms. I. Hutter, 'Das Bild der Frau in der byzantinischen Kunst', in W. Hörandner (ed.), *Byzantios. Festschrift für Herbert Hunger zum 70. Geburtstag dargebracht von Schülern und Mitarbeitern* (Vienna, 1984), 163–70.

[16] The Octateuchs are a special group of manuscripts within illustrated Byzantine texts. I believe they offer stories, events and characters that not only provide another past in contrast to that of the ancient mythological world, but also have a kind of 'epic' dimension that could provide entertainment to the reader.

[17] The complete diptych is published in A. Bank, *Byzantine Art in the Collections of Soviet Museums* (Leningrad, 1977), Figs 143–4.

[18] The earliest surviving visual examples come from the 10th c., mostly in small private icons in ivory and steatite. A. Goldschmidt and K. Weitzmann, *Die byzantinischen Elfenbeinskulpturen* II (Berlin, 1934). I. Kalavrezou, *Byzantine Icons in Steatite* I–II (Vienna, 1985).

mourners, the reference to birth is made quite explicit through the representation of her soul, which on leaving her body has taken the form of a newborn child. In the tenth-century *Life of St Basil the Younger* a woman named Theodora narrates how grateful she is for the life she learned to lead through the influence of Basil. When she speaks of a near-death experience that had a happy outcome, she describes it in this way: 'For when I was about to die and came to the point of separation from my pitiful and much suffering body – how will I describe, my sweetest child, the toil of death, what misery I experienced, what great force, how much sting from the boundless pain and baneful narrowness, until my soul might leave my body?'[19] Alice-Mary Talbot has seen the 'baneful narrowness', the channel through which the soul exits the body, as a metaphor of birth for the soul.[20] The soul is imagined to leave the body in the manner that a child would leave the body of his mother, in a reference not only to the difficult narrow passage but also to the pain suffered. This text provides the graphic narrative to the well-known illustrations of the moment of death when the soul leaves the body through the mouth.[21] It allows us to perceive the way Byzantines saw death and afterlife in relation to the human body. The infant is the visual indicator to let the viewer know that death has taken place. In the Koimesis the soul is already in Christ's salvific hands, the hope for all mankind. In both scenes birth is present in death. In the Lamentation image the reference to birth is projected visually through the Virgin's pose and gestures; in the Koimesis birth, or rather rebirth, and death are brought together into one moment through the presence of the infant soul. Christ now holds her in his arms, reversing the relationship of Mother to Son. In other words, *she* is the mother of the Incarnate *Logos*, *he* is the Saviour of her soul. In visual terms he is parenting her soul in ways parallel to images of her holding him. A visual language has thus been created through which the love and human emotions between Mother and Son make the divine plan intelligible to mankind. Complex theological themes could be understood through simple imagery, thus making them accessible to the viewer.

This Koimesis panel, as I have mentioned above, is accompanied by the panel with Christ's Death on the Cross and below in the narrow register a reduced Anastasis where only the raising of the dead from their tombs is shown (Fig. 9.6). The Crucifixion and especially the moment of Christ's death on the Cross is proof not only of his human nature and of the Incarnation but also of the redemption that has come to mankind through his sacrifice,[22] and the juxtaposition of these two themes together with the Resurrection makes the message even stronger.

The significance of Christ's Incarnation in visual terms is directly articulated through the scene of his birth. In another ivory diptych in Ravenna we find the juxtaposition of the Nativity

---

[19] *Vita S. Basilii Iunioris*, ed. A. Veselovskii, in *Sbornik Otdeleniia Russkago Yazyka i Slov. Imp. Akad. Nauk* 46, *Suppl.* 14 (St Petersburg, 1889), 14. English translation by Dumbarton Oaks Greek Reading Group, 2000.

[20] Based upon the discussion in the Reading Group. I would like at this point to thank B. Pentcheva for bringing this text to my attention.

[21] As, for example, in the Psalter Dionysiou, cod. 65, fol. 11v, of *c.* 1313. St. Pelekanides, P. Christou, Ch. Mavropoulou-Tsioumi and S. Kadas, *Οι θησαυροί του Αγίου Όρους, Α. Εικονογραφημένα χειρόγραφα* I (Athens, 1973), Fig. 121, 420.

[22] On icons and objects of personal devotion, the scenes most frequently found are first the Crucifixion, and then the Koimesis. These two representations of death dominate all other narrative scenes. Among the *c.* 230 ivory icons of the corpus, for example, there are 53 Crucifixions and 21 Koimeses. The only other subject of great popularity, second after the Crucifixion in number, with 32 examples, is the Virgin holding the Child.

with the Deposition and Threnos (Fig. 9.7),[23] the two moments in which his full humanity was clearly manifested. At the same time, reference is made to the life of every human being, defined by the moments of birth and death. Thus the images also directly resonate with individual experience since they depict the polar opposites that govern life. The Virgin Mary and Christ are the combined path to the Divine Economy. That this was well understood by the Byzantines was demonstrated by the frequent use of such juxtapositions, especially in devotional icons for personal use.

One such private icon is the Ravenna diptych. The Nativity, divided into sub-scenes, is densely packed with figures. Central emphasis is given to the Virgin and Child in the manger, who are surrounded by additional narrative elements which address and underline Christ's humanity. The joyous and celebratory moments featured on the left panel are coupled on the other side with scenes of death, pain and lament, as a polar opposite. In the centre of the Deposition in the upper register, Christ is lowered from the Cross by Joseph of Arimathea. The Virgin, standing to one side, kisses the hand of her dead son. In the register below, the Virgin's grief is expressed by her tender embrace of her son as she kneels next to him to hold his head on her lap.

The selection and distribution of scenes on such private icons varies. Another example, an icon in London where four scenes have been assembled within one panel, carries this point further (Fig. 9.8).[24] The placement of the subjects requires a vertical reading, as is often found in diptychs. On the left side, both upper and lower scenes depict Christ's death. The Crucifixion, which begins to resemble a Deposition, is above, with the Lamentation below. At the top right is the Anastasis and at the bottom the Koimesis. Both these scenes have the overall theme of resurrection and salvation: above Adam and Eve are raised from their tombs, below is the Koimesis. Thematically the diptych icon is tied together by death on the one side and the hope of salvation through the Resurrection and spiritual rebirth on the other. Visually there are also parallels and opposites. The top two scenes have a strong vertical emphasis, with Christ in the centre; the two bottom scenes are connected by the horizontal placement of the two bodies. It is the combination and juxtaposition of their iconographic themes and their format that provide the visual evidence to suggest their specific religious function. Clearly much thought has been given to the organization and visual structure of these icons and their images. They are intended to provoke the individual's response to the subject matter through a visual experience that becomes easily accessible. The invisible acquires visible form through images. Human emotions such as the mother–child relationship, from its most tender and loving expressions as found on the icon from Sinai with an enthroned Virgin and Child (Fig. 9.9),[25] to those of pain and grief as in the narrative scenes in Ravenna, become the vehicles or material form for the spiritual experience. This becomes attainable for most people through the knowledge of Christ's sacrifice, his death and resurrection in conjunction with the visual representation in the icon. By using understandable basic human emotions interposed with divine beings, salvation takes on a material form which can be perceived by humanity.

---

[23] L. Martini and C. Rizzardi (eds), *Avori Byzantini e Medievali nel Museo Nazionale di Ravenna* (Ravenna, 1990), no. 6, 69–70.
[24] Goldschmidt and Weitzmann, *Elfenbeinskulpturen* II, no. 209.
[25] Vassilaki, *Mother of God*, no. 28, 314–16 (T. Papamastorakis).

9.1 Rome, S. Maria ad Martyres.
Icon of the Virgin and Child
(source: Vassilaki, *Mother of God*, Pl. 199)

9.2 Moscow, Tretyakov Gallery.
Icon of the Virgin of Vladimir (12th c.)
(source: Vassilaki, *Mother of God*, Pl. 24)

EXCHANGING EMBRACE. THE BODY OF SALVATION 111

9.3 Nerezi, Church of St Panteleemon. Fresco of the scene of the Threnos (1164) (source: G. Subotić)

9.4 Kastoria, Byzantine Museum. Two-sided icon with the Man of Sorrows and the Virgin Hodegetria (12th c.) (source: Kastoria, Byzantine Museum)

9.5 Rome, Biblioteca Apostolica Vaticana, MS. gr. 747, fol. 46v. Rebecca giving birth (late 11th c.) (source: Biblioteca Apostolica Vaticana)

9.6 St Petersburg, The State Hermitage Museum.
Ivory diptych with the Crucifixion and the Koimesis (12th c.)
(source: The State Hermitage Museum)

9.7 Ravenna, Museo Nazionale. Ivory diptych with
the Nativity and the Deposition and Threnos (12th c.)
(source: Martini and Rizzardi, *Avori Byzantini*, no. 6)

9.8 London, private collection. Ivory panel icon with four scenes: Crucifixion, Threnos, Anastasis, Koimesis (source: Goldschmidt and Weitzmann, *Elfenbeinskulpturen* II, no. 209)

9.9 Mt Sinai, Monastery of St Catherine. Icon of the Virgin and Child with figures from the Old and New Testament (detail) (mid-12th c.) (source: Sinai)

The symbolism of the censer in Byzantine representations of the Dormition of the Virgin

Maria Evangelatou

In certain twelfth- and thirteenth-century Byzantine representations of the Dormition of the Virgin one of the officiating hierarchs is shown holding up to his face a censer and either pointing at it or blowing on the incense. This paper suggests that this unusual iconographical feature should be interpreted in the light of Byzantine theological beliefs regarding the Dormition, as expressed through the symbol of the censer in homilies and hymns.

Byzantine ecclesiastical writings and works of art on the subject of the Mother of God focus on two basic doctrines: the Virgin's role in the Incarnation of the Word and her subsequent intercession for the salvation of the faithful through her prerogative of direct communication with her son.[1] These are the main themes of Byzantine homilies and hymns celebrating her Dormition.[2] As a mere human being Mary had to face the inevitability of death,[3] and this also demonstrated the human nature of Christ himself.[4] But as Mother of God and the Source of Life her flesh could not be subject to corruption:[5] indeed she had the privilege of rendering back

---

[1] See D. G. Tsamis, 'Η Θεοτόκος στην Ορθόδοξη ευλάβεια και οι μεγάλες θεομητορικές εορτές', in *Εικοσιπενταετηρικόν. Αφιέρωμα στον Μητροπολίτη Νεαπόλεως και Σταυρουπόλεως κ. Διονύσιο* (Thessaloniki, 1999), 665–89. K. D. Kalokyris, *Η Θεοτόκος εις την εικονογραφίαν Ανατολής και Δύσεως* (Thessaloniki, 1972). I. Kalavrezou, 'Images of the Mother: When the Virgin Mary Became *Meter Theou*', *DOP* 44 (1990), 165–72. S. Der Nersessian, 'Two Images of the Virgin in the Dumbarton Oaks Collection', *DOP* 14 (1960), 69–86, esp. 71–5. Vassilaki, *Mother of God*. Numerous references to intercession by the Virgin can be found, for example, in: Andrew of Crete, *Magnus Canon*, *PG* 97, 1329–85. Joseph the Hymnographer, *Mariale*, *PG* 105, 983–1414.

[2] On Byzantine theology concerning the Dormition and Assumption of the Virgin, M. Jugie, *La mort et l'assomption de la Sainte Vierge. Étude historico-doctrinale* (Vatican City, 1944). A. Wenger, *L'assomption de la T.S. Vierge dans la tradition byzantine du VIe au Xe siècle. Études et documents* (Paris, 1955). M. van Esbroeck, *Aux origines de la Dormition de la Vierge* (London, 1995). Also B. E. Daley, '"At the Hour of Our Death": Mary's Dormition and Christian Dying in Late Patristic and Early Byzantine Literature', *DOP* 55 (2001), 71–89 (esp. 72 n. 3, for further bibliography). I. Zervou Tognazzi, 'L'iconografia della Koimisis della Santa Vergine, specchio del pensiero teologico dei Padri bizantini', *Studi e ricerche sull'Oriente cristiano* 8 (1985), 21–46, 69–90.

[3] Andrew of Crete, *In Dormitionem I–II*, *PG* 97, 1053A–B, 1073A, 1085C. Germanos I of Constantinople, *In Dormitionem I*, *PG* 98, 357B. John Mauropous, *In Dormitionem*, *PG* 120, 1097A.

[4] Germanos I of Constantinople, *In Dormitionem I*, *PG* 98, 345C–D. John Geometres, *In Dormitionem*, 47, ed. A. Wenger, *L'assomption*, 396.

[5] This basic doctrine of Byzantine theology is emphasized in virtually all homilies and hymns on the Dormition of the Theotokos. Cf. Pseudo-Modestos, *PG* 86 II, 3277–3312 (for the false attribution of the homily to Modestos see Jugie, *La mort et l'assomption*, 214–17). John of Damascus, *PG* 96, 704A, 713D, 716A–C, 720A, 725C–728C, 733C, 736C, 741A–C, 749B, 753C–D, 756A–D, 760B, 1364B, 1365A–D. Andrew of Crete, *PG* 97, 1053C–1056D, 1068B–1069C, 1073A, 1080C–D, 1081C–D, 1085C, 1088A–B, 1097B–C, 1100A. Germanos I of Constantinople, *PG* 98, 345A–349C, 357A–D, 361C. Theodore of Stoudios, *PG* 99, 724A, 728B–C. Joseph the Hymnographer, *PG* 105, 1000B–1001D. John Geometres, *PG* 106, 907B. Leo VI, *PG*

her soul into the hands of her Creator, whom she had once held as a baby in her arms.[6] And three days after her death, her incorruptible body was translated to heaven, where as Mother of God she will forever intercede on behalf of mankind.[7] The troparion which in accordance with the *Typikon of the Great Church* was chanted on the eve of the feast of the Dormition (14 August) eloquently sums up the theology on this subject: 'When giving birth you preserved your virginity, at your Dormition you did not abandon the world, O Virgin. You were translated to life, being the Mother of Life, delivering our souls from death through your intercessions.'[8]

Under the influence of hymns and homilies, the iconography of the Dormition in Byzantine art developed features which emphasize the mystery of the Incarnation. As Henry Maguire has noted, in Byzantine churches the Dormition is often depicted in a location which has a direct visual link with a representation of the Nativity or of the Virgin and Child, while certain iconographic details may provide a further connection between the two compositions.[9] A typical example is the Dormition scene in the Virgin Arakiotissa church in Lagoudera, Cyprus (Plate 6, Fig. 10.1).[10] In place of the conventional iconography which puts Christ at the very centre of the representation, the incarnated *Logos*, holding his mother's soul wrapped in swaddling clothes, can be seen just above the dead Virgin's head. He is thus closer to the figure of the Theotokos, who is depicted in the lower register of the wall painting, standing with the Christ-child in her arms. There is a further affiliation between the angel descending to receive Mary's soul and the two angels with the symbols of the Passion on either side of the Virgin and Child below.[11] All this places emphasis on the role of the Virgin in the Incarnation of the Word, born as man to redeem the world through his death and resurrection, while at the same time it marks her role in God's plan for the salvation of mankind as intercessor at her son's heavenly throne through her own death and assumption (*metastasis*). The Virgin's mediation is also the theme of the dedicatory inscription accompanying the portrayal of the Mother and Child, where the donor of the wall paintings invokes the protection of Mary for himself and his family, concluding with the words: 'For you alone,

---

107, 157C–172A. John Mauropous, *PG* 120, 1080B, 1081A–C, 1085A–C, 1093C–D, 1096C–1097A. Isidore of Thessaloniki, *PG* 139, 125C, 129A, 137D–140A, 141A–C, 156B.

[6] Cf. John Geometres, *PG* 106, 907A–B. Leo VI, *PG* 107, 164A. John Mauropous, *PG* 120, 1093D. See also H. Maguire, *Art and Eloquence in Byzantium* (Princeton, NJ, 1981), 59–68.

[7] The belief in Mary's resurrection in body and soul, and in the assumption of her incorruptible body separately from her soul after the Dormition, are both found in Byzantine theology (Jugie, *La mort et l'assomption*, 213–68, 315–53): see also the texts in n. 5 above. The intercession of the Virgin with her son on behalf of all Christians is a basic theme of Byzantine homilies and hymns on the Dormition, which emphasize the idea that after her assumption to heaven Mary's mediation became more powerful than before (Jugie, *La mort et l'assomption*, 185). See also T. Papamastorakis, Ἐπιτύμβιες παραστάσεις κατά τη μέση καὶ ὕστερη βυζαντινή περίοδο', *DChAE* 19 (1996/7), 285–304, for representations of the Virgin as intercessor for the deceased in funerary paintings and reliefs. Cf. Pseudo-Modestos, *PG* 86 II, 3301C–3304A. John of Damascus, *PG* 96, 713A, 717A–B, 721B–C, 1368A. Andrew of Crete, *PG* 97, 1105D–1108D. Germanos I of Constantinople, *PG* 98, 344B–345C, 349B, 352A, 357B–D, 360D, 361C–D, 368B, 372B–C. Theodore of Stoudios, *PG* 99, 721A–D, 729A. Isidore of Thessalonike, *PG* 139, 164C–D.

[8] J. Mateos (ed.), *Le Typicon de la Grande Église. Ms. Sainte-Croix n° 40, Xe siècle* I (Rome, 1962), 370.

[9] Maguire, *Art and Eloquence*, 59–68.

[10] For a detailed study of the wall paintings in this church, see A. Nicolaïdès, 'L'église de la Panagia Arakiotissa à Lagoudera, Chypre. Études iconographiques des fresques de 1192', *DOP* 50 (1996), 1–137.

[11] Maguire, *Art and Eloquence*, 64–5, Figs 59–60. Cf. also Nicolaïdès, 'Arakiotissa', 97–9.

Virgin of suppliants, have the faculty to offer to the ones who pray to you the desired salvation.'[12]

The Arakiotissa Dormition contains another iconographic feature which has often been mentioned in the literature, but never satisfactorily explained. This is the figure of the hierarch next to Christ, raising a censer to his face with his right hand and touching it with the forefinger of his left (Fig. 10.2). I shall attempt to show that this unusual detail should be interpreted as a symbol of the Incarnation and of the intercessory role of the Virgin – doctrines which, as I have mentioned, lie at the heart of the Byzantine theology of the Dormition.

Incense burning was of course an integral part of the burial rites of the Byzantine Church, as a host of texts and illustrations confirm,[13] and it is for this reason that in the iconography of the Dormition the apostle Peter is regularly shown standing at the Virgin's head holding a censer.[14] Similarly, one of the bystanders is generally found burning incense near the deceased in representations of the Dormition of other figures.[15] Byzantine liturgical rituals and ecclesiastical writings demonstrate the role of the censer as a vehicle for carrying the believers' prayers up to God[16] – for example verse 2 of Psalm 140(141), which played a central role in the *Typikon of the Great Church*: 'Let my prayer be set before thee as incense.'[17] Incense burning at funeral services is thus not merely a symbol of the respects paid to the deceased by the mourners but also an accompaniment to their prayers for the salvation of his soul and to their invocations to him to intercede before God on their behalf.[18]

This second element seems to be given special emphasis when in the Dormition of the Virgin, the paraclete for humanity par excellence, a figure raises the censer and breathes on it to intensify the burning and thus facilitate the ascent to heaven of the incense and the mourners' prayers. This rare iconographic detail is found in two thirteenth-century works in St Catherine's

---

[12] The complete inscription, with a French translation, can be found in Nicolaïdès, 'Arakiotissa', 5.

[13] Ch. Walter, *Art and Ritual of the Byzantine Church* (London, 1982), 137–44. See also E. Velkovska, 'Funeral Rites According to the Byzantine Liturgical Sources', *DOP* 55 (2001), 21–51, esp. 27.

[14] Walter, *Art and Ritual*, 140–1. For the iconography of the Dormition in general, see L. Wratislaw-Mitrović and N. Okunev, 'La Dormition de la Sainte Vierge dans la peinture médiévale orthodoxe', *BSl* 3 (1931), 134–74. Kalokyris, *Η Θεοτόκος*, 126–40.

[15] Walter, *Art and Ritual*, 141–3.

[16] A typical example of the use of incense as the vehicle to carry one's prayers to heaven is found in the 6th-century apocryphal narrative of the Dormition of the Virgin by Pseudo-John the Evangelist (the prayers of Mary or the apostles are accompanied by the burning of incense no less than seven times): John, *Liber de Dormitione Mariae*, 1, 4, 8, 9, 10, 26, 38, ed. C. Tischendorf, *Apocalypses Apocryphae* (Leipzig, 1866), 95, 96, 97, 98, 103, 107 (for the dating of the text, see Jugie, *La mort et l'assumption*, 117). For the function of incense in the Byzantine liturgy, cf. for example, R. F. Taft, *The Great Entrance. A History of the Transfer of Gifts and other Pre-Anaphoral Rites* (2nd edn, Rome, 1978), 149–59, esp. 150. K. Kallinikos, *Ο χριστιανικός ναός και τα τελούμενα εν αυτώ* (4th edn, Athens, 1969), 145–50. For a comprehensive study on the use of incense, see M. Pfeifer, *Der Weihrauch. Geschichte, Bedeutung, Verwendung* (Regensburg, 1997).

[17] Psalm 140(141) was regularly sung at Vespers, and Psalms 140(141):2 was used as *prokeimenon* at Vespers on 9 March (Feast of the Forty Martyrs), 25 March (Feast of the Annunciation) and the first Monday of Lent: see Mateos, *Typicon*, I, xxii, 246, 254; II, 14.

[18] Velkovska, 'Funeral Rites', 27. T. Avner, 'The Recovery of an Illustrated Byzantine Manuscript of the Early 12th Century', *Byz* 54 (1984), 5–25, esp. 13 with reference to Odes 8:2 of a Penitential Canon (*PG* 88, 764–81) 'in which the monks are cautioned to the advantage of harkening to the last words of the dying who, in the hereafter, can intercede with God in their interest and witness to their charitable behaviour'.

monastery, Sinai: a miniature in a sticherarion (cod. 1216, fol. 149r), where on the right of the representation the thurible is held at head height by Peter, who is apparently blowing on the incense (Fig. 10.3),[19] and an icon where on the left-hand side a hierarch blows on the incense while raising his eyes to heaven, a vivid recollection of the exhortation at the hour of prayer 'Let us lift up our hearts' (Fig. 10.4).[20] The open gates of heaven and the two angels descending to take up the soul of the Virgin, in combination with the upward movement of the incense and of the hierarch's gaze, make an eloquent reference to the intercessory role of the Theotokos, who in the fifth stanza of the Akathistos Hymn is hailed as the 'accepted incense of intercession'. Both the miniature and the icon may have been the work of western artists reproducing Byzantine models, as Galavaris and Weitzmann suggest.[21] However, the feature which interests us here is certainly of Byzantine origin, as it is found in the miniatures in three eleventh-century Byzantine manuscripts of the homilies of Gregory of Nazianzos, which Galavaris attributes to Constantinople.[22]

In his article on the wall paintings of the Arakiotissa, Andreas Nicolaides describes some of these works as iconographic parallels to the figure of the hierarch holding the censer in the Lagoudera Dormition.[23] However, in the Cypriot murals (Plate 6, Fig. 10.2) the figure is clearly not blowing on the incense as in the other examples (Figs 10.3–10.4), but touching it with his finger, exactly as in another icon from Sinai, which dates from the thirteenth century and is also well known in the literature (Figs 10.5–10.6).[24] Nicolaides suggests that the hierarch in the Arakiotissa is feeling the censer to find out if it is sufficiently heated for use in the funeral service.[25] It should be noted, however, that the burning of the incense depends on the temperature of the coal placed in the censer and not on the heating of the vessel itself. Moreover, in both the Cypriot wall paintings and the Sinai icon the hierarch is not looking at the vessel he is touching (as one would expect if he was involved in the preparation of the censer) but at the figures of Christ and at the Virgin's soul, as if intending to show that the significance of his gesture somehow involves them.

So what does this gesture in fact signify, if it cannot be interpreted in the same way as the hierarch's blowing on the censer to lift the prayers up to the Lord? The answer seems to be that

---

[19] G. Galavaris, Ζωγραφική Βυζαντινών χειρογράφων (Athens, 1995), 256, Fig. 199.
[20] K. Weitzmann, 'Icon Painting in the Crusader Kingdom', *DOP* 20 (1966), 65, Fig. 29. Id., *The Icon. Holy Images, Sixth to Fourteenth Century* (London, 1978), 118, Pl. 40 (in colour).
[21] Galavaris, Ζωγραφική χειρογράφων, 256, Fig. 199.
[22] Florence, Biblioteca Medicea Laurenziana, cod. Pluteus VII, 32, fol. 70r (Dormition of St Basil); Paris, Bibliothèque nationale, cod. Coislin 239, fol. 74r (Dormition of St Basil); Turin, University Library, cod. C. I.6, fol. 37v (Dormition of St Cyprian). G. Galavaris, *The Illustrations of the Liturgical Homilies of Gregory Nazianzenus* (Studies in Manuscript Illumination, 6) (Princeton, NJ, 1969), 218–20, Fig. 268; 246–8, Fig. 221; 259–60, Fig. 44.
[23] Nicolaïdès, 'Arakiotissa', 103 n. 916, Fig. 75 (the Sinai icon and codex, and the Turin codex). In n. 917, Fig. 76, he also mentions the Dormition of a monk in fol. 2r of a 12th-c. illustrated bifolio sold in Haifa and published by Avner, 'Recovery', 5–25. However, in the latter miniature a monk holds the censer close to and above the corpse, but without blowing on the incense (in a manner similar to Peter holding the censer above the Virgin on the Dormition ivory in the Bayerische Staatsbibliothek, Munich). For an illustration of the latter see A. Cutler, 'The Mother of God in Ivory', in Vassilaki, *Mother of God*, 173, Fig. 112.
[24] Weitzmann, 'Icon Painting in the Crusader Kingdom', 60, Figs 18–19; also mentioned by Nicolaïdès, 'Arakiotissa', 103.
[25] Nicolaïdès, 'Arakiotissa', 102.

he is here pointing to the censer to draw the attention of the other figures in the composition, and more especially that of the viewer, to the symbolic association of this liturgical vessel with the Virgin. The golden 'altar to burn incense upon' (θυσιαστήριον θυμιάματος) in the Holy of Holies of the Jewish Temple, described in detail in Exodus 30:1–10, is known to have been regarded by the Church Fathers as a type of the Virgin, together with the other sacred objects mentioned in Exodus 40 (in patristic texts this object is usually called simply 'censer' – θυμιατήριον). Although the gold censer is not mentioned as frequently as the other prefigurations of the Mother of God which are related to the Tabernacle of the Holy of Holies and the visions of the prophets,[26] there are clear references to it not only as a general Old Testament type of the Virgin[27] but also specifically as a symbol of the Incarnation. For example the homily on the Birth of the Virgin by Andrew of Crete contains the words 'Hail, the gold thurible of truly spiritual fragrances, in which Christ, the spiritual incense formed from the union of the divine and the human, displayed by the fire of divinity the fragrance of his animated spiritual flesh, unconfused and undivided.'[28] In his *kanon* for the feast of the Virgin the same author writes: 'You have become a gold thurifer, because the Word under the inspiration of the Holy Spirit planted the fire in your womb, and became visible in human form, O pure Mother of God.'[29] The third homily on the Dormition of the Virgin by John of Damascus refers to the grave which enclosed Mary's body for three days before its Assumption: 'This grave is more blessed than Moses' ark, since it was not in possession of forms and shadows but of the truth itself: wherefore it received ... the gold censer, the one (the Virgin) who was pregnant with the divine coal and made fragrant the whole creation.'[30] In his homily on the Dormition, Pseudo-Modestos, addressing the Virgin's deathbed, exclaims: 'O holy bed bearing the spiritual fragrance

---

[26] On the Old Testament prefigurations of the Virgin in Byzantine ecclesiastical literature, cf. J. Ledit, *Marie dans la liturgie de Byzance* (Paris, 1976), 64–97. S. Eustratiades, *Η Θεοτόκος εν τη υμνογραφία* (Paris, 1930), under the relevant entries. For depictions of such prefigurations in Byzantine art, cf. D. Mouriki, 'Αι βιβλικαί προεικονίσεις της Παναγίας εις τον τρούλλον της Περιβλέπτου του Μυστρά', *AD* 25 (1970), A-*Meletai*, 217–54, Pls 72–93. P. A. Underwood, *The Kariye Djami* I (Bollingen Series, 70) (Princeton, NJ, 1975), 223–37. T. Papamastorakis, 'Η ένταξη των προεικονίσεων της Θεοτόκου και της Υψώσεως του Σταυρού σε έναν ιδιότυπο εικονογραφικό κύκλο στον Άγιο Γεώργιο Βιάννου Κρήτης', *DChAE* 14 (1987/8), 315–28 (esp. 318 n. 16 for references to monumental paintings in which the censer appears among other biblical prefigurations of the Virgin; to these should be added the censer held by one of the high priests in the Tabernacle where other holy objects appear as types of the Virgin, in the Prothesis of the Protaton on Mount Athos: G. Millet, *Monuments de l'Athos I, Les peintures* (Paris, 1927), Pl. 32.3). H. L. Kessler, '"Pictures Fertile with Truth": How Christians Managed to Make Images of God without Violating the Second Commandment', *Journal of the Walters Art Gallery* 49/50 (1991/2), 53–65, esp. 59–60.

[27] Usually included in a list of other Old Testament prefigurations, as in the troparion known as Ἄνωθεν οἱ Προφῆται (Mouriki, 'Προεικονίσεις', 241). Andrew of Crete, *Homily IV, In Nativitatem B. Mariae*, PG 97, 868C. Id., *Canon in B. Annae Conceptionem*, PG 97, 1316B–C.

[28] Id., *In Nativitatem B. Mariae*, PG 97, 877D.

[29] Id., *Canon in B. Mariae Nativitatem*, PG 97, 1324C. See also the interpretation of the burning censer shown in the 12th-c. wall painting of the Annunciation in the Syrian monastery at Scetis, Egypt, which is considered to be a symbol of Mary's virginity and her intercessory role, and is also related to liturgical practices and preoccupations of the Coptic community of the time: L.-A. Hunt, 'The Fine Incense of Virginity. A Late Twelfth-Century Wall-Painting of the Annunciation at the Monastery of the Syrians, Egypt', *BMGS* 19 (1995), 182–232, esp. 193–6.

[30] John of Damascus, *Homily X, In Dormitionem B. Mariae III*, PG 96, 756D–757A; also id., *Homily VII, In Nativitatem B. Mariae* II, PG 96, 689C. The Theotokos is also called 'the censer of the divine coal' (Christ) by Joseph the Hymnographer, *Mariale*, PG 105, 1160B, 1397A; also Eustratiades, Θεοτόκος, 29 ('θυμιατήριον').

which filled the whole world with "the sweet savour of Christ"' (2 Corinthians 2:15).³¹ The golden censer as a type of the Virgin also appears in three homilies by Neophytos of Paphos,³² whom the painter of the Arakiotissa must have known personally (if he is correctly identified with Theodore Apseudes, who painted Neophytos' *enkleistra* in 1183).³³ Byzantine ecclesiastical writings also contain frequent references to the fragrant grace and purity of the Virgin, while her body which received God is likened to a vessel or a receptacle. Expressions of this kind (sometimes found combined, as in 'a receptacle of fragrance') exactly match the typology of the censer.³⁴

The hierarch who is shown in the Arakiotissa bending over the body of the Virgin, gazing at her and pointing at the censer which he holds in his hand, could be using precisely these expressions. The symbolism of his gesture is not lessened by the fact that the object is a simple Byzantine liturgical vessel and not the gold thurible of the Temple. In his *Ecclesiastical History*, Germanos describes this object:

> The censer demonstrates the humanity of Christ, and the fire his divinity. The sweet-smelling smoke reveals the fragrance of the Holy Spirit which precedes …. Again, the interior of the censer … is understood as the (sanctified) womb of the (holy) virgin (and Theotokos), who bore the divine coal, Christ, in whom 'the whole fullness of deity dwells bodily' (Colossians 2:9). All together, therefore, give forth the sweet-smelling fragrance.³⁵

The significance of the hierarch's gesture in the Arakiotissa Dormition is also demonstrated by his prominent position almost at the centre of the composition, above the body of Mary and next to Christ, who is placed off-centre, holding the soul of his mother. The hierarch is given even greater emphasis by his phelonion, covered in crosses unlike the garments worn by the other two hierarchs in the scene.³⁶ Nicolaides considers that he should probably be identified as Dionysios the Areopagite, in view of the inscription accompanying the similarly depicted hierarch in the Sinai icon (Figs 10.5–10.6).³⁷ A passage in the *Ecclesiastical Hierarchy* of Pseudo-Dionysios the Areopagite, which was greatly influential on Byzantine theological belief, gives prominence to the role of incense as a symbol of the active presence of God in liturgical rituals.³⁸ And it was the presence of God in the Virgin's womb (of which the censer was a symbol) that led to the Incarnation and the Passion of the *Logos* for the salvation of the world and which predetermined the presence of Christ at her Dormition in order to receive his mother's soul and translate her to heaven, where she was received as intercessor for mankind.

---

³¹ [Pseudo-]Modestos, *In Dormitionem SS Deiparae*, PG 86 II, 3309B.

³² In his homilies on the Presentation of the Virgin, 1, and the Annunciation, 5, and his catechesis on the Presentation of the Virgin, 1, published by E.M. Toniolo, 'Omilie e catechesi inedite di Neofito il Recluso (1134–1200 c)', *Marianum* 36 (1974), 210 lines 14–15, 244 line 127, 300 lines 15–17.

³³ M. Panayotidi, 'The Question of the Role of the Donor and of the Painter. A Rudimentary Approach', *DChAE* 17 (1993/4), 143–56. S. Sophocleous, *Panagia Arakiotissa, Lagoudera, Cyprus* (Nicosia, 1998), 49–50.

³⁴ See, for example, Eustratiades, Θεοτόκος, 18–9 ('δοχεῖον'), 24 ('εὐωδιάζουσα'), 46 ('μυροθήκη', 'μῦρον'), 71 ('σκεῦος').

³⁵ Germanos I of Constantinople, *Ecclesiastical History and Mystical Contemplation*, 30, ed. and trans. P. Meyendorff, *St Germanus of Constantinople on the Divine Liturgy* (New York, 1984), 78–81.

³⁶ Nicolaïdès, 'Arakiotissa', 101.

³⁷ Ibid., 102.

³⁸ [Pseudo-]Dionysios the Areopagite, *De ecclesiastica hierarchia*, III.3, PG 3, 428D–429B; commentary by H.-J. Schulz, *The Byzantine Liturgy. Symbolic Structure and Faith Expression* (New York, 1986), 25–6.

Thus the censer to which the hierarch is pointing also refers to the Virgin's mediatory and salvatory role after her Assumption: the incense contained in the vessel accompanies the prayers of the faithful to God, just as the intercessions of the Virgin accompany their invocations. As Joseph the Hymnographer proclaims: 'Mary, the golden censer, remove the odour of my sufferings, and strengthen what is shaken by the onslaughts of the cunning enemy'.[39]

Exactly the same doctrines – the Incarnation and the Virgin's intercession – are projected in the rest of the church's iconographic programme. I have already referred to the figures of the Virgin and Child below the Dormition, which emphasize the soteriological message of the Incarnation of the *Logos*, while the dedicatory inscription invokes the intercession of Mary (Fig. 10.1). It has been suggested that the manner in which the Virgin holds the child is a reference to the 'tongs' of the divine coal in Isaiah's vision (6:6).[40] This is a prefiguration of the Virgin often referred to in Byzantine ecclesiastical writing,[41] and may be considered comparable to the censer as a symbol of the virgin womb which receives the divine coal, as expressed in the texts mentioned above. It is therefore likely that these two unusual iconographic features – the censer in the Dormition scene and the Virgin in her prefiguration as tongs – were chosen to strengthen the theological significance of the two representations.

The north pier of the bema has a representation of the Virgin Eleousa, who through the text on her scroll addresses Christ Antiphonetes on the south pier as she pleads for the redemption of the world.[42] The soteriological message of the Incarnation is also emphasized by the sacred Mandylion on the arch above the conch of the sanctuary,[43] the medallion with Christ Emmanuel, between the angel and the Virgin in the Annunciation scene,[44] and the representation of the Nativity opposite the Resurrection, on the south and north part of the west vault of the church.[45]

Moreover the location of the Dormition in the church – on the south wall instead of in its usual position on the west wall[46] – places it in direct contact with the other three scenes which emphasize the pre-eminent role of the Mother of God in the Incarnation. To its right is the Nativity, on the south side of the west vault; in the south-east pendentive to the left of and above the Dormition is the portrayal of Mary in the Annunciation scene (Fig. 10.7), shown beside a staircase – according to Nicolaides, a feature unique in extant Byzantine wall painting – which is an obvious reference to the Old Testament prefiguration of Mary as Jacob's ladder (Fig. 10.8).[47] This symbol, harmoniously integrated into the composition and forming an organic part of it, bears some similarity to the censer of the Dormition scene, which symbolizes the Incarnation. But there is probably an even deeper conceptual link between the Annunciation and the censer of the Dormition. Byzantine commentaries on the Divine Liturgy often treat incense as a symbol of the presence or the visitation of the Holy Spirit,[48] and the censer in the

---

[39] Joseph the Hymnographer, *Mariale*, PG 105, 1189C.
[40] D. I. Pallas, *Die Passion und Bestattung Christi in Byzanz* (Munich, 1965), 176–7.
[41] Cf. Eustratiades, Θεοτόκος, 40–1 ('λαβίς'). Neophytos of Paphos, *Catechesis on the Presentation of Christ to the Temple* 1, ed. Toniolo, 'Omelie', 304 lines 26–8.
[42] Nicolaïdès, 'Arakiotissa', 105–8, Figs 9, 77–8.
[43] Ibid., 35–6, Fig. 34.
[44] Ibid., 70, Fig. 62.
[45] Ibid., 74–5, Figs 63, 68.
[46] Ibid., 97.
[47] Ibid., 70, Fig. 60.
[48] e.g. Germanos I of Constantinople, *Ecclesiastical History*, 30 and 37, ed. Meyendorff, 78–81 and 86–7. Symeon

Dormition scene might therefore be a symbolic depiction of the Virgin as the receptacle of the Holy Spirit, a concept given narrative form in the Annunciation scene, at the very moment when it comes to fruition. And finally, just opposite the Dormition is the Presentation of the Virgin, a subject which again refers to the role of Mary as a vessel of the Incarnation, and which together with the Dormition defines the beginning and the end of her public life (Fig. 10.7).[49] On her admission into the Temple, the place which housed the sacred objects of the Jewish faith prefiguring her, the future Mother of God is greeted as the living temple which through the grace of the Holy Spirit will be prepared to bear the incarnated *Logos*. Here again the symbolism of the censer can be found in ecclesiastical writings. In a homily on the Presentation of the Virgin, Tarasios addresses Zacharias in these words: 'O prophet, receive the censer of immaterial light ... lead her to the shrine, as she hastens to bear the invisible one in her womb ... establish in the man-made temple the one who will be the living temple of the Word.'[50] And James of Kokkinobaphos says in his homily on the subject: 'Today there is received into the Holy of Holies the golden censer, in which the *Logos* setting light to the flesh filled the world with its fragrance.'[51]

The artist who painted the Arakiotissa murals in 1192 enriched the theological symbolism of the Dormition and of the other associated portrayals of the Virgin by incorporating an original iconographic feature, which seems to have been created under the influence of the copious Byzantine hymns and homilies on the role of the Theotokos in God's plan for the Incarnation. The theological expertise of the artist or of his instructor is demonstrated in other features of the mural decoration, and in particular their location in the church and their unusual iconographic details.[52] This accords with the general trend in twelfth-century art of renewing iconography with elements inspired by hymnographic and homiletic texts in order to enrich its theological content.[53] In the particular case of representations of the Virgin this is demonstrated in celebrated works of art – for example the two illustrated manuscripts of the homilies of James of Kokkinobaphos,[54] and the well-known icon from Sinai with the Kykkotissa surrounded by the prophets who foretold her in their visions.[55] Similarly the famous late-twelfth-century icon of the Annunciation, also from Sinai, incorporates architectural and topographical elements which are not narrative innovations but symbols of the deeper theological content of the subject.[56] In such an artistic climate a symbolic interpretation for the hierarch who points to the censer in the Arakiotissa Dormition is especially plausible.

---

of Thessaloniki, *De Sacra Liturgia*, PG 155, 285C. Id., *De Sacro Templo*, PG 155, 308A, 317C. Id., *Expositio de Divino Templo*, PG 155, 705D, 721A.

[49] Nicolaïdès, 'Arakiotissa', 62.
[50] Tarasios, *In SS. Deiparae Praesentationem*, PG 98, 1489A–C.
[51] James of Kokkinobaphos, *Homily III, In Praesentationem SS. Deiparae*, PG 127, 609B. An almost identical phrase is used by George of Nikomedeia, *In SS. Deiparae Ingressum in Templum*, PG 100, 1424C (a possible source of inspiration for James of Kokkinobaphos).
[52] For another example of complex visual exegesis in the mural decoration of this church, Ch. Baltoyanni, 'Christ the Lamb and the ενώτιον of the Law in a Wall Painting of Araka on Cyprus', *DChAE* 17 (1993/4), 53–8.
[53] H. Belting, *Likeness and Presence. A History of the Image Before the Era of Art* (Chicago and London, 1994), 261–96.
[54] I. Hutter and P. Canart, *Das Marienhomiliar des Mönchs Jakobos von Kokkinobaphos. Codex Vaticanus Graecus 1162. Einführungsband und Faksimile* (Codices e Vaticanis Selecti, 79) (Stuttgart, 1991). H. Omont, *Miniatures des Homélies sur la Vierge du moine Jacques (ms. gr. 1208 de Paris)* (Paris, 1927).
[55] Vassilaki, *Mother of God*, no. 28, 314–16 (T. Papamastorakis), with bibliography.
[56] Evans and Wixom, *The Glory of Byzantium*, no. 246, 374–5 (A. W. Carr), with bibliography.

What then was the fate of this iconographic innovation? As an isolated work, the Sinai icon (Fig. 10.5) cannot be incorporated into a larger group which might have given us the answer. However the symbolic interpretation seems very probable in view of the close relationship between the figures of Christ and the Virgin's soul on the one hand and the hierarch with the censer on the other. The expressions of these figures suggest that they are involved in an intense dialogue on the symbolism of the object at which the priest is pointing. The artist successfully reproduced in this icon the message of his Byzantine model.[57] As it is generally accepted that the painter of the Arakiotissa brought strong Constantinopolitan influences to his work,[58] the probability is that now lost works from the capital followed the same iconography. An echo of this can perhaps be traced in a late twelfth- to early thirteenth-century icon from the Mavriotissa, Kastoria, in which a hierarch, looking intently at the face of the recumbent Virgin, raises a censer to his face and uncovers it as if to smell its incense (Fig. 10.9).[59] Similarly, in the Dormition in the Holy Trinity church, Sopoćani (1260–1265), a hierarch is shown gazing at the body of Mary and holding a fragrant, uncovered thurifer in the centre of the composition, between the body of the Mother of God and the figure of the incarnated *Logos* who holds her soul in his hands.[60] A different iconographic solution, but one with probably similar theological dimensions, is found on the west wall of the Protaton (*c.* 1290). This shows a large censer standing on the ground in front of the Virgin's bier and above Christ *Anapeson* in the lower register.[61] As a symbol of the Incarnation the censer is given a particularly appropriate place between the figures of the recumbent baby – depicted in an iconographic type referring to the Passion and the Resurrection[62] – and the recumbent Virgin who as Mother of God will be resurrected after death like her son.[63]

The representations of the Dormition in the Arakiotissa at Lagoudera and the comparable Sinai icon (Figs 10.1–10.2, 10.5–10.6) undoubtedly display the clearest and most emphatic use of the censer as a symbol encompassing the doctrines of the Byzantine church on the Dormition of the Virgin. It is perhaps not irrelevant that in the twelfth century two homilies appeared which placed exceptional emphasis on the resurrection of the Virgin, on the very grounds of her status as Mother of God.[64] The following words of John Phournes may well convey the thoughts of the hierarch who holds the censer: 'For you are truly the gold censer, in which the coal of divinity was placed, and when it had burnt the proffered flesh of Christ in the form of incense it filled the world with the fragrance from his body'.[65]

---

[57] It is likely that the artist of the Sinai icon was Byzantine himself (cf. for Weitzmann's doubts on this issue, 'Icon Painting in the Crusader Kingdom', 60–1).
[58] Nicolaïdès, 'Arakiotissa', 135–7. Sophocleous, *Arakiotissa*, 49–50.
[59] Published by E. Tsigaridas, 'Φορητές εικόνες στη Μακεδονία και στο Άγιον Όρος κατά το 13ο αιώνα', *DChAE* 21 (2000), 125, Fig. 5.
[60] M. Acheimastou-Potamianou, *Byzantine Wall-Paintings* (Athens, 1994), 233, Fig. 90.
[61] Millet, *Athos*, Pl. 30.1–2.
[62] Pallas, *Passion*, 181–96. B. Todić, 'Anapeson. Iconographie et signification du thème', *Byz* 64 (1994), 134–65.
[63] Cf. the homilies mentioned by Jugie, *La mort et l'assomption*, 323–6.
[64] Ibid.
[65] Λόγος περὶ τῆς Μεταστάσεως τοῦ πανσέπτου σώματος τῆς Θεοτόκου, ὅτι ἀνέστη ἐκ τῶν νεκρῶν πρὸ τῆς κοινῆς ἀναστάσεως, ed. G. M. Palamas, Θεοφάνους τοῦ Κεραμέως Ὁμιλίαι εἰς Εὐαγγέλια κυριακὰ καὶ Ἑορτὰς τοῦ ὅλου ἐνιαυτοῦ (Jerusalem, 1860), 276.

10.1 Cyprus, Lagoudera, church of the Virgin Arakiotissa, view of the south wall.
Upper register: Dormition of the Virgin.
Lower register: Virgin and Child (left) and Archangel Michael (right) (source: Sophocleous, *Panagia Arakiotissa*, Pl. 16)

10.2   Cyprus, Lagoudera, church of the Virgin Arakiotissa. Dormition of the Virgin; officiating hierarch holding a censer (detail) (source: Nicolaïdès, 'Arakiotissa', Fig. 74)

10.3   Mt Sinai, Monastery of St Catherine, cod. 1216, fol. 149r. Miniature with the Dormition of the Virgin (source: Galavaris, Ζωγραφική χειρογράφων, Fig. 199)

10.4 Mt Sinai, Monastery of St Catherine. Icon with the Dormition of the Virgin (source: Weitzmann, *The Icon*, Pl. 40)

THE SYMBOLISM OF THE CENSER 129

10.5 Mt Sinai, Monastery of St Catherine. Icon with the Dormition of the Virgin (source: Weitzmann, 'Icon Painting in the Crusader Kingdom', Fig. 18)

10.6 Mt Sinai, Monastery of St Catherine. Icon with the Dormition of the Virgin; officiating hierarch holding a censer (detail) (source: Weitzmann, 'Icon Painting in the Crusader Kingdom', Fig. 19)

10.7 Cyprus, Lagoudera, church of the Virgin Arakiotissa, view of the dome (source: Sophocleous, *Panagia Arakiotissa*, Pl. 8)

10.8 Cyprus, Lagoudera, church of the Virgin Arakiotissa. The Annunciation; the Virgin (detail) (source: Sophocleous, *Panagia Arakiotissa*, Pl. 12)

10.9 Kastoria, church of the Virgin Mavriotissa. Icon with the Dormition of the Virgin (source: Tsigaridas, 'Φορητές εικόνες στη Μακεδονία και στο Άγιον Όρος', Fig. 5)

11

The Portaitissa icon at Iveron monastery and the cult of the Virgin on Mount Athos

Kriton Chryssochoidis

During the reign of the iconoclast emperor Theophilos, an icon of the Virgin in the possession of a pious widow and her son from Nicaea in Bithynia was cast into the sea to save it from the destructive frenzy of its pursuers. Many years later it reappeared in the midst of a pillar of fire in the bay of St Clement's monastery, the future Iveron, on Mt Athos. The monks tried to approach it, but in vain, as the icon retreated out to sea. After the Virgin herself gave a sign to the abbot, the icon was taken to the katholikon of the monastery by a humble Georgian ascetic, Gabriel by name, who had walked across the waves to pick it up. Eventually, after another sign from the Theotokos, the icon was placed in the parekklesion, which had been built for this purpose at the entrance (πόρτα) to the monastery, to be its guardian and protector: whence it acquired the name 'Portaitissa' (Our Lady of the Gate).

This, in brief, is the story of perhaps the most celebrated Theotokos icon on Athos, which is still housed in Iveron and acts as the monastery's *palladium* (Plate 7, Fig. 11.1).[1] The Portaitissa is also, on present knowledge, the earliest recorded miracle-working icon on Athos, being first mentioned in the sources, indirectly but with certainty, in the Synodikon of Iveron between 1170 and 1183–1184, when Abbot Paul renovated the doors of the church (parekklesion) of the Portaitissa, which clearly housed the icon of that name. This is an indication that it had been constructed some years before, perhaps even in the eleventh century; certainly not before the middle of that century, however, as there is no reference to it in the Lives of the founders John and Euthymios or of Abbot George, who died in 1056.[2]

The icon itself was recently dated to the early eleventh or late tenth century, i.e. a few decades after the foundation of the monastery by the Iberians John, Euthymios and Tornikios (monk John) in 980.[3] It was previously attributed variously to the iconoclast period (ninth century), the early twelfth century and even much later, to the late thirteenth century.[4] However, by the thirteenth century the fame of the icon was such that even in formal documents the Iveron monastery is given the supplementary title 'Monastery of the most holy Theotokos who is called

---

[1] It is headed Ὑπόμνημα and was edited by J. Bury, 'Iveron and Our Lady of the Gate', *Hermathena* 10 (1897), 71–99 (text, 86–99).
[2] J. Lefort, N. Oikonomidès, D. Papachryssanthou, V. Kravari and H. Métrévéli (eds), *Actes d'Iviron* II (*Archives de l'Athos*, XVI) (Paris, 1990), 11, 38. Cf. eid., *Actes d'Iviron* I (*Archives de l'Athos*, XIV) (Paris, 1985), 63.
[3] P. Vocotopoulos, 'Note sur l'icône de la Vierge Portaïtissa', *Zograf* 25 (1996), 27–30. Id., 'Ἡ εἰκόνα τῆς Παναγίας Πορταΐτισσας τῆς Ἱερᾶς Μονῆς τῶν Ἰβήρων', in *Ἅγιον Ὄρος. Φύση – Ἱστορία – Τέχνη* II (Thessaloniki, 2001), 81–8, 273 (photo).
[4] Th. Steppan, 'Überlegungen zur Ikone der Panhagia Portaitissa im Kloster Iwiron am Berg Athos', in *Sinnbild und Abbild. Zur Funktion des Bildes, Kunstgeschichtliche Studien-Innsburg* (*Veröffentlichungen der Universität Innsburg*, 198), Neue Folge, 1 (1994), 23–49 (early 12th c.). For the datings, see Vocotopoulos, 'Ἡ εἰκόνα τῆς Παναγίας Πορταΐτισσας', 83–4.

Portaitissa'–'Portiatissa'–'Portiotissa'.[5] In 1355–1356, when Patriarch Kallistos I assigned the abbot's office (*hegoumeneia*) and the katholikon of the monastery to the numerically superior Greek monks, the church of the Portaitissa was entrusted to the Iberians to 'perform their sacred hymnodies there' (ἐκτελῶσι καὶ οὗτοι ἐν αὐτῇ τὰς ἱερὰς ὑμνωδίας).[6]

We do not know of any special liturgical typikon for the *akolouthiai* which were held in the church in the Byzantine era, though in the first years of the sixteenth century the monks were tonsured and presented with their mega schema in the parekklesion in front of the icon.[7] About the same time the icon was covered with a precious revetment, the gift of Ambrosi, a Georgian nobleman of royal descent,[8] and a few years later, around 1517, the wife of the ruler of Wallachia, Neagoe Bassarab, donated a valuable podea.[9] Its cult spread to the Balkans and to Russia, particularly after the sixteenth century, and a remarkably large number of copies of it were produced.[10]

The presence of a celebrated ancient icon called the Portaitissa might have been expected to give rise to the composition of hagiographical *Hypomnemata* (memoirs) or *Diegeses* (narratives) going back to the Byzantine times on the subject of its appellation and history, and also of Byzantine hymnographical texts dedicated to its cult.[11] However, as we shall see, surviving Greek hagiographical texts on the Portaitissa, whether in full or abridged versions, do not pre-date the early post-Byzantine era.

The narratives, in the abridged version, contain the story of the miraculous appearance of the icon and its installation in the Iveron monastery. Usually headed 'Περὶ τῆς Πορταϊτίσσης Θεοτόκου' or 'Περὶ τῆς μονῆς τῶν Ἰβήρων', with small variations between them, they form an organic part of a group of texts known as 'Πάτρια τοῦ Ἁγίου Ὄρους',[12] which contain descriptions of fantastic or historical events and records of pious traditions, and also brief accounts of the foundation of Athonite monasteries and of the miracle-working icons they housed.[13]

All the texts of the *Patria* without exception make their appearance in the manuscript tradition in the first years of the sixteenth century, certainly before 1516. We know this because one

---

[5] Lefort *et al.*, *Actes d'Iviron* III (*Archives de l'Athos*, XVIII) (Paris, 1994), 6 and documents no. 61 (year 1273), line 11; no. 62 (year 1283), line 63.

[6] Lefort *et al.*, *Actes d'Iviron* IV (*Archives de l'Athos*, XIX) (Paris, 1995), document no. 93, lines 65–6.

[7] K. Chryssochoides, 'Τὸ βιβλιογραφικό εργαστήριο τῆς μονῆς Ἰβήρων στὶς πρῶτες δεκαετίες τοῦ 16ου αἰώνα', in *Η ελληνική γραφή κατά τους 15° και 16° αιώνες* (*ΙΒΕ/ΕΙΕ, Διεθνή Συμπόσια*, 7) (Athens, 2000), 530: autobiographical note of prohegoumenos Dionysios of Iveron.

[8] Lefort *et al.*, *Actes d'Iviron* IV, 24 and 27. Z. Skhirtladze, *The Revetment of the Portaitissa Icon* (Tbilisi, 1994) (in Georgian). The same subject is comprehensively covered by Skhirtladze in an unpublished doctoral thesis submitted at the Tbilisi State University, which I have been unable to examine: 'The Portaïtissa Icon at Iveron and the Jakeli Family of Samtskhe' (in Georgian). See *Bulletin of British Byzantine Studies* 21 (1995), 40–1.

[9] P. Năsturel, *Le Mont Athos et les Roumains. Recherches sur leurs relations du milieu du XIVe siècle à 1654* (*Orientalia Christiana Analecta*, 227) (Rome, 1986), 107.

[10] For an indication of the extensive bibliography in Russian, see I. Bentchev, *Bibliographie der Gottesmutterikonen* (Bonn, 1992), 153–8.

[11] Cf. Lefort *et al.*, *Actes d'Iviron* I, 63 n. 6.

[12] M. Gedeon, *Ο Άθως. Αναμνήσεις – έγγραφα – σημειώσεις* (Constantinople, 1885), 303–4. S. Lampros, 'Τὰ Πάτρια του Αγίου Όρους', *NE* 9 (1912), 129–30.

[13] On the *Patria*, see the note by D. Papachryssanthou, *Ο Αθωνικός μοναχισμός. Αρχές και οργάνωση* (Athens, 1992), 30 n. 29.

group, which contains the narrative of the Portaitissa icon, was translated into Russian by Maximos the Greek, who must have become acquainted with the texts during his ten-year residence on Athos (1505 or 1506 to 1516), before he emigrated to Russia.[14]

The full versions of the Greek texts are transmitted independently and are classified as *Hypomnemata*[15] or *Diegeses*.[16] They contain small variants between them, and some are faithful paraphrases in simple language (εἰς ἁπλῆν φράσιν) of the original more literary texts. The earliest known manuscript of any version of the text dates from as late as 1599,[17] but one of the variants must have appeared in the manuscript tradition in the first decades of the sixteenth century – certainly before 1540, the year in which another *Hypomnema* on the Portaitissa was copied by Pachomios Rousanos, as we shall see below.

In the full version of the Greek text, the narrative itself, with the miraculous appearance of the icon, its installation in the monastery, and the miracles it performed in later times, is preceded by chapters which form an apparent hotchpotch of texts with content similar to that of the *Patria*. They refer to the triumph of Christianity under Constantine the Great and the presence of monks on Athos at that time, the arrival of St Peter the Athonite on the mountain at the instigation of the Theotokos, the founding of Lavra by St Athanasios the Athonite and the instruction received from him by John of Iveron, as well as the story of the foundation of Iveron and the work of its founder Tornikios.[18]

The manuscript tradition of all the Greek versions of the narrative of the Portaitissa icon thus goes back to the early post-Byzantine era and does not pre-date the early sixteenth century. References to the transmission in Byzantine manuscripts of the abridged texts contained in the *Patria* and of the full narratives are without exception based on erroneous dating. Two of the manuscripts which transmitted the text of the *Patria* are dated to the fifteenth century in published catalogues,[19] but a study of the manuscripts themselves has shown that both were written around the mid-sixteenth or early seventeenth century.[20] A manuscript in the Synodal Library in Moscow (MS. no. 404) with the full *Diegesis* and the *Akolouthia* for the Portaitissa was given a twelfth-century dating in the middle of the nineteenth century.[21] The library's

---

[14] A. Ivanov, *Literaturnoe nasledie Maksima Greka. Kharakteristika, atributsii, bibliografiia* (Leningrad, 1969), no. 278, 177–8, and no. 327, 196–7.

[15] Ὑπόμνημα περὶ τοῦ ἁγίου ὄρους Ἄθω καὶ περὶ τῶν κτιτόρων τῆς σεβασμίας καὶ βασιλικῆς μονῆς τῶν Ἰβήρων, καὶ περὶ τῆς ἁγίας καὶ προσκυνητῆς εἰκόνος τῆς Θεοτόκου τῆς Πορταϊτίσσης· καὶ ὅθεν καὶ ὅπως καὶ κατὰ τίνα τρόπον εἰσῆλθεν ἐν αὐτῇ τῇ μονῇ καὶ μερικὴ θαυμάτων διήγησις (BHG, 1070, 1070b).

[16] Διήγησις πάνυ ὡραία περὶ τῆς ἱερᾶς καὶ σεβασμίας εἰκόνος τῆς Πορταϊτίσσης, πῶς ἦλθεν εἰς τὸ Ἅγιον Ὄρος, εἰς τὴν ἁγίαν μονὴν τῶν Ἰβήρων (BHG, Auctarium, 1070).

[17] The manuscript Oxon. Lincoln College 10, containing the *Hypomnema*, was copied in Constantinople by Michael Anerestos in 1599 and used for Bury's edition, see 'Iveron and Our Lady', 75–6.

[18] Ibid., 77–8.

[19] For a catalogue of manuscripts of the *Patria*, see M. Rigo, 'La Διήγησις sui monaci athoniti martirizziati dai latinofroni (*BHG* 2333) e le tradizioni athonite succesive: alcune osservazioni', *Studi Veneziani*, n.s., 15 (1988), 78–9 n. 26.

[20] The manuscripts are: (i) Karakallou 66 (=1579): see S. Lampros, Κατάλογος τῶν ἐν ταῖς βιβλιοθήκαις τοῦ Ἁγίου Ὄρους ἑλληνικῶν κωδίκων I (Cambridge, 1895), 136; personal observation showed that it was copied around the mid-16th c. (ii) Lavra 1142 (I 58): see Spyridon Lauriotes and S. Eustrathiades, Κατάλογος τῶν κωδίκων τῆς Μεγίστης Λαύρας (Paris, 1925), 188; it cannot be dated before the early 17th c. as it contains *inter alia* works by Dionysios the rhetor, an Athonite intellectual of the late 16th and early 17th c.

[21] V. Langlois, *Le Mont Athos et ses monastères* (Paris, 1867), 17 (the manuscript is referred to by its former number, 436).

catalogue of manuscripts later attributed it to the sixteenth,[22] and this dating has recently been authoritatively revised to the seventeenth century.[23] However, the error is still being perpetuated and a recent study which dates the icon to the twelfth century attributes the text to the same period.[24]

This late dating of the Greek hagiographical texts on the Portaitissa icon obviously does not exclude the possibility of the composition of narratives or *akolouthiai* in Georgian during the Byzantine era. We know that at this time the icon was particularly venerated by the monastery's Georgian monks and that in 1355 or 1356 the church of the Portaitissa was assigned to them by Patriarch Kallistos for their exclusive liturgical use, after the katholikon was presented to the Greeks. Bury assumes the existence of an older Georgian text which served as a source for the Greek *Hypomnema* which he edited, without however providing any direct evidence or suggesting a date for its composition.[25]

A note in Iveron monastery manuscript no. 1864, which was copied in the late seventeenth century and contains the *Hypomnema* of Bury's edition, supports the view which the editor put forward a century ago.[26] Written in the copyist's hand, it reads

> It is said that after the Iberians abandoned the monastery, the Greeks who settled there wished to translate the present *Hypomnema* from the Iberian language into their own dialect. But there was no proper interpreter or writer. For this reason it seems to me that the composition has been corrupted in many places. For it is happy neither in its phrasing nor in its copying. And it has therefore been corrected by us, as far as possible, and adapted to a simpler form, as can be seen here.
>
> (Λέγεται ὅτι μετὰ τὸ καταλειφθῆναι τὴν μονὴν ὑπὸ τῶν Ἰβήρων, ἠθέλησαν οἱ ταύτην οἰκήσαντες Γραικοὶ μετενεγκεῖν ἐκ τῆς ἰβηρίδος φωνῆς εἰς τὴν ἰδίαν διάλεκτον τὸ παρὸν ὑπόμνημα· οὐκ ἔτυχον δὲ οὔτε ἑρμηνέως οὔτε συγγραφέως ὡς ἔδει· ὅθεν μοι δοκεῖ ἐν πολλοῖς διαφθαρεῖναι τὸ σύγγραμμα· οὔτε γὰρ φράσιν οὔτε ἀντιστοιχίαν ηὐμοίρει· διωρθώθη δ' οὖν ὅμως παρ' ἡμῶν, ὡς δυνατόν, καὶ μεταρρυθμίσθη [cod.: μεταρριθμήθη] εἰς τὸ ἁπλοϊκότερον, ὡς ὁρᾶται ἐνθάδε)

The anonymous copyist thus provides earlier evidence of a Georgian original of the *Hypomnema* and of an unreliable translation of it into Greek, which he himself tried to improve and to render in 'a simpler form' (i.e. in popular speech).

These comments are highly interesting and no doubt reflect reality, but they complicate the issue because, as previously mentioned, the *Hypomnema* must have been composed before 1540, although the earliest manuscripts date from 1599. We might suggest that by the word 'corrected' the author means rendering the text in popular speech. The question must remain open pending an examination of this new manuscript of the *Hypomnema* and, even more, research into the Georgian manuscript tradition of the history of the Portaitissa. The

---

[22] Archim. Vladimir, *Sistematicheskoe opisanie rukopisei Moskovskoi Sinodal'noi (Patriarshei) Biblioteki I. Rukopisi grecheskiia* (Moscow, 1894), 603–4.
[23] B. Fonkich and F. Poljakov, *Grecheskie rukopisi Moskovskoi Sinodal'noi Biblioteki. Paleograficheskie, kodikologicheskie i bibliograficheskie dopolnenia k katalogu archimandrita Vladimira (Filantropova)* (Moscow, 1993), 132.
[24] Steppan, 'Überlegungen zur Ikone der Panhagia Portaitissa', 37–8.
[25] Bury, 'Iveron and Our Lady', 77.
[26] The manuscript is uncatalogued. It has been numbered and described by monk Theologos, librarian of Iveron monastery, to whom I am most grateful for this information.

comment by L. Evseeva and M. Shvedova that the Georgian narrative on the icon dates from the thirteenth century is based on nineteenth-century Russian bibliography and is unpersuasive.[27]

A considerable period of time, about five centuries, also separates the appearance of the Portaitissa in the monastery from the earliest Greek hymnographical text devoted to her. A kanon bearing the acrostic 'Γαβριὴλ θύτης', transmitted in a seventeenth-century manuscript and formerly attributed to the celebrated tenth-century hymnographer Gabriel, has been proved to be a much later work, composed by a hymnographer of the same name, presumably a seventeenth-century Athonite hieromonachos.[28] We do not know the date of composition of an unpublished *akolouthia* relating to the Portaitissa which is transmitted in a manuscript in Iveron copied in the first half of the sixteenth century. In fact this is not an *akolouthia* with hymnographical texts but the 'Τυπικὸν τῆς ἀγρυπνίας' (Typikon of the Vigil), which was celebrated after the transfer of the icon from the parekklesion to the katholikon of the monastery in specific circumstances (e.g. drought) and the 'Τυπικὸν τῆς λιτανείας' (Typikon of the litany) which followed. It does not contain any hymnographical text specifically composed for the Portaitissa icon but has associations with the well-known paracletic kanon to the Theotokos.[29]

The story of the miraculous arrival of the icon at Iveron is also included in another text, particularly noteworthy for its scholarly and rhetorical qualities, whose style suggests that it was written in the Byzantine era. This is an unpublished *Hypomnema* (as it too is headed) on the Portaitissa icon. In fact it is not a narrative but a panegyric composed to be read during the *akolouthia* preceding the litany of the icon on 16 August, the day following the feast of the Dormition, which is also the official feast day of the Iveron monastery, when the icon was taken in procession to the katholikon. The text is transmitted in one unique manuscript, copied in Iveron in 1540 by the celebrated scholar and author, the monk Pachomios Rousanos.[30]

In this *Hypomnema*, or rather panegyric, the anonymous author deliberately ignores the legend of the settlement of Athos by monks in the reign of Constantine the Great, the arrival of Peter the Athonite and the patridographic texts (texts related to the *Patria*) on the foundation of Iveron monastery. It begins with a historical reference to the iconoclast emperors from Leo III the Isaurian to Theophilos and continues with the celebrated narrative of the icon and a

---

[27] L. Evseeva and M. Shvedova, 'Afonskiie spiski Bogomateri 'Portaitissy' i problema podobiia v ikonopisi', in A. Lidov (ed.), *Chudotvornaia ikona v Vizantii i Drevnei Rusi* (Moscow, 1996), 346–7 n. 1. I was unable to refer to the recent book by Timothy Gabashvili, *Pilgrimage to Mount Athos, Constantinople and Jerusalem, 1755–1759*, translated and annotated by M. Ebanoidze and J. Wilkinson, *Caucasus world. Georgian Studies on the Holy Land* I (Richmond, Surrey, 2001), which refers extensively to the journey of the Georgian bishop Timotheos to Iveron and to the narrative of the icon.

[28] P. Paschos, *Gabriel l'hymnographe. Kontakia et canons* (Paris and Athens, 1978–79), 81–7 and 262–77 (edition of the canon).

[29] MS. Iveron 847, fols 33–54. The text is headed: Ἀκολουθία συνταχθεῖσα ἐν τῇ σεβασμίᾳ μονῇ τῆς ὑπεραγίας Θεοτόκου τῆς Πορτιάτισσας καὶ ἐπικεκλημένης τῶν Ἰβήρων, ὅταν μέλλει γενέσθαι ἀγρυπνία εἰς τὴν Ὑπεραγίαν Θεοτόκον τὴν ὀξυτάτην βοήθειαν τοῦ γένους ἡμῶν τῶν χριστιανῶν, ἵνα ῥύσηται ἡμᾶς ἐξ ἐχθρῶν ὁρατῶν καὶ ἀοράτων καὶ δωρήσηται τῆς αὐτοῦ ἀγαθότητος τὸ ἔλεος.

[30] MS. Iveron 593, fols 223v–238r. The text is headed: Ὑπόμνημα περὶ τῆς τιμίας καὶ προσκυνητῆς εἰκόνος τῆς ὑπεράγνου δεσποίνης ἡμῶν Θεοτόκου τῆς ἐπικεκλημένης Πορταϊτίσσης, ὅπως τε κατήντησεν ἐν τῇ κατὰ τὸν

description of the miracles, exactly as in the other full texts. Instead of the history of the monastery, at the end of the text is a specific reference to its first abbot, John the Iberian, and his instruction by Athanasios the Athonite. Through the use of this ancient testimony, the author tries to demonstrate the special relationship between the two founders of Iveron and Lavra, and thus to promote the personality of John. With this aim he includes the following:

1. The virtually complete text of a document of 984, which we identify with a document of Athanasios the Athonite to Abbot John of Iveron dating from 984.[31] In this the founder of Lavra praises John, mentioning his evergetic activities in Constantinople on behalf of the Lavra monastery.
2. Extracts from the *Diatyposis* of the same Athanasios, which refers to the appointment of John as supervisor (*epitropos*) and spiritual leader of the monks of Lavra after his death.[32]

This text also, which is expressly stated to have been written in Iveron monastery, cannot in my opinion be attributed to the Byzantine era. The author is clearly aware of the full narrative text of the *Hypomnema*, whose earliest known manuscript, as previously stated, dates from 1599, and he uses it as a source, quoting many phrases verbatim. It therefore follows that a manuscript containing this text existed in the monastery before 1540.

All the evidence points to the anonymous author of the panegyric belonging to the circle of scholarly monks resident in the Iveron monastery at least during the 1530s. The only individual monk of whom we have definite knowledge at present is Pachomios Rousanos. Born in Zakynthos, he settled in the monastery no later than 1535 and remained there for about ten years until 1544, with intervals of absence when he undertook pastoral tours of duty outside Athos in the surrounding area.[33]

Following the bibliographical tradition created in the monastery in the previous decades[34] he undertook as his handiwork the task of copying manuscripts. By the year 1540 he had copied on the monastery's behalf at least ten manuscripts – some of considerable length – which are notable examples of his calligraphic skill.[35] He often inserts his own works into the texts he is copying; for example, the manuscript which contains the *Hypomnema* on the icon also includes two of his compositions, one of which is addressed to the monks of Iveron.[36]

After his lengthy residence in the monastery, Pachomios was thoroughly familiar with the contents of the library, as he often comments on the *anthivola* which he used, and he would certainly have been conversant with the Iveron archive which contained (as it still does today) the original document of Athanasios addressed to John of Iveron. He also knew the *Diatyposis*

Ἄθω σεβασμίᾳ μονῇ τῶν Ἰβήρων καὶ ὑπὸ τίνων αὕτη ἡ μονὴ ᾠκοδομήθη (*BHG*, 1070e). An annotated edition of the text by the present writer is in the course of preparation.

[31] Lefort *et al.*, *Actes d'Iveron I*, document no. 6, lines 1–21.
[32] Ph. Meyer (ed.), *Die Haupturkunden für die Geschichte der Athosklöster* (Leipzig, 1894; repr. Amsterdam, 1965), 124 line 27 – 125 line 7; 125 line 21 – 126 line 1; 127 lines 6–10; 128 lines 1–16.
[33] I. Karmiris, *Ο Παχώμιος Ρουσάνος και τα ανέκδοτα δογματικά και άλλα έργα αυτού νυν το πρώτον εκδιδόμενα* (Athens, 1935), 5–6.
[34] Chryssochoides, 'Το βιβλιογραφικό εργαστήριο της μονής Ιβήρων', 523–68.
[35] They are enumerated in the autograph catalogue which is inserted in MS. Iveron 593, fol. 301v (9 manuscripts). The catalogue edited by Lampros (*Κατάλογος* II (Cambridge, 1900), 179–80) should have included the present manuscript, which is omitted.
[36] Karmiris, *Παχώμιος Ρουσάνος*, 23 and 61–2.

of Athanasios the Athonite, as the testamentary documents of the saint (*Τυπικὸν* and *Διατύπωσις*) form the content of one of the manuscripts which he copied on behalf of the Iveron monastery.³⁷

The style and language of the text, which are not subjects for the present paper, and the very extensive use of passages from ancient Greek, hagiographic and patristic writings point to an author with considerable education and knowledge of ecclesiastical literature, and recall the literary manner and the grandiloquent, academic and often archaic style of Rousanos' writings. The most learned text devoted to the Portaitissa therefore does not belong to Byzantine literature, but should rather be considered a work of the fourth decade of the sixteenth century. It would probably not be over-bold to attribute it to the pen of Pachomios Rousanos himself and to include it in the catalogue of his writings for the first time. If this is so, all the Greek texts on the miraculous icon of the Portaitissa date from at least four centuries after its attested appearance at the very centre of worship in Iveron monastery.

The long interval separating the arrival of the icon in the monastery from the written narrative recording it is not unique to the Portaitissa. Exactly the same phenomenon occurs with another celebrated Athonite icon of the Virgin, the Theotokos Karyotissa (now known as the 'Ἄξιον ἐστί'), housed and venerated in the church of the Protaton at Karyes. Its dating is disputed: some consider it a late thirteenth-century work originating from the workshop of the painter of the Protaton, while others date it to the fourteenth century.³⁸ But apart from the question of dating, there is firm evidence for the existence of an icon in the Protaton with the appellation 'Μήτηρ Θεοῦ ἡ Καρεώτισσα' in the first decades of the thirteenth century.³⁹ Yet the narrative of the icon, which must certainly have been in circulation orally, as recently demonstrated, was only written down in the early sixteenth century by Serapheim, the Protos of Mt Athos, an active hieromonachos who composed *Lives* of Athonite contemporaries, making a systematic effort to prove them saints.⁴⁰

It is to just this time that a forged Athonite Typikon can be dated, the 'Νόμος καὶ Τύπος τοῦ ἁγίου ὄρους καὶ τοῦ Πρωτάτου', otherwise known as the 'Τυπικὸν τοῦ Μανουὴλ Β΄ Παλαιολόγου τοῦ 1394', as well as apocryphal compilations of documents of an administrative nature. These documents and the miraculous narrative of the Protaton icon were concocted, recorded or recollected from the past for the purposes of bolstering the declining institution of the Protos – in other words to serve the ideological and jurisdictional requirements of the central administration of Athos, based in the Protaton.⁴¹

As we have suggested above, this was also the period when the *Patria* of Mt Athos made their appearance. These effectively rewrote the history of the Mountain and of its monasteries, as the

---

37 MS. Iveron 754 (Lampros, *Κατάλογος* II, 179). The manuscript does not have a bibliographical note, but personal observation indicates that it is the work of Pachomios Rousanos.
38 I. Tavlakis, 'Ἡ Παναγία Ἄξιον Ἐστίν. Ἡ εικόνα', in *Τὸ Ἄξιον Ἐστίν, Παναγία ἡ Καρυώτισσα, ἡ ἐφέστια εικόνα τοῦ Πρωτάτου* (Mt Athos, 1999), 22–3 (considering it a product of the workshop of the painter of the Protaton). E. Tsigaridas, 'Ἡ εικόνα 'Ἄξιον Ἐστίν' τοῦ Πρωτάτου καὶ ἡ Παναγία Κυκκώτισσα', in *Πρακτικά Συνεδρίου, Ἡ Ἱερά Μονή Κύκκου στη βυζαντινή καὶ μεταβυζαντινή ἀρχαιολογία καί τέχνη* (Nicosia, 2001), 185–7 (dating it to the second half of the 14th c.).
39 S. Kissas, 'Dve Domentijanove beleske o Protatonu', *Hilandarski Zbornik* 6 (1986), 54.
40 K. Chryssochoides, 'Παραδόσεις καὶ πραγματικότητες στὸ Ἅγιον Ὅρος στὰ τέλη τοῦ ΙΕ΄ καὶ στὶς ἀρχές τοῦ ΙϚ΄ αἰώνα', in *Ὁ Ἄθως στοὺς 14ο – 16ο αἰώνες* (*Ἀθωνικά Σύμμεικτα*, 4) (Athens, 1997), 11–21.
41 Ibid., 99–108, 115–18.

monks required a history which would display a lengthy tradition, celebrated founders and miraculous icons with a glorious past; historical inaccuracies and blatant chronological inconsistencies and contradictions were of no great significance. The main aim was to confront the crisis and the decline which had emerged since the Ottoman occupation in the fifteenth century, so that the holy site could rediscover its past glory and prestige in the world of eastern Christianity.

This new legendary history traces the foundation of the monasteries back to the days of Constantine the Great, Theodosios and Pulcheria. Partly factual, but mainly imaginary foundation chronicles are here interwoven with old and new tales of the miraculous icons which had been circulating orally, perhaps for centuries. Their consistent aim is to glorify the monastic foundations, and it is to this branch of patridographic writing that the narrative of the Iveron Portaitissa, at any rate in its Greek written version, belongs.

These sixteenth-century patridographic texts give a prominent place to promoting the Theotokos as the protector, guardian and spiritual owner of the Athonite peninsula. We know that immediately after the arrival of a small group of anchorites on Athos, the Theotokos cult came to the fore, as the church common to all the inhabitants of Athos, the Protaton, which must have been functioning in the late ninth century, was dedicated to her from the time of its foundation. She is also the dedicatee of the katholika of the three great koinobia (Lavra, Iveron and Vatopedi) founded in the tenth century.

In the eleventh century, the author of the *Life of Peter the Athonite*, the first Athonite ascetic of the eighth–ninth century, witnessed the rising glory of Athos and made the Theotokos appear to the saint in a dream to foretell the radiant future of the Holy Mountain.[42] As the fame of the area grew, the Virgin's prophecy to Peter was extracted from the *Life* and, notably during Athos' fourteenth-century efflorescence, turned into an independent text entitled 'Ἐκ τοῦ βίου Πέτρου τοῦ Ἀθωνίτου'. This was copied many times and exploited by celebrated Athonite intellectuals such as Gregory Palamas in order to authenticate the Theotokos' prophecy.[43]

For the flourishing Athonites of the Byzantine era this modest, rather unpretentious tradition provided sufficient authority for the prosperity and glory of their holy site. The prophecy was of course included in the texts of the *Patria of the Holy Mountain*, but it could not bring consolation to the inhabitants of the Mountain in the immediate post-Byzantine period. Orally at first no doubt, it was remoulded and transformed into a legendary historical narrative incorporated within the patridographic cycle, which demanded the presence of the Theotokos herself on Athos to convert the idolatrous natives to Christianity and also an express declaration by her Son and Lord that the area should be exclusively assigned to her.[44] This declaration was supposedly ratified later by the first earthly Christian Lord, Constantine the Great, who 'called Athos the garden of the Theotokos and ordained that the mountain should everywhere be

---

[42] *The Life of Peter the Athonite*, ed. K. Lake, *The Early Days of Monasticism on Mount Athos* (Oxford, 1909), 25. See also D. Papachryssanthou, 'La vie ancienne de saint Pierre l'Athonite. Date, composition et valeur historique', *AnBoll* 92 (1974), 40–1.

[43] Papachryssanthou, 'La vie ancienne de saint Pierre l'Athonite', 20–1. Gregory Palamas, Λόγος εἰς τὸν θαυμαστὸν καὶ ἰσάγγελον βίον τοῦ ὁσίου ... Πέτρου τοῦ ἐν τῷ ἁγίῳ ὄρει τοῦ Ἄθω ἀσκήσαντος, *PG* 150, 1005 (*BHG*, 1506). Lampros, 'Τὰ Πάτρια', 135–7.

[44] Lampros, 'Τὰ Πάτρια', 124 line 20 – 126 line 2.

called holy' (περιβόλιον τῆς Θεοτόκου ἐπωνόμασε καὶ τὸ ὄρος προστάξας πανταχόθεν λέγεσθαι ἅγιον)⁴⁵ – an audacious statement aimed at launching the hopes of a revival of the monastic community and at restoring glory to the sacred space, which now existed in the new reality of an alien religious state.

The description of Athos as 'the garden of the Virgin', in widespread use up to the present day, has its origins at the dawn of the sixteenth century. And the icons of the Theotokos, with the miraculous narratives which we can trace in writings of the same period, are the flowers of that garden.

---

⁴⁵ Ibid., 127 lines 7–12.

11.1 Mt Athos, Holy Monastery of Iveron.
Icon of the Virgin 'Portaitissa'
(source: Holy Monastery of Iveron)

Part III

Female authority and devotion

12

The empress and the Virgin in early Byzantium: piety, authority and devotion*

Liz James

It has been said that empresses from Pulcheria and Eudokia to Sophia displayed a 'persistent devotion' to the cult of the Virgin.[1] How true was this? Did the cult of the Virgin have a special adherence among empresses? Did a special bond between the Virgin and the empress exist? Such questions are both relevant to the issue of female devotion and authority and perhaps contribute, albeit obliquely, to the debate about the relationship between women and icons.

In this context, the fifth-century empress Pulcheria is the case study par excellence. Pulcheria's lifestyle as a pious virgin has been described as 'infused with devotion to Mary' and, indeed, designed to emulate the Virgin. She has been seen as demonstrating a concentrated patronage of the Virgin, especially in her foundation of the three great Marian shrines of Constantinople: the Blachernai, Chalkoprateia and Hodegon. She is interpreted as claiming Marian dignity in order to add 'a potent element' to her sacral *basileia*.[2] These elements together – her apparent devotion to the cult of the Virgin, her status as virgin and her assimilation of the Virgin into imperial ceremony – have been seen as offering her a public arena for involvement in government and power.[3] Indeed, it has even been suggested that the rise of the Virgin depended on social dynamics associated with Pulcheria.[4]

Nevertheless, the evidence for these claims is not clear-cut. What contemporary sources record is that Pulcheria dedicated herself and her sisters to perpetual virginity at the start of her brother's reign, dedicating an inscribed altar in Hagia Sophia as a perpetual reminder of this act.[5] Her robe was accepted as an altar cloth in Hagia Sophia, her image placed above the altar and she was permitted to receive communion in the sanctuary, hitherto barred to women.[6] Patriarch Nestorios removed her portrait from above the altar in Hagia Sophia and her robe from the altar, and refused her entry to the sanctuary to receive communion. When Pulcheria

---

* The original title of my paper read at the Symposium was: 'Adorned with piety: authority, devotion and the empress in early Byzantium'.
[1] By, among others, J. Herrin, 'In Search of Byzantine Women: Three Avenues of Approach', in A. M. Cameron and A. Kuhrt (eds), *Images of Women in Antiquity* (London, 1983), 183. It is a view that has become in some ways a truism in scholarly literature. See, for example, L. Garland, *Byzantine Empresses. Women and Power in Byzantium AD 527–1204* (London, 1999), 96.
[2] By K. Holum, *Theodosian Empresses. Women and Imperial Domination in Late Antiquity* (Berkeley, 1982), 145.
[3] See ibid., esp. ch. 5. V. Limberis, *Divine Heiress. The Virgin Mary and the Creation of Christian Constantinople* (London, 1994), esp. ch. 3. J. Herrin, 'The Imperial Feminine in Byzantium', *Past and Present* 169 (2000), 3–35, esp. 12–19. L. James, *Empresses and Power in Early Byzantium* (Leicester, 2001), 153–4.
[4] As suggested by Limberis, *Divine Heiress*. Herrin, 'Imperial Feminine', suggests that the 5th-c. cult of the Virgin was a result of imperial, specifically female, impetus.
[5] Sozomenos, *H.E.*, 9.1.3–4, ed. J. Bidez and G. C. Hansen, *Kirchengeschichte* (Berlin, 1960).
[6] *Lettre à Cosme*, 5–7, trans. F. Nau, *PO* 13 (1919), 278.

insisted, with the claim, 'Have I not given birth to God?', Nestorios retorted 'You have given birth to Satan' and expelled her.[7] He refused to honour her as 'bride of Christ' in his public prayers for the imperial family because she had been involved in adulterous relations with various (one source suggests seven) men.[8] As a result of this and Nestorios' opposition to the title 'Theotokos' for the Virgin, Pulcheria engineered Nestorios' exile via the Council of Ephesus in 431.

These disparate elements have been woven together to present a narrative in which Pulcheria, as a pious virgin, 'could not resist the Mariology of contemporary preaching' which encouraged virgins to imitate Mary's purity and faith, and used her devotion to the Virgin to establish a symbolic role in the imperial family. She adopted the Virgin as the divine figure whose representative she was on earth and from whom she drew her earthly authority. She established Mary as her heavenly counterpart. In this context, her claim to have given birth to God is significant, for it is interpreted as a claim for Marian dignity and power and a reflection of actual Late Roman Marian ritual.[9] In this model, Nestorios' downfall is, in part, a result of challenging the conceptual basis of Pulcheria's standing.[10] Pulcheria, her power and the Virgin are interdependent.

Yet this is not what the texts say. There is no evidence of Pulcheria's response to contemporary preaching on the Virgin – preaching which did not aim to extol women but only to rid them of the curse of Eve.[11] A dedication to perpetual virginity in the fifth century was not an act that automatically associated a virgin with Mary; rather, such women were 'brides of Christ'.[12] Nor has any explanation been offered for why Pulcheria should have adopted the Virgin, who was not a particularly significant figure in Constantinople in the early fifth century, as her patron. It is perhaps Pulcheria's claim to be 'bride of Christ' rather than to have 'given birth to God' that offers an alternative scenario.[13] Rather than adopting and inventing a new female role model, it is conceivable that Pulcheria sought to associate herself with the most significant figure in Christian doctrine, Christ himself. She made her vows to Christ in a church dedicated to him as Holy Wisdom, and dedicated an altar there (to him?) at the same time. Her robe was

---

[7] Ibid., 8.
[8] *Bazaar of Herakleides*, 1.3, tr. G. R. Driver and L. Hodgson (Oxford, 1925), 96–7. Both the *Bazaar* and the late 6th-c. Syriac account of Barhadbeshabba (*H.E.*, 27, tr. F. Nau, *PO* 9 (1913), 564–5) attack Pulcheria for unchastity, as indeed does the *Epitome* of Theodore Lector. The *Souda* Lexicon (ed. A. Adler, *Suidae Lexicon* (Leipzig, 1928–1938), s.v. 'Pulcheria') says that Pulcheria hated Nestorios because he accused her of indecent behaviour with her brother.
[9] K. Cooper, 'Contesting the Nativity: Wives, Virgins, and Pulcheria's *Imitatio Mariae*', *Scottish Journal of Religious Studies* 19 (1998), 31–43.
[10] J. A. McGuckin, *St Cyril of Alexandria. The Christological Controversy. Its History, Theology and Texts* (Brill, 1994), sees the hand of Pulcheria behind events at Ephesus. See, for example, 40–1, the role of Pulcheria in moving the Council to Ephesus; 90, her lobbying of Theodosios. While these are plausible scenarios, there is little evidence besides plausibility to support them.
[11] Holum, *Theodosian Empresses*, 141. Holum suggests that Atticus' lost treatise *On Faith and Virginity*, addressed to the three daughters of Arkadios, connected faith and virginity specifically with the Virgin Mary Theotokos as archetypal virgin (ibid., 139).
[12] P. Brown, *The Body and Society* (London, 1988), 259–64, and esp. 274–6.
[13] Her reported claim to have 'given birth to Christ' comes in the Syriac *Letter of Kosmas*, a text whose date is not certain and whose authorship is unclear. In contrast, it is Nestorios' own account, preserved only in Syriac in the *Bazaar of Herakleides*, that says that the patriarch refused to honour her as 'bride of Christ'.

used as an altar cloth on his altar and her picture hung above it, both offering a perpetual reminder of her special bond with him. In taking Eucharist in the sanctuary, she entered into communion with Christ in a unique and distinctive context. 'Bride of Christ' suggests a very different relationship both with Christ himself and with the Virgin.[14] As Cooper has suggested, Pulcheria was well aware of the significance of the emperor being Christ's regent on earth. Rather than taking the Virgin, who was not a particularly significant figure at this time, as her divine counterpart, why not try to establish her own 'special relationship' with Christ? In underpinning Pulcheria's claims to imperial credibility and serving as an assertion of her piety and devotion, Christ, her 'husband', was surely a safer bet than his mother.

In this reading, any involvement Pulcheria might have had with the Council of Ephesus reflects a conflict with Nestorios over her own prestige and authority, which is what the written sources, with their stresses on the personalized nature of the dispute between the two, actually tell us. They do not tell us that Pulcheria and Nestorios were in dispute over the term 'Theotokos'.[15] Indeed, it has been well suggested that the Theotokos conflict had far more to do with the struggle for supremacy between the sees of Constantinople and Alexandria.[16]

As for Pulcheria's foundations of the three major Constantinopolitan shrines of the Virgin, these too are problematic.[17] Cyril Mango has shown that the textual attributions are late and misleading.[18] Contemporary written sources do not connect Pulcheria with shrines of the Virgin. Mango prefers Prokopios' ascription of the Blachernai church to Justin I. Indeed, in sixth- and seventh-century sources, Verina and Leo I, Justin I, Justinian I and Justin II, but not Pulcheria, are all described as founders of the Blachernai, and a text in the tenth-century *Menologion* of Basil II specifically ascribes it to Zeno, excluding any empress at all.[19] For the Chalkoprateia, the evidence linking it with Leo and Verina is more compelling than that linking it with Pulcheria.[20] The Hodegon does not appear in the historical record until the

---

[14] Space does not allow me to explore it here, but I wonder if her claim to have 'given birth to Christ' is also a claim that says more about the relationship between Pulcheria and Christ than Pulcheria and Mary. Indeed, Pulcheria's purported claims to be both mother and bride of Christ will be found echoed by later western female Christian mystics. See C. W. Bynum, *Holy Feast and Holy Fast* (Berkeley, 1987), e.g. 174–5 on the mystic marriages of Catherine of Alexandria and Catherine of Siena with Christ.

[15] Sokrates never mentions Pulcheria at any point in his history. Sozomenos has most about her, including the material on the dedication of her virginity and of her robe, but the last part of his history, covering 425–439, is lost. Marcellinus makes no mention of Pulcheria and the Virgin nor of Pulcheria as playing a role in the Nestorian crisis. Malalas makes no mention of her in this context, and nor does the *Chronicon Paschale*, though both contain other details about her. Evagrios ascribes the imperial role in the crisis to Theodosios. Theophanes, who has quite a lot on Pulcheria, including her influential role at court and her relics, does not mention her in the context of the Nestorian crisis. Philostorgios in Photios' *Epitome* says only that she directed the imperial rescripts. For some of the issues about the ways in which texts treat powerful women, see Cooper, 'Contesting the Nativity' and James, *Empresses and Power*, ch. 2.

[16] Holum, *Theodosian Empresses*, 152 and n. 27.

[17] Theodore Lector, *Epit.*, 363. Cf. also statements by Nikephoros Kallistos, *H.E.*, 14.2, 49 and 15.14. Though the evidence for this is late, scholars have tended to accept it uncritically: Holum, *Theodosian Empresses*, 142 n. 120.

[18] See C. Mango in the *Addenda* to the reprint of 'The Development of Constantinople as an Urban Centre', in his *Studies on Constantinople* (Aldershot, 1993), esp. 4, and also Mango, 'Blachernae Shrine', 61–76, and id., 'Theotokoupolis', 17–26.

[19] See W. Lackner, 'Ein byzantinisches Marienmirakel', *Byzantina* 13 (1985), 835–60. My thanks to Nadine Schibille.

[20] See Mango, 'Blachernae Shrine'.

ninth century.²¹ Pulcheria's association with relics of the Virgin – her icon painted by St Luke, her robe and her girdle – is equally complicated. Again, as with the churches, the accounts are late or preserved only in fourteenth-century sources, posing similar questions of authenticity.²²

Thus a relationship between Pulcheria and the Virgin is highly dubious, and Pulcheria's role in promoting the cult of the Virgin limited or even potentially non-existent. More general arguments about female imperial devotion to the Virgin tend to derive from a belief in empresses imitating the example of Pulcheria but, again, evidence of such a devotion is very limited.

Leo and Verina, if anyone, appear to be the key figures in the foundation of the Blachernai and the Chalkoprateia and the discovery of the Virgin's robe. As these events post-date the Council of Ephesus, they may reflect a growing cult of the Virgin Theotokos. Not only that, both Leo and Verina, originally raised to power by the Arian Aspar, may well have felt the need to establish their own credentials for orthodoxy.²³ In this context, it is worth remembering that Verina is supposed to have finished the church of St Irene in the Perama, begun in the reign of Pulcheria. Leo and Verina are recorded as writing on the costly chest in which they housed the Virgin's robe, 'by showing reverence here to the Theotokos, they secured the power of their *basileia*'.²⁴ Here, if anywhere, is the evidence of an emperor and an empress adding to their power through the Virgin. Otherwise the only evidence for a persistent devotion to the Virgin on the part of empresses is the prayer ascribed to the empress Sophia in Corippus' poem to Justin II. This prayer, however, serves as a pendant to Justin's prayer to Christ, so the Virgin appears to be a logical choice. In this context, we should note that donations to the Blachernai and Chalkoprateia churches are recorded in Justin's name alone.²⁵

It is not as if empresses during the fifth to eighth centuries were not involved in religious activities. Most played a part in church building, and the pattern of church dedications may thus offer some insights into religious devotion.²⁶ These indicate that the Virgin actually had a very minor role in the dedications of religious foundations by imperial women. In Constantinople, apart from the three churches that she is reputed to have dedicated to the Virgin, Pulcheria certainly built the church of St Laurence for the relics of that saint, and the church of

---

²¹ See Angelidi, 'Un texte patriographique', 113–49, who sees the link with Pulcheria as being made in the 12th c.
²² By Nikephoros Kallistos again. Both R. Wolff, 'Footnote to an Incident of the Latin Occupation of Constantinople: The Church and the Icon of the Hodegetria', *Traditio* 6 (1948), 323 and Ch. Walter, 'Iconographical Considerations', in J. A. Munitiz, J. Chrysostomides, E. Harvalia-Crook and Ch. Dendrinos (eds), *The Letter of the Three Patriarchs to the Emperor Theophilos and Related Texts* (Camberley, 1997), iv, suggests that it is odd that the story of the icon of the Virgin painted by St Luke and sent by Eudokia to Pulcheria is not mentioned elsewhere – in the iconophile Theophanes, for example. See also Angelidi, 'Un texte patriographique', 122–3.
²³ Mango, 'Blachernae Shrine', makes this case for Leo.
²⁴ A. Wenger, 'Notes inédites sur les empereurs Théodose I, Arcadius, Théodose II, Léon I', *REB* 10 (1952), 54–9. Holum, *Theodosian Empresses*, 227.
²⁵ Corippus, *In Laudem Iustini Augusti Minoris*, ed. and tr. A. M. Cameron (London, 1976), II.46–70. See A. M. Cameron, 'The Theotokos in Sixth-Century Constantinople: A City Finds its Symbol', *JThSt* 29 (1978), 79–108, esp. 82–5. The Virgin appears on weights from the reign of Justin (ibid., 97. Mango, 'Theotokoupolis', 21) and on seals from the reign of Maurice. Heraklios appropriates the Virgin as almost a warrior-goddess. For Justin's donations, see M. Jugie, 'L'église de Chalcoprateia et le culte de la ceinture de la Sainte Vierge à Constantinople', *EO* 16 (1913), 308. Also Janin, *Églises CP*, 169, 237.
²⁶ For church building as an imperial requirement, see L. Brubaker, 'Memories of Helena: Patterns in Imperial Female Matronage in the Fourth and Fifth Centuries', in L. James (ed.), *Women, Men and Eunuchs. Gender in Byzantium* (London, 1997), 52–75. James, *Empresses and Power*, ch. 9.

the Forty Martyrs for their relics, and began the church of the Prophet Isaiah and the chapel of St Stephen.[27] Together with Marcian, she also built the churches of St Menas and of St Mokios. Eudokia was responsible for the first church of St Polyeuktos in Constantinople and for foundations throughout the Holy Land, including the church of St Stephen and the church of St Peter in Jerusalem.[28] Verina and Leo are credited with building the Blachernai and the Chalkoprateia,[29] and with finishing the church of St Irene of Perama.[30] Ariadne, with Zeno, her first husband, founded the church of Elijah, and with Anastasios, her second, the church of St Euphemia at Pera, of St Stephen in Constantiniae, and of the Forty Martyrs at the Chalke.[31] Euphemia, the wife of Justin I, built the church and monastery of the Augusta, where she chose to be buried.[32] The church of St Panteleemon was reputedly built by Theodora, wife of Justinian I,[33] and Mango has argued convincingly for her major role in the founding of the church of Sts Sergios and Bakchos.[34] She is also linked with Justinian in Hagia Sophia. Sophia and Justin built churches dedicated to, among others, Sts Kosmas and Damianos, St Tryphon and St Thomas.[35] Anastasia and Tiberios, reigning after Justin, founded a church dedicated to the Forty Martyrs.[36] Constantina, wife of Maurice, Tiberios' heir, built St Paul in the Palace.[37] Anna, so-called wife of Leo III, founded St Anne's Monastery and the Spoudes monastery.[38] Irene, the first wife of Constantine V, founded the church of Anastasios the Persian and churches dedicated to Sts Euphemia and Euphrosyne.[39] Maria, first wife of Constantine VI, founded the monastery 'To Despoinon', and his second wife, Theodote, the monastery of St

---

[27] For Pulcheria's buildings in Constantinople, both religious and secular, see G. Dagron, *Naissance d'une capitale* (Paris, 1974), 97, 400–1. C. Mango, *Le développement urbain de Constantinople* (Paris, 1990), 52.

[28] *Greek Anthology*, I.105. For Eudokia's buildings in the Holy Land, see E. D. Hunt, *Holy Land Pilgrimage in the Later Roman Empire, AD 312–460* (Oxford, 1982), 239–42.

[29] C. Mango, 'The Chalkoprateia Annunciation and the Pre-Eternal Logos', *DChAE* 17 (1993/4), 165–70. Wenger, 'Notes inédites', 47–59. Text partially tr. in Mango, *Art of the Byz. Empire*, 34–5. Also see Jugie, 'L'église de Chalcoprateia', 308.

[30] Janin, *Églises CP*, 106.

[31] *Patria Constantinopoleos*, ed. T. Preger, *Scriptores Originum Constantinopolitanarum* (Leipzig, 1907), III.236–7 (Forty Martyrs, Stephen), 239–40 (Elijah, Euphemia). Janin, *Églises CP*, 126 (Euphemia), 137 (Elijah), 475 (Stephen), 485 (Forty Martyrs).

[32] *Patria Constantinopoleos*, III.273. Janin, *Églises CP*, 54. The *Parastaseis Syntomoi Chronikai*, ed. and tr. in A. M. Cameron et al. (eds.), *Constantinople in the Early Eighth Century* (Leiden, 1984), ch. 37, also credits her with the church of St Euphemia, but this may simply be by the association of names. This church is also linked to Eudokia and Galla Placidia: see Janin, *Églises CP*, 124.

[33] *Patria Constantinopoleos*, III.265. A. van Millingen, *Byzantine Constantinople. The Walls of the City and Adjoining Historical Sites* (London, 1899), 300.

[34] C. Mango, 'The Church of Saints Sergius and Bacchus at Constantinople and the Alleged Tradition of Octagonal Palace Churches', *JÖB* 21 (1972), 189–93. Id., 'The Church of Sts. Sergius and Bacchus Once Again', *BZ* 68 (1975), 385–92.

[35] Kosmas and Damianos: *Greek Anthology*, I.105. Tryphon: Pseudo-Kodinos, *PG* 157, 580B. Janin, *Églises CP*, 489. Thomas: Janin, *Églises CP*, 249.

[36] *Patria Constantinopoleos*, III.234. Janin, *Églises CP*, 483.

[37] Pope Gregory, *Epistle* 4, 30, *PL* 77, 701A. Janin, *Églises CP*, 393.

[38] St Anne's: *Patria Constantinopoleos*, III.251. Janin, *Églises CP*, 38. Spoudes: *Patria Constantinopoleos*, III.251. Janin, *Églises CP*, 470.

[39] Anastasius: *Patria Constantinopoleos*, III.219. Janin, *Églises CP*, 27. Euphemia: Theophanes, *Chronographia*, ed. C. de Boor (Leipzig, 1883–1885), tr. C. Mango and R. Scott, *The Chronicle of Theophanes Confessor: Byzantine and Near Eastern History AD 284–813* (Oxford, 1997), AM 6258. Janin, *Églises CP*, 121. Euphrosyne: *Patria Constantinopoleos*, III.243. Janin, *Églises CP*, 130–1.

Theodote.⁴⁰ Irene and Constantine founded the church of St Anastasios the Persian, and Irene built the monastery of Euphrosyne and rebuilt the church of the Virgin Pege, damaged in an earthquake.⁴¹ This is not an overwhelming patronage of or devotion to the Virgin in terms of church building by imperial women. Significantly as well, the sources for many of these attributions are not always contemporary, suggesting that there was no wide-scale rewriting-in of female imperial dedications to the Virgin. The same is true of relic-collecting: only the Virgin's robe features in an imperial feminine connection.⁴²

Neither building activity nor relic collection suggests a 'persistent devotion' to the cult of the Virgin on the part of any of these empresses, at least not in the public arena. Rather, there seems to be a more wide-ranging religious sensibility, covering a large number of saints, a sensibility that perhaps related to specific temporal circumstances and needs. Different relics at different times carried different significances.⁴³ The choices of saints and relics by different empresses were not random but related to particular circumstances. For example, in the case of Pulcheria and the rediscovery of the Forty Martyrs, the timing of this discovery is suggestive. According to Sozomenos, the Forty Martyrs were found in 434–446.⁴⁴ In *c.* 439 Pulcheria's rival, the empress Eudokia, returned from Jerusalem in a blaze of holiness after her pilgrimage there, offering a challenge to Pulcheria's piety and standing. The *Chronicon Paschale*, however, says that the relics were recovered in 451, which, coincidentally, was the year in which Pulcheria and Marcian were crowned.⁴⁵ This too would be an auspicious moment for the revelation of divine favour to Pulcheria, serving to underline her piety. It seems hard to believe that such timings were accidental. What the broader political significance of the Forty Martyrs might have been for Pulcheria – why she discovered them, rather than, say, Sergios and Bakchos – is unclear, but it seems plausible that the Forty themselves were of significance at this time to this empress. It may be important that the *Life of Peter the Iberian* records the relics of the Forty as being in the martyrion next to the church of the Ascension on the Mount of Olives, consecrated in the presence of Eudokia by Melania, who deposited the relics of St Stephen at the same time.⁴⁶ Thus the rediscovery of the Forty might potentially be construed as a further challenge to Eudokia's piety.

Rather than a 'special relationship' between empresses and the Virgin, the evidence of actual religious patronage suggests a more general form of religious piety. Indeed, it is emperors from Leo I onwards who display a more persistent devotion to the Virgin, in church buildings and dedications and even on imperial seals.⁴⁷ It was not until the sixth century that the Virgin held

---

⁴⁰ Virgin Pege: *Patria Constantinopoleos*, III.260. Janin, *Églises CP*, 223–4. Theodote: Janin, *Églises CP*, 146. 'Despoinon': Janin, *Églises CP*, 88.
⁴¹ For Irene, see R. Cormack, 'The Arts During the Age of Iconoclasm', in A. A. M. Bryer and J. Herrin (eds), *Iconoclasm* (Birmingham, 1977), 4.
⁴² For details of relic-gathering, see L. James, 'Bearing Gifts from the East: Imperial Relic-Hunters Abroad', in A. Eastmond (ed.), *Eastern Approaches to Byzantium* (Aldershot, 2000), 119–32.
⁴³ As I. Kalavrezou, 'Helping Hands for the Empire: Imperial Ceremonies and the Cult of Relics at the Byzantine Court', in H. Maguire (ed.), *Byzantine Court Culture from 829 to 1204* (Washington, DC, 1997), 53–80, illustrates.
⁴⁴ Sozomenos, *H.E.*, IX.2. For Eudokia's triumphant progress to and from the Holy Land and her building activities, see Sokrates, *Ecclesiastical History*, 7.47, ed. R. Hussey (Oxford, 1883).
⁴⁵ *CP*, yr. 451.
⁴⁶ *Vita* of Peter the Iberian, 37, in Hunt, *Holy Land Pilgrimage*, 232.
⁴⁷ See details in Mango, 'Theotokoupolis', 20–3, stressing the significance of Justinian's dedications to the Virgin.

the place scholars would like her to have occupied in the time of Pulcheria. By the ninth century, she was seen as the patron and protector of Constantinople. This is indeed the period when written sources begin to associate Pulcheria with the Virgin. As Christine Angelidi has well shown, this is more to do with the construction of Pulcheria as pious empress at this time than with fifth-century events.[48]

Why emperors rather than empresses? As the Virgin gained an increasingly significant and powerful position in public perceptions, it may have been too risky to associate the Virgin and the empress too closely. Byzantine imperial ideology does not seem to have had space for a queen of heaven paralleled on earth. Building a church was both a religious and a political act in Byzantium. Where you built, what you built, when you built it and whom you built it for were all significant. Eudokia's pilgrimages to and foundations in Jerusalem gained her a reputation for holiness and piety, an aura of being blessed and favoured by God, that may have outshone, briefly, Pulcheria's.[49] However, Eudokia's building work in Constantinople itself, the centre of imperial power, was limited, reflecting her position in relation to her husband. Pulcheria, on the other hand, based most of her patronage in Constantinople, where her buildings appeared as public monuments at the heart of empire.[50] Building empresses both gained in their lifetime and left behind a reputation for piety, virtue and orthodoxy. They did not also need a bridge to heaven via the Mother of God. Eudoxia, Eudokia and Pulcheria are all called 'most pious' by those authors whose faith had benefited from their building activities. Verina is another empress whose reputation as pious and faithful, 'beloved of God', indeed a second Helena, derives from her church-building activities.[51] The inscription inside Sts Sergios and Bakchos talks of 'God-crowned Theodora'.[52] These reputations enhanced the prestige and standing of an empress, acting as a form of symbolic capital. Piety in Byzantium equalled power and was an essential imperial virtue. To be perceived as possessing piety was a means of establishing status and authority, both useful tools for an empress. Building a church established an empress's piety in public. In building for the glory of God and the benefit of the subjects of the empire, both God's chosen emperor and his consort displayed their fitness to rule and sought to maintain harmonious relations with the deity who protected their empire. Building a church and dedicating it with relics was an act of piety but also one of power, about asserting the favour of God and the saints and placing oneself within the heavenly court.

In this context, if, as Kate Cooper has suggested, the contest over the title Theotokos in the reign of Theodosios II became a contest over who would mediate the power of Christ, the power of the Virgin was also a power requiring mediation.[53] Both the Virgin and the emperor

---

[48] For an important study and interpretation of the sources about Pulcheria, see Ch. Angelidi, 'De Aelia Pulcheria Augusta Eiusque Fortuna', *Diptycha* 5 (1991), 251–69 (in Greek; my thanks to Vassiliki Dimitropoulou for help with this article) and her *Pulcheria. La castità al potere (c. 399 – c. 455)* (Milan, 1998). Angelidi analyses how written sources create five versions of Pulcheria, including that of pious virgin and devotee of the Virgin, and how these roles were developed and changed over time.
[49] Hunt, *Holy Land Pilgrimage*, 439.
[50] Sozomenos, *H.E.*, IX.1 notes that it would take too long to describe all her buildings in the city.
[51] Mango, *Art of the Byz. Empire*, 34–5.
[52] Greek text in Van Millingen, *Churches*, 73, tr. by Mango, 'The Church of Saints Sergius and Bacchus at Constantinople', 190.
[53] Cooper, 'Contesting the Nativity', 42.

were bridges to Christ, mediating presences, his vice-regents on earth and in heaven. This left no place for the empress. It is notable that the Virgin is not shown dressed as an empress in Byzantine iconography, perhaps because this was too overt a link between earthly and heavenly powers, one that placed the empress in the heavenly hierarchy. The Virgin became too significant – too powerful and too potentially problematic – to associate with the empress alone. As patron of the city, if anyone, she needed to belong to the emperor. The empress's devotions were more general and less personal.

13

Female piety in context: understanding developments in private devotional practices*

Brigitte Pitarakis

'On account of Mary all women are blessed. No longer does the female stand accursed, for it has produced an offspring which surpasses even the angels in glory. Eve is fully healed.'[1] This passage from a homily on the Nativity of Christ by Proklos of Constantinople contains praise of women founded on their privileged bond with the Mother of God as second Eve. The purpose of this paper is to gather material evidence documenting this bond and subsequently to examine the broader issue of female piety in Byzantine society. Female piety is a topic which has received much scholarly attention in the past few years. The focus of this study, however, will be an aspect which has not been much investigated and which centres on private devotional practices. The study refers to individuals from the entire spectrum of Byzantine society, while the material consists mainly of metal objects of personal devotion which bear dedicatory inscriptions naming women or are described in written sources as belonging to women. These are the main categories of phylacteries from Early Christian times to the Middle Byzantine period. Instead of pilgrimage souvenirs marked with a specific message, I shall examine objects with polyvalent functions such as crosses, enkolpia of various kinds and cameos set in jewellery. As visual channels for proximity to God, these objects motivate a virtuous attitude and prayer. My purpose is not to contrast men and women in relation to their religious zeal, but to contextualize female piety by a functional approach to objects of devotion and religious iconography. Although the objects and their imagery are not gender-specific, their function and the context of their usage may be understood in terms of female ownership. Inscriptions accompanying objects of private devotion show that heavenly intercession is mainly asked for health and salvation. These are universal issues that are common to both genders. However, health and salvation also imply some important concerns that are specific to women. Fertility, successful procreation, and health of children and spouse are the key issues which will help us understand the relation of women to their objects of devotion and to religious imagery in general.

Objects of private devotion and female ownership

A gendered approach to metal objects of private devotion is difficult because of the limited number of objects that indicate the identity of their recipient. Many of them are universal

---

* I would like to thank Sharon Gerstel and John Nesbitt for their helpful suggestions and assistance in the preparation of this study. I am also grateful to Susan Boyd and Stephen Zwirn for allowing me access to the Dumbarton Oaks Collection.

[1] *PG* 65, 720B. N. Constas, *Proclus of Constantinople and the Cult of the Virgin in Late Antiquity, Homilies 1–5, Texts and Translations* (*Vigiliae Christianae Suppl.*, 66) (Leiden and Boston, 2003), 261 (Homily 5).

objects with standardized decoration intended for both genders and transferred from one gender to the other. Let us consider a few examples drawn from different periods. One of the earliest pieces of evidence for the use of a portion of the True Cross as a personal object of devotion concerns the death of Makrina, the sister of Gregory of Nyssa, at her convent in northern Cappadocia at the end of 379. While preparing the burial together with Gregory, a woman named Vetiana pulled a slender chain from around the neck of the deceased. On the chain hung an iron cross and a ring of the same material. This was Makrina's legacy, which Gregory decided to share with Vetiana. He kept the ring and gave the cross to the woman for her protection. Vetiana then told him that the bezel of his ring, engraved with a cross motif, was hollow and that it concealed a fragment of the wood of life. Makrina's reliquary ring thus became the property of her brother, while her pectoral cross remained in the possession of a female owner.[2] Another example can be drawn from the ninth-century *Vita* of Antony the Younger, in which we learn that the holy man entrusted his enkolpion to his sister, a nun, as a sign of his intention to renounce the world.[3] The will of the nun Maria, widow of Symbatios Pakourianos (1099) is a further important source for the study of female ownership of objects of private devotion. The list of her objects of devotion includes two enkolpia: one gold, containing a piece of the True Cross together with twenty-four fragments of relics; and the other with two closing wings, also holding a fragment of the True Cross. Maria bequeaths these enkolpia to two monks, named Saba and Basil.[4]

Examination of mass-produced artefacts such as rings and crosses shows that metal workshops had an output intended for a female clientele. Inscriptions accompanying these objects include standard formulae indicating both genders, while iconographic patterns do not seem to be gender-specific. A silver ring in the Museo Correr, Venice, decorated with the nielloed bust figure of Christ Pantokrator, bears a standard invocatory formula addressed to Christ by a woman named Eudokia: 'Lord help thy servant Eudokia (Κ(ύρι)ε βοήθι τῖς δ(ού)λι‹ς› σου Ἐβδοκήας).'[5] A sixth/seventh-century bronze ring in the Benaki Museum in Athens, decorated with the nielloed image of St George orans in military garb, bears the dedicatory inscription of a woman named Anastasia invoking the help of the saint (Ἅγιε Γεώργι(ε) βοήθ[ι] Ἀναστασίαν) (Plate 8, Fig. 13.1).[6] In the absence of a dedicatory inscription, nothing in the decoration of these objects preassigned them to a female owner. One of the largest categories of objects of private devotion used by both genders and all ages is represented by the mass-produced bronze pectoral reliquary crosses of the ninth to eleventh centuries. The most precious of these contained a fragment of the True Cross and bones of holy martyrs, while the several hundreds

---

[2] *PG* 46, 990. K. Corrigan, *The Life of Saint Macrina by Gregory, Bishop of Nyssa* (Toronto, 1989), 53–4. Grégoire de Nysse, *Vie de Sainte Macrine*, ed. P. Maraval (SC, 178) (Paris, 1971), 238–43 (ch. 30). See also L. Kötzsche-Breitenbruch, 'Zum Ring des Gregor von Nyssa', in *Tesserae. Festschrift für J. Engemann, JbAC* 18 (1991), 291–8.
[3] M. P. Vinson, 'Gender and Politics in the Post-Iconoclastic Period. The Lives of Antony the Younger, the Empress Theodora, and the Patriarch Ignatios', *Byz* 68 (1998), 473. For the Life and Conduct of St Antony the Younger, see A. Papadopoulos-Kerameus (ed.), in *Pravoslavnyi Palestinskii Sbornik* 19.3 (1907), 195 lines 10–14.
[4] J. Lefort, N. Oikonomidès, D. Papachryssanthou, V. Kravari and H. Métrévéli (eds), *Actes d'Iviron* II (*Archives de l'Athos*, XVI) (Paris, 1990), 179 line 29; 182 lines 56–7.
[5] A. Guillou, *Recueil des inscriptions grecques médiévales d'Italie* (Collection de l'École française de Rome, 222) (Rome, 1996), no. 61, 69.
[6] D. Papanikola-Bakirtzi (ed.), *Καθημερινή ζωή στο Βυζάντιο*, exh. cat., Thessaloniki, White Tower, October 2001 – January 2002 (Athens, 2002), no. 573, 438–9 (A. Drandakis).

of crosses in base metal probably held materials that were sanctified through contact with a primary relic. Bits of wood, pebbles, earth, pieces of cloth, residues of balsam, incense and fragrant substances are found among the remains of some of these crosses that have preserved their content. Discoveries from graves attest that pectoral reliquary crosses were used by men, women and children alike.[7] The iconography of these crosses includes representations of intercessory saints in orant attitude. St George is the most popular intercessor, followed by John, Peter, Archangel Michael and Stephen. Female saints are rarely attested on these crosses: I have only noted the figures of Paraskevi and Kyriaki, who are chosen to enhance the salvatory powers of the cross. These objects rarely bear personalized inscriptions. One example is the half of an eleventh-century reliquary cross found in Silistra, Bulgaria, decorated with the engraved figure of the Virgin orans. The inscription flanking the image identifies its recipient, a nun named Anna (Fig. 13.2).[8] A more precious version is a ninth- or tenth-century gold aniconic reliquary cross at Dumbarton Oaks. The cruciform inscription reads: 'Theotokos help Helen. Amen' (Θεοτόκε βοήθει Ἑλένης, Ἀμήν) (Fig. 13.3).[9] The small dimensions of this cross, which is only 2.5 cm high, might suggest that it was intended for a child. Its small suspension loop may originally have been sewn on to the clothing of a baby child for protection, as is common in present-day practice. Indeed, the chain that could slip into such a small loop would break very easily on the neck of an adult.

Piety is a collective phenomenon which has its roots in the family. A seventh-century bronze votive cross at Dumbarton Oaks bears a collective inscription that reads: 'Saint Thekla help Symionios, Synesios, Maria and Thekla' (Ἁγία Θέκλα, βοήθι Συμιονίου κ(αὶ) Συνεσίου καὶ Μαρία κ(αὶ) Θέκλα). The recipient of the invocation, St Thekla, is crudely sketched in *intaglio* in orant attitude at the top of the cross. The miracle-working saint was probably the privileged intercessor of the woman named Thekla and her family (Fig. 13.4).[10] Similarly, the iconography of imperial seals reveals devotional traditions that are specific to families. The Komnenoi, for instance, had a predilection for St George, while the Angeloi often chose the image of the Annunciation for their seals. However, the Mother of God remained the preferred device on seals issued by women.[11] Following the model of the Virgin, who obtained her intercessory

---

[7] B. Pitarakis, 'Les croix-reliquaires pectorales en bronze: recherches sur la production des objets métalliques à Byzance', PhD thesis, Université de Paris-I, Panthéon-Sorbonne, Paris, 1996, 37–40, 81–98, 134–5 (forthcoming in *Bibliothèque des CahArch*).

[8] G. Atanassov, 'Croix-encolpions proche-orientales de la région de la Dobroudja du Sud (Bulgarie)', in *Akten des XII. Internationalen Kongresses für Christliche Archäologie*, Bonn, 22–28 September 1991, *JbAC Ergänzungsband* 20.1 (Münster, 1995), 492, Fig. 5.4; 500, Pl. 59.5.

[9] M. C. Ross, *Catalogue of the Byzantine and Early Medieval Antiquities in the Dumbarton Oaks Collection* II (Washington, DC, 1965), no. 17, 22, Pl. XXII. Ross proposes a date in the 6th–7th c. for this cross. However, the epigraphic form of the Beta with an open loop, like a Latin capital R, rather points to the 9th–10th c., see N. Oikonomides, *A Collection of Dated Byzantine Lead Seals* (Washington, DC, 1986), 159.

[10] M. C. Ross, *Catalogue of the Byzantine and Early Medieval Antiquities in the Dumbarton Oaks Collection* I (Washington, DC, 1962), no. 67, 58, Pl. XL. For the anonymous *Life and Miracles* of St Thekla, see G. Dagron, *Vie et miracles de Sainte Thècle* (*Subsidia Hagiographica*, 62) (Brussels, 1978). In a recent study devoted to female pilgrimage, Alice-Mary Talbot has pointed out that the shrine of St Thekla near Seleukia on the southern coast of Asia Minor was very popular among women: A.-M. Talbot, 'Female Pilgrimage in Late Antiquity and the Byzantine Era', *Acta Byzantina Fennica*, n.s., 1 (2002), 77. See also S. Davis, *The Cult of Saint Thecla: A Tradition of Women's Piety in Late Antiquity* (Oxford, 2001).

[11] J.-C. Cheynet, 'Texte et image sur les sceaux byzantins', in N. Oikonomides (ed.), *Studies in Byzantine*

power from her role as Mother of God, women intercede for the protection of their family. The late ninth-century reliquary cross of Queen Khosrovanush of Georgia, decorated with a nielloed Crucifixion on the front, refers to the Queen and her two sons David and Bagrat, while the nielloed inscription of the reliquary cross of Queen Tamar, richly decorated with emeralds, rubies and pearls, and dated to the twelfth–thirteenth century, asks for protection for the king and for Queen Tamar.[12] In a similar tone, the dedicatory inscription on one of the reliquary boxes that Irene Doukaina Komnene offered to her convent of the Virgin Kecharitomene opens with the following words: 'The faith of the empress Irene gained protection for herself and her husband and children.'[13] On the other hand, in a poem written after the death of Maria Komnene, eldest daughter of Andronikos I, on behalf of her sorrowing husband, the Caesar John Dalassenos, we learn that John chose one of his deceased wife's pieces of gold jewellery, his favourite, to give to the Theotokos with prayers for their reunion in the afterlife.[14]

Devotional preferences of women in relation to their role as mothers and wives

In Byzantine society the essential goal of every marriage was procreation, and absence of procreation was a legal cause for divorce.[15] Written testimonies, especially miracle-stories from healing shrines, define childlessness as a shaming and disabling state, while women are considered solely responsible for sterility. In a society suffering from high infant mortality, a high morbidity rate among pregnant women, and a high proportion of women suffering from sterility, successful childbearing appears as the major concern conditioning devotional practices of women.[16] Images of the Virgin performed numerous miracles on behalf of women suffering from infertility.[17] Leo VI's fourth wife, Zoe Karbonopsina, became pregnant after wearing as a girdle a skein of silk that had been measured around an icon of the Virgin, called the Episkepsis, in the crypt of the church of Pege.[18] From the same anonymous tenth-century account we learn that Leo VI undertook a programme of embellishment of the crypt with fine mosaics and frescoes and that he restored the chapel of St Anne, whose cult also seems to be closely connected

---

Sigillography 4 (1995), 28–30. See also J. Cotsonis, 'Women and Sphragistic Iconography: A Means of Investigating Gender-Related Piety', in *Nineteenth Annual Byzantine Studies Conference, Abstracts of Papers* (Princeton, NJ, 1993), 59.

[12] N. Chichinadze, 'The True Cross Reliquaries of Medieval Georgia', *Studies in Iconography* 20 (1999), 29–30 and 34. A. Djavakhichvili and G. Abramichvili, *L'or et les émaux de Géorgie* (Paris, 1986), Fig. 86, 182–3.

[13] J. Thomas and A. Constantinides Hero (eds), *Byzantine Monastic Foundation Documents* II (Washington, DC, 2000), 714.

[14] S. P. Lampros, 'Ὁ Μαρκιανός κώδιξ 524', *NE* 8 (1911), no. 52, 21; discussed in L. Garland, '"The Eye of the Beholder": Byzantine Imperial Women and their Public Image from Zoe Porphyrogenita to Euphrosyne Kamaterissa Doukaina (1028–1203)', *Byz* 64 (1994), 286–7. For the role of women in the household, see A. P. Kazhdan, 'Women at Home', *DOP* 52 (1998), 10–13.

[15] G. Vikan, 'Art and Marriage in Early Byzantium', *DOP* 44 (1990), 154–5 n. 77.

[16] For a study focused on the attitude of Byzantine society towards newly born children, see M.-H. Congourdeau, 'Regards sur l'enfant nouveau-né à Byzance', *REB* 51 (1993), 161–76. See also A. Laiou, 'The Role of Women in Byzantine Society', *JÖB* 31.1 (1981), 236 (repr. in ead., *Gender, Society and Economic Life in Byzantium* (London, 1992), I).

[17] Several examples are documented in J. Herrin, *The Formation of Christendom* (Princeton, NJ, 1987), 308.

[18] Anonymous *Miracula* of Theotokos tes Peges, in *AASS*, Novembris III, 885E (ch. 26). A.-M. Talbot, 'Two

with childbearing.¹⁹ His inclusion of an image of the Virgin on coin iconography for the first time may thus be interpreted as a thanksgiving to the Mother of God for her intercession for the conception of his son Constantine (VII).²⁰ The devotional bond of Zoe Karbonopsina with the Theotokos is also reflected on a rare silver solidus pattern from her reign with her son Constantine VII, dated around 914, which introduces the Virgin Nikopoios surrounded by the invocative formula 'O Most Holy Mother of God, aid …' (Ὑπεραγία Θεοτόκε βοήθει …) (Fig. 13.5).²¹

In the light of the above examples, the function of personal phylacteries belonging to women and the relationship of women with their objects of private devotion can be seen in a new perspective. One of the rare amuletic objects of the sixth–seventh century with a dedicatory inscription permitting its attribution to a woman is a nielloed silver armband in the Royal Ontario Museum, Toronto. One medallion of the flat ribbon-like band bears the representation of the enthroned Virgin with the Christ-child, coupled with an invocation to the Virgin on behalf of a woman named Anna (Θεοτόκε βο(ήθει) Ἄννᾳ, χάρις). The latter has a parallel in the word 'health' (ὑγία) inscribed on another medallion decorated with the image of a Holy Rider with a cross staff. Protection and health, the main concerns of the female recipient of this armband, might be related to successful childbearing.²² Protection against ailments related to childbearing involved magical practices grounded in the belief in a female demon and evil spirits attacking newly born children.²³ A wide group of mediaeval amulets were intended for protection in contexts of childbirth, bleeding and various ailments, such as migraine and fever, thought to be caused by the roaming of the womb. These amulets often bear the conventional image of a face with rays, associated with apotropaic formulae. However, Christian imagery, including representations and invocations to the Virgin, is also attested.²⁴ The extensive range of materials from which these amulets were made illustrates their widespread use at all levels of Byzantine society. According to Psellos, for instance, after her marriage with Romanos III, Empress Zoe's hope of bearing a heir to the dynasty drove her to the use of amulets and other magical practices.²⁵

Accounts of Miracles at the Pege Shrine in Constantinople', in *Mélanges Gilbert Dagron*, TM 14 (2002), 607–8. Ead., 'The Anonymous *Miracula* of the Pege Shrine in Constantinople', in *For Professor Ihor Ševčenko on his 80th Birthday, Palaeoslavica* 10.2 (2002), 222–8.

19 *AASS*, Novembris III, 884 (ch. 18). For devotion to St Anne in the context of childbearing, see S. Gerstel, 'Painted Sources for Female Piety in Medieval Byzantium', *DOP* 52 (1998), 98.

20 P. Grierson, *Catalogue of the Byzantine Coins in the Dumbarton Oaks Collection and in the Wittemore Collection* III.2 (Washington, DC, 1973), no. 1, 512, Pl. XXXIV. See also discussion by V. Penna, 'The Mother of God on Coins and Lead Seals', in Vassilaki, *Mother of God*, 210.

21 A. Veglery and G. Zacos, 'A Unique Silver Coin of Constantine VII', *Numismatic Circular* 64 (1956), 379–80, 472. Eid., 'More About The Silver Coin of Constantine VII', *Numismatic Circular* 65 (1957), 195–6. Grierson, *Catalogue* III.2, no. 1, 541, Pl. XXXVI.

22 G. Vikan, 'Two Byzantine Amuletic Armbands and the Group to which they Belong', *The Journal of the Walters Art Gallery* 49/50 (1991/2), no. 22, 41; Fig. 5, 46. M. Mundell Mango, *Silver From Early Byzantium. The Kaper Koraon and Related Treasures* (Baltimore, 1986), no. 94, 266–7. Y. Israeli and D. Mevaorah (eds), *Cradle of Christianity*, exh. cat., Jerusalem, The Israel Museum (Jerusalem, 2000), 151, 163, 224.

23 See I. Sorlin, 'Striges et Géloudes. Histoire d'une croyance et d'une tradition', *TM* 11 (1991), 411–36. Further bibliographical references in Congourdeau, 'Regards', 170.

24 See J. Tuerk, 'An Early Byzantine Inscribed Amulet and its Narratives', *BMGS* 23 (1999), 25–42. J. Spier, 'Medieval Byzantine Magical Amulets and their Tradition', *JWarb* 56 (1993), nos 9, 13, 27–9, 54, 57.

25 Michael Psellos, *Chronographie*, ed. E. Renauld, I (Paris, 1926), 34.

As a model of divine motherhood, the Virgin of the Annunciation is the most popular image on devotional objects belonging to women. One example is the seventh-century gold ring in the Cabinet des médailles, Paris, inscribed with an invocation to the Virgin by a woman named Giora (Θεοτόκε β(ο)ήθι τὴν δούλιν σ(ου) Γιόρας) (Fig. 13.6).[26] Another interesting case in the same collection is a seventh-century sardonyx cameo with the Annunciation, the back of which was recarved in the tenth century with an intaglio of the Deesis surrounded by the inscription: 'Theotokos help thy servant Anna' (Θ(εοτό)κε βοήθι τὴν δούλιν σ(ου) Ἄνα) (Fig. 13.7).[27] An object of a different type, where the Annunciation is combined with the image of the Marriage at Cana on the other side, is a seventh-century gold medallion in Berlin, said to have been found in Antinoë, Egypt.[28] The medallion is surmounted by a smaller one which bears on both sides the inscription 'Christ help the wearer' in the feminine gender (Κύ(ριε) βοήθι τὲ φέρουσα). This could be a marriage medallion intended to ensure successful and healthy procreation for the married couple. The Byzantine marriage ceremony contains repeated references to childbearing in a formula based on biblical models. The miracle at Cana, according to the benediction, becomes a metaphor for abundant childbearing.[29] A concern with childbearing may also have influenced the decoration of the reliquary enkolpion in Maastricht, dated to the late eleventh or early twelfth century, showing the Virgin Hagiosoritissa on the front and the Annunciation on the back (Fig. 13.8).[30] On the basis of the inscription, a strong candidate for the ownership of this enkolpion is Irene Synadene, wife of Manuel Botaneiates, whose particular devotion to the Virgin is known from a lengthy epigram on her gravestone, dating from the 1130s, which was published by Lampros. We learn that in all her torments Irene finds refuge in the Virgin, of whom she asks intercession.[31] The epigram constantly reiterates Irene's distress at not having been able to hold her own child in her arms. Irene's and Manuel's fervent desire for a child is also reflected on their respective seals, both of which show the standing Virgin holding Christ on her right arm, a common type that takes on a new meaning in this context (Fig. 13.9).[32]

The messages of salvation and fertility in the image of the Annunciation are reinforced by its frequent association with the figure of John the Baptist, prophet of salvation, but also the miraculous offspring of a barren woman. Such a parallelism occurs on a sixth/seventh-century bronze votive cross at Dumbarton Oaks, bearing an inscription of a woman named Leontias,

---

[26] J. Durand (ed.), *Byzance. L'art byzantin dans les collections publiques françaises*, exh. cat., Musée du Louvre, 3 November 1992 – 1 February 1993 (Paris, 1992), no. 88, 133 (J.-Cl. Cheynet).

[27] Ibid., no. 184, 277–8 (J.-Cl. Cheynet).

[28] K. Weitzmann (ed.), *Age of Spirituality. Late Antique and Early Christian Art, Third to Seventh Century*, exh. cat., The Metropolitan Museum of Art, 19 November 1977 – 12 February 1978 (New York, 1979), no. 296, 319–21 (K. Reynolds Brown).

[29] G. Vikan, 'Art, Medicine, and Magic in Early Byzantium', *DOP* 38 (1984), 83 n. 122.

[30] H. Vogeler, 'Das Goldemail-reliquiar mit Darstellung der Hagiosoritissa im Schatz der Liebfrauenkirche zu Maastricht', Inaugural-Dissertation zur Erlagung der Doktorwürde der Philosophischen Fakultät der Rheinischen Friedrich-Wilhelms-Universität zu Bonn (Bonn, 1984). Evans and Wixom, *The Glory of Byzantium*, no. 113, 165 (A. W. Carr). D. Buckton, 'The Mother of God in Enamel', in Vassilaki, *Mother of God*, 180–1, Pl. 118 (cf. Aim. Yeroulanou, 'The Mother of God in Jewellery', ibid., 230).

[31] Lampros, 'Ὁ Μαρκιανὸς κῶδιξ 524', no. 75, 40.

[32] The seal of Sebaste Irene Synadene was found in 1970 at Pernik, Bulgaria. A second example of the same seal is in the Fogg Art Museum collection (no. F 17). See J. Jouroukova, 'Un sceau d'Irène Synadènos', *Byzanto-Bulgarica* 4 (1973), 221–6.

who asks for the remission of her sins (Fig. 13.10).³³ The Annunciation, the central image of the cross, is framed by the figure of John the Baptist and his father Zacharias holding a censer. The parallel between these two figures in combination with a representation of the Virgin of the Incarnation is a standard pattern in sixth/seventh-century art.³⁴ However, the relation between the object and its female owner may help to give a new perspective for the understanding of this imagery. Next to John the Baptist is the vessel of manna containing three shoots, referring to the rod of Aaron which miraculously blossomed.³⁵ The vertical bar of the cross combines the standing Christ with a stylite saint on top of his column. The absence of an inscription does not allow any precise identification of the stylite. However, a combination of this image with that of the censer held by Zacharias results in a recurrent motif found on a group of tokens with medicinal properties from the shrine of Symeon the Younger in the Wondrous Mountain, near Antioch.³⁶ The powers of the Virgin were invoked along with those of Symeon and Christ in the performance of miraculous cures, which include cases of healing miracles performed for women.³⁷ To complete the link between the decoration of the Leontias' cross and Symeon the Younger, let us remember that the latter was conceived after the prayers of his mother in the church of John the Baptist in Antioch. After successful incubation, she awoke with a ball of incense in her hand, with which she censed the entire church.³⁸

The protective power of John the Baptist in the context of childbearing is probably based on the biblical episode of the 'Visitation' (Luke 1:46–55) when, endowed with prenatal grace, he recognized Christ's divinity by leaping in his mother's womb. In a speech written for the first anniversary of the translation of the relic of the arm of the Prodromos from Antioch to Constantinople by Constantine Porphyrogennetos in 956, we read that by his mediations John the Baptist protected Constantine VII from the time he was in the womb.³⁹ Moreover, we know that the emperor's mother, Zoe Karbonopsina, was buried in the chapel dedicated to John the Baptist, in the monastery of St Euphemia τῆς Εὐμόρφου.⁴⁰ Also, on the dedicatory inscription of her reliquary cross, Queen Khosrovanush of Georgia asks John the Baptist to be

---

³³ J. Cotsonis, *Byzantine Figural Processional Crosses*, exh. cat., Dumbarton Oaks, 23 September 1994 – 29 January 1995 (Washington, DC, 1994), no. 9, 90–5, Fig. 33. Israeli and Mevorah, *Cradle of Christianity*, no. 90, 218.

³⁴ Among other examples, see the apsidal composition in the Eufrasius basilica, Poreč (c. 550): (J. Maksimović, 'Iconography and Program of Mosaics at Poreč (Parenzo)', in *Mélanges Georges Ostrogorsky*, ZRVI 8 (1964), 247–62. Similarly, on a late 6th-century pilgrim ampulla (pilgrim's flask) in Bobbio, John the Baptist and Zacharias flank the orant Virgin: A. Grabar, *Ampoules de Terre sainte (Monza-Bobbio)* (Paris, 1958), 43–4, 60–1). See also K. Corrigan, 'The Witness of John the Baptist on an Early Byzantine Icon in Kiev', *DOP* 42 (1988), 5, Figs 5–6.

³⁵ For discussion of Aaron's rod as a prefiguration of the Virgin, see P. A. Underwood, *The Kariye Djami, 1. Historical Introduction and Description of the Mosaics and Frescoes* (New York, 1966), 78–80.

³⁶ The censer is a prominent element in the iconography and invocations accompanying the tokens from the shrine of St Symeon the Younger. See Vikan, 'Art, Medicine, and Magic', 69–71.

³⁷ G. Vikan, *Byzantine Pilgrimage Art* (Washington, DC, 1982), 30, 33.

³⁸ Vikan, 'Art, Medicine, and Magic', 83 n. 122. P. van den Ven, *La vie ancienne de S. Syméon Stylite le Jeune (521–592)* (*Subsidia Hagiographica*, 32) (Brussels, 1962–1970), chs 2 and 3.

³⁹ Theodore Daphnopates, Λόγοι δύο, ed. V. V. Latyshev, in *Pravoslavnyi Palestinskii Sbornik* 59 (1910), 38, section 23. Translation and discussion in I. Kalavrezou, 'Helping Hands for the Empire: Imperial Ceremonies and the Cult of Relics at the Byzantine Court', in H. Maguire (ed.), *Byzantine Court Culture from 829 to 1204* (Washington, DC, 1997), 77–8.

⁴⁰ *De cerimoniis aulae byzantinae*, ed. J. J. Reiske (Bonn, 1829–1830), 647. Janin, *Églises CP*, 415. One should note, however, that burial chapels were often dedicated to John the Baptist.

an intercessor for her and her two sons.⁴¹ The above considerations invite us to consider in a new perspective the context of miracle-stories connected with John the Baptist. One should remember, for example, that the Constantinopolitan church in which St Artemios worked healing miracles, especially those related to diseases of the genitals, was dedicated to John the Baptist. The shrine, located in Oxeia, was often visited by women for the cure of their children.⁴²

A further illustration of devotion to John the Baptist from the perspective of a woman is given by an epigram in twelve-syllable verses, which accompanied a reliquary containing a bone fragment from his wrist.⁴³ The reliquary was kept in the Church of La Madeleine at Châteaudun, France, where it is said to have been brought after the Latin conquest of Constantinople, but it is lost today. The epigram reads:⁴⁴

> The wrist/fruit is bone, the hand is gold. From where?
> The wrist/fruit of the desert is from Palestine,
> the golden palm with golden fingers from elsewhere.
> Bone is the fruit from the tree of the Forerunner,
> But the hand was wrought by the skill and desire
> of Lady Anna, scion of the porphyra.

This epigram is one of the rare testimonies to the shape of Byzantine reliquaries of the hand of the Baptist.⁴⁵ Also lost today is the presumed reliquary of the Baptist's hand from the monastery of St John in Petra, preserved in a drawing displaying a roughly outlined hand with only a slightly protruding thumb.⁴⁶ It is commonly accepted that reliquaries in the shape of realistic hands with clearly defined fingers, such as the silver reliquary of the arm of John the Baptist in Topkapı Palace, Istanbul, belong to a western tradition.⁴⁷ The exact gesture of the hand on the

---

⁴¹ Chichinadze, 'True Cross Reliquaries', 29–31.
⁴² V. S. Crisafuli and J. W. Nesbitt, *The Miracles of St. Artemios* (Leiden, 1997).
⁴³ I would like to thank Jannic Durand for drawing my attention to this epigram. See E. Curtius and A. Kirchoff (eds), *Corpus Inscriptionum Graecarum* IV (Berlin, 1877; repr. 1977), no. 8719, 333–4. J. Ebersolt, *Constantinople. Recueil d'études d'archéologie et d'histoire* (Paris, 1951), 134.
⁴⁴
Ὁ καρπὸς ὀστοῦν, ἡ δὲ χεὶρ χρυσῆ πόθεν;
ἐκ τῆς ἐρήμου καρπὸς ἐκ Παλαιστίνης.
χρυσῆ παλαιστὴ χρυσοδάκτυλος ξένον.
ὀστοῦν ὁ καρπὸς ἐκ φυτοῦ τοῦ Προδρόμου,
τὴν χεῖρα δ' ὠ[ρ]γάνωσε τέχνῃ καὶ πόθος
Ἄννης ἀνάσσης, ἐκγόνου τῆς πορφύρας.

I am grateful to Michael Featherstone for his help with the English translation of this epigram.
⁴⁵ Usually pilgrim accounts mention metal strips and gems covering the bones that were exposed, but the latter seem to have been kept in box-shaped caskets; see Kalavrezou, 'Helping Hands', 68–9.
⁴⁶ More probably the relic was that of John, the 11th-century hegoumenos who restored the monastery. See J. Durand, 'À propos des reliques du monastère du Prodrome de Pétra à Constantinople. La relique de saint Christophe de l'ancien trésor de la cathédrale de Cambrai', *CahArch* 46 (1998), 152–4, Fig. 4.
⁴⁷ Kalavrezou, 'Helping Hands', 68–9. There are several examples of 13th–14th-c. Venetian hand-shaped reliquaries in the Treasury of St Mark's, Venice. See H. R. Hahnloser (ed.), *Il Tesoro di San Marco. Tesoro e Museo* (Florence, 1971), nos 145–7, 145–8. See also the 12th-c. reliquary hand of St Symeon in the treasury of St Denis Abbey, D. Gaborit-Chopin (ed.), *Le trésor de Saint-Denis*, exh. cat. (Paris, 1991), 47, Fig. 4. For other examples cf. C. Hahn, 'The Voices of the Saints: Speaking Reliquaries', *Gesta* 36.1 (1997), 20–31.

reliquary commissioned by the purple-born 'Lady Anna' cannot be inferred from the epigram.[48] The wording of the latter, however, if taken literally, suggests that hand-shaped reliquaries were also manufactured in Byzantium. The use of a single word meaning either 'wrist' or 'fruit' allows the poet to make a metaphorical reference to the biblical episode of John the Baptist preaching in the desert (Matthew 3:10–11; Luke 3:9–10). The style and content of the epigram, which underlines the imperial birth and rank of the recipient, match a body of poetic works from the Komnenian period.[49] Yet who can the recipient of this prestigious reliquary be? Such identification is not an easy task. Anna ranks first among the names of Komnenian princesses,[50] while the title *anassa*, feminine form of *anax* (ruler), is common in eleventh/twelfth-century poetic verses as an alternative formula for *basilissa*.[51] However, a series of convergent clues lead me to consider a figure who thus emerges as the strongest candidate. This is Anna Komnene (1110 or 1111 to after 1140, before 1176), second daughter of John II Komnenos and wife of Stephen Kontostephanos, frequently addressed in poetic verses.[52] The use of the title ἀνάσσῃ for her younger sister Theodora (1118–1143) might imply that it was also applied to her.[53] A further piece of evidence reinforcing this hypothesis is Anna Komnene's privileged devotional link with John the Baptist, reflected in a poem devoted to a liturgical veil that she offered to the altar of the church of St John Stoudios, repository of the relic of the head of John the Baptist.[54] Among the poems composed for Anna Komnene, one (attributed to Theodore Prodromos) bears similar metaphorical allusions to the biblical episode of John the Baptist preaching in the desert. In this poem Anna expresses her grief and revulsion over her husband's

---

[48] One might perhaps consider the word χρυσοδάκτυλος to be used here as a noun, intended to highlight one prominent finger, rather than as an adjective evoking a gold-fingered hand.

[49] See, for instance, G. Dagron, 'Nés dans la pourpre', *TM* 12 (1994), 105–7, 118–9. Garland, 'Byzantine Imperial Women', 261–313. P. Magdalino and R. Nelson, 'The Emperor in Byzantine Art of the Twelfth Century', *BF* 8 (1982), 123–83. See also the epigram engraved in niello on the reverse of a late 12th-c. reliquary enkolpion in Moscow, containing several relics, including the hair and a bone of John the Baptist. Evans and Wixom, *The Glory of Byzantium*, no. 115, 166–7 (S. Taft). I. Ševčenko, 'Observations Concerning Inscriptions on Objects Described in the Catalogue *The Glory of Byzantium*', *Palaeoslavica* 6 (1998), 246. A further parallel is the silver-gilt reliquary hand of St Marina in Museo Correr, Venice, dated before 1213. The use of the feminine participle in the dodecasyllables engraved on the side of the reliquary indicates that the donor was a woman. See Evans and Wixom, *The Glory of Byzantium*, no. 332, 496–7 (J. Folda). Ševčenko, 'Observations', 251–2.

[50] See K. Barzos, *Η γενεαλογία των Κομνηνών* (*Βυζαντινά κείμενα και μελέται*, 20a) I (Thessaloniki, 1984), 410 n. 32 and 716 (index).

[51] E. Bensammar, 'La titulature de l'impératrice et sa signification. Recherches sur les sources byzantines de la fin du VIIIᵉ siècle à la fin du XIIᵉ siècle', *Byz* 46 (1976), 289. E. A. Margarou, *Τίτλοι και επαγγελματικά ονόματα γυναικών στο Βυζάντιο. Συμβολή στη μελέτη για τη θέση της γυναίκας στη βυζαντινή κοινωνία* (Thessaloniki, 2000), 23–4.

[52] See Barzos, *Η γενεαλογία*, I, no. 77, 380–90. W. Hörandner, *Theodoros Prodromos, Historische Gedichte* (*Wiener byzantinische Studien*, XI) (Vienna, 1975), nos. XLVIII–LI, 436–43. E. Miller (ed.), *Recueil des Historiens des Croisades, Historiens Grecs* II (Paris, 1881; repr. 1969), 772–4. See also the metrical inscription on a seal issued by her son: Ἰωάννου σφράγισμα Κοντοστεφάνου τῆς πορφυραυγούσ(της) Ἄννης ἔγγονος γόνος. H. Bell, 'Byzantine Sealings', *BZ* 30 (1929/30), 636.

[53] In a poem addressed to her husband Manuel Anemas, see Hörandner, *Theodoros Prodromos*, no. LIV, 455 line 201.

[54] Lampros, 'Ὁ Μαρκιανός κώδιξ 524', no. 230, 151. P. Speck, 'Die Ἐνδυτή', *JÖB* 15 (1966), no. 12, 364. For the relics of John the Baptist in the Stoudios monastery see Janin, *Églises CP*, 435. J. Durand and M.-P. Laffite (eds), *Le trésor de la Sainte Chapelle*, exh. cat. (Paris, 2001), 79–80.

tragic death by stoning and asks that the hand which killed her husband be cut off and the tree from which the catapult was made be pulled out by the roots and burnt. She likens her bones to those of her husband, which have been broken in pieces.⁵⁵ Rather than being coincidental, similarities in the vocabulary of the two poems might be connected with the life-story of Anna Komnene, wife of Stephen Kontostephanos. If we accept her as the recipient of this reliquary, her devotion to John the Baptist may also be explained by his bearing the same name as her father, John II Komnenos, and her first son, also named John. We may perhaps assume that Anna Komnene commissioned the reliquary containing the Baptist's wrist bone to cast a spell on the evil hand which stoned her husband, and to ensure the salvation of the deceased. This epigram is thus an important testimony on the circulation of prestigious relics among women from imperial circles in Byzantium. It is also an evocative illustration of piety from the woman's perspective.⁵⁶

This study has focused on the life of devotional objects, illustrating the various aspects of their usage and their iconographic message in relation to the concerns and expectations of their female owners – mainly successful childbearing, health of children and spouse, and salvation. The human dimension that emerges from the study of objects of private devotion introduces a new perspective for the understanding of their imagery. Religious images are not only illustrations of biblical narratives or issues of dogma but also symbols with which viewers can identify. This study has helped to contextualize an important aspect of the interactive relationship between an object of devotion and its recipient. Protection involves multiple levels of intercession, and images have several layers of meaning according to their use and ownership. John the Baptist emerges as a powerful intercessor next to Christ and the Mother of God, who remains by far the most important intercessory figure among women. In parallel to her role as Mother of God, this study has brought out other maternal messages that she might have sent. The rare occurrence of female saints among the devotional objects discussed above is another point reflecting the individual role of personal phylacteria as compared with other types of devotional media such as icons and wall paintings.

---

⁵⁵ Miller, *Recueil*, 774 lines 261–5. Barzos, *Η γενεαλογία*, I, 389 n. 53.
… Καὶ τοῦ πετροβολήσαντος κοπείησαν αἱ χεῖρες!
Τὸ δένδρον ὅθεν ἔκοψαν τὸ μάγγανον ἐκεῖνο
Ἀπ' ἀστραπῆς ἐκτεφρωθὲν ῥιζόθεν ἐκσπασθείη,
Ὅτι συνέτριψαν ὀστοῦν ἐκ τῶν ὀστῶν μου μέγα
Καὶ στέφανον ἀτίμητον ἀπὸ τῆς κορυφῆς μου!

⁵⁶ Relics of the True Cross were most common among women of the Komnenian dynasty. See for instance a series of epigrams which accompanied True Cross reliquaries that belonged to the wife and daughters of Alexios I Komnenos (1081–1118): A. Frolow, *La relique de la Vraie Croix. Recherches sur le développement d'un culte* (Paris, 1961), nos 241 and 308 (Irene Doukaina), no. 249 (Maria), no. 312 (Eudokia). For an illustration of the reliquary cross of Maria Komnene, see also J. Lafontaine-Dosogne (ed.), *Splendeur de Byzance*, exh. cat. (Brussels, 1982), no. O.21, 152, 154.

FEMALE PIETY IN CONTEXT   163

13.1 Athens, Benaki Museum, inv. no. 11519. Bronze ring (6th–7th c.) (source: Benaki Museum)

13.2 Bulgaria, Silistra. Bronze pectoral reliquary cross (11th c.) (source: Atanassov, 'Croix-encolpions', Pl. 59.5)

13.3 Washington, DC, Dumbarton Oaks, inv. no. 53.12.22. Gold reliquary cross (9th–10th c.) (source: Byzantine Collection, Dumbarton Oaks)

13.4 Washington, DC, Dumbarton Oaks, inv. no. 52.5. Bronze votive cross (7th c.) (source: Byzantine Collection, Dumbarton Oaks)

FEMALE PIETY IN CONTEXT 165

13.5 Former A. Veglery Collection. Silver solidus pattern of Constantine VII and Zoe (source: Veglery and Zacos, 'A Unique Silver Coin', 379)

13.6 Paris, Bibliothèque nationale, Cabinet des médailles, inv. no. Schl. 131. Gold ring (7th c.) (source: *Byzance*, no. 88)

13.7 Paris, Bibliothèque nationale, Cabinet des médailles, Babelon 338. Cameo (7th c.) on the obverse and intaglio (10th c.) on the reverse (source: *Byzance*, no. 184)

13.8 Maastricht, Onze Lieve Vrouw. Enkolpion (late 11th–12th c.) (source: Evans and Wixom, *Glory of Byzantium*, no. 113)

13.9   Cambridge, Massachusetts, Fogg Art Museum, inv. no. F 17 (on loan to Dumbarton Oaks Collection). Seal of the Sebaste Irene Synadene (12th c.) (by kind permission of the Harvard University Art Museums Visual Resources)

13.10   Washington, DC, Dumbarton Oaks, inv. no. 69.75.
Bronze cross (6th–7th c.)
(source: Dumbarton Oaks)

14

The eyes of the Mother of God

Robin Cormack

The icon of the Virgin and Child between Archangels accompanied by two Saints from the monastery of St Catherine at Sinai (Fig. 14.1) is a key painting for the study of early Byzantine art. But much of the literature in which it has featured since the fundamental publications of Soteriou and Weitzmann has been based on photographs rather than on direct viewing of the panel itself.[1] The 'Mother of God' exhibition at the Benaki Museum has transformed that position and for viewers it was a dramatic opening image in the presentation. This enabled for example an appreciation of its substantial scale (68.5 × 49.7 cm) and that in section the painting layer is thicker at the top and progressively becomes thinner downwards – suggesting that it may have been intended for display at a relatively high position and was designed to be viewed from below. This might indicate that it was conceived as a public image for reverence and devotion. Currently, the larger icon of the Virgin and Child between Archangels (164 × 116 cm) is displayed high above the viewer in the church of S. Maria in Trastevere in Rome.

This paper focuses on an issue which both the photographic record and viewing at first hand seem to endorse: the fact that the Virgin at the centre of the picture looks away from the viewer. As is written in the catalogue, 'the eyes of the Virgin look to the right and do not meet the eyes of the viewer. She appears to look away from and beyond the person who contemplates the icon.'[2] The question to explore here is the significance of her gaze.

It is well known that certain famous faces in the history of art offer the opposite impression. As Robert Van Nice was fond of asking after his many years spent in Hagia Sophia at Constantinople looking at every detail: 'Why did the eyes of Christ in the Deesis mosaic always look directly at him, wherever he stood in the south gallery?' The artistic device to create the impression that the eyes in a portrait 'seem to follow you about everywhere' is perhaps most notorious in comments by viewers of the Mona Lisa, where the response seems to be universally agreed. However, a number of experiments in the nineteenth-century study of the phenomenon established that, although we as viewers are highly skilled in perceiving gaze direction, we are not infallible. It seems we do not base our judgement of gaze direction solely on the position of the iris and pupil relative to the whites of the eyes, but we need to take into account head direction also.[3] Nevertheless in the case of this particular icon, the position of the brown iris and black

---

[1] Ernst Kitzinger, for example, in a retrospective discussion on his writings on iconoclasm at a seminar at the Courtauld Institute of Art in 1986 commented that his published discussions of the icon and his dating to the seventh century all depended on the study of photographs alone. His archive is now held at the J. Paul Getty Museum in Los Angeles.
[2] Vassilaki, *Mother of God*, no. 1, 262 (R. Cormack).
[3] This question is discussed with reference to the experimental literature by V. Bruce and A. Young, *In the Eye of the Beholder. The Science of Face Perception* (Oxford, 1998), esp. 211–2.

pupil overrides the other features of the face, and gives the clear message that the central figure in the painting avoids eye contact with the viewer. The question – 'Why do the Virgin's eyes look away from the viewer, wherever they stand?' – seems to be a legitimate one to pursue in front of this icon. An indication that the mediaeval viewer would have been struck by the nature of the eyes and the gaze of the Virgin is given by a different example: a thirteenth-century panel of the Virgin and Child in the cathedral at Siena was specifically identified in fifteenth-century inventories as the 'Madonna degli occhi grossi'. In this case it was the size as much as the power of the eyes that had influenced the viewers.[4]

One problem has already inadvertently slipped into this present discussion of the panel. Since this icon has no title, and since it has been displayed as part of the Mother of God exhibition, we have catalogued it as an icon with the Virgin and Child between Archangels accompanied by two saints. Such a title is entirely opportunistic (and anachronistic), and may even disguise and distort the intended subject of the picture. It does not mention, for example, the highly prominent Hand of God in the centre at the top of the panel and the beam of light coming down from heaven. A title like 'The Incarnation of Christ' would considerably alter the spiritual response to the image, and make the viewer look to see Christ as the central figure among the figures. This response could indeed be supported by consideration again of the question of the gaze. The eyes of the Christ-child do indeed look out to make contact with the viewer, and, like the eyes of the two saints, they do follow the viewer 'wherever they stand'. Perhaps equally significant is a feature that has been analysed by measuring portraits painted by one hundred and seventy different western artists from the fifteenth to the twentieth century.[5] It was found that statistically one of the sitter's eyes is very often placed on the vertical centre line of the panel – it is the importance of the gaze and eye contact that determines the central axis of the painting. In the case of our icon, it is the right eye of Christ that is placed on the vertical centre line, and not either of the eyes of the Virgin. So it might be more correct if we were to read Christ as the central figure in the image, and the main subject of the icon.[6]

Nevertheless we can pursue the question of the position in the icon of the Virgin's gaze and the direction of her glance over the right shoulder of the viewer. The viewer might well ask if she is bestowing her attention on another person, who is behind and beyond the viewer. If she is in fact shown as declining to relate directly to the viewer, this is in sharp distinction with the two saints, who both stare forwards and strikingly make eye contact with the viewer. Her gaze does however echo that of the two archangels, whose eyes are also turned to one side, in their case clearly towards the 'invisible' God in heaven. In the radiating circle of faces around the Virgin, three (Christ and the saints) stare out at the viewer, while three (Mary and the archangels) gaze towards an unseen vision. This careful artistic balance together with the calm and symmetrical composition of the icon with the six figures framed within a semi-circular exedra or church apse reinforces the idea that the purpose of this icon is a devotional image, a peaceful setting for adoration and prayer on the part of the viewer. Yet the question remains of the dynamic of the

---

[4] B. Kempers, 'Icons, Altarpieces, and Civic Ritual in Siena Cathedral, 1100–1530', in B. A. Hanawalt and K. L. Reyerson (eds), *City and Spectacle in Medieval Europe* (Minneapolis and London, 1994), 89–136, esp. 107–10.
[5] See C. W. Tyler, 'An Eye Placement Principle in 500 Years of Portraits', *Investigative Ophthalmology and Visual Science* 38 (1997), quoted in Bruce and Young, *In the Eye of the Beholder*, 214–5.
[6] This is the approach of A. M. Lidov, *Byzantine Icons of Sinai* (in Russian) (Moscow and Athens, 1999), 38.

eyes of the figures and how the viewer was likely to respond to their gaze. How far is the glance of the Virgin part of a complex message to the viewer about the nature and channels through which prayer might pass through intercessors to God? How far is the glance of Mary a gendered gaze from the Mother of God?

When I first proposed a paper on the eyes of the Virgin, I was unaware that it was a subject about to generate a flurry of publication in the Byzantine field, notably the set of papers edited by Robert Nelson in *Visuality Before and Beyond the Renaissance* and the study of pilgrims in *The Memory of the Eyes* by Georgia Frank.[7] Their research considerably refines our frame of reference, both through the exploration of Byzantine thinking on optics and vision by Nelson, and the analysis of the conceptual nature of looking with the 'eye of faith' exposed in pilgrim texts by Frank. Another aspect raised by the frontal gaze is suggested by recent work on the perennial issue of the 'evil eye'. This idea, inherited from Antiquity, exercised early Church Fathers, who were not able to eliminate the belief that the eyes of the envious could harm a viewer, and that the devil operated through the gaze.[8]

The issue raised by the icon is whether we can understand the early Byzantine use of images by analysing the eyes of the figures in this painting. It is clear that while we have no direct texts which illuminate the mentality of the users of this particular icon, we do have a considerable number of Byzantine texts on the power of the image in the culture. It seems legitimate to apply the evidence of recorded statements from other places and other times, since there is no reason to think that the environment of the Sinai monastery was anything but representative of Byzantine mentality. After all, universally studied texts, such as those of John Klimax and Anastasios of Sinai, were actually written in the monastery and then circulated widely throughout the Orthodox world. We do not know where the Virgin and Saints encaustic icon was produced (Constantinople seems to remain the favoured provenance) nor when it arrived on Sinai (although its good condition suggests its arrival was earlier rather than later – it is a noticeable feature of the icons in the collection of St Catherine's on Sinai that a fine condition and the remarkable lack of craquelure can be used as an indication of an icon's long presence, if not manufacture, in the stable and dry environmental conditions of the monastery). Yet we can reasonably infer that Byzantine attitudes towards the icon would apply to this image as well.

From the period of the production of the Virgin and Saints icon (sixth century?), we have a text by Agathias about an icon of St Michael as well as an inscribed wall painting of St Michael (now in fragments) from the theatre at Aphrodisias (Plate 9, Fig. 14.2). These confirm that attention to the eyes of the holy figure was paramount in the viewing of the painting, and that a Byzantine painter could be expected to devote pictorial planning to this aspect.[9]

The sixth-century text of Agathias on St Michael can be translated as follows:

---

[7] G. Frank, *The Memory of the Eyes. Pilgrims to Living Saints in Christian Late Antiquity* (Berkeley, CA, 2000) and R. S. Nelson (ed.), *Visuality Before and Beyond the Renaissance* (Cambridge, 2000).

[8] M. W. Dickie, 'The Fathers of the Church and the Evil Eye', in H. Maguire (ed.), *Byzantine Magic* (Washington, DC, 1994), 9–34 and A. D. Vakaloudi, 'Deisidaimonia and the Apotropaic Magic Amulets', *Byz* 70 (2000), 182–210. Also R. Nelson, 'To Say and to See. Ekphrasis and Vision in Byzantium', in id., *Visuality*, 143–68, esp. 155.

[9] For the epigram by Agathias, see W. R. Paton (ed.), *The Greek Anthology*, ed. Loeb, I (Leipzig, 1916), no. 34, 20–3. Mango, *Art of the Byz. Empire*, 115. R. Cormack, 'The Wall-Painting of St. Michael in the Theatre', in R. R. R. Smith and K. T. Erim (eds), *Aphrodisias Papers* 2 (Ann Arbor, 1991), 109–22.

The wax remarkably has represented the invisible, the form of the bodiless chief of the angels. This achievement means that the earthly viewer of the icon can direct the mind to a higher contemplation. The viewer can directly venerate the archangel. With this perception of the features of the archangel in the mind, the viewer trembles as if in his actual presence. The eyes encourage deep thoughts; through art and its colours the innermost prayer of the viewer is passed to the imaged.

Such an ekphrasis needs treating with care if it is to be used in the interpretation of how a Byzantine viewer would actually have responded to a work of art. Nor can we assume that our reading of the reference to the eyes conforms with sixth-century assumptions on cognition and perception.[10] Nelson has discussed the difference between Byzantine optics and those of the post-mediaeval world in the West; he proposes that while the intromission theory became predominant in the late mediaeval West, in Byzantium both intromission and extramission theories were known, but Photios and other writers favoured extramission thinking. So Photios in his homily on the apse mosaics of Hagia Sophia in 867 assumed that optical rays emerged from the viewer's eyes, contacted the object of vision and then returned to the eye and conveyed the essence of the vision to the mind and memory. In the case of our epigram, we can understand on this theory how the viewer 'can directly venerate the archangel' as the features of the archangel are imprinted on the mind. The problem arises in interpreting when eyes meet eyes, as in the Aphrodisias wall painting of the archangel, and how far a frontal image sets up a more dynamic process. According to the extramission theory, the viewer is the active observer of the world. But in the wall painting, the viewer observes the process in reverse, where the archangel's receptive eyes indicate that 'the innermost prayer of the viewer is passed to the imaged'. This two-way situation underlies the complexities of the gazes in the Sinai Virgin and Saints icon, where it is the saints and not the Virgin Mary whose eyes meet the gaze of the viewer.

In the Sinai icon, the frontal gaze of the two saints invites the viewer to address prayers to them as intercessors, and to reverence the Virgin Mary as an object of love. Photios in his homily writes that the Virgin 'fondly turns her eyes on her begotten son in the affection of her heart'.[11] Although she does not in the Hagia Sophia mosaic actually appear to do this, the important point is that Photios communicates that the direct gaze is understood by him as an indication of love and adoration. In his analysis of this panel, Ernst Kitzinger introduced the notion of 'artistic modes' to explain the different stylistic means used to portray the martyr saints, the Virgin and the archangels.[12] He suggested that different manners or styles were deliberately chosen to indicate different 'orders of being' or different 'levels of reality' (later on, he refers to the latter as 'degrees of spirituality'). He argued that the 'abstract mode' was developed in the period between Justinian and iconoclasm as the most effective form for the portrayal of images 'that lent themselves to devotional use'; he calls such figures as the saint in the Sinai icon 'the first truly iconic figures in Byzantine art'.

---

[10] For a discussion of a slide from extramission to intromission theory, see also M. Camille, 'Before the Gaze. The Internal Senses and Late Medieval Practices of Seeing', in Nelson, *Visuality*, 197–223.
[11] See Nelson, 'To Say and to See', 149 for a discussion of this passage.
[12] E. Kitzinger, 'Byzantine Art in the Period Between Justinian and Iconoclasm', in *Berichte zum XI. Internationalen Byzantinisten-Kongress, München 1958* IV.1 (Munich, 1958), 1–50, repr. in W. E. Kleinbauer (ed.), *The Art of Byzantium and the Medieval West: Selected Studies by Ernst Kitzinger* (Bloomington and London, 1976), VI.

Kitzinger's theory of modes has been extremely influential in art-historical writing, but has recently come under increasing criticism.[13] However, John Haldon in his historical treatment of Byzantium in the seventh century builds a substantial argument from this theory of modes as a way of understanding cultural change before iconoclasm, when icons became increasingly a part of everyday life, offering a more immediate access to God.[14] Haldon follows Kitzinger in seeing 'different modes with the deliberate intention of thus signifying or suggesting different levels of symbolic reference'.[15] He suggests that the abstract mode assisted the desire for devotional and authoritative figures – figures that were both approachable and at the same time of high status, although he sees that it is hard to say how intentional the development was. The stylistic dichotomy, he argues, is between the illusionistic mode, which portrays figures within their own self-contained world, and the abstract mode where the portrayed figures look out and touch the world of the onlooker.[16] This application of the theory of modes to the cultural environment of the period extends Kitzinger's thinking – he had at the end of this paper drawn back from 'relating a major stylistic innovation to a vague and general Zeitgeist' and emphasized that such images as the Sinai icon 'were prayed to and expected to work miracles and were thought of as indwelt by the Holy Ghost'. In entering this debate, this paper has set out to suggest that a close attention to the pictorial treatment of the eyes may in part cut across this notion of modes. Whatever the stylistic means employed, the direction of the gaze will influence the perceptions of the viewers. The styles of the two saints and Christ are different, but all these figures make eye contact with the viewer. The status of the Virgin and archangels in the Christian order is different; here they are all three seen looking away from the viewer. The evidence of texts and images is that the gaze is a significant part of the meaning of the imagery of the Sinai icon of the Virgin and Child between Archangels accompanied by two Saints.

---

[13] On this see Vassilaki, *Mother of God*, no. 1, 262 (R. Cormack).
[14] J. Haldon, *Byzantium in the Seventh Century. The Transformation of a Culture* (Cambridge, 1990), esp. 405–35.
[15] Ibid., 409.
[16] Ibid., 422.

14.1 Mt Sinai, Monastery of St Catherine.
Icon of the Virgin and Child between Archangels
accompanied by two Saints (6th c.) (source: Sinai)

14.2 Turkey, Aphrodisias, wall painting at the theatre.
St Michael (6th c.)
(source: Cormack, 'The Wall-Painting of St. Michael', Fig. 1)

Zoe's lead seal: female invocation to the Annunciation of the Virgin

Vasso Penna

Representations of the Annunciation, like those of other feasts of the church calendar, were not particularly common in the iconography of lead seals, which were used by the Byzantines to secure the confidentiality of their correspondence.[1] Most of the surviving examples date from the eleventh and twelfth centuries, although the subject can be found on such seals from as early as the sixth century.[2]

In general the criteria for choosing a particular iconography on seals can be traced to details related to the social or professional status of the owner, as the accompanying inscriptions indicate. Thus the choice of the Annunciation for seals belonging to members of important Byzantine families, or civil or military officials, is associated with devotional objects such as portable icons or pictorial steatite plaquettes, which probably served private devotional needs and were kept in private places – residences or chapels – as family *palladia*. Lead seals of the Angelos family belong to this category,[3] and similar criteria perhaps influenced the iconography of the seals of the *symponos* Radenos,[4] the *vestes* and *oikistikos* Theodore Skleros,[5] the *sebastophoros* Christopher,[6] the *spatharokoubikoularios* Constantine Pepagomenos,[7] Stephen (unknown but presumably a member of a distinguished family),[8] and Theodora of the Komnenos family.[9] When seals of ecclesiastical dignitaries, monasteries and abbots contain a

---

[1] On trends in the iconography of Byzantine lead seals, J.-Cl. Cheynet and C. Morrisson, 'Texte et image sur les sceaux byzantins: les raisons d'un choix iconographique', in *Studies in Byzantine Sigillography* 4 (1995), 9–32. W. Seibt and M. L. Zarnitz, *Das byzantinische Bleisiegel als Kunstwerk, Katalog zur Ausstellung* (Vienna, 1997), esp. 103–78. V. Penna, 'Εικονογραφικά βυζαντινών μολυβδοβούλλων: ο αυτοκράτορας, η εκκλησία, η αριστοκρατία', *DChAE* 20 (1998), 261–74.

[2] On seals with the representation of the Annunciation from the 6th to the 10th c., see V. Laurent, *Les sceaux du Médailler Vatican* (Vatican City, 1962), nos 218 (6th c.) and 168 (7th–8th c.). V. Laurent, *Le corpus des sceaux de l'Empire byzantin, V, 1–3. L'église* (Paris, 1963–1972), nos 521 (10th c.), 701 (7th c.), 1083bis (6th–7th c.). G. Zacos and A. Veglery, *Byzantine Lead Seals* I, 3 (Basel, 1972), no. 2951 (550–650). J.-Cl. Cheynet, C. Morrisson and W. Seibt, *Les sceaux byzantins de la collection Henri Seyrig* (Paris, 1991), no. 367 (7th c.). J. Nesbitt and N. Oikonomides (eds), *Catalogue of the Byzantine Lead Seals at Dumbarton Oaks and in the Fogg Museum of Art* I (Washington, DC, 1991), nos 82.12, 82.23 (10th c.); II (Washington, DC, 1994), no. 2.3 (10th c.). Seibt and Zarnitz, *Das byzantinische Bleisiegel*, no. 4.2.1 (7th c.).

[3] Cheynet and Morrisson, 'Texte et image sur les sceaux byzantins', 30. Penna, 'Εικονογραφικά βυζαντινών μολυβδοβούλλων', 270. On lead seals of the Angelos family see Zacos and Veglery, *Byzantine Lead Seals*, nos 2738, 2741, 2743–4.

[4] V. Laurent, *Le corpus des sceaux de l'Empire byzantin, II. L'administration centrale* (Paris, 1981), no. 1083.

[5] Seibt and Zarnitz, *Das byzantinische Bleisiegel*, no. 1.2.6.

[6] K.M. Konstantopoulos, *Βυζαντιακά μολυβδόβουλλα του εν Αθήναις Εθνικού Νομισματικού Μουσείου* (Athens, 1917), no. 498, β.

[7] Ibid., no. 669.

[8] Ibid., no. 1147.

[9] Seibt and Zarnitz, *Das byzantinische Bleisiegel*, no. 3.1.7.

representation of the Annunciation, we cannot know whether the metropolitan church or the monastery was dedicated specifically to the Annunciation or to the Virgin generally.[10]

A group of tenth- and eleventh-century seals with this subject, which belonged to certain imperial *protospatharioi*, is particularly interesting.[11] If the choice of the Annunciation is not coincidental, it suggests that during these centuries there was a trend towards iconographic crystallization in the seals of these particular officials. This may derive from some feature of the office of imperial *protospatharios* that is associated either with its ceremonial practices[12] or with the social order of its holder.[13]

Also hard to interpret is the presence of the Annunciation on a seal which is probably attributable to Emperor Justinian I.[14] It is in a bad state of preservation, and the details of the design are so difficult to make out that even the identification of the Annunciation is problematic. But the fact that the formal declaration of 25 March as the feast day of the Annunciation coincides with the date of the seal is striking, and a surviving letter of Justinian clearly expresses the view that this is the fitting date for celebrating the Annunciation.[15]

A study of Byzantine seals with a representation of the Annunciation should not omit special mention of a seal belonging to a woman called Zoe, of whom nothing else is known,[16] which can be dated to the first half of the eleventh century (Plate 10, Fig. 15.1). It should be noted here that the number of lead seals belonging to women is small and, apart from nuns, the majority of those who owned seals were members of imperial or aristocratic families.

The obverse of the seal shows the Annunciation with the inscription Χαῖρε Κεχαριτωμένη (Hail, thou that art highly favoured) in a circular arrangement; this is exceptionally rare on lead seals with a representation of the Annunciation, which normally bear the inscription: Ὁ Χαιρετισμός (The Greeting).

---

[10] On seals of monasteries and ecclesiastical officials with a representation of the Annunciation after the 10th c., see Laurent, V, 1–3. *L'église*, nos 97 (12th c.), 215 (11th–12th c.), 468 (11th c.), 716 (11th–12th c.), 1158 (11th c.), 1972 (11th–12th c.), 1982 (11th–12th c.), 1495–6 (12th c.), 1497 (12th–13th c.), 1498 (14th c.). The last four seals belonged to Archbishops of Bulgaria, who generally favoured representations of the Annunciation.

[11] See Nesbitt and Oikonomides, *Catalogue of the Byzantine Lead Seals*, I, no. 82.12: Gregory, *basilikos protospatharios* and *strategos* of Cherson (10th c.); II, no. 2.3: Michael or Manuel, *basilikos protospatharios* of chrysotriklinos and *krites Nikopoleos* (10th c.). Laurent, *II. L'administration*, no. 877: Theoktistos, *protospatharios* of chrysotriklinos, *krites tou Hippodromou* (11th c.); no. 984: Bardas, *basilikos protospatharios* and *chartoularios tou droungou* (11th c.).

[12] As for example in the reign of Constantine VII: *De cerimoniis aulae byzantinae*, ed. J. J. Reiske, I (Bonn, 1829), 165, where the *protospatharioi* were given a place of exceptional honour next to the emperor during the Annunciation festivities in Constantinople.

[13] The *protospatharioi* belonged to two orders, 'bearded' and eunuchs, each with its own distinguishing uniform and insignia.

[14] I. Koltsida-Makri, Βυζαντινά μολυβδόβουλλα συλλογής Ορφανίδη-Νικολαΐδη Νομισματικού Μουσείου Αθηνών (Athens, 1996), no. 332, where the seal is attributed to Emperor Anastasios I or Justinian I. However, the monogram on the reverse resembles that of Justinian on the capitals of Hagia Sophia. The equivalent monogram of Anastasios, as found on coin types (W. Hahn, *Moneta Imperii Byzantini: Rekonstruktion des Prägeaufbaues auf synoptisch-tabellarischen Grundlage, 1. Von Anastasius I. bis Justinianus I.* (Wien, 1973), 40), shows variations, especially in the treatment of the left-hand section. For monograms of Anastasios, see also Seibt and Zarnitz, *Das byzantinische Bleisiegel*, no. 4.2.6. Two lead seal types of Justinian I's reign are known to date, one with a depiction of a winged Victory and the second aniconic, with a monogram of the emperor on one face and a three-line inscription with his name in Latin characters on the other.

[15] See the relevant entry in *ODB* 1, 106 (R. F. Taft and A. W. Carr).

[16] G. Zacos, *Byzantine Lead Seals* II (comp. and ed. J. W. Nesbitt; Berne, 1984), no. 771.

The reverse is completely filled with a five-line metrical inscription: Χαράν λαβοῦσα τῇ Ζωῇ χαράν δίδου (Thou who hast received joy, give joy to Zoe). A similar invocation for joy or personal happiness is found on the seal of the *symponos* Radenos expressed in the form: †Χαράν μαγίστρῳ Ῥαδηνῷ τῷ συμπόνῳ νέμοις, Πάναγνε, τῆς χαρᾶς τὸ χωρίον (May you give joy to *magistros* Radenos the *symponos*, O all-pure one, the place of joy). In spite of the similar wording the character of the two inscriptions is fundamentally different. Zoe's invocation is clearly informal and has no connection with the theological significance of the Annunciation. Her supplication is specific and very personal. It addresses the Virgin as a woman and contains an indirect request for the greatest blessing that can come to a woman, the birth of a child. Representations of the Annunciation had long been associated with fertility, and they are found on prophylactic rings, amulets, *eulogiai*, cameos and necklaces – objects used generally as charms for the protection of women, and in particular for the fulfilment of their desire to obtain a child.[17] For the Byzantines childlessness was a deep misfortune and a disgrace, a punishment from God for sinful behaviour. A barren woman was considered an object of shame and often met with cruel treatment at the hands of her husband, while the birth of a child brought harmony and happiness to the family and filled it with joy and pride.[18]

The choice of the Annunciation for Zoe's seal, when combined with the unusual invocational inscription, clearly places it within the spirit of the above objects. A lead seal, which authenticated the signature of the writer and sender of a letter, was obviously not a strictly personal object. However, its circulation depended on the quantity and frequency of the correspondence entered into by its owner, while the extent of its geographical coverage varied according to his professional activity and status. But the impression on a lead seal of a secret personal desire is surprising and may even seem rather audacious: probably it was not the owner's regular seal, but one for occasional use, restricted to personal and private correspondence addressed to a particularly intimate recipient, such as a counsellor of Zoe. A connection between the iconography of the seal and the content of the letter is therefore very probable.

Establishing the identity of this anonymous, audacious Zoe is not an easy task. The rarity of lead seals belonging to women implies a position in the higher social circles of the capital, while the richly formulated inscription on the obverse, together with the unusual metrical invocation on the reverse, point to a woman of some learning, with a striking personality.

This contribution to the 'Mother of God' conference could finish here. But I will continue with a rather bold suggestion as to the identity of this Zoe, since I believe that conferences like this should be a kind of workshop, a forum for the expression of preliminary views, in the hope of stimulating thought, provoking positive or negative reactions, and even sparking off ideas and exchanges of opinion. So, on the basis of the dating of this lead seal to the first half of the

---

[17] A. Yeroulanou, 'The Mother of God in Jewellery', in Vassilaki, *Mother of God*, 228, 231, which mentions a necklace from Antinoë, Egypt, probably a product of a Constantinopolitan workshop and now in Berlin, another necklace in the Chr. Schmidt collection, Munich, an agate seal-stone in the Benaki Museum, etc. See also three 6th–7th-c. cameos with representations of the Annunciation: J. Durand (ed.), *Byzance, L'art byzantin dans les collections publiques françaises*, exh. cat., Musée du Louvre, 3 November 1992 – 1 February 1993 (Paris, 1982), nos 40–1, 89 and no. 184, 277–8 (M. Avisseau); the third one indicates extended use until at least the 10th c., when a representation of the Deesis was engraved on the reverse. See also the amulet ring of Giora, also with the Annunciation, ibid., no. 88, 133 (J.-Cl. Cheynet).

[18] Ph. Koukoules, Βυζαντινῶν βίος καὶ πολιτισμός IV (Athens, 1951), 10.

eleventh century, I shall propose an identification of the owner of the seal as the empress Zoe Porphyrogenneta (1028–1050). Daughter of Constantine VIII, the last male member of the Macedonian dynasty, she was around fifty years of age when she married Romanos III Argyros. Michael Psellos gives a vivid description of the desire of Romanos to found a long-standing dynasty and the efforts of the imperial couple to obtain a child. Husband and wife both followed courses of therapy, and Zoe even resorted to magic, going about with gemstones, amulets and chains attached to her body.[19] In the context of this agonized longing for a child it seems entirely possible that Zoe became involved in a correspondence with specialists and counsellors, and that she ensured its confidentiality by using a seal with an appropriate design.[20]

---

[19] Michael Psellos, *Chronographie*, 3, 5, 5–17, ed. E. Renauld, I (Paris, 1926), 34–5. See also L. Garland, *Byzantine Empresses, Women and Power in Byzantium AD 527–1204* (London, 1999), 138.

[20] I would mention here the longing for a child of another Byzantine empress Zoe, in the 10th c. In her desperation to bear a child and to escape the shame of childlessness, Zoe Karbonopsina, the fourth wife of Leo VI, is said to have resorted to the church of the Virgin in Pege where there was a miraculous icon; there she took a silk cord of the same length as the icon of the Mother of God in Kataphyge, tied it round her waist and thus conceived the celebrated emperor Constantine VII. This showed that the Virgin had the power to break the bonds of childlessness and provide a barren womb with legitimate children (*AASS*, Novembris III, 885E). However, the seal discussed here cannot be attributed to Zoe Karbonopsina on chronological grounds. I should like to thank Christos Stavrakos for his suggestions on the dating of the seal to the first half of the 11th c.

15.1   Paris, Bibliothèque nationale, inv. no. BnF 3233.
Zoe's lead seal.
Annunciation (obverse) and inscription (reverse) (11th c.)
(source: J.-Cl. Cheynet)

Part IV

Public and private cult

16

Byzantine domestic art as evidence for the early cult of the Virgin

Henry Maguire

Images of the Virgin appear on many types of domestic objects in the early Byzantine period, particularly on clothing and jewellery. These objects raise some interesting questions about the unofficial, private cult of the Virgin in the early Byzantine period. Some of these issues have been raised already by historians, who have worked from the evidence of texts, but, to my knowledge, art historians, working from the material culture, have not addressed them. The questions that will be considered here are three in number. First, there is the problem of chronology. Was the visual cult of the Virgin, in the sense of people invoking her aid through images, a phenomenon that appeared first at the upper levels of society, and did it only subsequently trickle down to the popular level? Or was the movement the other way around, that is, was the visual cult of the Virgin in the first place a popular movement, which was only subsequently co-opted by the powerful and made an instrument of their authority? Alternatively, were the official and the popular cults of the Virgin both contemporary manifestations of the same cultural phenomenon?[1]

The second question is related to the first: during the early Byzantine period, how popular were images of the Virgin in the domestic arts – as opposed to other subjects, such as Old Testament scenes, or pagan iconography? In other words, how significant was her cult in the homes of ordinary people, at least insofar as it was expressed in the decoration of everyday objects?

The third question is that of gender specificity. Was the wearing of images of the Virgin in the early Byzantine period restricted to women – or especially espoused by women?

The domestic objects – the clothing and the jewellery – that bear images of the Virgin are notoriously difficult to date. Nevertheless, in several cases there is enough evidence to suggest approximate periods for their manufacture. With few exceptions, those dates do not fall before the second half of the sixth century. A well-dated example is a magnificent gold pectoral, which was discovered in Egypt and is now in Berlin. This piece consists of two parts. The upper portion incorporates fourteen gold coins on either side of a large imitation medallion depicting the bust of an emperor turned to the right. The emperor is framed by an inscription reading 'Lord, protect her who wears [this piece]'. At this period, coins and imitation coins were believed to have a protective, prophylactic value. The lower part of the pectoral consists of a large framed gold medallion depicting the Annunciation. The fourteen gold coins belong to the reigns of Justinian I, Justin II, Tiberios I and Maurice. The

---

[1] On the veneration of religious images, including those of the Virgin, as a 'horizontal' phenomenon within society, see A. M. Cameron, *Christianity and the Rhetoric of Empire* (Berkeley, 1991), 201–3.

last-named emperor reigned from 582 until 602, which gives us a *terminus post quem* for this pectoral of 582.[2]

Another magnificent gold medallion with a prophylactic inscription is preserved in the collection at Dumbarton Oaks (Fig. 16.1). It was mounted to be worn hanging from the neck by a chain. On the front side the Virgin sits enthroned between angels and holding the Christ-child on her lap. Below her, to the left, appear small scenes of the Nativity, including the child in the manger, and to the right the Adoration of the Magi. Around the upper half of the medallion is an inscription, framing the Virgin, which reinforces the message of the images: 'Christ our God, help us!'[3] This medallion was part of a treasure found near Kyrenia, on the island of Cyprus, in around 1900. As Philip Grierson has shown, technically and stylistically the medallion is very close to four consular medallions of Maurice, which belonged to the same treasure. The consular medallions were issued in 583, or in 602, when Maurice assumed the consulship for the second time. Like the consular medallions, the piece in Dumbarton Oaks with the Marian scenes was struck rather than cast.[4]

The Virgin also appears on humbler classes of jewellery, such as the silver bands that women wore around their arms. On one of these bands, which is now in Toronto, there is a crude engraving of the Virgin seated frontally on a lyre-backed throne with the Christ-child in front of her (Fig. 16.2). She is surrounded by an invocation on behalf of the wearer: 'Mother of God, help Anna. Grace'. Reportedly, this armband was discovered in eastern Turkey in a small hoard that included several coins of Justinian and also a ring and a spoon displaying cross monograms. Justinian reigned from 527 until 565, but, as Gary Vikan has argued, the presence of cross monograms indicates a date for the hoard late in Justinian's reign, after the middle of the sixth century.[5]

The Virgin also appeared on rings. For example, a gold ring in the Dumbarton Oaks collection has, engraved on its bezel, the Virgin standing between two crosses and holding her child on her left arm. This ring was part of a treasure that also contained objects datable to the sixth century, including a clasp for a necklace or a belt that frames two gold coins of Justinian. This may give us a sixth-century date for the ring, unless it was an heirloom when it was buried.[6]

The best known of the early Byzantine rings on which the Virgin appears are the octagonal gold marriage rings now preserved in London and Washington (Fig. 16.3). On the bezels of the rings in London and Washington, the Virgin is paired with Christ; they stand back to back, raising their right hands in order to bless, or to crown, the bride and the groom respectively. On each of the seven remaining facets of the hoops a different scene from the life of Christ is engraved, beginning on each of the rings with episodes in which the Virgin plays a prominent role, namely the Annunciation, the Visitation, and the Nativity. These marriage rings cannot be precisely dated, but the scenes on their hoops are related iconographically to the cycle of

---

[2] K. Weitzmann (ed.), *Age of Spirituality. Late Antique and Early Christian Art*, exh. cat., The Metropolitan Museum of Art (New York, 1979), no. 296, 319–21 (K. Reynolds Brown).

[3] M. C. Ross, *Catalogue of the Byzantine and Early Medieval Antiquities in the Dumbarton Oaks Collection* II (Washington, DC, 1965), 33–5, pls 28–9.

[4] Ph. Grierson, 'The Date of the Dumbarton Oaks Epiphany Medallion', *DOP* 15 (1961), 221–4.

[5] G. Vikan, 'Two Byzantine Amuletic Armbands and the Group to which they Belong', *The Journal of the Walters Art Gallery* 49/50 (1991/2), 33–51, esp. 38, 41.

[6] Ross, *Catalogue* II, 136–8, Pls 95, 98.

scenes that appears on the pilgrims' flasks preserved in Monza and Bobbio, which are generally assigned to the late sixth or the seventh century.[7]

The Virgin seems to have begun to make her appearance on pectoral crosses around the seventh century. One of the earliest examples is a gold cross engraved with the Virgin in the orant pose, which was discovered at Palermo together with a hoard of coins dated to the reigns of Tiberius II, Leo III and Constantine V. That means that the hoard, at least, was not buried before 741.[8] The earliest bronze pectoral crosses depicting the Virgin seem to date from the seventh or eighth centuries. Five bronze crosses survive bearing images of the Virgin in relief, standing with her hands placed on the shoulders of her child, who appears to be suspended in front of her body. The other side of these crosses shows the Crucifixion. As Brigitte Pitarakis has shown, several factors argue that this group of crosses should be dated to the seventh or the eighth centuries. For example, the depiction of Adam beneath the Crucifixion is an iconographic feature that does not appear in other works of art before the seventh century.[9]

Among the domestic arts, it is only in clothing that we find images of the Virgin occurring very occasionally before the second half of the sixth century. The principal exception to the chronological rule is provided by a fragment of draw-loom silk weaving dating to the late fourth or early fifth century. This scrap of what was originally a much larger textile was found in a grave in Egypt and is now in the collection of the Abegg-Stiftung near Bern. The silk was woven with repeated strips containing superimposed identical images of the early life of the Virgin. Several iconographic elements suggest that the silk has a fourth- or early fifth-century date. For example, in the scene of the Annunciation, the angel still has no wings. And in the episode of Christ's first bath, the water is identified by means of a personified nymph of the spring, a survival from pagan art that has no parallels in other portrayals of this episode.[10] It is very possible that this silk was originally part of a high-status garment, since a bishop of the late fourth century, Asterios of Amaseia, criticized rich people who wore silk clothing densely woven with scenes from the Gospels. He complained that 'when they come out in public dressed in this fashion, they appear like painted walls to those they meet'.[11]

It seems that the criticisms of Asterios of Amaseia, and of others who felt like him, may have been effective for some time, because by far the greatest number of pieces of clothing that survive with Christian scenes date to the seventh century or later. These include some subjects in which the Virgin plays an important part, such as the Visitation, the Nativity, and the Adoration of the Magi (Fig. 16.5). These tapestry-weaves showing Gospel scenes are closely related to another, larger group of tunic ornaments that illustrate the story of the Old Testament patriarch Joseph (Fig. 16.6). Both groups of textiles frequently have red grounds, which imitate silks, and the ornamental motifs in their borders are similar. The work of Laila Abdel-Malek has convincingly dated the Joseph textiles to the seventh century, primarily on the basis of their

---

[7] G. Vikan, 'Art and Marriage in Early Byzantium', *DOP* 44 (1990), 145–63, esp. 157–8.
[8] B. Pitarakis, 'Un groupe de croix-reliquaires pectorales en bronze à décor en relief attribuable à Constantinople avec le Crucifié et la Vierge Kyriotissa', *CahArch* 46 (1998), 81–102, esp. 101 n. 80.
[9] Ibid., 92–5.
[10] L. Kötzsche, 'Die Marienseide in der Abegg-Stiftung. Bermerkungen zur Ikonographie der Szenenfolge', *Riggisberger Berichte* 1 (1993), 183–94.
[11] Ibid., 193–4. *Homilia I*, PG 40, 168; tr. Mango, *Art of the Byz. Empire*, 50–1.

ornament. Among other pieces of evidence she makes effective use of comparisons with motifs found on Byzantine silverware dated by imperial stamps to the first decade of the seventh century.[12]

To sum up, it appears that the Virgin begins to play a significant role in the decoration of domestic objects in the latter half of the sixth century, and more prominently in the seventh. She appears earlier in the decoration of some domestic textiles, but by far the majority of surviving examples in this medium are seventh-century or later. From this conclusion we can see that the famous image of Theodora in San Vitale, wearing an embroidery of the Adoration of the Magi on the hem of her silk cloak in the mid-sixth century, was in the vanguard.[13] It was not until the following century that the ordinary people of Egypt were to incorporate this subject onto their clothing in the cheaper medium of tapestry weave (Fig. 16.5).[14]

If we turn from domestic objects to monumental art, we find that the Virgin was invoked as a protector in the officially sponsored art of churches well before she was invoked in the art of the home. In the late 460s she was portrayed in a now lost mosaic at Constantinople, which had been commissioned by the imperial family to fill the apse of the church of the 'Soros' at the Blachernai, the space which enshrined the precious relic of the Virgin's veil. The mosaic at the Blachernai reportedly depicted the Virgin on a throne and flanked by the emperor Leo I, his empress Verina, their daughter Ariadne, and their grandson Leo. The empress was holding the infant Leo while she bowed, or kneeled, before the Virgin. Although this work no longer survives, it is described in a sixth-century text that recounts the translation of the veil from Palestine to Constantinople.[15]

The mosaics of the Virgin that survive, or are recorded, from churches of the sixth century are well known.[16] The most impressive of them is the great apse of the basilica built by Bishop Eufrasius at Poreč, in Istria (Plate 11, Fig. 16.7). The mosaics at the Eufrasiana can be dated to the middle of the sixth century, although they were extensively restored in the late nineteenth century. Here we find the Virgin seated on a jewelled throne in the centre of the apse vault. She is flanked on the left by St Maurus, a former bishop of Parentium, followed by the current bishop, Eufrasius, followed by the archdeacon, Claudius, and by Claudius' young son, also named Eufrasius. Thus, as in the mosaic at the Blachernai, we have a parent presenting a child to the Virgin; in the mosaic at Poreč, the young Eufrasius is holding candles with long wicks as offerings.[17] The Virgin also appears with high-status supplicants in

---

[12] L. Abdel-Malek, 'Joseph Tapestries and Related Coptic Textiles', PhD thesis, Boston University, 1980, esp. 147–52, 161–73.
[13] F. W. Deichmann, *Frühchristliche Bauten und Mosaiken von Ravenna* (Baden-Baden, 1958), Pls 358, 360, 367.
[14] Abdel-Malek, 'Joseph Tapestries', 169–73, 227–9.
[15] Mango, 'Blachernae Shrine', 61–75, esp. 70–1.
[16] For surveys of them, see C. Rizzardi, 'Relazioni artistiche fra Ravenna e l'Istria: i mosaici parietali', *CorsiRav* 42 (1995), 817–36, esp. 825–30. R. Cormack, 'The Mother of God in Apse Mosaics', in Vassilaki, *Mother of God*, 91–105.
[17] A. Terry and H. Maguire, 'The Wall Mosaics at the Cathedral of Eufrasius in Poreč', *Hortus Artium Medievalium* 4 (1998), 199–221, Fig. 3; 6 (2000) 159–81, Figs 1, 21, 24, 29–31.

the now lost ex-voto mosaics of the inner north aisle of the church of St Demetrios at Thessaloniki, which may have dated to the first half of the sixth century.[18]

The evidence of these and other sixth-century mosaics suggests that during the fifth and much of the sixth centuries the Virgin was more prominently displayed as the recipient of supplications in the public art of churches than she was in the domestic art of people's homes. It is only in the course of the second half of the sixth century that the Virgin begins to appear on jewellery and apparel with any regularity. We can, indeed, propose a progression, from public monumental art to high-status jewellery and apparel, and from the items of attire worn by the rich to the adornments of the less wealthy. For example, we have seen that the two marriage rings, with their paired images of Christ and the Virgin crowning or blessing the groom and the bride, probably date to the end of the sixth century or the beginning of the seventh (Fig. 16.3). But they had a precedent in public, imperial art, which we can find in Paul Silentiarios' description of the lost gold-embroidered silks that once adorned the sanctuary of the reconstructed church of Hagia Sophia in Constantinople, which was rededicated in 562. These silks showed both Christ and the Virgin 'joining together' the imperial couple, Justinian and Theodora. Although Paul Silentiarios' description does not specify the precise nature of the composition on the silks, his text suggests that the imagery of Christ and the Virgin acting as a pair to bless a marriage had its origins in imperial art.[19] The art-historical evidence, therefore, strongly suggests that the visual cult of the Virgin began at the top, and only later filtered down to the everyday domestic objects used by ordinary people. The material culture provides little evidence for a horizontal explanation; that is, the beginnings of the visual invocation of the Virgin in the official and in the domestic contexts do not seem to have been contemporaneous.

The second question concerns the cult of the Virgin among the general population. To what extent was the cult of the Virgin during the later sixth and the seventh centuries truly popular – how frequently was she evoked as opposed to other Christian, or even pagan, holy figures? There are obvious difficulties in trying to answer this important problem from the material culture. Although a remarkable number of objects have survived from early Byzantine households, they are often small, and they are widely scattered in both public and private collections. Much of this material is uncatalogued, which makes it difficult to quantify. Nevertheless, some classes of material are well enough documented that one can make some preliminary observations concerning the relative popularity of images of the Virgin. For example, some interesting statistics can be drawn from Gary Vikan's recent catalogue of twenty-two surviving silver and bronze armbands that he dates to between the mid-sixth and the mid-seventh centuries. Starting with images of individual holy figures, as opposed to narrative scenes, we find only one portrayal of the Virgin: it is the engraving of the enthroned Virgin and Child that we have

---

[18] For a discussion of these mosaics and their patronage, see L. Brubaker, 'Elites and Patronage in Early Byzantium: the Evidence from Hagios Demetrios at Thessalonike', in J. F. Haldon (ed.), *Elites in Late Antiquity* (Princeton, NJ, forthcoming).

[19] *Descriptio S. Sophiae*, lines 802–4, ed. P. Friedländer, *Johannes von Gaza und Paulus Silentiarius* (Leipzig and Berlin, 1912), 249; tr. Mango, *Art of the Byz. Empire*, 89.

already seen on the band in Toronto (Fig. 16.2). Among the other motifs on the bands, there are six images of saints who are not the Virgin. One of these can be identified as Menas, since he is flanked by camels, and one is attired as a soldier. The other four saints, who appear to be male, are standing in the orant pose. In addition to these Christian saints, the armbands present ten images of the Holy Rider, a figure with both Christian and magical associations. Among the narrative scenes that involve the Virgin, the Annunciation is depicted six times on the bands. On the other hand, the Visit of the Women to the Tomb, a scene without the participation of the Virgin, occurs eight times. The Nativity occurs four times, the same number as for the Baptism and the Crucifixion, in which the Virgin is not shown on the bands. The Adoration of the Magi is found twice, and the Visitation not at all.[20] The conclusion must be that on the armbands, at least, images of the Virgin were not especially frequent. The most favoured subject was the Holy Rider, whose connotations were half-Christian at best.

A somewhat similar conclusion concerning the status of the Virgin in domestic art can be obtained from a survey of the surviving marriage rings, which have also been catalogued by Gary Vikan.[21] There are some twenty extant examples of marriage rings showing on their bezels the bride and groom standing beside Christ alone (Fig. 16.4), but only two rings feature the bride and the groom flanking both Christ and the Virgin (Fig. 16.3). These two are the already mentioned rings at Dumbarton Oaks and at the British Museum. It is perhaps not accidental that they are particularly expensive rings, with an elaborate figural decoration in niello, so that, in effect, they should count as high-status items.

As we have seen, there survives a group of tapestry weaves from tunics with narrative scenes involving the Virgin. These relatively inexpensive textiles have been catalogued by Laila Abdel-Malek, and, once again, the textiles with the Virgin are relatively few in number. Abdel-Malek lists four examples depicting the Visitation, three with the Nativity, and nine with the Adoration of the Magi (Fig. 16.5). On the other hand, she lists no fewer than fifty-four textiles with scenes from the life of Joseph (Fig. 16.6).[22] So this Old Testament subject was clearly more popular than any of the Gospel episodes in which the Virgin plays a role.

Our conclusion has to be that the Virgin did not play an especially large part in the decoration of apparel before iconoclasm – at least not among the general population.

The third question is that of gender specificity. As far as the evidence of images is concerned, we have seen that men as well as women invoked the protection of the Virgin through large-scale mosaics in churches – witness the apse mosaics at the Blachernai and at Poreč (Fig. 16.7). But what of the arts of the household: were images of the Virgin perhaps limited to items worn by women, or particularly associated with them? This is another difficult question to answer, but it can be said that in the early Byzantine period, when we find a personal name accompanying an image of the Virgin on an item of apparel, the name is usually, but not always, female. In the post-iconoclast period, on the other hand, there are a greater number of inscriptions on such objects that mention men.

---

[20] Vikan, 'Armbands', 40–1.
[21] Vikan, 'Art and Marriage', 145–63.
[22] Abdel-Malek, 'Joseph Tapestries', 200–29.

We have already cited two examples of objects with inscriptions naming women: the pectoral in Berlin, with its portrayal of the Annunciation and its gender-specific inscription: 'Lord, protect *her* who wears this piece', and the armband in Toronto, where the image of the enthroned Virgin and Child is accompanied by the inscription: 'Mother of God, help Anna' (Fig. 16.2). To these examples can be added a gold ring in Paris which has the Annunciation engraved on its bezel, and on its hoop the following invocation on behalf of a female wearer: 'Mother of God, help your servant Giora.'[23] There is also another published ring in Munich portraying the Hodegetria on the bezel with the inscription 'Mother of God, help Eustathia' on the hoop.[24]

With textiles, it is very difficult to determine the gender of the wearer of the garments, because most of the surviving pieces are only scraps of clothing obtained from unscientific excavations. Nevertheless, at San Vitale it is Theodora, not Justinian, who wears the Magi embroidered into her robe, even though both the emperor and the empress are portrayed bringing gifts.

There is, then, some support for the notion that the cult of the Virgin would have been especially attractive to women in domestic contexts, an attractiveness that must have been enhanced by the analogical potential of scenes such as the Visitation and the Nativity, which could function as exemplars of successful pregnancy and childbirth.[25] However, the statistical sample is still extremely small, so it may be unwise to draw firm conclusions from it. And there is no doubt that men also sought the Virgin's aid in their search for home remedies. This can be seen from a medical charm that is preserved on a fifth-century papyrus from Egypt, now in Berlin. In this amulet, which was probably designed to be worn around the neck, the Virgin is asked to 'stop the discharge, the pains of the eyes of Phoibammon, son of Athanasios', since she has 'received grace from' her 'only-begotten Son'.[26] A silver ring in Berlin portrays the Virgin and Child on its bezel, with the following inscription on the hoop: 'Mother of God, help Kosmas.'[27]

In summary, the Virgin and scenes from her life do not appear to have become popular subjects for depiction on jewellery and clothing until the second half of the sixth century, and even then she was not as popular as other Christian figures, or even subjects of pagan origin. There are very few portrait images of the Virgin in the silks and tapestry weaves intended for clothing or for domestic furnishings during the early Byzantine period, but there are a great many images of other women, for the most part beneficent and often sumptuously dressed personifications of pagan derivation, such as seasons, tyches, or the earth with her fruits. These 'wealthy women', with their jewellery and their rosy cheeks, had general connotations of good fortune, good health, and prosperity (Fig. 16.8).[28] In many respects the visual culture of the household was

---

[23] J. Durand (ed.), *Byzance, L'art byzantin dans les collections publiques françaises*, exh. cat., Musée du Louvre, 3 November 1992 – 1 February 1993 (Paris, 1992), no. 88, 133 (J.-Cl. Cheynet).
[24] Vassilaki, *Mother of God*, no. 13, 294–5 (J. Spier).
[25] H. Maguire, 'The Cult of the Mother of God in Private', in Vassilaki, *Mother of God*, 284–5.
[26] R. W. Daniel, F. Maltomini, *Supplementum Magicum* I (Opladen, 1990), no. 26, 72–3.
[27] W. F. Volbach, *Bildwerke des Kaiser-Friedrich-Museums, Mittelalterliche Bildwerke aus Italien und Byzanz* (Berlin and Leipzig, 1930), no. 6398, 133, Pl. 5 (with a 10th-century dating).
[28] E. D. Maguire, H. P. Maguire, and M. J. Duncan-Flowers, 'Designs in Context', in eid., *Art and Holy Powers in*

more conservative than the official art of church and state; the old pagan images lingered longer, and the new cult of the Mother of God penetrated more slowly.

With respect to gender specificity, there is certainly evidence that the cult of the Virgin held a particular appeal for women at home. Nevertheless, in the early Byzantine period, men also appealed to the Virgin for help in day-to-day problems. After iconoclasm, the invocations accompanying images of the Virgin on jewellery are as likely to be on behalf of men as of women, as in the case of the ring of Michael Attaleiates, the well-known historian and high Byzantine official who died around 1080. This piece has an enamelled bust of the Virgin on its bezel, and an inscription on the hoop reading 'Mother of God, help your servant Michael Attaleiates'.[29]

Finally, it should be emphasized that the conclusions presented in this paper are only preliminary. Completely accurate statistics will only become possible after a full publication and inventory of the various classes of material that have been surveyed here – and that goal is a long way away. My aim has been only to highlight the importance of these objects for what they may be able to tell us about changes in people's engagement with the supernatural, and the developing role of the cult of the Virgin. These domestic items – the jewellery and the scraps of clothing – speak about all members of Byzantine society; both the exalted, whose culture is comparatively better documented, and the humble, whose lives and concerns the written texts often failed to reach.

---

the *Early Christian House*, exh. cat., Krannert Art Museum (Urbana and Chicago, 1989), 2–3, 13–14, Figs 1, 10–14.

[29] Ross, *Catalogue* II, no. 156, 107, Pls E, 72. Aim. Yeroulanou, 'The Mother of God in Jewellery', in Vassilaki, *Mother of God*, 233–4, Pl. 182.

BYZANTINE DOMESTIC ART 191

16.1 Washington, DC, Dumbarton Oaks Collection. Gold medallion. Virgin and Child with the Nativity and the Adoration of the Magi (source: Dumbarton Oaks)

16.3 Washington, DC, Dumbarton Oaks Collection. Gold marriage ring. Christ and the Virgin between the groom and the bride (source: Dumbarton Oaks)

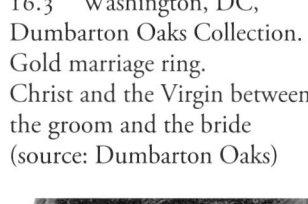

16.2 Toronto, Royal Ontario Museum. Silver armband. Virgin and Child (source: Royal Ontario Museum)

16.4 Richmond, Virginia Museum of Fine Arts. The Arthur and Margaret Glasgow Fund. Gold marriage ring. Christ between the groom and the bride (source: photo, Ron Jennings, © Virginia Museum of Fine Arts)

16.5 London, British Museum. Tapestry-woven medallion. The Adoration of the Magi (source: British Museum)

16.6 New York, The Metropolitan Museum of Art, Gift of Mr and Mrs Charles K. Wilkinson, 1963, 63.178.2. Tapestry-woven medallion. Scenes from the life of Joseph (source: The Metropolitan Museum of Art)

16.7 Poreč, Basilica of Eufrasius. Apse mosaic. The Virgin and Child with bishop Eufrasius and the child Eufrasius (detail) (source: A. Terry)

16.8 Washington, DC, The Textile Museum. Tapestry-woven panel. 'Wealthy woman' (source: The Textile Museum)

The 'activated' icon:
the Hodegetria procession and Mary's *Eisodos**

Bissera V. Pentcheva

Public liturgical processions in Constantinople developed in the context of the stational liturgy in the late fourth century.[1] Icons, however, were not included in these *litaniai* until after the end of iconoclasm.[2] By the eleventh century most of the established processions such as the *presbeia* at the Blachernai integrated painted panels as part of their train.[3] Along with the traditional *litaniai*, new processions were created for the explicit purpose of showcasing icons, for example the Tuesday ceremony with the Hodegetria.[4] The original Tuesday procession formed part of the stational liturgy; it covered a long route, starting in the early morning at the Hodegon, moving up the main thoroughfare of the city, the Mese, and culminating in a different church each week for the celebration of Mass. In the course of time this *litania* changed. By the fourteenth century the procession covered a very short route from the monastery to a square nearby, where most of the ceremony took place. Attention was focused on the action of the blindfolded man who carried the icon on his back and swayed to and fro under its burden (Fig. 17.1).

Icons carried in processions move in the time and space of the spectator. They engage the viewer mimetically and kinaesthetically and trigger a dramatic emotional response.[5] How can we gain access to this past experience; how can we reconstruct the processions? Many obstacles stand in the way, particularly as the Byzantines did not feel the necessity to describe and depict their processions with icons. By the end of the eleventh century they perceived these *litaniai* as manifestations of an established tradition that did not need to be recorded. Most of the evidence about Byzantine *litaniai* comes from the fourteenth century in the form of written accounts by foreign visitors to the capital, and of images depicting the Constantinopolitan *litaniai* as imitated and performed outside the empire in the neighbouring states.[6] Yet because the Palaiologan processions did not resemble their Middle Byzantine precedents, the use of this

---

* This paper is excerpted from my book entitled: *Icons and Power: the Mother of God in Byzantium* (University Park, PA, forthcoming).

[1] J. Baldovin, *The Urban Character of Christian Worship. The Origins, Development and Meaning of Stational Liturgy* (Rome, 1987).

[2] B. V. Pentcheva, 'The Supernatural Protector of Constantinople: The Virgin and Her Icons in the Tradition of the Avar Siege', *BMGS* 26 (2002), 2–41.

[3] J. Thomas and A. C. Hero (eds), *Byzantine Monastic Foundation Documents. A Complete Translation of Surviving Founder's Typika and Testaments* II (Washington, DC, 2000), 753–4. N. P. Ševčenko, 'Icons in the Liturgy', *DOP* 45 (1991), 45–57.

[4] Pentcheva, *Icons and Power*.

[5] S. V. Webster, *Art and Ritual in Golden Age Spain. Sevillian Confraternities and the Processional Sculpture of Holy Week* (Princeton, NJ, 1998), 58.

[6] N. P. Ševčenko, 'Servants of the Holy Icon', in C. Moss and K. Kiefer (eds), *Byzantine East, Latin West. Studies in Honor of Kurt Weitzmann* (Princeton, NJ, 1995), 547–53.

later material to reconstruct the early processions is problematic. Despite the fact that there are no visual representations recording the original Tuesday processions, by using the evidence of narrative scenes from the life of the Theotokos, especially her Entry into the Temple or *Eisodos*, this paper will reconstruct the *litania* with the Hodegetria icon in the Middle Byzantine period and explore its meaning.

Iconography of the Hodegetria icon

The Hodegetria icon displays a specific and easily recognizable iconographic type. It features the Virgin carrying the Child in her left arm and gesturing to him with her free right hand (Fig. 17.2). He answers to her intercessory prayer by raising his hand in blessing. The image-type expresses the notion of conversation silently conducted through the painted hands of the Mother and Child. The dialogue has the potential to expand in the physical space of the viewer when the same gestures are mimetically reproduced by the faithful in the process of prayer or in the train of the procession.

The early 'Hodegetria' visual formula is employed on seventh-century imperial seals (Fig. 17.3).[7] The image-type dominant in the period from the sixth to the tenth centuries shows Mary placing her right hand on the infant's knee. Rather than offering the Child, she keeps his body closer to hers and seeks physical and tactile contact with him.[8] It is this close physical link between the Mother and Child that dissolves in the representations after iconoclasm. Starting in the tenth century, a new image-type is formed, according to which the Virgin only gestures towards the Child and her embrace is loosened (Figs 17.2–17.3).[9] The new visual formula emphasizes the dogmatic or theological relationship in the way Mary pleads with and offers Christ.[10] It is this image-type that should be identified as the 'Hodegetria'.

In this post-tenth-century visual type, distinction should be made between images that merely exhibit the iconographic type and representations that display the visual formula along with the name 'Hodegetria' inscribed in the field. Only these named images were understood by their mediaeval audience as conscious copies of the original Hodegetria icon of the Hodegon monastery. An example is offered by the thirteenth-century panel from the Peribleptos church in Ohrid; it has the name 'Hodegetria' inscribed across the top.[11] Like the original Hodegetria, it is a two-sided panel featuring the Virgin and Christ on the front (Plate 12a, Fig. 17.4) and the

---

[7] Seal of Emperor Constantine IV (668–685): G. Zacos and A. Veglery, *Byzantine Lead Seals* I (Basel, 1972), no. 23. W. Seibt, 'Die Darstellung der Theotokos auf byzantinischen Bleisiegeln besonders im 11. Jahrhundert', *Studies in Byzantine Sigillography* 1 (1987), 35–56, esp. 37–8.

[8] For other images, see Vassilaki, *Mother of God*, no. 2, 264–5 (R. Cormack) and Pls 1, 3, 169, 199. The traditional identification of the pre-iconoclast type with the term 'Hodegetria' is problematic: see for instance H. Torp, 'Una Vergine Hodigitria del periodo iconoclastico nel "Tempietto Longobardo" di Cividale', in A. Cadei et al. (eds), *Arte d'Occidente, Temi e metodi. Studi in onore di Angiola Maria Romanini* II (Rome, 1999), 583–99.

[9] The icon from Mt Sinai is dated to the 8th to 9th c. by K. Weitzmann, *The Monastery of Saint Catherine at Mount Sinai. The Icons* (Princeton, NJ, 1976), no. B40, 67, and to the 10th c. by L. Brubaker, in J. Haldon and L. Brubaker, *Byzantium in the Iconoclast Era (ca. 680–850). The Sources: an Annotated Survey* (Birmingham and Aldershot, 2001), 70.

[10] Pentcheva, *Icons and Power*.

[11] V. Djurić, *Icônes de Yougoslavie* (Belgrade, 1961), no. 4, 85–6. *Trésors médiévaux de la République de Macédoine*,

Crucifixion on the back (Plate 12b, Fig. 17.5).[12] The Mother and Child on the obverse are gently brought together; they stand straight, composed, without overt embracing and tugging.

Both figures have one hand that speaks and another that carries an object. The speaking hand of Mary is visually juxtaposed with the speaking hand of Christ, forming the first pair of hands. The *Theometor* gestures to and implores the Child in a manner similar to the way she prays in the standard Deesis scenes. Christ answers by raising and blessing with his hand. In the second pair, the hand of each figure holds the *Logos*, and thus expresses the notion of the Incarnation. The Mother's arm carries the Word in the form of the Child, while Christ holds it in the form of a text scroll.

The position of the speaking hand of the Virgin mirrors the way the viewer would pray in front of the image. By depicting the very gesture that the faithful would use to carry out their communication with God, the painted image gives reassurance of the success of the prayer and the Virgin's intercession for humanity. Mary's gesture both elicits and enhances the response of the viewer. The supplication conveyed both through the painted hands in the icon and through the living hands of the faithful constitutes the main theme of the public processions: a communal intercession addressed to God.

The Tuesday procession in the texts and images

What did the Tuesday procession look like in the Middle Byzantine period? According to the eleventh-century life of St. Thomaîs of Lesbos, the Tuesday *litania* started in the early morning.[13] It passed through the Mese, making stops/stations at many churches along the way, and culminating at a different sanctuary each week for the celebration of the day's stational liturgy.[14]

The urban *litaniai* were usually led by crosses called *litanikoi stauroi*.[15] When decorated, these objects sometimes featured figures in intercessory gestures, thereby enhancing the mimetic response of the participants in the procession. In addition to the crosses, icons played a prominent role in the Tuesday *litaniai*. Many of these panels were carried on forked poles affixed to the bottom of their frames. Both the crosses and the icons were transported by means

---

exh. cat., Paris, Musée national du Moyen Âge – Thermes de Cluny, 9 February – 3 May 1999 (Paris, 1999), no. 19, 62–3 (V. Popovska-Korobar).

[12] *Pero Tafur. Travels and Adventures 1435–1439*, tr. M. Letts (London, 1926), 141–2. A. Vasiliev, 'Pero Tafur. A Spanish Traveller of the Fifteenth Century and his Visit to Constantinople', *Byz* 7 (1932), 75–122. R. González de Clavijo, *Embassy to Tamerlane 1403–1406*, tr. G. Le Strange (London, 1928), 83–5.

[13] P. Halsall, 'Life of Thomaïs of Lesbos', in A.-M. Talbot (ed.), *Holy Women in Byzantium. Ten Saints' Lives in English Translation* (Washington, DC, 1996), 291–322, esp. 311. For the 11th-c. date, see A. Kazhdan, *List of Saints, First to Tenth Centuries*, unpublished work, kept at Dumbarton Oaks.

[14] E. von Dobschütz, 'Maria Romaia. Zwei unbekannte Texte', *BZ* 12 (1903), 173–214. For a second recension of the same text, dated to the late 11th c., but reworked in the 13th c., see id., *Christusbilder. Texte und Untersuchungen zur Geschichte der altchristlichen Literatur* I–III (Leipzig, 1899), 233**–66**, esp. 258**.

[15] J. Cotsonis, *Byzantine Figural Processional Crosses*, exh. cat., Dumbarton Oaks, 23 September 1994 – 29 January 1995 (*Dumbarton Oaks Collection Publications*, 10) (Washington, DC, 1994), 14–24, esp. 23. See also the literature on the Cluny cross from the 11th c. displaying Marian iconography, J.-P. Caillet, 'La croix byzantine du musée de Cluny', *La Revue du Louvre et des musées de France* 3 (1988), 208–17.

of the same mechanism: a handle placed in a metal cup or a leather pouch with a sling suspended from the neck of the bearer (Fig. 17.6).[16]

A text written by a Latin pilgrim in the last quarter of the eleventh century offers the most detailed account of the procession:[17]

> There is another church, which is called the Hodegetria, in which resides the glorious icon of the Theotokos painted by St Luke the Evangelist, as the Greeks say. This icon is in the highest veneration in Constantinople, so that throughout the year on Tuesdays it is carried by the clergy with the greatest honour through the city, with an exceeding multitude of men and women walking in front of and behind it, singing praises to the Theotokos and carrying burning candles in their hands. You would witness in this procession that takes place, as I said, on Tuesday at all times many different examples of human veneration, and you would hear many sweet-sounding voices not only of the clergy but of the lay people, and, what you would marvel and delight at more, women dressed in silk clothes, singing religious chants behind the icon of the Theotokos, like maids after their mistress. And next to the voice of the Psalmist, youths and virgins, old and young men, give praise to the name of God who became incarnated in the Virgin for our sake. Preceding indeed this noble image of the Mother of God are numerous other icons from other churches, sacred and golden, as maids precede their mistress. [The icon] then follows the rest at the back, and like the mistress of all others she is recognised by her merciful face and gesture. Then in the church where the stational liturgy is scheduled for that day, festivities are celebrated by the people. The laymen gather there, and as the glorious image is brought with honour to the church allotted for the stational liturgy for the day, mass is celebrated. After the rites are duly performed the icon is taken back again to its own church with great honour.
>
> I have heard them relate a miracle about this holy image [the Hodegetria], when I was staying in the aforementioned city. When the aforesaid icon of the blessed Mother of God is carried through the city and passes by the church of Christ the Saviour [at the Chalke] in whose entry Jesus is eminently represented, the sacred Theotokos turns by itself to face her Son, independently of the one who carries the icon; and the image of the Mother turns to see the face of her Son [Christ at Chalke], wanting to gaze at and venerate the Son who made her Queen of the angels. I myself did not see this, because I did not look closely but I heard about it when staying there.[18]

---

[16] N. P. Ševčenko, 'The Limburg Staurothek and its Relics', in Θυμίαμα στη μνήμη της Λασκαρίνας Μπούρα I (Athens, 1994), 289–94.

[17] K. Ciggaar, 'Une description de Constantinople dans le *Tarragonensis* 55', *REB* 53 (1995), 117–40, esp. 128–31. The manuscript dates from the late 12th or early 13th c., yet the text itself is dated on internal topographical evidence to the period 1075–1098 or 1099.

[18] 'Est quoque alia ecclesia que Odigitria dicitur, in qua est gloriosa Dei genetricis ycona quam beatus Luchas euangelista, ut aiunt Greci, depinxit. Hec in summa veneratione est in Constantinopolitana urbe adeo ut per totum anni curriculum omni ebdomada feria .iii. defertitur a clericis per urbem cum maximo honore, preeunte ac subsequente permaxima virorum ac mulierum multitudine canentium laudes Dei genetrici ac cereos ardentes tenentium in manibus suis. Cerneres in hac processione que, ut dixi, tercia feria fit omni tempore multos et diversos cultus hominum, audires multas dulcisonas voces non solum clericorum verum et laicorum et quod magis mirareris et placeret mulieres oloscericis indutas vestibus clericales cantus canentes post Dei genetricis yconam et quasi famulas sequentes dominam. Et iuxta Psalmiste vocem iuvenes et virgines, senes cum iunioribus laudent nomen Domini qui pro nobis ex Maria carnem assumpsit. Precedunt vero hanc nobilem Dei genetricis ymaginem alie quam plurime ex aliis ecclesiis ymagines sancte auree quasi dominam famule. Ipsa autem retro sequitur ceteras sicut omnium earum domina clementi vultu sicut cognoscitur actu. Porro in ecclesia ad quam eo die fit statio celebratur festivitas a populo. Fit ibi concursus popularis et sicut cum honore gloriosa imago est delata ad ecclesiam in qua eo die habuit stationem, sic missa celebrata; omnibusque rite peractis cum magno honore iterum refertur ad suam sedem.
Audivi autem referre quoddam miraculum de eadem sancta ymagine positus in predicta urbe. Dum defertur

In this description of the procession, attention is focused on the icons and the entourage of women dressed in silk: clearly the two most prominent elements that caught the eye of the foreign visitor. The Hodegetria is like a mistress surrounded by her maids (the icons of the other Constantinopolitan churches), all sending off streams of golden light. The women dressed in silk garments enhance this opulence. It is the light of the gilded and metal-revetted icons and the shimmering silk gowns of the women that characterize the procession.

At the culmination of the ceremony the Hodegetria is brought to the altar of the designated church for the celebration of the liturgy. This ritual symbolically resembles the procession during the *Eisodos* of Mary. The Virgin is escorted like a bride by a train of Jewish maidens, received at the altar by the priest Zacharias, and welcomed at the Holy of Holies. In a similar manner, the Hodegetria icon is brought out from the Hodegon with a procession of maidens and icons and deposited on the altar of the church designated for the last station of the Tuesday *litania*. Moreover, like the child Mary sitting in the Holy of Holies, the Hodegetria panel was traditionally kept in the sanctuary of the Hodegon monastery during the week.[19]

Based on this affinity between the Tuesday Hodegetria processions and the feast of Mary's *Eisodos*, it is possible to use narrative scenes from this moment of Mary's life to shed light on the Tuesday icon *litaniai*. A miniature from the twelfth-century Kokkinobaphos manuscript Vat. gr. 1162, fol. 59v depicts a procession from the Virgin's Entry into the Temple (Fig. 17.7).[20] The *litania* is headed by the Jewish maidens carrying candles. Following the young girls is the three-year old Mary placed in the middle of the upper register. Her parents Anna and Joachim and a group of middle-aged men appear at the back. At the bottom, the crowds of men, women, and children split in order to let the procession pass through their midst.[21] The perception of space changes from the upper to the lower frieze; while the direction goes from left to right at the top, the procession should be imagined as cutting straight through the centre of the congregation at the bottom.

The miniature presents the diversity of the crowd; people come from all walks of life. Most of them raise their hands in prayer, replicating the very gesture the Virgin makes both in the frieze above and on the Hodegetria icon (Figs 17.4 and 17.7). The miniature suggests by analogy that during the regular Tuesday procession the raised hands of the faithful were in

---

beate Dei genetricis supradicta imago per urbem et transit iuxta basilicam Sancti Salvatoris, in cuius introitu idem Ihesus est egregie effigiatus, sponte sua dei genetrix sancta vertit se ad filium velit nolit ille qui portat eam, et matris imago se convertit ad videndum vultum filii, volens cernere et honorare filium qui fecit eam reginam angelorum. Hoc quidem ego non vidi quia non consideravi sed ibi manens audivi'. From Ciggaar, 'Tarragonensis 55', 127.

[19] The icon was kept in the sanctuary, while a copy was set for veneration in the naos, as discussed in a late 14th- or early 15th-c. text. Angelidi, 'Un texte patriographique', 113–49, esp. 147. G. Ralles and M. Potles (eds), Σύνταγμα των θείων και ιερών κανόνων των τε αγίων και πανευφήμων αποστόλων και των ιερών οικουμενικών Συνόδων και των κατά μέρος αγίων πατέρων (Athens, 1952), 467.

[20] I. Hutter, 'Die Homilien des Mönches Jakobus und ihre Illustrationen, Vat. gr. 1162 und Paris. gr. 1208', PhD thesis, University of Vienna, 1970, 125–38. For the most recent facsimile, see ead. and P. Canart, *Das Marienhomiliar des Mönches Jakobos von Kokkinobaphos. Codex Vaticanus Graecus 1162* (*Codices ex Vaticanis selecti*, 79) (Zurich, 1991). For issues of patronage, see J. Anderson, 'A Twelfth-Century Leaf from the Byzantine Courtly Circle in the Freer Gallery of Art', *Gesta* 35 (1996), 142–8. Id., 'The Seraglio Octateuch and the Kokkinobaphos Master', *DOP* 36 (1982), 83–114. Id., 'The Illustrated Sermons of Saint James the Monk: Dates, Order, and Place in the History of Byzantine Art', *Viator* 22 (1991), 69–120.

[21] The same reading also in Hutter, 'Die Homilien des Mönches Jakobus', 129.

harmony with the painted hands of the Virgin on the icon. Similarly, the people depicted in this scene with their faces raised to view Mary evoke the way participants in the procession saw the Hodegetria raised above their heads.

The Tuesday procession and Mary's *Eisodos*

No Middle Byzantine depiction of the Tuesday processions exists. The illustrated *menologia* do not include *litaniai* with icons.[22] Their miniatures only feature processions established in the pre-iconoclast period which do not include panels but merely crosses and tapers (Fig. 17.6).[23] It is therefore necessary to turn to another source of visual evidence. As already suggested by the Latin pilgrim's account, an affinity existed between the Tuesday Hodegetria procession and the feast of Mary's *Eisodos*. The Byzantines rarely depicted scenes from daily life, but they were capable of reading elements of their contemporary reality in the scenes from the *vitae* of the Virgin and Christ. This section will focus on the origins and development of the scene of Mary's *Eisodos* and explore the symbolic connection between this narrative image and the Tuesday Hodegetria *litania*.

Jacqueline Lafontaine-Dosogne has studied the iconography of Mary's Entrance into the Temple.[24] She has not, however, addressed the issue of the relationship between the narrative scene and the reality of Byzantine processions. A fifth-century ivory book-cover in the cathedral treasury in Milan is among the earliest extant examples (Fig. 17.8).[25] Mary's *Eisodos* is carved on the top right; it features the Virgin standing in front of a staircase leading to a church. The angel points with his finger to a star in Heaven. There is a total absence of processional elements; the image only depicts the encounter of the Virgin with the angel. The character of this early composition is not surprising, particularly as this moment of Mary's life was defined as a feast only in the eighth century by Patriarch Germanos I (715–730).[26]

The Entrance of the Virgin into the Temple develops into an image of a procession in the post-iconoclast period.[27] Several ninth- and tenth-century frescoes from Cappadocia depict the *Eisodos* of Mary as a *litania*, in which Anna and Joachim escort their child to the high priest Zacharias.[28] The iconography of this scene is gradually expanded with the addition of the

---

[22] *Il menologio di Basilio II* I–II (Turin, 1907). Evans and Wixom, *The Glory of Byzantium*, no. 55, 100–1 (D. G. Katsarelias), with recent bibliography.
[23] *Il menologio di Basilio II*, pp. 142, 350. J. Baldovin, 'A Note on the Liturgical Processions in the *Menologion* of Basil II (MS. Vat. gr. 1613)', in E. Carr, S. Parenti, A. Thiermeyer and E. Velkovska (eds), *Eulogema. Studies in Honor of Robert Taft S.J.* (*Studia Anselmiana*, 110, *Analecta liturgica*, 17) (Rome, 1993), 25–37.
[24] J. Lafontaine-Dosogne, *Iconographie de l'enfance de la Vierge dans l'Empire byzantin et en Occident* I (Brussels, 1964; repr. 1992), 136–67.
[25] F. Volbach, *Elfenbeinarbeiten der Spätantike und des frühen Mittelalters* (Mainz, 1976), no. 119.
[26] Lafontaine-Dosogne, *Iconographie de l'enfance de la Vierge* I, 137.
[27] Hutter has argued for a connection between Mary's *Eisodos* and wedding processions. The same parallel is drawn by Photios in his Homily VII. Photios urges his listeners to imagine the Feast of the Annunciation as a wedding procession (Hutter, 'Die Homilien des Mönches Jakobos', 128 n. 6).
[28] Church of Joachim and Anna at Kizil, 9th c.; chapel of the Theotokos, Göreme, 10th c. Lafontaine-Dosogne, *Iconographie de l'enfance de la Vierge* I, 136–67, esp. 138. C. Jolivet-Lévy, *Les églises byzantines de Cappadoce. Le programme iconographique de l'abside et de ses abords* (Paris, 1991), 46–50, 109–11.

figures of seven maidens holding burning tapers.²⁹ The presence of these young women emphasizes the processional aspect of the image.

The *Eisodos* of Mary in the *Menologion* of Basil II (Vat. gr. 1613, fol. 198) offers an example of the standard post-iconoclast iconography (Fig. 17.9).³⁰ A procession of seven maidens with tapers appears in the far left. They are led by Anna and Joachim, who present their eager child to Zacharias. The tremulousness and pious excitement of the high priest is expressed through the agitation of his drapery and his long stride. At the upper right the Virgin sits in the sanctuary and accepts manna from the angel.³¹

The Presentation in the Temple is unique among the feast scenes because it allots special importance to the virgins. The Latin description of the Hodegetria procession quoted above also emphasizes the presence of young women. Dressed in silk, singing religious chants, they walk behind the icon like maidens after their mistress. In a similar way, in the scene of Mary's *Eisodos*, the maidens embody purity, which in turn opens the doors of Salvation. The immaculate Virgin is at the pinnacle of chastity, on account of which she is admitted to the Holy of Holies. The maidens are described in the twelfth-century homily of James of Kokkinobaphos as follows:

> A chorus of maidens came forth in a well-arranged harmony and presented a sweet spectacle with their ordered step and with the blossoming beauty of spring. The Virgin, attended on all sides by the maidens carrying candles, was unusual as regards her age and also her exterior appearance. For their blossoming faces were obscured by her brightest beauty, as the ray of the sun outshines the brightness of the stars. For her thoughtfulness veiled by joy revealed the greatness of her soul.³²

The spectacle is unusual. Although it was late autumn, the procession of maidens and the Virgin causes the blossoming beauty of spring to come forth.³³ Harmony, rhythm and beauty characterize the advance of the virgins. In their midst, Mary is like the sun's rays among stars. In a similar way, the Hodegetria outshines the other icons and the maidens walking in the procession. Light and purity ensures the coming Salvation.

Conclusion

A series of coincidences emerges from this discussion: the processional scene of Mary's *Eisodos* develops in the tenth century at the time when the iconographic type of the Hodegetria icon

---

²⁹ Ivory plaque with the *Eisodos* in Berlin. A. Effenberger and H.-G. Severin, *Das Museum für Spätantike und Byzantinische Kunst* (Berlin, 1992), no. 130, 224–5.

³⁰ *Il menologio di Basilio II*, p. 198. Lafontaine-Dosogne, *Iconographie de l'enfance de la Vierge* I, 143–4. For a fuller discussion of the development of the iconography of the *Eisodos*, see B. V. Pentcheva, 'Images and Icons of the Virgin and their Public in Middle Byzantine Constantinople', PhD thesis, Harvard University, 2001, 150–63.

³¹ With small modifications, the same scene is depicted in a number of 11th-c. images in Asia Minor at Çemil and Sariça kilise in Cappadocia and in Grotto V of Stylos monastery in Latmos. In all of them the train of the procession consists of seven maidens carrying candles. Jolivet-Lévy, *Les églises byzantines de Cappadoce*, 157–60, with bibliography. J. Lafontaine-Dosogne, 'Sariça kilise en Cappadoce', *CahArch* 12 (1962), 263–84. T. Wiegand (ed.), *Der Latmos* (Milet, III.1) (Berlin, 1913), 208–9.

³² *PG* 127, 612B–C.

³³ The feast of the *Eisodos* on November 21 is in the late autumn. Thus the comparison juxtaposes Mary's beauty, recalling spring, with the cold weather of late November.

consolidates and when *litaniai* with icons become a prominent feature in the urban life of Constantinople. Contrary to the previously established theory which argued for the presence of painted panels in public processions as early as the late sixth century,[34] it is in fact in the late tenth century that the characteristic Byzantine identity linked to icons emerges.[35] The Hodegon monastery fully exploited these new developments. While the initial focus of its cult was placed on the holy spring, by the late tenth century devotion centred on the Hodegetria icon and its Tuesday *litaniai*.[36] The success of the icon was due to its weekly urban processions. In this way the Hodegetria was catapulted to the position of the *palladium* of Constantinople. During its Tuesday procession the image was perceived to be animated or *empsychos*, turning, for instance, of its own accord to face the icon of Christ at the Chalke gate.[37] The weekly Tuesday *litania* gave the faithful a glimpse into the sacred history of the life of the Virgin. The borders of time dissolved, allowing the people walking in procession to perceive the 'activated' icon as the Mother of God in person and to become participants in her *Eisodos*. It is the narrative scene of Mary's Entrance into the Temple that remains today as a mimetic visual template of this Byzantine processional practice.

---

[34] A. M. Cameron, 'The Theotokos in Sixth-Century Constantinople: A City Finds its Symbol', *JThSt* 29.1 (1978), 79–108. Ead., 'Images of Authority: Élites and Icons in the Late Sixth-Century Byzantium', in M. Mullett and R. Scott (eds), *Byzantium and the Classical Tradition. University of Birmingham Thirteenth Spring Symposium of Byzantine Studies, 1979* (Birmingham, 1981), 205–34, repr. in ead., *Continuity and Change in Sixth-Century Byzantium* (London, 1981), XVIII.

[35] Pentcheva, 'The Supernatural Protector', 2–41.

[36] Angelidi, 'Un texte patriographique', 113–49. Ead. and T. Papamastorakis, 'The Veneration of the Virgin Hodegetria and the Hodegon Monastery', in Vassilaki, *Mother of God*, 373–87. Pentcheva, *Icons and Power*.

[37] Ciggaar, '*Tarragonensis 55*', 127.

THE 'ACTIVATED' ICON 203

17.1 Arta, Blacherna monastery. Tuesday ceremony with the Hodegetria (after Vassilaki, *Mother of God*, Pl. 211)

17.2 Washington, DC, Dumbarton Oaks, inv. no. DO 55.1.253. Seal. Pre-iconoclast visual type of the Virgin (7th c.) (source: Dumbarton Oaks)

17.3 Cambridge, Massachusetts, Fogg Art Museum, inv. no. Fogg 340, (on loan to Dumbarton Oaks Collection). Seal, showing the Hodegetria type identified with the name *Nikopoios* (second half of the 11th c.) (by kind permission of the Harvard University Art Museums Visual Resources)

17.4 Ohrid, church of St Clement (the Virgin Peribleptos). Two-sided icon: front side, the Virgin Hodegetria (source: Vocotopoulos, *Βυζαντινές εικόνες*, Fig. 67)

17.5 Ohrid, church of St Clement (the Virgin Peribleptos).
Two-sided icon: back side, the Crucifixion
(source: Vocotopoulos, *Βυζαντινές εικόνες*, Fig. 68)

17.6 Vatican City, Biblioteca Apostolica Vaticana. MS. gr. 1613, Basil II's *Menologion*, p. 142. Liturgical procession (source: Biblioteca Apostolica Vaticana)

17.7 Vatican City, Biblioteca Apostolica Vaticana. MS. gr. 1162, sermons of James of Kokkinobaphos, fol. 59v. The *Eisodos* of Mary (source: Biblioteca Apostolica Vaticana)

17.8 Milan, Museo del Duomo. Ivory book-cover (detail). The *Eisodos* of Mary (source: Fabbrica del Duomo di Milano)

17.9 Vatican City, Biblioteca Apostolica Vaticana. MS. gr. 1613, Basil II's *Menologion*, p. 198. Entry of Mary into the Temple (source: Biblioteca Apostolica Vaticana)

18

Picturing the spiritual protector: from Blachernitissa to Hodegetria

Christine Angelidi and Titos Papamastorakis

Ἀπόρθητον τεῖχος of the Empire, σκέπη κραταιά of the Oecumene, the poetic attributes of the Virgin, recorded in the late fifth and early sixth century,[1] express strong belief in the Theotokos as protector of the earthly realm of her Son. In this spiritual Empire, Constantinople held an outstanding place. By the late fifth century, Leo I and Verina had founded the Marian churches at Chalkoprateia and at Blachernai, the latter being at the time a suburb outside the Theodosian Land Walls. Next to the church the emperors built the Hagia Soros chapel, where they deposited the Virgin's maphorion, the Marian relic transferred to Constantinople from Palestine.[2] A third Marian church built by Justinian I, the Theotokos at Pege, again *extra muros* west of the Land Walls, strengthened the relationship of the Virgin with Constantinople. The symbolic location of the two Theotokos churches outside the Land Walls is explicitly stated by Prokopios: '[they] chance to be near the end of the line of fortifications, in order that both of them may serve as invincible defences to the circuit-wall of the city'.[3] By the early seventh century the dedication of Constantinople to the Virgin was established and the city became 'Theotokoupolis'.[4] Among the Marian churches, Blachernai was, according to Theodore Synkellos, 'the head, the metropolis, the Virgin's most divine dwelling'.[5] Synkellos' wording reflects a number of early seventh-century realities. Blachernai housed the maphorion, a relic of unique importance, and the inscription allegedly incised by Leo and Verina on the reliquary stated that the Theotokos' garment guaranteed the safety of the Empire.[6] Moreover, in 588 the Emperor Maurice instituted a weekly *lite* or *panegyris* in the Blachernai.[7]

The development of the public cult of the Theotokos, patron of Constantinople and protector of the Empire, has a long historiographic story, Byzantine as well as modern and contemporary. Many of its aspects have been thoroughly studied, but there is still much to be

---

[1] *Akathistos Hymn*, strophe 23, verse 13, ed. C. A. Trypanis, *Fourteen Early Byzantine Cantica* (Vienna, 1968), 9. Romanos, *On the Nativity*, strophe 23, verse 6, ed. P. Maas and C. A. Trypanis, *Sancti Romani Melodi Cantica* (Oxford, 1963), 8.
[2] Mango, 'Blachernae Shrine', 61–76, esp. 71 and 75.
[3] Prokopios, *On the Buildings*, I.3. Prokopios' association of the Pege with the Golden Gate is, of course, not topographically correct.
[4] On the consecration of Constantinople, see Mango, 'Theotokoupolis', 17–25.
[5] Theodore Synkellos, *In Depositionem Pretiose Vestis*, ed. F. Combefis, *Historia Haeresis Monothelitarum* (Paris, 1648), 774.
[6] A. Wenger, *L'Assomption de la Vierge dans la tradition byzantine du VIe au Xe siècle* (Paris, 1955), 300. Cf. Mango, 'Blachernae Shrine', 73.
[7] Theophanes, *Chronographia*, I, ed. C. de Boor (Leipzig, 1883), 265 line 28 – 266 line 2. Cf. A. Berger, *Untersuchungen zu den Patria Konstantinupoleos* (Bonn, 1988), 537. The *lite* described in Constantine VII, *De cerimoniis aulae byzantinae*, I.27, ed. J. J. Reiske (Bonn, 1829), 156, is not to be identified with the Friday *panegyris* at the Blachernai, as Berger assumes.

done. In this paper we shall explore the representations of the Virgin on the icons that symbolized her protection over the reigning city, the Empire, and the imperial rule in peace and war. We shall accordingly discuss the typology of 'emblematic' representations of the Theotokos, which specifically functioned as signs of protection, with particular reference to the chronological sequence of their appearance.

I

The earliest account involving the icon of the Virgin in a military context refers to an event in 610, when Herakleios used a Marian panel in his expedition against Phokas. Pisides' wording does not make clear whether he refers to a particular representation, and later sources merely record an icon of the Virgin being attached to the mast of the ship that conveyed Herakleios to Constantinople.[8] However this may be, Herakleios' reign seems to represent an important stage in the development of the Virgin's public cult. Escaping from the unexpected Avar attack in 623, the emperor prayed for the salvation of the city in the church of the Virgin Jerusalem,[9] a gesture that combined the reminiscence of the restoration of the Holy realm of the Son with the protection of his Mother over the earthly Empire.

A decisive step in the iconic representation of the spiritual protection of Constantinople dates from the long period of the Avar wars. The salvation of the city from the siege of 625–626 has – wrongly – been associated with the procession of a Marian panel. We shall not discuss here in detail the disparity of the accounts of the siege nor the procession on the walls, in which the patriarch Sergios allegedly carried either the icon of the Virgin or her maphorion, both of which were kept in the Blachernai.[10] However, a procession of the maphorion did indeed take place in Constantinople, though in 623, when Sergios removed the reliquary from Blachernai to secure it from the Avar siege. Once the enemy retreated, the holy relic was transferred back to the shrine.[11] But the only icon mentioned in sources contemporary with the events of 626 is an 'acheiropoietos' of Christ carried by Sergios in procession on the eve of the decisive enemy attack.[12]

Still, it is with reference to this siege that seventh-century sources mention for the first time representations of the Mother of God being placed on the walls of the city, thereby serving as a visual mark of her protection. In his account of the Avar and Persian assault on Constantinople,

---

[8] Latest discussion of the sources by B. Pentcheva, 'The Supernatural Protector of Constantinople: the Virgin and her Icons in the Tradition of the Avar Siege', *BMGS* 26 (2002), 15–16.

[9] Synkellos, *In Depositionem Vestis*, ed. Combefis, 774; ed. Chr. Loparev, in *VV* 2 (1895), 594. For the date see C. Mango and R. Scott, *The Chronicle of Theophanes Confessor* (Oxford, 1997), AM 6110 n. 1.

[10] For a discussion of the sources and the bibliography, cf. Pentcheva, 'Supernatural Protector', 4–27. It is a widespread commonplace that Sergios carried a Marian panel on the walls of the city. The icon was identified as an 'acheiropoietos', a Nikopoios, a Blachernitissa (discussion in I. van Dieten, *Geschichte der Patriarchen von Sergios I. bis Johannes VI* (Amsterdam, 1972), 174–8), and even a Hodegetria panel.

[11] Synkellos, ed. Combefis, 775; ed. Loparev, 596–602.

[12] S. Szadecsky Kardoss, T. Dér and T. Olajos, 'Breviarium Homeliae Theodori Synkelli *De Obsidione Avarica Constantinopoli* (*BHG* 1078m)', *AnBoll* 108 (1990), 163–4; cf. also George Pisides, *Bellum Avaricum*, vv. 370–9, ed. A. Pertusi, *Giorgio di Pisidia, Poemi* (Ettal, 1959), 193. On the identification of this icon with the Kamouliana, see Van Dieten, *Geschichte der Patriarchen*, 176.

Theodore Synkellos relates that the patriarch Sergios 'made representations of the Virgin, holding in her arms the Lord to whom she gave birth' on the western gates of the city.[13] The importance of the image of the Virgin functioning as the decisive weapon against the impious enemy is reflected in the account of the siege in the *Chronicon Paschale*. There we are told that at the crucial moment of the battle, the Avar Chagan saw the figure of a woman in dignified garments running alone along the walls of the city.[14] The text does not specify the exact location of the miraculous – for the Byzantines – vision, but we suggest that the anonymous author is here alluding to a legend that developed soon after the events, which already connected the apparition with the Blachernai shrine. The same legend seems to be at the background to an epigram of George Pisides, in which the Virgin of the Blachernai is praised for defeating the barbarian enemy through her mere appearance.[15] The wording employed by Pisides in the epigram is very close to that of Theodore Synkellos, who described the Marian image in the narthex of the Hagia Soros, representing the Virgin 'holding in her arms the Lord'. Evidence drawn from other sources confirms that at least two representations of the enthroned Virgin and Child existed in the Hagia Soros in the sixth century, and probably from the late 460s.

The long version of the *Galbius and Candidus Legend* is the main source for the *inventio* of the maphorion in Palestine, its *translatio* to Constantinople and its deposition in the Hagia Soros chapel by Leo I and Verina. Although transmitted by three manuscripts dated from the tenth to the twelfth/thirteenth centuries, it has been established that the text goes back to the sixth century.[16] The *Legend* records two icons offered by the emperors to the Hagia Soros. The first, a large, probably mosaic icon placed in the diakonikon or between the two diakonika, represented the Virgin flanked by two angels and two saints, John the Baptist and Conon; Galbius and Candidus were shown in an attitude of prayer.[17] In the second, a mosaic placed in the apse (above the bema of the Soros), the Virgin was seated on a throne and surrounded by two angels and the imperial family: Leo I, Verina holding the infant Leo II, and Ariadne.[18]

Literary descriptions are often insufficiently reliable evidence for the reconstruction of works of art. Yet it is obvious that the testimonies refer to the same representation of the enthroned Virgin and Child, placed over the bema, in the diakonikon, and in the narthex of the Hagia Soros, and in the 620s over the – western – gates of Constantinople. The image was not specifically linked with the Blachernai shrine, since in the sixth century it was already commonly used for panels and apse decoration in the eastern as well as the western part of the Empire. However, the Virgin and Child seems to function as a constant visual expression of the relationship between the Mother of God and the protected city. Evidence from literary sources and iconography supports our hypothesis.

---

[13] Theodore Synkellos, Περὶ τῆς τῶν ἀθέων βαρβάρων καὶ Περσῶν κατὰ τῆς θεοφυλάκτου ταύτης πόλεως μανιώδους κινήσεως, ed. L. Sternbach, *Analecta Avarica* (Cracow, 1900), 106 [304], 5–8.
[14] *Chronicon Paschale*, ed. Dindorf (Bonn, 1832), 725 lines 10–11.
[15] *Anthologia Graeca*, I.120, and L. Tartaglia, *Carmi di Giorgio di Pisidia* (Turin, 1998), no. 95, 496.
[16] Mango, 'Blachernae Shrine', 73.
[17] Text in Wenger, *L'Assomption*, 302 and 135 (commentary); cf. Mango, 'Blachernae Shrine', 71 and 76 (for a hypothetical reconstruction of the chapel).
[18] Text in Wenger, *L'Assomption*, 300–2 and 133–4 (commentary); cf. Mango, 'Blachernae Shrine', 70–1.

In the second half of the ninth century, to give a visual parallel to the praise of Holy Sion in the 86th Psalm, miniaturists of the Psalters chose to represent it as a city suggested by an 'abbreviated' depiction of its ramparts. They portray an equally 'abbreviated' image of the Virgin and Christ, both in frontal pose (Fig. 18.1).[19] In an extended form, the same representation was used in 867 to decorate the apse of Hagia Sophia as a celebration of the victory over the impious iconoclasts.[20]

A century later, the Arab attack on Constantinople in 717–718 is recorded in the *Synaxarion of Constantinople* under the date of 16 August. The account borrows several elements from the narratives of the 625–626 siege – or rather presents a different arrangement of identical legendary components. It repeats the story about the impious barbarian chieftain awe-struck by the vision of the Virgin, but in this case the Theotokos appears in the form of a mosaic icon of the Mother of God and Child placed over the Gate of Bosporion. Following archaic models or merely serving the notion of continuity, the image of the Virgin and Child summarized her protection over Constantinople and the imperial rule. This belief acquired its visual counterpart in the mosaic of the south-west vestibule of Hagia Sophia, representing Constantine I offering the city of Constantinople to the Virgin and Child (Fig. 18.2).[21]

II

However by the tenth century a new set of practices was starting to develop, based partly on older cultic elements. There is, firstly, the highly symbolic gesture of Romanos Lecapenos, who in 924 visited the Hagia Soros and wrapped himself in the maphorion as θώρακα ἀδιάρρηκτον before meeting Symeon, on the eve of the Bulgarian attack on Constantinople.[22] There is also the *Diegesis ophelimos*, which connects the miraculous salvation of 626 with the celebration of the Akathistos Hymn. The text states that two processions took place: the first with an icon of the Virgin and Child, and the second with the 'acheiropoietos' of Christ, the maphorion and the Holy Cross relics.[23] Finally, in the late tenth century, the *Menologion* of Basil II commemorates the defeat of the Persians and Avars (in 626), and records the procession of the icon of the Virgin in which all hope for victory was invested.[24] A strong relationship was thus established between the Virgin *strategos*, her icon, the maphorion, and the Blachernai shrine.

In 971, John Tzimiskes began his campaign against the Bulgarians with a ceremonial visit first to Hagia Sophia and then to the Blachernai church. On his return to Constantinople, Tzimiskes placed the icon of the Virgin and Child at the head of his triumphal procession since,

---

[19] T. Papamastorakis, 'Ένα εικαστικό εγκώμιο του Μιχαήλ Η´ Παλαιολόγου', *DChAE* 15 (1989/90), 224. For illustrations, see K. Corrigan, *Visual Polemics in the Ninth-Century Byzantine Psalters* (Cambridge, 1992), Figs 99–100.

[20] C. Mango and E. J. W. Hawkins, 'The Apse Mosaic of Saint Sophia at Istanbul', *DOP* 19 (1965), 125, 143–4, Figs 1–3.

[21] R. Cormack, 'The Emperor at St. Sophia: Viewer and Viewed', in J. Durand (ed.), *Byzance et les images* (Paris, 1994), 237, Figs 8–10.

[22] Theophanes Continuatus, ed. B. G. Niebuhr (Bonn, 1838), 406 line 19 – 407 line 7; abbreviated version in Skylitzes, ed. I. Thurn, *Ioannis Skylitzes, Historia* (Berlin and New York, 1973), 219 lines 31–5.

[23] *PG* 92, 1354 (for the Akathistos), 1356–7.

[24] *PG* 117, 576, from the Grottaferrata copy of the Vatican MS.

according to Leo the Deacon, this was the most glorious of the spoils seized on the campaign; and because, adds Skylitzes, the Virgin was the protector of the imperial city. His triumphal procession ended at Hagia Sophia where the emperor dedicated to God the crown of the Bulgarian tsar Boris, having first stripped him of his regalia in the Forum.[25]

Tzimiskes' triumph is the first instance in which we encounter an icon of the Virgin being carried in a public ceremony, thus stressing the shift from the public cult of relics to the public cult of Marian icons in a military context.[26] For our purposes we shall focus on a few details concerning the representation of the Theotokos and Child.

In describing the captured icon, Leo the Deacon employs the expression τὴν τῆς θεομήτορος εἰκόνα, ἐνηγκαλισμένην τὸν θεάνθρωπον λόγον, which seems to allude to a particular representation of the Virgin and Child. We shall tentatively interpret Leo's wording as referring to the so-called Eleousa type. The twelfth-century illuminated manuscript of Skylitzes supports this hypothesis. The miniature illustrating Tzimiskes' triumph shows the Marian panel placed on the top of the imperial chariot: the Virgin is holding on her right arm the Child, who leans down towards his Mother's head. The gesture could be rendered by the expression ἐνηγκαλισμένην, and the panel, which according to Skylitzes represented the patron of Constantinople, can undoubtedly be identified with a Theotokos Eleousa (Fig. 18.3).[27]

From 971 onwards, the sources record several cases involving Marian icons in battle or important military events. In 989, Basil II clasped the icon of the Theotokos as a shield against the onslaught of his opponent, the usurper Bardas Phokas.[28] In 1030, Romanos Argyros abandoned the Byzantine camp to the Arab plunderers. When he returned, the Marian icon was the sole object rescued from the devastation. This image, says Psellos, was habitually carried by the Roman emperors on campaign ὥσπερ στρατηγὸν καὶ τοῦ παντὸς στρατοπέδου φύλακα, and Romanos addressed to the icon his prayers for the safety of his army, recalling its past support of the Roman Empire in times of trouble.[29] Referring to a Marian panel in the context of a divine judgement performed in the presence of Romanos IV Diogenes during his campaign against the Turks, Attaleiates is the first to make the connection between the icon accompanying the emperor on his expedition as ἀπροσμάχητον ὅπλον and the Blachernai shrine, expressly defining it as Βλαχερνίτισσα.[30]

Can we deduce that the icon mentioned by Skylitzes as participating in Tzimiskes' triumph was the same as the panel of Argyros' campaign at Antioch or the icon functioning as arbitrator in the 1070s? Were these icons kept in the Blachernai shrine, and did they all represent the Virgin as Eleousa? What do we know about Marian icons of the Blachernai?

The tenth-century *De cerimoniis* records a number of Marian icons in the Hagia Soros and the Holy Bath of the Blachernai shrine. When visiting the Blachernai for the ritual of bathing,

---

[25] Leo the Deacon, *History*, VIII.1 and IX.12, ed. C. Hase (Bonn, 1828), 129 lines 7–9 and 158 lines 10–13. Skylitzes, ed. Thurn, 310 lines 60–2. On Tzimiskes' triumph, see M. McCormick, *Eternal Victory* (Paris and Cambridge, 1986), 170–4.
[26] Pentcheva, 'Supernatural Protector', 20, 29.
[27] Matritensis II (Matritensis gr. Vitr. 26-2), fol. 152v.
[28] Michael Psellos, *Chronography*, I.16, ed. S. Impellizzeri, *Michele Psello, Imperatori di Bizanzio* I (Milan, 1984), 26 lines 3–5.
[29] Id., ibid., III.10–11, ed. Impellizzeri, I, 84 lines 23–7 and 86 lines 5–7.
[30] Michael Attaleiates, *Historia*, ed. W. Brunet de Presle and I. Bekker (Bonn, 1853), 139.

the emperor first entered the Hagia Soros, in which the text mentions an icon of the Mother of God located between the 'episkepsis'[31] and the *metatorikion*. The text gives no additional indication, but it is plausible to assume that it refers to the large (mosaic?) icon of the Virgin and Child described in the *Galbius and Candidus Legend*. In the Holy Bath, the emperors lit candles in the eastern conch, where the silver icon of the Mother of God stood over the basin, and then turned to the left to venerate the impression of the Theotokos' hand. In the inner vault the emperors lit candles before the marble icon of the Mother of God, from whose hands the holy water flowed[32] – thus, probably an orans. The *De cerimoniis* mentions only fixed Marian images:[33] but the Blachernai shrine also contained panels of the Theotokos.

In 1030–1031 an icon of the Virgin and Child painted on wood was discovered in the sanctuary of the Blachernai church, and Skylitzes' account clearly indicates that the ancient panel represented the Nikopoios type.[34] By the late eleventh century another Marian image, the covered icon of the 'usual miracle', was displayed in the church. The miraculous act of the lifting of the veil was invested with attributes of divine judgement; moreover, Alexios Komnenos demanded from it an answer to his prayers before departing on campaign.[35] Although Psellos describes in detail the mechanism of the 'usual miracle', he does not give any clear indication about the representation of the covered icon.[36] From a Latin text of the late eleventh century we learn that the lifted veil disclosed the Theotokos holding Christ in her arms. The vague description does not, in our opinion, allow for any identification of the representation.[37] Does the Skylitzes manuscript reproduce a third important icon kept in the Blachernai by depicting an Eleousa?

Iconographic evidence attests that in the late eleventh century an Eleousa icon was displayed in the Blachernai shrine. The earliest indication, the Sinai hexaptych, dated to the early twelfth century, presents a variant of the Eleousa type with the inscription Ἡ Βλαχερνίτισσα (Fig.

---

[31] *De cerimoniis*, II.12, ed. Reiske, 553 line 6. On the term 'episkepsis' originally designating the reliquary, see Mango, 'Blachernae Shrine', 63.

[32] *De cerimoniis*, II.12, ed. Reiske, 554 line 21 – 555 line 3 and 555 lines 6–10. On the marble icon, cf. K. N. Ciggaar, 'Une description de Constantinople dans le *Tarragonensis 55*', *REB* 53 (1995), 122 lines 135–9; the text is vague about the location of the icon.

[33] On these icons, cf. I. Zervou Tognazzi, 'L'iconografia e la "vita" delle miracolose icone della Theotokos Brefokratoussa: Blachernitissa e Odighitria', *BollGrott* 40 (1986), 266 ff. For another monumental representation of the Virgin at the Hagia Soros in the 10th c., see L. Rydén, *The Life of St Andrew the Fool* II (Uppsala, 1995), 254 n. 6. Chr. Belting-Ihm, *Sub Matris Tutela. Untersuchungen zur Vorgeschichte der Schutzmantelmadonna* (Heidelberg, 1976), 44, 50–1, 60–1, identifies the representation with an Orans.

[34] Skylitzes, ed. Thurn, 384 lines 21–6; E. Trapp, 'Eine wiedergefundene Ikone der Blachernen Kirche', *JÖB* 35 (1985), 193–5, and W. Seibt, 'Der Bildtypus der Theotokos Nikopoios', *Βυζαντινά* 13.1 (1985), 551–64.

[35] Anna Komnene, *Alexias*, XIII.1, 2, ed. D. Reinsch and A. Kambylis (Berlin and New York, 2001), 384 lines 13–20.

[36] Michael Psellos, Λόγος ἐπὶ τῷ ἐν Βλαχέρναις γεγονότι θαύματι, ed. E. Fisher, *Michaeli Pselli Orationes Hagiographicae* (Stuttgart and Leipzig, 1994), 204 line 112 – 206 line 146 and 209 lines 220–37. On Psellos' description, see E. Papaioannou, 'The "Usual Miracle" and an Unusual Image', *JÖB* 51 (2001), 183–4, 185.

[37] V. Grumel, 'Le "miracle habituel" de Notre Dame des Blachernes à Constantinople', *EO* 30 (1931), 134–5; cf. also 130. Grumel rightly rejects Kondakov's identification with a Nikopoios (ibid., 132–3); Zervou Tognazzi, 'L'iconografia', 270–2, suggests an Eleousa, whereas Papaioannou, 'The "Usual Miracle" and an Unusual Image', 188, returns to the Nikopoios. On the icon, see Ciggaar, '*Tarragonensis 55*', 121 lines 103–7; the text places the icon in the Hagia Soros chapel.

18.4).³⁸ In the late twelfth-century Enkleistra, St Stephen the Younger is depicted holding an icon of the Virgin Eleousa (Plate 13, Fig. 18.5). The representation most probably alludes to the vision the saint's mother had during the Friday celebration in the Blachernai,³⁹ and the miniature in the twelfth-century manuscript of Skylitzes therefore correctly represents, in our opinion, an Eleousa. The image follows the text by connecting the Marian panel with the ceremonial visit of Tzimiskes to the Blachernai shrine before the Bulgarian campaign, where he probably prayed before the most important icon in the church, dubbed Blachernitissa by the anonymous artist of the Sinai hexaptych.

An additional example from the twelfth century supports this hypothesis. Around the year 1130 an icon of the Virgin Eleousa was presented to the prince of Kiev (Fig. 18.6). First kept in Kiev, and then in Vladimir and Moscow, the Marian panel was invested with the attributes of the Theotokos at Blachernai. The Virgin of Vladimir was venerated as patron of the city, of the principality and of the prince himself. Moreover the icon was carried on campaign, was celebrated on 1 August, and performed miracles, exactly as the Blachernai Theotokos did. From the fifteenth century onwards, the Vladimir icon was attributed to the brush of the apostle Luke,⁴⁰ a tradition already widespread in Constantinople from the late eleventh century for another icon, the miraculous image of the Virgin at the Hodegon.

While referring to 'ancient' ceremonies and practices, which cannot be identified with certainty, narrative sources have no record of the cult of the Hodegon icon before the late eleventh century. The texts emphasize that it was executed by Luke and record the splendour of its weekly procession.⁴¹ The monastery of Hodegon and the icon were particularly venerated by the Komnenos family. In accordance with John Komnenos' wishes, the icon was transferred to the Pantokrator monastery, and it was deposited in St Michael's chapel during the commemoration offices for the deceased members of the imperial family. Moreover, numerous epigrams inscribed on or accompanying donations presented to the Hodegon by members of the Komnenos family show that the monastery and its most precious icon gained a particular importance during the twelfth century.⁴² From the available evidence, however, it is not possible to deduce which icon was placed at the head of the triumphs of John and Manuel Komnenos.⁴³ Was it a Blachernai Eleousa, according to the tradition, or a Hodegetria?

The function of the Hodegetria icon as ἀμάχου ὀχυρώματος καὶ ἀναλώτου χαρακώματος is first recorded in 1186, when Isaac Angelos carried it on the walls to confront the usurper

---

38 Zervou Tognazzi, 'L'iconografia', 263–4. The central place in the upper zone is reserved for the 'archetypal' representation of the enthroned Virgin and Child.
39 Stephen the Deacon, *Life of St Stephen the Younger*, 4, ed. M.-F. Auzépy, *La Vie d'Étienne le Jeune* (Aldershot, 1997), 92 lines 9–14. R. Cormack, *Painting the Soul. Icons, Death Masks and Shrouds* (London, 1997), Fig. 7.
40 L. A. Schennikova, 'Tsar'gradskaia sviatynia "Bogomater' Odigitriia" i ee pochitanie v moskovskoi Rusi', in *Drevnerusskoe istkusstvo. Vizantiia u drevnaia Rus'* (St Petersburg, 1999), 329–46; O. E. Etinhof, *Obraz Bogomateri. Ocerki vizantiiskoi ikonografii XI–XII vv.* (Moscow, 2000), 127–56; cf. M. Bacci, *Il pennello dell'Evangelista* (Pisa, 1998), 181–7.
41 Chr. Angelidi and T. Papamastorakis, 'The Veneration of the Virgin Hodegetria and the Hodegon Monastery', in Vassilaki, *Mother of God*, 378–9. Cf. Bacci, *Il pennello*, 114–29.
42 Angelidi and Papamastorakis, 'The Veneration of the Virgin Hodegetria', 379–82.
43 The panel was probably carried in battle by the emperors. Choniates, ed. I. Van Dieten, *Nicetas Choniates, Historia* (Berlin and New York, 1975), 15 lines 87–93. For the triumphs, see Choniates, ed. Van Dieten, 19 lines 89–92 [John Komnenos; cf. also P. Magdalino, *The Empire of Manuel Komnenos, 1143–1180* (Cambridge,

Branas.⁴⁴ Yet the use of the Hodegetria in this particular context has no precedent either in Choniates' History or in any other earlier historiographic account. It is thus impossible to know which of the emperors' συστράτηγος icons Alexios V Doukas lost to the Crusaders in 1204 (Fig. 18.7),⁴⁵ but two centuries later, Joseph Bryennios explicitly mentions the Hodegetria ἄμαχον ὀχύρωμα καὶ ἀνάλωτον χαράκωμα leading the battle against the Ottomans in 1453.⁴⁶ It is not easy to assert whether Bryennios records a reality or merely follows Choniates' wording referring to a similar event, but, however this may be, in the period between the two sieges a new dynasty had established its own relationship with the Hodegetria.

Michael Palaiologos' entry into Constantinople in 1263 was marked by two deliberate choices: the date – 15 August, the commemoration of the Virgin's Dormition – and the use of the Hodegetria icon, placed at the head of his triumphal procession. Both choices would determine the bond of the dynasty with the Virgin Hodegetria. Andronikos II dedicated the month of August to the Virgin, to be celebrated with lengthy ceremonies in three churches of Constantinople; the church of Hodegon is listed in the first place, followed by Hagia Sophia and the Blachernai shrine. Through the reform of the liturgical calendar and a topographical arrangement that remodelled the hierarchy of the Marian churches of Constantinople, the Hodegon church and its icon became pivotal to the cult of the Virgin patron of the city. The annual ἐπιδημία of the Hodegetria to the palace of Blachernai introduced the icon's cult into the imperial ritual.⁴⁷ The fourteenth-century *De officiis* preserves the detailed regulations of the ceremony. The icon reached the palace in time for the celebration of the *Megas Kanon*. Followed by the emperor, the Hodegetria was deposited in the chapel of the Nikopoios and remained there until Easter Sunday. On its departure, a procession was formed with the emperor at its head and a memorial service for the deceased emperors was performed in the passage leading to the Blachernai church.⁴⁸ It was probably on this occasion that the *Diegesis ophelimos* was rewritten to form the 'historical' background to the Akathistos celebration.⁴⁹

For Andronikos II, Andronikos III and John VI Kantakouzenos it was the Hodegetria icon that symbolized the protection of the Virgin over their righteous reigns, and it was to this icon

---

1993), 425] and 158 lines 66–7 [Manuel Komnenos]. In Van Dieten's edition of Choniates these instances are recorded under the heading 'Hodegetria'.
⁴⁴ Choniates, ed. Van Dieten, 382 lines 53–60.
⁴⁵ Ibid., 567 lines 48–50. On Venetian traditions identifying the icon with the Nikopoios preserved in San Marco, Venice, see Chr. Maltezou, 'Βενετία καὶ βυζαντινὴ παράδοση. Ἡ εἰκόνα τῆς Παναγίας Νικοποιοῦ', in *Μνήμη Δ. Α. Ζακυθηνοῦ*, *Σύμμεικτα* 9.2 (1994), 7–20; cf. M. Schultz, 'Die Nicopea in San Marco. Zur Geschichte und zum Typ einer Ikone', *BZ* 91 (1998), 475–92.
⁴⁶ Ἰωσὴφ μοναχοῦ τοῦ Βρυεννίου, Τὰ εὑρεθέντα II, ed. E. Voulgari (Leipzig, 1768), 409.
⁴⁷ Angelidi and Papamastorakis, 'The Veneration of the Virgin Hodegetria', 383–5.
⁴⁸ *Pseudo-Kodinos, Traité des Offices*, ed. J. Verpeaux (Paris, 1966), 231 lines 1–12; cf. 238 lines 1–3. Verpeaux dates the *De Officiis* to John VI Kantakouzenos, but we may suppose that the compiler used already accumulated material, part of which originated from the reigns of Andronikos II and Andronikos III.
⁴⁹ *PG* 92, 1348–53. P. Speck, *Zufälliges zum Bellum Avaricum des Georgios Pisides* (Munich, 1980), 59 n. 320, suggests the attribution of the text to Nikephoros Kallistos Xanthopoulos. An early example, the illustration of *Messinensis San Salvatore*, 27, fol. 202r (11th c.), presents a Hodegetria *dexiokratousa* accompanying the reading of the *Diegesis ophelimos* on 25 March. On the Constantinopolitan origin of the script of the manuscript and its 'provincial' illustration, see N. P. Ševčenko, *Illustrated Manuscripts of the Metaphrastian Menologion* (Chicago and London, 1990), 77, 82 n. 161. The choice of this particular representation is merely due to the name of the monastery for which the manuscript was destined, the Hodegetria in Calabria.

that they dedicated their victories. Moreover, the Tuesday *lite* during which the large Hodegetria icon was carried by members of the *diakonia* of the Hodegon is the only procession described by travellers in fourteenth- and fifteenth-century Constantinople. Imperial ceremonial and public ritual converge in endowing the Hodegetria with emblematic features (Fig. 18.8).[50] The image became the visual counterpart of the supernatural protection of the Virgin commemorated in the Akathistos, the hymn celebrating the salvation of Constantinople – head and soul of the Empire – from the Avar siege of 626.[51]

The relationship established between the emperor, the Empire and the Hodegetria by the Palaiologoi is reflected in the figurative rendering of the Akathistos' last stanzas. The Byzantine imperial veneration of the Hodegetria is sumptuously represented in monasteries founded by members of the Serbian royal family (Figs 18.9–18.10).[52] However, it is noteworthy that the artists of the Markov Manastir placed side by side the Hodegetria and the Eleousa, the two successive aspects of the *palladium* of Constantinople and the Empire.

---

[50] The icon in the British Museum, dated around 1400 and representing the Triumph of Orthodoxy, depicts the empress Theodora and Michael III. A Hodegetria icon occupies the centre of the panel. On the icon, see Vassilaki, *Mother of God*, no. 32, 340–1 (R. Cormack).

[51] It is difficult to accept the hypothesis of Pentcheva, 'Supernatural Protector', 35–7, who, relying on a misinterpretation of Ciggaar, '*Tarragonensis 55*', 128 lines 377–400, thinks that by the late 11th c. the Hodegetria was already connected with the salvation of Constantinople from the Avar siege. It should also be noted that the date of the *Tarragonensis* should be reconsidered.

[52] A. Pätzold, *Der Akathistos-Hymnos. Die Bilderzyklen in der byzantinischen Wandmalerei des 14. Jahrhunderts* (Stuttgart, 1989), 71 ff., Figs 46, 50a–50b (Dečani), 66a–66b, 69, 70a–70b, 73, 76a–76b (Matejć), 112, 113, 114 (Markov).

18.1   Moscow, State Historical Museum,
MS. 129, Khludov Psalter, fol. 86v (9th c.)
(source: Cutler and Spieser, *Byzance médiévale*, Fig. 38)

18.2 Constantinople, Hagia Sophia. South-west vestibule, mosaic lunette over the doorway into the inner narthex (10th c.) (source: Studio Kontos)

18.3 Madrid, National Library, cod. gr. Vitr. 26-2, fol. 172v (a). John Tzimiskes' triumph (12th c.) (source: Vassilaki, *Mother of God*, Pl. 207)

18.4 Sinai, Monastery of St Catherine, Hexaptych (12th c.). The Virgin Blachernitissa (detail of the upper zone) (source: Vassilaki, *Mother of God*, Pl. 88)

18.5 Cyprus, Paphos, Enkleistra of St Neophytos (late 12th c.). St Stephen the Younger holding the icon of the Virgin (source: Cormack, *Painting the Soul*, Fig. 7)

PICTURING THE SPIRITUAL PROTECTOR 221

18.6   Moscow, Tretyakov Gallery.
The Virgin of Vladimir
(Constantinople, *c.* 1130)
(source: Vassilaki, *Mother of God*, Pl. 24)

18.7   Venice, San Marco.
The Virgin *Nikopoios*
(Constantinople, 12th c.)
(source: Vassilaki, *Mother of God*, Pl. 208)

18.8 London, British Museum.
Icon of the Triumph of Orthodoxy
(Constantinople, c. 1400)
(source: Vassilaki, *Mother of God*, no. 32)

18.9 Skopje, Markov Manastir (14th c.). 23rd stanza of the Akathistos Hymn, procession with the icon of the Virgin Eleousa (source: Pätzold, *Der Akathistos-Hymnos*, Fig. 113)

18.10 Skopje, Markov Manastir (14th c.). 24th stanza of the Akathistos Hymn, procession with the icon of the Virgin Hodegetria (source: G. Subotić)

The image of the Virgin Zoodochos Pege: two questions concerning its origin*

Natalia Teteriatnikov

In memory of Vladimir Teteriatnikov

Introduction

The purpose of this paper is twofold: to re-evaluate when the image of the Virgin with the epithet 'Zoodochos Pege' was created and to discuss why this Virgin, who appears with her hands raised and a frontal image of the Christ-child against her chest, sometimes with and sometimes without a miraculous spring, was chosen to represent an iconographic type known as Zoodochos Pege for the Pege monastery in Constantinople.

Zoodochos Pege simply means 'life-bearing source'. A pictorial image with this name was created for the Pege monastery during the reign of Andronikos II Palaiologos (1282–1328).[1] According to legend, Emperor Leo I (457–474) founded the monastery in the fifth century on the site of a miraculous spring outside the walls of Constantinople near the Silivri Gate.[2] Later, during the reign of Andronikos II Palaiologos, the monastery underwent renovation, and during this period an inauguration feast, for which Nikephoros Kallistos Xanthopoulos wrote a liturgical *akolouthia*, was established on the first Friday after Easter.[3]

Scholars suggest that a new image labelled Zoodochos Pege was probably created for the monastery in the first decades of the fourteenth century in the Pege shrine.[4] This view had its origin in Xanthopoulos' description of a mosaic in the dome above the miraculous fountain: the Virgin is shown with the Christ-child as he rises from the water below, symbolic of the source of life. Xanthopoulos describes this image as follows:

> For the whole place [the Kataphyge] has all sorts of icons in mosaic – exceptional are the [ones] of Christ and the Mother of God.... In the picture[,] which is in the middle of the dome, where there is the ceiling of the church, the artist perfectly depicted with his own hands the life-bearing Source [Zoodochos Pege], who bubbles forth from Her bosom the most beautiful and eternal infant [i.e., Christ] in the likeness of transparent and drinkable water which is alive and leaping; upon seeing it one

---

* I would like to thank Alice-Mary Talbot for her assistance during the preparation of this paper.
[1] See D. Medaković, 'Bogoroditsa "Zhivonosnii Istochnik" u cruckoj umesnosti', *ZRVI* 5 (1958), 203–18. T. Velmans, 'Iconographie de la "Fontaine de Vie" dans la tradition byzantine à la fin du moyen âge', in *Synthronon. Art et archéologie de la fin de l'Antiquité et du Moyen Âge* (Bibliothèque des CahArch, 2) (Paris, 1968), 119–34. D. I. Pallas, 'Ἡ Θεοτόκος Ζωοδόχος Πηγή', *AD* 26 (1971), *A-Meletai*, 201–24.
[2] [E. Gedeon], *Ἡ Ζωοδόχος Πηγή καὶ τὰ ἱερὰ αὐτῆς προσαρτήματα* (Athens, 1886). Misn [M. Is. Nomides], *Ἡ Ζωοδόχος Πηγή* (Istanbul, 1937). S. Bénay, 'Le monastère de la Source à Constantinople', *EO* 3 (1899), 223–8. Janin, *Églises CP*, 223–8. A.-M. Talbot, 'Epigrams of Manuel Philes on the Theotokos tes Peges and Its Art', *DOP* 48 (1994), 135–65. Ead., 'Miracle-Working Images at the Church of Zoodochos Pege in Constantinople' (in Russian), in A. M. Lidov, *Chudotvornaia Ikona v Vizantii i Drevnei Rusi* (Moscow, 1996), 117–22.
[3] See *Πεντηκοστάριον χαρμόσυνον* (Venice and Athens, *s.a.*), 16–22. Talbot, 'Epigrams', 135–65.
[4] Talbot, 'Epigrams'.

might liken it [the Source] to a cloud making water flow down gently from above, as if a soundless rain; and from there [sc. above] looking down toward the water in the *phiales* and rendering it [the water] active [or effective], incubating it, one might say, and rendering it [the water] fertile; and this [Source] I at least would call at present *the spirit of God floating over the water*. For at any rate when the plug opposite the image [of the Virgin] is raised so as to stop the water flow, and the shadowy [image] reflects on the water, one might see, as if in a mirror, the *Theometor* herself floating in the living water and emitting supernatural sparkling, so that one might wonder which is more believable [i.e. which is the real image not the reflection], whether out of the water the image is transferred to above, rebounding marvellously by means of the perceptible sunlight which strikes down [on the water], and is preserved on the ceiling ....[5]

When was this image created?

Fortunately sources exist which help clarify the question of when this image of the Virgin was created. There is a well-known fresco called 'Zoodochos Pege' in the church of the Aphendiko in Mistra (Fig. 19.1). This church, built some time before 1311, has frescoes in the narthex that were probably painted soon after the church was built. Two imperial decrees were issued to the monastery and were then painted on the wall above the entrance to the south-west chapel of the narthex (1312–1313 and 1322).[6] The frescoes can be generally assigned to the period between these dates. The image represents the Virgin, again with hands raised and with a frontal figure of the Christ-child depicted in front of her chest. Below Christ's figure is a stream of water painted in blue. At the Virgin's side are her parents, Joachim and Anna, and on both sides of her nimbus is the inscription 'Zoodochos Pege'. The Aphendiko image is the earliest known with this name. Its presence at Mistra soon after the year 1312–1313 suggests that the hegoumenos of the monastery, Pachomios, the founder of the church of the Virgin Hodegetria (Aphendiko), had obtained a copy of an image from an already existing one in the Pege monastery.

There are strong similarities between the Aphendiko image and the one that Xanthopoulos describes in the shrine of Pege. The Virgin in the church of Aphendiko is depicted in an almost three-quarter-length pose with raised hands; the Christ-child, rising from an invisible basin, rests against her upper body. Unfortunately, the lower portion of the lunette fresco and the frescoes on the walls below have been destroyed, and therefore the entirety of the original composition is not known. On the left side below the Virgin is a fragment of a curved line, which is hardly visible. Since there was no space, the artist depicted a curve, presumably to represent the top of the phiale, but it is difficult to be sure. Thus the dates 1312–1313 and

---

[5] Xanthopoulos, *Logos*, 13–14. Cf. Talbot, 'Miracle-Working Images', 120. Ead., 'Epigrams', 137.

[6] G. Millet, *Monuments byzantins de Mistra* (Paris, 1910), Pls 92–104. S. Dufrenne, *Les programmes iconographiques des églises byzantines de Mistra* (Paris, 1970), 8, 41 and n. 425. D. Mouriki, 'Revival Themes with Elements of Daily Life in Two Palaeologan Frescoes Depicting the Baptism', in *Okeanos: Essays Presented to Ihor Ševčenko on His Sixtieth Birthday, Harvard Ukrainian Studies* 7 (1983), 458–74. M. Chatzidakis, *Mystras: The Medieval City and the Castle* (Athens, 1992), 59–67. Chatzidakis points out that these narthex frescoes, probably executed soon after 1311, are the most archaic stylistically and are the earliest frescoes in the church. He suggests that they are close in style to Kariye Çamii in Istanbul.

1328 establish a *terminus ante quem* for the creation of the image of Zoodochos Pege in Constantinople.

Other relevant information comes from Xanthopoulos' *Logos*, a collection of miracles. In Miracle 60, he describes an important event that took place in the twenty-fourth year of the reign of the pious Emperor Andronikos [i.e. 1306].[7] Numerous pilgrims had converged on the shrine of Kataphyge, and it was so crowded that a staircase leading to the shrine collapsed:

> Thus all the building was full so that not even a coin thrown with force could reach the floor of the church, and an unintelligible murmur was stirred up everywhere [of people] of almost every age …

> At that time as they were being jostled on the staircase (which was built of [??] blocks of marble), crowding and pushing each other, a column which was set up as a support for the balustrade of the staircase was broken off its base by the weight pressing from above and fell down. Striking the water basin which is in front [of the spring], it knocked it off its base and cast it to the ground with a great crash, while people more numerous than grains of sand were filling vessels and drawing water from it (the phiale).

> Although it shattered into countless pieces and scattered all over the shrine, it resulted in no harm to anyone, causing no injury at all.[8]

The shrine was probably in poor condition. It is known that Emperor Justinian I had rebuilt it, and Basil I and Leo VI had renovated it after the 869 earthquake.[9] Since the damage from the collapse of the staircase was severe, its renovation must have taken place immediately after 1306. This shrine played an important role in curing the sick, so the renovation was probably done as quickly as possible. The first passage from Xanthopoulos quoted above describes the mosaics of the dome in Kataphyge as if the image had just recently been placed there.[10] He mentions that 'the artist with his own hands' depicted the image as if he actually saw this. Xanthopoulos's description of the dome mosaics gives the impression that he is talking about a new image suited to the contemporary concept of the Virgin holding Christ the *Logos*, as well as a metaphor of the Virgin as 'floating over the water'. It is unlikely that new mosaics were installed prior to the renovation of the shrine.

Alice-Mary Talbot offers important information on the epigram of Manuel Philes on the water reservoir dedicated to the Life-bearing Source, which was commissioned for the Pege monastery by the monk Hilarion Kanabes. It has been established that the spring was located in Kataphyge.[11] The renovation of the spring and the shrine may have taken place between 1306 and 1312–1313, the date of the Aphendiko fresco, and since the Pege shrine was a pilgrimage site, it is possible that it was renovated shortly after 1306. The shrine certainly would not have closed for an extended period. Furthermore, Talbot suggests that Xanthopoulos's *Logos* was completed between 1308 and 1320[12] and that the *Logos* promoted the use of the name

---

[7] Xanthopoulos, *Logos*, 85–6.
[8] Ibid.
[9] A.-M. Talbot, 'Two Accounts of Miracles at the Pege Shrine in Constantinople', in *Mélanges Gilbert Dagron*, TM 14 (2002), 606–7.
[10] Talbot, 'Miracle-Working Images', 120–1.
[11] Ead., 'Epigrams', 142, table 1 and 147–8.

Zoodochos Pege. In addition, Xanthopoulos wrote an *akolouthia* for the inauguration feast, which probably took place before the *Logos* was completed.

I would further suggest that in Miracle 60 Xanthopoulos describes this new feast day at the Pege monastery:

> It is necessary to relate [an event] which I almost forgot, even though it is not insignificant but rather familiar [?] and very important. It was already the twenty-fourth year of the reign of the pious emperor Andronikos [i.e. 1306]. And since [the fame of] the miracles spread everywhere in his empire, a countless number [of pilgrims] streamed in on the commemoration day of water, so that even one who rejoiced exceedingly in numbers could not enumerate their multitude. And one might liken the church of the Pege to a beehive and the throngs to a swarm of bees, not storing up the honey by flying around everywhere, but rather by everyone striving openly to carry off the sweet water and deposit it in the storage chambers of their soul, and thereby harvest a cure.[13]

Xanthopoulos first states that the event is significant, and took place during the reign of Andronikos II (1306), and he then indicates that it took place after 'the miracles spread everywhere in his empire'. If the feast day of the Pege monastery was already well established, Xanthopoulos would not have included this historical note, which suggests that the feast was recently established. Furthermore, the day of the commemoration of water could not have taken place on the feast of Epiphany: if it had, he would have specifically stated this. Epiphany is usually celebrated by the parishioners of each church. The reason the day of the Pege feast is not mentioned in Miracle 60 is that it was established on the Friday after Easter, and hence it was a movable feast. If this new feast was established in Pege monastery in 1306 (or a few years earlier), the *akolouthia* was read during the church service.

Both the *akolouthia* and the *Logos* contributed to the popularity of this epithet for the Virgin, and this also suggests that the liturgical hymns were in use before the *Logos*. Although an anonymous tenth-century text refers to the icons of the Virgin in the monastery chamber (*Kataphyge*), it is difficult to reconstruct the details of the image.[14] It is unlikely that a new image would have been created during the Latin occupation of the monastery between 1204 and 1261. Talbot argues that, although the epithet *Zoodochos Pege* first appeared in hymnography, it was not used in representations of the Virgin until the fourteenth century, and thus it would have coincided with the shrine's renovation.[15] Here I would suggest that the mosaics were created in the dome of *Kataphyge* and above the *hagiasma* after the renovation of the shrine and its miraculous spring soon after 1306.

Because the Aphendiko image was painted soon after 1312–1313 and the *Logos* was completed between 1308 and 1320, the image known as the Zoodochos Pege probably appeared soon after 1306 and before 1320. Once it had appeared, the image was incorporated soon after in the church decorative programmes of Byzantium.[16] From the third decade of the fourteenth century, however, the surviving fresco programmes in Serbian and Russian churches frequently

---

[12] Ead., 'Two Accounts of Miracles', 609. Ead., 'Epigrams', 136 n. 3.
[13] Xanthopoulos, *Logos*, 85–6.
[14] Talbot, 'Miracle-Working Images', 121.
[15] Ead., 'Two Accounts of Miracles', 609.
[16] S. Gabelić, *Manastir Lesnovo. Istoria i slikarstvo* (Belgrade, 1998), 173. Churches containing the image of

include this image. Examples include the church of the Virgin at Peć (*c.* 1330), Lesnovo (*c.* 1349),[17] Ravanica (*c.* 1380),[18] and the churches of the Saviour and Transfiguration[19] and the church of the Assumption in Novgorod.[20] No images labelled Zoodochos Pege have been found in Byzantine or provincial art prior to the Aphendiko fresco of the Virgin.

A new iconographic type

The second question I address is why this particular iconography of the Virgin was chosen as a new image for the renovated Pege shrine. Many scholars have discussed the various types of *Zoodochos Pege* images, and their meanings and functions in Byzantine art,[21] but the identity of this early image type, as it appears in monuments of the first decades of the fourteenth century, has been overlooked. This type is usually called a Blachernitissa or Platytera, a later epithet,[22] and the fourteenth-century images of the Virgin Zoodochos Pege resemble the Virgin Blachernitissa. Both Virgins are orans, and differences lie only in the representation of the Christ-child. The Zoodochos Pege has a frontal figure of him, whereas the Blachernitissa depicts him within a medallion suspended over the Holy Mother's breast, as in the twelfth-century apse fresco of the church at Trikomo, Cyprus (Plate 14, Fig. 19.2). The half-figure of the Virgin with raised hands and a frontal figure of the Christ-child without the epithet *Zoodochos Pege* existed in Byzantine art prior to the fourteenth century, and, although rare, it is found in early Byzantine art; for example, in a fifth-century fresco from the catacombs of S. Maria Maggiore, Rome[23] and the fifth- or sixth-century lead ampulla from the Archaeological Museum in Bologna.[24] After iconoclasm in the eleventh and twelfth centuries, the use of sacred images in Byzantine art increased. Several examples of the Virgin orans existed in Constantinople during this period, but only two images of the Virgin orans from the Blachernai church have been identified: (a) the Virgin orans without the Christ-child and (b) the Virgin orans with the Christ-child within a medallion suspended from her breast.[25] Both types were popular in Byzantine art, as attested by an abundance of frescoes, mosaics, and portable objects. According to the *Book of Ceremonies*, there was a relief marble icon of the Virgin orans without the Christ-child in the *hagiasma* of the Blachernai monastery, inside the imperial bath close to the chapel of St Photeinos.[26] This was located near the holy fountain, and the Virgin was portrayed with

---

Zoodochos Pege during this period were Kariye Çamii in Istanbul, St Theodore in Mistra, Aliveri in Euboea, and others.

[17] Gabelić, *Manastir Lesnovo*, 172–5, Pl. XLV.
[18] M. Belović, *Ravanica: History and Painting* (Belgrade, 1999), 152–4, Fig. 37.
[19] G. I. Vzdornov, *Freski v tserkvi Spasa Preobrazhenia v Novgorode*, 128–9, Figs 117–8.
[20] G. I. Vzdornov, *Volotovo: Freski tserkvi Uspenia na Volotovom pole bliz Novgoroda* (Moscow, 1989), no. 168, 52–4.
[21] Medaković, 'Bogoroditsa "Zhivonosnii Istochnik"', 203–18. Velmans, 'Iconographie de la "Fontaine de Vie"', 119–34; Pallas, 'Η Θεοτόκος Ζωοδόχος Πηγή', 201–24. For images of Zoodochos Pege in the narthexes of Byzantine churches, see Gabelić, *Manastir Lesnovo*, 172–5, Pl. XLV.
[22] For discussion of types, see 'Virgin Blachernitissa', in *ODB* 3, 2170–1 (N. P. Ševčenko).
[23] G. A. Wellen, *Theotokos. Eine ikonographische Abhandlung über das Gottesmutterbild in frühchristlicher Zeit* (Utrecht and Anvers, 1961), 152, Fig. 28, b.
[24] A. Grabar, *Ampoules de Terre Sainte (Monza-Bobbio)* (Paris, 1958), no. 9, a in Pl. X.
[25] Ševčenko, 'Virgin Blachernitissa'.

pierced hands through which water flowed. Every Friday, the emperor and members of the clergy bathed here after services. A number of marble relief icons of the Virgin orans have pierced hands: for example, those in the Archaeological Museum in Istanbul (Fig. 19.3),[27] St Mark's in Venice,[28] and the Museum of Byzantine Culture in Thessaloniki.[29] These icons may have been copies of the famous marble icon at the Blachernai *hagiasma*.[30] It is possible that a similar image also existed in the Kataphyge in the Pege monastery during the Middle Byzantine period. According to Bissera Pentcheva and other recent scholars, the second image-type – the Blachernitissa, the Virgin orans with the Christ-child in a medallion suspended over her breast, which dates from the end of the twelfth century – was associated with the miracle of the veil, which took place every Friday in the *naos* of the Blachernai church.[31] Numerous copies of this image were made and disseminated in Byzantine art.

As for the type of the Virgin orans with the frontal image of the Christ-child in the iconography of Virgin Zoodochos Pege, no examples exist in church murals or icons of the eleventh to the thirteenth centuries. These sacred images were primarily depicted in portable artworks, and they appear consistently on ecclesiastical seals of the eleventh and twelfth centuries (Fig. 19.4),[32] with a few dating from the thirteenth century.[33] The owners of these seals were mainly church officials: metropolitans, archbishops, priests, and *economoi* from different monasteries. Moreover, this image also appeared on the coins of Basil II and Alexios I Komnenos.[34]

This image of the Virgin was depicted on metal medallions[35] and crosses of the eleventh and twelfth centuries, suggesting that it was part of popular Byzantine devotion.[36] It appears as a headpiece for the Magnificat in the twelfth- or thirteenth-century Psalter, cod. 851, fol. 190 of the Vatopedi monastery, Mt Athos.[37] The image also appears on small portable objects, as attested by the thirteenth-century jasper cameo from the Hilandar monastery,[38] the twelfth-century cameo from the Victoria and Albert Museum[39] and the thirteenth-century

---

[26] *De cerimoniis aulae byzantinae*, 555.8–10.
[27] R. Lange, *Die byzantinische Reliefikone* (Recklinghausen, 1964), Figs 1 and 47.
[28] Ibid., 51–4, Figs 2 and 6.
[29] Ibid., 76 and Fig. 20.
[30] Ibid., 43–4.
[31] E. S. Smirnova, 'Novgorodskaia ikona "Bogomater' Znamenie": nekotorye voprosy bogorodichnoi ikonografii XII v.', in *Drevnerusskoe iskusstvo. Balkany, Rus'* (St Petersburg, 1995), 288–309. B. Pentcheva, 'Rhetorical Images of the Virgin: the Icon of the "usual miracle" at the Blachernai', *Res. Anthropology and Aesthetics* 38 (2000), 34–55.
[32] V. Laurent, *Le corpus des sceaux de l'Empire byzantin, I. L'Église* V, Planches (Paris, 1965), no. 59, Pl. 9; no. 85, Pl. 12; no. 110, Pl. 16; no. 623, Pl. 84; no. 801, Pl. 109; no. 1240, Pl. 158; no. 1245, Pl. 159; no. 1305, Pl. 166.
[33] G. Zacos and J. W. Nesbitt, *Byzantine Lead Seals* II, Plates (Berne, 1985), no. 364, Pl. 39; no. 385, Pl. 40; no. 445, Pl. 45; no. 473, Pl. 48; no. 547, Pl. 55.
[34] M. F. Hendy, *Coinage and Money in the Byzantine Empire 1081–1261* (DOS, XII) (Washington, DC, 1969), Pl. 2, Figs 15–16.
[35] J.-P. Caillet, *L'antiquité classique, le haut moyen âge et Byzance au Musée de Cluny* (Paris, 1985), no. 166, 242 (inv. no. Cl. 17702).
[36] B. Pitarakis, 'À propos de l'image de la Vierge orante avec le Christ-Enfant (XIe–XIIe siècles): l'émergence d'un culte', *CahArch* 48 (2000), 45–58.
[37] A. Cutler, *The Aristocratic Psalters in Byzantium* (Paris, 1984), 31.
[38] B. Radojković, 'The Treasury', in G. Subotić (ed.), *Hilandar Monastery* (Belgrade, 1998), 331 (the proposed date for this cameo to the 10th–11th c. cannot be acceptable on stylistic grounds).

jasper cameo from the Tretyakov Gallery (Fig. 19.5),⁴⁰ which were probably worn by church officials. Two jasper liturgical cups (*panagiaria*) from the Hilandar monastery, Mt Athos, have this image carved in relief at the centre of their interior (Fig. 19.6).⁴¹

The presence of this image in artwork, and especially on coins and seals, strongly suggests that in the Middle Byzantine period another venerable image existed at Blachernai. The absence of this image in church murals of this period indicates that it could have been made of different material – it is difficult to know. Its limited use in artwork prior to the renovation of the Pege monastery raises the question as to why this image, which was not popular in Byzantine art of the thirteenth century, was the one finally chosen to decorate the dome above the miraculous fountain.

I offer two suggestions. First, in the thirteenth century the image was depicted on portable objects such as *panagiaria*, cameos and seals, all of which were associated with ecclesiastical use. *Panagiaria* were used for the elevation of the pieces of Eucharistic bread called the *Panagia* which were offered to monks before meals or the *orthros* service. This rite was introduced in the eleventh century.⁴² Interestingly, *panagiaria* were decorated with images of the Virgin orans alone or the Virgin orans with a medallion of the Christ-child. However, the Virgin with the frontal figure of the Christ-child, as seen in early images of the Zoodochos Pege, was the most appropriate choice, as it suited the content of the image of Christ rising from the *phiale* like 'living water'. The concave shape of the *panagiarion* resembles the shape of the *phiale*. Court poet Manuel Philes wrote a poem on the Virgin of the Source, which was depicted on a stone *panagiarion*:

> The stone bears the earth, the earth bears grain,
> The grain is the nourisher of souls, the earth is the Virgin;
> Or rather seeing the spring of giving waters,
> O faithful one, suckle grace from the stone.⁴³

This type of Virgin orans image was combined with the frontal figure of the Christ-child as a means of expressing the theological concept of the Incarnation. Through his Incarnation, Christ symbolizes the eternal *Logos* and is the source of eternal life. During the Latin occupation of Constantinople, the monastery followed the Latin rite. Therefore, after the renovation of the Pege shrine, it was important to choose an image that related specifically to Orthodox ritual and the revival of the miraculous power of the Pege fountain.

Second, the Zoodochos Pege resembles the images of the Virgin from the Blachernai shrine. Two fourteenth-century images of the Zoodochos Pege present iconographic elements that show how similar they are to images of the Virgin orans with the Christ-child within a medallion from the Blachernai shrine. For example, in the lunette above the door in the narthex of the

---

39 Inv. no. A.4-1982. Evans and Wixom, *The Glory of Byzantium*, no. 134, 179–80 (R. Ousterhout).
40 Inv. no. 12658. L. I. Iovleva (ed.), *Gosudarstvennaia Tretjakovskaia Gallereia, Katalog Sobrania. Drevnerusskoe iskusstvo X – nachala XV veka* (Moscow, 1995), no. 110, 209 (T. V. Bruk).
41 Radojković, 'The Treasury', 331.
42 J. Yiannias, 'The Elevation of the Panaghia', *DOP* 26 (1972), 227–36.
43 Talbot, 'Epigrams', 145. Cf. also I. Kalavrezou-Maxeiner, *Byzantine Icons in Steatite* I (Vienna, 1985), nos 131–2, Pls 64–5.

monastery church of the Virgin at Peć (*c.* 1330)⁴⁴ (Fig. 19.8) the Virgin, amid angels, is placed between Bishop Danilo on her left and St Nicholas on her right. Here she is shown standing with raised arms in a pose similar to monumental images of the Blachernitissa. Although there is no inscription, the trilobed phiale on the Virgin's breast, from which the Christ-child emerges, allows positive identification as the Zoodochos Pege. The monumental composition of the standing image of the Virgin orans of the Christ Emmanuel type (blessing with both arms in the company of angels) resembles well-known images of the Virgin in apse compositions. One such representation in the church in Lesnovo (*c.* 1348) depicts the Virgin above the phiale, orans and without the Christ-child. It is similar to the Virgin Blachernitissa without Christ, found on the coinage of Emperor Andronikos II Palaiologos (Fig. 19.7).⁴⁵

Another example is a mosaic image of the Virgin Zoodochos Pege in the *arcosolium* of the inner narthex in Kariye Çamii dated *c.* 1340 (Fig. 19.9).⁴⁶ This mosaic depicts a half-figure image of the Virgin without the Christ-child. The Christ-child, however, appears in the apex of the *arcosolium* vault. He is holding a scroll and offering a blessing with both hands. His image is contained within a medallion. Only a fragment of this mosaic has survived, but it is likely that these iconographic features refer to the famous image of the Virgin, the Blachernitissa.

Why was it necessary to choose an image of the Virgin for Pege that resembled the Blachernai? To understand the connection between these two images, the Zoodochos Pege and the Virgin at Blachernai, an understanding of their role and function at their respective monasteries is of primary importance. Both shrines were established in the fifth century about two miles apart, outside the city walls. This location predetermined their role as protectors of the city. In *On the Buildings*, the sixth-century historian Prokopios describes the churches of Constantinople, including the Virgin Mary at Blachernai and the monastery of Pege, as follows:

> Both of these churches are built outside the city walls, the one at the place where the wall starts from the sea-shore, the latter close to what is called the Golden Gate, which is near the further end of the fortification, in order that both of them might form impregnable defences for the city walls.

Thus Prokopios considered both churches defenders of the city.⁴⁷ Moreover, there was a connection between the religious feasts of both monasteries. For example, both celebrated a feast to mark the saving of the city from the Avars in the month of August. The Blachernai monastery (7 August) had played a crucial role in the Byzantine victory over the Avars when the Pege shrine as well as the whole city was saved. Another connection concerns the establishment of the Inauguration feast on the Friday after Easter which celebrated the renewal of the Pege shrine. Significantly, Friday was also the day of the miracle of the veil in Blachernai and the day when the emperor and high-ranking clergy bathed in the holy pool there. The establishment of an Inauguration feast on the same Friday at Pege reinforced the connection between the two and linked them in the mind of the public as being central to imperial ritual. Furthermore, the emperors established, supported and embellished both shrines. The *Book of Ceremonies*

---

44 V. Djurić et al., *Pećka Patrijaršija* (Belgrade, 1990), 132–40, Fig. 76.
45 Hendy, *Coinage*, Pl. 45, Figs 14–16.
46 P. A. Underwood, *The Kariye Djami* (New York, 1966), I, 295–9; III, Figs 550–2.
47 Prokopius, *On the Buildings of Justinian*, tr. A. Stewart (London, 1886), 16–17. See also Prokopios, *On Buildings*, I.III, ed. J. Haury, IV (6th edn, Leipzig, 1964), 20–1.

describes an imperial procession to the Pege monastery on the feast of the Ascension.[48] On that morning there was a traditional ceremony of the acclamation of the factions in which the Greens and the Blues chanted supplications to the Mother of God. The Greens chanted: 'You are the source of Life of the Romans, the Virgin, the Mother of God, the Word. Protect your sovereigns who are in purple.'[49]

Several miracles show that the holy spring at the Pege monastery saved many members of the royal family (e.g. Justinian I, Leo I, Leo VI, John Komnenos, and Empress Theophano and Empress Irene).[50] Both shrines were established on the site of a holy spring and hence had a miraculous *hagiasma* associated with the cult of the Virgin. Pege was renowned for curing the sick.

The creation of a new image of the Virgin in the Pege monastery is thus better understood within the historical context of the Zoodochos Pege and Blachernai monasteries. It reflected the political situation during the reign of Andronikos II, which followed the Latin occupation of Constantinople and the pro-Latin policy of his father, Michael VIII. The latter had supported union with the Latins and the policy of the Council of Lyons in 1274.[51] In 1285, a second council at Blachernai condemned the pro-Latin policy of Patriarch John XI Bekkos and restored Orthodoxy.[52]

It is notable that the shrine's restoration coincided with disastrous events during a year-long period that spanned 1306 and 1307. It was a time of famine, food shortages, and high death rates.[53] Growing poverty and a general lack of provisions forced Patriarch Athanasios to call for reform and promote tangible reminders that would restore Byzantium's glorious past. It was therefore important symbolically to choose an effective image for this miraculous shrine, which would make manifest its origin in the Orthodox rite and return power to Pege. In Constantinople at this time, one of the most powerful images of the Virgin was the Blachernitissa, and it was believed to possess defensive properties. Significantly, the coins of Andronikos II reproduced an image of the Virgin orans without the Christ-child, which was associated with Blachernai shrine (Fig. 19.7). Here the Virgin orans in the centre, surrounded by the walls of Constantinople, appears as protector of the city. The Virgin Zoodochos Pege as orans, which resembles the famous images of the Virgin from Blachernai, was a fortunate choice for the Pege monastery. It strikingly links the Virgin's image with the holy water below, thus stressing its ability to heal the sick. This in turn strengthened the popularity of the Zoodochos Pege image throughout the Palaiologan period.

---

[48] Talbot, 'Two Accounts of Miracles', 607.
[49] *Le Livre des cérémonies*, ed. A. Vogt, I (Paris, 1935), 50–1.
[50] A.-M. Talbot, 'The Anonymous *Miracula* of the Pege Shrine in Constantinople', *Paleoslavica* 10.2 (2002), 223–5.
[51] A. Laiou, *Constantinople and the Latins: The Foreign Policy of Andronicus II, 1283–1328* (Cambridge, MA, 1972), 32–7.
[52] Ibid.
[53] Ibid., 195–6.

19.1 Mistra, church of the Aphendiko. Narthex
(source: Millet, *Monuments byzantins de Mistra*, Pl. 97, 2)

19.2 Cyprus, Trikomo, church of the Virgin. Apse conch
(source: Dumbarton Oaks)

19.3 Istanbul, Archaeological Museum.
Marble relief. The Virgin orans
(source: T. F. Mathews, Dumbarton Oaks)

19.4 Zacos Collection. Lead seal of the nun Maria (source: Zacos and Veglery, *Byzantine Lead Seals* I.3, Pl. 177, Fig. 2682a)

19.5 Moscow, Tretyakov Gallery. Jasper cameo (source: Iovleva, *Gosudarstvennaia Tretiakovskaia Gallereia, Katalog Sobrania*, no. 110, 209)

19.6 Mt Athos, Hilandar Monastery Treasury. *Panagiarion* (source: Subotić, *Hilandar Monastery*, 331)

19.7 Washington DC, Dumbarton Oaks, inv. no. 60.125.84. Coin of Andronikos II Palaiologos (source: Dumbarton Oaks)

19.8 Peć, monastery church.
East wall of the narthex, lunette above the main door
(source: Djurić *et al.*, *Peća Patriarshia*, Fig. 76)

19.9 Istanbul, Kariye Çamii.
Narthex, north wall, *arcosolium*
(source: Dumbarton Oaks)

The cult of the Virgin Zoodochos Pege at Mistra*

Rhodoniki Etzeoglou

The monastery of the Zoodochos Pege at Constantinople, erected outside the Land Walls on the site of a natural spring, was a place of worship much favoured by the Byzantines. The spring was identified with the Virgin, who bestowed her grace on the water which possessed miraculous qualities for the healing of many types of disease.[1] A tenth-century text describes forty-eight miracles effected at the monastery of the Mother of God 'at the spring'; many of these involved the cure of emperors or members of the imperial family or the court.[2] Nikephoros Kallistos Xanthopoulos, writing in the early fourteenth century, adds another fifteen miracles which occurred in his own time.[3]

The foundation of the original house of prayer by the spring is attributed to Leo I (457–474),[4] but it was Justinian who built the celebrated church and monastery beside a dense cypress grove, a flowery meadow, 'a paradise fertile in beauty, a spring gushing forth peaceful water, good to drink'.[5]

All the emperors paid honour to the monastery by restoring or extending buildings, or donating ecclesiastical treasures, while on Ascension Day, the feast day of the church, the emperor processed there with his entourage and participated in a special ceremony.[6] During the period of Latin occupation the church adopted the Latin rite and the Virgin ceased to work miracles at the spring.[7] Andronikos II (1282–1328) restored the Orthodox rite to the church and it was at this time, and particularly from the beginning of the fourteenth century, that the

---

* This article is based on my detailed study of the iconographic programme of the narthex of the Aphendiko in Mistra to be published in the series Τετράδια Βυζαντινῆς Ἀρχαιολογίας καὶ Τέχνης by the Christian Archaeological Society.

[1] Select bibliography on the church and the shrine of Zoodochos Pege: S. Bénay, 'Le monastère de la Source à Constantinople', *EO* 3 (1899), 222–8, 295–300. J. Ebersolt, *Sanctuaires de Byzance* (Paris, 1921), 61–5. Misn [Miltiades Nomides], *Ἡ Ζωοδόχος Πηγή* (Istanbul, 1937). Janin, *Églises CP*, 223–8. *ODB* 3, 1616 (C. Mango and N. P. Ševčenko).

[2] *AASS*, Novembris III, 878–89.

[3] Xanthopoulos, *Logos*, 66–94.

[4] Although it has been argued that written testimony on the foundation of the church by Leo I derives from a later tradition (*ODB* 3, 1616), evidence exists which in my view indicates that Leo was responsible for initiating the basic cult of the Virgin at the spring. See *AASS*, Novembris III, 878, and Janin, *Églises CP*, 224. Moreover, a recent study notes that the reign of Leo I saw the first wave of church-building dedicated to the Virgin: Mango, 'Theotokoupolis', 23.

[5] Prokopios, *De aedificiis*, I.3.6–10: 'παράδεισος εὐφορῶν τὰ ὡραῖα, πηγὴ βλύζουσα γαληνὸν τὸ ὕδωρ καὶ πότιμον'.

[6] Janin, *Églises CP*, 224–5. Constantine VII, *De cerimoniis aulae byzantinae,* I.18, ed. J. J. Reiske, I (Bonn, 1829), 108–14.

[7] Information on the church and the shrine of Zoodochos Pege mainly derives from the works of Nikephoros Kallistos Xanthopoulos (*c.* 1256–1335). On the author, *ODB* 3, 2207 (A.-M. Talbot).

holy spring attained its zenith; indeed Nikephoros Kallistos Xanthopoulos wrote two works specially devoted to the Zoodochos Pege, one a history of the foundation of the church and the miracles performed by its holy waters,[8] and the other an *akolouthia* for the feast of the Zoodochos Pege, which since then is celebrated on the Friday after Easter (*Diakainisimos* week).[9] The same author probably wrote two poems for the feast day, which were set to music by John Koukouzeles.[10] At this time Manuel Philes composed epigrams on icons of the Virgin associated with the veneration of the Spring,[11] and the epithet 'Zoodochos' was added to the name of the church, which had previously been the Virgin 'of the spring' (τῆς Πηγῆς) or 'at the spring' (ἐν τῇ Πηγῇ).[12] And during the same period the iconographic type of the Zoodochos Pege appeared with its many variants, great and small, in which the dominant feature is always water.[13]

The earliest of these representations still extant is at Mistra, in the church of the Virgin Hodegetria of the Brontocheion monastery, known as the Aphendiko (Plate 15, Fig. 20.1). It can be found in the east tympanum of the narthex, above the entrance door to the main church, and dates from around 1315. The Virgin is shown in frontal pose, waist-length and with her hands open in supplication. In front of her, Christ – also depicted frontally – holds in his left hand a closed scroll and raises his right in a gesture of blessing. Below Christ the ruffled water is painted in light blue tones. To the left and right stand Joachim and Anna, turned three-quarters to the Virgin. On either side of the Virgin's head are two miniature flying angels. Above the Virgin's shoulder on the left is the two-line inscription Ἡ Ζωο/δόχος while the word Πηγή, which would have been written on the right, has disappeared. There is an interesting treatment of the water below Christ: continuous circles of white against a blue background, with spiral motifs drawn inside them, give an impression of bubbling water gushing from the spring (Fig. 20.2). This detail provides the link between the Aphendiko representation and the depiction of the Virgin in the dome of the shrine in Constantinople, as described by Nikephoros Kallistos Xanthopoulos: 'in the middle of the dome, where there is the ceiling of the church, the artist perfectly depicted with his own hands the life-bearing Source who bubbles forth from her bosom the most beautiful and eternal infant in the likeness of transparent and drinkable water, which is alive and leaping'.[14]

---

[8] Xanthopoulos, *Logos*, 1–99.
[9] This *akolouthia* is included in all the *Pentekostaria* of the Orthodox Church: see Πεντηκοστάριον, ed. Apostoliki Diakonia of the Church of Greece (Athens, 1959), 15–21.
[10] S. Eustathiades, 'Ἰωάννης ὁ Κουκουζέλης, ὁ μαΐστωρ καὶ ὁ χρόνος ἀκμῆς αὐτοῦ', *EEBS* 14 (1938), 11–12, 41.
[11] A.-M. Talbot, 'Epigrams of Manuel Philes on the Theotokos tes Peges and its Art', *DOP* 48 (1994), 135–65.
[12] The origin of this epithet lies in earlier hymnological texts referring to the Virgin, but its incorporation into the name of the building derives from the work of Xanthopoulos, Ἀκολουθία εἰς τὴν Ὑπεραγίαν Κυρίαν καὶ Δέσποιναν Θεοτόκον, τὴν Ζωοδόχον Πηγήν.
[13] Publications on the iconographic type of the Zoodochos Pege are: G. Medaković, 'Théotokos "Ζωοδόχος Πηγή" dans l'art serbe', *ZRVI* 5 (1958), 203–18 (in Serbian with French summary). T. Velmans, 'L'iconographie de la "Fontaine de Vie" dans la tradition byzantine à la fin du Moyen Âge', in *Synthronon. Art et archéologie de la fin de l'Antiquité et du Moyen Âge* (Bibliothèque des CahArch, 2) (Paris, 1968), 119–34. D. I. Pallas, 'Ἡ Θεοτόκος Ζωοδόχος Πηγή', *AD* 26 (1971), *A-Meletai*, 201–24.
[14] Xanthopoulos, *Logos*, 13: 'Τῇ γε μὴν μέσῃ θόλῳ ἢ ὄροφος καθίσταται τῷ νεῷ αὐτὴν ὁ πλάστης τὴν ζωηφόρον πηγὴν χερσὶν ἰδίαις ἀρίστως διέγραψε, τὸ πάγκαλον βρέφος καὶ προαιώνιον, ὡς διειδές τι καὶ πότιμον ὕδωρ, ζῶν καὶ ἁλλόμενον, τῶν κόλπων ἀναμορμύρουσαν'. The English translation is taken from Talbot, 'Epigrams', 137.

This mosaic image at Constantinople was probably contemporary with Xanthopoulos' description, and as it was located above the water of the spring, the Virgin was reflected in it bestowing her divine grace.[15] In the roughly contemporary representation at Mistra the water is painted in a free style in order to suggest the association of Christ with the 'transparent and drinkable water' that emerges from the Virgin's bosom, and to emphasize the association of the image with the spring. The Aphendiko painter may thus have been aiming at a symbolic depiction of the Virgin Zoodochos Pege, perhaps with knowledge of the image at Constantinople or even under the inspiration of Xanthopoulos' literary description.

The church of the Virgin Hodegetria of the Brontocheion was erected and decorated with wall paintings between 1310 and 1320 as the katholikon of the monastery of that name in the newly established city of Mistra.[16] Abbot Pachomios, the founder of the monastery, who was granted the title of Great Protosynkellos and archimandrite of the Peloponnesos, was a man who enjoyed the absolute confidence of Andronikos – indeed the emperor issued three chrysobulls granting great privileges to the monastery, which he declared 'royal' and independent of all local ecclesiastical authority.[17]

Anyone examining the paintings in the Aphendiko finds himself faced by a problem: why, in a church dedicated to Virgin Hodegetria, is a prominent position – the first representation facing one on entering the church – devoted to the Virgin Zoodochos Pege and not to the Hodegetria? A detailed study of the iconography of the narthex reveals the probable answer: the Zoodochos Pege is the basic concept around which the whole iconographic programme is planned.

The narthex is divided into three parts; the central section is covered by a cross-vault supported on two arches and the side sections by transverse vaults. The wall paintings which survive in whole or in part are arranged in the following manner:[18] on the cross-vault four angels, and on the arches four full-length prophets; on the east tympanum the Virgin Zoodochos Pege with her parents (Fig. 20.1); on the west tympanum six figures of healing saints in bust (Fig. 20.3); on the vaults and on the side tympana nine scenes from Christ's public ministry – on the north vault, the meeting of Christ and the Woman of Samaria at Jacob's well, the turning of water into wine at the Marriage at Cana in Galilee (Fig. 20.4), the healing of the man blind from birth at the pool of Siloam and the healing of Peter's wife's mother (Fig. 20.5); on the north tympanum, the healing of the man with dropsy (Fig. 20.6); on the south vault, the healing of the paralytic at the pool of Bethesda, the cure of the woman with an issue of blood (Fig. 20.7) and the rarely-depicted healing of the halt and the blind in Solomon's Temple; on the south tympanum, Christ with the Elders in the Temple.

---

[15] The view that the mosaic representation of the Virgin above the spring was a work contemporary with the revival of the cult in the church under Andronikos II is also supported by Talbot, who in the introductory section of her study on Philes' epigrams makes general observations on the church and the sacred waters of the Zoodochos Pege: Talbot, 'Epigrams', 136–7.

[16] M. Chatzidakis, *Mystras. The Medieval City and the Castle. A Complete Guide to the Churches, Palaces and the Castle* (Athens, 1981), 47–8, 63–7.

[17] G. Millet, 'Inscriptions byzantines de Mistra', *BCH* 23 (1899), 100–18 (esp. 102, 104–6, 113, 116).

[18] S. Dufrenne, *Les programmes iconographiques des églises byzantines de Mistra* (Paris, 1970), Pl. 13 (Fig. IX), which records the representations known before the conservation work on the murals in the 1970s. On this work, see R. Etzeoglou, *AD* 28 (1973), B2-Chronika, 241. Ead., *AD* 29 (1973/4), B2-Chronika, 416–18.

A detailed study of these representations confirms that the whole programme is linked symbolically, and that the Gospel scenes are associated with the cult of the Zoodochos Pege. This conclusion is corroborated by contemporary written sources, in particular the first of Nikephoros Kallistos Xanthopoulos' works mentioned above, which describes miraculous cures at the Zoodochos Pege similar to those of Christ depicted in the Aphendiko, and sometimes makes specific reference to the miracles worked by Christ.

Thus the first miracle, which relates to the healing of a blind man, contains a comparison with the man blind from birth at the pool of Siloam.[19] In the fourth and sixth, which describe cures of women with haemorrhages, there is a reference to the woman with an issue of blood.[20] The seventh, twentieth, twenty-second, twenty-eighth and twenty-ninth miracles describe high fevers cured by the grace of the holy water of the Pege.[21] The fifty-seventh miracle concerns the cure of the Varangian John Rodolphos who suffered from the dropsy,[22] and the sixty-first the cure of 'a long-time paralytic'.[23] After the sixty-third and final miracle, Xanthopoulos compares the water of the spring with other waters noted for their coolness and clarity, and concludes that the holy water of the Zoodochos Pege is superior to all ('τῶν ἄλλων ἁπάντων ὑπερηκόντισεν, ὕδωρ τὸ τῆς πηγῆς'), mentioning the spring of Paradise, the water struck from the rock by Moses, the water of Siloam, the well of the Woman of Samaria and the sheep pool at Bethesda.[24]

Further references to miracles depicted in the Aphendiko can be found in the other work of Xanthopoulos, the *akolouthia* for the feast day of the Zoodochos Pege. This service, which is read on the Friday of *Diakainisimos* week, includes a *kanon* of the Virgin with the acrostic 'Νικηφόρου Καλλίστου τοῦ Ξανθοπούλου' and the verse: 'The fleece, the Manna, Siloam, the water struck from the rock and Solomon's portico, the waters of Jordan and the spring of the Woman of Samaria told of your grace'; other verses are: 'May you cure my sufferings, O Maiden, who dries up the source of haemorrhage and shivering, the lighting of the fire [i.e. fever]' and 'The Spring of divine and venerable water flows from you, O Virgin. For it checks the flow of the dropsy'.[25]

As all these references indicate, the episodes of the Woman of Samaria, the blind man at the pool of Siloam, the paralytic at the portico of Bethesda, the woman with an issue of blood, the man with dropsy and Peter's wife's mother, sick of a fever, all have links with the Zoodochos Pege; however, this does not apply to the Marriage at Cana, Christ with the Elders, and his miracles at the Temple. The Miracle at Cana occurs only in St John's Gospel (2:1–10), as does Christ's meeting with the Woman of Samaria (4:5–42), the healing of the paralytic at the pool of Bethesda (5:1–16) and of the blind man at the pool of Siloam (9:9–38). These last three

---

[19] Xanthopoulos, *Logos*, 10.
[20] Ibid., 18, 21–2.
[21] Ibid., 22–3, 43, 44, 49.
[22] Ibid., 78–82.
[23] Ibid., 87.
[24] Ibid., 94–6.
[25] 'Ἱστόρησε πόκος τὸ Μάννα, καὶ Σιλωὰμ καὶ ἡ πέτρα πηγάζουσα, Σολομῶντος ἡ στοὰ τὴν χάριν σου, τὰ ἰορδάνεια νάματα, καὶ ἡ πηγὴ Σαμαρείτιδος.' 'Τὰ πάθη μου Κόρη ἰάσαις, τῆς αἱμορροίας πηγὴν ἡ ξηράνασα καὶ τὸ ῥῖγος, τῆς φλογὸς τὴν ἄναψιν.' 'Θεῖον ἡ Πηγὴ καὶ σεβάσμιον ὕδωρ, προρρέει σου Παρθένε· ὑδρωπικῶν γὰρ τὸ ῥεῦμα ἀναχαιτίζει σφοδρῶς ....' *Πεντηκοστάριον*, 17–20.

incidents are known to have symbolic associations with the sacrament of Baptism.[26] The Miracle at Cana, which is often shown together with the Woman of Samaria – as in the Aphendiko – is also connected with Baptism; for example, it is depicted in the Baptistery of San Giovanni in Fonte[27] and on a tenth-century liturgical scroll which contains the services of Baptism and of the *Great Hagiasmos*.[28] But these two ceremonies – Baptism and *Hagiasmos* – are for the Byzantines comparable, with similar prayers and similar designations, as G. Millet has shown in an exhaustive study of the *Phiale* of the Great Lavra monastery on Mt Athos.[29] The link between the two ceremonies is based on the concepts of purification and protection from every evil, which are the special qualities of Baptism and are renewed by *Hagiasmos*. And, as is well known, the same day, 6 January, sees the celebration by the church of the Baptism of Christ, with the Great Blessing of the Waters following on afterwards in the open air.[30]

According to a sacramentary dated 1027, the service of *Hagiasmos* also took place on other days of the year, on Sundays and feast days, within the church and especially in the narthex: Ἑτέρα ἀκολουθία καὶ τάξις ἁγιασμοῦ γινομένη εἰς διαφόρους ἐκκλησίας ταῖς κυριακαῖς καὶ ἑορταῖς ἐν τῷ νάρθηκι ἢ καὶ ἑτέρῳ μέρει τῆς ἐκκλησίας, φιάλης οὔσης ἢ λεκανίου'.[31] In fact, evidence for the celebration of *Hagiasmos* in the narthex has been noted in many churches. A. Xyngopoulos in his study on the subject observes that the depiction of the Baptism of Christ often found on the east wall of the narthex, apparently unconnected with the rest of the decoration, is proof of this, as in many of these a *phiale* for *Hagiasmos* is kept in front of the representation of the Baptism.[32] Such depictions of the Baptism can be found in the narthex of the churches of St Stephen, St Nicholas Kasnitzes and the Mavriotissa in Kastoria, of St Peter in Kalyvia Kouvara, Attica, of the Theotokos in Gračanića, and in the chapel of St George in the St Paul monastery, Mt Athos, where the Baptism is in the north conch of the east wall of the narthex, while in the corresponding south conch is a depiction of the Virgin Zoodochos Pege.[33] This suggests that the narthex at the Aphendiko was used for the celebration of *Hagiasmos* and that the iconographic programme based on the Zoodochos Pege, surrounded by appropriate

---

[26] P. Underwood, 'Some Problems in Programs and Iconography of Ministry Cycles', in P. Underwood (ed.), *The Kariye Djami* 4 (Princeton, NJ, 1975), 257–62.

[27] J.-L. Maier, *Le baptistère de Naples et ses mosaïques* (Fribourg, 1964), 33–4. Among the monuments of the Palaiologan era where the Woman of Samaria and the Marriage at Cana are represented together, one may mention St Nicholas Orphanos in Thessaloniki and St Nicholas in Ljuboten: see A. Tsitsouridou, *Ο ζωγραφικός διάκοσμος του Αγίου Νικολάου Ορφανού στη Θεσσαλονίκη* (Thessaloniki, 1986), 299. G. Millet and T. Velmans, *La peinture du Moyen-Âge en Yougoslavie* 4 (Paris, 1969), Pl. 3.

[28] M. Avery, *The Exulted Rolls of South Italy* (Princeton, NJ, 1936), 28–9.

[29] G. Millet, 'Phiale et simandre à Lavra', *BCH* 29 (1905), 105–23. The terms 'βαπτίσματα' and 'φωτίσματα' are used equally for Baptism and Hagiasmos, while the vessel used in both ceremonies is called 'βαπτιστήριον', 'φωτιστήριον' and 'κολυμβήθρα' indiscriminately: ibid., 112, 115.

[30] *Μηναῖον Ἰανουαρίου*, ed. Apostoliki Diakonia of the Church of Greece (Athens, 1970), 144, 149.

[31] A. Dmitrievskii, *Opisanie liturgicheskikh rukopisei II. Εὐχολόγια* (Kiev, 1901), 1051.

[32] A. Xyngopoulos, 'Αἱ ἀπολεσθεῖσαι τοιχογραφίαι τῆς Παναγίας τῶν Χαλκέων Θεσσαλονίκης', *Μακεδονικά* 4 (1955/60), 2–3. To the examples mentioned by Xyngopoulos several more have been added by recent scholars: N. Coumbaraki-Pansélinou, *Saint Pierre de Kalyvia-Kouvara et la chapelle de la Vierge de Mérénta*, (Thessaloniki, 1976), 59–60. It should be noted that at the Aphendiko there is no conclusive evidence of a permanently fixed *phiale*.

[33] G. Millet, *Monuments de l'Athos, I. Les peintures* (Paris, 1927), Pl. 190. M. Chatzidakis, 'Notes sur le peintre Antoine de l'Athos', in *Studies in Memory of David Talbot Rice* (Edinburgh, 1975), 85, repr. in id., *Études sur la peinture post-byzantine* (London, 1976), VII.

images, aimed at giving expression to the spirit of this particular ritual. Moreover there is an obvious link between the Zoodochos Pege and *Hagiasmos*, since the spring with the holy water (the *hagiasma*) was the main reason for the existence of the shrine in Constantinople.

We may also note that several *akolouthiai* of *Hagiasmos* contain special prayers for its celebration in churches dedicated to the Virgin. In particular, a thirteenth-century sacramentary contains the service of *Small Hagiasmos* which is almost exclusively dedicated to the Virgin and was probably directed to be celebrated in churches of the Virgin, as certain prayers suggest. This *Hagiasmos* also contains a long prayer which commemorates the Virgin's parents and all the Anargyroi as intercessors.[34] In this context we may recall that the Virgin Zoodochos Pege on the east tympanum of the narthex at the Aphendiko is flanked by the figures of Joachim and Anna, while directly opposite on the west tympanum are six figures of Anargyroi (healing saints).

The two representations which have no apparent connection with the Zoodochos Pege are the scenes of Christ with the Elders and the healing of the halt and the blind. Both take place in Solomon's Temple, to which Christ likens himself according to St John's Gospel: 'Destroy this temple, and in three days I will raise it up ... but he spake of the temple of his body'. These lines appear in a section entitled 'On those cast out from the temple' (John 2:12–22) which is read in church on the Friday of *Diakainisimos* week, the feast day of the Zoodochos Pege,[35] and we may therefore assume that the two scenes are associated with it.

All this suggests that the Zoodochos Pege is the central idea behind the iconographic programme of the narthex, because of its specific role as the location for celebrating *Hagiasmoi* in honour of the Theotokos, on the pattern of churches of the Theotokos in Constantinople. The Aphendiko thus preserves a complete programme on the veneration of the Zoodochos Pege, which to my knowledge cannot be found in any other monument in the capital or in its sphere of influence. Probably even the shrine in Constantinople did not contain such a full programme, as the church was in continuous use for many centuries and the decoration was carried out gradually over a long period of time.

The cult of the Zoodochos Pege, which spread to Mistra from the capital in the context of the imperial policy of establishing the Orthodox faith with particular emphasis on the cult of the Virgin,[36] was observed in the Byzantine capital of the Peloponnese at least until the end of the fourteenth century, as can be gathered from representations in two other churches there.

The chapel of Ai-Yannakis ('small St John') just outside the walls of the lower city contains another iconographic type of the Zoodochos Pege.[37] It is located on the west side of the templon, above the arch of the altar gate, and has been only partially preserved (Fig. 20.8). It shows the pool of water surrounded by miniature figures of three believers who are drawing water from the spring. The wall painting in the upper register is completely destroyed, and we

---

[34] J. Goar, *Euchologion sive rituale Graecorum* (Venice, 1730; repr. Graz, 1976), 358–62.

[35] Θείον και Ιερόν Ευαγγέλιον, ed. Apostoliki Diakonia of the Church of Greece (Athens, 1968), 11.

[36] It is well known that unlike his pro-Union father Michael VIII, Andronikos II displayed a particular attachment to Orthodoxy and tried hard to impose Orthodox worship on the entire empire. Less familiar perhaps is the particular devotion shown to the Virgin by this emperor, who by special decree dedicated the entire month of August to her honour: see V. Grumel, 'Le mois de Marie des Byzantins', *EO* 31 (1932), 257–69.

[37] N. Drandakis, 'Ο Άϊ-Γιαννάκης του Μυστρά', *DChAE* 14 (1989), 61–82, esp. 64, 72. Pallas, 'Ζωοδόχος Πηγή', 208–9, Pl. 47.

do not know if it contained a representation of the Virgin alone or with Christ; however, D. Pallas and A.-M. Talbot in their studies on this subject associate the representation with epigrams of Manuel Philes entitled 'On an Icon of Pege' and claim that the poet was referring to an icon showing the Virgin and Christ in a basin from which waters flow into a cistern below, and other figures receiving miraculous blessings from the holy water.[38] This suggests that the type was known from the first thirty years of the fourteenth century, since Philes died in the 1330s,[39] but the representation in Ai-Yannakis which dates from c. 1370–1375[40] is the only such example surviving from that century.

In the apse of the south-east chapel of the church of Sts Theodore is another representation of the Zoodochos Pege dating from c. 1400.[41] It contains in its crystallized form the iconographic type of the two figures within the basin, familiar from all later representations of the Zoodochos Pege. The Virgin with her hands spread out in prayer stands in a basin, with Christ in front of her making a gesture of blessing. On either side of the basin are two full-length venerating angels (Fig. 20.9). Extant fourteenth-century examples depict either the Virgin alone in the basin (in the south chapel of the katholikon of Chora monastery and the narthex of the church of the Archangels in Lesnovo) or Christ in the basin in front of the Virgin's breast (in the apse of the churches of the Lesser Anargyroi in Ohrid, of St Nicholas in Psača and of the Dormition of the Virgin in Aliveri).[42] The representation of the Zoodochos Pege in the chapel at Sts Theodore, on the side walls of which there are portraits of two Byzantine officials, suggests that this iconographic type was created in Constantinople towards the end of the fourteenth century and transferred to Mistra by those officials who were responsible for the decoration.[43]

To sum up: the Hodegetria at Mistra contains an original iconographic type in a part of the church which contains a complete programme honouring the Zoodochos Pege; in Ai-Yannakis a prominent position is given to the densely populated type showing the faithful surrounding the holy water; and in Sts Theodore the crystallized iconographic type is found with the two figures inside a basin. All this suggests that the cult of the Zoodochos Pege was well established in Mistra and that one factor contributing to this was the extensive iconography in the narthex of the Aphendiko, which would have been fully comprehensible to fourteenth-century believers.[44] Thus Mistra offers important features which enrich our knowledge, otherwise based mainly on written sources, of the cult of the Zoodochos Pege in Constantinople.

---

[38] Pallas, 'Ζωοδόχος Πηγή', 207–8. Talbot, 'Epigrams', 142–4, 158–9.
[39] Talbot, 'Epigrams', 139.
[40] Drandakis, 'Ὁ Ἀϊ-Γιαννάκης τοῦ Μυστρᾶ', 81–2.
[41] Chatzidakis, *Mystras*, 51.
[42] On variants of the representations of the Virgin Zoodochos Pege, see Velmans, 'Fontaine de Vie', 128–34 (with photographs and drawings) and Pallas, 'Ζωοδόχος Πηγή', Pls 46–51.
[43] R. Etzéoglou, 'Quelques remarques sur les portraits figurés dans les églises de Mistra', in *Akten des XVI. Internationalen Byzantinistenkongresses*, Vienna, 4–9 October 1981, *JÖB* 32.5 (1982), 515–16.
[44] There is another interesting reference in the work of Nikephoros Kallistos Xanthopoulos. The forty-ninth miracle – the first in the reign of Andronikos II, contemporary with the writer – concerns a sick man from Lakedaemonia: 'ἀνήρ τις Λακεδαιμόνιος, ἔμπορος μὲν τὸν βίον, Γεώργιος Μαιούλιος ἐπώνυμον' (Xanthopoulos, *Logos*, 66). Presumably this was a merchant from Lakedaemonia who had settled in the capital, since Xanthopoulos' description does not suggest that the sick man was brought to Constantinople from the Peloponnese.

20.1   Mistra, church of the Hodegetria (Aphendiko). The Virgin Zoodochos Pege (source: author)

20.2   Mistra, church of the Hodegetria (Aphendiko). The Virgin Zoodochos Pege (detail) (source: author)

20.3   Mistra, church of the Hodegetria (Aphendiko). Sts Anargyroi (source: author)

20.4 Mistra, church of the Hodegetria (Aphendiko). Christ and the woman of Samaria; the Marriage at Cana (source: author)

20.5 Mistra, church of the Hodegetria (Aphendiko). Healing of the man blind from birth; healing of Peter's wife's mother (source: author)

20.6 Mistra, church of the Hodegetria (Aphendiko). Healing of the man with dropsy (source: author)

20.7 Mistra, church of the Hodegetria (Aphendiko). Healing of the paralytic at Bethesda; cure of the woman with issue of blood (source: author)

20.8 Mistra, chapel of Ai-Yannakis. The Virgin Zoodochos Pege (source: Millet, *Monuments byzantins de Mistra*, Pl. 107.2)

20.9. Mistra, church of Sts Theodore. The Virgin Zoodochos Pege (source: Millet, *Monuments byzantins de Mistra*, Pl. 90.2)

The Virgin, the Christ-child and the evil eye*

Vassiliki Foskolou

The wall painting illustrated in Plate 16 and Fig. 21.1, from the Omorphi Ekklesia, Aigina,[1] and dated on epigraphical grounds to 1289,[2] might at first glance appear to be a standard Nativity scene typical of late Byzantine 'provincial' art. A closer look, however, reveals a number of unusual iconographic features, which suggest that first impressions are wrong, and that it is actually rather an unconventional treatment of the subject.

One significant variation is the depiction of the Virgin with the Christ-child at her breast. While the Galaktotrophousa type is obviously not unusual in itself – its development, diffusion and theological symbolism have been frequently discussed[3] – it was adopted mainly in works of a devotional nature, and seldom occurs in narrative scenes until the end of the thirteenth century.[4]

But as one looks at the painting, what catches the attention is the treatment of the Cave of Bethlehem, the birthplace of the incarnated *Logos*, which is shown as a rocky mass fringed by a corrugated band with six eyes depicted on it. These eyes encompass the Virgin and her new-born child, and are focused on the interior of the cave, seeming to follow the drama which unfolds within it. This composition with the Galaktotrophousa and the watching eyes is unique in Byzantine art, and in this paper I shall be suggesting that the clue to its interpretation lies in the popular belief in the evil eye.

Let us begin by considering another iconographic oddity, which at first glance seems to be a standard genre feature. This is the figure of the dog on the right; with its long claws and gaping jaws the barking animal exudes an air of menace. Ferocious dogs of this kind appear in murals in

---

* This study was carried out during post-doctoral research supported by a grant from the State Scholarships Foundation (I.K.Y.).
[1] On the church and its wall paintings, G. Soteriou, 'Ἡ Ὀμορφη Ἐκκλησιά Αἰγίνης', *EEBS* 2 (1925), 243–76. V. Foskolou, 'Ἡ Ὀμορφη Ἐκκλησιά στην Αἴγινα. Εικονογραφική και τεχνοτροπική ανάλυση των τοιχογραφιών', PhD thesis, University of Athens, 2000.
[2] S. Kalopissi-Verti, *Dedicatory Inscriptions and Donor Portraits in Thirteenth-Century Churches of Greece* (VTIB, 5) (Vienna, 1992), 85.
[3] L. Mirković, 'Die nährende Gottesmutter (Galaktotrophusa)', in *Atti del V Congresso Internazionale di Studi Byzantini* II (Rome, 1940), 297–304. V. Lazareff, 'Studies in the Iconography of the Virgin', *ArtB* 20 (1938), 27–36. E. Papatheophanous-Tsouri, 'Εικόνα Παναγίας Γαλακτοτροφούσας από τη Ρόδο', *AD* 34 (1979), A-Meletai, 1–14. A. Cutler, 'The Cult of the Galaktotrophousa in Byzantium and Italy', *JÖB* 37 (1987), 335–50. Cf. also the paper of E. Bolman in this volume, 13–22.
[4] The Nativity scene in the Omorphi Ekklesia is the earliest known example of such a scene in wall painting depicting the Virgin Galaktotrophousa; it is followed by two 14th-c. representations, in St John at Kroustas Merambellou, Crete (1347–1348) (K. Gallas, K. Wessel and M. Borboudakis, *Byzantinisches Kreta* (Munich, 1983), 438, Fig. 412) and in St Nicholas tes Steges, Cyprus (A. and J. Stylianou, *The Painted Churches of Cyprus* (London, 1985), 68–71, Fig. 28).

the churches of San Pietro in Otranto, southern Italy[5] and of Sts Anargyroi in Kipoula, Mani (1265),[6] while a strange creature resembling a dragon rather than a dog can be found in the church of the Archangel Michael in Kouneni, Crete (Figs 21.2–21.3).[7] The inclusion of this fierce creature in four near-contemporary Nativity scenes is unlikely to be a coincidence, and in view of the generally negative attitude to dogs held by the Byzantines, its presence here raises a number of questions.

The Scriptures tend to take an unsympathetic view of dogs and to associate them with impious, savage and dangerous men.[8] This attitude is clearly illustrated in Psalms 21:17 ('Many dogs have encircled me, a band of evil men has surrounded me'), which Byzantine theological commentaries and Psalter illustrations[9] link with the betrayal and arrest of Christ.[10] A particularly interesting instance of the latter is found in the so-called marginal Psalters, which for Psalm 21 depict men with dogs' heads coming to arrest Christ[11] (Fig. 21.4).

As the dog is the personification of impiety, canine disguise is also assumed by the Devil and his followers – in fact demonic possession in a dog is usually betrayed by barking.[12] In hagiological and theological literature, descriptions of saints confronting the Devil in canine form[13] and frequent comparisons of the Evil One to a dog[14] suggest that this was a widely accepted belief in Byzantine society. The purpose of including such ferocious animals in Nativity scenes seems therefore to be a reminder that on the margins of this joyful event lurked the evil presence of a demonic creature.[15] Why should this be so?

In Orthodox theology, Christ's Nativity marks the start of the fulfilment of God's plan for the salvation of mankind, and it also represents the first important step in the overthrow of the agents of evil.[16] Statements such as 'Today the ancient bond was broken, the Devil disgraced, the demons put to flight and death defeated' are a common topos in Christmas sermons.[17] And

---

[5] L. Safran, *San Pietro at Otranto. Byzantine Art in South Italy* (Rome, 1992), 88, Fig. 39.

[6] N. B. Drandakis, Βυζαντινές τοιχογραφίες της Μέσα Μάνης (Athens, 1995), 323–4, Pl. XIV, 73.

[7] K. Lassithiotakis, 'Δύο εκκλησίες στο νομό Χανίων', *DChAE* 2 (1960/1), Pl. 5, a.

[8] See the entry 'Hund', in *LCI* 2 (1970), 334 (P. Gerlach). D. Forstner, *Die Welt der christlichen Symbole* (Innsbruck, Vienna and Munich, 1977), 266–8.

[9] J. J. Tikkanen, *Die Psalterillustration im Mittelalter* (2nd edn, Utrecht, 1975), 55–6. S. Duffrenne, *Tableaux synoptiques de 15 psautiers médiévaux* (Paris, 1978), Psalms 21:17.

[10] See, for example, Euthymios Zigabenos, *Commentarius in Psalterium*, *PG* 128, 281: 'And he calls the Roman soldiers dogs, being unclean according to the law and without shame'.

[11] Khludov Psalter: K. Corrigan, *Visual Polemics in the Ninth-Century Byzantine Psalters* (Cambridge, 1992), Fig. 6. Barberini Psalter: Tikkanen, *Psalterillustration*, Fig. 71. London Add. 19352 (1066): S. Der Nersessian, *L'illustration des psautiers grecs du moyen-âge* II (Paris, 1970), Fig. 41.

[12] C. D. G. Müller, 'Von Teufel, Mittagsdämon und Amuletten', *JbAC* 17 (1974), 95. R. P. H. Greenfield, *Traditions of Belief in Late Byzantine Demonology* (Amsterdam, 1988), 86–7. Demons also appear in canine form in modern popular superstition: Ch. Stewart, *Demons and the Devil. Moral Imagination in Modern Greek Culture* (Princeton, NJ, 1991), 156 n. 28.

[13] P. P. Joannou, *Démonologie populaire – démonologie critique au XI*^e* siècle: la vie inédite de S. Auxence par M. Psellos* (Wiesbaden, 1971), 12.

[14] Greenfield, *Demonology*, 133–4.

[15] The depiction of a dog as a symbol of evil is also relatively common in the art of the Roman West. H. Schade, *Dämonen und Monstern* (Regensburg, 1962), 74 ff., Fig. 22. V. von Blankenburg, *Heilige und dämonische Tiere* (Cologne, 1975), 122–5, 303, 311, Figs 29, 31.

[16] Greenfield, *Demonology*, 56.

[17] John Chrysostom, *Homilia in Natalem Christi Diem*, *PG* 56, 391. In another homily on the Incarnation of the Saviour the writer not only refers to the connection with the defeat of evil but also 'illustrates' it with a text

according to Orthodox Christian tradition the devil, powerless against the new-born Christ but ever on the watch for opportunities to cause harm, was the inspiration behind the Massacre of the Innocents; in the words of Gregory of Nyssa, 'Add to the catalogue of the offshoots of evil Herod's slaughter of children.'[18] A text of Eusebios of Emesa is particularly enlightening in this regard; in it the devil, conversing with Hades, assures him that there is no need for concern about the Baptist's message heralding Christ, since he knows his identity and that of his parents, and adds: 'When he was born, Herod sought to kill him … if he escaped my clutches then, he will fall into them now', and he continues by revealing his plan for the Crucifixion of Christ.[19]

Byzantine theologians also suggest that as the Devil knew of Isaiah's prophecy of the birth of Christ to the Virgin (7:14), it lay within his power and his intent to injure her and to prevent the birth. The solution found to ensure the fulfilment of God's Plan was the betrothal of Mary to Joseph, as indicated by writers of all periods. In the words of Basil the Great: 'The betrothal to Joseph was planned so that the virginity of Mary should go unobserved by the Prince of this world.'[20] And as Euthymios Zigabenos was later to declare: 'the Virgin was betrothed so that the birth of Christ would go unnoticed by the Devil.'[21]

The same explanation for the Virgin's betrothal is also given in a homily by James of Kokkinobaphos. What concerns us here, however, is that in the two famous illustrated manuscripts of his homilies the passage is accompanied by a miniature entitled 'How the Virgin was preserved unharmed from the weapons of evil by an unseen power'; this shows the enthroned Virgin surrounded by angels, with in the lower section angels armed with spears warding off demons in a gloomy cavern (Fig. 21.5).[22]

All this indicates that the Devil's threat to the Virgin and to the Christ-child is clearly part of Orthodox belief, and it also provides a possible explanation of the inclusion of the rabid dog as a symbol of evil in the Nativity scene. However, we obviously cannot establish how far this 'standard Orthodox' tradition influenced 'alternative' traditions (i.e. popular religious beliefs and practices), and furthermore how far Byzantine thinking generally was influenced by each of these.[23] In other words, it is very difficult to know what the ordinary person in the Byzantine

---

giving a visual image of the Nativity: 'it was a great wonder to behold, the Babe in swaddling clothes under the star, the magi worshipping and offering gifts. There were also shepherds receiving the tidings and demons being chastised and God among men', Ch. Martin, 'Un florilège grec d'homélies christologiques des IVe et Ve siècles sur la Nativité. Par. gr. 1491', *Muséon* 53 (1940), 45.

[18] Gregory of Nyssa, *In Natalem Salvatoris*, in W. Jaeger et al. (eds), *Gregorii Nysseni Opera* X.2 (Leiden, 1996), 241. In the apocryphal Acts of Thomas, the Devil himself appears to the apostles and he mentions the Massacre of the Innocents among his evil deeds: E. Hennecke, *Neutestamentliche Apokryphen* II (Tübingen, 1964), 199, 322. For further references on the subject, see Greenfield, *Demonology*, 57.

[19] Eusebios of Emesa, *De adventu Joannis in Infernum*, PG 86, 520.

[20] Basil the Great, *In Sanctam Christi Generationem*, PG 31, 1464.

[21] Euthymios Zigabenos, *Interpretatio Evangelii Lucae*, PG 129, 865. See also Greenfield, *Demonology*, 56–7.

[22] I. Hutter and P. Canart, *Das Marienhomiliar des Mönchs Jakobos von Kokkinobaphos. Einführungsband zur Faksimileausgabe des Cod. Vat. gr. 1162* (Cologne, 1992), 52 (fol. 92). On the miniature in the second manuscript, Par. gr. 1208 (fol. 123), see Th. Provatakis, *Ο Διάβολος εις την Βυζαντινήν τέχνην* (Thessaloniki, 1980), Fig. 59. Similar expressions are found in other Marian homilies, e.g. of John of Damascus (P. Voulet (ed.), *J. Damascène, Homélies sur la Nativité et la Dormition* (Paris, 1961), 62) and of Patriarch Tarasios of Constantinople (PG 98, 1493).

[23] More generally on the problem of our lack of knowledge of the 'alternative' tradition in matters of demonology and its diffusion among the Byzantines: Greenfield, *Demonology*, 153–5. Id., 'Contribution to the Study of Palaeologan Magic', in H. Maguire (ed.), *Byzantine Magic* (Washington, DC, 1995), 150–3.

world actually believed about the dangers encountered by the new-born Christ. An idea, or at least some clues, as to how the Orthodox view might have been 'transformed' can be gathered from apocryphal writings such as the Arabic gospel of John, which relates how angels linked their wings from heaven to earth to protect and conceal the cave of the Nativity.[24]

The confrontation of the Christ-child with the agents of evil is also found in the Christmas liturgy itself. The prophecy par excellence of the coming of the Messiah (Isaiah 11:1–8) describes the co-existence of wild and tame animals ('then the wolf also shall graze with the lambs') in verses 6–8, which end with the passage 'and he shall play while giving suck at the hole of the asps and being weaned he shall raise his hand to the face of the basilisk'.[25]

The theological message of the passage is easy to interpret: the child 'giving suck' is identified with Christ, whose peaceable kingdom will gain the victory and crush the forces of evil.[26] But the special interest of the passage lies not in this interpretation but rather in the fact that the evil powers take on a specific form. They assume the guise of asps and basilisks, two fantastic creatures which are described in several biblical passages as symbols of the Devil and which were associated in the Byzantine mind through theological commentary and pagan myth with certain aspects of the activity of the Evil One.[27]

The basilisk, the king of reptiles, could according to legend cause death with his glance. This belief, which has its roots in Roman times and is found in early Christian texts, spread throughout the Byzantine world, as is clear from references in literature[28] and from illustrated manuscripts of zoological treatises depicting this fantastic creature with its huge head and terrifying eyes.[29] The myth of its deadly gaze led to the basilisk being linked with the popular belief of the evil eye (βασκανία), i.e. the harm caused by envy through the power of the gaze. This connection is clearly expressed in the commentary on the Psalter by Euthymios Zigabenos. Writing about Psalms 90(91):13 ('You will overcome the asp and the basilisk and tread down the lion and the dragon'), Zigabenos, like other commentators,[30] says that these

---

[24] R. Stichel, *Die Geburt Christi in der russischen Ikonenmalerei* (Stuttgart, 1990), 24 n. 47. Cf. the episode in the cave with the dragons on the flight into Egypt in Pseudo-Matthew, ed. W. Schneemelcher, *Neutestamentliche Apokryphen* I (5th edn, Tübingen, 1987), 367. In the entrance to the Cave of the Nativity in Bethlehem there is a 5th-c. mosaic pavement with the acronym ΙΧΘΥΣ and the knots of Solomon, symbols which were often depicted in doorways throughout the eastern Mediterranean in early Byzantine times for apotropaic purposes, to prevent the admission of evil: E. Kitzinger, 'The Threshold of the Holy Shrine. Observations on Floor Mosaics at Antioch and Bethlehem', in P. Granfield and J. A. Jungmann (eds), *Kyriakon. Festschrift für Johannes Quasten* II (Münster, 1970), 641–5, Figs 2–5. J. Engemann, 'Zur Verbreitung magischer Übelabwehr in der nichtchristlichen und christlichen Spätantike', *JbAC* 18 (1975), 42–6. Cf. H. Maguire, 'Magic and Geometry in Early Christian Floor Mosaics and Textiles', *JÖB* 44 (1994), 267–8.
[25] The text in the Septuagint is: 'καὶ παιδίον νήπιον ἐπὶ τρώγλην ἀσπίδων καὶ ἐπὶ κοίτην ἐκγόνων ἀσπίδων τὴν χεῖρα ἐπιβαλεῖ' ('And an infant child shall put his hand on the hole of the asps and on the nest of the offspring of asps'). The version given in the paper comes from the translation of Symmachos (2nd c.): see *Septuaginta, Vetus Testamentum Graecum, XIV. Isaias*, ed. J. Ziegler (Göttingen, 1967).
[26] Hesychios of Jerusalem, *PG* 93, 1372. For a pictorial interpretation of this passage in an early 14th-c. Tree of Jesse, see M. D. Taylor, 'A Historiated Tree of Jesse', *DOP* 34/5 (1980/1), 131–2, Fig. 5.
[27] See also the entries on 'Basilisk' in *RAC* 1 (1950), 1260–1 (F. Eckstein) and in *LCI* 1 (1970), 251–3 (L. Wehrhahn-Stauch). Forstner, *Die Welt der christlichen Symbole*, 291. On the asp, see Provatakis, *Διάβολος*, 234–7 and the entry 'Aspis' in *LCI* 1 (1970), 191–3 (L. Wehrhahn-Stauch).
[28] E. Piccolomini, 'Intorno ai collectanea di Massimo Planude', *Rivista di Filologia* 2 (1874), 158.
[29] Z. Kádár, *Survivals of Greek Zoological Illuminations in Byzantine Manuscripts* (Budapest, 1978), 71–2, Pl. 101, 3.
[30] Athanasios of Alexandria, *PG* 27, 404. Cyril of Alexandria, *PG* 69, 1224. Nikephoros Blemmydes, *PG* 142, 1542.

fearful monsters are symbols of the Devil, and then he adds: 'The basilisk is the baskania (evil eye), for just as he has destruction in his eyes, so baskania causes destruction through the eyes'.[31]

Inherited from the Graeco-Roman world, belief in the evil eye was particularly widespread in Byzantine society.[32] The pagan belief in the maleficent power of the envious gaze[33] was 'translated' by the early Christian Fathers into new religious language: thus it is no longer the human eye which causes harm, but the Devil and his demons acting through it.[34] At the same time, in accordance with the idea that one of the Devil's basic motives is envy, the epithet βάσκανος is often used in ecclesiastical literature to describe the agent of evil and his followers.[35] Eventually even ecclesiastical writers identified *baskania* – always associated with demons – with the popular belief in the evil eye.[36]

Like many other peoples throughout history,[37] the Byzantines believed that it was pregnant mothers and new-born children who were most susceptible to the workings of the envious eye because of the risks and dangers arising from pregnancy and childbirth.[38] A whole series of apotropaic practices relating to babies and children indicates how widespread this belief was: red ribbons, for example, were tied to babies' arms 'as amulets to provide protection against diseases and the evil eye'.[39] On the other hand, although the church officially condemned such unorthodox religious practices, it offered prayers for the protection of mothers in labour and new-born children which – it is no coincidence – contained references to the evil eye.[40] One may therefore wonder whether the Orthodox beliefs in the threat to the new-born Christ from

---

[31] *PG* 128, 941–4. Psalm 90(91) is considered to be apotropaic and its first two verses are found on amulets against the evil eye: E. Peterson, *ΕΙΣ ΘΕΟΣ. Epigraphische, formgeschichtliche und religionsgeschichtliche Untersuchungen* (Göttingen, 1926), 91–2. C. Bonner, *Studies in Magical Amulets Chiefly Greco-Egyptian* (Ann Arbor, 1950), 50, 219 ff.

[32] On the evil eye in Byzantium, Ph. Koukoules, Βυζαντινῶν βίος καὶ πολιτισμός I.1 (Athens, 1948), 244–8. Provatakis, Διάβολος, 294–5. H. Maguire, *The Icons of their Bodies. Saints and their Images in Byzantium* (Princeton, NJ, 1996), 106 ff.

[33] Generally on belief in the evil eye in the Graeco-Roman world, see Chr. Veikou, Κακό μάτι. Η κοινωνική κατασκευή της οπτικής επικοινωνίας (Athens, 2000), 50–9.

[34] Greenfield, *Demonology*, 111–12. M. W. Dickie, 'The Fathers of the Church and the Evil Eye', in Maguire, *Byzantine Magic*, 9–33. Th. Rakoczy, *Böser Blick, Macht des Auges und Neid der Götter* (Tübingen, 1996), 216 ff.

[35] G. Bartelink, 'ΒΑΣΚΑΝΟΣ. Désignation de Satan et des démons chez les auteurs chrétiens', *Orientalia Christiana Periodica* 49 (1983), 390–406. Müller, 'Von Teufel', 93, 101–2. Greenfield, *Demonology*, 42–3.

[36] Bartelink, 'ΒΑΣΚΑΝΟΣ', esp. 393–4.

[37] S. Seligmann, *Der böse Blick und Verwandtes* I (Berlin, 1910), 190–4. E. A. Wallis Budge, *Amulets and Superstitions* (Oxford, 1930), 354. Cl. Maloney (ed.), *The Evil Eye* (New York, 1976), 44, 80, 105–6.

[38] In Byzantium the fears and dangers relating to pregnancy and childbirth were reflected in taboos and purificatory rituals for new mothers, in ideas about the vulnerability of babies and in the belief that unbaptized infants were easy prey for demons: Koukoules, Βυζαντινῶν βίος καὶ πολιτισμός VI (Athens, 1957), 33. I. Sorlin, 'Striges et Géloudes. Histoire d'une croyance et d'une tradition', *TM* 11 (1991), 432. M.-H. Congourdeau, 'Regards sur l'enfant nouveau-né à Byzance', *REB* 51 (1993), 161–76. Cf. D. de F. Abrahamse, 'Magic and Sorcery in the Hagiography of the Middle Byzantine Period', *BF* 8 (1982), 12–14.

[39] Koukoules, Βυζαντινῶν βίος καὶ πολιτισμός I.2 (Athens, 1948), 247 n. 4. The popularity of such superstitions is mainly confirmed by indirect evidence. A typical example is the reference in Theodore of Stoudios to a funerary speech for his mother, which states that, unlike all other women, she never turned to amulets and spells for the protection of her children, and this was proof of her virtue: *PG* 99, 884–5.

[40] e.g. the prayer uttered on the day of birth of a child: 'O God our Lord and Master ... preserve them from all the tyranny of the devil ... from envy and jealousy and the evil eye'. J. Goar (ed.), *Euchologion sive rituale Graecorum* (Venice, 1730; repr. Graz, 1960), 261.

the Devil and in the Devil as the prime source of the evil eye were somehow amalgamated to create a tradition that the Virgin and the holy infant were in danger from the evil eye, like any other mother in labour or new-born child.[41]

It is obviously hard to give a definite answer to this, but a particularly interesting piece of evidence is an exorcism against the Yello or Gylou, the female demon who endangers the life of new-born children and women during pregnancy and labour. Popular belief in this demonic figure must have been especially widespread in the Byzantine world, to judge from literary references and from the survival of similar female child-harming demons in Balkan folk tradition up to the present day.[42]

In an apotropaic text on the demon's confrontation with Archangel Michael and her defeat at his hands, she gives a description of her powers, in accordance with the concept that in order to resist unfamiliar evil spirits one must first recognize their strengths: 'I enter someone's house in the form of a snake, a serpent ... I go to wound women; wherever I go I cause them pain in their heart, and I dry up their milk ... I kill infants.' And she concludes: 'When the holy Mary gave birth to the Word of truth, I went there to delude her, but I failed and was myself turned away deluded.'[43]

Such apotropaic texts, although not officially accepted by the church, must have been in wide circulation, to judge from numerous written records from the fifteenth right up to the twentieth century. Their content does not display great variety: the demon appears to St Michael or to St Sisinnios, who overpowers her by reciting the secret names which represent her various forms and evil qualities, and this makes the exorcism effective.[44]

As one of the Gylou's appellations is given as 'Baskosyne' (Βασκοσύνη) and a basic motive for her actions is envy, she is identified with *baskania*, the evil eye.[45] This is clearly demonstrated in a sixth-century wall painting from the monastery of St Apollo at Bawīṭ in Egypt depicting St Sisinnios in the act of spearing a female demon, while just above her an eye is shown being attacked by various animals and weapons, a common visual device for protection against the evil eye[46] (Fig. 21.6); it is also confirmed by a large group of apotropaic amulets, one

---

[41] In modern Greek folklore, divine figures are susceptible to the evil eye, as indicated by a number of spells uttered against the evil eye which relate that even the Virgin was its victim: L. Arnaud, 'La baskania ou le mauvais œil chez les Grecs modernes', *EO* 15 (1912), 385–94, 514–7. This shows both the gravity of the danger – since the power of good itself is imperilled – and also how through ritual acts the transposition from the human to the spiritual world is accepted and fully understood in contemporary popular superstition. See Chr. Veikou, 'Τελετουργικός λόγος και συμβολική μετατόπιση στο ξεμάτιασμα', *Αρχαιολογία* 72 (September, 1999), 18–19.

[42] Sorlin, 'Striges et Géloudes', 411–36. Greenfield, *Demonology*, 182–8. Provatakis, *Διάβολος*, 115–19. On the survival of such superstitions, see D. B. Oikonomides, 'Η Γελλώ εις την Ελληνικήν και Ρουμανικήν Λαογραφία', *Λαογραφία* 30 (1975/6), 246–78.

[43] K. N. Sathas, *Μεσαιωνική βιβλιοθήκη* V (Venice, 1876), 576.

[44] R. Greenfield, 'Saint Sisinnios, the Archangel Michael and the Female Demon Gylou: The Typology of the Greek Literary Stories', *Βυζαντινά* 15 (1989), 83–141. According to Greenfield, the fact that the exorcism is recorded over a wide geographical area and a long period of time suggests that the texts are part of an extensive oral tradition (ibid., 139–41).

[45] P. Perdrizet, *Negotium Perambulans in Tenebris. Études de démonologie gréco-orientale* (Strasbourg, 1922), 24–31. Müller, 'Von Teufel', 101–2. Sorlin, 'Striges et Géloudes', 428–9. Similarly in an exorcism against the evil eye it is called Yello, A. Delatte, *Anecdota Atheniensia* I (Liège, 1927), 248–9.

[46] E. Dauterman-Maguire, H. P. Maguire, and M.-J. Duncan-Flowers (eds), *Art and Holy Powers in the Early Christian House*, exh. cat., Krannert Art Museum of the University of Illinois at Urbana-Champaign 1989 (Urbana and Chicago, 1989), 27, Fig. 23.

side of which depicts the Holy Rider overcoming a female demon and the other the 'much-suffering eye'[47] (Fig. 21.7).

The reference in the exorcism to the attack on the Virgin, though probably a magical formula expressing the demon's strength and immunity, which can only be overcome by the powers of God,[48] could have suggested the idea of danger to the Christ-child from the forces of evil and in particular the evil eye. The fact that the boundaries between Orthodox beliefs and practices on the one hand and magical rituals and superstitions on the other are not always recognized by the general public or sometimes even by priests lacking in theological knowledge makes this a very plausible theory.[49]

To return to the placing of eyes around the cave of the Nativity in the Omorphi Ekklesia, this should be interpreted as an apotropaic practice against envy and the Devil's evil eye. The representation of an eye as a protection against *baskania* follows a basic apotropaic rule, in which the very thing which provokes the evil is used to destroy it.[50] The fact that Christ is depicted at his mother's breast supports this interpretation, since although this image basically emphasizes the doctrine of the Incarnation, it is at the same time a representation of an intimate and human moment in the life of the incarnated *Logos*, who is here no different from any other new-born infant; Christ is shown as an ordinary baby needing protection from the perils of the evil eye.[51]

Finally, the interpretation of the eyes around the cave may also lie in the symbolism given to the sacred birthplace in ecclesiastical hymnography and homilies. In addition to its associations

---

[47] There is a considerable bibliography on this type of amulet: Bonner, *Studies in Magical Amulets*, 208 ff. Ch. Walter, 'The Intaglio of Solomon in the Benaki Museum and the Origins of the Iconography of Warrior Saints', *DChAE* 12 (1989/90), 33–42. *Art and Holy Powers*, 25–8, and *passim*. J. Spier, 'Medieval Byzantine Magical Amulets and their Tradition', *JWarb* 56 (1993), 33–8. T. Matantséva, 'Les amulettes byzantines contre le mauvais œil du Cabinet des médailles', *JbAC* 37 (1994), 111–21. J. Russell, 'The Archeological Context of Magic in the Early Byzantine Period', in Maguire, *Byzantine Magic*, 40–1. In general the use of such charms is thought to have originated in Syria and Palestine and later to have spread from the North African coast to that of Asia Minor and the Crimea. From the chronological point of view these amulets are thought to be Byzantine and have survived until the 7th c., though as most belong to private collections and museums and are without archaeological context, accurate dating is difficult. Evidence of this problem, which at the same time suggests a lengthy period of use for the amulets, is provided by an amulet found in a 12th- or 13th-c. house in Cherson in the Crimea: Matantséva, 'Les amulettes byzantines', 113 n. 27. As regards their use, G. Vikan considers that amulets of this type, in particular those made of haematite, must have been intended for pregnant women, to ensure safe childbirth and protect against miscarriages: 'Art, Medicine, and Magic in Early Byzantium', *DOP* 38 (1984), 79–81.

[48] R. Reitzenstein associates the motif of the threat against the Virgin with a contemporary popular tradition from the Holy Land, in which she could not breastfeed until she had obtained a miraculous cure (*Poimandres. Studien zur griechisch-ägyptischen und frühchristlichen Literatur* (Leipzig, 1904), 297–9, 367). Conversely F. Pradel considers that the subject of the demonic threat contains an echo of Revelation 12:4 and 20:8 (*Griechische und süditalienische Gebete. Beschwörungen und Rezepte des Mittelalters* (Giessen, 1907), 28, 89). Greenfield believes that it reflects the fact that the evil actions of the Gylou are specifically turned against mothers and children ('Saint Sisinnios', 123).

[49] C. Stewart in a study of the boundaries between magical and Orthodox Christian practices mentions the case of a priest from Naxos who was summoned before the Metropolitan of Paronaxia and reprimanded because he read the χαρτί της Γελούς ('Μαγεία και ορθοδοξία', *Αρχαιολογία* 72 (September, 1999), 10–11).

[50] Seligmann, *Der böse Blick*, 144 ff. In the Testament of Solomon the demon who provokes the evil eye says 'I am called Phthenoth and bring the evil eye to every man. Therefore the engraved much-suffering evil eye destroys me' (Provatakis, *Διάβολος*, 292 n. 22). On the Testament of Solomon, see Greenfield, *Demonology*, 158 ff. Some of the amulets against the evil eye have the shape of an eye; cf. Bonner, *Studies in Magical Amulet*, 218–19.

[51] A similar feature is found in 14th- and 15th-c. Italian paintings, which show a coral hanging from the neck of

with Paradise and Heaven and with the cave of the Burial and Resurrection, the cave of the Nativity is also likened to the 'dark underground life of mortals'.[52] This comparison is extended in hymns to the individual figure of the hymnographer and thence to that of the believer, who is characterized as a cave, and specifically a cave of robbers, i.e. demons.[53] Christmas homilies associate the idea of the believer as a 'cave of devils' with the Cave of the Nativity, as in this later text: 'The Lord was born in a poor, humble cave, to transform man who is the cave and dwelling of the robber and the murderous demon, the fearful evil devil, into the temple and house of the Holy Spirit.'[54] It was thus the belief that the Cave of the Nativity was to be compared with sinful and demon-dominated man, and more generally that caves were the haunt of demons, that led to the placing of these apotropaic symbols at the cave mouth.

I should like to conclude this attempt at interpreting a unique iconographic feature with a general comment. It seems that this is yet another instance which demonstrates how the iconography of humble churches of the Byzantine world can hold many meanings, not necessarily of an exclusively theological nature, and that it can provide a means of access to the barely explored world of popular beliefs.

---

the Christ-child, as worn in the West even today as an amulet against the evil eye. S. A. Callisen, 'The Evil Eye in Italian Art', *ArtB* 19 (1937), 450–62.
[52] Gregory of Nyssa, *In Natalem Salvatoris*, ed. Jaeger *et al.*, 257. See also J. Daniélou, 'Le symbole de la caverne chez Grégoire de Nysse', *JbAC Ergänzungsband* 1 (1964), 43–51.
[53] E. Benz, 'Die heilige Höhle in der Ostkirche', *Eranos Jahrbuch* 22 (1953), 404–5, 416. On the comparison of demons to robbers, see Greenfield, *Demonology*, 134 n. 444. The cave as a place of demons is a common topos in hagiographical writing; see Joannou, *Démonologie*, 10–11.
[54] In a homily of Archbishop Anthimos of Athens (late 14th c.). K. I. Dyovouniotis, 'Ἀνθίμου Ἀθηνῶν, λόγος ἀνέκδοτος εἰς τὴν Γέννησιν τοῦ Χριστοῦ', *EEBS* 7 (1930), 45.

THE VIRGIN, THE CHRIST-CHILD AND THE EVIL EYE 259

21.1   Aigina, Omorphi Ekklesia (1289). The Nativity (source: author)

21.2   Otranto, San Pietro. The Nativity; barking dog (detail) (third quarter of the 13th c.) (source: Safran, *San Pietro at Otranto,* Fig. 39)

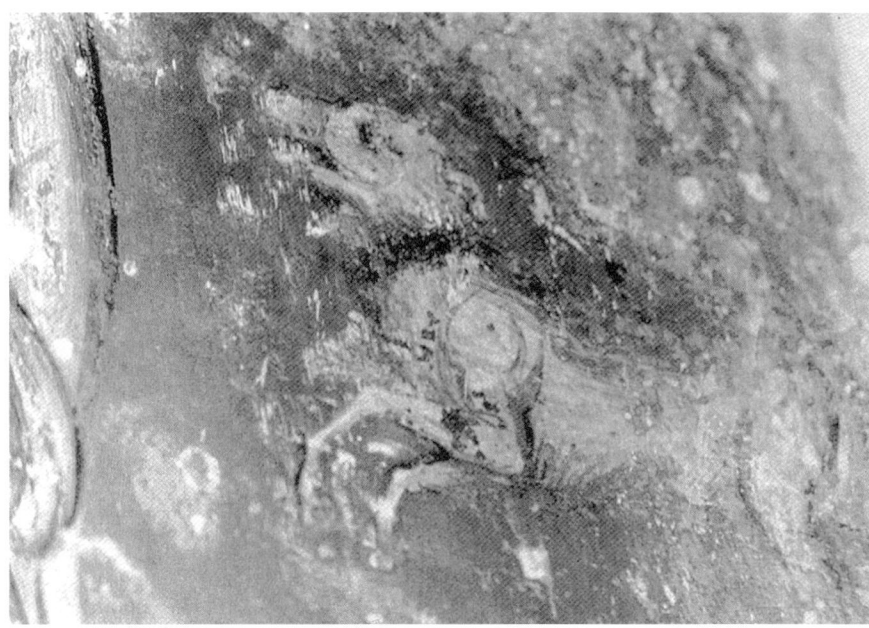

21.3 Crete, Kouneni,
Church of Archangel Michael. The Nativity
(source: Lassithiotakis, 'Δύο εκκλησίες', Pl. 5, a)

21.4 Moscow, State Historical Museum,
MS. gr. 129, fol. 19v, Khludov Psalter.
Miniature of Psalms 21:17
(source: Corrigan, *Visual Polemics*, Fig. 6)

21.5 Paris, Bibliothèque nationale, MS. gr. 1208, fol. 123r
(Homilies of James of Kokkinobaphos).
'How the Virgin was preserved unharmed from the weapons
of evil by an unseen power' (source: Cutler and Spieser,
Das mittelalterliche Byzanz, Fig. 303)

21.6 Egypt, Bawīṭ. Monastery of St Apollo. St Sisinnios piercing a female demon (6th c.) (source: Dauterman-Maguire, Maguire and Duncan-Flowers, *Art and Holy Powers in the Early Christian House*, 27, Fig. 23)

21.7 Paris, Bibliothèque nationale, Cabinet des médailles. Bronze amulet. The Holy Rider piercing a female demon and the 'much-suffering eye' (source: Matantséva, 'Les amulettes byzantines', Fig. 14, b)

Praying for the salvation of the empire?

Maria Vassilaki

The subject of this paper is an icon, the Freising 'Lukasbild', which, though it has long been well known to art historians[1] (Plates 17 and 18a, Fig. 22.1), still continues to withhold many of its secrets. It is for this reason perhaps as much as any other that, at a conference held under the auspices of the Benaki Museum's 'Mother of God' exhibition, I chose to talk not about one of the items on view there, but rather about one that was not. I should for the record, though, mention that we originally intended to bring this icon to the Benaki Museum and indeed made every effort to do so, through visits to Freising, discussions with Dr Peter Steiner, director of the city's Diözesanmuseum, and consultation with the Archbishop of Munich and Freising, Cardinal Friedrich Wetter. All seemed to be going well until, at the very end of May 2000, we were notified of the Freising museum's condition report, which stated that some of the icon's enamel medallions had begun to disintegrate. This obviously put an end to any further discussion, as we could not think of bringing the icon to Athens in these circumstances. However, it should not be thought that the choice of this icon for my paper was made merely out of frustration. The truth is that I wanted to set down a few of the thoughts that occurred to me at various times during the preparation of the exhibition, especially as I had the opportunity to observe and study the icon at close hand when it was on view in the exhibition 'Rom und Byzanz' at the

---

[1] J. Sighart, *Der Dom zu Freising. Eine kunstgeschichtliche Monographie mit artistischen Beilagen* (Landshut, 1852), 68–73. M. Kalligas, 'Φορητή εικών εν Freising', *AE* (1937), 501–6, Pl. A', Figs 1–3. A. Xyngopoulos, *Σχεδίασμα ιστορίας της θρησκευτικής ζωγραφικής μετά την Άλωσιν* (Athens, 1957), 17–18, Pl. 1.2. S. Benker, *Philipp Dirr und die Entstehung des Barock in Baiern* (Munich, 1958), 95, 183–4, Fig. 27. *Byzantine Art, an European Art*, exh. cat., Athens, Zappeion Exhibition Hall (Athens, 1964), no. 214, 260–1 (A. Xyngopoulos). C. Wolters, 'Beobachtungen am Freisinger Lukasbild', *Kunstchronik* 17 (1964), 85–91, Figs 1–4. J. Deér, 'Die byzantinisierenden Zellenschmelze der Linköping-Mitra und ihr Denkmalkreis', in *Tortulae, Studien zur altchristlichen und byzantinischen Monumenten* (*Römische Quartalschrift, Supplementheft*, 30) (Rome, Freiburg and Vienna, 1966), 49–64, esp. 59 n. 36. K. Wessel, *Die byzantinische Emailkunst vom 5. bis 13. Jahrhundert* (*Beiträge zur Kunst des christlichen Ostens*, 4) (Recklinghausen, 1967), no. 65, 196–8, fig. on p. 196. A. Grabar, *Les revêtements en or et en argent des icones byzantines du moyen âge* (*Bibliothèque de l'Institut Hellénique d'Études Byzantines et Post-byzantines de Venise*, 7) (Venice, 1975), 7, no. 16, 41–3, 44, 46, 48–9, Figs 39–41. F. Fahr, H. Ramisch and P. B. Steiner (eds), *Diözesanmuseum Freising. Christliche Kunst aus Salzburg, Bayern und Tirol, 12. bis 18. Jahrhundert* (*Diözesanmuseum für christliche Kunst des Erzbistums München und Freising, Kataloge und Schriften*, II) (Freising, 1984), 244–51 (S. Benker). A. Legner (ed.), *Ornamenta Ecclesiae. Kunst und Künstler der Romanik*, exh. cat., Cologne, Schnütgen Museum (Cologne, 1985), no. H.69, 171–2, colour pls on pp. 169–70 (P. Steiner). F. Fahr, H. Ramisch and P. B. Steiner (eds), *Freising. 1250 Jahre Geistliche Stadt* (*Diözesanmuseum für christliche Kunst des Erzbistums München und Freising, Kataloge und Schriften*, IX) (Freising, 1989), no. IV.1, 298–9 (S. Benker). R. Baumstark (ed.), *Rom und Byzanz. Schatzkammerstücke aus bayerischen Sammlungen*, exh. cat., Munich, Bayerisches Nationalmuseum (Munich, 1998), no. 84, 244–9 (M. Restle). D. Buckton, 'Byzantine Enamels in Bavaria', *Mitteilungen zur spätantiken Archäologie und byzantinischen Kunstgeschichte* 2 (2000), 93–105, esp. 97–9. Id., 'Enamelled Metal Icons of the Twelfth and Thirteenth Centuries', in M. Vassilaki (ed.), *Byzantine Icons: Art, Technique and Technology*, International Symposium, Gennadius Library, Athens, 20–21 February 1998 (Heraklion, 2002), 313–17, Pl. XXI.2, Fig. 1.

Bayerisches Nationalmuseum, Munich in 1998–1999,[2] and on two separate visits to the Freising Diözesanmuseum.

The dimensions of the icon are relatively small; 27.8 cm in height and 21.5 cm in width. The central panel depicts the Virgin in the Hagiosoritissa iconographic type,[3] accompanied by the abbreviations Μή(τη)ρ Θ(εο)ῦ and the inscription Ἡ Ἐλπὶς τῶν Ἀπελπισμένων, 'Hope of the Hopeless'. The background and the Virgin's halo are covered by an elaborate revetment made from a gilded silver sheet, repoussé, chased and pierced. The frame consists of a parcel-gilt silver sheet and was originally adorned with ten enamel medallions, nine of which still survive intact; these show (top row) the *Hetoimasia* (Preparation of the Throne) between the archangels Michael and Gabriel; (second row) the apostles Peter (left) and Paul (right); (third row) Sts George (left) and Demetrios (right); (bottom row) Sts Kosmas, Panteleemon and, on the missing medallion, Damianos, as the surviving inscription indicates. These medallions alternate with rectangular plaques containing an inscription in enamelled lettering, which reads as follows:

top row
Ψυχῆς πόθος ἀργυρὸς καὶ χρυσὸς τρίτος
σοὶ τῇ καθαρᾷ προσφέρονται Παρθένῳ
ἄργυρος μέντοι καὶ χρυσοῦ φύσις ὄντως
δέξαιντο ῥύπον ὡς ἐν φθαρτῇ οὐσίᾳ

right side
ἐκ δὲ ψυχῆς ὁ πόθος ὢν ἀθανάτου
οὔτ' ἄ(ν) σπῖλον δέξαιτο, οὔτε μὴν τέλος
κἂν γὰρ λυθεῖ τὸ σῶμα τοῦτ' Ἅδου τόπῳ

left side
τοῦ τῆς ψυχῆς οἴκτου σὲ δυσωπῶν μένει
Κανστρίσιος ταῦτα σοὶ προσφέρων λέγει
Μανουὴλ Δισύπατος τάξει λεβίτης

bottom row
καὶ ταῦτα δέξαι συμπαθῶς, ὦ Παρθένε
τὸν ῥευστὸν τοῦτον ἀντιδιδοῦσα βίον
ταῖ[ς σαῖς] διελθεῖν ἀνώδυνον πρεσβείαις
ὡς ἡμέρας δείξειας καὶ φωτὸς τέ[λος].[4]

---

[2] For full reference, see n. 1.
[3] The Hagiosoritissa iconographic type is connected with the devotional icon of the same name, associated with the Hagia Soros and the holy 'relics' of the Theotokos, her girdle and her mantle, housed respectively in the Chalkoprateia church and the Blachernai monastery in Constantinople. *ODB* 3, 1929 (A. W. Carr). The image of the Virgin Hagiosoritissa is found in all Byzantine media: icons, marble relief plaques, steatites, enamels, coins, lead seals, etc. *ODB* 3, 2171 (N. P. Ševčenko). For numerous examples, see Vassilaki, *Mother of God*, nos 14, 21, 38 and Pls 87, 90, 113, 118–20, and 191. See most recently, A. W. Carr, 'Icons and the Object of Pilgrimage in Middle Byzantine Constantinople', *DOP* 56 (2002), 75–92, esp. 78–80.
[4] Kalligas read the final word of this inscription as τέκνον (child). Kalligas, 'Βυζαντινή εικών', 505. Grabar

The soul's yearning, silver and thirdly gold are offered to you, the pure Maiden. But silver and the nature of gold may suffer taint, being of a transitory substance. Yet yearning, being of an immortal soul, will never be unclean, nor know an end. For though this body suffers dissolution in Hades, the soul's sorrow, it remains imploring you. In offering this to you, Manuel Dishypatos, Kanstresios and of the Levite order, addresses you as follows. Take it graciously, Maiden, and in return allow us to pass this transitory life free from pain, thanks to your supplications; may you show [this joy] to the end of day and light.

According to the inscription, the donor of the icon was the deacon Manuel Dishypatos, whom M. Kalligas identified with the Metropolitan of Thessaloniki of that name who held office from 1258 to 1261.[5] This identification and a consequent dating to the third quarter of the thirteenth century are totally consistent with the icon – at least as regards the frame with the medallions, since the representation of the Virgin in the centre is thought to be a late fourteenth-century overpainting, and X-ray examination during its restoration (Fig. 22.2) confirmed this: an earlier layer of paint lies under the surface visible today.[6] The revetment of the central panel is considered to be contemporary with the over-painting.[7]

The special interest of this icon lies in its alleged connection with the emperor Manuel II Palaiologos and his travels in Europe. It is well known that between 1399 and 1403 Manuel, in a desperate search for economic and military assistance from Europe to confront the Ottoman threat during the siege of Constantinople by Bayezid I (1399–1402), set out on a journey that would take him to Venice, Padua, Milan, Paris – even as far as London.[8] On his return to the troubled capital of his empire he sent an illuminated manuscript containing the works of Pseudo-Dionysios the Areopagite[9] as a gift to the abbey of St Denis, where he had attended a liturgy together with King Charles VI of France.[10] A full-page miniature in the manuscript (Paris, Musée du Louvre, Département des Objets d'Art, MR 416, fol. 2) portrays the emperor and his family under the Virgin's protection (Fig. 22.3), while the colophon states that it was delivered to the abbey of St Denis in 1408 on behalf of the emperor Manuel

---

adopted the reading τέλος suggested to him by M. Manoussacas, which makes better sense. Grabar, *Les revêtements*, 43. Strangely enough, Kalligas' reading is still used by German scholars. Legner, *Ornamenta Ecclesiae*, 171 (P. Steiner). Baumstark, *Rom und Byzanz*, 246 (M. Restle).

[5] Kalligas, 'Βυζαντινή εικών', 506. For information on Manuel Dishypatos, see *PLP* 3 (1978), nos 5543–4, 54. P. Gounaridis, *Το κίνημα των Αρσενιατών (1261–1310). Ιδεολογικές διαμάχες την εποχή των πρώτων Παλαιολόγων* (Athens, 1999), 62–4, and *passim*. George Pachymeres makes a specific reference to an alleged miracle that occurred in 1258 during a vigil organized at the Akapniou monastery in Thessaloniki by the Metropolitan Manuel Dishypatos. The miracle, which took the form of a mysterious loud voice that pronounced the incomprehensible word ΜΑΡΠΟΥ, was taken as prophesying the ascent of the Palaiologoi family to the throne of Constantinople. George Pachymeres, *De Michaele Palaeologo* I, *PG* 143, 460–2; ed. I. Bekker (Bonn, 1835), I.27–8; ed. A. Failler (Paris, 1984), I.46–9.

[6] Wolters, 'Beobachtungen', 85–91. Buckton, 'Enamelled Metal Icons', 316. Buckton, however, says that the central painted panel appears in the X-ray photograph to be earlier than the mid-thirteenth enamelled frame. This view is also expressed by S. Benker, who gives a date *c.* 1200 in his entry in the catalogue Fahr, Ramisch and Steiner, *Diözesanmuseum Freising*, 244–51.

[7] Baumstark, *Rom und Byzanz*, 249 (M. Restle). Buckton, 'Byzantine Enamels', 99.

[8] J. W. Barker, *Manuel II Palaeologus (1391–1425): A Study in Late Byzantine Statesmanship* (New Brunswick, NJ, 1969), 123–99, esp. 171–99.

[9] *Byzance. L'art byzantin dans les collections publiques françaises*, exh. cat., Paris, Musée du Louvre, 3 November 1992 – 1 February 1993 (Paris, 1992), no. 356, 463–4 (J. Durand).

[10] Barker, *Manuel II Palaeologus*, 181.

Palaiologos by Manuel Chrysoloras, who was responsible for composing the text of the colophon.[11]

Absolute confirmation of the manuscript's connection with Manuel Palaiologos is thus contained in the colophon, while, in the case of the icon, support comes from later evidence alone. This evidence takes the form of a Latin inscription engraved on the baroque-style altarpiece in Freising cathedral (Fig. 22.4), where the icon was placed in the seventeenth century (1629);[12] it reads as follows:

> Hanc Virginum Virginis Iconem
> Penicili St Lucae ab Imperatore
> Orientis Ioannes Galeacius Insubrum Dux
> Accepit, ab isto Comes Anglade Chent, ab hac
> Bronorius de la Scala, qui dono misit fratri
> Suo Nicodemo Frisingensium Episcopo A[nn]o 1440
> 23 Septemb[ris]. Ex inhic, colitur, non donatur;
> Nec alij donassent, si satis novissent
> Vitus adamus Frisingensium
> Episcopus Ec[clesiae] Dei Matrem Dei
> Matri posuit A[nn]o MDCXXIX.

This icon of the Virgin of Virgins, painted by St Luke, was received from the Emperor of the East by Giangaleazzo Duke of the Insubres, and from him by the Earl (*comes*) of Kent in England, and from her [*sic*] by Brunoro della Scala, who sent it as a gift to his brother Nicodemo, the bishop of Freising, on 23 September 1440. From henceforth it is an object of veneration, and not a gift: nor would others have given it, if they had been sufficiently knowledgeable. Veit Adam, the Bishop of the church of Freising, placed the Mother of God on behalf of the Mother of God, 1629.

The Virgin in prayer of the Freising icon may be thought to be in perfect sympathy with the purpose of Manuel II Palaiologos' visit to Europe, and this view is strengthened by her appellation 'Hope of the Hopeless', to the left and right of the halo, which exactly describes the psychological climate in which he undertook the journey. But are these clues sufficient to link the icon with Manuel when there is no specific reference to him in the inscription, which merely states that the icon was presented to Giangaleazzo Visconti by 'The Emperor of the East', i.e. an

---

[11] 'Τὸ παρὸν βιβλίον ἀπεστάλη παρὰ τοῦ ὑψηλοτάτου βασιλέως / αὐτοκράτορος Ῥωμαίων κυροῦ Μανουὴλ τοῦ Παλαιολόγου εἰς τὸ μο/ναστήριον τοῦ Ἁγίου Διονυσίου τοῦ ἐν Παρυσίῳ τῆς Φραγγίας ἢ Γαλατίας / ἀπὸ τῆς Κωνσταντινουπόλεως, δι' ἐμοῦ Μανουὴλ τοῦ Χρυσολωρᾶ, πεμ/φθέντος πρέσβεως παρὰ τοῦ εἰρημένου βασιλέως. Ἔτει ἀπὸ κτίσεως κόσμου, ἑξακισχιλιοστῷ ἐννεακοσιοστῷ ἑξκαιδεκάτῳ, ἀπὸ σαρκώσεως / δὲ τοῦ Κυρίου, χιλιοστῷ τετρακοσιοστῷ ὀγδόῳ: / ὅστις εἰρημένος βασιλεὺς ἦλθε πρότερον εἰς τὸ Παρύσιον πρὸ ἐτῶν τεσσάρων'. Translated in Barker, *Manuel II Palaeologus*, 264, as 'The present book was sent by the most excellent Basileus and Autokrator of the Romans, lord Manuel Palaiologos, to the Monastery of Saint Dionysios in Paris of Phrangia, or Galatia, [France] from Constantinople through me, Manuel Chrysoloras, who has been sent as ambassador by the said Basileus, in the year from the Creation of the Universe, the six thousandth nine hundredth sixteenth, and from the Incarnation of the Lord, the thousandth four hundredth and eighth. The said Basileus himself came formerly to Paris four years before'. A transcription of the Greek text also in Barker, *Manuel II Palaeologus*, Appendix XXIV, no. 4.

[12] The altarpiece was made for the 'Elisabethaltar', constructed at the same time on the initiative of the Freising bishop Veit Adam von Gepeckh, and is the work of Philipp Dirr. Benker, *Philipp Dirr*, 95, 183–4.

anonymous Byzantine emperor? Of course the fact that Giangaleazzo was Duke of Milan at the time of Manuel Palaiologos' visit to the city[13] might be considered support for the theory that the icon was one of the gifts which the Byzantine emperor brought with him to Europe. Moreover, we know that Manuel was welcomed in Milan by Giangaleazzo Visconti, who promised to give aid to the emperor and even to go to Constantinople in person, if this should prove necessary.[14] It is also recorded that during his stay at the court of Giangaleazzo, Manuel offered him a precious relic of the Passion, one of the thorns from the crown worn by Christ on the Cross.[15] Giangaleazzo's connections with the arts are well known and consequently the emperor's gift of a Byzantine icon would have been directed to a recipient who was fully capable of appreciating it.[16]

According to its Latin inscription, the icon passed from Giangaleazzo to an anonymous Earl (*comes*) of Kent in England, but this figure has always remained obscure. No attempt has ever been made to identify this person and clarify the conditions under which he obtained the icon. However, Veit Arnpeck in his late fifteenth-century history of the bishops of Freising, *Liber de Gestis Episcoporum Frisingensis* speaks of the 'countess' of Kent, that is, a woman: '… Que ymago prius donata fuit per ilustrissimum principem Grecorum imperatorem Constantinopolitanum Johanni Galiatz, tandem duci Mediolanensi, post cujus mortem prescripta ymago pervenit ad manus cujusdam comitisse de Chent et partibus Anglie ….'[17] C. Meichelbeck in his *Historiae Frisingensis* of 1724 and 1729 also states '… post cujus obitum Matrona quaedam nobilis ex Anglorum Regno Comitissa de Chent dicta eadem veneranda imagine…'.[18] This may explain the discrepancy of the Latin inscription on the altarpiece, which after mentioning the 'Earl' of Kent, goes on to say *ab hac* (from her), which denotes a female. This woman must have been Lucia, sister-in-law of Giangaleazzo Visconti, who in 1407 married Edmund Holland, the Earl of Kent.[19] By that time Giangaleazzo was dead, as was his wife Caterina (†1404), the sister of

---

[13] Giangaleazzo Visconti was co-lord of Milan and its dominions from 1378 to 1385, sole lord from 1385 to 1395, and the first Duke of Milan from 1395 to his death in 1402. D. M. Bueno de Mesquita, *Giangaleazzo Visconti, Duke of Milan (1351–1402). A Study in the Political Career of an Italian Despot* (Cambridge, 1941).

[14] Barker, *Manuel II Palaeologus*, 171–2.

[15] 'De deux épines possédées par la cathédrale de Pavie, où elles entrèrent le 2 septembre 1499, l'une venait de Philippe de Valois, qui l'avait détachée de la couronne de Paris … L'autre avait été donnée au duc Jean Galeazzo Visconti, en 1400, par Manuel II Paléologue, empereur de Constantinople, lors de son séjour à Pavie'. F. de Mèly, *Exuviae Sacrae Constantinopolitanae* (Paris, 1904), 268, 342. See also S. Mergiali-Sahas, 'Byzantine Emperors and Holy Relics. Use, and Misuse, of Sanctity and Authority', *JÖB* 51 (2001), 56.

[16] G. A. dell'Acqua, 'I Visconti e le arti', in M. Bellonci, G. A. dell'Acqua and C. Perogalli, *I Visconti a Milano* (Milan, 1977), 123–217, esp. 165–90. Giangaleazzo is mainly known for his passion for manuscripts. The first inventory of the Visconti library, made in 1426, included 988 volumes, most of which had probably entered the collection by the time of Giangaleazzo's death in 1402. E. W. Kirsch, *Five Illuminated Manuscripts of Giangaleazzo Visconti* (University Park and London, 1991), 1–2. See also M. Meiss and E. W. Kirsch, *The Visconti Hours. Biblioteca Nazionale, Florence* (London, 1972), for a richly illuminated manuscript especially commissioned by Giangaleazzo, and K. Sutton, 'Giangaleazzo Visconti as Patron: a Prayerbook Illuminated by Pietro da Pavia', *Apollo* 137 (1993), 89–96.

[17] Veit Arnpeck, *Sämtliche Chroniken herausgegeben von Georg Leidinger, Quellen und Erörterungen zur Bayerischen und Deutschen Geschicthe* (Munich, 1915; repr. Darmstadt, 1969), 896.

[18] C. Meichelbeck, *Historiae Frisingensis, tomus II. Posteriora quinque ab adventu S. Corbiniani I episcopi saecula seu res ab anno Christi MCCXXIV usque ad anno MDCCXXIV Frisingae gestas exhibens* (Augustae Vindelicorum, 1729), 224.

[19] *Storia di Milano, VI. Il Ducato Visconteo e la Republica Ambrosiana (1392–1450)* (Milan, 1955), tavola genealogica della famiglia Visconti – II. See also D. Hay and J. Law, *Italy in the Age of the Renaissance 1380–1530*

Lucia. It seems probable therefore that the icon was already in Lucia's possession at the time of her marriage in 1407. Edmund Holland died in September 1408 and Lucia in 1424.

According to the Latin inscription, the next owner of the icon was Bronorius (Brunoro) della Scala, a member of the former ruling family of Verona, who was resident at the court of Vienna.[20] We do not know under what circumstances and on whose initiative the transfer was made – whether, for example, it was by Lucia herself before her death (1424), or on some occasion afterwards. In any case, the icon must have been given to Brunoro and passed on by him to his brother by 1437, the year of Brunoro's death. Nicodemo della Scala was appointed bishop of Freising in 1421 and he held the office until his death in 1443.[21] As mentioned in the Latin inscription, Nicodemo presented the icon to the cathedral of Freising on 23 September 1440. It has remained in Freising ever since, first in the cathedral treasury, then from 1629 on the altarpiece, and since 1974 in the city's Diözesanmuseum, just opposite.[22]

The Latin inscription seems to provide the Freising icon with a historically authenticated provenance from the time it reached Europe. It remains therefore to try to piece together the various stages in the icon's history before 1400. Kanstresios Manuel Dishypatos of the order of Levites (i.e. a deacon), who is mentioned on the frame, has been identified with Manuel Opsaras Dishypatos, Metropolitan of Thessaloniki from 1258. If this identification is correct, the icon must have been commissioned by Manuel Dishypatos before 1258, since he is referred to as a priest and not a metropolitan. André Grabar, who discussed the icon's revetment, acknowledged that, although from the stylistic point of view the enamels on the frame could date from the fourteenth century, the dedicatory inscription makes the mid-thirteenth century the most likely date.[23] At the same time he expressed doubts as to whether the revetment of the central panel was contemporary with the frame, and seems rather to have believed that the central representation of the Virgin Hagiosoritissa, the halo, the revetment of the background and the inscriptions Μή(τη)ρ Θ(εο)ῦ and Ἡ Ἐλπὶς τῶν Ἀπελπισμένων post-dated the frame. However, the information then available to him did not permit him to take the argument further and put an exact date to those elements of the icon which he considered to be of a later period. David Buckton has studied the icon and was also able to consult the technical data which emerged during the icon's restoration and X-ray examination at the Doerner-Institut in Munich in 1964.[24] He too concludes that the icon contains features dating from different periods and dates the entire frame to the mid-thirteenth century, since on the basis of the analysis of the glass used for the enamel he confirms that its technical features permit a certain dating around the middle of the thirteenth century. I would myself also place great significance on his remark that, while the letters of the inscription on the frame are made of enamel, the pounced black and red letters of the appellation (Ἡ Ἐλπὶς τῶν Ἀπελπισμένων) and of the abbreviations (Μή(τη)ρ Θ(εο)ῦ) are composed of pigment in an organic binding medium.

(London and New York, 1989), 240. The husband of Lucia is mistakenly called Edward and not Edmund Holland.

[20] *Dizionario biografico degli Italiani* 37 (Rome, 1989), 389–93.
[21] *Meichelbeck's Geschichte der Stadt Freising und ihrer Bischöfe. Neu in Druck gegeben und fortgesetzt von A. Baumgärtner* (Freising, 1854), 162–8. *Dizionario biografico*, 453–6.
[22] Fahr, Ramisch and Steiner, *Diözesanmuseum Freising*, 244–51.
[23] Grabar, *Les revêtements*, 41–3.
[24] Buckton, 'Byzantine Enamels', 97–9. Id., 'Enamelled Metal Icons', 315–16.

As revealed by X-ray examination, the original layer of the paint surface does not permit any significant stylistic analysis, but the second, visible, layer displays similarities with works of the second half of the fourteenth century.[25] I would in particular mention the two-sided icon in the Pantokrator monastery on Mt Athos with John the Baptist on one side and the Virgin and Child with the Baptist on the other (Plate 18b, Fig. 22.5), which has been associated with the monastery's foundation and dated to 1363;[26] the icon of the Virgin and Child in the Tretyakov Gallery (Fig. 22.6), from the last third of the fourteenth century;[27] and the Virgin from the Crucifixion scene in the two-sided icon of Christ Psychosostis and the Crucifixion from the Virgin Peribleptos, Ohrid (now in the Icon Museum there), with a possible date of the late fourteenth century.[28] Stylistically the face of the Virgin in the Freising icon belongs to this tradition of painting.

If we believe that this icon was a gift from Manuel Palaiologos to Duke Giangaleazzo Visconti, what arguments can be adduced to support a link with Thessaloniki on the one hand and Manuel Palaiologos on the other? Manuel was twice resident at Thessaloniki, first as governor (despot) of the city from 1369 to 1373 and then as co-emperor from 1382 to 1387.[29] During his term as despot he resorted to the sale of church treasures in order to provide economic assistance to his father, Emperor John V, and during both periods he was accused of disposing of ecclesiastical property belonging to monasteries and to the metropolis of Thessaloniki for the city's defence requirements against the Turks. These charges and his well-attested ruthlessness are strong indications that in times of crisis he did not hesitate to take advantage of his direct access to ecclesiastical estates and treasures to appropriate some of their contents; it is thus entirely possible that this particular icon, which had very probably been donated by Manuel Dishypatos to some church in Thessaloniki, came into his possession in this manner. It should also be noted that the Virgin's appellation, 'Hope of the Hopeless',[30] used in the Freising icon but rarely elsewhere, also occurs in a fourteenth-century icon now in the icon-stand in the narthex of the church of the Acheiropoietos in Thessaloniki.[31]

The reign of Manuel Palaiologos was associated with the practice aptly characterized by John Barker as 'reliquary diplomacy'[32] – in other words, he made use of venerable relics to serve his diplomatic activities throughout his desperate attempts to secure assistance from the West. Particular mention may be made of his dispatching of relics to Henry III of Castile, Charles III

---

[25] Restle in his entry on the Freising icon suggests comparisons with the Poganovo icon of c. 1395, and the diptych with the Virgin and Christ (Akra Tapeinosis) in the Transfiguration monastery, Meteora, and consequently dates the central panel of the icon to the last decade of the 14th c. Baumstark, *Rom und Byzanz*, 249.

[26] M. Acheimastou-Potamianou, 'Παρατηρήσεις σε δύο αμφιπρόσωπες εικόνες της Μονής Παντοκράτορος στο Άγιον Όρος', *DChAE* 20 (1998/9), 309–16, Fig. 4. T. Papamastorakis, 'Icons 13th–16th Century', in *Icons of the Holy Monastery of Pantokrator* (Mt Athos, 1998), 52, 62–70.

[27] *Vizantiia, Balkani, Rus'. Ikoni kontsa XIII–pervoi polovinii XV veka, XVIII Mezhdunarodnomu Kongressu Vizantinistov*, exh. cat., Moscow, Tretyakov Gallery (Moscow, 1991), no. 74, 243–4 (O. Korina and G. Sidorenko).

[28] *Trésors médiévaux de la République de Macédoine*, exh. cat., Paris, Musée national du Moyen Âge – Thermes de Cluny, 9 February – 3 May 1999 (Paris, 1999), no. 27, 78–9 (V. Popovska Korobar).

[29] G. T. Dennis SJ, *The Reign of Manuel II Palaeologus in Thessalonica, 1382–1387* (Rome, 1960).

[30] This comes from a prayer to the Virgin for supplication, read at the Great and Small Apodeipnon: 'ἡ τῶν ἀπελπισμένων μόνη ἐλπίς, καὶ τῶν πολεμουμένων βοήθεια'.

[31] As far as I am aware, this icon is unpublished.

[32] Barker, *Manuel II Palaeologus*, 265. Mergiali-Sahas, 'Byzantine Emperors', 41–60, esp. 47, 52, 55–9.

of Navarre, John I of Portugal, Martin I of Aragon,[33] and even Pope Boniface IX.[34] The Spanish ambassador Ruy Gonzalez de Clavijo tells us that Manuel himself held the keys of the treasury of St John's church near the Blachernai monastery.[35]

Yet Manuel's religious devotion cannot be called into question. As well as the testimonies of his contemporaries (Demetrios and Manuel Chrysoloras, Demetrios Kydones and Isidore Glavas, Metropolitan of Thessaloniki), his own letters and speeches provide a clear indication of his deep theological erudition and devoutness.[36] In this context it is of particular significance that he composed a 'paracletic canon to the holiest Mother of God for the present situation'[37] – a situation which was none other than the siege of the city by the Turks (1399–1402). And the raising of Bayezid's siege in 1402 was considered to have occurred through a miraculous intervention by the Virgin, as is joyously proclaimed in the thanksgiving addressed 'to the holy Virgin' by Manuel's close associate, Demetrios Chrysoloras,[38] and in the elegant narrative on the subject, attributed to the same author.[39]

All the above seems to point to the following conclusion. The Freising icon came into the possession of Manuel Palaiologos during the period he spent in Thessaloniki. He then had the central panel over-painted and covered with a revetment. A precious work like this would have been ideally suited to Manuel's suppliant diplomacy towards a European ruler like Duke Giangaleazzo Visconti of Milan, who was a great enthusiast for the arts. It also seems that from very early times the icon was credited with the legend of having been painted by St Luke,[40] and was therefore considered almost a relic. Lastly, the Virgin as 'Hope of the Hopeless' is the perfect expression of the psychological climate of the endangered capital, which also dictated the emperor's political initiatives. And we should not forget Manuel's special relationship with the Virgin, whom he implores for the safety of the capital in the paracletic canon which he composed in her honour. If we interpret the Freising icon in this way, the question mark attached to the title of this paper is no longer required. I think it is now clear that in the icon the Virgin is praying for the salvation of the empire.

---

[33] Barker, *Manuel II Palaeologus*, 176–83.
[34] G. T. Dennis, 'Two Unknown Documents of Manuel II Palaeologus', *TM* 3 (1968), 397–404.
[35] Barker, *Manuel II Palaeologus*, 408 n. 22.
[36] *The Letters of Manuel II Palaeologus*, ed. G. T. Dennis (*Dumbarton Oaks Texts*, IV) (Washington, DC, 1977).
[37] É. Legrand, *Lettres de l'empereur Manuel Paléologue publiées d'après trois manuscrits* (Amsterdam, 1962), 94–102.
[38] P. Gautier, 'Action de grâces de Démétrius Chrysoloras à la Théotokos pour l'anniversaire de la bataille d'Ankara (28 juillet 1403)', *REB* 19 (1961), 340–57.
[39] P. Gautier, 'Un récit inédit du siège de Constantinople par les Turcs (1394–1402)', *REB* 23 (1965), 100–17.
[40] The Latin inscription ('Hanc Virginum Virginis Iconem Penicili Sanctae Lucae opus'), Veit Arnpeck ('ymaginem gloriose virginis, quam Beatus Lucas evangelista propriis manibus laboravit') and C. Meichelbeck ('hanc Imaginem Gloriosissima[e] Virginis Mariae, Beati Evangelistae Lucae manibus depictam') all speak of the icon as painted by St Luke. They seem to repeat an old legend created around the icon.

PRAYING FOR THE SALVATION OF THE EMPIRE?   271

22.1   The Freising 'Lukasbild' (source: Freising, Diözesanmuseum)

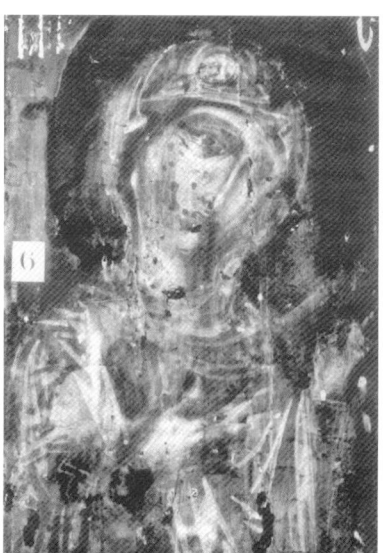

22.2   The Freising 'Lukasbild'. X-ray photograph (source: Freising, Diözesanmuseum)

22.3 Paris, Musée du Louvre.
Département des Objets d'Art, MR 416, fol. 2
(source: Cutler and Spieser, *Byzance médiévale*, Fig. 356)

22.4 The Freising 'Lukasbild' in its baroque setting
(source: Freising, Diözesanmuseum)

22.5 Mt Athos, Pantokrator monastery. Detail from a two-sided icon of the Virgin and Child (source: Mt Athos, Pantokrator monastery)

22.6 Moscow, Tretyakov Gallery. Detail from an icon of the Virgin and Child. (source: Moscow, Tretyakov Gallery)

Part V

Between East and West

Thoughts on Mary east and west*

Annemarie Weyl Carr

On the brink of the First Crusade a Latin priest in Constantinople recorded a procession of the Hodegetria.[1] On one occasion, he wrote, as it passed the chapel of Christ, the great icon paused and bowed to her son. The detail is striking for its kinship to the 15 August processions in Rome.[2] It is perhaps more striking for its contrast to the behaviour customarily assigned to great icons in Constantinople. In the 'usual miracle' of the veiled icon at the Virgin's church at Blachernai, described with theatrical flair by Michael Psellos in 1075,[3] as also in Anthony of Novgorod's description of the Hodegetria itself a century later,[4] the Holy Spirit is said to descend upon the icon, as if to allegorize both its and Mary's own role as a bridge between heaven and earth.[5] In these accounts Mary does not bow before Christ; she looms behind him, a bridge between humanity and God. Was the bow, then, a western motif, appealing to the imagination of the western author? Or was it Byzantine in origin? Among the themes of the symposium 'Mother of God' was that of Mary east and west, observing the ways in which the imagery of Mary both served and differentiated Byzantine and western European conceptions of her in the Middle Ages. This is the theme of the present essay. It takes as its focus the Mother of God in the crucible of the Crusades. Mary is not a figure strongly associated with the Crusades, and her role in Crusader art has been examined only episodically. Yet it is hard to believe that the Crusades cannot help to illuminate the convergence of cultures upon that potent construct

---

* This article is based on a paper entitled 'The Virgin Mary, East and West: Introduction', read in the symposium 'Mother of God' at the National Research Foundation in Athens on 14 January 2001. I owe my warmest thanks to Maria Vassilaki for the invitation to participate in both the symposium and the present publication. As always, I am grateful to the Dumbarton Oaks Center for Byzantine Studies for library resources.

[1] K. N. Ciggaar, 'Une description de Constantinople dans le *Tarragonensis* 55', *REB* 53 (1995), 127: 'Audivi autem referre quoddam miraculum de eadem sancta ymagine positus in predicta urbe. Dum defertur beate Dei genetricis supradicta imago per urbem et transit iuxta basilicam Sancti Salvatoris, in cuius introitu idem Ihesus est egregie effigiatus, sponte sua Dei genetrix sancta vertit se ad filium suum velit nolit ille qui portat eam, et matris imago se convertit ad videndum vultum filii volens cernere, volens et honorare filium qui fecit eam reginam angelorum. Hoc quidem ego non vidi quia non consideravi sed ibi manens audivi'.

[2] The Roman miracle has been studied extensively; see in particular G. Wolf, *Salus Populi Romani. Die Geschichte römischer Kultbilder im Mittelalter* (Weinheim, 1990), 37–78 and *passim*. H. Belting, 'Icons and Roman Society in the Twelfth Century', in W. Tronzo (ed.), *Italian Church Decoration of the Middle Ages and Early Renaissance* (Baltimore, 1989), 27–41.

[3] V. Grumel, 'Le "miracle habituel" de Notre-Dame des Blachernes', *EO* 30 (1931), 136–8.

[4] *Kniga Palomnik, Skazanie mest sviatykh. Vo Tsaregrade Antoniia Arkhiepiskopa Novgorodskogo*, ed K. M. Loparev, *Pravoslavnyi Palestinskii Sbornik* 17.3 (1899), 21. I am indebted to George Majeska for this reference and look forward to his published translation.

[5] Thus Psellos (Grumel, 'Le "miracle habituel"', 137), says: '... καὶ ἔστι τὸ πρᾶγμα τοῖς μὲν μὴ ἰδοῦσιν ἄπιστον, τοῖς δὲ ἰδοῦσι παράδοξον καὶ τοῦ θείου ἄντικρυς κάθοδος'. Anthony, as translated by Janin, *Églises CP*, 212, says: '... l'image de la Très Sainte Vierge Odighitria, peinte par le saint apôtre Luc, qu'on porte à travers la ville par le chemin de Pierre patrice, aux saintes Blachernes; le Saint Esprit descend en elle'. As George Majeska points out, this may mean simply that the Spirit descends in the church at Blachernai.

called Mary. The text that follows will use the theme of Mary in the Crusades to pose five questions that underlie any inquiry into Marian imagery east and west.

The first question, introduced already by the ceremony of Mary's bow, is one of geography: what is 'east'; what is 'west'? The icon procession is something that has seemed quintessentially to belong to eastern Christendom, and in the western mediaeval compendia of Marian miracles the stories involving panel paintings are characteristically associated with Constantinople.[6] But mediaeval Italy, and especially mediaeval Rome, often offers clearer evidence of icon processions than Byzantium does.[7] Is Italy, then, 'east'?

The opposite question is posed by the most formidable Marian icon associated with the Crusades. This is the icon of Saidnaya near Damascus, known in the West as Sardenay.[8] Venerated by Christians of all creeds and by non-Christians alike, this icon exuded copious oil from breasts that blossomed from its wooden surface. One could touch the breasts; they felt like flesh, a Latin visitor reported.[9] The icon of Saidnaya figured prominently in western European and especially transalpine collections of Marian miracle stories, and it was initially illustrated with an image not of an icon but of a statue.[10] As the earliest known Middle Eastern description of its miraculous properties coincides almost exactly in date with the earliest spate of western European reports,[11] it is easy to suppose that the breasts were a response to the Crusader presence, accommodating the European preference for tangible three-dimensionality.[12] Recently, however, Daniel Baraz has shown that the 'incarnate icon' of

---

[6] See A. W. Carr, 'East, West and Icons in Twelfth-Century Outremer', in V. P. Goss and C. V. Bornstein (eds), *The Meeting of Two Worlds. Cultural Exchange Between East and West During the Period of the Crusades* (*Studies in Medieval Culture*, 21) (Kalamazoo, 1986), 349–50, drawing upon A. Mussafia, 'Studien zu den mittelalterlichen Marienlegenden', *Sitzungsberichte der phil.-historischen Klasse der kaiserlichen Akademie der Wissenschaften* 113 (1886), 917–94; 115 (1887) 5–93; 119 (1889), section IX. The miracles with panel paintings include, in 113 (1886), 942, no. 33, on the story of the icon of Christ Antiphonetes at the church of the Chalkoprateia; 944, no. 42, on the 'usual miracle'; 963, no. 31, on the Saracen in possession of a Marian icon that responds to his scepticism about the virgin birth by sprouting breasts that flow with oil – a version of the Saidnaya story; 971, nos 26–8, the icon of Mary thrown in a latrine, also narrated by Arculf about an icon that he venerated in Constantinople; and in 115 (1887), 33, no. 47, and 88, no. 67, both versions of the Antiphonetes story; 89, no. 75, the story of the bleeding Crucifix from Beirut, housed in Hagia Sophia in Constantinople.

[7] On the Roman processions see H. Belting, *Likeness and Presence. A History of the Image Before the Era of Art* (Chicago, 1994), 311–29. Wolf, *Salus Populi Romani*, 37–170; see also his contribution in this volume, 23–49.

[8] D. Baraz, 'The Incarnated Icon of Saidnaya goes West. A Re-examination of the Motif in the Light of New Manuscript Evidence', *Muséon* 108 (1995), 181–91 with earlier bibliography, especially P. Peeters, 'La légende de Saidnaia', *AnBoll* 25 (1906), 137–57.

[9] Thus Thietmar in his *Cité de Jérusalem* of 1187, in Brussels, Bibliothèque Royale, II 1146, says: 'Cepit autem Dei genitricis imago carnis mammillas emittere et carne vestiri. Que scilicet imago, ut a Fratribus Templi testantibus qui eam viderunt, scilicet Fratre Thoma, qui cum digito suo palpavit, et pluribus qui eam viderunt, didicimus, a mammillis deorsum carne videtur induta; ex qua carne liquor ille manat'. See P. Devos, 'Les premières versions occidentales de la légende de Saïdaia', *AnBoll* 65 (1947), 255. This said, it is perhaps worth noting that Burchard, whose account of Saidnaya was composed at much the same time, wrote that 'nunquam tamen predicta tabula tangere audetur, videri autem omnibus conceditur' (ibid., 265).

[10] The miracle was included in the *Miracles of the Virgin* by Gautier de Coincy, a text that was often illuminated. The earliest of the illuminated versions, St Petersburg, Saltykov–Shchedrin State Public Library, fr. F v 14, shows the figure as a statue: S. Ringbom, *Icon to Narrative* (Abo, 1965), Fig. 1. In the late-thirteenth-century version in Paris, Bibliothèque nationale, fr. 1533, fol. 100v, however, the figure is shown as a painting.

[11] The earliest European reports about the icon are those of Guido Chat of 1174 and Thietmar of 1186; the earliest Arabic report is that of Amba Mikhail of 1184. See J. Nasralleh, 'La Vierge Hodigitria (La Vierge conductrice ou Al-Hadia)', *PrOC* 38 (1988), 245, 249.

Saidnaya was in fact rooted in Middle Eastern tradition.[13] Elizabeth Bolman has shown in conjunction with the recurrence of the Virgin Lactans in Egyptian apses that Mary's lactation was linked by the monastic fathers of Egypt with the miraculous nourishment of the Host.[14] The icon at Saidnaya was in fact located in the apse. Thus its palpable lactation may reflect less western European materialism than a distinctively Middle Eastern theology of grace. Under these conditions, Byzantium and Rome with their fastidious rituals of intangible encounter coalesce together into a world of the West, and the East begins to the east of Constantinople. What, then, *are* east and west?

A second question concerns movement across these categories: what are we seeing when we see Byzantine elements in the art of others: do they tell us of Byzantium, or do they tell us of the borrower? This question might be posed by the pilgrim votives painted on the massive columns of the church of the Nativity at Bethlehem. Of the four paintings displaying the Virgin Mary, three are notable for the tenderness of their imagery: one shows her as a child in her mother's arms, one shows her nursing her own child, and the earliest of all shows her caressing Christ in the familiar pose of the Glykophilousa.[15] The Glykophilousa was installed by a Latin family in 1130. Contrasting its tender posture with stark contemporary images of Mary in the West, Gustav Kühnel has emphasized its Byzantine character.[16] Jaroslav Folda, on the other hand, spoke of its westernness; its Italianate sweetness.[17] All three of the Marian images on the columns at Bethlehem emphasize maternity. This is appropriate to the setting where Mary bore Jesus. But how are we to read their sweetness? Is it the sensibility of Byzantium that we are reading in these overtly tender postures? Or is it the sensibility of the borrowers, who have elected – among the many Orthodox images of Mary – exclusively those that express maternal meekness? And when we reach the Catholic home countries of the Franks, might the patterns of Byzantine borrowing that we see there be a far more telling index to what is 'western' than they are to what is 'eastern' in the image of Mary?

How treacherous it can be to assign Byzantine values to the images espoused in western Europe might be illustrated by the powerful Galaktotrophousa in Cosenza known as the *Madonna del Pilerio* (Fig. 23.1).[18] Striking here is the discourse of clothing, the Child dressed in a diaphanous shirt of transparent linen, and his mother adorned with a red veil that falls at a conspicuous, canted angle over her traditional maphorion. The Child's clothing uncovers more of his body than usual while his mother is more clothed, suggesting a visual dialectic of the naked vulnerability of the flesh with which she clothes his divinity. Individually their garments

---

[12] Thus for instance the cult of the Saidnaya icon is treated entirely as an aspect of western European behaviour in G. Signori, *Maria zwischen Kathedrale, Kloster und Welt. Hagiographische und historische Annäherungen an eine hochmittelalterliche Wunderpredigt* (Sigmaringen, 1995), 260.
[13] Baraz, 'The Incarnated Icon', 181–91.
[14] E. Bolman, 'Food for Salvation: The Coptic *Galaktotrophousa*', in *Twentythird Annual Byzantine Studies Conference, Abstracts of Papers* (Madison, WI, 1997), 89; cf. also her contribution in this volume, 13–22.
[15] G. Kühnel, *Wall Painting in the Latin Kingdom of Jerusalem* (Berlin, 1988), 14–32, Pls III–VI (Glykophilousa), VII–III (Galaktotrophousa), IX (St Anne with the child Mary).
[16] Ibid., p. 19 on the Glykophilousa, p. 25 on the Galaktotrophousa, p. 32 on the image of St Anne.
[17] J. Folda, *The Art of the Crusaders in the Holy Land, 1098–1187* (New York, 1995), p. 95 on the Glykophilousa as a work by a South Italian painter; p. 283 on the St Anne.
[18] M. P. di Dario Guida, *Icone di Calabria e altre icone meridionali* (Messina, 1993), 57–86, Pls XI, XII, XV, with earlier bibliography.

can be paralleled readily in Greek comparanda. The Cosenza icon exploits in particular the transparent linen of the Christ-child's garment, a motif familiar in Byzantine images like the roughly contemporary Presentation in the Temple in the Rockefeller–McCormick New Testament.[19] The motif captured the imagination not only of Italian but of transalpine painters, and we find it again in a French illuminated Bible of the late twelfth century (Fig. 23.2).[20] Here the veiled mother caresses her exposed Child in the 'O' at the opening of the Song of Songs, adorning the passionate phrase 'Let him kiss me with the kisses of his mouth'. The content is no less passionate than that of the Cosenza icon. Yet it literally reverses the kisses in the Byzantine rhetoric. Rather than kissing her son and so functioning actively to enfold his suffering in hers, Mary becomes the object, even the abject, of his passion. Thus the initial transforms the image. A visual language used to convey one kind of message in Byzantium is adopted with attentive appreciation in western Europe, but in the service of a radically different content. And if the motifs that were selected from the Byzantine repertoire prove to be so fundamentally reinterpreted, how significant are the omissions – the images not adopted? The images of Mary with the clipeate Child on her breast that are so prevalent in Byzantium seem rarely to have spoken to western sensibilities.[21] Yet they are believed to have conveyed messages at the very heart of Byzantine Mariolatry, including those of protection and eternal victory.[22] This image had only a meagre life in the West. About whom, then, do migrant forms speak?

The images of the Mother of God clipeate, highly public images circulated on the gold coins of rulers and the lead seals of courtiers, can lead into our third question. This concerns the relation of Mary as a gendered figure to the body politic. In the world of the Crusades this is a theme one might approach through great tombs. The Crusader states were dominated by the tomb of Christ; it was here, in the church of the Holy Sepulchre, that the kings of Jerusalem were buried,[23] and Mary was strangely mute in that great burial place of men.[24] The Mary who figured there was the Magdalene, whose meeting with Christ in the Garden was marked by the

---

[19] On this image and its rich content see H. Maguire, 'The Iconography of Symeon with the Christ-child in Byzantine Art', *DOP* 34/35 (1980/1), 268.

[20] Lyon, Bibliothèque municipale, MS. 410, fol. 207v. See Fr. Avril, X. Barral I Altet and D. Gaborit-Chopin, *Le Temps des Croisades* (Paris, 1982), Fig. 161. *Les manuscrits à peintures en France du VIIe au XIIe siècle*, exh. cat., Paris, Bibliothèque nationale (2nd edn, Paris, 1954), no. 330, Pl. XXXI.

[21] S. H. Steinberg, 'Abendländische Darstellungen der Maria Platytera', *ZKirch* 51 (1932), 514–16, points out the persistent but remarkably thin thread of this motif's tradition in western European imagery.

[22] On the significance assigned to the image of the Virgin with the medallion bust of Christ in Byzantium, see most recently B. V. Pentcheva, 'Rhetorical Images of the Virgin: The Icon of the "Usual Miracle" at the Blachernai', *Res. Anthropology and Aesthetics* 38 (2000), 34–55. J. Cotsonis, 'The Virgin with the "Tongues of Fire" on Byzantine Lead Seals', *DOP* 48 (1994), 221–7 (both with earlier bibliography).

[23] Folda, *Art of the Crusaders*, 74–5 (tomb of Baldwin I), 114–15 (tomb of Baldwin II), 328 (tomb of Baldwin III), 461 (tomb of Baldwin IV), 39 and 467–9 (tomb of Baldwin V).

[24] The person of the Mother of God was included in the 11th-century mosaics of the rotunda, where an image of the Annunciation flanking the bema entrance survived the 12th-century destruction of the apse (J. Wilkinson, *Jerusalem Pilgrimage, 1099–1185* (London, 1988), 280–1, quoting Theoderich); an icon of her was retained in the Crusader apse (ibid., 281); and she figured in the scenes on the outside of the tomb aedicula and in the Calvary chapel (ibid., 278, 286). See also M.-L. Bulst-Thiele, 'Die Mosaiken der "Auferstehungskirche" in Jerusalem und die Bauten der "Franken" im 12. Jahrhundert', *Franziskanische Studien* 13 (1979), 451 on the scenes of the Entombment and Myrrhophores on the aedicula, and 464 for the Crucifixion and Deesis with Mary in the Calvary Chapel. But aside from the Armenian chapel of the Mother of God outside of the western

Omphalos at the centre of the Crusader addition, and depicted on the building's main, south façade.[25] But Jerusalem in fact embraced not one but two great empty tombs, as one sees in the even-handed balance of the murals in the Hospitaller church at Abu Ghosh, where the nave is adorned with monumental compositions of the Crucifixion on the south wall and the Koimesis on the north.[26] The Church of the Koimesis, where pilgrims venerated the empty sepulchre of God's Mother, was the chosen burial place of the great Crusader Queen Melisende (ruled 1131–1152).[27] If the kings lay in the shadow of Christ, she sought eternity by the empty tomb of Mary. Her choice points to our question: how does the gendering of Mary in public play across the geography of mediaeval politics?

The even-handed justice of the Crusader burials – the men with God and Melisende with Mary – feels familiar enough in Byzantium: among the famous images of the Virgin with the clipeate Christ in a conspicuously political context is the one selected for the obverse of their gold coinage by the joint empresses Zoe and Theodora (1042) (Fig. 23.3).[28] The figure is labelled 'Blachernitissa'. The name Blachernitissa linked it with the church of the Virgin at Blachernai, repository of the relic of Mary's veil and the site associated since the seventh century with her supernatural defence of Constantinople. The choice of this potent and protective female figure for the gold currency of women rulers seems governed by gender. Theodora surely used the Mother of God as an emblem of her authority, as seen on a silver weight in the British Museum with her portrait on one side and the Virgin orans on the other.[29] Especially when labelled as Blachernitissa, thus evoking the reliquary shrine of Mary's veil, these images linked the empresses with the Virgin's potent protection of the empire as its 'undefeatable general' and guarantor of its eternal victory.

As an image of women rulers veiled by Mary's power, the coin compares interestingly with an almost exactly contemporary image from faraway England. This is the first of the three full-page frontispieces to the *Liber Vitae* of Hyde Abbey, Winchester (Fig. 23.4).[30] Here, too,

---

door of the church mentioned by Theoderich (Wilkinson, *Jerusalem Pilgrimage*, 283), we hear of no spaces in the building that were sacred especially to her. N. da Poggibonsi, *Libro d'Oltramare (1346–1350)* (Jerusalem, 1945), 14, speaks of a very much abraded image of the Virgin and Child in the tympanum of the south façade, but none of the 12th-c. travellers, including the careful Theoderich, speaks of it: see Bulst-Thiele, 'Die "Auferstehungskirche"', 446 n. 16.

[25] Folda, *Art of the Crusaders*, 214. The Magdalene figured as well in the mosaics of the tomb aedicula and Calvary chapel described by Theoderich (see above, n. 24).

[26] Kühnel, *Wall Painting*, 159–71, Pls XLIX, 86 (Koimesis) and LVI, 99 (Crucifixion).

[27] Folda, *Art of the Crusaders*, 324–8. B. Hamilton, 'Women in the Crusader States: The Queens of Jerusalem (1100–1190)', in D. Baker (ed.), *Medieval Women* (Oxford, 1973), 149–57. H. E. Mayer, 'Studies in the History of Queen Melisende of Jerusalem', *DOP* 26 (1972), 95–182. Melisende's mother, Queen Morphia, had been buried here as well.

[28] P. Grierson, *Catalogue of the Byzantine Coins in the Dumbarton Oaks Collection and in the Whittemore Collection, 3. Leo III to Nicephorus III, 717–1081, Part 2. Basil I to Nicephorus III (867–1081)* (Washington, DC, 1973), Pl. LVIII, AV 1, beautifully reproduced in colour in A. W. Carr, 'The Mother of God in Public', in Vassilaki, *Mother of God*, 327, Pl. 206. On the reign of the sisters, see L. Garland, *Byzantine Empresses. Women and Power in Byzantium, A.D. 527–1204* (London, 1999), 136–7, 161–7. B. Hill, *Imperial Women in Byzantium, 1025–1204. Power, Patronage and Ideology* (Harlow and New York, 1999), 51–8.

[29] Vassilaki, *Mother of God*, no. 43, 364 (C. J. S. Entwistle); C. J. S. Entwistle and M. Cowell, 'A Note on a Middle Byzantine Silver Weight', in Θυμίαμα στη μνήμη της Λασκαρίνας Μπούρα I (Athens, 1994), 91–3. On Theodora, see most recently K.-P. Todt, 'Die Frau als Selbst Herrscher: Kaiserin Theodora, die letzte Angehörige der Makedonischen Dynastie', *JÖB* 50 (2000), 139–71.

an exceptionally eminent queen, Emma, is confirmed in power by a figure of Mary who extends a veil over her, balancing the crown that St Peter extends to her spouse. In each, Mary's protection veils a woman ruler. Notable, however, is the range of the veil's protection. Recurrently in the Latin images of rulership, sacred protection is divided, Christ or a male saint protecting male rulers and Mary protecting females. Exemplary is the ivory in the Castello Sforzesco in Milan showing the imperial couple, Otto II (973–983) and Theophano (973–991), flanking the enthroned Christ.[31] As her husband is presented to Christ by St Maurice, Theophano kneels below Mary, her infant offspring emerging from her garments as if in proof of the fertility she shares with Mary. The unmarried Mathilda of Tuscany actually portrayed herself in the enthroned and frontal posture of a Maria Regina. This mimetic possibility exists in the English image, too, in that the veil that Mary offers Emma may be Mary's own. Such mimesis is out of the question in Byzantium. Just as male rulers assumed the robes not of Christ himself but of the heavenly hosts who served him,[32] so female rulers did not assume the form of Mary. Equally uncharacteristic of Byzantium is the gendered division in the rhetoric of state. Here sacred protection, like the state itself, is unpartible, and Mary, if singled out, protects the state regardless of the sex, or sexes, of its heads. The realm of coinage that had offered the image of Zoe and Theodora under the protective figure of the Virgin illustrates this, for the numismatic formulae of Mary move from ruler to ruler without regard to gender.[33] The identity conferred by Mary's presence is one not of gender but of office. Here, where Mary functioned as a bridge not merely between humans and Jesus but between humankind and God, she seems to have been conceived as 'Queen of Heaven'. In the West she was conceived as Christ's queen; thus she could echo earthly queens, and quickly transformed even the Byzantine-looking Hodegetrias of the Italian city states into crowned ingenues, as one can watch in Siena as Simone Martini rethinks Duccio's mighty Maestà in the terms of gracious Gothic queenship in the Palazzo Pubblico (Figs 23.5–23.6). Thus the character of Mary's gendered role in the civic order offers a third question in pursuing Mary east and west.

---

[30] London, British Library, Stowe 944, fol. 6r. On this great miniature's very extensive bibliography, see most recently E. C. Parker, 'The Gift of the Cross in the New Minster *Liber Vitae*', in E. Sears and T. Thomas (eds), *Reading Medieval Images* (Ann Arbor, 2002), 177–86. A. W. Carr, 'Threads of Authority: The Virgin Mary's Veil in the Middle Ages', in S. Gordon (ed.), *Robes and Honor. The Medieval World of Investiture* (Boston, 2001), 59–61, 74–9. P. Stafford, *Queen Emma and Queen Edith* (Cambridge, MA, 1997), 175–9.

[31] P. Corbet, 'Les impératrices ottoniennes et le modèle marial. Autour de l'ivoire du château Sforza de Milan', in D. Iogna-Prat, E. Palazzo and D. Rosso (eds), *Marie. Le culte de la Vierge dans la société médiévale* (Paris, 1996), 109–35. P. Ernst Schramm and F. Mütherich, *Denkmale der Deutschen Könige und Kaiser. Ein Beitrag zur Herrschergeschichte von Karl dem Grossen bis Friedrich II, 768–1250* (Munich, 1962), no. 75, 75 and 144–5.

[32] H. Maguire, 'The Heavenly Court,' in id. (ed.), *Byzantine Court Culture from 829–1204* (Washington, DC, 1997), 149–57.

[33] Thus the clipeate half-length Virgin adorns the obverse not only of Zoe and Theodora's coins, but of two earlier gold issues of Zoe's husband, Romanos III (Grierson, *Catalogue*, Pl. LVII, 2.1 and 2.2), and later ones of Michael VII (ibid., Pl. LXVI, 3). Those of Romanos show only his figure on the reverse; those of Michael VII, like Zoe and Theodora's, show two figures on the reverse, but these are now male and female, Michael and Maria of Alania. Theodora's issues from her reign as sole ruler, in turn, show Christ on the obverse and on the reverse the Mother of God crowning Theodora (ibid., Pl. LXII, AV 1a, 1b, 1c). This formula was used by Romanos III (ibid., Pl. LVI, AV 1a.2, 1b, 1c, 1d), and before him by Nikephoros II Phokas and John Tzimiskes.

Along with devotional forms and civic forms, pilgrimage offers a matrix within which to explore the conceptions of Mary in the Crusader world. We know that western pilgrims brought home with them Byzantine images. Thus, the Koimesis Church in Jerusalem, where Queen Melisende was buried, was adorned above Mary's tomb with an image of the Koimesis which, though 'eastern', was in no sense mute to Frankish pilgrims.[34] It was echoed at Abu Ghosh; one sees it again if one returns to far-away England, to the miniatures of the Winchester Psalter.[35] The Psalter opens with an extensive multiple frontispiece illustrating the history of salvation from Adam and Eve's expulsion to the Last Judgement. In between the scenes of Christ's saving life on earth on the one hand and those of the impending Last Judgement on the other, the manuscript presents a discreet, Byzantine-looking diptych of leaves displaying Mary's Dormition on one side and her frontally enthroned and orans image on the other. Interpreted as showing Mary's elevation to be the greatest intercessor at the Judgement, the scenes are labelled not with the Byzantine terminology of the Koimesis, but with the western terminology of Mary's Assumption.[36] Given their western content, their Byzantine form stands out sharply, begging explanation. A solution is offered, I believe, by the translation of the customary little footstool by Mary's bier into a far larger, open sarcophagus. This must reflect her empty tomb in Jerusalem. It may have been included here because Winchester had a relic of Mary's sepulchre.[37] But its aptness was probably intensified by contemporary debate in England over the issue of Mary's bodily assumption.[38] The sight in Jerusalem of Mary's empty tomb must have stood as an indelible witness to English pilgrims of the verity of her assumption, and it must have been this sight that prompted the miniatures' Byzantinism here, attesting on the basis of Jerusalem's visual evidence the Virgin's presence as queen and intercessor in heaven. This raises a fourth question for our consideration, and this is the way the convergence of Christianities in the Crusading era affected Mary's role as an object of pilgrimage. Pilgrimage, which drew Orthodox and Catholic alike to the shrines of Christianity's holiest figures, affected both Churches profoundly; how did it affect their perception of Mary?

Here the orientation of our inquiry changes, for the striking evidence here is the overwhelming predominance of western European over Byzantine or Middle Eastern sources. This

---

[34] It is cited by John of Würzburg and very fully described by Theoderich (Wilkinson, *Jerusalem Pilgrimage*, 299): 'Also on the ceiling over the steps by which one goes down into the crypt the journey of Our Lady is painted, in which her beloved Son, our Lord Jesus Christ, accompanied by a multitude of angels, carries her soul and transfers it to heaven. The Apostles stand by mourning, and showing devoted loyalty to her. For when a Jew wished to tear away the veil which was placed on her body, which was lying on a bier, an angel with a sword struck off both his hands, and they fell to the ground, and left his arms handless'.

[35] London, British Library, Cotton Nero C IV, fols 29r and 30r. The so-called Byzantine diptych, now bound as successive rectos, is widely reproduced and has been the subject of considerable recent discussion. See U. Nilgen, 'Byzantinismen im westlichen Hochmittelalter. Das "Byzantinische Diptychon" im Winchester-Psalter', in B. Borkopp and T. Steppan (eds), Λιθόστρωτον. *Studien zur byzantinischen Kunst und Geschichte, Festschrift für Marcell Restle* (Stuttgart, 2000), 173–90. H. A. Klein, 'The So-Called Byzantine Diptych in the Winchester Psalter, British Library, Cotton Nero C IV', *Gesta* 37 (1998), 26–43. Evans and Wixom, *The Glory of Byzantium*, no. 312, 474–5 (A. W. Carr). F. Wormald, *The Winchester Psalter* (London, 1973), Pls 4, 32, 33, 88.

[36] The Dormition is labelled 'ICI EST LA SUMPTION DE NOSTRE DAME'; the enthroned Virgin with angels is labelled 'ICI EST FAITE REINE DEL CIEL'.

[37] W. de Gray Birch, FSA (ed.), *Liber Vitae: Register and Martyrology of New Minster and Hyde Abbey, Winchester* (London, 1892), 148: 'de Sepulcro Sancte Marie'.

[38] C. Edmondson Haney, *The Winchester Psalter: An Iconographic Study* (Leicester, 1986), 44–6, 125 and *passim*.

is true of the pilgrimage sites in Constantinople itself, for the Russian travellers – so valuable for the fourteenth century – are sparse still in the twelfth and thirteenth;[39] it is true of the Holy Land, where the Abbot Daniel and John Phokas offer lone Orthodox voices amid a chorus of western accounts;[40] and it remains true as the monastic pilgrimage sites of late Byzantine fame begin to emerge into visibility in Latin travellers' reports. The late Byzantine pilgrimage sites are overwhelmingly Marian, served by miracle-working icons that drew devotees to the monasteries in which they resided. It is extremely difficult to document such sites before the Crusading era itself, and they seem genuinely to have become more widespread in Byzantium in the wake of western religious tourism in the thirteenth and fourteenth centuries.[41] Westerners could not have brought the Marian enthusiasm, but they may have brought a type of pilgrimage to which the icon cults responded. Distinctive about pilgrimage icons are the inventories of miracles assembled around them, a kind of inventory first evidenced in the eleventh- or twelfth-century *Vita* of the Maria Romaia icon in Constantinople.[42] In time they were also distinguished by the generation of replicas: that is, icons of icons.[43] We have one very provocative record of this process that comes from the Crusader context. This is the huge panel with Mary and Carmelite devotees in Nicosia.[44] Jaroslav Folda has argued, I think compellingly, that this is an image of an image, most probably of a great golden statue of Mary.[45] It is surrounded in the manner of a *Vita* icon with scenes in which a similar golden figure interacts with humans in scenes of miraculous interventions. The image, then, is apparently surrounded by scenes of its own miracles. This is a formula that would appear only later in Orthodox images, with a miracle-worker – not a miracle-working saint but a miracle-working icon – surrounded by scenes of its miraculous life.[46] The golden Mary represented in the icon in Nicosia cannot have been an Orthodox cult object – with its Carmelite devotees, it must have been a Catholic one. If Jaroslav Folda is right, it was not even an icon. Yet it offers precocious evidence of a visual formula – and with it a charismatic formula – that would emerge from the Crusading era in Byzantium, too. I believe that the western patterns of religious tourism played a role in shaping the habits of pilgrim devotion that sustained the icon cults of late Byzantium, and pose that as fourth question for our consideration.

The fifth question might best be posed with the narrative of Mary's life. Different episodes assumed centrality in different communities: we have seen already in the Winchester Psalter how the image used in Byzantium as the Koimesis was adapted in the West to the Assumption. This was true already of the very earliest instances of the Koimesis in western art, and there can

---

[39] The key source on the Russian pilgrims is G. P. Majeska, *Russian Travelers to Constantinople in the Fourteenth and Fifteenth Centuries* (DOS, XIX) (Washington, DC, 1984).
[40] See Wilkinson, *Jerusalem Pilgrimage*, 2–23 ('Introduction to the Texts').
[41] On the Byzantine pilgrimage icons, see A. W. Carr, 'Icons and the Object of Pilgrimage in Middle Byzantine Constantinople', *DOP* 56 (2002), 75–92.
[42] E. von Dobschütz, 'Maria Romaia. Zwei unbekannte Texte', *BZ* 12 (1903), 173–214.
[43] G. Babić, 'Il modello e la replica nell'arte bizantina delle icone', *Arte Cristiana* 76.724 (1988), 61–78.
[44] A. Papageorghiou, *Icons of Cyprus* (Nicosia, 1992), Pl. 31.
[45] J. Folda, 'Problems in the Iconography of the Art of the Crusaders in the Holy Land: 1098–1291/1917–1997', in C. Hourihane (ed.), *Image and Belief. Studies in Celebration of the Eightieth Anniversary of the Index of Christian Art* (Princeton, NJ, 1999), 17.
[46] On this very interesting development see O. Gratziou, 'Μεταμοφώσεις μίας θαυματουργής εικόνας. Σημειώσεις στις παραλλαγές της Παναγίας του Κύκκου', *DChAE* 17 (1993/4), 317–29.

be little doubt but that the image addressed different issues there.[47] In the West it allegorized Mary's entry into grace, a theme conceived rather differently in Byzantium and visualized in the scene of Mary's entry into the Temple,[48] an event little developed in the West. The theme illustrated in Byzantium in the Koimesis – the nature of the body Mary offered as vehicle for God – was in turn allegorized in the West through the very different idea of her immaculate conception. Thus different scenes assumed different degrees and inflections of significance. Along with the themes, the shapes of Mary's life differed. As seen in the Byzantine Dodekaorton, which opens with Mary's birth or Annunciation and closes with her Koimesis, Mary's life in Byzantium literally embraces that of her son, as if his life were encompassed within her body. A similar pattern unfolds in monumental cycles, as the Virgin in the apse conch faces her Koimesis on the western wall. How differently the cycle of Mary functions in Giotto's Arena Chapel, where scenes of her son bracket her life, as he arranges her election and birth on the east wall, and adjudicates at the Last Judgement on the west.

By the time we reach Giotto, the forms of Marian representation had criss-crossed the boundaries of the churches: the Assumption was often seen in Byzantine art;[49] Mary had found a place on Latin coins;[50] her Presentation in the Temple was a feast in the Latin Churches of Jerusalem and Cyprus, from which it would be introduced in 1372 to the Church of Rome;[51] and Byzantium itself was leaving behind the abstract images like the so-called Platytera in favour of evocative images of Mary's intimacy with her child of the sort that had proved so riveting to European viewers.[52] A fourteenth-century icon from Cyprus illustrates this interpenetrating of imagery vividly (Plate 19, Fig. 23.7).[53] Its compelling image of Mary caressing Jesus' erect but lifeless body echoes the exactly contemporary *Pietà* of 1365 by Giovanni da Milano (Fig. 23.8). And yet: where can the motif of her enfolding maphorion have emerged but in Byzantium, where Mary's potent will looms over and enfolds Christ's mortality? And so the fifth question that intrigues me: does this ever-greater interchange of imagery imply greater convergence or mask divergence in the understanding of Mary?

Five questions, then, to ponder as we think of Mary east and west: where *is* east, where is west; about whose conception of Mary do motifs borrowed across these borders speak – about the culture that created the motif or the one that borrowed it; how does Mary's gendering play

---

[47] R. Kahsnitz, 'Koimesis – Dormitio – Assumptio. Byzantinisches und Antikes in den Miniaturen der Liuthargruppe', in P. Bjurström *et al.* (eds), *Florilegium Carl Nordenfalk* (Stockholm, 1987), 91–122.

[48] H. Maguire, '*Abaton* and *Oikonomia*: St Neophytos and the Iconography of the Presentation of the Virgin', in N. P. Ševčenko and C. Moss (eds), *Medieval Cyprus. Studies in Art, Architecture, and History in Memory of Doula Mouriki* (Princeton, NJ, 1999), 95–116.

[49] B. Todić, *Serbian Medieval Painting. The Age of King Milutin* (Belgrade, 1999), 114–21. C. D. Kalokyris, 'La Dormition et l'Assomption' de la Théotokos dans l'art de l'église orthodoxe', *EEThSPTh* 19 (1974), 133–43.

[50] Before the Pisan coins of the mid-13th c. the Virgin Mary appeared only rarely on western European coins: see P. Grierson, *Monnaies du Moyen Âge* (Paris, 1976), 163 and Pl. 300 for the Pisan coin; 143 and Pl. 259 for a coin of Stephen IV of Hungary (1162–1163) with the enthroned Virgin and a sceptre on the reverse; 107–9 and Pl. 167 for a coin of Roger I of Sicily (1072–1101) with the Virgin and Child on the reverse; and 86 for the German coins of the 11th c. from Speyer imitating the gold coins of Zoe and Theodora with the Virgin clipeate on the obverse.

[51] W. E. Coleman (ed.), *Philippe de Mézières' Campaign for the Feast of Mary's Presentation* (Toronto, 1981).

[52] Ch. Baltoyianni, *Icons. The Mother of God in the Incarnation and the Passion* (Athens, 1994).

[53] S. Sophocleous (ed.), *Cyprus the Holy Island. Icons through the Centuries, 10th–20th Century*, exh. cat., London, Hellenic Centre, 1 Nov. – 17 Dec. 2000 (Nicosia, 2000), no. 30a–b, 178–81.

across conceptions of community and power; how did conceptions of pilgrimage shape the forms of Marian veneration; and did greater interchange bring with it a convergence in conceptions of Mary, or did it mask an ever-deeper divergence? In concluding, I'll indulge in a sixth. That Byzantium left the West an indelible image of Mary is evident still in the frame that Robert Mapplethorpe selected for publication from a long, feisty photo-session with the sculptor Louise Bourgeois. It shows the confident and smiling Bourgeois holding on her right arm her phallus-shaped sculpture, *Fillette*. The portrait has a classic quality: showing the formative maternal figure with her male issue firmly on her arm, it echoes the Hodegetria. Erect and firm, it reflects the authority of the creator before the one she creates. Mignon Nixon published the image under the title, 'Bad Enough Mother';[54] she used it to exemplify the opprobrium attached to the self-willed mother. The maternal figure of autonomous will has fitted uncomfortably in western European sentiment, which has chosen as its preferred paradigm the wife, governed by her husband's will, and not the woman of autonomous will. Uncomfortable in the West, too, has been the severe form of the Hodegetria, so often modified to a gentler grace in the West, as we have seen in Simone Martini's bridal *Maestà*. And so a final question: is the Mary whom we see in Byzantium in fact a product of doctrine? Or is it a product of art? Presenting very God for human contemplation, Mary figures here as a the ultimate icon, the matter that bears the conceived Word – that is, the image. Might Byzantium's Marian icons, then, have done what western art found so difficult: to present the female body not as the object of the gaze, but as the bearer of the image?

---

[54] M. Nixon, 'Bad Enough Mother', *October* 71 (1995), 71–92.

23.1   Cosenza, Cathedral. *Madonna del Pilerio* (source: Di Dario Guida, *Icone di Calabria e altre icone meridionali*, Pl. XII)

23.2   Lyon, Bibliothèque municipale, MS. 410, fol. 207v.
Opening of Song of Songs
(source: Bibliothèque municipale de Lyon, Didier Nicole)

23.3 Washington, DC, Dumbarton Oaks. Gold nomisma. The empresses Zoe and Theodora (source: Dumbarton Oaks)

23.4 London, British Library, MS. Stowe 944, fol. 6r. Opening of *Liber Vitae* of New Minster and Hyde Abbey, Winchester (source: Walter Grey, *Register and Martyrology of New Minster and Hyde Abbey*, frontispiece)

23.5 Siena, Museo del Opera del Duomo.
Duccio, *Maestà*; Mary from the central panel (detail)
(source: Alinari/Art Resource, NY)

23.6 Siena, Palazzo Pubblico.
Simone Martini, *Maestà*; Mary (detail)
(source: Alinari/Art Resource, NY)

23.7 Kalopanagiotis, Monastery of St John Lampadistes, Icon Museum. Diptych; *Pietà* (detail) (source: G. Philotheou, Dept. of Antiquities, Cyprus)

23.8 Florence, Accademia. Giovanni da Milano, *Pietà* (source: Scala/Art Resource, NY)

24

The Kahn and Mellon Madonnas and their place in the history of the Virgin and Child Enthroned in Italy and the East

Rebecca W. Corrie

Undoubtedly one of the most intriguing problems in thirteenth-century Mediterranean art is presented by two images of the Virgin and Child Enthroned, now known as the Kahn and Mellon Madonnas (Plate 20, Fig. 24.1 and Fig. 24.2). The two panels surfaced together in 1912 at auction in Madrid and after passing through different private collections were reunited in the National Gallery in Washington, DC, where they now hang side by side.[1] Perhaps as much as any, these images stand between east and west in art history's version of thirteenth-century events and offer us an opportunity to explore the relationship between Byzantine and Italian images and painters. Published early on by Bernard Berenson, who called them Constantinopolitan, they have also been attributed variously to Venice, Sicily, Siena, Cyprus, and Thessaloniki.[2] A tradition which added Calahorra, Spain, by way of Sicily, to their provenance has recently been discredited and so we are left with remarkably little information about their history.[3]

Twice in the last two decades I have addressed the issue of the Kahn and Mellon Madonnas; in 2000 in the catalogue for the 'Mother of God' exhibition and in 1985 at the College Art Association Conference in Los Angeles, where I presented a paper which has remained unpublished, but which Jaroslav Folda has kindly cited in his publications.[4] In part my reluctance to publish the Los Angeles paper was based on the uncertainty I felt about localizing their

---

[1] F. R. Shapley, *Catalogue of Italian Paintings* II (Washington, DC, 1979), 96–7.
[2] E. B. Garrison, *Italian Romanesque Panel Painting* (Florence, 1949), 44, 48. B. Berenson, 'Due dipinti del XII secolo venuti da Constantinopoli', *Dedalo* 2 (1921/2), 285–304. Id., 'Two Twelfth-Century Paintings from Constantinople', in *Studies in Medieval Painting* (New Haven, 1930), 1–16. O. Demus, 'Zwei Konstantinopler Marienikonen des 13. Jahrhunderts', *JÖBG* 7 (1958), 87–104. Id., *Byzantine Art and the West* (New York, 1970), 212–18. *La pittura in Italia: Il Duecento e il Trecento* II (Milan, 1986), Fig. 717. J. H. Stubblebine, 'Two Byzantine Madonnas from Calahora, Spain', *ArtB* 48 (1966), 379–81. H. Belting, 'The "Byzantine" Madonnas: New Facts About Their Italian Origin and Some Observations on Duccio', *Studies in the History of Art* 12 (1982), 7–22. J. Polzer, 'Some Byzantine and Byzantinizing Madonnas Painted During the Later Middle Ages, Part I', *Arte Cristiana* 87.791 (1999), 83–90. Id., 'Some Byzantine and Byzantinizing Madonnas Painted During the Later Middle Ages, Part II', *Arte Cristiana* 87.792 (1999), 167–82. Id., 'The "Byzantine" *Kahn* and *Mellon Madonnas*: Concerning their Chronology, Place of Origin, and Method of Analysis', *Arte Cristiana* 90.813 (2002), 401–10. Evans and Wixom, *The Glory of Byzantium*, no. 262, 396–7 (J. Folda).
[3] Belting, 'The "Byzantine" Madonnas', 7, 21 n. 2.
[4] R. W. Corrie, 'Tuscan Madonnas and Byzantine Masters', *73rd Annual Meeting, College Art Association of America, Abstracts and Program Statements for Art History Sessions*, 14–16 February 1985 (Los Angeles, 1985), 46 and Vassilaki, *Mother of God*, no. 68, 438–9 (R. W. Corrie). J. Folda, 'The Kahn and Mellon Madonnas: Icon or Altarpiece', in C. Moss and K. Kiefer (eds), *Byzantine East, Latin West. Art-Historical Studies in Honor of Kurt Weitzmann* (Princeton, NJ, 1995), 501–6, and id., 'Icon to Altarpiece in the Frankish East: Images of the Virgin and Child Enthroned', in V. M. Schmidt (ed.), *Italian Panel Painting of the Duecento and Trecento* (Studies in the History of Art, Center for Advanced Study in the Visual Arts, Symposium Papers, XXXVIII) (Washington, 2002), 122–45.

production. Unlike Folda, who recently has argued for the East, or Hans Belting and Joseph Polzer, who have argued for Italy, I saw merit in both positions.[5] While to me the painters appear to be Greek, trained either at Thessaloniki or Constantinople, the connections to images produced in Italy in the later thirteenth century are also clear. But in this paper I would like to argue more strenuously on the Greek side, for an array of elements that have been described by some as Italian on the contrary seem to have had their origins in Byzantine painting. Most importantly, I would argue that we need to separate the production of these images from that of the enthroned Virgins of Duccio and Cimabue painted around 1285, a connection stressed by Stubblebine, Belting and Polzer. In turn the work of Duccio and Cimabue may emerge as part of a much larger Mediterranean world once we cut them loose from the Washington panels and set all of these images into a wider visual repertoire. Moreover, this is a repertoire vastly enriched in the last few years by a dazzling array of exhibitions, including those in New York, Thessaloniki, Athens and St Petersburg, and by publications on the painting of Greece and Serbia.[6]

In part owing to its relatively good condition, I begin with the larger of the two images, usually called the Kahn Madonna (Fig. 24.1). Art historians who have argued for the training of this painter in Constantinople have offered a series of convincing comparisons. Unquestionably the brilliant and extensive chrysography argues that its style is based in the brilliant painting at Constantinople around 1200; and indeed among the early comparisons offered for this image were the frescoes painted by a Constantinopolitan painter at St Demetrios at Vladimir, dated around 1195.[7] Otto Demus' even more convincing comparison with the Deesis mosaics from Hagia Sophia at Constantinople pushed the date to shortly after 1261.[8] Here are remarkably similar facial types, especially in eye and mouth shapes and deep shadows along the necks. The bodies retain the slender form found at Vladimir, but like the Kahn Madonna include a three-dimensionality not seen there. The handling of the chrysography also argues for this later date. For example, in both Washington images the mantle of the Virgin falls into sharp folds just above her elbow and omits the gold fringe usually found there in icons. This chrysographic treatment is found extensively in Palaiologan painting, especially in fresco and mosaic, as in the Christ of the Hagia Sophia Deesis.[9] The gold stripes on the Virgin's headpiece are also typical of mosaic work.[10] This Byzantine chrysography differs from that in contemporary Italian

---

[5] Polzer, 'Part I' and 'Part II'. Belting, 'The "Byzantine" Madonnas'. Folda, 'Madonna and Child'. Id., 'Kahn and Mellon'. Id., 'Icon to Altarpiece' and id., 'Icon or Altarpiece? Reflections on the Kahn and Mellon Madonnas', *Ideas* 6.1 (1999), downloaded 29 July 2002 from *www.nhc.rtp.nc.us:8080/ideasv61/folda.htm*.

[6] Evans and Wixom, *Glory of Byzantium. Treasures of Mount Athos*, exh. cat., Thessaloniki, Museum of Byzantine Culture (Thessaloniki, 1997). Vassilaki, *Mother of God*. Y. Piatnitsky, O. Baddeley, E. Brunner and M. M. Mango (eds), *Sinai, Byzantium, Russia. Orthodox Art from the Sixth to the Twentieth Century*, exh. cat., London, Courtauld Institute of Art, 19 Oct. 2000 – 4 Feb. 2001 (St Petersburg, 2000). *The Holy and Great Monastery of Vatopaidi. Tradition – History – Art* I–II (Mount Athos, 1998). *Hilandar Monastery* (Belgrade, 1998). B. Todić, *Serbian Medieval Painting: The Age of King Milutin* (Belgrade, 1999). R. D'Amico (ed.), *Tra le due sponde dell'Adriatico: la pittura nella Serbia del XIII secolo e l'Italia* (Ferrara, 1999).

[7] V. Lazarev, *Old Russian Murals and Mosaics* (London, 1966), 81–91, esp. Figs 60–3. For sources and discussion, see T. Velmans, *La peinture murale byzantine à la fin du moyen âge* I (Paris, 1977), 117–21.

[8] Demus, 'Zwei Konstantinopler', and id., *Byzantine Art*, 218.

[9] Vassilaki, *Mother of God*, Pl. 69, and no. 74, 465 (M. Acheimastou-Potamianou). L. James, *Light and Colour in Byzantine Art* (Oxford, 1996), Pls 16, 59. See also the frescoes at Boiana in Bulgaria, dated 1259: R. J. Crampton, *A Concise History of Bulgaria* (Cambridge, 1997), Fig. 2.3.

[10] James, *Light and Colour*, Pl. 28.

painting, which makes extensive use of short, broad cross-hatching not seen here.[11] Like the lavender and blue palette, such comparisons place the painter of the Kahn Madonna in the mainstream of Byzantine painting and pull him away from Italy, and support a localization at Thessaloniki or at Constantinople, probably after 1261.[12]

My impression that this is a Greek painter was only increased by Belting's article in 1982. The small angels in red roundels, with jewelled collar loros, pearl diadems, and blue orbs (Fig. 24.3) fit Byzantine art after 1260 well. Indeed, the loros with pearl pendants finds exact parallels in frescoes at Mt Athos and Arilje dated around 1290 and attributed to painters from Thessaloniki.[13] But Belting provided a detail of the left angel from the Kahn panel, and I was struck by the similarity of its facial type, including small upper eyelid folds, to that of the attending virgins in an icon of the Presentation of the Virgin in the Temple on Mt Athos, usually dated to 1300 or slightly later, and given to a painter from Thessaloniki, creating another connection to Greek painters of that era.[14]

Since Berenson and Demus a number of scholars, including Irmgaard Hutter and Annemarie Weyl Carr, have commented that Constantinople was a likely location for the training of this painter.[15] But a different question has been raised by scholars such as Belting and Polzer, and that is whether the training of the Kahn painter and the production of the image necessarily took place in the same city or region. A series of characteristics considered Italian by some have been raised as barriers to an attribution to Constantinople. For example, some argue that full-length enthroned images function as altarpieces and thus have little role in the Byzantine world, and are more at home in Italy with the Cimabue and Duccio Madonnas and many subsequent images. But in fact there are numerous Byzantine examples, from the Sinai panel of the sixth or seventh century to the Byzantine stone relief usually dated to the thirteenth century, now in the chapel of San Zeno at San Marco.[16] By the thirteenth century, smaller scale, personal images of the Virgin and Child Enthroned were produced in metal or as painted icons.[17] Indeed, the contexts for images of the Virgin and Child Enthroned seem to have been more varied in the Byzantine orbit than we have assumed. A panel such as the Mellon Madonna might have been made for private devotion, or even as part of an iconostasis perhaps, as we find in later, post-Byzantine examples on Patmos, and the larger Kahn Madonna could have functioned in a pair of despotic icons such as those from around 1300 preserved at the Protaton in Karyes on Mt Athos, and of course Folda's theory of a Latin patron remains an option.[18]

---

[11] Polzer, 'Part I', Figs 2–3.
[12] Vassilaki, *Mother of God*, Pls 19–20, 56, 69, 74–7, 79, 101.
[13] P. Sherrard, *Athos: The Holy Mountain* (London, 1982), Fig. 17. Todić, *Serbian Medieval Painting*, Fig. 1. For the diadems, see Piatnitsky *et al.*, *Sinai, Byzantium, Russia*, 237, 251. For the orbs, see K. Weitzmann *et al.*, *The Icon* (New York, 1982), 181–2, 255.
[14] Todić, *Serbian Medieval Painting*, 360–1, esp. Fig. 189. *Hilandar*, 283, and *Treasures*, 79–80. See also the St Demetrios icon, ibid., 76–7.
[15] I. Hutter, *Early Christian and Byzantine Art* (New York, 1971), 156 and A. W. Carr, 'Byzantines and Italians on Cyprus: Images from Art', *DOP* 49 (1995), 352 n. 71.
[16] Vassilaki, *Mother of God*, no. 1, 262–3 (R. Cormack). V. Lasareff, 'Studies in the Iconography of the Virgin', *ArtB* 20 (1938), Figs 15, 16, 44.
[17] Weitzmann, *The Icon*, 66, 98.
[18] Chapel of the Panaghia: M. Chatzidakis, *Icons of Patmos: Questions of Byzantine and Post-Byzantine Painting*

The despotic icon on Mt Athos brings another motif to our attention: a gesture in which the Virgin touches the child's knee with slightly spread fingers. Here too is a motif which appears in Cimabue's S. Trinità Madonna and Duccio's Rucellai Madonna, which have been fielded as evidence of the dependence of the Kahn and Mellon Madonnas on Italian images. But in fact the motif is found throughout the history of Byzantine art.[19] Similarly, the child in a long tunic of red and gold with blue or grey straps ranges from Cyprus to Rome to a twelfth-century manuscript on Mount Athos.[20] A standing Virgin from Naxos, attributed to Constantinople in the later thirteenth century, includes the gesture, the child type, and the Virgin's mantle open at the neck.[21]

One element has troubled all of us who see this image as eastern: the halo decoration. Scholars have found it to be an indication of an Italian provenance or at least the taste of an Italian patron. Recently Joseph Polzer argued that the Kahn haloes are not only Italian, but Sienese, and he proposed that our painter had worked in Siena itself.[22] But the first such decorated halos in Tuscany may well be in works dated around 1260 by the very Byzantinizing painter Coppo di Marcovaldo and his contemporary Guido da Siena. Moreover the halo motifs used by the Kahn Madonna's painter and Coppo are versions of a lotus and palmette motif, which also appears on the throne back.[23] Indeed, while it appears in Italian art, it is one of the most common motifs in Byzantine painting.[24] Similarly, the second halo motif cited by Polzer, a repeated heart pattern, is also standard in Byzantine art.[25] It seems likely that the use of such motifs is a Byzantine rather than a Tuscan invention, for decorated haloes appear in various forms from Russia and Bulgaria to Cyprus and Sicily.[26] Indeed, in the Madrid sacramentary, probably made at Messina and variously dated between 1190 and 1220, we find Guido's halo.[27] Interesting and telling is a small image of the Virgin attributed to a Greek painter of the thirteenth century, now at Ohrid, which has an incised halo.[28]

Unquestionably the element which led Belting as well as Stubblebine to attribute both panels to Italy or at least to see them as dependent on Tuscan painting is the chair throne. But as I pointed out in 1985, the chair throne found in the Kahn Madonna, while new to Italy, has a

---

(Athens, 1985), Pl. V. The Enthroned Virgin and Child and Enthroned Christ: Sherrard, *Athos*, Figs 77–8. Folda, 'Icon to Altarpiece'. The different sizes of the two panels do argue that the Mellon Madonna (81.5 × 49.0 cm, 32⅛ × 19⅜ in) may well have been intended as a personal image, while the Kahn Madonna (131.1 × 76.8 cm, 51⅝ × 30¼ in) was not.

[19] Vassilaki, *Mother of God*, Pls 3, 107, 169, 199.
[20] M. Bacci, 'La Panaya Odighitria e la Madonna di Costantinopoli', *Arte Cristiana* 84.772 (1996), Fig. 1. A. M. Cerioni and R. del Signore, *The Basilica of Saint Paul Outside the Walls* (Rome, 1991), Fig. 52. Vassilaki, *Mother of God*, Pls 51, 102. A. Cutler, *The Aristocratic Psalters in Byzantium* (Paris, 1984), 103–6, Fig. 364.
[21] Vassilaki, *Mother of God*, no. 67, 434–7 (Ch. Baltoyanni).
[22] Polzer, 'Part II'.
[23] R. W. Corrie, 'The Political Meaning of Coppo di Marcovaldo's Madonna and Child in Siena', *Gesta* 29.1 (1990), Fig. 3.
[24] Weitzmann, *The Icon*, 174–5. Evans and Wixom, *Glory of Byzantium*, no. 58, 103 (D. Katsarelias).
[25] Polzer, 'Part II', Fig. 21. Corrie, 'Political Meaning', Fig. 2.
[26] Evans and Wixom, *Glory of Byzantium*, no. 75, 128 (R. W. Corrie); no. 198, 295 (O. Z. Pevny); no. 203, 300 (O. Z. Pevny); fig. on p. 323; no. 316, 480 (R. W. Corrie); no. 330, 494 (M. L. Coulson). Vassilaki, *Mother of God*, no. 33, 342–3 (E. Tsigaridas); no. 36, 350–3 (A. Papageorgiou). Cf. also V. Pace, 'Between East and West', ibid., 431, Pls 221–3.
[27] Evans and Wixom, *Glory of Byzantium*, no. 316, 480 (R. W. Corrie).
[28] Weitzmann, *The Icon*, 162.

long Byzantine heritage. Fine examples used for evangelist portraits appear in illuminated manuscripts as early as the eleventh century.[29] Its use for the Virgin and Child in a manuscript dated 1274, probably produced in Constantinople and now on Sinai, is a good indication that Byzantine examples of the type preceded Cimabue's work.[30] Indeed, variations of this chair throne, usually without the silk cloth of Cimabue's panels, continue in fourteenth-century wall painting, for example at Ohrid, Žiča and Staro Nagoričino.[31]

In sum, while Stubblebine and Belting saw this version of the chair throne of the Kahn Madonna as dependent on those of Cimabue or Duccio, what seems most likely is that all are variations of a shared type. The lathe-turned chair throne had become common in northern Europe as well as Byzantium by the early thirteenth century, as in the Goslar Evangeliary of about 1240, perhaps copied from other images but also from actual chairs, a few of which still survive, such as the English Hereford throne from the late twelfth century.[32] It seems likely that our throne with its finials, open arches, and back with carved decoration reflects carpentry techniques for elaborate wooden furniture produced throughout the Mediterranean in that period. The recently published minbar from the Kutubiyya Mosque at Marrakesh, produced in Morocco in the twelfth century, offers a striking comparison for painted thrones in some Italian and Byzantine images.[33]

When we turn from the Kahn to the much-restored Mellon Madonna we find a throne that is similarly Byzantine in its origins (Fig. 24.2). Certainly it has been convincingly argued that the Mellon Madonna is not the work of our Greek painter, but of a colleague or follower. Some have argued that the combination of a cherry red mantle and light blue tunic is Italian rather than Byzantine.[34] But the red mantle rarely appears in Italian images. The Virgin wears it much more often in Byzantine images, in sites as varied as Cyprus and Sinai and even in Constantinople.[35] And the distinctive folds resting on the knees of both the Virgin and the Child can be seen on the enthroned St John the Evangelist at Sopoćani painted between 1263 and 1265.[36]

But it may well be the throne that places the Mellon image most emphatically in the ambient of Byzantine painting after 1250. The tub chair, as it has been called, had existed since Late Antiquity. It appears in a Roman relief, and is best known in the ivory throne of Maximian in Ravenna, an idea that Folda has recently expanded.[37] But there seems to have been a revival of

---

[29] J. C. Anderson, 'The Past Reanimated in Byzantine Illumination', in Moss and Kiefer, *Byzantine East, Latin West*, Figs 4, 5. Evans and Wixom, *Glory of Byzantium*, no. 58, 103 (D. Katsarelias).
[30] Sinai, cod. gr. 61: Cutler, *Aristocratic Psalters*, 112–15, Fig. 411. Folda, 'Kahn and Mellon', Fig. 5.
[31] Velmans, *La peinture murale*, Fig. 45. E. Tsigaridas, 'The Mother of God in Wall-Paintings', in Vassilaki, *Mother of God*, 132, Pl. 78.
[32] *Das Goslarer Evangeliar* (Graz, 1991), fol. 10v. E. Lucie-Smith, *Furniture: A Concise History* (London, 1997), Fig. 36.
[33] J. M. Bloom, A. Toufiq, S. Carboni, J. Soultanian, A. M. Wilmerihg, M. D. Minor, A. Zawacki and E. Hbibi, *The Minbar from the Kutubiyya Mosque* (New York, 1998), Fig. 1.
[34] Belting, 'The "Byzantine" Madonnas', 12–13.
[35] Vassilaki, *Mother of God*, Pl. 103 and no. 28, 314–16 (T. Papamastorakis); no. 33, 342–3 (E. Tsigaridas); no. 61, 402–4 (A. Nitič); no. 63, 408–9 (Ch. Baltoyanni). Evans and Wixom, *Glory of Byzantium*, figs on pp. 4 and 116. Weitzmann, *The Icon*, 319, 338, 370. The orange and green robes of the child also belong to an Eastern context as in Vassilaki, *Mother of God*, no. 62, 406–7 (A. Papageorgiou).
[36] D'Amico, *Tra le due sponde*, 71, Fig. 35.
[37] Lucie-Smith, *Furniture*, Figs 23–5. Folda, 'Icon to Altarpiece', 132–7, 143–4.

the type in the thirteenth century. Many examples of the round-backed throne occur in Constantinople. Folda and others noted it in a miniature of the Annunciation in Paris gr. 54, usually attributed to Constantinople after 1261.³⁸ And we find the throne in Byzantine evangelist portraits of the later thirteenth century.³⁹ Most important may be an image of an enthroned Joshua from the Mt Athos Octateuch, Vatopedi cod. 602, attributed to a Constantinopolitan painter working in an imperial atelier after 1261.⁴⁰

Recent publications of frescoes in Greece and the Balkans show us how often the round throne was used for the Virgin in Palaiologan frescoes, uses which must be reflected in the Mellon image. For example, the round-backed throne with arches occurs in a fresco fragment with the Virgin and Child with Angels dated between 1280 and 1310 in the Vatopedi monastery on Mt Athos and attributed to a painter from Constantinople or Thessaloniki.⁴¹ Another damaged fresco dated to the 1280s at Porta Panaghia near Trikala in Thessaly depicts the founder, John Komnenos Doukas, presented to a Virgin and Child on a curved-back throne which includes hand knobs and small knobs along the back.⁴² Like the use of the throne for Joshua in Vatopedi 602, the frequent use of this throne type in the apse decorations of Palaiologan fresco programmes suggests a reference to Byzantine imperial imagery, whether at Thessaloniki or Constantinople, or subsequently in the circles of King Milutin of Serbia at Studenića and Staro Nagoričino.⁴³ Indeed, the Virgin and Child on a round-backed throne in the apse of St Euthymios at Thessaloniki belongs to a fresco cycle commissioned by powerful and pious relatives of the Byzantine emperor, Andronikos II.⁴⁴

Thus on the basis of facial types, details such as halo ornament, palette, type of chrysography, gesture, and above all the types of thrones and even the footstools, and despite the relative delicacy of the figures, these images of the Virgin and Child appear to fit most comfortably in Palaiologan Constantinople or Thessaloniki in the second half of the thirteenth century, or perhaps in a nearby centre such as Mt Athos or Sopoćani or Arta. They do not require the work of Cimabue or Duccio to explain their types or composition. In other words, evaluated on their own, they were most likely produced in the East and remained there until around 1912. And we can stand this question on its head. Does the development of Italian painting require the presence of these works in Italy? More likely the Kahn and Mellon panels show us the style and

---

38 Folda, 'Kahn and Mellon', Fig. 6, and id., 'Icon or Altarpiece?', part 3 of 3.
39 H. Buchthal and H. Belting, *Patronage in Thirteenth-Century Constantinople: An Atelier of Late Byzantine Book Illumination and Calligraphy* (Washington, DC, 1978), Pls 6b, 15, 27, 87b.
40 P. Huber, *Bild und Botschaft* (Zurich and Freiburg, 1973), 33–40, Fig. 78. *Treasures*, 241.
41 E. N. Tsigaridas, 'The Mosaics and the Byzantine Wall-Paintings', in *The Holy and Great Monastery of Vatopaidi*, 234–5, Fig. 193.
42 A. Tsitouridou, 'Les fresques du XIIIᵉ siècle dans l'église de la Porta-Panaghia en Thessalie', in *Actes du XVᵉ Congrès international d'Études byzantines*, Athens, September 1976, II (Athens, 1981), 863–78, Fig. 9.
43 S. E. J. Gerstel, *Beholding the Sacred Mysteries: Programs of the Byzantine Sanctuary* (Seattle and London, 1999), Figs 46, 49. Todić, *Serbian Medieval Painting*, Figs 28, 62, 82, 142, 159. Another Palaiologan curved throne with niches is at Pelendri on Cyprus, before 1375: Carr, 'Lusignan Kings', Fig. 13. Less three-dimensional are examples on Crete: K. Kalokyris, *The Byzantine Wall Paintings of Crete* (New York, 1973), Figs BW 12, BW 13, and BW 79.
44 Th. Gouma-Peterson, 'The Frescoes of the Parekklesion of St. Euthymios in Thessaloniki: Patrons, Workshop, and Style', in S. Čurčić and D. Mouriki, *The Twilight of Byzantium: Aspects of Cultural and Religious History in the Late Byzantine Empire* (Princeton, NJ, 1991), 111–29. The round throne appears in the apse, the Annunciation, and Christ Teaching in the Temple, Figs 2, 5, 8, 12.

repertoire of painters whose work functioned as models for images in Pisa, Perugia, Florence and Siena, possibly through the project of the mosaic decoration at the Baptistery in Florence or through the work of Giunta Pisano, or slightly later at Bologna through Venice.

There is still much to be explored, such as the larger history of the thrones, on which I have only made a start here. Although I have argued that the thrones we see depict actual chairs and types common in painting, it is possible that our images reflect much older painted thrones as well. I am intrigued by similarities between the curved thrones in later Byzantine painting and those in Carolingian painting, which in turn probably reflect examples from antiquity or from early Byzantine images.[45] Indeed, in his recent book on Cimabue, Luciano Bellosi put an important example on the scholarly table: a round-backed throne in the Gospel of Lothair which, I note, finds an astonishing match in the round throne of the Virgin at Ohrid dated 1379.[46] Horst Janson observed that the throne of the Mellon Madonna resembles the Colosseum.[47] And the circular wall-like treatment of the Mellon throne finds a remarkable parallel in the background wall in an icon of the Dormition of the Virgin now in St Petersburg, originally from Mt Athos and dated around 1300 (Fig. 24.4).[48] And the deep niches separated by foliate ornament in the Mellon throne appear in the architecture of the Presentation of the Virgin icon on Athos which provided comparisons for the angel in the Kahn Madonna.[49] In connection with a suggestion that early Byzantine images might lie behind the Palaiologan thrones, can we make anything of the Mellon throne's similarity to the walls such as that behind St John in the Carolingian Gospel of St Emmeran, with its deep niches and finials or knobs?[50] And finally, do these comparisons signal complex Byzantine meanings as well as the origins of this throne type: imperial, Solomonic or mariological, or all three?[51]

And what of the provenance of the panels? Although they surfaced together in 1912, recent writers have tended to separate their production. In contrast, I would support Bellosi's recent observation that they have far more in common with each other than they do with anything else, and thus I would conclude that they are likely to be from the same workshop at about the same time.[52] I wonder whether the 1912 date offers us any help, however circular in argument. 1912 was of course a year of great change and upheaval in Balkan history and in the history of Mount Athos, a coincidence that suggests that investigating the history of sales and collections at that time might tell us whether these panels could have reached Spain together in the possession of someone fleeing war or political change.[53]

For me, at the present moment, what we know about Italian and Byzantine painting argues that the two Washington panels fit well into Byzantine painting, probably by artists trained at

---

[45] J. Hubert, J. Porcher, and W. F. Volbach, *The Carolingian Renaissance* (New York, 1970), Figs 66–7 and 79.
[46] L. Bellosi, *Cimabue* (New York, London and Paris, 1998), 103–4. Velmans, *La peinture murale*, Fig. 77, and V. J. Djurić, *Byzantinische Fresken in Jugoslavien* (Munich, 1976), Fig. 85.
[47] H. Janson, *History of Art* (2nd edn, New York, 1977), 214.
[48] Piatnitsky *et al.*, *Sinai, Byzantium, Russia*, 152–3.
[49] *Treasures*, 179.
[50] Hubert, Porcher and Volbach, *Carolingian Renaissance*, Fig. 106.
[51] Jaroslav Folda and I have separately come to the same conclusion that the Mellon throne refers to the Throne of Solomon, although we see this reference in different contexts. Folda, 'Icon or Altarpiece?', and 'Icon to Altarpiece'. Corrie, 'Panel of the Madonna and Child'.
[52] Bellosi, *Cimabue*, 57–8.
[53] Crampton, *Concise History*, 135–40.

Constantinople or Thessaloniki, and that these two panels were never in Italy. Oddly though, while taking these images out of Italy, my recent look at this question has left me with an even stronger sense of the closeness of the art of Constantinople, Thessaloniki, and Serbia, Cyprus and Italy than I have had before, and an enlarged sense of the Byzantine role in the painting of the second half of the thirteenth century in Italy. And Cimabue and Duccio, no longer the source of the Washington panels, now seem even more a part of the mainstream of Mediterranean art.

24.1 Washington, National Gallery of Art, 1949.7.1. (1048)/PA.
Enthroned Madonna and Child (13th c.).
Gift of Mrs Otto H. Kahn
(Image © Board of Trustees, National Gallery of Art, Washington)

24.2 Washington, National Gallery of Art, 1937.1.1.(1)/PA.
Madonna and Child on a Curved Throne (13th c.).
Andrew W. Mellon Collection
(Image © Board of Trustees, National Gallery of Art, Washington)

24.3 Washington, National Gallery of Art, 1949.7.1.(1048)/PA. Enthroned Madonna and Child (13th c.) (detail). Gift of Mrs Otto H. Kahn (Image © Board of Trustees, National Gallery of Art, Washington)

24.4 St Petersburg, The State Hermitage Museum, I-286. Icon with the Dormition of the Virgin (first half of the 14th c.) (source: The State Hermitage Museum)

Representations of the Virgin in Lusignan Cyprus*

Sophia Kalopissi-Verti

In this paper I shall be commenting on some portrayals of the Virgin which seem to me representative of particular aspects of the art and culture of Lusignan Cyprus.

The first group of these is to be found in the mural decoration of the narthex of the church of Panagia Phorbiotissa in Asinou,[1] which was founded in 1105–1106. The narthex[2] was added slightly later and was decorated in the last decades of the twelfth and in the late thirteenth century. In 1332–1333 a new layer of painting was added, although certain dedicatory murals from the earlier layers were left uncovered.

The fourteenth-century paintings include on the north side of the entrance to the church a figure of the Virgin with the inscription 'Eleousa', rendered in the iconographic type generally called the Paraklesis (Figs 25.1–25.2). In this she is portrayed turned towards Christ, who is depicted in the corresponding position on the south side of the entrance, and she holds a scroll on which are inscribed prayers for the salvation of mankind in the form of a dialogue with her son.

The Paraklesis is a variant of the supplicating Hagiosoritissa,[3] which lays particular emphasis on the Virgin's intercessory role, for which she was venerated in Constantinople from the sixth/seventh century onwards.[4] This role, which is based on her maternal relationship with Christ, receives emphasis in ecclesiastical writings of the eighth and ninth centuries, and is the inspiration for a great number of liturgical hymns.

---

* Research for this paper was carried out while on a fellowship at Dumbarton Oaks in Autumn 2000.

[1] M. Sacopoulo, *Asinou en 1106 et sa contribution à l'iconographie* (Bibliothèque de Byz, 2) (Brussels, 1966), with earlier bibliography. A. and J. Stylianou, *Παναγία Φορβιώτισσα, Ασίνου* (Nicosia, 1973). Eid., *The Painted Churches of Cyprus* (London, 1985), 114–40. D. C. Winfield, *Asinou. A Guide* (s.l., s.a.). Chr. Hadjichristodoulou, *Ο ναός της Παναγίας της Ασίνου. Οδηγοί Βυζαντινών μνημείων της Κύπρου* (Nicosia, 2002).

[2] A. Papageorghiou, 'The Narthex of the Churches of the Middle Byzantine Period in Cyprus', in L. Hadermann-Misguich and G. Raepsaet (eds), *Rayonnement grec. Hommages à Charles Delvoye* (Brussels, 1982), 442–4.

[3] On the Hagiosoritissa, N. P. Kondakov, *Ikonografiia Bogomateri* II (St Petersburg, 1915), 294–315. M. Vloberg, 'Les types iconographiques de la mère de Dieu dans l'art byzantin', in S. J. d'Hubert du Manoir (ed.), *Maria. Études sur la Sainte Vierge* II (Paris, 1952), 422–5. S. Der Nersessian, 'Two Images of the Virgin in the Dumbarton Oaks Collection', *DOP* 14 (1960), 71–86. M. Andaloro, 'Note sui temi iconografici della Deesis e della Haghiosoreitissa', *RIASA*, n.s., 17 (1970), 85–153, esp. 128–43. E. Kitzinger, *The Mosaics of St. Mary's of the Admiral in Palermo* (DOS, XXVII) (Washington, DC, 1990), 199–206. Ch. Baltoyanni, 'The Mother of God in Portable Icons', in Vassilaki, *Mother of God*, 147–9. A. Mitsani, 'Βυζαντινή εικόνα της Παναγίας Δεομένης στην Καταπολιανή Πάρου', *DChAE* 23 (2002), 180–5.

[4] A. M. Cameron, 'The Theotokos in Sixth-Century Constantinople: A City finds its Symbol', *JThSt* 29 (1978), 79–108. Ead., 'The Early Cult of the Virgin', in Vassilaki, *Mother of God*, 12–14. P. Magdalino, 'The History of the Future and Its Uses: Prophecy, Policy and Propaganda', in R. Beaton and C. Roueché (eds), *The Making of Byzantine History. Studies dedicated to Donald M. Nicol* (Aldershot, 1993), 13–14.

One of the earliest representations of the Paraklesis[5] type is preserved in a mosaic in the basilica of St Demetrios in Thessaloniki,[6] which has been dated to between the seventh and the eleventh centuries, most persuasively perhaps to the seventh.[7] K. Weitzmann dates to the same period the original phase of an icon of the Virgin Paraklesis in Sinai, where traces of encaustic work have been noted on the Virgin's face, hands and scroll.[8]

A kanon on the Mother of God by Theodore of Stoudios[9] and two epigrams in a southern Italian codex of c. 900[10] testify to the existence of the type and to the form of the Virgin's dialogue with Christ at a time when no pictorial evidence seems to exist. In art the type is again found fairly frequently in icons and murals of the Komnenian era, and from around the end of the twelfth century and during the Palaiologan era the Virgin Paraklesis variant was crystallized and remained a constant feature of the iconography of the eastern pillars or pilasters of the templon.[11]

In connection with the representation of the Virgin Paraklesis at Asinou I would emphasize the significance of the choice of an iconographic type, deeply rooted in Byzantine tradition, which is the prime expression of the communal supplication of the entire world for the salvation of mankind. This involvement of the whole of humanity is made clear in the conventional, recurrent inscription on the Virgin's scroll, which in most examples of the type calls for the salvation of mortals ('βροτῶν σωτηρίαν').

From early times, however, the type is also used in isolated cases for individual supplication. The mosaic portrait in the basilica of St Demetrios was, according to the inscription, dedicated by one person, even though the Virgin's scroll states 'that I pray for the world' (ὅτι ὑπὲρ τοῦ κόσμου δέομαι).[12] In the twelfth century this iconographic type was used for individual

---

[5] On the type, Der Nersessian, 'Two Images', 81 ff. M. Tatić-Djurić, 'Steatitska ikonica iz Kursumlije', *ZLU* 6 (1966), 76 ff. For a detailed analysis of the type and parallels, S. Kalopissi-Verti, 'The Wall Paintings of the Narthex', in A. W. Carr and A. Nicolaidès (eds), *The Church of Panagia Phorbiotissa and its Paintings* (forthcoming).

[6] G. and M. Soteriou, *Ἡ βασιλικὴ τοῦ Ἁγίου Δημητρίου Θεσσαλονίκης* (Athens, 1952), 195–6, Pl. 66. J.-M. Spieser, *Thessalonique et ses monuments du IVᵉ au VIᵉ siècle* (Paris, 1984), 165–214. I. Phountoules, 'Τὸ ψηφιδωτὸ τοῦ ναοῦ τοῦ Ἁγίου Δημητρίου Θεσσαλονίκης μὲ τὴν παράσταση τῆς Παναγίας καὶ τοῦ Ἁγίου Θεοδώρου. Προσπάθεια ἑορτολογικῆς ἑρμηνείας', in *Χριστιανικὴ Θεσσαλονίκη, Γ΄ Ἐπιστημονικὸ Συμπόσιο ἀπὸ τῆς Ἰουστινιανείου ἐποχῆς ἕως καὶ τῆς Μακεδονικῆς δυναστείας, 1989* (Thessaloniki, 1991), 177–84.

[7] J. Anderson, 'A Note on the Sanctuary Mosaics of St Demetrius, Thessalonike', *CahArch* 47 (1999), 55–65. See also recently G. Belenes, 'Ταυτίσεις προσώπων σὲ ψηφιδωτὰ τοῦ Ἁγίου Δημητρίου Θεσσαλονίκης', in *XXᵉ Congrès International des Études Byzantines, 19–25 août 2001, Pré-actes, III. Communications libres* (Paris, 2001), 308.

[8] K. Weitzmann, *The Monastery of Saint Catherine at Mount Sinai. The Icons, I. From the Sixth to the Tenth Century* (Princeton, NJ, 1976), 21–3, Pls VI, XLVII. Kitzinger questions the early dating (Kitzinger, *The Mosaics of St Mary's of the Admiral*, 203). Belting dates the icon to c. 1100 (H. Belting, *Bild und Kult. Eine Geschichte des Bildes vor dem Zeitalter der Kunst* (2nd edn, Munich, 1991), 271). The overpainting has been dated to the 13th c. (G. and M. Soteriou, *Εἰκόνες τῆς Μονῆς Σινᾶ* (Athens, 1956–1958), I, Fig. 173 and II, 160–1).

[9] S. Eustratiades, *Θεοτοκάριον* (Chennevières-sur-Marne, 1931), 84–7, no. 26. S. Salaville, 'Marie dans la liturgie byzantine ou gréco-slave', in D'Hubert du Manoir, *Maria*, I, 315–16.

[10] R. Browning, 'An Unpublished Corpus of Byzantine Poems', *Byz* 33 (1963), 296. M. Lauxtermann, *The Byzantine Epigram in the Ninth and Tenth Centuries* (Amsterdam, 1994), 33–5.

[11] Cf. Der Nersessian, 'Two Images', 82. On the subject see recently, I. M. Djordjević and M. Marković, 'On the Dialogue Relationship Between the Virgin and Christ in East Christian Art', *Zograf* 28 (2000/1), 13–48.

[12] Soteriou, *Ἡ βασιλικὴ τοῦ Ἁγίου Δημητρίου*, 195.

supplication by celebrated individuals, such as George of Antioch in the Martorana, Palermo (1143) and the Grand Duke Andrej Bogoljubski in a dedicatory icon (1158).[13]

The fact remains that in the vast majority of examples the Virgin Paraklesis is the prime representative of communal supplication, through which individual prayers may also be expressed. The type was chosen by the donors of the painted decoration of 1332–1333 depicted in the narthex at Asinou – monks and laymen, men and women, representatives of the 'common people', as the dedicators' inscription states[14] – to unite their prayers for their personal salvation.

In the semi-dome of the south apse of the narthex at Asinou, the Virgin is depicted enthroned between three supplicants in an ex-voto which has been dated *c.* 1300 (Plate 21 and Figs 25.3–25.4).[15] As clearly indicated by the garments of the dedicators, a young woman and her two sons kneeling to the right and left of the figure of the Virgin, this is an offering commissioned by westerners.

The Virgin belongs to an iconographic type not found in Byzantium, but known in the West as the *Madonna della Misericordia* or *Schutzmantelmadonna*.[16] She spreads out her mantle to her right to enfold the dedicatress in a protective gesture. The creation of this type in the thirteenth century and its dissemination in Italy has been linked with the religious orders who believed in the physical and spiritual protection offered by the Virgin's mantle. One of the earliest surviving examples in the West is the very well-known small Madonna of the Franciscans by Duccio, now in the Pinacoteca Nazionale in Siena, which is variously dated around 1280 and in the 1290s.[17]

Even before this Italian example, the iconographic type of the Virgin of Mercy is encountered in the art of the south-eastern Mediterranean. It is found in two Armenian manuscripts from Cilicia, the famous Gospels of Prince Vasak (Fig. 25.5) in the Armenian Patriarchate, Jerusalem (no. 2568, fol. 320), dated shortly after 1272, and in a miniature (Fig. 25.6) from the Gospel book of Marshal Ōshin (1274, New York, Pierpont Morgan Library, MSS. M. 740 and 1111).[18] The spread of the type in the east has been associated with the activity of western

---

[13] Kitzinger, *The Mosaics of St Mary's*, 197–206, 316–7, Pls XXII, XVIV, XXVI, Figs 119, 123–5, 170. Vloberg, 'Les types iconographiques', 439–42. I. Bentchev and E. Haustein-Bartsch, *Gottesmutterikonen* (Recklinghausen, 2000), 146–7. Cf. also the Iviron cod. 5 (13th c.): I. Spatharakis, *The Portrait in Byzantine Illuminated Manuscripts* (Leiden, 1976), 84–7, Figs 53–4.

[14] A. and J. Stylianou, 'Donors and Dedicatory Inscriptions, Supplicants and Supplications in the Painted Churches of Cyprus', *JÖBG* 9 (1960), 104–5. S. Kalopissi-Verti, 'Painters in Late Byzantine Society. The Evidence of Church Inscriptions', *CahArch* 42 (1994), 145.

[15] On the representation, cf. S. Hatfield Young, 'Byzantine Painting in Cyprus During the Early Lusignan Period', PhD thesis, Pennsylvania State University, 1983, 342–72. A. W. Carr, 'Correlative Spaces: Art, Identity and Appropriation in Lusignan Cyprus', *Modern Greek Studies Yearbook, University of Minnesota*, 14/15 (1998/9), 59–80. On popular ex-votos in 13th- and 14th-c. Italy, cf. M. Bacci, *'Pro remedio animae'. Immagini sacrae e pratiche devozionali in Italia centrale (secoli XIII e XIV)* (Pisa, 2000), 202–26.

[16] Ch. Belting-Ihm, *'Sub matris tutela'. Untersuchungen zur Vorgeschichte der Schutzmantelmadonna* (Heidelberg, 1976), with bibliography. Belting, *Bild und Kult*, 398–400.

[17] Fr. Deuchler, *Duccio* (Milan, 1984), 41, 208, Figs 42–3. A. Bagnoli *et al.* (eds), *Duccio. Alle origini della pittura senese*, exh. cat., Siena, S. Maria della Scala and Museo dell'Opera del Duomo (Milan, 2003), no. 24, 158–61. V. M. Schmidt, 'La "Madonna dei francescani" di Duccio: forma, contenuti, funzione', *Prospettiva* 97 (2000), 30–44, points to an even earlier example, the enamel decoration of a chalice in the Cistercian abbey of Mehrerau in Bregenz (3rd quarter of the 13th c.), ibid., 136, Fig. 11. I wish to thank A. W. Carr for pointing out this article to me.

[18] Formerly in the Feron–Stoclet collection, Brussels. S. Der Nersessian, 'Deux exemples arméniens de la Vierge

monastic orders in the Crusader east: for example a Franciscan monastery had been founded in Sis, the capital of Little Armenia, and the Armenian prince of Cilicia, Het'um II, had joined the Franciscan order before he came to the throne in 1289.[19] The same iconographic type of the Virgin of Mercy is also found in the famous late thirteenth-century icon from Cyprus, where the Virgin spreads out her maphorion protectively over a group of Carmelite monks (Fig. 25.7).[20] The wall painting in the south conch at Asinou has closest affiliations with this Cypriot icon and with the miniature of the Marshal Ōshin Gospels, since in those examples the Virgin is shown enthroned.

In Byzantium the idea of the protection for the faithful offered by the Virgin's maphorion[21] has been associated with the 'usual miracle' which was enacted each Friday evening in the church of the Blachernai monastery in Constantinople, as described by Michael Psellos in a homily of 1075:[22] 'For the Mother of God the sacred veil is ineffably raised so that She may embrace the entering crowd inside Her as in a new innermost sanctuary and inviolate refuge.' Psellos is admittedly referring to the peplos which covered the icon and not to the Virgin's maphorion itself, though Andrew the Fool, according to his tenth-century *Vita*, had seen in a vision the latter spread protectively over the faithful: '... her veil ... it was large and awe-inspiring .... (She) spread it over all the people standing there.'[23] Perhaps in the minds of the faithful there could have been confusion between the veil which covered the icon and the maphorion kept as a precious relic in the same monastery, and between the Virgin herself as described in Andrew's vision and her representation in the miraculous icon. The sources do not indicate in what type the Virgin was depicted in the 'veiled' icon and varying opinions can be found in the bibliography, but it is certain that apart from the representation in the apse, the Blachernai monastery would have contained more than one icon of the Virgin. The iconographic variants of the praying Virgin with raised hands – either without Christ (Orans) or with the Christ-child in a clipeus in front of her breast (Blachernitissa, Episkepsis) – in which the maphorion is depicted spread out behind the Virgin as she raises her arms are those which seem best to correspond to the written sources and pictorial testimony as well as the concept of the protective powers of the outspread maphorion.[24] The cult of the Virgin's maphorion and the

---

de Miséricorde', *REArm* 7 (1970), 187–202. Ead., *Miniature Painting in the Armenian Kingdom of Cilicia from the Twelfth to the Fourteenth Century* (*DOS*, XXXI) (Washington, DC, 1993), I, 158–9 and II, Pls 646–7. H. C. Evans (ed.), *Byzantium. Faith and Power (1261–1557)*, exh. cat., The Metropolitan Museum of Art (New Haven and London, 2004), no. 30, 60–1.

[19] Der Nersessian, 'Deux exemples', 196–7.

[20] A. Papageorghiou, *Icons of Cyprus* (Nicosia, 1992), 46–9, Fig. 31. D. Mouriki, 'Thirteenth-Century Icon Painting in Cyprus', *The Griffon*, n.s., 1/2 (1985/6), 42–7, Figs 49–50, 55. J. Folda, 'Crusader Art in the Kingdom of Cyprus, ca. 1275–1291: Reflections on the State of the Question', in N. Coureas and J. Riley-Smith (eds), *Cyprus and the Crusades* (Nicosia, 1995), 216–21, Pls 7–8. A. W. Carr, 'Art in the Court of the Lusignan Kings', ibid., 242.

[21] On the association of the two types, Belting-Ihm, '*Sub matris tutela*', 55 ff. and Belting, *Kult und Bild*, 399.

[22] Michael Psellos, Λόγος ἐπὶ τῷ ἐν Βλαχέρναις γεγονότι θαύματι, ed. E. Fischer, *Michaelis Pselli, Orationes hagiographicae* (Stuttgart and Leipzig, 1994), no. 4. On the 'usual miracle', see V. Grumel, 'Le "miracle habituel" de Notre Dame des Blachernes à Constantinople', *EO* 30 (1931), 129–46. Recently, E. Papaioannou, 'The "Usual Miracle" and an Unusual Image', *JÖB* 51 (2001), 177–88 with bibliography, from which the English translation is taken, 185.

[23] L. Rydén (ed.), *The Life of St Andrew the Fool* II (Uppsala, 1995), 254–5. Cf. Belting, *Kult und Bild*, 567.

[24] Belting-Ihm, '*Sub matris tutela*', 38–57. On the Blachernitissa, M. Tatić-Djurić, 'Vrata slova. Ka liku i značenju

idea of the protection of the faithful within it, as in Andrew's vision, was especially prevalent in Russia from the twelfth century onwards.[25]

In any case this iconographic type of the praying Virgin with or without Christ is not associated in Byzantium with the portrayal of specific donors. The abstract and symbolic nature of this type in Byzantine art and its regular location in the conch of the apse give to the portrayal an ecumenical dimension which relates to the whole congregation, exactly as described in the life of Andrew the Fool and the narrative of Psellos. At the same time, however, each individual believer, as a discrete member of the whole, receives the divine protection of the maphorion.

It should be noted that the praying Virgin with Christ on a clipeus in front of her breast and with the appellation Phorbiotissa is depicted in bust in the narthex at Asinou on the tympanum of the entrance door to the main church (Fig. 25.1). It formed part of the original decoration of the church as an external wall painting (1105–1106), and subsequently it was harmoniously incorporated into the later mural decoration of the narthex.

By contrast with the communality expressed by the Virgin in the two Byzantine types, the Paraklesis and the Orans (praying in frontal pose) and its variations, the Virgin of Mercy with the outspread maphorion – at least in the surviving examples in the Crusader East – has a private devotional character. It is used to ensure protection either for specific fraternities, such as the Carmelites in the Cypriot icon, or for families, as in the Armenian manuscripts or in Asinou, where the location of this dedicatory portrait in the semi-dome of the south apse of the narthex suggests that this small area was used as a kind of private chapel for personal devotion. This private character is also reflected in the other representations in the conch which were executed at different periods, such as the St George (second half of the twelfth century), a donation of Nikephoros, 'healer of horses' according to the inscription, and the St Anastasia Pharmakolytria, commissioned by a woman of the same name (end of the thirteenth century).[26]

More problematic perhaps is the presence of a dedicatory portrait of a Latin family, clearly western in iconography and style, in an Orthodox monastery whose decoration follows conventional iconographic and stylistic models of the Byzantine tradition. This suggests peaceful coexistence and mutual religious tolerance between the two main ethnic groups in Cyprus, the Orthodox Greek-Cypriot majority and the ruling Catholic Latin minority.

Asinou is not unique in this regard. The donation of a large icon by the knight Ravendel to the church of St Nicholas tes Steges at Kakopetria after the fall of Acre (1291)[27] and the depiction of Jean de Lusignan, brother of king Peter I, and his wife in the scene of the Incredulity of

---

Vlahernitise', *ZLU* 8 (1972), 61–88 and *ODB* 3, 2170–1 (N. P. Ševčenko). See also I. Tognazzi Zervou, 'L'iconografia e la "Vita" delle miracolose icone della Theotokos Brefokratoussa: Blachernitissa e Odighitria', *BollGrott* 40 (1986), 262–87. A. W. Carr, 'The Mother of God in Public', in Vassilaki, *Mother of God*, 327.

[25] On this subject, see Belting-Ihm, *Sub matris tutela*, 58–61. L. Rydén, 'The Vision of the Virgin at Blachernae and the Feast of Pokrov', *AnBoll* 94 (1976), 63–82. O. Etinhof, 'The Virgin of Vladimir and the Veneration of the Virgin of Blachernai in Russia', in M. Vassilaki (ed.), *Byzantine Icons. Art, Technique and Technology* (Herakleion, 2002), 63–73. J. Stuart, 'The Deposition of the Virgin's Sash and Robe, the Protection of the Mother of God (Pokrov) and the Blachernitissa', ibid., 75–84.

[26] Cf. Carr, 'Correlative Spaces', 59–80.

[27] Papageorghiou, *Icons of Cyprus*, 46–9, Fig. 32. Mouriki, 'Thirteenth-Century Icon Painting', 42–7, Fig. 48. Folda, 'Crusader Art in the Kingdom of Cyprus', 216–21, Pl. 6. Carr, 'Art in the Court of the Lusignan Kings', 242. N. Ševčenko, *The Life of Saint Nicholas in Byzantine Art* (Turin, 1983), 38, no. 14.

Thomas in the north aisle of the church of the Holy Cross in Pelendri[28] (third quarter of the fourteenth century) show that the Latins did not hesitate to make offerings to Orthodox churches. This is also confirmed by written sources referring to pecuniary donations made by Latins, and especially by the Lusignan court, to Orthodox religious establishments during the fourteenth century.[29]

The next representation of the Virgin on which I should like to comment is an icon (1.69 × 0.69 m) from the Phaneromeni collection in Nicosia (Fig. 25.8), which is currently exhibited in the Byzantine Museum of the Archbishop Makarios III Foundation. It has been variously dated to the late fourteenth–early fifteenth century and to the fifteenth century.[30]

The Virgin is depicted in the enthroned Brephokratousa type. She wears a blue speckled chiton and a purple maphorion with a reddish-gold border and a fringe on the left shoulder. The maphorion is embellished with two gold star-shaped rosettes on the forehead and the left shoulder. She is turned slightly to the left and holds Christ in her right arm while pointing to him with her left hand. Christ stands upright in the Virgin's arms wearing a red chiton with gold striations, and he raises his left hand to his mother's neck clutching the collar of her chiton, while extending his right in a gesture of blessing.

At the Virgin's feet are four figures. On the left the two supplicants, husband and wife, evidently with one of their daughters, kneel with hands raised in supplication. On the right is the barely visible figure of a young woman, portrayed frontally and on a larger scale, wearing a gold peplos and with a pearl necklace around her neck. The frontal pose, formal costume and size of her portrait indicate that this is the deceased daughter of the couple depicted on the left.

The icon has no extant inscriptions, but comparisons with other Cypriot funerary icons indicate that it must have been donated by a Greek-Cypriot Orthodox family. Icons with a similarly long, narrow shape and a frontal portrait of a dead person or persons dating from the second half of the fourteenth century can be found in the same museum in Nicosia; one has recently been studied by A. W. Carr.[31]

The choice of the Virgin and Child for a funerary composition is totally consistent with the funerary icons and wall paintings of the Middle and Late Byzantine eras, when ecclesiastical literature, hymnography and art treat the Virgin as the intercessory figure par excellence for the salvation of the soul.

---

[28] Stylianou, *Painted Churches*, 223–32. A. W. Carr, 'Byzantines and Italians on Cyprus: Images from Art', *DOP* 49 (1995), 347–8. Ead., 'Art in the Court of the Lusignan Kings', 245–6. I. Christoforaki, 'An Unusual Representation of the Incredulity from Lusignan Cyprus', *CahArch* 48 (2000), 71–87.

[29] The court contributed funds towards the foundation of the monastery of the Holy Cross Faneromenos at Lefkara, 1340–1350: G. Hill, *A History of Cyprus* III (Cambridge, 1948), 1077–8. Queen Eleanor of Aragon, wife of Peter I, gave economic support to the rebuilding of Kykkos monastery after its destruction by fire in 1365: C. N. Constantinides and R. Browning, *Dated Greek Manuscripts from Cyprus to the Year 1570* (Nicosia, 1993), 11 nn. 57–8, 203. On relations between the Latin and Orthodox church in Cyprus, cf. recently N. Coureas, *The Latin Church in Cyprus, 1195–1312* (Aldershot, 1997), 251–317.

[30] A. Papageorgiou, *Ikonen aus Zypern* (Munich, 1969), pl. on p. 39. A. W. Carr, 'A Palaiologan Funerary Icon from Gothic Cyprus', in Πρακτικά του Τρίτου Διεθνούς Κυπρολογικού Συνεδρίου, Λευκωσία, 16–20 Απριλίου 1996 II (Nicosia, 2001), 599–619.

[31] Papageorgiou, *Ikonen aus Zypern*, pl. on p. 38. Id., *Icons of Cyprus*, 62–3, Figs 39–41. A full analysis in Carr, 'A Palaiologan Funerary Icon', 599–619.

More unusual is the iconographic type of the Virgin with Christ upright in her arms, often with his legs astride. This type seems to have originated in Constantinople as a variant of the Glykophilousa. The earliest representation of which I am aware is found in the celebrated eleventh-century hexaptych in Sinai (Fig. 25.9), dedicated by the monk John.[32] The upper register shows four devotional icons of the Virgin from churches in Constantinople, of which the first on the left has the appellation Blachernitissa and portrays Christ upright in the arms of the Virgin who embraces him in the iconographic type known as the Glykophilousa.

Although, as the Sinai icon suggests, it reproduced one of the important devotional icons of the capital in the eleventh century, this type is not very common in Byzantium. It has been suggested that this variant was portrayed on certain lead seals of the Metropolitans of Athens in the second half of the twelfth–early thirteenth century, but the identification is not certain.[33] Christ appears depicted in an upright pose in a Glykophilousa icon in Episkopi, Mesa Gonia in Santorini (early thirteenth century).[34] The same iconographic type is found in a thirteenth-century marble relief icon built into a wall of St Mark's, Venice, with the appellation ἡ Ἀνίκητος (Invincible),[35] and in an icon of the second decade of the fourteenth century from Thessaloniki, now in the Museum of Byzantine Culture there.[36] The variant of the Glykophilousa with Christ upright in the Virgin's arms spread throughout the East; examples are an icon in the church of the Saviour in Adiš, Svaneti, Georgia[37] and another from the Tolga monastery near Yaroslav, dating from the last quarter of the thirteenth century and now in the Tretyakov Gallery, Moscow.[38]

This iconographic variant of the Glykophilousa,[39] with Christ upright in the Virgin's arms, reached the West as early as the twelfth century, as indicated by an Exultet scroll written and

---

[32] Soteriou, *Εικόνες της Μονής Σινά* I, Figs 146–9 and II, 125–8. Baltoyanni, 'The Mother of God in Portable Icons', 144, Pls 82, 87, 88. N. Trahoulia, 'The Truth in Painting: a Refutation of Heresy in a Sinai Icon', *JÖB* 52 (2002), 271–85. A. W. Carr, 'Icons and the Object of Pilgrimage in Middle Byzantine Constantinople', *DOP* 56 (2002), 77–81. Cf. A. Grabar, 'Les images de la Vierge de Tendresse. Type iconographique et thème', *Zograf* 6 (1975), 25–30, Fig. 3.

[33] V. Laurent, *Le Corpus des sceaux de l'Empire byzantin* V.1 (Paris, 1963), 450–3, nos 605, 607, Pl. 82. Cf. N. Chatzidakis, 'A Fourteenth-Century Icon of the Virgin Eleousa in the Byzantine Museum of Athens', in Ch. Moss and K. Kiefer (eds), *Byzantine East, Latin West. Art-Historical Studies in Honor of Kurt Weitzmann* (Princeton, NJ, 1995), 497. Vassilaki, *Mother of God*, no. 80, 478 (A. Tourta).

[34] M. Georgopoulou-Verra, *AD* 30 (1975), B2-*Chronika*, 336, Pl. 242. Mitsani, 'Βυζαντινή εικόνα', 193, Fig. 17. Ead., 'Παναγία η Δαμασκηνή: μία βυζαντινή εικόνα στην ιπποτοκρατούμενη πόλη της Ρόδου', in *Δεκαπέντε χρόνια έργων αποκατάστασης στη μεσαιωνική πόλη της Ρόδου*, Ρόδος 14–18 Νοεμβρίου 2001 (forthcoming).

[35] O. Demus, *The Church of San Marco in Venice* (DOS, VI) (Washington, DC, 1960), 121, 187–8, Fig. 35. R. Lange, *Die byzantinische Reliefikone* (Recklinghausen, 1964), no. 39, 109–10. A. Grabar, *Sculptures byzantines du Moyen Âge (XIIe–XIVe siècle)* II (Paris, 1976), no. 123, 123, Pl. XCIV. Belting, *Bild und Kult*, 224–6, Fig. 118.

[36] Chatzidakis, 'A Fourteenth-Century Icon', 495–8. Vassilaki, *Mother of God*, no. 80, 478–9 (A. Tourta).

[37] 12th c., according to N. Thierry, 'La Vierge de la Tendresse à l'époque macédonienne', *Zograf* 10 (1979), 69, Fig. 16, but more probably 13th c., in my opinion.

[38] V. Lazarev, *The Russian Icon* (Collegeville, 1997), no. 25, 367. O. E. Etinhof, *Obraz Bogomateri* (Moscow, 2000), 73–4, Fig. 40.

[39] On the iconographic type, see A. Grabar, 'Sur les origines et l'évolution du type iconographique de la Vierge Éléousa', in *Mélanges Charles Diehl* II (Paris, 1930), 29–42. V. Lazareff, 'Studies in the Iconography of the Virgin', *ArtB* 20 (1938), 26–65. M.-L. Concasty, 'Vierge Éléousa d'une Bible romane', in *Actes du XIIe Congrès International d'Études Byzantines, Ochride 1961* III (Belgrade, 1964), 31–4. M. Tatić-Djurić, 'Eleousa', *JÖB* 25 (1976), 259–67. G. Kühnel, *Wall Painting in the Latin Kingdom of Jerusalem* (Berlin, 1988), 20–1. M. Panayotidi,

illustrated in Fondi near Rome between 1100 and 1117 (Paris, Bibliothèque nationale, nouv. acq. lat. 710)[40] and the 'Lyon' Bible (Bibliothèque municipale, MS. 410, fol. 207v),[41] the work of a Latin painter probably based on a Byzantine icon, and dated *c*. 1180. At the same time it appears in mosaic form in the apse of S. Francesca Romana (S. Maria Nova) in Rome (second half of the twelfth century), with Christ held upright in the Virgin's arms, but without embracing her neck as in the Glykophilousa type, and with Christ's torso and head erect.[42]

This iconographic type was particularly widespread in Italy towards the end of the thirteenth and the first half of the fourteenth century, mainly in two regions – northern Italy (in particular Tuscany), in panels of exceptional quality, and Apulia, in more popular work. The most common Tuscan variant in the decade 1280–1290 shows Christ upright in his mother's arms or embracing her tenderly with his cheek pressed against hers, as in the Byzantine Glykophilousa type (a painting of 1285–1290 by Duccio in the Kunstmuseum, Berne)[43] or raising his hand in a childish gesture to touch her face and neck (the *Madonna di Varlungo* of 1280–1285 in the Metropolitan, New York[44] and the pala by Cimabue (*c.* 1280) in the church of the Servi, Bologna).[45] The type of the upright Christ in his mother's arms continues in northern Italian art during the fourteenth century, as in the *Maestà* by Filippo di Pace (1310) in the Musée du Petit Palais, Avignon,[46] in a picture of the Virgin with saints and donors by Bernardo Daddi (mid-fourteenth century) in the Museo Bigallo, Florence,[47] in a triptych in the Benaki Museum (inv. no. 3740),[48] etc.

However, the variant iconographically closest to the Cypriot icon can be found in the *Madonna Gualino* of 1280–1282 (Fig. 25.10), now in the Galleria Sabauda, Turin.[49] Here Christ is upright in the Virgin's arms, extending his left arm towards his mother's neck, while the Virgin supports the baby in her right arm and gestures towards him with her left, just as in the Cypriot icon.

Similar representations exist in Apulia in more primitive compositions, e.g. the crypt at Urgento (Glykophilousa type, late thirteenth–early fourteenth century) and the church of the Immaculate Virgin in Novoli, near Lecce (first half of the fourteenth century?) (Fig. 25.11).[50] They can also be found in areas which had direct contacts with Italy, such as Dalmatia (a

---

'Η εικόνα της Παναγίας Γλυκοφιλούσας στο μοναστήρι του Πετριτζού (Bačkovo) στη Βουλγαρία', in *Ευφρόσυνον. Αφιέρωμα στον Μανόλη Χατζηδάκη* II (Athens, 1992), 461–4. The above bibliography does not distinguish between the upright and sitting postures of Christ. On epithets accompanying the representations of the Virgin, G. Babić, 'Epiteti Bogorodice koju dete grli', *ZLU* 21 (1985), 261–75.

[40] Grabar, 'Sur les origines', 37. Lazareff, 'Studies in the Iconography of the Virgin', 41. Concasty, 'Vierge Éléousa', 33, Fig. 2. Kühnel, *Wall Painting in the Latin Kingdom*, 21, Fig. 12.

[41] Concasty, 'Vierge Éléousa', 31–2, 34, Fig. 1. Kühnel, *Wall Painting in the Latin Kingdom*, 20, Fig. 11.

[42] W. Oakeshott, *The Mosaics of Rome* (London, 1967), 252–4, Fig. 174. G. Matthiae, *Mosaici medievali delle chiese di Roma* (Roma, 1967), I, 315–21 and II, Pls 269, 271.

[43] Deuchler, *Duccio*, 208, Pls 40–1. Bagnoli *et al.*, *Duccio*, no. 27, 184–7.

[44] L. Marques, *La peinture du Duecento en Italie Centrale* (Paris, 1987), 195, Fig. 243.

[45] L. Coletti, *Die frühe italienische Malerei, I. Das 12. und 13. Jahrhundert – Giotto* (Vienna, 1941), Pl. 53. Marques, *La peinture du Duecento*, 194–5, Fig. 241. Bagnoli *et al.*, *Duccio*, 126, Fig. 20.

[46] Bacci, 'Pro remedio animae', no. 21, 461.

[47] P. Toesca, *Florentine Painting of the Trecento* (Florence and Paris, 1929), 47, Fig. 86.

[48] Unpublished.

[49] Coletti, *Die frühe italienische Malerei*, Pl. 52. Bagnoli *et al.*, *Duccio*, 126–7, Fig. 21. Deuchler, *Duccio*, 24, Fig. 22. Marques, *La peinture du Duecento*, 195–6, Fig. 242.

[50] A. Medea, *Gli affreschi delle cripte eremitiche Pugliesi* (Roma, 1939), 55, Fig. 87. Concasty, 'Vierge Éléousa', 33, Fig. 3. M. Falla Castelfranchi, *Pittura monumentale bizantina in Puglia* (Milan, 1991), Fig. 220.

thirteenth-century icon of the Glykophilousa type in Zadar).⁵¹ The same type of the Glykophilousa with Christ upright in his mother's arms is depicted in a thirteenth-century icon in St Catherine's monastery, Sinai, which is thought to show Italian influences.⁵²

I believe that, as with the *Madonna della Misericordia* at Asinou, it is late-thirteenth- century Tuscan models which the Cypriot icon follows since, as mentioned earlier, the Glykophilousa type predominated in Byzantium and the East generally, while in Italian works the type of the Virgin with Christ upright in her arms – either in the variant of the Glykophilousa (Christ embracing his mother's neck) or with Christ's head and torso erect – exist side by side.

By comparison with funerary representations of the later phase of the Byzantine empire,⁵³ the Virgin's gesture in the Cypriot icon is an unusual feature. In nearly all other such representations she extends her hand palm outwards to the deceased person depicted therein, while in the Cypriot icon from the Phaneromeni collection the Virgin gestures towards Christ with her hand, as in the Hodegetria type. Conversely, Christ's gesture of extending his arm in blessing to the dead person is often found in Byzantine funerary representations.

It seems therefore that, for a conventional mediaeval Cypriot funerary icon, an iconographic type was chosen which derives from the Byzantine tradition but was used in its Italian variant and enriched with secondary elements, such as the Virgin's speckled chiton, also of western European origin.⁵⁴ It was combined with the figures of the supplicants and the dead girl, who was depicted frontally in accordance with a tradition inspired by Latin funerary relief slabs, which have been found in large numbers in Cyprus⁵⁵ and other areas under Latin occupation.⁵⁶ This type with the deceased in frontal pose, normally with the arms crossed over the breast, was very common in painted works of a funerary nature among the native population of Latin-occupied areas of the Byzantine empire, such as Crete⁵⁷ and Rhodes.⁵⁸

We can thus draw the following conclusions from these Cypriot representations of the Virgin. In the narthex at Asinou, in the late thirteenth century and the first decades of the fourteenth,

---

51 I. Petricioli, 'Novootkrivena ikona Bogorodice u Zadru', *Zograf* 6 (1975), 11–13, Fig. 1.
52 Soteriou, Εικόνες της Μονής Σινά I, Fig. 201 and II, 182. Evans, *Byzantium. Faith and Power*, no. 209, 350.
53 On Byzantine funerary portraiture, see N. Thierry, 'Le portrait funéraire byzantin. Nouvelles données', in Ευφρόσυνον. Αφιέρωμα στον Μανόλη Χατζηδάκη II (Athens, 1992), 582–92. A. Semoglou, 'Contribution à l'étude du portrait funéraire dans le monde byzantin (14ᵉ–16ᵉ siècle)', *Zograf* 24 (1995), 5–11. T. Papamastorakis, 'Επιτύμβιες παραστάσεις κατά τη μέση και ύστερη βυζαντινή περίοδο', *DChAE* 19 (1996/7), 285–303. Id., 'Ioannes "Redolent of Perfume" and His Icon in the Mega Spelaion Monastery', *Zograf* 26 (1997), 65–73.
54 See, for instance, S. Francesca Romana (S. Maria Nova) (12th c.): Matthiae, *Mosaici*, Fig. 271. S. Maria in Trastevere (12th c.): Oakeshott, *The Mosaics*, Pl. XXV. Margarito d'Arezzo (2nd half of the 13th c.): Marques, *La peinture du Duecento*, Figs 113, 117. An icon in a private collection in Venice (14th c.): Belting, *Kult und Bild*, 398, Fig. 214.
55 T. J. Chamberlayne, *Lacrimae Nicossienses* (Paris, 1894), *passim*. F. A. Greenhill, *Incised Effigial Slabs* I–II (London, 1976), *passim*. Carr notes this connection, 'Byzantines and Italians on Cyprus', 341. Ead., 'A Palaiologan Funerary Icon', 603.
56 On Rhodes, G. Konstantinopoulos, Μουσεία της Ρόδου, Ι. Αρχαιολογικό Μουσείο (Athens, 1977). E. Kollias, *The City of Rhodes and the Palace of the Grand Master* (Athens, 1988), Fig. 66. A. M. Kasdagli, 'Τρεις ταφόπλακες της Ιπποτοκρατίας στη Ρόδο', *AD* 44/46 (1989/91), A-Meletai, 191–3, Pl. 77.
57 G. Gerola, *Monumenti Veneti nell'isola di Creta* II (Venice, 1908), 333, 335, nos 19, 32, 37, Pls 10.3–4, 11.2 and 12.2.
58 I. Bitha, 'Ενδυματολογικές μαρτυρίες στις τοιχογραφίες της μεσαιωνικής Ρόδου (14ᵒˢ αι.–1523)', in Ρόδος

two portrayals of the Virgin – one a Byzantine iconographic type which expresses communal supplication, and the other western and indicative of private devotion and entreaty – were placed side by side. The presence of these clearly contrasted iconographic and stylistic types in the same location reflects a community of varied ethnic traditions but also of mutual tolerance.

The slightly later fifteenth-century icon, which portrays the individualized supplication of a family for the salvation of the soul of their dead daughter and sister, unites features from western and Byzantine iconography to express the gradual assimilation of different traditions and the progressive osmosis of the ethnic groups resident and active in Cyprus. In art, as in language,[59] Byzantine and Frankish characteristics are brought together to create a special idiom which, though dominated by the Greek element, expresses the multi-ethnic, multi-cultural nature of late mediaeval Cyprus.

2400 χρόνια. Η πόλη της Ρόδου από την ίδρυσή της μέχρι την κατάληψη από τους Τούρκους (1523). Διεθνές Επιστημονικό συνέδριο, Ρόδος 1993, Πρακτικά II (Athens, 2000), 429–48, Figs 1, γ', θ'–ι', ιστ', Pls 169a, 170a, 171b and 173. I. Christoforaki, 'Χορηγικές μαρτυρίες στους ναούς της μεσαιωνικής Ρόδου (1204–1522)', ibid., 449–64.

[59] Cf. recently, A. Nikolaou-Konnari, 'Η γλώσσα στη Κύπρο κατά τη Φραγκοκρατία (1192–1489). Μέσο έκφρασης φαινομένων αλληλεπίδρασης και καθορισμού εθνικής ταυτότητας', *Βυζαντιακά* 15 (1995), 347–87.

25.1   Asinou, church of the Virgin Phorbiotissa.
Narthex, east wall (source: author)

25.2   Asinou, church of
the Virgin Phorbiotissa.
The Virgin Eleousa,
in the Paraklesis type
(source: author)

25.3 Asinou, church of the Virgin Phorbiotissa. Narthex, south conch (source: author)

25.4 Asinou, church of the Virgin Phorbiotissa. The Virgin of Mercy with donors (source: author)

REPRESENTATIONS OF THE VIRGIN IN LUSIGNAN CYPRUS 317

25.5 Jerusalem, Armenian Patriarchate, MS. 2568, fol. 320. The Virgin of Mercy praying for Prince Vasak and his sons (source: Der Nersessian, *Miniature Painting in the Armenian Kingdom of Cilicia*, Fig. 647)

25.6 New York, Pierpont Morgan Library, MS. M. 1111. The Virgin of Mercy with Marshal Ōshin and his sons (source: Der Nersessian, *Miniature Painting in the Armenian Kingdom of Cilicia*, Fig. 646)

25.7 Nicosia, Byzantine Museum, Archbishop Makarios III Foundation. Icon of the enthroned Virgin with a group of Carmelite monks (source: Papageorgiou, *Ikonen aus Zypern*, fig. on p. 34)

25.8 Nicosia, Byzantine Museum, Archbishop Makarios III Foundation. Icon of the enthroned Virgin with a family of donors and a dead girl (source: Papageorgiou, *Ikonen aus Zypern*, fig. on p. 39)

25.9 Mt Sinai, Monastery of St Catherine. Hexaptych; the Virgin Blachernitissa (detail) (source: Vassilaki, *Mother of God*, Fig. 88)

25.10 Turin, Galleria Sabauda. The Virgin and Child, known as 'Madonna Gualino' (source: Deuchler, *Duccio*, Fig. 22)

25.11 Novoli, church of the Virgin Immacolata. The Virgin and Child (source: Falla Castelfranchi, *Pittura monumentale bizantina in Puglia*, Fig. 220)

The legacy of the Hodegetria:
holy icons and legends between east and west*

Michele Bacci

The 'Mother of God' exhibition at the Benaki Museum included an entire section devoted to an exceptionally famous image, the Hodegetria of Constantinople, whose cult developments were excellently outlined in the catalogue by Christine Angelidi and Titos Papamastorakis.[1] Here, as a kind of gloss to their work, I should like to draw the reader's attention to some circumstantial evidence of the renown of that miracle-working icon in other parts of the Mediterranean world, in order to stress its striking adaptability to differing historical and geographical contexts. A photograph taken near a shrine devoted to *sa Itria* (the corrupt southern Italian version of Hodegetria) in the hills near Gavoi in inland Sardinia well illustrates this point (Fig. 26.1). This remote place, whose village festival is held yearly in July with extended feasting and drinking, does not house any ancient image; devotional practices consist exclusively of participation in fairs and public rituals and seem haunted by persistent echoes of an ancient past, as indicated by the proximity of the church building to a prehistoric menhir entitled 'Our Lady of the Good Path' (*Nostra Signora del Buon Cammino*), a rough translation of 'Hodegetria' (Fig. 26.2).[2] So the question is: how should we interpret the curious relationship between this genuine folkloric manifestation and its noble Constantinopolitan ancestor, the most holy Hodegetria?

As scholars have pointed out, the icon housed in the Hodegon monastery underwent several functional transformations between the ninth century, when the church was founded, and 1453, when the panel was destroyed by Mehmet II's janizaries. Originally rooted in the public worship of certain healing springs and waters, the cult centred around a painted image, which

---

* I should like to thank Father Stylianos of Machairas Monastery, Cyprus; Father Francesco Trolese of the Library of S. Giustina, Padua; and Prof. Giovanni Vitolo, Naples, for their helpful suggestions.
[1] Chr. Angelidi and T. Papamastorakis, 'The Veneration of the Virgin Hodegetria and the Hodegon Monastery', in Vassilaki, *Mother of God*, 373–85. Several studies have been devoted to the cult of the Hodegetria in recent years: see esp. I. Zervou Tognazzi, 'L'iconografia e la "Vita" delle miracolose icone della Theotokos Brefokratoussa e Odighitria', *BollGrott* 40 (1986), 215–87. Angelidi, 'Un texte patriographique', 113–49. G. Babić, 'Les images byzantines et leur degrés de signification: l'exemple de l'Hodegetria', in J. Durand (ed.), *Byzance et les images* (Paris, 1994), 189–222. N. P. Ševčenko, 'Servants of the Holy Icon', in C. Moss and K. Kiefer (eds), *Byzantine East, Latin West. Art-Historical Studies in Honor of Kurt Weitzmann* (Princeton, NJ, 1995), 547–53. M. Tatić-Djurić, 'L'icône de l'Odigitria au XVIᵉ siècle', ibid., 557–68. M. Bacci, *Il pennello dell'Evangelista. Storia delle immagini sacre attribuite a san Luca* (Pisa, 1998), 114–29. B. Zeitler, 'Cults Disrupted and Memories Recaptured: Events in the Life of the Icon of the Virgin Hodegetria in Constantinople', in *Memory and Oblivion. Proceedings of the XXIXth International Congress of the History of Art, held in Amsterdam, 1–7 September 1996* (Amsterdam, 1999), 701–8. See also the paper by Ch. Angelidi and T. Papamastorakis in the present volume, 209–223.
[2] M. Pittau, *La Sardegna nuragica* (Sassari, 1977), 195–6, Fig. 66. On Sardinian cults of the Itria, see F. Cherchi Paba, *La Chiesa Greca in Sardegna. Cenni storici – culti – tradizioni* (Cagliari, 1962), 79. L. Neccia, 'Il convento agostiniano di N. Signora d'Itria in Illorai', *Analecta augustiniana* 61 (1998), 151–70. For local legends, see also A. Piras and A. Sanna, *Il culto della Vergine d'Itria a Villamar, dall'Oriente ai paesi di Sardegna* (Cagliari, 2001).

was gradually invested with new roles and meanings until it eventually became interpreted as the true *palladium* of Constantinople and of the Empire itself. The climax of this metamorphosis was the claim of authorship by the evangelist Luke, and the perception of the image as a true-to-life portrait of the Virgin Mary, venerated in her city shrine since the time of Empress Pulcheria, who received it as a gift from Eudokia after its fortuitous discovery in Antioch.

This reference to Antioch, St Luke's homeland, as the place of origin of the holy icon was most likely suggested by the monastery's close institutional relationship with that city; in fact, since the time of John Tzimiskes, the Hodegon buildings belonged to the jurisdiction of the Antiochene Patriarchate, and in the twelfth century were the actual see of the exiled Patriarch.[3] In a curious text whose inner core dates from *c.* 1422,[4] the monk Gregory of Kykkos places emphasis on this ownership: according to him, during the iconoclast controversies the Patriarch of Constantinople persuaded the Hodegon hegoumenos to commit the holy icon to the waves, which carried it to the Syrian shore near Antioch. Forewarned by an angel, the Patriarch, followed by the entire population, came to the beach, where the icon jumped out of the water straight into the prelate's arms. In this way, sheltered in the town cathedral, the Hodegetria escaped destruction at the hands of the iconoclasts; but after the final restitution of icons, when the Constantinopolitans demanded back their *palladium*, the whole of Antioch gave a firm refusal. Quarrels ensued, which were resolved only by means of a compromise: it was decided that the entire Hodegon monastery and all its properties and revenues should be ceded to the Patriarch of Antioch.

It is likely that such stories represent, in a kind of mythic form, real dissensions between the two Patriarchates over the possession of the precious image.[5] Another late legend brings on to the scene the disagreement between the Antiochene church and the emperors, who in Palaiologan times wanted to appropriate the cult of the Hodegetria for themselves: according to this version, it was Pulcheria herself who, wishing to recover her wicked husband Marcian, sailed to Antioch and stole the image from the wise people of that town by a trick.[6] The relationship between the monastery and the Antiochene Patriarchate was so close as to justify of itself the attribution of the Hodegetria to St Luke, one of Antioch's most illustrious citizens. In the documents available to us, however, there is no evidence for the growth of an autonomous cult of the

---

[3] K. G. Pitsakis, 'Η έκταση της εξουσίας ενός υπερορίου πατριάρχη. Ο πατριάρχης Αντιοχείας στην Κωνσταντινούπολη τον 12ο αιώνα', in N. Oikonomides (ed.), *Byzantium in the 12th century. Canon Law, State and Society* (Athens, 1991), 119–33. O. Kresten, *Die Beziehungen zwischen den Patriarchaten von Konstantinopel und Antiocheia unter Kallistos I. und Philotheos Kokkinos im Spiegel des Patriarchatsregisters von Konstantinopel* (Stuttgart, 2000), 379–82.

[4] The text is known from two 18th-century copies preserved in the library of the Phaneromeni church in Nicosia, Cyprus, and the Patriarchal Library in Alexandria, Egypt, as well as from an 18th-century edition by Ephraim of Athens: cf. K. Spyridakis, 'Η περιγραφή της μονής Κύκκου επί τη βάσει ανεκδότου χειρογράφου', *KyprSp* 13 (1949), 1–29, and K. Chatzipsaltis, 'Το ανέκδοτο κείμενο του αλεξανδρινού κώδικος 176 (366). Παραδόσεις και ιστορία της μονής Κύκκου', *KyprSp* 14 (1950), 39–69. For the dating to 1422, based on internal evidence provided by the text, see ibid., 45–6. See also the most recent publication, K. N. Konstantinidis, *Η Διήγησις της θαυματουργής εικόνας της Θεοτόκου Ελεούσας του Κύκκου κατά τον Ελληνικό κώδικα 2313 του Βατικανού* (Nicosia, 2002).

[5] Spyridakis, 'Η περιγραφή', 18–20. Chatzipsaltis, 'Το ανέκδοτο', 54–6.

[6] S. Lambros, 'Τρεις παραδοξογραφικαί διηγήσεις περί Πελοποννήσου, Πουλχερίας, και Θεοδοσίου του Μικρού', *NE* 4 (1907), 129–51, esp. 138–9.

Hodegetria in that city, although we know that a miracle-working icon was venerated within its cathedral in Frankish times.[7]

There can be no doubt that by the twelfth and thirteenth centuries the fame of the Constantinopolitan *palladium* was already widespread outside the capital: not only were several replicas of the icon reproduced in the decoration of churches and on painted panels, but also the rituals and the cultic life associated with it began to be imitated. The case of Thessaloniki is obviously of particular interest. In the second city of the Empire, where several liturgical practices of the capital were reproduced in the twelfth century, an icon of the Virgin entitled the Hodegetria was housed in an annexe of the great church of St Sophia. It was brought to the metropolis daily for both the morning and evening offices and was exhibited to the west of the ambo; like its archetype in Constantinople it was involved in a solemn procession on Tuesdays and was credited with oracular properties.[8] During the terrible Norman siege in 1185, the Hodegetria showed itself unwilling to return to its chapel after the procession, using supernatural power to ward off the bearers: this was unquestionably an ill omen, as the citizens were forced to admit some days later when the city was pillaged.[9] More than a mere cultic phenomenon, the Thessalonikan Hodegetria imitated the political role of its archetype: it was a *palladium* of the city and a collective symbol for all the citizens, especially on the eve of great calamities.

Another identical copy of the Hodegetria was described at about the same time (*c.* 1177) by the Greek pilgrim John Phokas in his account of the monastery of St Mary of Kalamon on the river Jordan. According to him, on the right side of the katholikon was

> a tiny vaulted church, erected in the times of the Apostles (as it is said), where in the apse is painted an image of the Theotokos holding Christ the Saviour in Her arms; it displays the figure, colour and size of the most holy icon of the Hodegetria in the capital. It is said by ancient traditions that this one was painted by the hand of the Apostle and Evangelist Luke: the frequent miracles and the awe-inspiring scent coming out of the icon persuade one to believe such a renown …[10]

How should we interpret such a passage? The pilgrim simply remarks that an image of the Virgin and Child adorned a church dating back to apostolic times: its striking likeness to the

---

[7] Cf. Wilbrand of Oldenburg, *Journey to the Holy Land (1211–1212)*, I.14, ed. S. de Sandoli, *Itinera Hierosolymitana crucesignatorum (saec. XII–XIII)* III (Jerusalem, 1979–1984), 215.

[8] J. Darrouzès, 'Sainte-Sophie de Thessalonique d'après un rituel', *REB* 14 (1976), 45–78, esp. 59. D. I. Pallas, 'Le ciborium hexagonal de Saint-Démétrios de Thessalonique. Essai d'interprétation', *Zograf* 10 (1979), 44–58, esp. 50–1.

[9] Eustathius of Thessaloniki, Συγγραφὴ τῆς κατ' αὐτὴν ἁλώσεως, ed. S. Kyriakides (Palermo, 1961), 142.

[10] John Phokas, *Description of the Holy Land*, PG 133, 953: 'Ἀλλὰ καὶ ἡ τοῦ Καλαμῶνος μονή, καὶ αὕτη ὑπὸ πύργων καὶ κορτίνων, ἀπὸ τετραγώνου λαξευτοῦ λίθου ἀνωκοδόμηται, καὶ ὁ ναὸς μέσον αὐτῆς ἐγχώρηγος τρουλλωτὸς ἵδρυται ἐν κυλινδρωτοῖς θόλοις ἐπικαθήμενος. Τούτου συνέζευκται ἐν τῷ δεξιῷ μέρει ναὸς ἕτερος θολωτὸς πάνυ σμικρώτατος, ἐν τοῖς χρόνοις, ὡς λέγεται, τῶν Ἀποστόλων ἀνεργερθείς, ἐν ᾧ ἐν τῷ μύακι εἰκὼν τῆς Θεοτόκου ἱστόρηται, ἐν ἀγκάλαις φερούσης τὸν Σωτῆρα Χριστόν, τὸ σχῆμα, καὶ τὸ χρῶμα, καὶ τὸ μῆκος ἐμφαίνουσα τῆς ἐν τῇ Βασιλευούσῃ Ὁδηγητρίας ὑπεραγίας εἰκόνος. Λέγεται δὲ ἐκ παλαιῶν παραδόσεων, ὡς ἱστόρηται αὕτη χειρὶ τοῦ ἀποστόλου καὶ εὐαγγελιστοῦ Λουκᾶ. Καὶ πιστεύεται τὴν φήμην πείθουσι τά τε συχνὰ θαύματα, καὶ ἡ φρικωδεστάτη ἐκ τῆς εἰκόνος ἐξερχομένη εὐωδία […]'. The Russian pilgrim Daniel of Kiev had already remarked in 1108–1111 that 'up to the present day, the Holy Ghost descends to an image of the Blessed Virgin': see text in B. de Khitrowo, *Itinéraires russes en Orient* (2nd edn, Paris, 1966), 31. Cf. A. Külzer, *Peregrinatio graeca in Terram Sanctam. Studien zu Pilgerführen und Reisebeschreibungen über Syrien, Palästina und den Sinai aus byzantinischer und metabyzantinischer Zeit* (Frankfurt am

Hodegetria, that is to say to the oldest and most true-to-life portrait painted by St Luke, indicated that it was a very ancient painting, probably as ancient as its architectural surroundings. It was of course to be expected that a meticulous copy made in the Evangelist's lifetime would best convey the miracle-working powers of the archetype, and we know that at least one other icon was venerated by Palestinian Christians as a replica of Constantinople's patroness: as we learn from an *Act* issued by Pope Honorius III in 1226, an icon called the *Deitria*, which the Venetians had illicitly appropriated, was worshipped in the basilica of Bethlehem.[11]

Although it is known that correspondence between the epithet and the iconographic theme was not universally followed – as we see in the case of the Agitria church in the Mani, where an image of the Virgin and Child in a medallion is labelled as the 'Hodegetria'[12] – the Constantinopolitan *palladium* was certainly the Byzantine icon which could boast the greatest number of meticulous copies. One of these was the image venerated in the monastery of S. Maria del Patir near Rossano in Calabria, founded by the Italo-Greek monk Bartholomew of Simeri (c. 1050–1130). As one of the most important religious establishments in Byzantine Italy, the monastery church was endowed with *vasa sacra*, icons and other adornments by Emperor Alexios Komnenos (the blessed Bartholomew himself went to Constantinople in order to obtain these gifts);[13] a document dated 1103 refers to it as the Rossano *Odigitria*, an appellation which was already pronounced *Neodigitria*, i.e. the 'New Hodegetria', eight years later, in 1111.[14] It was probably in this way that the Greek monks managed to introduce an already famous cultic manifestation from the capital to Calabrian believers in Rossano – where a famous twelfth-century preacher, Philagathos of Cerami, praised the most holy icon painted by St Luke and preserved in the 'Great Town'.[15]

The titular icon of the *Neodigitria* church was an exact copy of its archetype. Unfortunately this image has been lost, but we can obtain an idea of it by looking at the seal of a hegoumenos – the so-called 'St Nilus' ring' – dating from the twelfth century, which displays a Virgin *aristerokratousa*.[16] Indeed, we are even more fortunate, since an actual reproduction of the Rossano icon is displayed on a votive panel, now housed in the local museum, which was painted in the fifteenth century for Athanasios Chalkeopoulos, an Italo-Greek archimandrite and later bishop of Gerace in Calabria, who died in 1497 (Figs 26.3–26.4).[17] Although its style is reminiscent of the Italian Renaissance, its iconography and composition with a Crucifixion

---

Main, 1994), 170. D. Pringle, *The Churches of the Crusader Kingdom of Jerusalem. A Corpus* II (Cambridge, 1993–1998), 197–201.

[11] *Acta Honorii III et Gregorii IX*, ed. A. L. Tàutu (*Pontificia Commissio ad Redigendum Codicem Iuris Canonici Orientalis. Fontes, Series* III) (Rome, 1950), III, 187–8. I should like to thank my wife Barbara Ciampi, who first drew my attention to this important document.

[12] N. V. Drandakis, Βυζαντινές εκκλησίες της Μέσα Μάνης (Athens, 1995), 238, Fig. 13 and Pl. 54; an image of the Glykophilousa in the narthex bears the same epithet (ibid., 252, Fig. 30).

[13] G. Zaccagni, 'Il Βίος di san Bartolomeo da Simeri (*BHG* 235)', *RSBN* 33 (1996), 193–274, esp. 222–3.

[14] See P. Batiffol, *L'abbaye de Rossano. Contribution à l'histoire de la Vaticane* (Paris, 1891), 6–7. W. Holtzmann, 'Die älteste Urkunden des Klosters S. Maria del Patir', *BZ* 26 (1926), 238–330.

[15] Philagathus of Cerami, *Homilies*, 20, *PG* 132, 440.

[16] M. P. di Dario Guida, *Icone di Calabria e altre icone meridionali* (Soveria Mannelli, 1992), 36, Fig. 12.

[17] Ibid., 166–7, Figs 100–1. The image of the Virgin and Child is labelled as ἡ Νέα Ὁδηγήτρια; an inscription on the lower edge reads: Ἀθανάσιος Φιλίππου Χαλκεόπουλος ἀρχιμανδρίτης τῇ μητρὶ τοῦ Θεοῦ σωτηρίας τῶν προσερχομένων χάριν'. On Chalkeopoulos see M. Laurent and A. Guillou, *Le 'Liber Visitationis' d'Athanase Chalkéopoulos (1457–1458). Contribution à l'histoire du monachisme grec en Italie méridionale* (Vatican City, 1960).

on the reverse reproduce the features of the earlier icon and can even be regarded as indirect evidence for the appearance of the archetype. This association of the Virgin and Child with an image of Christ's sacrifice, so widespread in Middle Byzantine piety and religious art, was also to be noted in the icon of the Hodegon monastery. A late eyewitness, the often-quoted Catalan traveller Pero Tafur, who was in Constantinople in 1437, wrote that

> there [i.e. in the Hodegon monastery] is an image of Our Lady the Virgin Mary, made by St Luke, and on the opposite side is Our Lord Crucified, painted on stone and bearing a silver revetment on the borders and the background.[18]

The icon was large enough to be carried by a man with outstretched arms and was also fairly heavy – this is the explanation, in my opinion, for the term *losa*, 'stone', which is employed elsewhere by Tafur to describe another large holy icon, that of the Saviour in the Roman sancta sanctorum.[19] As it was involved in a weekly procession through the city streets, the image anyway needed to be a two-sided one. Further evidence is provided by the Cypriot monk Gregory's *Description of the Kykkos monastery*: according to him, St Luke, inspired by the archangel Gabriel,

> painted the purest image of the Hodegetria, and Christ Crucified on the opposite side of the icon, as well as, on both sides, Gabriel and Michael censing Jesus.[20]

Gabriel, who had also provided Luke with a panel 'not cut by human hands' (ἀχειρότμητος), had explicitly asked to be represented in the image; such a request can be explained as a corollary of the frequent inclusion of angels in the iconographic type of the Hodegetria in the Middle and Late Byzantine era, exactly as with the Crucifixion scene.

Elsewhere in Italy the imitation of the Constantinopolitan icon and its ritual life seems to have occurred at an early date. It was natural to expect that even after the end of imperial domination in 1071, Apulia would be greatly affected by Byzantine devotional practices: processions involving a Marian icon are recorded in Otranto as early as the eleventh century,[21] and we find a sculpted copy of the Hodegetria, commissioned by the local *turmarches* Delterios in the 1030s or 1040s, inside a church in Trani.[22] In that town the cathedral was dedicated to both the Virgin Mary and St Nicholas the Pilgrim, a monk from Hosios Loukas who died there in the eleventh century, and whose public cult was in competition with that of Nicholas of Myra in Bari; since we know that this saint's icon has long been displayed in the crypt, we can assume that this could also have been the location for a titular image of the Theotokos, who was

---

[18] Pero Tafur, *Andanças é viajes por diversas partes del mundo avidos*, tr. and ed. G. Bellini (Rome, 1986), 174–5.
[19] Ibid., 29.
[20] Spyridakis, 'Ἡ περιγραφή', 16; Chatzipsaltis, 'Τὸ ἀνέκδοτο', 51–2: 'καὶ ἱστόρησε δὲ τὴν ἄχραντον εἰκόνα τῆς Ὁδηγητρίας, ὄπισθεν δὲ τῆς εἰκόνος τὸν Ἰησοῦν ἐσταυρωμένον, ἔνθεν [δὲ] καὶ ἔνθεν τὸν Γαβριὴλ καὶ Μιχαὴλ θυμιάζοντας τὸν Ἰησοῦν'.
[21] *De vita S. Nicolai in Graecia*, III.19, ed. *AASS*, Iunii, I.237–43, esp. 241: 'Erat autem consuetudo civibus Hydruntinis Virginis gloriosae imaginem, cum processione psalmis et hymnis, de ecclesia in ecclesiam transportare, pro peccatis ipsorum et omnium indulgentiam postulantes'.
[22] P. Belli d'Elia (ed.), *Alle sorgenti del Romanico. Puglia XI secolo*, exh. cat. (Bari, 1975), no. 84, 71. R. Lange, *Die byzantinische Reliefikone* (Recklinghausen, 1964), no. 10, 56. The inscription reads: 'Κ(ύρι)ε βοΐθη τὸν δοῦλο(ν) σου Δελτέριον το(υ)ρμάρχη'.

Nicholas' pendant in the bishop's seals from the late twelfth century.²³ Indications of a deep-rooted veneration of the Hodegetria in Trani are provided by its reproduction on Barisano of Trani's twelfth-century bronze doors and on a thirteenth-century panel from the church of San Giovanni della Penna; moreover, a fifteenth-century pilgrim's account informs us of the veneration in the town cathedral of an autograph work by the evangelist Luke and adds:

> In fact St Luke painted thirteen images of Our Lady, each one of which can be called a *decatria*, being one of thirteen. We have seen many of these here and there in various places.²⁴

In my opinion²⁵ this passage records a popular etymology of the term Hodegetria, spelled *decàtria* with aphaeresis of the initial 'O': we should bear in mind that in the dialect of the Italo-Greek communities in the Salento area (the so-called *griko*), as in native Greek, *decatría* – with accented iota – is the neuter form of the cardinal number thirteen (*decatrì*), which cannot be other than plural.²⁶

Southern Italy was a cross-cultural area, and it is only natural that it should be one of the main gateways for the introduction of the Hodegetria cult into the West. Other vehicles were the accounts of travellers to Constantinople, translations of Byzantine religious literature (such as those by John of Amalfi in the eleventh century²⁷), and especially the collections of Marian miracles, which were widely circulated throughout Europe in the twelfth and thirteenth centuries. Here the Hodegetria, often confused with the icon of the Blachernai church, was mainly celebrated as the patron of Constantinople during a terrible siege by the 'Saracens'; the story naturally drew on the narration in the final strophes of the Akathistos Hymn (referring to the Avar–Persian attack in 626), and that of the August *Menaia* concerning the Arab raid in 717. A thirteenth-century Norwegian poem, the *Maríu Saga*, related that the Virgin *Odiguria* had rescued the city at the time of the *keisar* Leo, i.e. Leo III the Isaurian.²⁸ Vincent of Beauvais, writing his *Speculum historiale* in the same century, added further details, such as the location of the monastery 'close to the Palace, next to the sea', St Luke's authorship, and the custom of performing weekly processions on Tuesdays, as well as a correct etymology of the term Odigitria as 'deductrix', i.e. 'guide', because of the miracle of the two blind men. On the occasion of the Arab siege, the Constantinopolitans, acting as if in a northern European ritual of *humiliatio sanctorum*, threatened the Virgin Mary that they would throw her image into the sea

---

²³ Cf. M. Falla Castelfranchi, 'Riflessioni su una mostra: *Icone di Puglia e Basilicata dal Medioevo al Settecento*, Bari, Pinacoteca Provinciale, 9 ottobre 1988 – 7 gennaio 1989', *Arte Medievale* 2 (1991), 203–7. Generally on icon veneration in 11th- to 13th-c. Apulia, cf. P. Belli d'Elia, 'Fra tradizione e rinnovamento. Le icone dall'XI al XIV secolo', in *Icone di Puglia e Basilicata dal Medioevo al Settecento*, exh. cat., Bari, Pinacoteca Provinciale, 9 October 1988 – 7 January 1989 (Milan, 1988), 19–30. Id., 'L'icona nella cattedrale tra XI e XIII secolo: ipotesi a confronto nel contesto pugliese', in N. Bux (ed.), *L'Odegitria della cattedrale. Storia, arte, culto* (Bari, 1995), 11–23.
²⁴ J. Heers and G. de Groër (eds), *Itinéraire d'Anselme Adorno en Terre Sainte* (Paris, 1978), 394: '[...] Sanctus enim Lucas tredecim ymagines Nostre Domine pinxit, quarum unaqueque quasi una ex tredecim decatria appellari potest. De hiis multas hinc inde diversis in locis vidimus.'
²⁵ Bacci, *Il pennello*, 286–7.
²⁶ M. Cassoni, *Vocabolario griko-italiano*, ed. S. Sicuro and G. Schilardi (Lecce, 1999), 157.
²⁷ John of Amalfi, *Liber de miraculis* (Heidelberg, 1913).
²⁸ C. R. Unger, *Maríu Saga. Legender om jomfru Maria og hendes Jertegn* (Christiania, 1871), 1033–4.

if she would not consent to drive away their enemies; and when they began to dip the Hodegetria into the water, the entire navy was destroyed.[29]

Nourished by the *contaminatio* of various Byzantine legends, the cult of Constantinople's *palladium* developed in late mediaeval Italy. According to the seventeenth-century historian Giuseppe Richa, the dedication of a Florentine church to *Santa Maria Edigitria* or *Odigitria* was evidenced by now lost twelfth-century archive documents.[30] In Naples, an ancient chapel overlooking the entrance to the poet Virgil's tomb – which was to become the famous church of the *Madonna di Piedigrotta* – is recorded as *Santa Maria dell'Itria* in certain documents of the 1310s and 1320s, and there are some grounds for supposing that this originated when people began worshipping a copy of the Constantinopolitan icon there.[31] In southern Italian dialects, *Itria* is the standard abbreviated form of *Hodegetria*; in the very same years (1308–1310) this term is also evidenced in the name of a church in the neighbourhood of Catania (*Ecclesia Sancte Marie de Idria Eupli*).[32] In the second half of the fourteenth century, such dedications seem to have been increasingly popular in Sicily: a Benedictine monastery of the Itria in Sciacca was founded by Queen Eleanor of Aragon in 1370, and in the 1390s both a hospital and a chapel were dedicated to her in Palermo, the capital of the island.[33]

An even more interesting indication is provided by the so-called 'Constantinopolitan Madonna' of Padua, whose public veneration developed from the fourteenth century onwards.[34] The local Benedictine abbey of S. Giustina had boasted ownership of St Luke's relics since the twelfth century; gradually a thirteenth-century icon of the Virgin and Child exhibited near the Evangelist's tomb began to be venerated as a work by his hand (Fig. 26.5). A late legend claimed that the image had been transferred to Padua from the Constantinopolitan church of the Holy Apostles during the reign of Julian the Apostate or Leo the Isaurian; nonetheless a text dating from the early fourteenth century, the Abbey lectionary, now in Berlin, bears witness to an earlier stage of development which focused on the commemoration of the Byzantine Hodegetria itself. An odd story is included in the liturgical reading for the feast of St Luke on 18 October: the canonical text is expanded with a narration set in the time of Julian the Apostate, who is portrayed as a cruel iconoclast and leipsanoclast. One day – a Tuesday – the Emperor gave orders to burn all the icons in Constantinople, but one of them, representing the Mother of God, miraculously jumped out of the flames and ran away across the waves. The people of Constantinople were

---

[29] Vincent of Beauvais, *Speculum historiale* (Douai, 1624), 950.
[30] G. Richa, *Notizie istoriche delle chiese fiorentine divise ne' suoi Quartieri* VII (Florence, 1758), 319–20. The epithet was another title of the church of S. Maria in Capitolio.
[31] *Cronache de la Inclita Città di Napoli emendatissime. Con li Regni de Puzolo* (Naples, 1526), fol. 11r: '[Virgilio] fo portato in Napoli e fo sepelito in quello locho, dove se chiama sancta Maria dellitria, al presente Santa Maria de pedigrotta'. Cf. F. Lo Parco, 'Dell'antico titolo 'Dell'Itria o Idria' attribuito alla Madonna di Piedigrotta. Nuove indagini e deduzioni storico-filologiche', *Atti della Accademia Pontaniana* 53 (1923), 32–60. The custom of performing votive masses in honour of *Sancta Maria de ill'Itria* is evidenced by a testamentary bequest of the lady Sichelgaita Orimina dated 4 March 1316: see R. Bevere, 'Suffragi, espiazioni postume, riti e cerimonie funebri dei secoli XII, XIII e XIV nelle province napoletane', *Archivio Storico per le province napoletane* 21 (1896), 119–32, esp. 119.
[32] P. Sella (ed.), *Rationes Decimarum Italiae nei secoli XIII e XIV. Sicilia* (Vatican City, 1944), no. 945, 73.
[33] G. Bresc Bautier, *Artistes, patriciens et confréries. Production et consommation de l'oeuvre d'art à Palerme et en Sicile occidentale (1348–1460)* (Rome, 1979), 73–4.
[34] Cf. M. Bacci, 'La 'Madonna Costantinopolitana' nell'abbazia di Santa Giustina di Padova', in G. Mariani Canova (ed.), *Luca Evangelista. Parola e immagine tra Oriente e Occidente*, exh. cat. (Padua, 2000), 405–7.

astonished at seeing Julian's soldiers totally powerless to reach and strike it; then a pious woman, speaking as the *coryphaeus* of all the believers, promised that they would abstain from meat every Tuesday if God would rescue this holy *Dimitria*. This vow was immediately fulfilled: the icon jumped into the woman's arms and the miracle was subsequently celebrated in Constantinople and the whole of the Empire by means of a solemn procession on Tuesdays:

> That is why the Greeks do not eat meat on Tuesdays right up to today, and on Tuesdays they always carry that *Dimitria* through Constantinople with a procession and great rejoicing; in honour of holy Mary icons are carried everywhere in the Greek Empire, in towns, castles and villages.[35]

These words suggest a deep fascination with Byzantine devotional customs and a sound knowledge of the world of eastern Christianity; the allusion to minor centres imitating the weekly procession of the icon is of special interest, since there is good reason to suppose that the rituals of refugee communities from Turkish-occupied lands in the Balkans gave new life to the already extant cult of the Hodegetria, most often named *Madonna dell'Itria* or *Madonna di Costantinopoli*, in fifteenth- and sixteenth-century southern Italy. Some of these groups took with them their own *palladia* and set up 'national' shrines in their new homeland: refugees from mainland Albania, settling in a small village in Molise, Portocannone, in 1468, began to venerate there 'Our Lady of Constantinople', whose feast falls even today on the Tuesday after Pentecost;[36] refugees from Koroni in Messenia after its conquest by the Ottomans in 1533 took with them their icons of the Hodegetria; an Albano-Greek group took up residence in Barile, Calabria, and erected a shrine in honour of its own *Madonna di Costantinopoli*;[37] certain Greek notables arrived in Messina, where they collected around the church of S. Niccolò dei Greci and, as stated in a Latin inscription, placed in it a replica of the Hodegetria archetype in Constantinople, which was 'the only consolation' for that unfortunate people;[38] and finally,

---

[35] Berlin, Staatsbibliothek, Preußischer Kulturbesitz, MS. lat. fol. 480, fols 34v–35r (I include here the full text from the woman's prayer to the final remarks): 'Fortissime Deus spirituum universe carnis demitte hanc noxam nobis et, si voluntas tua est ut sacre picture remaneant in ecclesia iugiter, fac nos habere per tuam misericordiam hanc sanctam Dimitriam, ita quod omnia que hodie deleta sunt per nos restaurentur et insuper pro hoc delicto causa penitentie nunquam in die martis carnes comederemus. Cumque omnis populus clamasset: "Fiat, fiat!", statim cucurrit in brachio illius sancte mulieris et illa cum universo populo cum laudibus et hymnis et canticis et magno gaudio tulerunt eam in civitatem. Quapropter Greci non comedunt carnes in die martis usque hodie et, semper in die martis, portant illam Dimitriam cum processione et magno gaudio per Constantinopolim. Et pro reverentia sancte Marie per totum regnum Grecorum et per civitates et castella sive villulas portantur singule ancone.' Cf. the text edited by E. Necchi, 'Reliquie orientali e culto di martiri a Santa Giustina di Padova', *ItMedUm* 42 (2001), 91–118, esp. 112–13. See also F. G. B. Trolese, 'Un antico lezionario trecentesco del monastero di Santa Giustina in Padova', ibid., 63–89. This scene was also included in Giovanni Storlato's frescoed decoration of St Luke's chapel in S. Giustina (1436–1441): cf. A. de Nicolò Salmazo, 'Le reliquie di san Luca e l'epistola di Santa Giustina a Padova', in Mariani Canova, *Luca Evangelista*, 155–86, esp. 173–4.

[36] M. Flocco, *Studio su Portocannone e gli Albanesi in Italia* (Foggia, 1985), 108–9.

[37] C. Korolevskij, 'Le vicende ecclesiastiche dei paesi italo-albanesi della Basilicata e della Calabria, I. Barile', *Archivio Storico per la Calabria e la Lucania* 1 (1931), 43–68, esp. 54–5 and 62. M. Camaj (ed.), *Racconti popolari di Greci (Katundi) in provincia di Avellino e di Barile (Barili) in provincia di Potenza* (Rome, 1972), xix. It is significant that the cult of the *Madonna di Costantinopoli* developed in the area inhabited by immigrants from Koroni and was unconnected with the Catholic Albanians from Scutari who had been settled in the same village since the late 15th c.

[38] P. Samperi, *Iconologia della Madre di Dio, protettrice di Messina* (Messina, 1644), 536. C. Guarna Logoteta, *Ricerche storiche sul titolo d'Itria dato a Maria SS. e il culto a Lei prestato nel Regno di Napoli* (Reggio Calabria,

Thomas, the son of the last despot of Mistra, Demetrios Asan Palaiologos, sought refuge in Naples, where, by 1523, he had founded a votive chapel in the church of S. Giovanni Maggiore dedicated to St Luke's most famous icon.[39]

From the first half of the sixteenth century onwards the *Madonna d'Itria* also enjoyed a wide popularity among Latin believers throughout the whole viceroyalty of Naples and elsewhere in Italy.[40] Shrines spread everywhere: the Sicilians invoked the Virgin Hodegetria as their own *palladium* and in 1595 dedicated to her their national church in Rome;[41] Naples chose her as a patron against natural disasters, and a convent was founded in 1603 to 'honour the sacred image on Tuesdays according to the rules established by St Pulcheria in Constantinople';[42] lay confraternities were dedicated to the *Madonna di Costantinopoli* in Campania and Apulia, and the Calabrians and Sicilians took up the custom of celebrating her on Tuesdays, especially on the Tuesday after Easter, by renouncing the eating of meat, as in the usages described in the Paduan lectionary.[43]

Above all, the Hodegetria had become an ideological model, because of its role as the supernatural defender of the imperial city. Gradually the *Itria* was transformed into one of the several *Madonnas* of post-Tridentine devotion, performing the specific role of protecting towns against various kinds of calamities, such as sieges, droughts, plagues and volcanic eruptions; it was this very precise function that brought about its popularity and which, outside Sicily and Calabria, finally became much more important than any historical reminiscence of its Byzantine origins. After the *Madonna d'Itria*'s help was invoked in Naples during the famous pestilence of 1630, chapels dedicated to her were erected everywhere from Campania to the Marches near the burial place of the plague victims; elsewhere, the pastoral concerns of the Reformed clergy made use of the epithet to provide a local, paganistic cult manifestation with an official Roman Catholic stamp – as probably happened in the Sardinian shrine of *sa Itria*.

At the same time, no canonical iconography was worked out during these centuries, nor did all painters remain loyal to the ancient *aristerokratousa* type. In this respect, a curious

---

1845), 30, quoting the inscription: 'Virgini Odigitriae ex archetypo Constantinopolitano divi Lucae effictae olim Corone cultae demum ab eius optimatibus Messanam anno MDXXXIII. Non sine gratiarum foenore adsportatae, unico suae coloniae solatio Coronei cives'.

[39] D. Ambrasi, 'In margine all'immigrazione greca nell'Italia meridionale nei secoli XV e XVI. La Comunità greca di Napoli e la sua Chiesa', *Asprenas* 8 (1961), 156–85.

[40] On this point, cf. B. Cappelli, 'Iconografie bizantine della Madonna in Calabria', *BollGrott* 6 (1952), 185–206, esp. 190–5. W. von Rintelen, *Kultgeographische Studien in der Italia Byzantina. Untersuchungen über die Kulte des Erzengels Michael und der Madonna di Costantinopoli in Süditalien* (Meisenheim am Glan, 1968). C. Gelao, 'L'iconografia della Madonna di Costantinopoli in Terra di Bari. Culto confraternale e devozione', in L. Bertoldi Lenoci (ed.), *Le confraternite pugliesi in età moderna* (Fasano di Puglia, 1990), 63–90. M. Bacci, 'La Panayia Hodighitria e la Madonna di Costantinopoli', *Arte Cristiana* 84.772 (1996), 3–12. Id., *Il pennello*, 403–20.

[41] G. M. Croce, *L'Arciconfraternità di S. Maria Odigitria dei Siciliani in Roma, Profilo storico (1593–1970)* (Rome, 1994).

[42] C. d'Engenio Caracciolo, *Napoli Sacra* (Naples, 1623), 218–20. Guarna Logoteta, *Ricerche*, 34. G. Galasso, 'Napoli nel viceregno spagnuolo dal 1648 al 1696', in *Storia di Napoli* III (Naples, 1976), 273–661, esp. 312. D. Sinigalliesi, 'L'iconografia della Madonna di Costantinopoli', in V. Martini and A. Braca (eds), *Angelo e Francesco Solimena. Due culture a confronto* (Naples, 1994), 63–7.

[43] Bacci, *Il pennello*, 406.

composition deserves to be noticed, which probably originated in the cultural contacts between the Greek and Latin communities and provides further evidence of the westerners' fascination with Byzantine traditions. Usually it depicts the half-length Virgin Mary either in an Italianate variant of the Hodegetria or in the orans pose with the Child upright; in any event, she is always shown inside a case held by two men in religious dress. Such a type is first evidenced in a late-fourteenth-century fresco in Agrigento cathedral, Sicily (Fig. 26.6), probably commissioned by a private donor, who is represented in the middle of the scene next to the Cross.[44] In the image the Virgin Mary stands erect with upheld arms and with the Child in a medallion, and she is carried by two bearded men wearing caps and odd liturgical dress, a kind of chasuble and stole. We may wonder if this latter detail was meant to suggest vaguely the appearance of Greek priests or others who served the holy icon in Constantinople; certainly similarly shaped caps are known from representations of members of the confraternity of the Hodegetria (the so-called *hodegoi*).[45]

We do not know if the same design was used for the *Madonna d'Itria* painted on the external wall of the church of S. Margherita in Palermo, which the painter Tommaso de Vigilia was commissioned to copy in 1457.[46] In any case, no other examples are known from before c. 1530, when we find it again in two twin panels now in Polistena, Calabria (Plate 22, Fig. 26.7) and the Musei di Capodimonte, Naples.[47] This new image is more western in character and displays the Child upright and two old men dressed as Italo-Greek (or 'Basilian') monks, against the background of a seashore. In the seventeenth and eighteenth centuries this type, exported to other regions of the Neapolitan state and to the Papal territories, enjoyed widespread popularity and was often adapted to local circumstances, e.g. by substituting for the monks (the so-called *calogeri*) representatives of the Franciscan or Augustinian orders (Fig. 26.8); it is significant, however, that the original iconography was more carefully preserved in Calabria and Sicily (Fig. 26.9).

But what is the exact meaning of this iconography? The question is highly controversial, but nobody will fail to notice that the type of the Virgin orans with the Child upright is a revised Italianate variant of that with Christ in a medallion, found in Byzantine portable icons from the eighth/ninth centuries onwards and reproduced in the Agrigento fresco.[48] We may suppose that an image of this kind, brought to southern Italy by refugee communities from Greece, began to be venerated and exhibited inside a pictorial frame, as often happened in churches of the early modern era. A reminiscence of this archetype was preserved by the now lost *Madonna d'Itria*, once housed in the church of the same name in Messina, which was formerly in the hands of Greek clergy before being handed over to a Latin confraternity in 1578. As we learn from a seventeenth-century engraving (Fig. 26.10), the image showed a genuine icon with the

---

[44] P. Santucci, 'La produzione figurativa in Sicilia dalla fine del XII secolo alla metà del XV', in *Storia della Sicilia* V (Naples, 1981), 139–230, esp. 162–3 and Fig. 19. Santucci's dating of the fresco to the early 14th c. seems rather odd; stylistic affinities to certain scenes by the 'Master of Solomon's Judgement' in the Steri Palace, Palermo, may indicate execution in the last decades of the 14th c.

[45] See Angelidi and Papamastorakis, 'The Veneration of the Virgin Hodegetria', 379 and Pl. 213 (14th-century icon in the State Museum of the Moscow Kremlin).

[46] M. C. di Natale, *Tommaso de Vigilia* (Palermo, 1974), 20.

[47] Di Dario Guida, *Icone di Calabria*, 201.

[48] Ch. Baltoyanni, 'The Mother of God in Portable Icons', in Vassilaki, *Mother of God*, 139–53, esp. 139–41.

initials of Μήτηρ Θεοῦ being carried by two *calogeri* in a case.⁴⁹ In this way the painters managed to illustrate the association of the type with processional customs, imitating the procession of the Hodegetria which the islanders had inherited from Greek refugees: the nineteenth-century scholar Giuseppe Pitrè was still able to see and describe a solemn feast being performed on the Tuesday after Easter in Palazzolo Acreide, Sicily, when two men dressed as Greek monks carried a case containing the *Madonna d'Itria* image through the streets of the village.⁵⁰

As at Palazzolo, many local feasts of the *Madonna d'Itria* fell on the Tuesday after Easter, corresponding to the Tuesday τῆς Διακαινησίμου of the Orthodox Church. Probably this date had already played a role in Byzantine ritual life: it fell during a very solemn week, and we know that in Palaiologan times the normal weekly processions were restored only on that day, since during the previous fortnight, from Tuesday before Palm Sunday to Monday after Easter, the Hodegetria was kept inside the Imperial Palace of Blachernai.⁵¹ A new cycle in the ritual life of the icon started when it returned to its ordinary location; unequivocal evidence of such a custom is provided by one of the manuscripts with Gregory of Kykkos' text, where it is stated that the icon was to be venerated in every town and village on Tuesdays from the *Διακαινήσιμος* week onwards.⁵² In this respect, the southern Italian celebrations of the 'Constantinopolitan Virgin' may be reminiscent of a particular annual ritual in honour of the most holy Hodegetria.

---

⁴⁹ T. Pugliatti, 'La "Vergine Odigitria" di Alessandro Allori. Vicenda critica e iconologia', in *Scritti in onore di Vittorio Di Paola* (Messina, 1985), 283–308. See also the revised version of this article in M. A. Pavone (ed.), *Modelli di lettura iconografica. Il panorama meridionale* (Naples, 1999), 159–76.

⁵⁰ G. Pitrè, *Spettacoli e feste popolari siciliane* (Palermo, 1881), 63–6: 'The case where the sacred image stands upright is that usually represented in every image of the Hodegetria, carried on the shoulders by two *calogeri*: the former with long beard, bald head, and an ascetically severe look, the latter with short beard, lively eyes and a passionate and gentle look. They are unknown *calogeri*; nonetheless, in Palazzolo they are nicknamed "St Sufficient" [*San Bastante*] and "St Assistant" [*Sant'Aiutante*] and in the Contea they go by the peculiar name of "Saint Go" [*Santo Va*] and "Saint Come" [*Santo Vieni*]. The entire night was devoted to a sacred merrymaking, since the procession was interspersed with lights, bonfires, rides, masquerades of both men and women and, even worse, of priests [...].'

⁵¹ Pseudo-Kodinos, *Traité des Offices*, ed. J. Verpaux (Paris, 1966), 231. Cf. Zervou Tognazzi, 'L'iconografia', 245.

⁵² Spyridakis, 'Ἡ περιγραφή', 16: 'Οἱ ἅγιοι πατέρες, πῶς ἐστάλη ὁ ἄγγελος Κυρίου ἐν ἡμέρᾳ Τρίτῃ κομίζων τὰς ἀχειροτμήτους εἰκόνας, ἔταξαν λιτανεύειν καθ' ἑκάστην Τρίτην τὴν εἰκόνα τῆς Θεομήτορος εἰς ἴασιν τῶν Χριστιανῶν ἀπὸ τὴν Τρίτην τῆς Διακαινησίμου ἕως τῆς ἑνδεκάτης τοῦ Νοεμβρίου μηνὸς ἐν ταῖς ὁδοῖς καὶ πλατείαις τῶν πόλεων' ('As indicated by the Lord's angel who had brought the icons not cut by human hand on Tuesday, the holy Fathers prescribed for the cure of Christians the celebration of the icon of the Mother of God in the streets and squares of towns on Tuesdays from that in *Diakainesimos* week to 11 November'). The liturgical association of Tuesdays after Easter with the Holy Virgin is already evidenced in some ancient typika (11th–12th c.): cf. A. Dmitrievskii, *Opisanie liturgicheskikh rukopisei* I (Kiev, 1895), 175, 362. In present-day practice, a *theotokion* is said at vespers: see Πεντηκοστάριον (Rome, 1883), 30. Another important Marian feast falls on the Friday after Easter, when the Zoodochos Pege is celebrated, cf. N. Nilles, *Kalendarium Manuale utriusque Ecclesiae Orientalis et Occidentalis* (Innsbruck, 1897), 335–6. In Cyprus, a very solemn office is held on Tuesdays after Easter in honour of the miraculous icon of Machairas Monastery.

26.1   Sardinia, Gavoi, the hill of *sa Itria*.
The annual feast day (31 July).
Photograph taken in 1994 (source: author)

26.2   Sardinia, Gavoi, the hill of *sa Itria*.
Prehistoric menhir known as
Nostra Signora del Buon Cammino
(source: Pittau, *La Sardegna nuragica*, Fig. 66)

26.3 Rossano Calabro, Museo Diocesano. Two-sided icon of *Our Lady the Neodigitria*. The Virgin and Child (obverse, late 15th c.) (source: author)

26.4 Rossano Calabro, Museo Diocesano. Two-sided icon of *Our Lady the Neodigitria*. The Crucifixion (reverse) (source: author)

26.5 Padua, Benedictine Abbey of S. Giustina. Icon of the *Madonna Costantinopolitana* (late 13th c.) (source: after *Luca Evangelista*, 407)

26.6 Agrigento, Cathedral. Fresco of the *Madonna dell'Itria* (late 14th c.) (source: author)

THE LEGACY OF THE HODEGETRIA 335

26.7 Calabria, Polistena, parish church. Panel of the *Madonna dell'Itria* (c. 1530) (source: author)

26.8 Umbria, Bugian Piccolo, parish church. Panel of the *Madonna di Costantinopoli* (early 17th c.) (source: author).

26.9 Messina, church of S. Caterina di Valverde (from the church of Santissima Trinità).
A. Riccio, *Madonna di Costantinopoli*, oil on canvas (*c.* 1570) (source: author)

26.10 Engraving with the icon of the *Madonna d'Itria* church in Messina (17th c.)
(source: Samperi, *Iconologia della Madre di Dio*, pl. between 491–2)

A Byzantine icon of the *dexiokratousa* Hodegetria from Crete at the Benaki Museum

Nano Chatzidakis

An important icon of the Virgin with the Christ-child on her right arm (dimensions: 85 × 63 × 3 cm) has been recently acquired by the Benaki Museum (Plate 23, Figs 27.1–27.2).[1] The main subject is surrounded on three sides by a wide raised border, decorated along the top with the busts of five figures forming the Deesis, and on the two vertical sides with four pairs of saints in bust (Figs 27.2–27.8). The icon was in a poor state of preservation and the original surface was overpainted during the nineteenth century (Fig. 27.1).[2] Following conservation in the laboratories of the Benaki Museum, the original representations (Fig. 27.2) now appear against a uniform dark blue ground which covers the entire surface of the panel, even the border and the haloes, with no surviving inscriptions and no use of gold.[3] The most notable technical feature of the icon is the carving in plain relief of the haloes of the main figures. Although the painted surface has suffered considerable damage, the colours which survive reflect a high level of mastery, most apparent in the modelling of the small-scale figures on the border, where the underlying freehand preliminary design and incisions are visible (Figs 27.6–27.7).[4]

Iconography

THE VIRGIN AND CHILD ON THE CENTRAL PANEL

The Virgin – half-length, in a quasi-frontal position, turned slightly to the left – supports the Christ-child on her right arm while holding the left in an attitude of prayer (Fig. 27.2). She wears a brownish-red maphorion with a narrow yellow strip on the hem, which is visible on her left arm and shoulder. Her head must originally have been slightly inclined, as is indicated by the scant remnants of the original paint on the drapery folds of the maphorion around her head. The Christ-child, in an upright three-quarter pose with the upper part of his body in a frontal position, gazes at the spectator, though his head is turned to the right; his legs are parallel to each other – not crossed – and are depicted sideways on. He holds a white closed scroll in his left hand and blesses with his right. A long orange-ochre tunic covers his torso and also his left leg,

---

[1] Inv. no 32650. The icon was found in eastern Crete. A first version of this paper was presented at the conference *Griechische Ikonen* in Marburg on 30 June 2000.
[2] The facial features of the Virgin, now removed, were designed by the former owner of the icon.
[3] See K. Milanou, 'Εικόνα Παναγίας Βρεφοκρατούσας με προτομές αγίων. Τεχνική εξέταση', *Μουσείο Μπενάκη* 1 (2001), 41–58, Figs 1–31. All overpainting has been removed.
[4] Ibid., Figs 9, 10, 23 (printed in reverse).

and a dark blue himation his left arm and right leg; the toes of both feet can be seen below the hem of the garments.

The iconographic type of the Virgin supporting the Christ-child at her side on either her left or right arm has been classified as the Hodegetria, even in those cases where the accompanying inscription does not correspond to this epithet.[5] The type is represented down the centuries with considerable inventive skill; in order to avoid mere repetition, Byzantine artists gave great variety to the pose and the gesture of both figures, depicting them either frontally, looking towards the spectator, or in three-quarter view, thus expressing the varying relationship between Mother, Child and viewer. Particular diversity can be observed in the pose, gesture and garments of the Child. Although a study of the details of the Hodegetria iconography is an elusive task because of the multiplicity of possible interpretations, attempts at distinguishing particular versions may be useful, particularly when they can be associated with a precise location which indicates their provenance and/or diffusion.[6]

The type of the *dexiokratousa* (right-handed) Hodegetria has been widely discussed in the past, particularly by Kondakov, Lazarev and Grabar, who pointed out its Byzantine origin.[7] The earliest known example is found in the sixth-century icon of the Virgin from S. Maria Nova (S. Francesca Romana) in Rome.[8] One of the most important Middle Byzantine examples occurs in the mosaic in Hosios Loukas,[9] while the mosaic icon from Sinai (c. 1200)[10] displays an iconography identical to that on certain Sinai icons from later in the thirteenth century,[11] whose high technical and stylistic quality are indicative of metropolitan painters.

---

[5] For the use of the term Hodegetria indiscriminately for the left-handed or the right-handed type, see V. Lazarev, 'Studies in the Iconography of the Virgin', *ArtB* 20 (1938), repr. in id., *Studies in Byzantine Painting* (London, 1995), 226: 'the Hodegetria type became firmly established as a half-length figure of the Virgin holding the Infant on either the left or the right arm'. For the lack of correspondence between epithets and iconographic types of the Virgin and Child, see A. Grabar, 'Remarques sur l'iconographie byzantine de la Vierge', *CahArch* 26 (1977), 169–78 (with previous bibliography).

[6] N. Kondakov, *Ikonografiia Bogomateri* (St Petersburg, 1915), I, 152–62; II, 274 ff., Figs 150 ff. Lazarev, 'Iconography of the Virgin', 226–48. E. Sandberg-Vavalá, *L'iconografia della Madonna col bambino nella pittura italiana del Dugento* (Siena, 1934), 42–54. R. L. Freytag, *Die autonome Theotokosdarstellung* I (Munich, 1985), 264–75. See also M. Tatić-Djurić, 'L'icône de la Vierge Peribleptos, son origine et sa diffusion', in *Sbornik Svetozar Radojčić* (Belgrade, 1969), 335–54. D. Mouriki, 'A Thirteenth-Century Icon with a Variant of the Hodegetria in the Byzantine Museum of Athens', *DOP* 41 (1987), 403–14, and ead., 'Variants of the Hodegetria on Two Thirteenth-Century Sinai Icons', *CahArch* 39 (1991), 153–82.

[7] See above, nn. 5 and 6, and A. Grabar, 'Note sur l'iconographie ancienne de la Vierge. 1: Découverte à Rome d'une icône de la Vierge à l'encaustique', *Les Cahiers techniques de l'art* 3.1 (1954), 531–3, repr. in id., *L'art de la fin de l'Antiquité et du moyen âge* (Paris, 1968), 21, 529–34, where the author traces its models to Constantinopolitan seals with a Palestinian origin (ibid., 532 n. 1 and 533). See collected examples and bibliography in Freytag, *Theotokosdarstellung*, 262 ff. ('Hodegetria typus, buste rechte'). See also Mouriki, 'Variants of the Hodegetria', 153 ff. The *dexiokratousa* type could also be connected with the archetype icon painted by St Luke and housed in the Hodegon Monastery in Constantinople (M. Bacci, 'With the Paintbrush of the Evangelist Luke', in Vassilaki, *Mother of God*, 79–89). In a 13th-c. manuscript, St Luke is shown painting an icon of the Virgin *dexiokratousa*: Vassilaki, *Mother of God*, no. 55, 390–1 (B. Pentcheva).

[8] Grabar, 'Découverte à Rome', 531 ff. See also G. Wolf, *Salus Populi Romani, Die Geschichte römischer Kultbilder im Mittelalter* (Weinheim, 1990). See collected bibliography in Freytag, *Theotokosdarstellung* I, 262 ff.

[9] N. Chatzidakis, *Hosios Loukas, Byzantine Art in Greece* (Athens, 1997), 33, Fig. 32.

[10] K. Weitzmann, *The Icon* (New York, 1978), Pl. 32. Id., 'Icon Painting in the Crusader Kingdom', *DOP* 20 (1966), Fig. 66. Mouriki, 'Variants of the Hodegetria', Fig. 16.

[11] Mouriki, 'Variants of the Hodegetria', Fig. 17.

The distinctive features of the Benaki icon, such as the frontality of the configuration broken by the slight turn to the right of the Virgin's body and the inclination of her head, as well as by the Child's three-quarter pose (although the upper part of his body is represented frontally), can be associated with a series of large-scale icons located in Cyprus and attributed to local workshops from the late twelfth to the early fourteenth century. Among the most representative of these are an icon from Laneia[12] with a wide raised frame decorated with plaster reliefs, another from Doros[13] and a recently published icon from the Panagia at Moutoullas,[14] painted on a red ground; these icons present a similar configuration with the Christ-child clad in a long tunic and a himation covering both legs. An even closer example is found on an icon from Hagios Theodoros (Fig. 27.9), which shows the Child in a similar attitude, represented frontally with his legs parallel and in three-quarter view.[15]

The Benaki icon presents a significant variation from this group in the colour and the arrangement of Christ's himation, which on the Cypriot icons is usually red or yellow-ochre and covers both legs. The covering of only one leg by the himation is found on another more prestigious series of icons with the Hodegetria, where the Child usually appears with his feet extended horizontally, such as the left-handed Panagia Arakiotissa[16] as well as two Sinai icons.[17] This iconographic device is also reproduced on icons located in Italy, with a provenance from Cyprus or the eastern Mediterranean, such as the *dexiokratousa* Hodegetria (*Madonna di sotto gli organi*) in the Duomo at Pisa,[18] where the Christ-child holds an open Gospel book, the *Madonna di Ciurcitano* and the *Madonna della Fonte*.[19] Certain other icons from the same region provide examples of the unusual dark blue colouring of the Child's himation, as on the Benaki icon, which thus recalls the himation of Christ Pantokrator, as portrayed in the small-scale bust on the frame (Figs 27.2–27.3). Even more closely related to the Benaki icon as far as this feature is concerned is the left-handed Hodegetria in the Pinacoteca Provinciale, Bari (Fig. 27.10), where a dark blue himation covers only one leg of the Child. This icon, which reproduces the iconography of the Virgin

---

[12] For a brief account see S. Sophocleous, *Icons of Cyprus 7th – 20th Century* (Nicosia, 1994), Fig. 11 (last quarter of the 12th c.).

[13] A. Papageorgiou, Εικόνες της Κύπρου (Nicosia, 1991), 28, Fig. 16. Sophocleous, *Icons*, Fig. 18 (first decades of the 13th c.).

[14] P. Vocotopoulos, 'Three Thirteenth-Century Icons at Moutoullas', in N. P. Ševčenko and C. Moss (eds), *Medieval Cyprus. Studies in Art, Architecture, and History in Memory of Doula Mouriki* (Princeton, NJ, 1999), 161–7, Pl. 10, Figs 1, 3; the icon is dated to the last quarter of the 13th c.

[15] Sophocleous, *Icons*, 87, Fig. 22 (13th c.); Christ wears a blue embroidered tunic; the colour of his himation has flaked off.

[16] See below, n. 41.

[17] See examples in Mouriki, 'Variants of the Hodegetria', Figs 2, 7, 13, 15, 24, 28. See also Tatić-Djurić, 'L'icône de la Vierge Peribleptos'.

[18] The icon is affiliated to Cypriot, Sinaitic or eastern Mediterranean workshops of the Crusader period. See M. Bacci, 'Due tavole della Vergine nella Toscana occidentale del primo duecento', *Annali della Scuola Normale Superiore di Pisa*, Serie IV, 2.1 (1997), 36–53, Fig. 25. The icon, first published by Garrison in 1943, was attributed to Berlinghiero; for its *fortuna critica* see Bacci, 'Due tavole', 37 ff. and notes. See also V. Pace, 'Between East and West', in Vassilaki, *Mother of God*, 426, Pls 214, 216.

[19] P. Belli d'Elia (ed.), *Icone di Puglia e Basilicata dal Medioevo al Settecento*, exh. cat., Bari, Pinacoteca Provinciale, 9 October – 11 December 1988 (Bari, 1988), no. 6, 106–7 (colour fig. on p. 47) (M. Millela Lovecchio) and no. 8, 109 (colour fig. on p. 49) (M. Millela Lovecchio), with further bibliography; they are dated to the end of the 13th c.

from Andria, is also attributed to an eastern Mediterranean workshop of the first half of the fourteenth century.[20]

A similarly posed Virgin *dexiokratousa*, with the same gesture of prayer, but with significant differences in the pose and garments of Christ, who wears a short tunic and reclines on his Mother's arm, is found on another group of icons also associated with workshops of the eastern Mediterranean; this includes an icon from Thessaloniki[21] (c. 1200), the *Madonna Costantinopolitana* from Padua (Fig. 27.11), dated to the second half of the thirteenth century,[22] and the *Madonna della Neve* from Barletta (Bari), dated probably to the late thirteenth or early fourteenth century.[23]

In conclusion, the iconography of the *dexiokratousa* Hodegetria in the Benaki icon, distinguished by the semi-frontal pose of the Child, with the legs parallel and turned to the side, one covered by the yellow-ochre chiton and the other by the dark blue himation, can be associated with an established metropolitan model, widespread during the thirteenth and the early fourteenth century in Cyprus and in Italy in icons connected with eastern Mediterranean workshops.

THE SMALL-SCALE FIGURES ON THE BORDER

The three sides of the raised frame are decorated with half-length holy figures – originally, it would appear, five along the top and four pairs of saints on the two vertical sides. Four busts of saints are visible on the right side but only three on the left, as the original paint layer does not survive intact in this area. In the lower part of the icon there are no traces of paint nor of a relief border.

At the centre of the upper part is the well-preserved bust of Christ (Plate 24a, Fig. 27.3), presented frontally holding a scroll bound with a red ribbon in his left hand and blessing with his right hand in front of his breast, in the well-known 'closed' type of Pantokrator, reproduced on a whole series of fine icons such as those of Christ from Hilandar and from the Byzantine Museum, Athens.[24] He wears a red tunic and a grey-blue himation with multiple linear folds, rendered in lighter tones of blue. On the left, the badly damaged figure of the Virgin can be

---

[20] Belli d'Elia, *Icone di Puglia*, no. 11, 110–1 (colour fig. on p. 53) (R. Lorusso Romito). See also no. 16, 115 (colour fig. on p. 56) (P. Belli d'Elia).

[21] Because of its Italianate character the icon has been attributed to a Crusader or to a Cypriot workshop. *Byzantine Art, an European Art, 9th Exhibition of the Council of Europe*, exh. cat., Athens, Zappeion Megaron 1964 (Athens, 1964), Supplement, no. 714, 575. A. Tourta, 'Εικόνα δεξιοκρατούσας Παναγίας στη Θεσσαλονίκη', in *Ευφρόσυνον. Αφιέρωμα στον Μανόλη Χατζηδάκη* 2 (Athens, 1992), 609–15. Tsigaridas proposes a Thessaloniki workshop during the Latin occupation of the city. E. Tsigaridas, 'Φορητές εικόνες στη Μακεδονία και το Άγιον Όρος κατά το 13° αιώνα', *DChAE* 21 (2000), 148–9, Fig. 38, with previous bibliography.

[22] Monastery of S. Giustina (88 × 63 cm). The Child turns his head to the opposite side. G. Canova Mariani (ed.) *Luca Evangelista. Parola e imagine tra oriente e ocidente*, exh. cat. (Padua, 2000), no. 75, 405–7 (M. Bacci), with previous bibliography. See below, n. 67, and also the paper of M. Bacci in this volume, 321–336.

[23] The icon originally had a decorated border; the Child's legs are uncovered and parallel to each other, as in the Benaki icon. Belli d'Elia, *Icone di Puglia*, no. 13, 112–13 (R. Lorusso Romito); see also no. 14, 113–14 (M. Millela Lovecchio) (*Madonna di Ripalta*, right-handed Hodegetria, enthroned).

[24] This iconographic type of the Pantokrator stems from the 6th-century model known from the Sinai encaustic icon; see M. Chatzidakis, 'An Encaustic Icon of Christ at Sinai', *ArtB* 49.3 (1967), 197–208. *Treasures of Mount Athos*, exh. cat. (Thessaloniki, 1997), no. 2.9, 67–70 (E. Tsigaridas). *A Mystery Great and Wondrous, Year of*

distinguished, turned to the right in a three-quarter pose of prayer towards Christ, and dressed in a dark brown maphorion. Presumably the corresponding area of the painted surface on the right, now missing, would have contained the half-figure of St John the Baptist, as is usual in the Deesis.[25] On the corners are two angels turned in prayer towards the central figure of Christ. The angel on the right (Plate 24b, Fig. 27.4) is well preserved, with multi-coloured, open wings carefully rendered in a free design of brown, blue, white and bright red brushstrokes. A notable feature is the precision of the contours of his face, turned three-quarters to the left, and the fine modelling of the flesh with warmer tones. His garments, a red tunic and grey-blue himation, are rendered in the same linear manner. His right arm is placed on his breast in prayer, and his left hand is closed as if holding an object, probably a sceptre. The angel on the left side is almost completely destroyed, and only the lower part of his left wing is preserved. Below, three pairs of saints placed symmetrically on the vertical sides are preserved in fairly good condition. Nothing remains of the original inscriptions, but the following names from the nineteenth-century repainting were visible in small cursive script: 'ὁ ἅγιος ἀπόστολος Πέτρος', 'ἅ(γιος) ἀπόστολος (Π)αῦ(λος)', 'ὁ ἅγιος Ἰωά(ννης) ὁ Χρισόστομος', 'ὁ ἅγιος Βασίλειος', 'ὁ ἅγ.ος ιγν...ς .ντ...', 'ὁ ἅγιος Γρηγόριος ὁ θεολόγος'. (St Peter, St Paul, St John Chrystostom, St Basil, St Ignatios of Antioch (?) and St Gregory the Theologian) (Fig. 27.1).

In the first row, the two saints are turned slightly towards the centre, thus participating in the scheme of the Deesis above. The saint on the left (Fig. 27.5) with himation and chiton has his left arm extended in prayer, while the clenched fingers of his right hand hold a cylindrical brown object, probably keys and/or a scroll. His facial features, with short curly white hair and beard, identify him as St Peter;[26] a schematic circular shape for the curls on St Peter's forehead has been associated by Weitzmann with the 'Roman' type, found also on a 'Crusader' epistyle from Sinai[27] and on the Vatican icon of Sts Peter and Paul, a thirteenth-century Serbian icon displaying Latin influences.[28] The half-figure on the right side (Fig. 27.2), with high forehead and long brown beard, can be identified as St Paul despite the alteration of the facial features through the flaking of the paint.[29] His right hand is extended in prayer, and in his left he holds a book decorated with polychrome stones and pearls – St Paul is usually depicted holding indiscriminately either a closed scroll, as on a thirteenth-century icon from Cyprus[30] where he has similar facial features, or a book, as on the already mentioned Vatican icons and the 'Crusader' epistyle at Sinai.[31]

Salvation 2000, Exhibition of Icons and Ecclesiastical Treasures, exh. cat., Athens, Byzantine and Christian Museum, 28 May – 31 July 2001 (Athens, 2002), no. 52, 188–9 and no. 54, 192–4 (N. Chatzidakis).

[25] From the extensive bibliography see: Ch. Walter, 'Two Notes on the Deësis', *REB* 26 (1968), 311–36. Id., 'Further Notes on the Deësis', *REB* 28 (1970), 161–87. Id., 'Bulletin on the Deësis and the Paraclesis', *REB* 38 (1980), 261–9, with previous bibliography.

[26] K. Weitzmann, *The Saint Peter Icon of Dumbarton Oaks* (Washington, DC, 1983), 21–8, 33–40, Figs 25–6, 32.

[27] Ibid., 21–8. K. Weitzmann, G. Alibegashvili, A. Volskaja, G. Babić, M. Chatzidakis, M. Alpatov and T. Voinescu, *Les icônes* (Paris, 1982), colour pl. on p. 229 (late 13th c.).

[28] Weitzmann, *Saint Peter*, 21–8, Figs 4, 25, 31. Weitzmann et al., *Les icônes*, colour pl. on p. 156. The icon is an offering of the Serbian kings Jelena and Dragutin and dated to the late 13th c.

[29] For the iconography of St Paul, see Weitzmann, *Saint Peter*, 33–4.

[30] Papageorghiou, Εικόνες της Κύπρου, Fig. 33.

[31] See above, nn. 27–8. For more examples on Sinai icons, see Weitzmann, *Saint Peter*, Figs 26, 32, 34, 36, 38, 39, 42, 44.

The other two pairs of saints belong to a different order; they are hierarchs and they have a frontal pose. On the left, we can recognize St John Chrysostom (Fig. 27.6) with his characteristic emaciated triangular face and a short, sparse beard,[32] holding the Gospel book in his left hand and a finely designed red cross in his right. On the right St Basil (Fig. 27.7), identifiable by his long, thick brown beard, holds the book diagonally with his right hand placed reverently on it.[33] In the next row the bishop on the right has a long greyish-white beard, a typical feature of St Gregory the Theologian (Fig. 27.8), though with a slight variation in the lower part, which is usually rounded;[34] the saint holds in his left hand a Gospel book and in his right a red cross. The figure of the saint in the same row on the left is mostly destroyed, though part of his face is preserved displaying the features of an old man with a long, finely shaped, greyish-white beard; he wears a dark brown phelonion but no other trace of his vestments or gesture can be distinguished. He could be a bishop or a desert ascetic, and his facial features, as well as the remnants of the nineteenth-century repainted inscription (ιγν…ς..ντ….), may permit his identification as St Ignatios of Antioch,[35] a hypothesis enhanced by the fact that the other inscriptions correspond to the identifications suggested above (Fig. 27.1).

CHOICE OF SUBJECT, DISPLAY AND FUNCTION OF THE ICON

The choice of subject and the arrangement of the saints on the border around the main figure of the Virgin present an interesting combination of themes closely related to the Incarnation, thus conferring on this icon a religious content associated with the iconography and the liturgy of the Sanctuary, where the Virgin on the conch of the apse is often surrounded by the hierarchs on the lower part, and where, in some famous Middle Byzantine monuments, such as Hosios Loukas and St Sophia in Kiev, there is a small-scale depiction of the Deesis. The connection between the prayer of intercession, the office of the *Proskomide* and the iconography of the Virgin surrounded by angels and saints in Byzantine manuscripts and icons such as fol. 4v of the former Pantokrator cod. 49 (now in Washington, DC) and a later Palaiologan 'composite icon' from Blatadon Monastery, Thessaloniki, has been widely discussed in the past.[36]

---

[32] Dionysios of Fourna, Ἑρμηνεία τῆς ζωγραφικῆς τέχνης, ed. P. Papadopoulos-Kerameus (St Petersburg, 1909), 154. O. Demus, 'Two Palaeologan Mosaic Icons in the Dumbarton Oaks Collection', *DOP* 14 (1960), 110–19. N. Drandakis, Η εικονογραφία των Τριών Ιεραρχών (Ioannina, 1969), 12–13. For the iconography of the hierarchs, see H. Buchthal, 'Some Notes on Byzantine Hagiographical Portraiture', *Gazette des Beaux Arts* 62 (1963), 81–90 and Drandakis, Η εικονογραφία των Τριών Ιεραρχών, 8 ff.

[33] Buchthal, 'Hagiographical Portraiture', 81–90. Drandakis, Η εικονογραφία των Τριών Ιεραρχών, 8–11. For the Byzantine origin of this gesture of respect, similar to that of the Virgin Hodegetria touching the foot of Christ, see A. Vassilaki-Karakatsani, 'Σημειώσεις σε μια εικόνα Βρεφοκρατούσας της Μονής Βατοπεδίου', *DChAE* 5 (1969), 203 ff.

[34] Dionysios of Fourna, Ἑρμηνεία, 267. Buchthal, 'Hagiographical Portraiture', 81 ff. Drandakis, Η εικονογραφία των Τριών Ιεραρχών, 8–11.

[35] The inscription was discernible on the yellow ground, see 341 above, Fig. 27.2. For the iconography of St Ignatios of Antioch, see Th. Chatzidakis-Bacharas, *Les peintures murales de Hosios Loukas. Les chapelles occidentales* (Τετράδια Χριστιανικής Αρχαιολογικής Εταιρείας, 2) (Athens, 1982), 101–2, Figs 49–50.

[36] K. Weitzmann, 'Byzantine Miniature and Icon-Painting in the Eleventh Century', in *Thirteenth International Congress of Byzantine Studies* (Oxford, 1966), 8–9, Pl. 22, with a comprehensive treatment of the impact of the liturgy on iconography from the 11th c. onwards, and A. Xyngopoulos, 'Une icône byzantine à Thessalonique',

Icons with the Deesis and saints surrounding a holy figure appear on some fine Middle Byzantine works, among them the precious enamel book cover in the Biblioteca Marciana, Venice, and the icon of St Nicholas from St Catherine's Monastery, Sinai (late tenth century), where there are further resemblances in the choice of saints on the upper part of the frame, which is decorated with the busts of Christ flanked by Sts Peter and Paul turned in prayer.[37] On another Deesis icon from Sinai (early twelfth century) the upper part of the border contains two angels in prayer, as in the Benaki icon, flanking the *Hetoimasia*.[38] There are further similarities on a Crucifixion icon, dated to the same period, whose raised border contains the Deesis with St John in the centre flanked by two angels and Sts Peter and Paul, turned slightly to the centre, while on the sides are two pairs of hierarchs: St Basil and St John Chrysostom, and St Nicholas and St Gregory the Theologian.[39] Finally, busts of saints are also found on the border of some later 'Crusader' Sinaitic icons dated to the second half of the thirteenth century, such as a Crucifixion with Christ in the centre of the upper part, flanked by the Virgin and St John, and fifteen busts of various saints, among them Sts Peter and Paul and the hierarchs John Chrysostom and Basil.[40]

The large dimensions of our icon (85 × 63 cm) indicate its function as the main cult icon of a church, either as the despotic icon for the templon or for display on a *proskynetarion*. Among the earliest known examples of this type of large-scale icon is the Christ from the church of Panagia tou Arakos, Cyprus (c. 1192),[41] similarly surrounded on the border by two full-length pairs of hierarchs, of whom only St John Chrysostom and St Gregory the Theologian on the left side survive. However, the well-known left-handed Hodegetria, which forms a pair with the icon of Christ, does not have figurative decoration on the border.[42] The Benaki icon is further related to an icon of the Virgin Eleousa from Santorini,[43] where the main subject is painted on a red ground. Although the iconographic type of the Virgin (a Glykophilousa) is different, there is close similarity in the choice of three pairs of hierarchs depicted full-length on the border. Its

---

CahArch 3 (1948), 114 ff., Fig. 1. A. Tourta, 'Αμφιπρόσωπη εικόνα στη Μονή Βλατάδων', Κληρονομία 9.1 (1977), 133 ff., Pls 1, 3. P. Vocotopoulos, 'Composite Icons', in E. Haustein-Barch and N. Chatzidakis (eds), *Griechische Ikonen, Greek Icons, Proceedings of the Symposium in Memory of Manolis Chatzidakis* (Athens and Recklinghausen, 1998), 6–7. In the icon from Thessaloniki, the Virgin Hodegetria, flanked by an angel and St John, is shown under the protection of Christ between two angels in the upper part, while on the later frame (15th c.) Sts Peter and Paul are depicted among other saints in bust.

[37] Weitzmann *et al.*, *Les icônes*, colour pl. on 410–11. K. Weitzmann, *The Monastery of Saint Catherine at Mount Sinai I. The Icons, 1: From the Sixth to the Tenth Century* (Princeton, NJ, 1976), no. B.61, 101–2, Pl. XXXVIII: on the sides are depicted two pairs of military saints and below three physician-saints (Kosmas, Panteleemon and Damianos).

[38] Weitzmann *et al.*, *Les icônes*, colour pl. on p. 49: on the vertical sides of the border we find a full-length hierarch and a monk.

[39] Weitzmann, *The Icon*, 90–1, Pl. 26.

[40] Weitzmann *et al.*, *Les icônes*, colour pl. on p. 211.

[41] The paint on the upper part of the border has not survived; the lower part contained three busts of saints, of which only two remain: St Theodore and St George. A. Papageorghiou, 'Εικών του Χριστού εν τω ναώ της Παναγίας του Άρακος', *KyprSp* 32 (1968), 45–55. Id., Εικόνες της Κύπρου, Fig. 10.

[42] Papageorghiou, 'Εικών του Χριστού', Fig. 11. Vassilaki, *Mother of God*, no. 62, 406–7 (A. Papageorgiou) (the border is decorated with lozenges).

[43] M. Georgopoulou-Verra, 'Βυζαντινά και μεταβυζαντινά μνημεία Κυκλάδων, Συντήρηση τοιχογραφιών-εικόνων', *AD* 30 (1975), B2-Chronika, 336, Pls 242–4. A. Mitsani, 'Βυζαντινή εικόνα της Παναγίας Δεομένης στην Καταπολιανή της Πάρου', *DChAE* 23 (2002), 193, Fig. 17.

dating around 1200 suggests a close association with the fresco decoration of the church of the Episkopi, where the icon was found.[44]

To this group can be added a series of icons where the Virgin is surrounded on the border by small-scale holy figures of different orders. We find the busts of the apostles on the frame of the Virgin at Jerusalem,[45] dated probably to the twelfth or the thirteenth century, as well as later on the Palaiologan icon of the Hodegetria from the Pantokrator Monastery, Mt Athos.[46] Prophets appear on the frame of two important late fourteenth-century examples, the Hodegetria in the National Gallery of Ireland and the Glykophilousa from Nesebŭr at Sofia,[47] as well as on an icon from Dories, Crete, dating from the early fifteenth century.[48] Another interesting variation in the choice of the saints for the border is found on a fourteenth-century icon from Cyprus, in the church of Panagia Faneromeni, where the Virgin in the Hodegetria type is surrounded by six standing hymnographers.[49]

This general review of the iconography of the *dexiokratousa* Hodegetria enables us to conclude that the origin of the Benaki icon can be positively attributed to a greatly venerated Constantinopolitan model, widely diffused during the thirteenth and early fourteenth century in the periphery, and particularly in Cyprus and eastern Mediterranean workshops. Furthermore the subject, taken in conjunction with the large dimensions, indicates that it was destined for public worship within a church dedicated to the Virgin.

Technique

WOOD AND COLOURS

Many of the technical features of the Benaki icon are indicative of its provincial provenance. The roughness of the paint surface, together with the dark blue of the ground, which extends even to the haloes, reveals a lack of more expensive materials and confers on this icon the texture of a wall-painting. This is enhanced by the thick (3 cm), rough wooden panel with its border and haloes carved in relief. Panels of this quality and similarly crude execution are a regular feature of icons from northern Greece, Macedonia and Thrace, as well as on those from Cyprus and Italy.

---

[44] For the dating of the Episkopi frescoes see M. Chatzidakis, 'Aspects de la peinture murale du XIIIe siècle en Grèce', in *L'art byzantin du XIIIe siècle, Symposium de Sopoćani, 1965* (Belgrade, 1967), 59–73, repr. in id., *Studies in Byzantine Art and Archaeology* (London, 1972), XIII.

[45] P. Vocotopoulos, 'Δύο παλαιολόγειες εικόνες στα Ιεροσόλυμα', *DChAE* 20 (1998/9), 297–300, Fig. 4. On the upper part of the raised borders the throne of the *Hetoimasia* is flanked by two angels in prayer.

[46] E. Tsigaridas, 'Τοιχογραφίες και εικόνες της Μονής Παντοκράτορος Αγίου Όρους', *Μακεδονικά* 18 (1968), 197–8. T. Papamastorakis, 'Icons 13th–16th century', in *Icons of the Holy Monastery of Pantokrator* (Mt Athos, 1998), 86, 88, Fig. 39.

[47] D. Talbot Rice and T. Talbot Rice, *Icons. The National Gallery of Ireland* (Dublin, 1968), no. 1, 13–18. K. Paskaleva, *Die Bulgarische Ikonen* (Sofia, 1981), no. 5, 70–1.

[48] M. Borboudakis (ed.), Εικόνες Κρητικής Τέχνης, exh. cat. (Herakleion, 1993), no. 156, 510–1 (M. Borboudakis); the figures on the lower part of the border are mostly repainted.

[49] Papageorghiou, Εικόνες της Κύπρου, 67, Fig. 47a. The icon was repainted in the 16th c. The figure of the Virgin is accompanied by the epithet Faneromeni.

However, the dark blue ground is an unusual feature even in provincial icons, such as those from the regions of Veroia, Kastoria and Cyprus, where the use of silver, yellow-ochre or red on the ground and the haloes is more common.[50] However, a dark blue ground, reminiscent of fresco decorations, is not unknown, and can be found on some rare examples from northern Greece, such as a thirteenth-century icon with St Nicholas in a private collection in Athens[51] and a fifteenth-century icon of Christ from the Prespa region in the Byzantine Museum, Athens.[52] It appears to be more frequent on icons painted under western influence, such as the 'Crusader icons' at Sinai – the Virgin Blachernitissa (c. 1224), and the Anastasis[53] – as well as icons found in Italy and associated with similar eastern Mediterranean workshops. Among these are the Virgin *Lactans* from Pisa (c. 1260–1280)[54] and icons from the region of Bari, such as the Virgin from the church of S. Maria della greca (first half of the fourteenth century),[55] the *Madonna della Neve*[56] and the Virgin from the Pinacoteca Provinciale, Bari (Fig. 27.10; first half of the fourteenth century) – the last already noted above for its dark blue colouring on the himation of the Christ-child.[57]

THE HALOES, CARVED IN PLAIN RELIEF

The haloes of the Virgin and Child, painted in the same dark blue colour, with no trace of additional decoration, are discernible only by their rendering in relief, while those of the saints on the border can be distinguished only by a very thin line of red around the edge (Figs 27.5–27.8). This feature, which rarely occurs on Byzantine icons, must be considered as a separate and distinct technique from that of raised haloes decorated with rich ornamentation in plaster relief, which are fairly common on the icons from Cyprus and southern Italy, already mentioned in connection with the iconography of our icon. The latter, generally regarded as imitations in simple materials of richly ornamented silver mounts, have often been associated with the increased influence of Crusader or Italian art on the icon-painting of this region.[58]

---

50 See examples in Papageorghiou, Εικόνες της Κύπρου, passim. Sophocleous, Icons, passim. Th. Papazotos, *Byzantine Icons of Verroia* (Athens, 1995), passim.
51 Vassilaki, *Mother of God*, no. 35, 346–9 (I. D. Varalis). This is a rare case where the blue colour also extends onto the halo, which is modelled in gesso relief and adorned with a simple floral motif.
52 *Mystery Great and Wondrous*, no. 58, 202–3 (N. Chatzidakis).
53 D. Mouriki, 'Icons from the 12th to the 15th Century', in K. A. Manafis (ed.), *Sinai. Treasures of the Monastery of Saint Catherine* (Athens, 1990), Figs 48, 64.
54 Vassilaki, *Mother of God*, no. 70, 442–3 (M. Bacci). For post-Byzantine examples, see N. Chatzidakis, *Icons. The Velimezis Collection* (Athens, 1997), no. 13, 148 and no. 22, 245, Figs 64, 145.
55 Belli d'Elia, *Icone di Puglia*, no. 20, 118–19 (colour fig. on p. 60) (R. Lorusso Romito).
56 Ibid., no. 13, 112–13 (colour fig. on p. 54) (R. Lorusso Romito).
57 See above, 340 n. 20, and Belli d'Elia, *Icone di Puglia*, no. 11, 110–11 (colour fig. on p. 53) (L. Lorusso Romito).
58 D. Talbot-Rice, 'Cypriot Icons with Plaster Relief Backgrounds', *JÖB* 21 (1972), 269–78. M. S. Frinta, 'Raised Gilded Adornment of the Cypriot Icons and the Occurrence of the Technique in the West', *Gesta* 20 (1981), 333–47. Id., 'Relief Decoration in Gilded Pastiglia on the Cypriot Icons and Its Propagation in the West', in Πρακτικά του Δευτέρου Διεθνούς Κυπρολογικού Συνεδρίου II (Nicosia, 1986), 539–44. For painted decoration on haloes in Macedonia and on Cretan frescoes, see Tsigaridas, Σχέσεις βυζαντινής και δυτικής τέχνης στη Μακεδονία από τον 13ο έως τον 15ο αιώνα', in Εταιρεία Μακεδονικών Σπουδών, Εορταστικός τόμος, 50 χρόνια, 1939–1989 (Thessaloniki, 1992), 160–1, Fig. 4, and M. Vassilakis-Mavrakakis, 'Western Influences on the Fourteenth-Century Art of Crete', in *Akten des XVI. Internationalen Byzantinistenkongresses* II.5 (Vienna, 1981), *JÖB* 32.5 (1982), 303.

The haloes in our icon are considerably different, as they are carved in plain relief without any kind of ornamental imitation of metal mounts; on the contrary, they are associated with wood-carving workshops, such as those which produced certain famous thirteenth-century relief icons from northern Greece: the St George from Kastoria, now in the Byzantine Museum, Athens,[59] and two other carved icons of St George and St Demetrios from the same region,[60] where the saints have similar haloes in plain relief. Even closer in view of its subject and technique is another early fourteenth-century wood-carved relief icon of the Virgin in the Hodegetria type, from Alexandroupolis in Thrace.[61]

Although the origins of wood-carved icons have often been attributed to the influence of a western practice adopted by artists working in territories under Latin occupation,[62] another plausible hypothesis is a relationship with metropolitan practices, particularly that of carving relief icons on marble panels.[63] The rendering of haloes in carved plain relief on a painted panel, as on the Benaki icon, is unusual though not unknown, and is not necessarily connected with a western practice. One icon with the Virgin Eleousa from Thessaloniki, formerly in the Byzantine Museum of Athens,[64] presents a fine example of early Palaiologan art, displaying no western influences, in which the raised haloes in plain relief are similar to those of the Benaki icon although painted in a yellow-ochre colour.[65] Two other examples by different artists suggest the diffusion of this technique to a wider area by the late thirteenth–early fourteenth century. One is the Virgin Faneromeni from the monastery of St John Chrysostom at Koutsovendis (Fig. 27.12),[66] painted in a rather schematic and linear local style, where the rendering of the haloes in plain relief seems to be an exception to the prevailing technique of Cypriot icons. The other, the *Madonna Costantinopolitana*, a Virgin *dexiokratousa*

---

[59] R. Lange, *Die byzantinische Reliefikonen* (Recklinghausen, 1964), no. 49, 121–3. This icon with its clear western influences has been attributed to a Cypriot or Crusader workshop; see M. Chatzidakis, in K. Weitzmann, M. Chatzidakis and S. Radojčić, *Icons* (New York, s.a.), 68–70. Weitzmann, *The Icon*, 109, Pl. 35. See also Tsigaridas, 'Φορητές εικόνες', 151–3 nn. 99 and 106, for a discussion of the previous literature.

[60] Both icons are displayed in the church of St George at Omorphe Ekklesia, Gallista. Tsigaridas, 'Σχέσεις βυζαντινής και δυτικής τέχνης στη Μακεδονία', Figs 2–3. Tsigaridas, 'Φορητές εικόνες', 149–51 n. 87, Fig. 39. See also a large relief icon of St Clement at Ohrid: Lange, *Reliefikonen*, no. 51, 124.

[61] Ch. Pennas, 'Ξυλόγλυπτη βυζαντινή εικόνα Οδηγήτριας από την Αλεξανδρούπολη', in *Αφιέρωμα στη μνήμη Στυλιανού Πελεκανίδη* (*Μακεδονικά, Παράρτημα*, 5) (Thessaloniki, 1983), 397–440, Pls 1–3a.

[62] As Thessaloniki, Arta, Cyprus and Sinai. For previous literature, see above, nn. 59–61. For a discussion on the provenance of 13th-century wood-carved icons, see Tsigaridas, 'Φορητές εικόνες', 149–53 and corresponding notes.

[63] A Constantinopolitan origin for wood-carved icons was proposed by G. Sotiriou, 'La sculpture sur bois dans l'art byzantin', in *Mélanges Charles Diehl* II (Paris, 1930), 179–80. For Constantinopolitan marble relief icons, see A. Grabar, *Sculptures byzantines du moyen âge (XIe–XIVe siècle)* II (Paris, 1976), Pls Ia, XCIIIa, XCIV, CVI, CVIII–CIXd (cf. also Pls IIb, XCII). Lange, *Reliefikonen*, nos 5, 7–8, 22, 31, 33b, 39–40. K. Loverdou-Tsigarida, 'The Mother of God in Sculpture', in Vassilaki, *Mother of God*, 237–49, Pls 186, 188–9, 192.

[64] The icon, now in the Museum of Byzantine Culture, Thessaloniki, belonged to the Byzantine Museum of Athens from 1914 to 1995; N. Chatzidakis, 'A Fourteenth-Century Icon of the Virgin Eleousa in the Byzantine Museum of Athens', in C. Moss and K. Kiefer (eds), *Byzantine East, Latin West. Art Historical Studies in Honor of K. Weitzmann* (Princeton, NJ, 1995), 495–8, Figs 1–2. Vassilaki, *Mother of God*, no. 80, 478–9 (A. Tourta).

[65] On another icon of St Nicholas, probably from western Macedonia and dated to the late 13th c., the halo in plain relief was painted with a simple decorative motif; see above, n. 51.

[66] Papageorgiou, *Εικόνες*, 42, Fig. 27 (dating probably from the 14th c.). The Virgin kisses the hand of her son and the background is yellow ochre. The whereabouts of this icon have been unknown since the Turkish occupation of 1974.

from Padua (Fig. 27.11), was most probably painted by a Byzantine artist with higher aspirations.[67]

This short review allows us to conclude that the use of wood-carved relief haloes on the Benaki Hodegetria may be linked with metropolitan workshops; however, the use of rough materials excludes a provenance from a wealthy artistic centre, and suggests an attribution to some local workshop on the periphery – most probably in the eastern Mediterranean, with which the icon has iconographic associations, as already mentioned above.

Style

The monumental and hieratic configuration of the Virgin and Child is characterized both by the flat and linear treatment of the drapery and by the use of a limited range of colours, most conspicuously dark blue, brick-red, and bright red, while the modelling of the flesh, as on the Virgin's fingers, is rendered with thick, vivid, brownish and olive-green brushstrokes. Furthermore, the broad, flat shaping, as well as the ill-proportioned treatment of the Child's facial features, constitute a stylistic device which is also found on the series of icons already discussed in terms of iconography and technique: the Cypriot icons of the Hodegetria from Laneia, Doros, Hagios Theodoros and Koutsovendis (Figs 27.9 and 27.12)[68] and the icons located in Italy and attributed to eastern Mediterranean workshops, such as those in Padua, Pisa and Bari (Figs 27.10–27.11).[69]

Further observations can be formulated regarding the small-scale figures on the frame, which are in a much better state of preservation (Figs 27.3–27.8). They are distinguished for their vivid spirituality, as in the case of St John Chrysostom, who looks to the side, and for their variety of pose and costume; while their faces, rendered with rapid brushstrokes in a skilful technique also found in the freehand preliminary design and incisions, and the meticulous decorative motifs with pearls and multi-coloured precious stones on the books and garments (Figs 27.6–27.8), reveal the hand of an accomplished master of icon-painting.

The bust of Christ (Fig. 27.3), with its prominent masses and its distinctive rendering of the neck muscles with precise small brushstrokes forming a reversed triangular pattern permits further associations. It can be compared to some important examples of 'Crusader' icons from Sinai, such as the Christ Pantokrator,[70] and even with the vivid face of Christ on the border of the icon of the Crucifixion, already mentioned above for its iconographic associations with the Benaki icon. This is also a feature of some interesting configurations on Cretan frescoes, such as those with the Deesis in the central nave of the church of Panagia Kera at Kritsa,[71] where we

---

[67] See Canova Mariani, *Luca Evangelista*, no. 75, 405–6 (M. Bacci). The icon can be dated to the late 13th c. and attributed to an early Palaiologan workshop of the Thessaloniki region. Its appellation 'Costantinopolitana', which is much later (after the Council of Trent), probably betrays its provenance from a Byzantine region, possibly Constantinople. For further comments, see above, 340, n. 22.

[68] See above, n. 12 (Laneia), n. 13 (Doros) and n. 65 (Koutsovendis).

[69] See above, n. 18 (Pisa), n. 20 (Bari), nn. 22 and 66 (Padua).

[70] *Mystery Great and Wondrous*, no. 53, 190–1 (N. Chatzidakis). See also a 15th-c. icon from Prespa, ibid., no. 58, 202–3 (N. Chatzidakis).

[71] Second layer of frescoes dated around 1300. In this church there are three painted layers dated on stylistic

find not only the same figure type of Christ (Fig. 27.13), but also a similar arrangement and colouring of his garments – a red tunic and a blue himation – covering a small part of his right shoulder and his left arm.

The angel on the right (Fig. 27.4), with its round face and wide open eyes, modelled with warm ochre-red brushstrokes on an olive-green ground, presents an almost identical figure type to that found on the icon of the Virgin from Mega Spelaion, Peloponnese, dated to the thirteenth century.[72] Similar treatment of the flesh and wings of the angels also occurs on another thirteenth-century icon with the Crucifixion from the Pantokrator Monastery, Mt Athos,[73] painted on a red ground. The affiliations can be extended to the wall paintings of the church of Kritsa, where we find a similar rendering of the angels, shown in a three-quarter view, in the Nativity of Christ and in the scene of the Prayer of Joachim in the garden (Fig. 27.14).[74]

The Sts Peter and Paul display a linear treatment similar to that of the same saints on the icon from the Vatican and the 'Crusader' epistyle from Sinai, already linked to our icon through their iconography, while St Paul may be compared with the thirteenth-century Cypriot icon of the same apostle.[75] Lastly, the vivid facial features and the modelling of the flesh of St Gregory the Theologian (Fig. 27.8) can be compared to certain similar faces of aged hierarchs at Kritsa[76] (Fig. 27.15).

Wider stylistic affiliations are also to be noted in the varied and detailed decoration of the costumes and the attributes of the saints on the border, in particular those of John Chrysostom, Basil and Gregory the Theologian (Figs 27.6–27.8). They recall the ornamentation with pearls and precious stones on the costumes of certain saints on the border of the thirteenth-century Sinai icon with the Crucifixion, where we find a similar treatment of Sts Peter and Paul and the hierarchs, and furthermore those found in various small Cretan churches dated to the first decades of the fourteenth century, such as Sts George and Constantine at Pyrgos Monofatsiou (1314–1315) and the church of the Archangel at Archanes (1314–1315);[77] an even closer relationship can be observed in the ornamentation of the garments of the saints in the Panagia Kera at Kritsa, as well as on the wall paintings of the neighbouring church of St John the Baptist.[78] The already noted close relationship between the rendering of the figures on the border of the

---

grounds as follows: first layer, late 13th c.; second layer, early 14th c.; third layer, second half of the 14th c. See M. Chatzidakis, 'Τοιχογραφίες στη Κρήτη', *KretChron* 6 (1952), 59–91. S. Papadaki-Oekland, 'Η Κερά της Κριτσάς', *AD* 22 (1967), *A-Meletai*, 87–111. K. Gallas, K. Wessel and M. Borboudakis, *Byzantinisches Kreta* (Munich, 1983), 428–33, plan in Fig. 407. M. Borboudakis, *Παναγία Κερά, Βυζαντινές Τοιχογραφίες στην Κριτσά* Athens (without date and numbering of the pages and with good colour photos), Fig. 28.

[72] A. Xyngopoulos, 'Icônes du XIIIe siècle en Grèce', in *L'art byzantin du XIIIe siècle*, 75 ff., Fig. 1.
[73] Papamastorakis, 'Icons 13th–16th century', 46, Figs 2, 19–20.
[74] Borboudakis, *Κριτσά*, Figs 24, 43.
[75] See above, 341, n. 30.
[76] Borboudakis, *Κριτσά*, Fig. 35.
[77] Gallas, Wessel and Borboudakis, *Kreta*, Figs 126–8 (St George and St Constantine, Pyrgos Monofatsiou, 1314–1315). I. Spatharakis, *Dated Byzantine Wall Paintings of Crete* (Leiden, 2001), Figs 33, 35–6 (Archangel Michael, Archanes, 1315–1316). See also K. Kalokyris, *The Byzantine Wall Paintings of Crete* (New York, 1973), Fig. C7 (St Nicholas, Meronas), Figs C9, BW86 (St George, Vathyako), Fig. BW110 (Our Lady Skafi-Prodromi, 1347).
[78] Borboudakis, *Κριτσά*, Figs 30, 46, 51, 57. St John the Baptist of the Nekrotapheion at Agios Nikolaos (ibid., Fig. 62, St Photeini). For the church, dated to 1370, see Gallas, Wessel and Borboudakis, *Kreta*, 434–5, Figs 408–9.

Benaki icon and the frescoes at Kritsa is enhanced by an astonishing similarity between the Virgin holding the Christ-child on her right arm on our icon and the figure of St Anne at Kritsa, in a similar pose, holding the young Virgin on her right arm (Fig. 27.16);[79] this fresco additionally contains a halo decorated in plaster relief comparable with those found on Cypriot and south Italian icons, thus demonstrating the western influences often detected in Cretan frescoes of the later Byzantine period and the Venetian occupation after the fall of the island in 1204.[80]

All the above-mentioned affiliations point to an experienced painter, associated in some way with the first layers of the fresco decoration of the church at Kritsa, Crete, around the year 1300.

Conclusion

The individual stylistic features as well as the technique and iconography of the Benaki Museum *dexiokratousa* are, as we have seen, characteristic of a series of icons which have been attributed to an artistic current widespread in thirteenth- and fourteenth-century icon-painting in areas of the eastern Mediterranean under Latin occupation, and often given the designation 'Crusader art'.[81] The various methods by which the trends of eastern Mediterranean art, and particularly those of Cypriot icons, arrived in Italy have been re-examined by scholars in recent years.[82] The existence of a common artistic language for icon-painting, characterized by a specific technique, iconography and style throughout the Latin-occupied Byzantine world is beyond any doubt, but the question of its origin and its relationship with metropolitan workshops still remains open and subject to discussion.[83]

The number of known thirteenth-century icons in mainland Greece and the islands has greatly increased in recent years with the publication of many icons from northern Greece and Cyprus which reflect the art of local workshops and sometimes betray a close contact with western art and an association with icons found in Italy.[84] From the Cycladic islands, however, only two thirteenth-century icons have been recorded: an icon of the Virgin from Santorini and

---

79 Borboudakis, Κριτσά, Fig. 23.
80 See Vassilaki, 'Western influences'. Among the frescoes at Kritsa is one representing St Francis (Borboudakis, Κριτσά, Fig. 38). For ornamented haloes on Cretan frescoes see Kalokyris, *Wall Paintings of Crete*, Figs BW19, C23, BW71. Spatharakis, *Dated Byzantine Wall Paintings of Crete*, Fig. 38.
81 Among the extensive bibliography, Weitzmann, 'Icon Painting in the Crusader Kingdom'. Id., 'Crusader Icons and "maniera greca"', in I. Hutter (ed.), *Byzanz und der Westen. Studien zur Kunst des europäischen Mittelalters* (Vienna, 1984), 149–51. L.-A. Hunt, 'Art and Colonialism: The Mosaics of the Church of the Nativity in Bethlehem (1169) and the Problem of "Crusader" Art', *DOP* 45 (1991), 69–85.
82 V. Pace, 'Presenze e influenze cipriote nella pittura duecentesca italiana', *CorsiRav* 32 (1985), 259–98. Bacci, 'Due tavole', 20 ff. (with further bibliography).
83 J. Folda, 'The Saint Marina icon; "maniera cypria", lingua franca, or crusader art?', in B. Davezac (ed.), *Four Icons in the Menil Collection* (Houston, 1992), 107–33. A. W. Carr, 'Byzantines and Italians on Cyprus: Images from Art', *DOP* 49 (1995), 339–57. M. Panayotidi, 'Η ζωγραφική του 12ου αιώνα στην Κύπρο και το πρόβλημα των τοπικών εργαστηρίων', in Πρακτικά Γ´ Διεθνούς Κυπρολογικού Συνεδρίου (Nicosia, 2001), 421–5.
84 From a more extensive bibliography see Xyngopoulos, 'Icônes du XIIIe siècle en Grèce'. Tsigaridas, 'Φορητές εικόνες στη Μακεδονία και το Άγιον Όρος', 123–55. Papageorghiou, Εικόνες της Κύπρου. Sophocleous, *Icons*. For icons found in Italy and attributed to eastern Mediterranean or Cypriot artists, see above, nn. 82–3.

another icon of the Virgin from Paros.[85] The remnants of the Virgin's face, incorporated in a later icon with the full-length Virgin *dexiokratousa*, provide valuable evidence of a twelfth-century icon of the *dexiokratousa* Hodegetria, venerated in an unknown church in Candia, repainted in the year 1657, and brought to Zakynthos by Cretan refugees after 1667;[86] as far as I know, however, this is the only Byzantine icon recorded in Crete before the late fourteenth century or the first decades of the fifteenth.[87]

Considered in this context, the Benaki Museum *dexiokratousa* acquires an additional interest. The foregoing iconographic and stylistic examination has demonstrated its close relationship with the frescoes at Kritsa, the most important church of the Merambello region, which exerted a great influence on the wall paintings of the small churches of the area.[88] The icon's large dimensions, as well as its subject, indicate its destination as the main *proskynesis* icon for an unknown church of the Virgin. Lastly, its provenance from eastern Crete[89] provides us with one more argument for its attribution to a painter working in the area of Merambello during the late thirteenth century or the first decades of the fourteenth. The regressive aspect of the late thirteenth- and fourteenth-century frescoes in the small churches of Crete, and particularly at Kritsa, may explain the conservative nature of this icon, which nevertheless reveals in its iconography, technique and style an aspiration to reproduce some established metropolitan prototype.

---

[85] Mitsani, 'Εικόνα της Παναγίας Δεομένης', 177–97.
[86] M. Chatzidakis, 'Παναγία η Επισκοπιανή. Μία βυζαντινή εικόνα στη Ζάκυνθο', *Thesaurismata* 16 (1979), 387–91, Pls 22–3. According to the dedicatory inscription, the worshippers at Candia reproduced the iconography of a damaged original icon of the Virgin.
[87] This fact is even more remarkable as 900 fresco decorations are preserved in the churches of the island, and 95% of them date from the 13th and 14th centuries: M. Chatzidakis, 'Η μνημειακή ζωγραφική στην Ελλάδα. Ποσοτικές προσεγγίσεις', *Πρακτικά της Ακαδημίας Αθηνών* 56 (1981), 381. See also M. Borboudakis, 'Η βυζαντινή τέχνη ως την πρώιμη Βενετοκρατία' and 'Πρώιμη Βενετοκρατία, 14ος αιώνας', in M. Dettorakis (ed.), *Κρήτη, Ιστορία και πολιτισμός* (Herakleion, 1988), 47–74 and 74–100.
[88] This is apparently the case with the church of St John the Baptist at the Nekrotapheion: see above, n. 78.
[89] See above, 337, nn. 1–2.

27.1 Athens, Benaki Museum.
Icon of the Virgin Hodegetria
dexiokratousa with the Deesis and Saints
on the border (before conservation)
(source: Benaki Museum)

27.2 Athens, Benaki Museum. Icon of the Virgin Hodegetria *dexiokratousa* with the Deesis and Saints on the border (after conservation) (source: Benaki Museum)

AN ICON OF THE DEXIOKRATOUSA HODEGETRIA 353

27.3 Christ, detail of Fig. 27.2.
(source: Benaki Museum)

27.4 The Angel on the right,
detail of Fig. 27.2.
(source: Benaki Museum)

Details of Fig. 27.2 (source: Benaki Museum)

27.5   St Peter

27.6   St John Chrysostom

27.7   St Basil

27.8   St Gregory the Theologian

27.9 Cyprus, Hagios Theodoros.
Icon of the Virgin Hodegetria
dexiokratousa
(source: Sophocleous, *Icons*, Fig. 22)

27.10 Bari, Pinacoteca Provinciale.
Icon of the Virgin Hodegetria
(source: Belli d'Elia, *Icone di Puglia*,
fig. on p. 53)

27.11 Padua, S. Giustina.
Icon of the Virgin *dexiokratousa*,
Madonna Costantinopolitana
(source: M. Bacci)

27.12 Cyprus, formerly in the church of
St Chrysostomos Koutsovendis.
Icon of the Virgin *Faneromeni* (source:
Papageorgiou, Εικόνες της Κύπρου, Fig. 27)

27.13 Crete, Kritsa, Panagia Kera.
Christ from the Deesis. Wall-painting
(source: Borboudakis, Κριτσά, Fig. 28)

27.14 Crete, Kritsa, Panagia Kera.
Angel from the Prayer of Joachim. Wall-painting
(source: Borboudakis, Κριτσά, Fig. 43)

27.15 Crete, Kritsa, Panagia Kera.
Unidentified saint. Wall-painting
(source: Borboudakis, Κριτσά, Fig. 35)

27.16 Crete, Kritsa, Panagia Kera.
St Anne holding the Virgin. Wall-painting
(source: Borboudakis, Κριτσά, Fig. 23)

Epilogue

Epilogue

Maria Vassilaki

As I write the Epilogue to this book, I feel that I have reached the end of a long journey, which began seven years ago in 1997 when I started organizing the 'Mother of God' exhibition at the Benaki Museum. The exhibition was inaugurated on 20 October 2000, and when it closed on the following 15 January the journey seemed to be over. Before long, however, we were on our way again, for the decision was taken to publish the proceedings of the conference held during the final days of the exhibition, between 13 and 15 January 2001, and the result is the book which you now hold in your hands.

Epilogues tend to take the form of a valediction, and in this present case this valediction is, sadly, an actual as well as a metaphorical one, for not only are we taking leave, for the present at least, of a subject with which we have lived for seven years, but also we have said our last farewell to two individuals who were in their different ways associated with the conference and the book, Nicolas Oikonomides and Michel van Esbroeck. Nicolas Oikonomides was the first to leave us, before the opening of the conference which he had welcomed with such enthusiasm. He is mentioned several times in the opening pages of this book, in Angelos Delivorrias' Foreword, Evangelos Chrysos' Preface and my own Acknowledgements: more than this, however, the whole volume is dedicated to his memory.

Michel van Esbroeck is responsible for the paper entitled 'The Virgin as the True Ark of the Covenant', which he originally wrote in French for the conference. With his customary diligence and efficiency, he presented me with the text, in publishable form complete with footnotes, before he left Athens. We communicated by electronic mail from time to time and when I informed him of our choice of English as the common language for all the essays in the volume, he lost no time in sending me the translation of his text. Our last exchange was on 27 June 2003, when I returned his paper to him after the editing process was completed. His acknowledgement ended with the words 'With God's blessing and the Virgin's'. Michel van Esbroeck left us on 21 November 2003, the feast of the Presentation of the Virgin, and I trust that the Virgin's blessings accompanied him on his final journey.

This volume originated in a conference which was held in conjunction with an exhibition, and its point of departure was naturally the visual evidence surrounding the figure of Mary in her identity both as Mother of God (Theotokos) and as Virgin. But a glance at the exhibition catalogue will show that visual evidence alone is insufficient to interpret the complex phenomenon of the Virgin's cult, and the dimension it acquired throughout the life of Byzantium.[1] This is why the catalogue of what was basically a visual event contains essays such as those by

---

[1] Vassilaki, *Mother of God*.

Averil Cameron,[2] Cyril Mango,[3] Niki Tsironis,[4] Savvas Agouridis[5] and Ioannis Karavidopoulos.[6] The aims intimated in the catalogue took a more concrete form with the holding of the conference and the publication of its proceedings. Art historians may dominate this volume numerically, but, as the title of the book makes clear, it was our aim to examine the perceptions of the Theotokos in Byzantium through the images of the Mother of God, and even the art historical papers for the most part combine both visual and textual evidence.

The contributions to this volume from art historians, philologists, historians and feminist historians represent an attempt to formulate new arguments and to suggest new interpretations of the Virgin's cult and of the visual material which was created to serve it. Sometimes celebrated works are viewed from a fresh angle and make the subject of original readings. In other cases neglected, obscure examples are brought to light and their meaning extracted in order to enhance our understanding of the era and the conditions in which they were produced. The varied approaches to the visual material and the diverse readings of the texts found in all the papers aim at making an individual contribution to the lively debate which has centred around the personality and the cult of the Virgin in recent years.

I should like to conclude this Epilogue in the same way that I brought the conference to an end three years ago, with a reference to an unexpected use of the appellation 'Hodegetria' by a contemporary Greek football club. I discovered the Hodegetria club by chance, through an exhibition of the work of the photographer Thanassis Stavrakis at the Cultural Centre of the City of Athens. The team is based at Tabouria in Piraeus an area with a strong leftist tradition. They adopted the name 'Hodegetria' in the troubled years of the junta (1967–1974), when they addressed the Virgin and sought her aid in facing the political problem of the club's survival in difficult times. It did survive, and it continues to use the name Hodegetria to this day (Figs E1–E2). The role of the Virgin in the political life of Byzantium is well known and has been widely interpreted, but her role in contemporary Greek political life may offer an equally interesting dimension of the phenomenon, and is a subject that could well reward further study.

---

[2] A. M. Cameron, 'The Early Cult of the Virgin', in Vassilaki, *Mother of God*, 3–15.
[3] Mango, 'Theotokoupolis'.
[4] N. Tsironis, 'The Mother of God in the Iconoclastic Controversy', in Vassilaki, *Mother of God*, 27–39.
[5] S. Agouridis, 'The Virgin Mary in the Texts of the Gospels', in Vassilaki, *Mother of God*, 59–65.
[6] I. Karavidopoulos, 'On the Information Concerning the Virgin Mary Contained in the Apocryphal Gospels', in Vassilaki, *Mother of God*, 67–76.

E1 The 'Hodegetria' football team. At the training grounds.
(source: Th. Stavrakis, Athens)

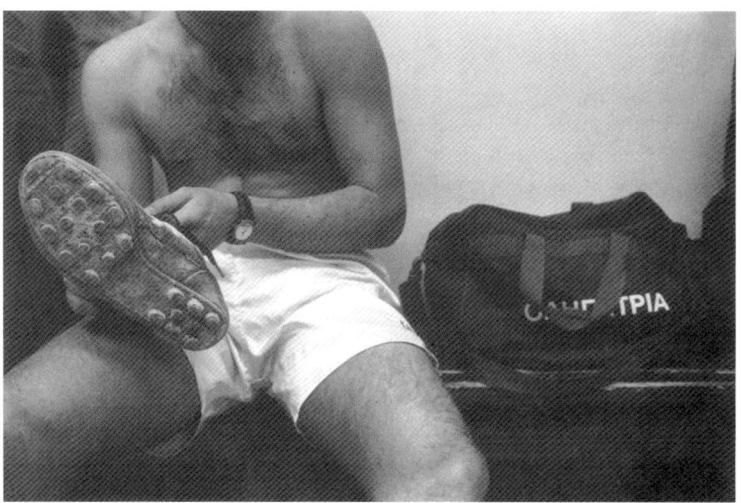

E2 The 'Hodegetria' football team. In the dressing room.
(source: Th. Stavrakis, Athens)

Index

Aaron, prophet 63, 65
abandonment, of children 15
abbots, seals of 175–6
Abraham, prophet 64
Abydos 78
Acre 309
acronym 254n
acrostic 69, 137, 242
Acts of John 3
Acts of St Marina of Antioch 83
Acts of Thomas 253n
Adam 73, 185, 283
Agathias 169–70
Akathistos hymn xxviin, xxviii, xxxi, 78, 79, 84, 85, 105, 120, 209n, 212, 216, 217, 223, 326, Figs 18.9–10
akolouthia see liturgy
Albania 328
　Scutari 328n
Alexios I Komnenos, emperor 162n, 214, 230, 324
Alexios V Doukas, emperor 216
allegory 69, 73, 75, 76, 78
allusion 78
Ambrose, St xxviii
Ambrosi, Georgian nobleman 134
Amon 5
ampulla (pilgrim flask) 159n, 185, 229
amulets 157, 177, 178, 189, 255, 256, 257n, 258n
Anargyroi, Sts 244; *see also* Kosmas, Damianos, saints, healing
Anastasia, empress 149
Anastasia, owner of a ring 154
Anastasia Pharmakolytria, St 309
Anastasios, Patriarch 86
Anastasios I, emperor 63, 68, 149, 176n
Anastasios of Sinai 72, 169
Andrew, St, in Crisi 84
Andrew of Crete 92, 121
Andrew the Fool, St 308–9
Andronikos I Komnenos, emperor 156

Andronikos II Palaiologos, emperor 216, 225, 227, 228, 232, 233, 236, 239, 241, 244n, 298
Andronikos III Palaiologos, emperor 216
Anemas, Manuel 161n
Angeloi, family 155, 175
　lead seals of 175n
angels 3, 4, 37, 40, 51, 64, 66, 78, 119, 120, 184, 185, 198, 200, 201, 211, 232, 240, 241, 245, 254, 283n, 295, 298, 322, 325, 341, 343, 348, Plate 24b, Fig. 27.4
　archangels 167, 170, 172, Fig. 14.1
　ranks of 51, 58, Figs 4.2–3
animals, wild and tame 254
Anna, *anassa* possibly Komnene 160–2
Anna, empress 149
Anna, nun 155
Anna, owner of an armband 157
Anna, owner of a sardonyx cameo 158
Anne, St 156–7, 199, 200, 201, 226, 240, 279n, 349, 356, Fig. 27.16
Anthimos, archbishop of Athens 258n
Anthony of Novgorod 277
Antioch 159, 213, 322
　church of St John the Baptist 159
　Patriarchate 322
Antony the Younger, St 154
Aphrodisias 169–70, 173
Aphrodite 4
Apocalyptic Vision of Esdras 18
Apophthegmata Patrum 16
aporia 82
Apostles 65, 73, 75, 82, 283n, 323
apotropaic practices 254n, 256, 257
Arabs 27, 86n, 212, 213, 326
archimandrite 241
arcosolium 232, 238
Arculf 278n
Ariadne, empress 149, 186, 211
Arios 93
Ark of the Covenant 63–5, 66, 68, 73
armband 157, 184, 187, Fig. 16.2

364 INDEX

Armenia 68
Armenia, Little 308
  Sis 308
Armenian manuscript illumination 13, 307, 309
Artabasdos 86
Artemis 83
Artemios, St 160
asp 254
Aspar 148
Asterios of Amaseia 185
Athanasios, mentioned in an amulet 189
Athanasios of Alexandria 254n
Athanasios, Patriarch 233
Athanasios, St, the Athonite 135, 137, 138, 139
Athos *see* Greece, Mt Athos
Attaleiates, Michael 190, 213
Augustine 30
aurum coronarium 27
Austria
  Bregenz, abbey of Mehrerau, chalice 307n
  Vienna 268
Avars 210, 212, 232
  Avar assault (siege) 210, 217, 326
  Chagan 211

Babylon, three children of 67
Bagrat, son of Khosrovanush 156
Baldwin I, king of Jerusalem 280n
Baldwin II, king of Jerusalem 280n
Baldwin III, king of Jerusalem 280n
Baldwin IV, king of Jerusalem 280n
Baldwin V, king of Jerusalem 280n
Balkans 134
balsam 155
bands *see* armbands
banners 51
Baptism 18, 19, 243
Bardas, *basilikos protospatharios* 176n
Barisano of Trani 326
Bartholomew of Simeri 324
Basil, monk 15
Basil I, emperor 79–80, 227
Basil II, emperor 147, 201, 212, 213, 230
Basil the Great 253n, 341, 342, 343, 348, 354,
    Fig. 27.7
basileia 145, 148
basileus 88
basilisk 254, 255
Basiliskos, martyr 73
basin 214, 227
baskania 254–5, 256, 257
Baskosyne 256

Bassarab, Neagoe 134
Bayezid I, sultan 265, 270
Bazaar of Herakleides 146n
Belgium
  Brussels, Feron–Stoclet collection 307n
belt 184
Bethlehem *see* Palestine
Bethlehem, son of Caleb 64, 65
Birth Houses *see Mammisi*
Bithynia 133
Blemmydes, Nikephoros 254n
Blues *see* factions
Bogoljubski, Andrej, Grand Duke 307
Boniface III, Pope 31
Boniface IV, Pope 28, 30, 36
Boniface IX, Pope 270
Boris, tsar 213
Botaneiates, Manuel 158
Bourgeois, Louise, sculptor 286
bracelet 103
Branas, Alexios, 216
breast 6, 9, 16–17
  of a Marian icon 278n
  of the Saidnaya icon 278–9
breast-feeding 15, 257n
'bride of Christ' 146, 147
Bronorius della Scala 266, 268
Bulgaria 296
  Boiana church 294n
  Pernik 158n
  Silistra, bronze pectoral cross, 155, 163,
    Fig. 13.2
  Sofia, National Art Gallery
    icon of the Virgin Glykophilousa 344
    Poganovo icon 269n
Bulgarian attack 212
bushel 63
Byzantium xxvii, xxxi, xxxii, 23, 30, 73, 89, 96,
    162, 228, 233, 279, 282, 284, 285, 359

cakes
  dedicated to the Virgin 16
  prepared by Sara 64
Caleb son of Jephoniah 64, 65, 66–7
calogeri 330, 331
cameos as phylacteries 153–62, 177, 230, 231
Canada
  Toronto, Royal Ontario Museum, silver
    armband 157, 184, 187–8, 189, 191, Fig. 16.2
Candidus 211
candles 3, 186, 214
Canons of Hippolytus 18

Cappadocia 154
  Göreme, Tokalı kilise, New Church 96, 101, Fig. 8.3
  chapel of the Theotokos 200n
  Kizil, church of Joachim and Anna 200n
Carmelite monks 284, 308, 309, 318, Fig. 25.7
Caterina, wife of Giangaleazzo Visconti 267–8
Catherine, St, of Alexandria 18, 147n
Catherine, St, of Siena 147n
Catholicossate of Armenia 68
cave
  of demons 254n, 258
  of the Nativity of Christ 251, 254, 257, 258
  of the Burial of Christ 258
Cecilia, martyr 73
cell, monastic 4, 16
censer 117–25, 159
chains, attached 178
Chalcedon, council of *see* Councils, Ecumenical
Chalkeopoulos, Athanasios 324
chancel screen *see* templon screen
chapels, burial 159n
chariot, imperial 213
charis 74
Charles III of Navarre 269–70
Charles VI, king of France 265
charms 177, 189, 257n
chartoularios 176n
chastity 87n
chasuble 330
childbearing 156, 157, 162, 189, 257n
childhood 15
childlessness 156, 177, 178n
children 15, 18, 153, 155, 156, 160, 162, 178n, 199, 257n
  new-born 15, 156n, 157, 255, 256
Choniates, Niketas 216
Christ xxviii, 4, 9, 13, 17, 18, 19, 23, 28, 38, 64, 65, 66, 72, 75, 103, 146, 148, 159, 167, 168, 184, 185, 187, 188, 191, 196, 197, 198, 200, 202, 210, 212, 214, 225, 226, 227, 229, 230, 231, 232, 233, 240, 241, 242, 243, 244, 245, 247, 251, 252, 253, 254, 255, 257, 258n, 267, 269 282, 305, 311, 312, 313, 337, 340, 347, 348
  blood of 17, 18, 81
  as blossom 75
  bread 64, 81
  epithets and types of
    Anapeson 125
    Antiphonetes 123, 278n
    Emmanuel 87, 123, 232
    Man of Sorrows (King of Glory, 'Akra Tapeinosis') 105, 111, 269, Fig. 9.4
    New Adam 75
    Pantokrator 9, 154, 339, 340, Plate 24a, Fig. 27.3
  Gospel scenes
    Baptism 188, 243
    Christ with the elders in the Temple 241, 242, 244, 298n
    Crucifixion 93, 94, 96, 98, 102, 106, 107, 108, 109, 113, 114, 185, 188, 197, 253, 280n, 281, 324–5, Plate 12b, Figs 8.4, 9.6, 9.8, 17.5, 26.4
    cure of the woman with an issue of blood 241, 242, Fig. 20.7
    death on the Cross 108
    Deposition 94, 95, 109, 113, Fig. 9.7
    Entombment 280n
    Epiphany 228
    Flight into Egypt 254n
    healing of Peter's wife's mother 241, Fig. 20.5
    healing of the halt and the blind in the Temple 241, 242, 244
    healing of the man blind from birth 241, 242, Fig. 20.5
    healing of the man with dropsy 241, 242, Fig. 20.6
    healing of the paralytic at Bethesda 241, 242, Fig. 20.7
    Lamentation (Threnos) 94, 105, 106, 108, 109, 111, 113, 114, Figs 9.3, 9.7–8
    Marriage at Cana 158, 241, 242, 243, Fig. 20.4
    Massacre of the Innocents 253
    Meeting of Christ and Mary Magdalene in the Garden 281
    Meeting of Christ and the Woman of Samaria 241, 242, 243, Fig. 20.4
    Nativity 103, 104, 108, 109, 113, 118, 123, 184, 185, 188, 189, 191, 251, 259–60, 348, Plate 16, Figs 9.7, 16.1, 21.1–3; first bath 185
    Passion 93, 96, 99, 105, 118, 122, 125, 267
    Resurrection (Anastasis) 107, 108, 109, 114, 123, 125, Fig. 9.8
    Visit of the Women to the Tomb (Myrrhophores) 188, 280n
icons
  'acheiropoietos' 210, 212
  at the Chalke gate 202
  held by Augustine 30
  in Lateran 28, 33, 34, 35, 40, 325
  as light and Sun 52–3, 93

as the *Logos* 17, 18, 19, 23, 53–6, 81, 82, 83, 85, 87, 94, 106, 108, 118, 122, 123, 124, 125, 197, 231, 251, 257
nursing 14, 16–17, 279
source of life 225–6, 231
Christology 72
Christopher, *sebastophoros* 175
Chronicon Paschale 147n, 150, 211
chrysobulls (imperial decrees) 226, 241
chrysography 294
Chrysoloras, Demetrios 270
Chrysoloras, Manuel 266, 270
Church, doctrine and liturgy 98–9
Cilicia 307
Cimabue 294, 295, 296, 297, 298, 299, 300, 312
clasp 184
Claudius, archdeacon of Parentium 186
Clement of Alexandria 17–18, 19
clothing 183, 185, 186, 189
 pieces of cloth 155
coal 120, 121, 122, 123
coins 183–4, 281, 282n, 285
 iconography of 157, 230, 232, 236, 281, 289, Figs 19.7, 23.1
 prophylactic value 183
collecta 33
colophon 265–6
column, honorary 31
Communion 145, 147
Conon, St 211
Constantina, empress 149
Constantine I the Great 135, 137, 140, 212, Fig. 18.2
Constantine V, emperor 56, 80n, 84, 85, 88, 149, 185
Constantine VI, emperor 149
Constantine VII Porphyrogennetos 157, 159, 165, 178n, 209n
Constantine VIII, emperor 178
Constantine Pepagomenos 175
Constantinople xxvii, xxviii, xxx, xxxi, 25, 27, 31, 36, 40, 68, 147, 148, 159, 186, 187, 195, 198, 202, 209, 210, 211, 212, 215, 217, 227, 231, 233, 239, 240, 241, 264n, 265, 266n, 267, 277, 278, 279, 281, 284, 294, 295, 296, 297, 298, 300, 305, 308, 311, 322, 324, 325, 326, 327, 343
 churches and monasteries of
  Anastasios the Persian 149, 150
  Anne 149, 156
  Augusta 149
  Blachernai 29, 68, 145, 147, 148, 149, 186, 188, 195, 209, 210, 211, 212, 213, 214, 215, 216, 229, 231–2, 233, 270, 277, 281, 308, 326; Bath 213, 214, 229; *hagiasma* 229–30, 233; palace 331; St Photeinos chapel 229–30; Soros chapel 209, 211, 212, 214, 264n
  Chalkoprateia 68, 145, 147, 148, 149, 209, 264n, 278n
  Chora (Kariye Çamii) 226n, 232, 238, 245, Fig. 19.9
  Christ at Chalke 198, 277
  Elijah 149
  Euphemia at Pera 149
  Εὐφημία τῆς εὐμόρφου (en Petriō) 159
  Euphrosyne 149, 150
  Forty Martyrs 149
  Hagia Sophia 9, 95, 100, 145, 146, 149, 167, 170, 176n, 187, 212, 213, 216, 219, 278n, 294, Figs 8.1, 18.2
  Hodegon 145, 147, 195, 196, 199, 202, 215, 216, 321, 322, 325; *diakonia* 217, 330
  Holy Apostles 327
  Irene in Perama 148, 149
  Isaiah 149
  John Stoudios 161
  John the Baptist at Oxeia 160
  John the Baptist in Petra 160
  John near the Blachernai monastery 270
  Kosmas and Damianos 149
  Laurence 148
  Menas 149
  Mokios 149
  Nikopoios' chapel 216
  Panteleemon 149
  Paul 149
  Polyeuktos 149
  Sergios and Bakchos 149, 151
  Spoudes 149
  Stephen 149
  Theodote 149–50
  Thomas 149
  'To Despoinon' 149
  Tryphon 149
  Virgin Jerusalem 210
  Virgin Kecharitomene 156
  Virgin tes Peges xxx, 150, 156, 178n, 209, 225, 227–8, 231, 232, 233, 239, 240; Kataphyge 178n, 225, 227, 228, 230; miraculous cures 233, 239, 242ff.; *phiale* 226, 227, 231, 232
 Forum 213
 Great Palace 53, 216

Chalke gate 53, 54, 55, 149, 198, 202
chrysotriklinos 176n
Hippodrome 176n
liturgical processions 195, 277–8
Mese 195, 197
walls 209, 210, 211, 239
    Gate of Bosporion 212
    Golden Gate 232
    Silivri Gate 225
    western gates 211
Constantinos Tios 87n
Coppo di Marcovaldo 296
Coptic art
  paintings 13–22, 13n
Copts 14
  Coptic monks 14, 16
Corippus xxxn, 148
Council
  of Blachernai 81, 233
  of Hiereia 81
  of Lyons 233
  of Quinisext 56
  Vatican I 70
Councils, Ecumenical, 98
  Chalcedon xxviin, 14
  Constantinople III 69
  Ephesus xxi, xxviin, xxviii, xxix, xxxi, 65, 67, 69, 81, 104, 146, 147, 148
  Nicaea II 81, 85, 88
Creed, Nicene 87
crib 33, 65
Croatia
  Poreč, basilica Eufrasiana 105n, 159n, 186, 188, 193, Plate 11, Fig. 16.7
  Zadar 312–13
Cross 51, 54–6, 86, 98
cross, as phylactery 153–62
  litanikoi stauroi 197, 200
  pectoral 185, 230
  reliquary 154–5, 163, 164
  votive 164, 166
crown 213
Crusades, Crusaders 216, 277, 278, 280
  Crusader milieu 278, 280, 282, 283, 284, 308, 309, 340n
  Crusader art 277, 339n, 340n, 341, 343, 345, 346n, 347, 348, 349
cult, term xxix, 91
Cyprus 293, 296, 297, 300, 305–16
  churches and museums
    Asinou, church of Panagia Phorbiotissa 305–16
    Doros, icon of the Virgin Hodegetria 339, 347

    Hagios Theodoros, icon of the Virgin Hodegetria 339, 347, 355, Fig. 27.9
    Kakopetria, church of St Nicholas tes Steges 251n, 309
    Kalopanagiotis, St John Lampadistes monastery, Icon Museum, diptych 285, 292, Plate 19, Fig. 23.7
    Keryneia 184
    Kition, Chruch of the Virgin Angeloktisti 105n
    Koutsovendis, St John Chrysostom monastery, icon of the Virgin Faneromeni 346, 347, 355, Fig. 27.12
    Kykkos monastery 310n
    Lagoudera, Church of the Virgin Arakiotissa 118, 120, 122, 124–7, 130, Plate 6, Figs 10.1–2, 10.7–8; icon of Christ 343
    Laneia, icon of the Virgin Hodegetria 339, 347
    Lefkara, monastery of Holy Cross Faneromenos 310n
    Machairas monastery 321n, 331n
    Moutoullas, church of the Panagia, icon of the Virgin Hodegetria 339
    Nicosia, Byzantine Museum, Archbishop Makarios III Foundation, icon with the Virgin and the Carmelite monks 284, 308, 318, Fig. 25.7; icon of the enthroned Virgin 310, 318, 344, Fig. 25.8; Faneromeni church 322n
    Paphos, Enkleistra of St Neophytos 122, 215, 220, Plate 13, Fig. 18.5
    Pelendri 298n; church of the Holy Cross 309–10
    Trikomo, church of the Virgin 229, 234, Plate 14, Fig. 19.2
  coexistence of ethnic groups 309, 314
  Latin church 285, 310n
Cyril of Alexandria xxviin, xxix, 4, 17–18, 76, 254n
Cyril of Jerusalem 66

da Milano *see* Giovanni da Milano
Daddi, Bernardo 312
Damianos, St 264, 343n
Daniel, abbot 284, 323n
Danilo, bishop 232
David, son of Khosrovanush 156
daughter of Zeus 83
De Locis Martyrum 38, 39
de Lusignan, Jean 309
De officiis 216
de Vigilia, Tommaso 330

death
  depiction of 108
  of children 15
decree 226, 244n
Deesis 158, 280n, 294, 337, 340, 342, 343
Definition (*Horos*) 81, 82, 84, 87, 88
dekatría 326
della Scala *see* Bronorius della Scala, Nicodemo della Scala
Delterios, *turmarches* 325
Demeter and Kore 5
Demetrios, St 264, 346
Demetrios Asan Palaiologos 329
Demetrios Kydones 270
demonology 253n
demons 35, 41, 252n, 253, 255, 256, 257, 262, Figs 21.6–7
Dendera 18–19, 22
  temple complex of Hathor 22
Devil, the 252–7
  symbols of 254
  Satan 83, 145
devotion, term xxix
di Pace, Filippo, 312
Diakainisimos week 240, 242, 244, 331
diakonia see Constantinople, churches and monasteries, Hodegon
diakonikon 211
'diataxeis' 97
Diatyposis 138
Diegesis 134, 135
Diegesis ophelimos 212, 216
dignitaries, ecclesiastical 175
Dionysios the Areopagite 122
Dionysus
  Dionysiac subjects 4
Dioscuri 5
Dishypatos Kanstresios, Manuel 265, 268
doctrine, Trinitarian *see* Trinity
dog 251–2
donor 4, 309, 312, 316, 318, 330
Dorotheos of Tyre 65
dragons 254n
droungos 176n
dropsy 242
drowning, of children 15
Duccio 282, 290, 294, 295, 296, 297, 298, 300, 307, 312, Fig. 23.5
Durantus Gullielmus 35

earth 155
  personifications of 189

Ecloga 88
economoi of monasteries, seals of 230
Edessa 36
Edmund Holland, Earl of Kent 267–8
Egypt 4–6, 8, 13–22, 67, 69, 121n, 158, 183, 185, 186, 189
  Alexandria 4, 10, 147
    Patriarchal Library 322n
  Antinoë 158, 177n
  Bawīṭ
    monastery of St Apollo 4, 5, 256, 262, Fig. 21.6
    monastery of Apa Jeremiah 17, 20
  Cairo, Coptic Museum 20
  Dakhleh oasis 7–8, 11
    temple of Tutu 8, 11
  Fayyūm 4, 5, 6
  Karanis 5, 9, 10
  Kellis 7, 11
    Isis panel 7–8, 11, Fig. 1.5
  Kom el-Dikka 4, 6, 10
  Saqqara 20
  Scetis, monastery of the Syrians 121n
  Sinai 3–4, 5, 6, 25, 73, 74, 104n, 167, 169, 297
    icons 8, 32, 115; Anastasis 345; Annunciation 23, 124; Christ Pantokrator 347; Crucifixion 343, 347, 348; 'Crusader' epistyle 341, 348; Deesis 343; Dormition of the Virgin (13th c.) 120, 128, Fig. 10.4; Dormition of the Virgin (13th c.) 120, 125, 129, Figs 10.5–6; Hexaptych (12th c.) 214–5, 220, 311, 319, Figs 18.4, 25.9; St Nicholas 343; St Panteleemon 32; Virgin and Child between Archangels (encaustic) 3–4, 5–8, 104n, 167–72, 295, Fig. 14.1; Virgin Blachernitissa 345; Virgin Glykophilousa with Christ 313; Virgin Hodegetria (mosaic icon) 338; Virgin Kykkotissa enthroned 109, 115, 124, Fig. 9.9; Virgin Paraklesis 306; Virgin with Christ-child (encaustic, in Kiev) 8, 25, 32; Virgin with Christ-child (no B40) 8, 196n; Virgin with Christ-child (no B48) 8
    manuscripts 119–20; cod. gr. 61 297; gr. 1216 119–20, 127, Fig. 10.3
  Wadi Natrun, monastery of the Virgin Mary 21
eipha 63
Eisodos see Virgin, episodes of life and feasts
ekphrasis 95
Elamon 63, 64
Eleanor of Aragon 310n, 327
Elevation of the Cross, feast of 73
Elisabeth 65

Emma, queen 282
Emmanuel *see* Christ
Empire
  Byzantine *see* Byzantium
  Frankish-Saxon xxii
enkleistra see Cyprus, Paphos
enkolpia, as phylacteries 103, 153–62, 165
Ephraim of Athens 322n
Ephrata 64
Ephrem the Syrian xxviii, 105
epigrams 306
Epiphanios of Cyprus 63–5, 66, 67
'episkepsis' (reliquary) 214
epitropos 138
Esau 107
Esdras 18
Euchaita 78
Eucharist 17, 19, 82, 105, 147; *see also*
  Communion
Eucharistic bread 231
Eudokia, empress 145, 150, 151, 322
Eudokia, owner of a ring 154
Eudokia Komnene 162n
Eudoxia, empress 151
Eufrasius, bishop 186, 193, Fig. 16.7
Eufrasius, son of archdeacon Claudius 186, 193, Fig. 16.7
eulogiai 177
Eunomios 93
Euphemia, empress 149
Europe 96
Eusebios of Caesarea 3
Eusebios of Emesa 253
Eustathia, owner of a ring 189
Eustathios of Thessaloniki 323n
Euthymios, founder of Iveron monastery 133
Euthymios Zigabenos 252n, 253, 254
Evagrios 147n
Eve xxvii, 146, 153, 283
evil eye 254–8
exegetical theology 75–6
exorcism 256, 257
exposure, of children 15

factions 233
fertility 153, 177
figurines 5
fire [fever] 242
footstool 3
Fortuna 4
Forty Martyrs, relics of 150
fragrance 121, 122

fragrant substances 155
France
  Avignon, Musée du Petit Palais, Filippo di Pace's *Maestà* 312
  Châteaudun, Church of La Madeleine, reliquary 160
  Lyons, Bibliothèque municipale, Bible, MS. 410 280, 288, 312, Fig. 23.2
  Paris 265
    Bibliothèque nationale, cod. fr. 1533 278n; cod. Coislin 239 120n; cod. gr. 1208, Homilies of James of Kokkinobaphos 253n, 261, Fig. 21.5; nouv. Aq. Lat. 710 311–12; Zoe's lead seal 179, Fig. 15.1
    Cabinet des médailles, bronze amulet 262, Fig. 21.7; gold ring of Giora 158, 165, 189, Fig. 13.6; sardonyx cameo 158, 165, 177n, Fig. 13.7
    Musée du Louvre, MR 416 265, 272, Fig. 22.3
  St Denis monastery 265, 266n
Franks 279
Friday
  after Easter, day of the feast of the Virgin Zoodochos Pege (celebration day of the Virgin tes Peges monastery) 225, 228, 232, 240, 242, 244, 331n
  bath of the emperor and high-rank clergy at the Blachernai bath 230, 232
  day of the 'usual miracle' at Blachernai 209n, 215, 230, 232, 308
funerary representations 313
furniture 297

Gabriel, archangel 264, 325
Gabriel, Georgian ascetic 133
Gabriel, hymnographer 137
Gaipha 64
Galbius 211
Galbius and Candidus Legend 211, 214
gates of heaven 120
Gazouba 64
gemstones 178
George, abbot of Iveron 133
George, St 155, 264, 309, 343n, 346
George Maioulios, merchant 245n
George of Antioch, admiral 307
George of Nikomedeia 94, 95, 97, 98, 105
George Pachymeres 265n
George Pisides 210, 211
George Scholarios 70
Georgia
  Svaneti, Adiš, church of the Saviour 311

Germanos I, Patriarch 52, 83, 84, 92, 93, 96, 98, 122, 200
Germanos II, Patriarch 92
Germany
  Berlin
    Staatliche Museen zu, Preußischer Kulturbesitz:
    Ägyptisches Museum 6, 10; Isis panel 6–7, 11 Fig. 1.3;
    Antikenabteilung, pectoral with gold medallion 158, 183–4, 189;
    Kaiser-Friedrich-Museum (Bodemuseum), silver ring 189;
    Museum für Spätantike und Byzantinische Kunst (Bodemuseum), ivory diptych 105n; limestone icon of the Virgin Galaktotrophousa 104n
    Staatsbibliothek, Preußischer Kulturbesitz, MS. lat. fol. 480 328n
  Freising 266, 268, 270, 271, 273;
    Diözesanmuseum, 'Lukasbild' 263–71, 273, Plates 17, 18a, Figs 21.1–2, 22.4
  Munich
    Bayerisches Nationalmuseum 264
    Chr. Schmidt collection, necklace 177n; ring 189
Giangaleazzo Visconti, duke of Milan 266–7, 269, 270
Gideon, prophet 72–3
Giora, owner of a gold ring 157, 189
Giotto 285
Giovanni da Milano 285, 292, Fig. 23.8
Giunta Pisano 299
Glavas, Isidore, metropolitan of Thessaloniki 270
Godhead 74
  represented by Gospel book, dove and cross 52
Goslar Evangeliary 297
Gospel of John, Arabic 254
Gospel of Lothair 299
Gospel of St Emmeran 299
Graptoi brothers 80n, 94
'Great Virgin' 4
Greece 294
  Aigina, Omorphi Ekklesia 251, 259, Plate 16, Fig. 21.1
  Arta 298
    Blacherna monastery 203, Fig. 17.1
  Athens 294, 311
    Academy of Athens xxi
    Benaki Museum xix, xxi, xxiv, xxvii, 24, 101, 167, 321, 359; agate seal-stone 177n; bronze ring 154, 163, Plate 8, Fig. 13.1; icon of the *dexiokratousa* Hodegetria 337–54, Plates 23–4, Figs 27.1–8; icon of the Lamenting Virgin 101, Fig. 8.2; triptych 312
    Byzantine Museum, icon of Christ from the Prespa region 345; icon of Christ Pantokrator 340; icon of St George 346
    Hellenic National Research Foundation xix, xxi
    Institute for Byzantine Research, xxi, xxiii
    private collection, icon of Christ 345
  Attica, Kalyvia Kouvara, church of St Peter 243
  Crete 298n, 313
    Archanes, church of the Archangel Michael 348
    Dories monastery, icon of the Virgin Hodegetria 344
    Kouneni, church of Archangel Michael 252, 260, Fig. 21.3
    Kritsa, church of the Panagia Kera 347–50, 356, Figs 27.13–16; church of St John the Baptist 348, 350n
    Kroustas Merambellou, church of St John 251n
    Merambello 350
    Pyrgos Monofatsiou, church of Sts George and Constantine 348
  Euboea, Aliveri, church of the Dormition of the Virgin 229n, 245
  Kastoria 345
    Byzantine Museum, two-sided icon 105, 111, Fig. 9.4
    churches:
      Mavriotissa, icon of the Dormition of the Virgin 125, 131, Fig. 10.9; scene of the Baptism 243
      St Nicholas Kasnitzes 243
      St Stephen 243
    Gallista, Omorphe Ekklesia, icons of St George and St Demetrios 346
  Lakedaimonia 245n
  Lesbos 197
  Mani, Hagia Kyriaki, church of the Agitria 324; Kipoula, church of Sts Anargyroi 252
  Mega Spelaion monastery, icon of the Virgin 348
  Messenia, Koroni 328
  Meteora, Transfiguration monastery, diptych with the Virgin and Christ 269n
  Mistra 226, 229n, 234, 239, 240, 241, 244, 245, 246–9;
    Brontocheion monastery, church of the Aphendiko 226, 234, 240, 242, 243, 244, 246–8, Plate 15, Figs 19.1, 20.1–7; church of Sts Theodore 229n, 245, 249, Fig. 20.9
    chapel of Ai-Yannakis 244, 249, Fig. 20.8

Mt Athos 133–42, 299
  Great Lavra monastery 138, 140; cod. 1142 135n; *phiale* 243
  Hilandar monastery, icon of Christ 340; icon of the Presentation of the Virgin 295, 299; icon of St Demetrios 295n; jasper cameo 230; two jasper *panagiaria* 231, 236, Fig. 19.6
  Iveron monastery (St Clement) 133–42; cod. 5 307n; cod. 593 138n
  Karakallou monastery, cod. 66 135n
  Pantokrator monastery, cod. 49 342; icon of the Crucifixion 348; two-sided icon 269, 274, 344, Plate 18b, Fig. 22.5
  Protaton 125, 139, 140, 295
  St Paul monastery, chapel of St George 243
  Vatopedi monastery 140; fresco fragment with the Virgin and child with Angels 298; Octateuch, cod. 602 298; Psalter, cod. 851 230
Naxos 257n, 296
  Roman Catholic Cathedral, two-sided icon 296
Paros, icon of the Virgin 350
Patmos 295
Peloponnese 241, 244, 245n
Phokis, Hosios Loukas monastery 96, 102, 325, 338, 342, Fig. 8.4
Rhodes 313
Santorini, Mesa Gonia, Episkopi, icon of the Virgin Eleousa 311, 343–4, 349
Veroia 345
Thessaloniki 265, 268, 269, 270, 293, 294, 295, 298, 300, 323
  Akapniou monastery 265n
  Blatadon monastery, 'composite' icon 342, 343n
  church of Acheiropoietos, icon of the Virgin 269
  church of St Demetrios 187, 306
  church of St Euthymios 298
  church of St Nicholas Orphanos 243n
  church of St Sophia 323
  liturgical practices 323
  Museum of Byzantine culture:
    icon of the Virgin Glykophilousa 311, 346; icon of the Virgin *dexiokratousa* 340; marble icon of the Virgin 230
Thessaly 298
  Trikala, Porta Panaghia church 298
Thrace
  Alexandroupolis, icon of the Hodegetria 346
Zakynthos 138; icon of the Virgin 350
Greens *see* factions
Gregory, *basilikos protospatharios* 176n
Gregory I 39

Gregory II, Pope, letters of 88
Gregory III, Pope 27, 30–31, 33, 35, 36, 37, 41
Gregory of Kykkos 322, 325, 331
Gregory of Nazianzos 120
Gregory of Nyssa 15, 154, 253, 258n, 341, 342, 343, 348, 354, Fig. 27.8
Gregory of Tours 35, 68
Gregory Palamas 140
Guido da Siena 296
Gylou 256, 257n

Hades 253, 265
haematite 257n
haemorrhage 242
hagiasma 228, 229, 233, 244
Hagiasmos see liturgy
halo 5, 6, 8, 9
hand of God 51, 52
Harpocrates *see* Horos
Hathor 22
health 153, 162
Helen, owner of a reliquary cross 155
Henotikon 68
Henry III of Castile 269
Herakleios, emperor 210
Herod, king 253
Heron 5, 9
Hesychios of Jerusalem 76, 254n
Hetoimasia 51, 52, 59, 264, 343, Plate 17, Figs 4.4, 21.1
Het'um II, prince of Cilicia 308
hierarch, blowing the censer 119–20
  officiating 117, 127, 129, Figs 10.2, 10.6
  pointing to the censer 120
Hiero 78
hieromonachos 137
Hikelia 65
Hilarion Kanabes, monk 227
History of Aur 19
Holland *see* Edmund Holland, Lucia, countess of Kent
Holy Rider 157, 188, 257, 262, Fig. 21.7
honey 18
Honorius III, Pope 324
hooks, metal 4
Horos (definition), *see* Definition
Horos (Harpocrates) 4, 5, 6, 10
houses
  birth houses 18, 22
  late antique 4, 5
  worship inside 3
Ḥûr 64

Hyakinthos, hegoumenos 51
hymnography 69–76, 77, 228, 257, 258
Hypomnema 134, 135, 136, 137, 138

Iberians 133–4, 136
iconoclasm xxxi, xxxii, 26, 40, 51, 53, 77–89, 91, 103, 190, 195, 229
iconoclasts 53, 56, 77–89, 212, 327
iconolatry 84
iconophiles xxx, 54, 77–89, 93
icon screen *see* templon screen
icons
  acheirograptos 36, 38
  acheiropoietos 25, 34, 38, 39, 40, 210
  acheirotmetos 325
  aspasmos of 3
  carrying of 197–8, Fig. 17.6
  concordia of 35
  cult of 3, 23, 24, 91
  as ex-votos 25
  as images 23, 30
  in *litaniai* 195, 197
  marble 214, 229–30, 325
  mosaic 211, 212, 214, 338
  proskynesis of 3, 36
  restoration of 79
  veneration of 3, 30, 82–3, 91n, 95
idolatry 82, 84
idols 28, 30
Ignatios, Patriarch 53, 56
Ignatios of Antioch, St 341, 342
illness, of children 15
imago 23
imitatio dei 79
incense 3, 68, 117–25, 155
infants 256
inventio 211
Ireland
  National Gallery, icon of the Virgin Hodegetria 344
Irenaeus 3
Irene, empress wife of Constantine V 149
Irene Doukaina Komnene, empress 156, 162n, 233
Irene Synadene 158, 166
Irene the Athenian, empress xxx, 78–9
Isaac, exarch 31
Isaac II Angelos, emperor 215
Isaiah, prophet 7, 253
  vision of 123
Isis 4, 5, 6, 7, 8, 11, 104n
  attributes 5–9

'Isis look' 7–8
Lactans 5, 9
panel paintings 6, 11, Figs 1.3–5
sculptures 6
wall paintings 5, 6
Istria *see* Croatia
Italy
  Apulia 312, 325, 329
    Andria, icon of the Virgin 339–40
    Bari 325; church of S. Maria della Greca, icon of the Virgin 345; Pinacoteca Provinciale, icon of the Virgin Hodegetria 339, 345, 347, 355, Fig. 27.10
    Barletta, icon of the *Madonna della Neve* 340, 345
    Lecce 312
    Novoli, church of the Immaculate Virgin 312, 319, Fig. 25.11
    Otranto 325; church of San Pietro 252, 259, Fig. 21.2
    Salento 326
    Trani 325–6; church of San Giovanni della Penna 326
    Urgento, crypt 312
  Bologna 299
    Archaeological Museum, lead ampulla 229
    church of the Servi, Cimabue's pala 312
  Calabria 216n, 324, 328, 329, 330
    Barile 328
    Cosenza, cathedral, icon of the Madonna del Pilerio 279, 287, Fig. 23.1
    Gerace 324
    Polistena, parish church, panel of the *Madonna dell'Itria*, 330, 335, Plate 22, Fig. 26.7
    Rossano, monastery of S. Maria del Patir (the Rossano *Odigitria* or *Neodigitria*) 216n, 324; Museo Diocesano, two-sided icon of the Virgin *Neodigitria* 324, 333, Figs 26.3–4
  Campania 329
  Catania, *Ecclesia Sancte Marie de Itria Eupli* 327
  Florence 299
    Accademia, Giovanni da Milano's Pietà 285, 292, Fig. 23.8
    Baptistery 299
    Biblioteca Medicea Laurenziana, cod. Pluteus VII, 32 120n
    church of *Santa Maria Egitria* or *Odigitria* 327
    church of S. Marco 37
    Museo Bigalo, Bernardo Daddi's Virgin with saints and donors 312
  Grottaferrata, monastery of 70

Latium 34
Milan 265
  Castello Sforzesco, ivory with Otto II and Theophano 282
  Museo del Duomo, ivory book-cover 200, 207, Fig. 17.8
Molise, Portocannone 328
Naples 329
  baptistery of San Giovanni in Fonte 243
  chapel of *Santa Maria dell'Itria* (church of the *Madonna di Piedigrotta*) 327
  church of San Giovanni Maggiore 329
  Museo di Capodimonte 330
Padua 265
  Arena chapel 285
  monastery of Santa Giustina, icon of the *Madonna Costantinopolitana* 327, 334, 340, 346–7, 355, Figs 26.5, 27.11
Pavia
  Bobbio 159n, 185
  Monza 185
Perugia 299
Pisa 299
  coins of 285n
  Duomo, icon of the *Madonna di sotto gli organi* 339, 347
  icon of the Virgin *Lactans* 345
Ravenna 31
  Museo Archivescovile, throne of Maximian 297
  Museo Nazionale, ivory diptych 108–9, 113, Fig. 9.7
  San Vitale, image of Theodora 186, 189
Rome xxvii, 23–49, 277, 278, 285, 296
  ancient monuments: *Campus Martius* 30, 41; Colosseum 299; *Curia* 33; *Forum Romanum* 28, 31, 33, 34, 43, Fig. 3.2; Mausoleum of Hadrian 35; Pantheon 24, 28–31, 37, 41, 43, 44, Fig. 3.3
  catacombs of S. Maria Maggiore, fresco 229
  chapels: Cappella Altemps 47; Cappella Paolina 31, 34, 45–6; chapel of John VII 37; St Caesarius 31; Theodotus chapel 24
  churches: Lateran 28, 31, 34; S. Adriano 33; S. Maria Antiqua 23–4, 27, 31, 32; S. Maria in Aracoeli 49; S. Maria del Rosario 24, 48; S. Maria in Tempulo 40; S. Maria in Trastevere 24, 37–8, 47; S. Maria Maggiore 'ad praesepe' 24, 25, 28, 31–7, 45–6; S. Maria Nova 27–8, 33, 42, 312, 338; S. Maria Odigitria dei Siciliani 329; S. Sisto Vecchio 40; St Peter's 35, 37; *titulus Julii et Callistii* 37, 39

hills: Capitoline 41; Esquiline 34; Monte Mario 40, 48; Palatine 31
liturgy and ceremonials: *diaconiae* 33; feast of the Virgin's Presentation to the Temple 285; *laetania septiformis* 36; processions on Marian feast days 33, 277; *see also* Virgin, feasts, Assumption
Marian icons 33;
  Madonna della Clemenza 24, 37–9, 40, 47, 104n, 167, Fig. 3.8; Madonna di S. Sisto xxxii, 24–5, 39–41, 48, Fig. 3.9; Madonna in Aracoeli 41, 49, Fig. 3.10; Madonna of the Pantheon 26, 28–31, 32, 44, 110, Figs 3.3, 9.1; metalwork icon in the chapel 'ad praesepe' 33; of S. Maria Maggiore 'Salus Populi Romani', 'Regina coeli' 25, 31–7, 41, 45–6, Plates 2, 3a–b, Figs 3.5–7; Virgin with Christ-child in S. Maria Nova 8, 25, 27–8, 29, 32, 33, 42, 312, 338, Fig. 3.1
  palaces and treasuries: Imperial palace 31; Papal palace 28, 34; *Sancta sanctorum* 34, 40, 325
Sardinia
  Cagliari 30
  Gavoi, *sa Itria* 321, 329, 332, Figs 26.1–2
Sicily xxvii, 293, 296, 327, 329
  Agrigento, cathedral 330, 334, Fig. 26.6
  Messina 296, 328; church of the *Madonna dell'Itria* 330, 336, Fig. 26.10; church of S. Caterina di Valverde, Riccio's *Madonna di Costantinopoli* 336, Fig. 26.9; church of S. Niccolò dei Greci 328; cod. Mes. San Salvatore 27 216n
  Palazzolo Areide 331
  Palermo 185; church of S. Margherita 330; hospital and chapel of the Itria 327; Martorana 307
  Sciacca, monastery of the Itria 327
Siena 293, 296, 299
  cathedral, Madonna degli occhi grossi 168
  Museo del Opera del Duomo, Duccio's *Maestà* 282, 290, Fig. 23.5
  Palazzo Pubblico, Simone Martini's *Maestà* 282, 291, Fig. 23.6
  Pinacoteca Nazionale, Duccio's Madonna of the Franciscans 307
Turin
  Galleria Sabauda, Madonna Gualino 312, 319, Fig. 25.10
  University Library, cod. C. I.6 120n
Tuscany 296, 312
Umbria, Bugian Piccolo, parish church, panel of the *Madonna di Costantinopoli* 335, Fig. 26.8

Vatican City
  Biblioteca Apostolica Vaticana: Barberini Psalter 252n; cod. gr. 1162, Homilies of James of Kokkinobaphos 199, 206, Fig. 17.7; *Menologion* of Basil II 201, 206, 207, Figs 17.6, 17.9; Octateuch cod. gr. 747 107, 112, Plate 5, Fig. 9.5
  Musei Vaticani, icon of Sts Peter and Paul 341, 348
Verona 268
Venice 265, 293
  Biblioteca Marciana, enamel book cover 343
  Museo Correr, silver ring 154; silver-gilt reliquary of St Marina 161n
  San Marco
    chapel of San Zeno, marble icon of the Virgin enthroned 230, 295; marble icon of the Virgin Glykophilousa 311;
    Treasury 160n, icon of the Virgin Nikopoios 216n, 221, Fig. 18.7

Jacob, prophet 72–3, 107
Jacobus de Voragine 35n
James of Kokkinobaphos 124, 199, 201, 206, 253
janizaries 321
Jephoniah 66–7; *see also* Virgin, episode of Jephoniah
Jephonias 64, 65
  unnamed Jew 283
Jeremiah 65
Jerusalem *see* Palestine
Jesus *see* Christ
jewellery 153, 183, 187, 189, 190
Joachim, father of the Virgin 199, 200, 201, 226, 240
John, founder of the Iveron monastery 133, 135, 137
John, hegoumenos of the monastery of St John in Petra 160n
John, monk donor of the Sinai hexaptych 311
John, St, the Baptist 65, 158–62, 211, 253, 341, 343
John, St, the Evangelist 18, 94, 155, 297, 299
John I of Portugal 270
John I Tzimiskes, emperor 212, 213, 215, 219, 282n, 322, Fig. 18.3
John II Komnenos, emperor 161, 162, 215, 233
John V Palaiologos, emperor 269
John VI Kantakouzenos, emperor 216
John VII, Pope 37
John XI Bekkos, Patriarch 233

John Chrysostom 252n, 341, 342, 343, 347, 348, 354, Fig. 27.6
John Dalassenos, Caesar 156
John Klimax 169
John Komnenos Doukas 298
John Kontostephanos 161n, 162
John Koukouzeles 240
John of Amalfi 326
John of Damascus 72, 74, 76, 94, 121, 253n
John of Thessaloniki 68
John Phokas 284, 323
John Phournes 125
John Rodolphos 242
John Rufus 63, 67
John Thekaras 74
Joseph, husband of the Virgin 253
Joseph, Old-Testament patriarch 185
  Joseph textiles 185–6, 188, 192, Fig. 16.6
Joseph Bryennios 216
Joseph of Arimathea 109
Joseph the Hymnographer 123
Joshua bar Nun 64, 67
Julian the Apostate, emperor 66, 327
Justin I, emperor 147, 149
Justin II, emperor xxx, 27, 147, 148, 149, 183
Justinian I, emperor 15, 63, 147, 149, 176, 183, 184, 187, 189, 209, 227, 233, 239
Juvenal of Jerusalem 65, 68

Kallistos I, Patriarch 134, 136
Kanstresios, Manuel *see* Dishypatos Kanstresios, Manuel
kanon 69, 71, 72, 73, 74, 75, 121, 137, 242, 306
  apolytikion 72
  heirmos 73
  idiomela 72
  kathisma 71, 75
  kontakion 76, 97, 98
  Megas Kanon 216
  ode 72, 73, 74, 81
  sticheron 69, 71, 76
  theotokion 69, 71, 72, 74, 94, 97, 331n
    dogmatikon theotokion 72, 74
    staurotheotokia 69, 97
  troparion 69, 75, 76, 118
Kaphrata 64
Khosrovanush, queen of Georgia 156, 159
Khurus 13n, 21
killing, of a child 15
Koimesis see Virgin, Dormition
Kokkinobaphos *see* James of Kokkinobaphos

Kollyridians 16
kommerkia 78
Komnenoi, family 155, 215; Komnenian dynasty 162n
Kosmas, owner of a ring 189
Kosmas, St 264, 343n
Kosmas of Maiouma 94
krites 176n
Kyriaki, St 155

lamps 4
Last Judgement 18, 283
Late Antiquity 4, 5
laudes marianae 69
Lebanon
 Beirut, bleeding Crucifix 278n
Legenda aurea see Jacobus de Voragine
leipsanoclast 327
Leo I, emperor 147, 148, 149, 150, 186, 209, 211, 225, 233, 239
Leo II, emperor 186, 211
Leo III, emperor 87, 88, 92, 137, 149, 185, 326, 327
Leo III, Pope 87
Leo V, emperor 80n, 88
Leo VI, emperor 79, 156, 178n, 227, 233
Leo the Deacon 213
Leontia 31
Leontias, owner of a bronze votive cross 158–9
Leontios of Jerusalem 72
Letter of Kosmas 146n
Liber Pontificalis 26, 27, 29, 30, 31, 34
Life of John Kolobos 67
Life of Michael Synkellos 83
Life of Peter the Athonite 140
Life of Peter the Iberian 150
Life of Prophet Jeremiah 65
Life of St Basil the Younger 108
light 84
Lippi, Filippino xxii
litania see liturgy, litany and procession
lite see liturgy
liturgy 3, 18, 34, 91–2, 96–9, 119n, 195, 199
 akolouthia 134, 135, 136, 137, 225, 228, 240, 242, 244
 antiphons 76
 Apodeipnon, Great and *Small* 269n
 chairetismoi xxviii, 74
 funeral service 119
 hagiasmos 243–4
  Great Hagiasmos 243
  Small Hagiasmos 244

litany (*litania*) 137, 195, 199, 200, 202, 206, Fig. 17.6
lite 209, 217
orthros 231
panegyris 209
Paraklesis, Mikra 69
Proskomide 342
stational 195
typikon 134, 137
vespers 119n
vigil 137
Logos see Christ
Lucia, countess of Kent 267–8
Luke, St 23n, 25, 28, 35, 40, 41, 148, 198, 215, 266, 270, 322, 323, 324, 325, 326, 327, 328
Lykourgos 5

Macedonia, Former Yugoslav Republic of
 Lesnovo monastery 229, 232, 245
 Markov Manastir 217, 223, Figs 18.9–10
 Nerezi, church of St Panteleemon 105, 106–7, 111, Fig. 9.3
 Ohrid 296, 297, 299
  church of Lesser Anargyroi 245
  church of Virgin Peribleptos, two-sided icon of Christ Psychosostis and the Crucifixion 269; two-sided icon of the Hodegetria and the Crucifixion 196, 204–5, Plate 12a–b, Figs 17.4–5; small icon of the Virgin 296
 Staro Nagoričino 297, 298
Madonna *see* Italy, Rome, Marian icons, Virgin, epithets and types of
Maestà see France, Avignon and Italy, Siena
magic 16–17, 178, 188
 magical rituals 257
Magical Book of Mary and the Angels, The 17
magicians 19
magistros 177
Magna Mater 4
Makarios of Pelekete 80n
Makedonios 93
Makrina 154
Malalas 147n
Mammisi (Birth Houses) 18, 22
Mamre, oak of 64
Mandylion 36, 39, 123
manger *see* crib
manna 63–4, 66, 72–3, 201
Manuel, owner of a seal 176n
Manuel I Komnenos, emperor 215
Manuel II Palaiologos, emperor 265, 266n, 269–70

Mapplethorpe, Robert 286
Marcellinus 147n
Marcian, emperor 149, 150, 322
Maria, empress 149
Maria, nun 154
Maria, owner of a cross 155
Maria Komnene, daughter of Andronikos I 156
Maria Komnene, daughter of Alexios I 162n
Maria of Alania, empress 282n
Marina, St 83
Maríu Saga, poem 326
marriage 87n, 187
  ceremony 158
  rings 184–5, 187, 188, 191, Figs 16.3–4
Martin I of Aragon 270
Martini, Simone 282, 286, 291, Fig. 23.6
martyrs 82
Mary *see* Virgin
Mary Magdalene 280–1
Mathilda of Tuscany 282
Maurice, emperor 68, 149, 183, 184, 209
Maurice, St 282
Maurus, St 186
Mavrikios, *chartoularios* 31, 33
Maximos the Confessor 76
Maximos the Greek 135
medallion 103, 157, 158, 183, 184, 191, 230, Fig. 16.1
Mehmet II, sultan 321
Melania, nun 150
Melisende, queen of Jerusalem 281, 283
Melkites 14n
melourgos 98
Menaia 97, 326
Menas, St 188
Menologion 147, 200, 201, 212
metatorikion 214
Methodios, Patriarch 81, 83
Metrophanes, hymnographer 73
metropolitan, seals of 230, 311
  of Athens 311
  of Paronaxia 257n
  of Thessaloniki 265, 268, 270
Michael, archangel 35, 126, 155, 169–70, 256, 264, 325, Plates 9, 17, Figs 10.1, 14.2, 22.1
Michael, owner of a seal 176n
Michael III, emperor 217n
Michael VII Doukas, emperor 282n
Michael VIII Palaiologos, emperor 216, 233, 244n
milk 15, 17–19, 256
Milutin, king of Serbia 298

Mocha 65
modes, eight 71
  first 73, 74, 75
  second 74
  second plagal 72, 74, 75
  third 73
  fourth 74
  fourth plagal 69, 72, 73
  seventh 73
  eighth 72
modios 63–4
monks 5, 13, 14, 16, 70, 84, 86, 87n, 119n, 120n, 133, 134, 135, 136, 137, 138, 140, 154, 227, 231, 307, 308, 311, 318, 322, 324, 325, 330, 331, 343
Monophysites 14
Monothelitism 92
morbidity, of women 156
Morocco
  Marrakesh, Kutubiyya Mosque, minbar 297
Morphia, queen of Jerusalem 281n
mortality, infant 156
mosaics 9, 37, 51–3, 56–9, 95, 96, 100, 156, 159, 167, 170, 186, 187, 188, 193, 211, 212, 214, 219, 225, 227, 228, 229, 232, 241, 280, 281n, 294, 299, 306, 312, 338
Moses, prophet 25, 63, 65, 67, 73–5, 242
  staff of 73
'Mother of God'
  conference xix, xxi, xxiii, xxiv, xxvii, 177, 263, 277
  exhibition xix, xxi, xxiii, xxiv, xxviin, 3, 8, 24, 91, 167, 168, 263, 293, 321, 359
motherhood 15
Mravalthavi 65
mummy portrait 6, 8
myrrh 65
mysticism 70
Mytilenaios, Christophoros, poet 79n

Nahum, prophet 73
narthex 211, 226, 232, 234, 237–8, 240, 243, 244, 305, 307, 309, 313
necklace 177, 184
Neophytos of Paphos 122
Nero, emperor 22
Nestorios, Patriarch xxix, 93, 145–6, 147
Netherlands, The
  Maastricht, Onze Lieve Vrouw, reliquary enkolpion 158, 165, Fig. 13.8
Nicaea (Iznik) 86n, 133
  Koimesis church 51–3, 56–9

niche 4, 5
Nicholas, St 232, 325, 343
Nicholas the Pilgrim, St 325
Nicodemo della Scala, bishop of Freising 266, 268
Nika revolt 68
Nikephoros, healer of horses 309
Nikephoros I, Patriarch 80, 84, 85, 87
Nikephoros II Phokas, emperor 282n
Niketas of Medikion 77, 87
Nikopolis 176n
Nixon, Mignon 286
nomos 74, 75
Normans, siege of 323
nursing, image and methodology 13–16, 18, 22
  duration 15–16
nymph, of a spring 185

Octateuchs 107, 298
oikistikos 175
Oktoechos 69, 72
omer 63
Oneirokritika 78
Opsaras *see* Dishypatos Kanstresios, Manuel
Opsikion, theme of 86n
Ôr 64
Origen 4
Orimina, Sichelgaita 327n
Orthodox tradition xxvii, xxviii
Orthodoxy xxii, xxix, 91, 233, 244n
Ōshin, Marshal, Gospels of 307, 308, 317, Fig. 25.6
Otto II, king 282
Oziah 66

Pachomios, hegoumenos of the Brontocheion monastery 226, 241
Pakourianos, Symbatios 154
Palaiologoi 217, 265n
Palestine xxxii, 24, 186, 209, 211, 257n
  Bethlehem 33, 64, 65–6, 68, 254n, 279
    cave of the Nativity 251, 254n, 258
    church of the Nativity 254n, 279, 324
  Hebron 64, 65
  Jerusalem 27, 65, 68, 150, 151
    Armenian Patriarchate, cod. 2568, Gospels of Prince Vasak 307, Fig. 25.5
    Bethesda 242
    churches: Abu Ghosh, Hospitaller church 281, 283; Ascension 150; Forty Martyrs' martyrion 150; Gethsemane 65, 68; Holy Sepulchre 280; Armenian chapel of the Virgin 280n; Calvary chapel 280n; Omphalos 281; Rotunda apse, bema 280n; Holy Sion 68; Koimesis church 281, 283; 'Nea' Maria church 68; St Peter 149; St Stephen 149
    Greek Orthodox Patriarchate, icon of the Virgin 344
    Jewish temple 121, 122; Holy of Holies 199, 201
    Latin Church 285
    Liturgy of the Dormition 68
    Monastery of St Chariton (Palaea Lavra) 65
    Mount of Olives 68, 150
    Siloam 242
    Sion 65–6, 212
  Jordan, monastery of St Mary of Kalamon 323
  Kathisma, church 65, 68
palladium (icon) 29, 35, 133, 175, 202, 217, 322, 323, 327, 328, 329
panagiarion 231, 236, Fig. 19.6
panegyris see liturgy
panel paintings, pagan 5, 6
Panteleemon, St 264, 343n
Paradise 18, 258
Paraskevi, St 155
Parentium *see* Croatia, Poreč
parresia 94
Patria, of Mt Athos 134, 135, 137, 139, 140
Paul, abbot of Iveron 133
Paul, St 18, 264, 341, 343, 348, 354, Fig. 27.5
  Pauline theology 75
Paul Silentiarios 187
pebbles 155
Pentekostarion 240n
Persia 67; Persian assault 210, 326; Persians 212
personifications 189
Peter, St 119, 155, 264, 282, 341, 343, 348, 354, Fig. 27.5
Peter, St, the Athonite 135, 137
Peter I Lusignan, king of Cyprus 309
Peter the Iberian 67
Pharaoh 18, 74
Pharisees 64
phelonion 122
phiale 243; *see also* Constantinople, churches and monasteries, Virgin tes Peges
Philagathos of Cerami 324
Philes, Manuel 227, 231, 240, 245
Philippikos Bardanes, emperor 92
Philostorgios 147n
Phoibammon, mentioned in an amulet 189
Phokas, Bardas 213
Phokas, emperor 28, 30, 31, 210
Photeinos, St 230

Photios, Patriarch 76, 95, 147n, 170, 200n
Phthenoth, demon 257n
phylacteries 153, 157, 162
pilgrimage 150, 151, 153, 155n, 198, 200, 227, 228, 281, 283, 284, 286, 323, 326
Pius XII, Pope 70
Plerophories 63, 67
pneuma-gramma 75
poem 79, 240
poetry, ecclesiastical 69, 75, 91
pregnancy 189, 255–6
  pregnant women 156, 255, 257n
presbeia procession 195
priest
  emperor as 88
  in liturgy 3
  seals of 230
priesthood, pagan 5
procession
  of the emperor on the feast of Ascension 233, 239; *see also* triumph, of emperor
  of an icon
    of Christ 210
    of the Virgin 210, 223, 277, 278, 325, Figs 18.9–10
    Tuesday procession of the Hodegetria icon 195, 196, 197–202, 203, 215, 325, 328, 331, Fig. 17.1
  pagan 5
  wedding 200n
  see also liturgy, litany
procreation 153, 156, 158
Prodromos *see* John, St, the Baptist
Proklos of Constantinople xxviin, xxviii, xxx, 73, 92–3, 153
Prokopios, historian 209, 232
prophets 82, 241
proskynetarion 9
Protevangelium of James xxviii, 66, 75
protospatharios 176
  basilikos protospatharios 176n
protosynkellos, great 241
protypsis 74
Psalm 51, 52, 65, 76, 85, 119, 212, 252, 254, 255n, 260, Fig. 21.4
Psalter 76, 254
  illustration of 108n, 212, 218, 230, 252, 260, 283, 284
Psellos, Michael 157, 178, 213, 214, 277, 308, 309
Pseudo-Dionysios the Areopagite 122, 265
Pseudo-John the Evangelist 119n

Pseudo-Kodinos 149n, 216n, 331n
Pseudo-Matthew 254n
Pseudo-Modestos 121–2
Pulcheria, empress xxviii, xxx, 140, 145–8, 150–1, 322, 329

Quiricus and Julitta, Sts 24

Radenos Symponos 175, 177
Raphael xxii
Rationale Divinorum Officiorum see Durantus Gullielmus
Ravendel, knight 309
Rebecca 107, 112
Red Sea 73–4
refrains 76
regalia 213
relics
  of Holy Cross 212
  of martyrs 29
  thorn of the crown of Christ 267
  'reliquary diplomacy' 269–70
reliquary 103, 160
Renaissance 96
  'Macedonian' 32
revolt 68
Riccio, A. 336
ring 103, 154, 158, 163, 165, 177, 184, 187, 188, 189, 190, Figs 16.3–4
  'St Nilus' ring 324
Rockefeller–McCormick New Testament *see* United States of America, Chicago, University Library
Roger I, king of Sicily 285n
Romanos I Diogenes, emperor 213
Romanos I Lekapenos, emperor 212
Romanos III Argyros, emperor 157, 178, 213, 282n
Romanos the Melode 98, 105, 209n
Rotunda *see* Rome, Pantheon
Rousanos, Pachomios 135, 137, 138, 139
Rubens xxii
Russian Federation 134, 135, 296, 309
  Kiev 215
    St Sophia cathedral 342
  Moscow
    State Historical Museum, MS. gr. 129, Khludov Psalter 218, 252n, 260, Figs 18.1, 21.4
    State Museum of the 'Moscow Kremlin', icon with the Akathistos cycle 330n; reliquary enkolpion 161n

Synodal Library, MS. no 404 135
Tretyakov Gallery, icon of the Virgin and Child 269, 274, Fig. 22.6; icon of the Virgin of Tolga 311; icon of the Virgin of Vladimir 105, 106, 110, 215, 221, Figs 9.2, 18.6; jasper cameo 231, 236, Fig. 19.5
Novgorod, church of the Assumption 229; churches of the Saviour and Transfiguration 229
St Petersburg 294
  Saltykov–Shchedrin State Public Library, cod. fr. F v 14 278n
  The State Hermitage Museum, icon of the Dormition of the Virgin 299, 303, Fig. 24.4; ivory diptych 107, 113, Fig. 9.6
  Vladimir 215, 294
    church of St Demetrios 294
Ruy Gonzalez de Clavijo 270

Saba, monk 154
sacramentary 243
sacrifices, pagan 5
Sadducees 66
sagoma 23
saints
  healing 241, 244, 343n, Fig. 20.3
  military 3, 38
Salma 65
Salome 66
Salomon 64
Salvation 23, 153, 162, 252, 306, 310
sanctuary 12, 145, 147
  bema 211
Sara 64
Satan *see* Devil
schema, mega 134
screen *see* templon screen
Saracens 326
Sarapis 7, 9
seals, iconography of 155, 158, 166, 175–8, 196n, 230, 231, 236, 324, 326, Figs 15.1, 19.4
  of archbishops 230
  of church officials 230
  of monasteries 175–6
seasons, personifications of 189
sebastophoros 175
Seknebtunis 5
Septuagint, translation of 63
Serapheim, Protos of Mt Athos 139
Serbia 294, 300
  Arilje 295
  Dečani monastery 217n
  Gračanića monastery 243
  Ljuboten monastery 243n
  Matejć monastery 217n
  Psača, St Nicholas church 243
  Peć, church of the Virgin 229, 232, 237, Fig. 19.8
  Ravanica monastery 229
  Sopoćani, church of the Holy Trinity 125, 297
  Studenića 298
  Žiča 297
Serbian royal family 217
Serenus of Marseilles 30
Sergios, Patriarch 210, 211
Sergios and Bakchos, Sts 150
Sergius I, Pope 33
serpent 256
Severos of Antioch 68
shelf 5
shivering 242
shrine, domestic 5, 9
silks *see* textiles
silverware 186
Sion *see* Palestine, Jerusalem
Sisinnios, St 256, 262, Fig. 21.6
Six Books' Redaction 66
Sixtus III, Pope 33
Skleros, Theodore 175
Skylitzes, John 213, 214, 215
Smaragdus, exarch 31
smothering, of children 15
snake *see* serpent
Sokrates, historian 147n
solidus 157, 165, Fig. 13.5
Solomon
  knots of 254n
  Testament of 257n
  Throne of 299n
Sozomenos, historian 147n, 150
Sophia, empress xxx, 145, 148, 149
Sophronios of Jerusalem 76
Souda lexicon 146n
soul
  leaving the body 108
  of the Virgin 118, 122, 125
Spain 299
  Calahorra 293
  Madrid 293
    Biblioteca Nacional, cod. 52 296; cod. gr. Vitr. 26-2, Skylitzes' *Synopsis* 219, Fig. 18.3
spatharokoubikoularios 175
spells 16, 19, 255n, 256n

spoon 184
spring, miraculous *see* Constantinople, churches and monasteries, Virgin tes Peges
statue
  of the king 67
  pagan 6
sterility 156
Stephanus III, Pope 31
Stephen, owner of a seal 175
Stephen, St, 150, 155
Stephen, St, the Younger 215, 220, Plate 13, Fig. 18.5
Stephen IV, king of Hungary 285n
Stephen Kontostephanos 161, 162
Stephen the Deacon 80n
Sticherarion 72
Sticherokathismatarion 69
stole 330
strategos 176n, 212
Sunday of Orthodoxy 97
superstition 252, 255n, 256n, 257
Switzerland
  Bern, Abegg-Stiftung, silk weaving 185;
  Kunstmuseum, Duccio's Madonna 312
Symeon of Bulgaria 212
Symeon the Younger, St 159
Symionios, owner of a cross 155
Symmachos 254n
symponos 175
synagogue 30
Synaxarion of Constantinople 212
Synesios, owner of a cross 155
Synodikon 133
synthronon 28, 34
Syria 257, 322
  Damaskus, Saidnaya 278

tablets of stone 73
Tafur, Pero 325
Tamar, queen 156
tapers, in processions 200, 201
Tarasios, Patriarch 124, 253n
Tebtunis 5, 6
teleiosis 76
telos 76
templon screen 3, 9
textiles 103, 185–6, 187, 192–3, 198, 199, Figs 16.5–6, 16.8
Theadelphia 5
Thekla, owner of a cross 155
Thekla, St 155
Theoderich 280n, 281n, 283n

Theodora, empress, wife of Justinian I xxx, 149, 151, 187, 189
Theodora, empress, wife of Theophilos and saint 217n
Theodora, third daughter of Constantine VIII, empress 281, 282, 285n
Theodora, mentioned in the *Life of St Basil the Younger* 108
Theodora Komnene 161, 175
Theodore, Pope 27, 31
Theodore II Laskaris, emperor 74
Theodore Apseudes 122
Theodore Graptos *see* Graptoi brothers
Theodore Lector 146n
Theodore of Studios 54–6, 75, 78, 79n, 80, 85, 94, 255n, 306
Theodore Prodromos 161
Theodore Stratelates, St 78, 343n
Theodore Synkellos 209, 211
Theodosios II, emperor 140, 147n
Theodote, empress 149
Theodotos of Ankyra xxi–xxii, 70
Theoktistos, *protospatharios* 176n
theologoumenon 4
Theophanes, historian 78, 86, 87, 147n, 209n
Theophanes Graptos *see* Graptoi brothers
Theophano, empress 79, 233
Theophano, princess and queen xxii, 282
Theophilos, emperor 80n, 133, 137
Theophylaktos of Ohrid 75
Theosteriktos of Stoudios 69, 71, 77
Theotokos *see* Virgin
Thomaïs, St, of Lesbos 197
Thomas Palaiologos 329
throne
  as attribute of the Virgin 3, 4, 5, 6, 9, 37, 297–8, 299
  of Hereford 297
  of the Hetoimasia 51–2, 59, 264, 343, 344n
  of Solomon 299
Tiber 30, 35
Tiberios I, emperor 149, 183
Tiberios II, emperor 185
Timotheos, Georgian bishop 137n
Timotheos Ailouros 67, 68
Titian xxii
topos 84
Tornikios (monk John), founder of Iveron monastery 133, 135, 138
Trajan 22
Transitus Mariae xxix, 65, 66
translatio 211

Tree of Jesse 254n
triduum 68
Trinity, Holy 64
  doctrine 53, 56
Triodion 96, 97
triptych 6
Trisagion hymn 51
triumph
  of an emperor 212, 213, 215, 216, 219, Fig. 18.3
  of Orthodoxy 95, 217n, 222, Fig. 18.8
Tropologion 69
True Cross 154, 162n
Tuesday
  abstention of meat 328, 329
  processions of icons of the Virgin Hodegetria 195, 196, 197–202, 203, 215, 325, 328, 329
Turkey
  Istanbul
    Archaeological Museum, marble icon of the Virgin 230, 235, Fig. 19.3
    Kariye Çamii, 226n, 232, 238, Fig. 19.9
    Topkapı Palace, silver reliquary 160
  Prinkipo, monastery of the Virgin xxx
Turks 269, 270
turmarches 325
Tyche 4, 189
Typikon, athonite 139
typology 73–4, 76, 93, 94

Ukraine
  Crimea, Cherson 176n, 257n
  Kiev 8, 25
United Kingdom
  England 30, 267, 281, 283
  Kent 266, 267
  London 184, 265
    British Museum, marriage ring 184, 188; silver weight 281; tapestry-woven medallion 192, Fig. 16.5; icon of the Triumph of Orthodoxy 217n, 222, Fig. 18.8
    British Library, Add. 19352 252n; Cotton Nero C IV, Winchester Psalter 283, 284; cod. BMO 6782 17–18; cod. Stowe 944 282, 289, Fig. 23.4
    private collection, ivory panel 109, 114, Fig. 9.8
    Victoria and Albert Museum, cameo 231
  Oxford
    Oxon. Lincoln College 10 135n
  Winchester, New Minster and Hyde Abbey 282, 283, 289, Fig. 23.4

United States of America
  Cambridge, Massachusetts, Fogg Art Museum, seal 203, Fig. 17.3; seal of Sebaste Irene Synadene 158n, 166, Fig. 13.9
  Cleveland, The Cleveland Museum of Art 8; tapestry icon 8, 104n
  Chicago, University Library, Rockefeller–McCormick New Testament cod. 965 280
  Los Angeles 293
    The J. Paul Getty Museum 7, 8, 9, 11; Isis panel 7, 9, 11, Fig. 1.4
  New York 294
    Pierpont Morgan Library, MSS. M. 740 and 1111, Gospel book of Marshal Ōshin 307, 308, 317, Fig. 25.6
    The Metropolitan Museum of Art, Madonna di Varlungo 312; tapestry-woven medallion 192, Fig. 16.6
  Richmond, Virginia Museum of Fine Arts, gold marriage ring 191, Fig. 16.4
  Washington DC
    Dumbarton Oaks: bronze votive cross 155, 164, Fig. 13.4; bronze votive cross 158–9, 166, Fig. 13.10; coin of Andronikos II Palaiologos 236, Fig. 19.7; gold nomisma with empresses Zoe and Theodora 289, Fig. 23.3; gold marriage ring 184, 188, 191, Fig. 16.3; gold medallion 184, 191, Fig. 16.1; gold reliquary cross 155, 164, Fig. 13.3; gold ring with the Virgin between crosses 184; seal 203, Fig. 17.2; seal 203, Fig. 17.3; seal of Sebaste Irene Synadene 166, Fig. 13.9
    National Gallery of Art, Kahn and Mellon Madonnas 293–302, Plate 20, Figs 24.1–3
    The Textile Museum, tapestry-woven panel 193, Fig. 16.8
upbringing, of children 15
urn, of manna 63–4, 67

Vasak, prince 307, 317, Fig. 25.5
Veit Adam von Gepeckh, bishop of Freising 266
Venus 4
Verina, empress 147, 148, 149, 151, 186, 209, 211
Veronica, St 39
vestes 175
vestibule 212
Vetiana 154
Victory 176n
Vincent of Beauvais 326

Virgil, tomb of 327
Virgin
  apocryphal accounts xxviii, xxix, 103
  archetypal virgin, woman and mother xxi, 78, 79, 146n
  attributes
    girdle xxviii, 148, 264n
    impression of hand 214
    palm, of Life 68
    robe (maphorion, veil, mantle) xxviii, 29, 148, 150, 186, 209, 210, 211, 212, 264n, 281, 307, 308–9
    staff 37, 39
    throne 3, 4, 5, 6, 9, 37
  bride of Christ 34
  cult
    cakes of the Kollyridians 16
    cult and devotion xxix, xxx, 16–17
    East and West xxii, xxx, 277–86, 293–300
    female piety 153–62
    model for noblewomen and empresses 78, 145–52
    official policy and individual piety xxxi–xxxii
    personal or private objects 103, 153–62, 175
    private and public xxix, 183–90
    second Eve 153
    spells 16
    'usual miracle' 214, 230, 277, 278n, 308; see also Constantinople, churches and monasteries, Blachernai
    women's piety xxix–xxx, 16, 145–52
  doctrine
    Assumption xxii, 70
    habitaculum of Christ 38
    Immaculate Conception xxii, 285
    Incarnation 4, 23, 52–3, 56, 64, 72, 81, 83, 84, 85, 93, 94, 95, 97, 103, 104, 105, 108, 117, 121, 122, 123, 124, 159, 197, 231, 257, 342
    prohibition of depiction 82
    'Theotokos' dispute 147, 151
  episode of Jephoniah 66; see also Jephoniah
  episodes of life and feasts
    Adoration of the Magi 103, 184, 185, 186, 188, 189, 191, 192, Figs 16.1, 16.5
    Annunciation 23, 27, 33, 103, 104, 123, 130, 155, 158, 159, 175–9, 184, 185, 188, 189, 200n, 280n, 285, 298n, Figs 10.8, 13.8, 15.1
    Assumption 33, 34, 35, 36, 40, 65, 117n, 118, 121–2, 283, 284
    Birth 285
    Dormition (Koimesis) xxix, 28, 33, 34, 63, 65–6, 68, 107–8, 109, 113, 114, 117–31, 137, 216, 281, 283, 284, 299, Figs 9.6, 9.8
    Entry into the Temple (*Eisodos*) 124, 196, 199, 200–2, 206, 207, 285, 295, Figs 17.7–9
    Metastasis 118
    Prayer of Joachim 348, 356, Fig. 27.14
    Purification 33
    Visitation 103, 159, 184, 185, 188, 189
  epithets and types of
    Arakiotissa 339
    Advocata 41, 48, Figs 3.9–10
    Aristerokratousa 324, 329
    Blachernitissa 210n, 212, 213, 215, 220, 229, 230, 232, 233, 281, 289, 308, 311, 319, Figs 18.1, 18.4, 23.3, 25.9
    Brephokratousa xxi, 104, 105n, 310, 323, Fig. 9.1
    Deitria 324
    Deomene xxi
    Dexiokratousa 158, 216n, 337–40, 349–52, Plate 23, Figs 13.9, 27.1–2
    Dimitria 328
    Eleousa 101, 123, 213, 214, 215, 217, 305, 315, 343, Plate 13, Figs 8.3, 9.2, 18.3, 18.5–6, 25.1–2
    Enthroned 96, 100, 104, 184, 186, 211, 283, 285n, 293, 295, 301–2, 307, Plates 11, 21, Figs 8.1, 14.1, 16.1, 16.7, 24.1–2, 25.3–4
    Episkepsis 156, 308
    Galaktotrophousa xxi, 13–21, 104n, 251, 279, 287, Plate 1, Figs 2.1–2, 23.1
    Glykophilousa xxi, 96, 99, 279, 311–12, 343
    Hagiosoritissa 40, 158, 264, 268, 305, Plates 17, 18a, Figs 13.8, 21.1, 21.4
    Hodegetria xxi, xxvii, xxxi, xxxii, 9, 25, 95, 96, 104, 105, 111, 195, 196–7, 198, 199, 201, 203, 210n, 215–16, 217, 226, 240, 241, 277, 282, 286, 313, 321–31, 338–40, 360, Figs 9.4, 17.2–4, 18.8–10, 27.1–2
    Hope of the Hopeless 264, 269, 270
    Kahn Madonna 293–301, Plate 20, Fig. 24.1
    Karyotissa 139
    Kykkotissa xxi
    Lamenting 95, 99
    Madonna dell'Itria 328–30
    Madonna del Pilerio 279, 287, Fig. 23.1
    Madonna della Misericordia (Schutzmantelmadonna) 307, 313
    Madonna di Costantinopoli 328
    Maria Regina 27, 37–9
    Maria Romaia 284
    Mellon Madonna 293–301, Fig. 24.1

of Mercy 307–8, 309, 316–17, Figs 25.3–6
Nikopoios 157, 210n, 214, 221, Figs 13.5, 18.7
Nostra Signora del Buon Camino 321
Odiguria 326
Orans 185, 214n, 229, 231, 232, 233, 235, 281, 283, 308, 309, Fig. 19.3
Paraklesis 305, 306–7, 309, 315, Figs 25.1–2
of the Passion xxi
Phorbiotissa 309, 315, Fig. 25.1
Platytera xxi, 229, 285
Portaitissa 133–42, Plate 7, Fig. 11.1
Queen of Heaven 282, 283
Queen of the angels 198
Regina xxi, 282
sa Itria 321
of the Source (Spring) 231, 240
Strategos 212, 281
of Tenderness 95
of Vladimir 105, 106, 110, 215, 221, Figs 9.2, 18.6
Zoodochos Pege 225–33, 239–45, 249, 331n, Plate 15, Figs 19.1, 20.1–2, 20.8–9
homiletic xxvii, xxxi, 69, 70, 92–5, 97, 124, 257
hymnography xxi, xxvii, xxxi, 69–76, 124, 209, 228, 257, 310
identification with Isis 4
nursing 5, 13, 19
poetry xxxi, 81, 92–5, 97, 209
portrayal xxi, xxii, 9, 118
prefigurations, typological images 72, 121n
 ark of the Covenant 65, 74
 bridge 73
 bright cloud 94
 burning bush 25, 74, 94
 candle 73
 censer 121, 124
 city 81
 fleece 72–3, 94, 242
 gate, closed 72–3
 ladder 72–3, 94, 123, Fig. 10.8
 lamp 94
 loom 73, 75
 manna 242
 palace 73
 paradise 75
 portico 242
 rod of Aaron 159
 spring of the woman of Samaria 242
 tabernacle 121
 table, living 79
 tablet, inscribed 74, 75
 tent, sacred 74
 throne 73
 tongues of divine coal 123
 urn (jar) of Manna 63, 66, 72, 94, 159
 water struck from the rock 242
role
 bridge 277
 in dialectic of light and darkness 84–6
 helper of man 81, 97
 intercessor 81, 82, 87–8, 94, 97, 104, 118, 122, 123, 162, 283, 310
 motherly 91, 95, 162, 279
 personification of the destruction of idols 82–3
 protection 16, 97, 118, 156, 157, 177, 188, 216, 265, 282, 329; of Constantinople 210, 212, 217, 329; of the empire 281
 statues of 13, 278, 284
 tomb in Gethsemane 65, 121, 283
 womb 122, 123, 124, 159
Virginity, perpetual 145, 146
Visconti *see* Caterina, Giangaleazzo Visconti
von Gepeckh, bishop of Freising *see* Veit Adam von Gepeckh

Wallachia 134
'wealthy woman' 189, 193, Fig. 16.8
wedding
 ceremonies 86
 processions 200n
wet nurse 15
Winchester Psalter *see* United Kingdom, London, British Library
wood 155
workshops
 icon painting 339–40
 ivory and bone carvings 4
 wood-carving 346

Xanthopoulos, Nikephoros Kallistos 147n, 148n, 216n, 225–8, 239, 240, 241, 242, 245
xestoi 64

Yello *see* Gylou

Zacharias 124, 159, 199, 200, 201
Zara 64, 65
Zeno, emperor 67, 68, 147, 149
Zeus 5, 9, 83
Zoe, empress, wife of Romanos III 157, 178, 281, 282, 285n
Zoe, owner of a seal (possibly Zoe, empress) 176–9
Zoe Karbonopsina, wife of Leo VI 156–7, 159, 165, 178n